TREATISES
ON THE
SACRAMENTS

CATECHISM OF THE CHURCH OF GENEVA,
FORMS OF PRAYER,
AND CONFESSIONS OF FAITH.

TRACTS BY
JOHN CALVIN

TRANSLATED FROM THE ORIGINAL
LATIN AND FRENCH BY
HENRY BEVERIDGE

CHRISTIAN HERITAGE
MMII

Christian Focus Publications

publishes books for all ages

Our mission statement –
STAYING FAITHFUL
In dependence upon God we seek to help make His infallible word,
the Bible, relevant. Our aim is to ensure that the Lord Jesus Christ is
presented as the only hope to obtain forgiveness of sin, live a useful
life and look forward to heaven with Him.

REACHING OUT
Christ's last command requires us to reach out to our world with His
gospel. We seek to help fulfill that by publishing books that point
people towards Jesus and help them to develop a Christ-like maturity.
We aim to equip all levels of readers for life, work, ministry and mission.

Books in our adult range are published in three imprints.
Christian Focus contains popular works including biographies,
commentaries, basic doctrine, and Christian living.
Mentor focuses on books written at a level suitable for Bible College
and seminary students, pastors, and other serious readers. The
imprint includes commentaries, doctrinal studies, examination of
current issues, and church history.
Christian Heritage contains classic writings from the past.

ISBN 1- 85792-725- 7

Foreword © Copyright MMII Joel R. Beeke

Published in 2002
in the Christian Heritage imprint by
Christian Focus Publications Ltd,
Geanies House, Fearn,
Ross-shire, IV20 1TW, Great Britain
and
Reformation Heritage Books,
2919 Leonard St, NE Grand Rapids, MI 49525
Tel.: 616 977 0599/ Fax: 616 977 0889
email: rhbookstore@aol.com/ web: www.heritagebooks.org

Cover design by Alister MacInnes

Printed and bound by W.S. Bookwell, Finland

www.christianfocus.com

FOREWORD

Calvin as Shepherd and Promoter of Piety

This reprinting of Calvin's treatises on the sacraments is a most welcome addition to the works of Calvin currently on the market for today's readers. The author needs no introduction to Reformed Christians, of course; John Calvin (1509-64) was surely among the giants of all time as a thinker and theologian. He is constantly invoked as an authority (or adversary!) in discussions and debates on nearly everything. Calvin is well known as a scholar, dogmatician, and polemicist.

Calvin as Shepherd of God's Sheep

This volume introduces a Calvin few of us know, and yet one well worth knowing, viz., Calvin, the shepherd of God's sheep. As a minister of the Word and sacraments, Calvin was fully engaged in the life and work of the local congregation. In this book, we follow him into the classroom to hear him instruct new believers and children of the covenant with his *Catechism of the Church of Geneva*. He leads us in prayer at home and in church. He administers the sacraments and solemnizes marriages. He visits the sick and comforts the dying. For his fellow pastors, he adds, "If the minister has anything whereby he can console and give bodily relief to the afflicted poor, let him not spare, but show all a true example of charity."

Calvin puts his skill as a dogmatician to work for individual believers with his *Brief Confession of Faith*. He does the same for the churches of his homeland with the more extensive *Confession of Faith of the Reformed Churches of France*. He labors

A

long and tirelessly to unite the churches of the Reformation regarding the way in which believers partake of Christ in the Holy Supper by holding forth *The Best Method of Obtaining Concord.*

In all these ways, Calvin is shown to be much more than a mere academic. Indeed, these writings remind us that Calvin was first of all a true Christian, and second only to that, a faithful preacher, teacher, and pastor. He devoted all of his many gifts and abilities to the service of Jesus Christ and the members of His church, even those whom Christ called "the least of these my brethren" (Matt. 25:40).

Readers of Calvin's Catechism can't fail to notice how much it influenced later works such as the Heidelberg Catechism, and the Larger and Shorter Catechisms of the Westminster Divines. Members of congregations in the Dutch Reformed tradition will discover how much their own historic liturgy owes to Calvin's *Forms of Prayer, Form of Administering the Sacraments, Visitation of the Sick,* and his *Form and Manner of Celebrating Marriage* (omitted from the Table of Contents for no apparent reason; it begins on page 123).

Turning to the array of treatises on the sacraments, we call attention to the fact that Calvin's true views on the sacraments are not what some today seem to think they were. Calvin clearly subordinates the administration of the sacraments to the preaching of the Word. The sacraments are "appendages of the gospel" (p. 312). They "effect nothing by themselves" (p. 216). They "do not confer grace" (p. 217). "Believers before, and without the use of the sacraments, communicate with Christ" (p. 218). "No local presence must be imagined" (p. 218). "The body of Christ [is] locally in heaven" (p. 220). "It is not lawful to affix Christ in our imagination to the bread and wine" (p. 220).

Those who may be troubled in conscience, lest they partake of the Lord's Supper unworthily (1 Corinthians 11:27), will find much help in the *Short Treatise on the Lord's Supper.* Indeed, every communicant member of the church will profit from reading this presentation of the purposes and reasons for the institution of the Holy Supper, and the benefits to be received from it.

B

Given the volatility of the issue of the sacraments in Calvin's day, we are not surprised that Calvin engages many of his contemporaries in spirited debate—usually respectfully, but sometimes not. In a lengthy treatise, *Last Admonition to Joachim Westphal* (pp. 346-494), Calvin turns the blazing fire of his polemical guns on Westphal (1510-1574), the German Lutheran who did his best to intensify and harden the growing divide over the sacrament of the Lord's Supper between Swiss and German Reformers. Readers are advised to research the views and careers of such a man, and ask if Calvin's invective was not justified as an expression of righteous anger.

Throughout this book, Calvin clearly and concisely touches on nearly every aspect of the sacraments. In this brief introduction, I wish to focus on Calvin's frequently overlooked emphasis on piety *(pietas)* in the sacraments—especially in the Lord's Supper.

Calvin as Promoter of Piety

Throughout this volume, and elsewhere in his corpus of writings, Calvin views the sacraments as "exercises of piety." He defines them as testimonies "of divine grace toward us, confirmed by an outward sign, with mutual attestation of our piety toward him."[1] The sacraments Foster our faith, strengthen it, and help us offer ourselves as a living sacrifice to God.

For Calvin, as for Augustine, the sacraments are the visible Word. The preached Word comes through our ears; the visible Word, through our eyes. The sacraments hold forth the same Christ as the preached Word but communicate Him through a different mode. We don't get a better Christ in the sacraments, but sometimes we get Christ better.

In the sacraments, God accommodates Himself to our weakness, Calvin says. When we hear the Word indiscriminately proclaimed, we may wonder: "Is it truly for me? Does it really reach me?" However, in the sacraments God reaches out and touches us individually, saying, "Yes, it's for *you*. The promise extends to *you*." Thus, the sacraments minister to our weakness by personalizing the promises for those who trust Christ for salvation.

In the sacraments, God comes to His people, encourages them, enables them to know Christ better, builds them up, and nourishes them in Him. Baptism promotes piety as a symbol of how believers are engrafted into Christ, renewed by the Spirit, and adopted into the family of the heavenly Father.[2] Likewise, the Lord's Supper shows how these adopted children are fed by their loving Father. Calvin loves to refer to the Supper as nourishment for the soul. "The signs are bread and wine which represent for us the invisible food that we receive from the flesh and blood of Christ," he says. "Christ is the only food of our soul, and therefore our heavenly Father invites us to Christ, that refreshed by partaking of him, we may repeatedly gather strength until we shall have reached heavenly immortality."[3]

As believers, we need constant nourishment. We never reach a place where we no longer need to hear the Word, to pray, or to be nurtured by the sacraments. We must constantly grow and develop. As we continue to sin because of our old nature, we are in perpetual need of forgiveness and grace. The Supper, along with the preaching of the Word, repeatedly says to us: We need Christ, we need to be renewed in Christ and built up in Him. The sacraments promise that Christ is present to receive us, bless us, and renew us.

For Calvin, the word *conversion* doesn't only mean the initial act of coming to faith; it also means daily renewal and growth in following Christ. The sacraments lead the way to this daily conversion, Calvin says. They tell us that we need the grace of Christ every day. We must draw strength from Christ, particularly through the body that He sacrificed for us on the cross.

As Calvin writes, "For as the eternal Word of God is the fountain of life so his flesh is the channel to pour out to us the life which resides intrinsically in his divinity. For in his flesh was accomplished man's redemption, in it a sacrifice was offered to atone for sin, and obedience yielded to God to reconcile him to us. It was also filled with the sanctification of the Holy Spirit. Finally having overcome death he was received into the heavenly glory."[4] In other words, the Spirit sanctified Christ's body, which Christ offered on the cross to atone for sin. That body was raised from the dead and received up into heaven. At every stage of our redemption, Christ's

D

body is the pathway to God. In the Supper, then, Christ comes to us and says: "My body is still given for you. By faith you may commune with me and my body with all of its saving benefits."

Calvin teaches that Christ gives not only His benefits but Himself to us in the Supper, just as He gives us Himself and His benefits in the preaching of the Word. Christ also makes us part of His body as He gives us Himself. Calvin cannot precisely explain how that happens in the Supper, for it is better experienced than explained.[5] However, he does say that Christ does not leave heaven to enter the bread. Rather, in the Holy Supper, we are called to lift up our hearts on high to heaven, where Christ is, and not cling to the external bread and wine.

We are lifted up through the work of the Holy Spirit in our hearts. As Calvin writes, "Christ, then, is absent from us in respect of his body, but dwelling in us by his Spirit, he raises us to heaven to himself, transfusing into us the vivifying vigor of his flesh just as the rays of the sun invigorate us by his vital warmth."[6] Partaking of Christ's flesh is a spiritual act rather than a carnal act that involves a "transfusion of substance."[7]

The sacraments can be seen as ladders by which we climb to heaven. "Because we are unable to fly high enough to draw near to God, he has ordained sacraments for us, like ladders," Calvin says. "If a man wishes to leap on high, he will break his neck in the attempt, but if he has steps, he will be able to proceed with confidence. So also, if we are to reach our God, we must use the means which he has instituted since he knows what is suitable for us. God has then given us this wonderful support and encouragement and strength in our weakness."[8]

We must never worship the bread because Christ is not *in* the bread; rather, we find Christ *through* the bread, Calvin says. Just as our mouths receive bread to nourish our physical bodies, so our souls, by faith, receive Christ's body and blood to nourish our spiritual lives.

When we meet Christ in the sacraments, we grow in grace. That is why they are called means of grace. The sacraments encourage us in our progress toward heaven. They promote confidence in God's promises through Christ's "signified and sealed" redemptive death. Since the sacraments are covenants, they contain promises by which "consciences may be roused to an assurance of salvation," Calvin says.[9] The sacraments offer "peace of conscience" and "a special assurance" when the Spirit enables the believer to "see" the Word engraved upon the sacraments.[10]

Finally, the sacraments promote piety by prompting us to thank and praise God for His abundant grace. The sacraments also require us to "attest our piety toward him." As Calvin says, "The Lord recalls the great bounty of his goodness to our memory and stirs us up to acknowledge it; and at the same time he admonishes us not be ungrateful for such lavish liberality, but rather to proclaim it with fitting praises and to celebrate [the Lord's Supper] by giving thanks."[11]

Two things happen in the Supper: the receiving of Christ and the surrender of the believer. The Lord's Supper is not eucharistic from God's perspective, Calvin says, for Christ is not offered afresh. Nor is it eucharistic in terms of man's merit, for we can offer God nothing by way of sacrifice. But it is eucharistic in terms of our thanksgiving.[12] That sacrifice is an indispensable part of the Lord's Supper which, Calvin says, includes "all the duties of love."[13] The Eucharist is an *agape* feast in which communicants cherish each other and testify of the bond that they enjoy with fellow believers in the unity of the body of Christ.[14]

We offer this sacrifice of gratitude in response to Christ's sacrifice for us. We surrender our lives in response to the heavenly banquet God spreads for us in the Supper. By the Spirit's grace, the Supper enables us, as befits a royal priesthood, to offer ourselves as a living sacrifice of praise and thanksgiving to God.[15]

The Lord's Supper thus prompts both piety of grace and piety of gratitude, as Brian Gerrish has shown. The Father's liberality and His children's grateful response are a recurrent theme in Calvin's theology. "We should so revere such a father with grateful piety and burning love," Calvin admonishes us, "as to devote ourselves wholly to his obedience and honor him in everything."[16] The Supper is the liturgical enactment

F

of Calvin's themes of grace and gratitude, which lie at the heart of his piety.[17]

In the Lord's Supper, the human and divine elements of Calvin's piety are held in dynamic tension. In that dynamic interchange, God moves toward the believer while His Spirit consummates the Word-based union. At the same time, the believer moves toward God by contemplating the Savior who refreshes and strengthens him. In this, God is glorified and the believer edified.

Here, then, is a book for readers of many kinds, but especially for believers who need a pastor's help as they take beginning steps in the Christian life, as well as for experienced Christians who desire to experience more deeply the partaking of the Holy Supper as a means of communing with the living and heavenly Christ whom they love and serve.

2919 Leonard NE   *Joel R. Beeke*
Grand Rapids, Michigan   *October, 2002*

[1] *Calvin's Institutes,* 4.14.1 [hereafter, Inst.].

[2] Inst. 4.16.9; Ronald S. Wallace, *Calvin's Doctrine of the Word and Sacrament* (London: Oliver and Boyd, 1953), pp. 175-83. Cf. H.O. Old, *The Shaping of the Reformed Baptismal Rite in the Sixteenth Century* (Grand Rapids: Eerdmans, 1992).

[3] Inst. 4.17.8-12.

[4] Ibid.

[5] Inst. 4.17.24, 33.

[6] Inst. 4.17.12.

[7] *CO* 9:47, 522.

[8] Inst. 4.14.18.

[9] *Commentary* on 1 Corinthians 11:25.

[10] *Commentary* on Matthew 3:11; Acts 2:38; 1 Peter 3:21.

[11] *OS* 1:136, 145.

[12] Inst. 4.18.3.

[13] Inst. 4.18.17.

[14] Inst. 4.17.44.

[15] Inst. 4.18.13.

[16] *OS* 1, 76.

[17] Brian A. Gerrish, *Grace and Gratitude: The Eucharistic Theology of John Calvin* (Minneapolis: Fortress Press, 1993), pp. 19-20.

G

" CALVIN WAS AN ILLUSTRIOUS PERSON, AND NEVER TO BE MENTIONED WITHOUT A PREFACE OF THE HIGHEST HONOUR."—*Bishop Andrews.*

" CALVIN'S COMMENTARIES REMAIN, AFTER THREE CENTURIES, UNPARALLELED FOR FORCE OF MIND, JUSTNESS OF EXPOSITION, AND PRACTICAL VIEWS OF CHRISTIANITY." —*Bishop of Calcutta, (Wilson.)*

[Entered at Stationers' Hall.]

" THE VENERABLE CALVIN." " I HOLD THE MEMORY OF CALVIN IN HIGH VENERATION. HIS WORKS HAVE A PLACE IN MY LIBRARY; AND IN THE STUDY OF THE HOLY SCRIPTURES HE IS ONE OF THE COMMENTATORS I MOST FREQUENTLY CONSULT." —*Bishop Horsley.*

" A MINISTER WITHOUT THIS IS WITHOUT ONE OF THE BEST COMMENTARIES ON THE SCRIPTURES, AND A VALUABLE BODY OF DIVINITY."—*Bickersteth.*

EDINBURGH: PRINTED BY T. CONSTABLE, PRINTER TO HER MAJESTY.

CONTENTS.

		PAGE
TRANSLATOR'S PREFACE, . .		vii
I. CATECHISM OF THE CHURCH OF GENEVA, .		33
II. FORMS OF PRAYER, ...		95
III. FORM OF ADMINISTERING THE SACRAMENTS, .		114
IV. VISITATION OF THE SICK, . . .		127
V. BRIEF CONFESSION OF FAITH, . . .		130
VI. CONFESSION OF FAITH OF THE REFORMED CHURCHES OF FRANCE, ...		137
VII. SHORT TREATISE ON THE LORD'S SUPPER, .		163
VIII. MUTUAL CONSENT AS TO THE SACRAMENTS, .		199
IX. SECOND DEFENCE OF THE SACRAMENTS, .		245
X. LAST ADMONITION TO JOACHIM WESTPHAL, .		346
XI. TRUE PARTAKING OF THE FLESH AND BLOOD OF CHRIST, ...		495
XII. BEST METHOD OF CONCORD ON THE SACRAMENTS,		573

TRANSLATOR'S PREFACE.

THE TRACTS contained in the present Volume discuss subjects which are of the highest importance in themselves, and to some of which special circumstances give an unusual degree of interest at the present time. They conduct us over a very extensive field, presenting us both with general summaries of The Truth, in its most elementary form, and also with learned and profound disquisitions on more recondite points, particularly on the nature of our Saviour's Presence in the Supper—a question which, in employing the pens, has unhappily too often disturbed the equanimity of the most gifted Theologians.

The first Tract in the Volume is THE CATECHISM OF THE CHURCH OF GENEVA, which was first published in French in 1536, and in Latin in 1538. In its original form, it differed very much both in substance and arrangement from the Catechism which is here translated, and which was likewise published both in French and in Latin—in the former in 1541, and in the latter in 1545.

The careful revisions which the work thus underwent, and the translations of it not entrusted to other hands, as was usually done, but executed by CALVIN himself, bespeak the importance which he attached to it, and naturally lead us to inquire what there is in a CATECHISM, considered in itself, and what there is in this Catechism in particular, to justify the anxious care which appears to have been bestowed upon it?

At first sight we are apt to suppose that a Catechism is necessarily one of the humblest of literary labours. Being intended principally for the young, it must deal with those truths only which can be made intelligible to youthful minds ; and hence, as it seems, by its very nature, to exclude everything like profound and original discussion, it may be thought that when such a man as CALVIN engaged in it, he must have regarded it more as a relaxation than a serious employment. In opposition to this hasty conclusion, a slight consideration might convince us that the task which CALVIN undertook in framing his Catechism was every way worthy of his powers—a task, alike delicate, difficult, and important, in which he could not fail without doing serious mischief, nor succeed without conferring a valuable boon, not merely on the limited district which formed the proper sphere of his labour, but on the Christian world.

In regard to all the ordinary branches of knowledge, it has too long been the custom to leave the composition of elementary treatises to those whose names had never before been mentioned in connection with the subjects of which they treat. It would seem to have been regarded as a chief recommendation that they themselves knew little more than the elements, and were thus effectually prevented by their ignorance from overleaping the bounds within which it was meant to confine them. But surely when we consider that an elementary treatise is a representation in miniature of the whole subject of which it treats—a condensation in which every fundamental truth is distinctly expressed, and yet occupies no more space than its relative importance entitles it to claim—it seems to follow of course, that it requires for its right performance, not a mere smattering of knowledge, but such thorough mastery as may place its possessor on a kind of vantage-ground, from which the whole field can be at once accurately and minutely surveyed.

The thorough knowledge, so desirable in framing an elementary work on any ordinary subject, becomes still more essential when the work in question is a general summary from which Christian Societies are to receive their earliest notions, and hence, in all probability, their deepest impres-

sions of religious truth. Here the increased importance of
thorough knowledge arises not merely from the higher order
of the subject, but from another consideration to which it
is of consequence to attend. In the ordinary branches of
knowledge, neither the omission of truths which ought to
have been stated, nor the expansion of others to a greater
degree than their relative importance justifies, can lead to
very disastrous results. The worst which happens is, that
the learner is left ignorant of something with which he ought
to have been made acquainted, and has his mind fatigued,
or it may be perplexed with details which ought to have
been reserved for a later stage of his progress.

In religion, the effect produced is of a more fatal nature.
Here the omission of fundamental truth is equivalent to the
inculcation of deadly error, while the giving of undue pro-
minence to points of comparatively trivial importance is
unquestionably a principal cause of the many controversies
by which Christians, while essentially agreed, have been
unhappily divided. When such points not only find their
way into Catechisms, but stand forth so prominently as to
become a kind of centre round which the whole system of
Theology is made to turn, the natural consequence is, that
the persons into whose early training they so largely enter,
either regard them with a reverence which, in proportion as
it attracts them to their own particular community, repels
them from all others, or on discovering their comparative
insignificance discard them, and too often along with them,
other things which though of far higher moment, had not
been so carefully inculcated.

Christian communities have not been inattentive to the
important purposes for which a Catechism is designed, or to
which it may be made subservient; and accordingly we find
not only that the use of them is generally diffused, but also
that particular Catechisms have been so admirably framed,
that the Churches to which they belong justly regard them
as the most valuable of human compositions. It is unnecessary, and might be invidious to particularize; but it cannot
detract from the due merits of any to say, that while this
CATECHISM OF GENEVA is unquestionably superior to all which

previously existed, the best of those which have since appeared, owe much of their excellence to the free use of its materials, and still more to the admirable standard which it sets before them.

Without attempting anything like a complete analysis of this celebrated Catechism, it may not be improper briefly to glance at its contents, and the manner in which they are arranged.

The general division of the Catechism is into five heads, which treat respectively of Faith, The Law, Prayer, The Word of God, and the Sacraments.

The first head, viz., FAITH, after laying down the fundamental principles, that the chief end of human existence is to know God so as to confide in him, and that this knowledge is to be found only in Christ, contains an exposition of The Apostles' Creed, which, for this purpose, is divided into four parts; the first relating to God the Father, the second to Christ the Son, the third to The Holy Spirit, and the fourth to The Church, and the divine blessings bestowed upon her.

Under the second general head, viz., THE LAW, an exposition is given of The Decalogue, each commandment being taken up separately, and considered not only in its literal sense but in accordance with the enlarged and spiritual views which have been opened up by The Gospel.

The third general head, viz., PRAYER, after carefully explaining that God is the only proper object of prayer, that though the tongue ought usually to be employed, the mind is the only proper instrument, and that, to pray aright, we must pray both under a deep sense of our wants, and full confidence of being heard through the merits of Christ, concludes with an exposition of The Lord's Prayer, which, it is stated, though not the only prayer which we may lawfully use, is undoubtedly the model according to which every prayer should be framed.

The fourth head, viz., THE WORD OF GOD, treats briefly of the authority of Scripture, inculcating the duty of receiving it with full persuasion of heart as certain truth come down from heaven, and of exercising ourselves in it, not only by private reading and meditation, but also by diligent and reverential attendance on the public services at which it is regularly expounded.

The last general head, which treats of THE SACRAMENTS, contains a full explanation of the nature of these solemn Ordinances, and of the most important questions to which they have given rise. Nothing which is essential to the truth seems to be withheld, but at the same time it is impossible not to perceive how careful CALVIN here is to avoid giving unnecessary offence, and how ready he ever was to make all possible sacrifices to gain the great object on which his heart was bent—the establishment of a visible and cordial Union among all true Protestants.

The primary object which CALVIN had in view in preparing his Catechism undoubtedly was to provide for the wants of the district in which Providence had called him to labour. The practice of CATECHISING, which had early been established in the Church, and is indeed of such antiquity that some think they can trace an allusion to it in the first verse of St. Luke's Gospel, in which the word for " instructed " might have been rendered " catechised," had before the Reformation fallen into such neglect, that, according to CALVIN, it was either altogether omitted, or, when in use, was only employed in teaching and thereby perpetuating absurd and puerile superstitions. One of the first and most laudable efforts of the Reformers was to revive the practice, and restore it to its pristine vigour and purity ; and hence, in many instances, when a Church was regularly constituted, catechising was regarded as part of the Public Service. This practice seems to have been nowhere more regularly and systematically observed than in The Church of Geneva under CALVIN, and accordingly in the early French editions of the Catechism we find distinct markings on the margin specifying the different portions allotted for each day's examination. In this way, the whole Catechism was gone over in fifty-five Sundays, the children coming regularly forward to be examined by their Pastor, under the eye of the congregation, on that part of the Catechism which they were understood to have previously prepared.

It seems difficult to imagine a course of training more admirably fitted to imbue all the Members of a Community, young and old, with the whole System of Religious Truth. The previous preparation, the public examination at which parents would naturally be anxious to prove that the due training of their children had not been neglected, and the many opportunities of incidental instruction which each lesson would afford to the Examinator, more especially on those days when that office was performed by Calvin in person, all must have contributed powerfully to the desired result, and made The Church of Geneva, what indeed it was then admitted to be, one of the most enlightened Churches in Christendom.

But though the fruits which Calvin might thus expect to reap from his Catechism, within the district of Geneva, were valuable enough to justify the anxious care which he appears to have expended on it, it is impossible to read the Dedication without perceiving higher aims, and admiring the lofty aspirations with which Calvin's mind was familiar. While he occupied the comparatively humble office of a Pastor of Geneva, and discharged all its duties with minute fidelity, as if he had had no other sphere, if ever it could have been said of any man, it may be emphatically said of him, that his field was the world. He could not even write a Catechism without endeavouring to employ it as a bond of general Christian Union.

In one part of the Dedication he speaks despondingly of the prospects of Christendom, and almost goes the length of predicting a speedy return to barbarism. It is not difficult to account for these feelings. In contending with the colossal power of ROME, which, though at one time apparently paralyzed, had again brought all her forces into the field, Protestants could not hope either to make new conquests or secure those which they had made, without being united. And what was there to prevent their union? Agreed on all points of primary importance, there was common ground on which they could league together, and there was also enough of common danger to call for that simple exercise of wisdom which consists in sinking minor differences on the approach of an exterminating foe. In such circumstances, it must have been galling beyond description to a mind constituted like CALVIN's to see the Truth, which might have been triumphant, not only arrested in its course, but in danger of being trampled in the dust, because those who ought to have combined in its defence, and so formed an invincible phalanx, were with strange infatuation wasting all their energies on petty intestine disputes.

Still, how gloomy soever the prospect might be, CALVIN knew well that the course of duty being plain, the only thing which remained for him was to follow it, and humbly submit to whatever might be the result. He had laboured incessantly to promote Christian Union, and would labour still, seizing every opportunity of promoting it with as much alacrity as if he had felt assured of its success. Hence, in the midst of all this despondency, we see him quietly engaged in what must at any time have been rather an irksome task, in translating his own French into Latin, because he had reason to believe, that by thus securing a more extensive use of his Catechism, he might promote the cause of Union.

The thought even appears to have passed through his mind, Might it not be possible for all sound Protestants to concur in using one common Catechism? He distinctly affirms that nothing could be more desirable; but immediately after, with that good sense which never allowed him amidst his loftiest imaginings to lose sight of what was practicable, he adds, that it were vain to hope that this object, how desirable soever it might be, could ever be attained, that every separate division of the Church would for many reasons desire to have its own Catechism, and that, therefore, instead of striving to prevent this, the wisest course was for each to prepare its own Catechism, guarding, with the utmost care, against error, and then, on interchanging Catechisms, and learning how much they were one in fact, though not in form, cultivate that mutual respect and good will which constitutes the essence of true Union, and is indeed far more valuable than mere Visible Unity.

Though CALVIN could thus easily part with the idea of a

universal Catechism, he must certainly have been gratified with the wide circulation which his Catechism obtained ; and we can easily understand his feeling of honest pride, when rebuking a writer who had affected to sneer at his adherents as insignificant in number, he tells him more than once of the three hundred thousand who had declared their assent to his Catechism.

In mentioning this specific number, CALVIN seems to refer to THE PROTESTANT CHURCH OF FRANCE, which, after full discussion in its Synods, came to the resolution of adopting CALVIN'S CATECHISM unchanged. The resolution was not less wise in them than it was honourable, and must have been gratifying to him. Obliged to flee from his country for his life, he had ever after continued in exile, but thousands and tens of thousands rejoiced to receive the law from his mouth ; and now, by a formal act, expressing their admiration of his talents, and perfect confidence in his integrity, resolved, that The First Elements of Religious Truth should be communicated to their children in the very words which he had taught them. In adverting to this Resolution, we are reminded of the sad changes which afterwards took place, when the Reformed Church of France, not so much through the persecution of her enemies, atrocious though it was, as by her own voluntary declension from the faith, became almost annihilated. If she is again to become what she once was, it can only be by retracing her steps and returning to her first faith. In adopting this better course, one of her earliest proceedings should be the formal resumption of CALVIN'S CATECHISM.

The next TRACTS of the present volume are LITURGICAL, and possess a considerable degree of interest, both as exhibiting the FORM OF CHURCH SERVICE, which, under the auspices of CALVIN, was adopted at GENEVA, and also as containing at least the germ of what still appears to some a very important desideratum—a regular FORM OF PUBLIC WORSHIP, with such a degree of latitude in the use of it as leaves full scope for ministerial freedom.

Next follow two CONFESSIONS OF FAITH—the one general,

intended as a Compendium for common use, and furnishing us, within very narrow limits, with an admirable SUMMARY OF FUNDAMENTAL ARTICLES ; the other, a particular CONFESSION OF THE CHURCH OF FRANCE, intended to be employed on a special occasion, and still justly regarded as a document of great intrinsic value and deep historical interest.

The latter CONFESSION, as its title bears, was written in 1562, during the War, with the view of being presented to a Diet of the German Empire, held at FRANKFORT—a design, however, which could not be accomplished, in consequence of the way being closed.

The War here referred to was the Civil War which broke out in France between the PROTESTANTS, headed by the Prince of Condé, and the CATHOLICS, headed by the Duke of Guise. In 1562, shortly after the celebrated CONFERENCE OF POISSY, and partly in consequence of it, the Protestants had obtained an Edict which allowed the free exercise of their Religion. Trusting to the legal security thus guaranteed, they laid aside the concealments to which they had often been compelled to resort, and held their meetings in the face of day. Whether or not the Court, ruled as it was by a CATHERINE DE MEDICIS, ever intended to give fair effect to an Edict which owed its existence much more to fear than to liberal policy, it is needless here to discuss. The fact is certain, that the Edict had scarcely been published when the Duke of Guise broke in with armed force on a numerous meeting of Protestants assembled for Public Worship at Vassy, under the protection of the law, and perpetrated an indiscriminate massacre. Instead of attempting to deny the atrocity, he openly gloried in it, and appeared at Court like one who had, by a distinguished service, merited new marks of favour.

THE PROTESTANTS had now no alternative. The law, which had been most rigidly enforced, so long as it made sanguinary enactments against them, had become a dead letter the moment it pretended to take them under its protection ; and, therefore, it was clear that they must either submit to utter extermination or take up arms in their own defence.

Thus, not from choice, but from the powerlessness of the law, or the treachery of those who administered it, the Protestants were hurried into war. In order to maintain it, they did not confine themselyes to the forces which they might be able to bring into the field, but naturally looked abroad, and endeavoured to make common cause with the Protestants of other countries. Accordingly, they not only despatched an agent to the Diet of the German Empire, which was then about to meet at Frankfort, in order to secure the countenance of the Protestant Princes, whose sympathy with them on other occasions had more than once been substantially expressed ; but they also, probably through the instrumentality of BEZA, obtained the aid of CALVIN, who, aware of the prejudices which their enemies had endeavoured to excite against them by a gross misrepresentation of their doctrinal views, employed his pen in drawing up the admirable CONFESSION which is here translated ; and which, while disdaining to conciliate favour by suppressing any part of the truth, possesses the merit of stating it in its least offensive form.

It has been already mentioned, that the existence of the War rendered it impossible to forward the document in time for presentation to THE DIET, and hence, as a cessation of hostilities took place shortly after, it may be thought that the publication of the Document in such circumstances, was not only unnecessary but unseasonable, as only tending to keep alive feelings which every lover of peace must now have been anxious to suppress. It is not difficult, however, to find sufficient ground to justify the publication, not only in the value of the document itself, but also in the conviction which CALVIN, in common with the most of his party, appears to have entertained, that the peace which had been too hastily patched up would not prove of long duration. The CONFESSION thus published became a kind of *manifesto*, proclaiming the Religious System which THE PROTESTANTS OF FRANCE entertained, and by which they were determined in future and at all hazards to abide.

The publication of some such Manifesto was indeed imperatively required, in order to counteract the crafty policy which their enemies had pursued. Taking advantage of the serious differences which existed among Protestants, they began to profess a great respect for THE CONFESSION OF AUGSBURG, and to insinuate that if the Protestants of France would consent to adopt it as their National Confession, the chief obstacles to their distinct recognition by the State would be removed.

The hollowness of this device is very apparent, and yet it is impossible to deny that it was dexterously fitted to accomplish the end which its unprincipled contrivers had in view. It flattered the prejudices of those who were strenuous in maintaining the Augsburg Confession, amusing them with the fond hope of one day seeing that Confession publicly recognised as the Religious Standard of all great Protestant communities; and it repressed the sympathy which they naturally felt for their suffering brethren in France, by suggesting a doubt whether these sufferings, instead of being endured in the common cause of Protestantism, were not rather the result of a bigoted attachment to the peculiarities of their own creed. On the other hand, the very mention of the Augsburg Confession, as an universal Standard, aroused suspicion in the minds of those who were not disposed to embrace it, and made them backward in soliciting the expression of a sympathy which in return for any present relief might ultimately have the effect of subjecting them to a galling yoke. It was necessary, therefore, that the idea of compelling the Reformed Church of France to adopt the Augsburg Confession should at once be set at rest; and it clearly appears, both from the preface to this CONFESSION drawn up by CALVIN, and from other documents, that this was not the least important of the objects which CALVIN contemplated in now publishing it. In addition to its intrinsic worth, the interest which it excites is heightened by the fact that the life of its distinguished author was drawing to a close, and that he was already suffering from that accumulation of diseases under which, though his mind retained all its vigour, his body gradually sunk.

The next TRACT of the Volume introduces us to one of the most difficult questions in the whole compass of Theology—one in regard to which, after centuries of discussion, the Christian world is as far as ever from being agreed. There is certainly something very mysterious in the fact, that the most solemn and affecting Ordinance of our Religion, instituted by our Saviour on the very night in which he was betrayed, and expressly intended to unite his followers in the closest bonds of fellowship with himself, and with one another, should not only have given rise to the most conflicting opinions, but been converted into a kind of party badge, Communities employing their particular views of it as tests of Christian brotherhood, admitting those who subscribed to their views, and of course repelling all who declined to subscribe to them.

At one extreme, we have the Church of Rome, under pretence of adhering to the literal sense, inventing the dogma of TRANSUBSTANTIATION, and supplanting the simple Ordinance of Scripture by THE MASS, in which none of its original features can be recognised; while, at the other extreme, we have a body of most respectable Religionists not only avowedly abandoning the literal sense, but, under the pretext of spiritualizing it, objecting to every form of external celebration. Between these extremes we have a great variety of views, which seem however to admit of being reduced to three great classes,—the views, *First*, of those who regard the Elements of The Supper merely as Memorials of our Saviour's death and Signs of his spiritual blessings; *Secondly*, of those who regard them not merely as Signs but also as Seals, holding that Christ, though not bodily, is spiritually present, and is in an ineffable manner actually received, not by all who communicate, but only by those who communicate worthily: And *Thirdly*, of those who, though rejecting the dogma of Transubstantiation, which asserts that after consecration the Elements are no longer Bread and Wine, but material flesh and blood, still strenuously contend for such a literal sense as makes Christ bodily present in the Elements, and consequently gives him, under the Elements, to all who partake of them—to the unworthy as well as the worthy—though with benefit only to the latter.

The wide difference between the first and the third views early led to a very violent controversy, in which the most distinguished Reformers were ranged on opposite sides, and too often forgot the respect which they owed both to themselves and to one another. Whether ZUINGLIUS ever meant to maintain that The Sacraments are nothing more than empty Signs is very questionable. If he did not mean to maintain this, his language in his earlier Writings is very unguarded; but there is philosophy as well as charity in the observation of CALVIN, that both ZUINGLIUS and ŒCO-LOMPADIUS, while intent on the refutation of the Mass, which they regarded as the worst of the Papal corruptions, not only carried their arguments as far as they could legitimately go, but sometimes, through misconstruction, seemed to impugn views which they unquestionably entertained.

It is not fair to lay hold of incidental expressions which a writer may have employed in discussing one subject, and interpret them as if they had been uttered calmly and dispassionately for the avowed purpose of conveying his sentiments on some other subject. There are few writers who could bear to be subjected to such rigorous and disingenuous treatment, and who might not be made by means of it to countenance sentiments which they would be the first to disavow. True it is, however, that expressions thus incidentally used have too often proved the sparks from which conflagrations have arisen, and the peace of the Christian world has again and again been disturbed, because great Theologians, when essentially at one, have first brooded over imaginary differences, and then allowing their passions to become inflamed, have unfitted themselves for either giving or receiving candid explanations.

CALVIN was convinced that something of this kind had occurred in regard to the unhappy controversy between ZUINGLIUS and LUTHER and their respective followers. He was not unaware that points of great importance were involved, and nothing would have been more foreign to

his character than to represent these differences as trivial
and unworthy of serious consideration; but believing them
to be neither so numerous nor so vital as was supposed, he
imagined it possible, by means of an honest and faithful
statement on the subject, to furnish a kind of rallying point
for all men of moderate views, and at the same time gradually calm down the violence of those who were most deeply
committed in the strife.   He accordingly published his
TREATISE ON THE LORD'S SUPPER, a translation of which
enriches the present Volume, and with such success that it
was not only generally welcomed but received commendation in quarters from which it was least to have been expected—even LUTHER speaking of it in terms alike honourable to himself and gratifying to the heart of CALVIN.

In this Treatise CALVIN advocates the *second* Class of
views to which we have above referred.   He distinctly
asserts a True and Real Presence of Christ in The Supper—
a Spiritual Presence by which Christ imparts himself and
all His blessings, not to all indiscriminately, but to those
only whom a living faith prepares to receive Him.   To enjoy
this presence, we must not seek him in earthly Elements,
but raise our thoughts to heaven, and comply with the
well-known injunction of the primitive Church—SURSUM
CORDA.   CALVIN seems to recoil with a kind of instinctive
abhorrence from the idea that Christ is, in any sense of the
term, Eaten by the ungodly; and when the startling question is asked, How, then, can it be said that unworthy Communicants are " guilty of the body and blood of the Lord ?"
he replies, that Christ being offered to them, as He is to all,
their guilt consists not in receiving Christ, (an act which
must always bring the richest blessings along with it, and
to which no man can ever owe his condemnation,) but in
refusing to receive Him, their evil heart of unbelief precluding the only means of access, and so pouring contempt
on His holy Ordinance.

In opposition to those who rigidly insist on what is called
the literal sense of The Words of Institution, CALVIN shows
that throughout The Sacred Volume, whenever Sacraments
are mentioned, a peculiar form of expression is employed—

the name of the thing signified being uniformly given to
the sign—and that, therefore, to interpret without reference
to this important fact is at once to betray great ignorance of
Scripture phraseology and deviate from the analogy of faith.

When he proceeds to consider the modern controversies
by which Protestant Bodies have been so unhappily divided,
he adopts the most pacific tone, and speaks a language
which it is impossible not to admire. Touching with the
utmost tenderness on any errors of judgment or asperities
of temper into which the great luminaries of THE REFORMA-
TION had been betrayed, he gladly embraces the opportunity of paying a due tribute to their great talents and
distinguished services. He bids us reflect on the thick
darkness in which the world was enveloped when they first
arose, and then cease to wonder that the whole Truth was
not at once revealed to them. The astonishing thing is, that
they were able to deliver themselves and others from such a
multitude of errors. Considering the invaluable blessings
which they have been instrumental in bestowing upon us, it
were base ingratitude not to regard them with the deepest
reverence. Our true course unquestionably is, not indeed
to imitate but tread lightly on their faults, and at the same
time labour diligently in the imitation of their virtues.

The doctrine which CALVIN inculcates in this Treatise,
and which he ever steadily maintained, has been adopted by
some of the most distinguished Churches of Christendom,
and in particular seems to be identical with that which is
contained in The Public Confessions of this country. Accordingly, BISHOP COSENS, in his celebrated History of
Transubstantiation, quotes at considerable length from CAL-
VIN's Writings—among others, from this Treatise on The
Supper—and distinctly declares (Chapter ii. § 20) that CAL-
VIN's "words, in his Institutions and elsewhere, are such, so
conformable to the style and mind of The Ancient Fathers,
that no Catholic Protestant would wish to use any other."

The attempt at conciliation which CALVIN had thus so
admirably begun he never afterwards lost sight of. It became a kind of ruling passion with him; and hence, whenever in other countries men of like minds felt desirous to

co-operate in this truly Christian labour, they invariably applied to CALVIN.

Among those who thus distinguished themselves must be mentioned ARCHBISHOP CRANMER, who held the most liberal and enlightened views on the subject of Protestant Union, which he laboured anxiously to promote. Among the Zurich Letters, published by the Parker Society, are several from him, addressed to the leading Reformers, and urging them to take a lesson even from their enemies. He reminds them how the Romish Church had convoked her COUNCIL OF TRENT, and was vigorously endeavouring to regain what she had lost by infusing new vigour into her corrupt system ; and he asks, in the particular Letter which he addressed to CALVIN, " Shall we neglect to call together a Godly Synod for the Refutation of Error, and for Restoring and Propagating the Truth ? They are, as I am informed, making Decrees respecting the Worship of the Host ; wherefore we ought to leave no stone unturned, not only that we may guard others against this Idolatry, but also that we may ourselves come to an Agreement on The Sacrament. It cannot escape your prudence, how exceedingly The Church of God has been injured by dissensions and varieties of opinion concerning the Sacrament of Unity ; and though they are now in some measure removed, yet I could wish for an Agreement on this doctrine, not only as regards the subject itself, but also with respect to the words and forms of expression. You have now my wish, about which I have also written to MASTERS PHILIP (MELANCTHON) and BULLINGER, and I pray you to deliberate among yourselves as to the means by which this Synod may be assembled with the greatest convenience."

In the above extract the ARCHBISHOP speaks of Dissensions and varieties of Opinion concerning The Sacrament of Unity as having been in some measure removed. This undoubtedly refers to the celebrated CONSENSUS TIGURINUS, which had been recently drawn up, and to which, as forming the next TRACT in our present Series, it will now be proper briefly to refer.

Though THE CHURCHES OF SWITZERLAND were substantially agreed as to THE SACRAMENTS, there were shades of difference which, so long as they were not properly defined, it was easy for the ill-disposed to exaggerate, and which even the well-disposed regarded with uneasiness, as tending to unsettle their minds, and suggesting doubts with reference to a solemn ordinance on which it was most desirable that their views should be clear and decided.

As usual CALVIN became the leader in this work of conciliation, and that nothing might interfere to prevent or retard its accomplishment, though then suffering from the severest of domestic calamities, he resolved, in company with his venerable colleague FAREL, to undertake a journey to ZURICH. The very minuteness of many of the points which it was proposed to settle, made them unfit to be the subject of an epistolary correspondence. Such points, by the mere fact of being committed to writing, and formally discussed, acquire an importance which does not properly belong to them. It cannot be doubted, therefore, that CALVIN acted with his wonted tact and practical wisdom in determining on a personal interview.

It would be most interesting to seat ourselves along with the distinguished men by whom THE CONFERENCE was conducted, and follow it out into all its details ; but we must content ourselves with a simple statement of the result. The respect which they had previously felt for each other soon rose to the warmth of friendship ; all obstacles melted away, and an AGREEMENT was drawn up, consisting of a Series of Articles, in which all points of importance relating to The Sacraments are clearly and succinctly defined. The issue of The Conference gave general satisfaction, and CALVIN and FAREL returned home with the blessing of peacemakers on their heads.

It is scarcely congruous to talk of victory, when, properly speaking, there was no contest, and the only thing done was the establishment of peace ; and yet it is but justice to CALVIN to remark, that if any who subscribed the Agreement must be understood by so doing to have changed the views which they previously entertained, he was not of the number, as there is not one of the Articles which he had not maintained in one or other of his Works.

After the Agreement was drawn up, CALVIN urged the immediate publication of it. Certain parties, from prudential considerations, would fain have delayed ; but this only made him more anxious to proceed, and place the great object which had been gained beyond the reach of danger. The important results anticipated from the publication of the Agreement he thus states in a Letter to Viret, (Henri's Life of Calvin by Stebbing,)—" The hearts of good men will be cheered by that which has taken place : our constancy and resolution will derive more strength from it, and we shall be better able to break the power of the wicked. They who had formed an unworthy opinion of us will see that we proposed nothing but what is good and right. Many who are still in a state of uncertainty will now know on what they ought to depend. And those in distant lands who differ from us in opinion, will soon, we hope, offer us their hand." He adds, " Posterity will have a witness to our faith which it could not have derived from parties in a state of strife ! but this we must leave to God."

The important service which The Agreement performed by extinguishing strife in the Swiss Church, was only part of the grand result which CALVIN was contemplating. The attempt which had once been made to reconcile ZUINGLIUS and LUTHER having lamentably failed, had had the contrary effect of widening the breach between their adherents ; and hence a general idea among the Lutherans was, that THE SWISS did not acknowledge any Real Presence of Christ in The Sacrament. So long as that idea existed, it operated as an insuperable barrier to any Union between these Churches. That barrier, however, was now removed, as THE AGREEMENT which had been placed before the world distinctly recognised, and of course bound every one who subscribed it to recognise a Real Presence and Actual Participation of Christ in the Sacrament. Hence CALVIN appears to have reverted at this time more hopefully than ever to the practicability of effecting that General Protestant Union on which his heart had long been set, and in regard to which we have already seen him in communication with an admirable coadjutor in the person of ARCHBISHOP CRANMER. CALVIN may have been rendered more sanguine by the fact that his views on THE SACRAMENT were shared by the noblest intellect in Germany. MELANCTHON had long felt dissatisfaction with LUTHER'S views on this subject, but his natural timidity, increased by the ascendency of LUTHER, had prevented him from giving public expression to it. If any scruples still remained, it was understood that THE AGREEMENT OF ZURICH had removed them ; and it was therefore hoped, more especially as his great master had been called to his reward, that he would now come manfully forward, and avowing the belief which he undoubtedly entertained, that The Real Presence which The Agreement of Zurich recognised was the only presence which it was essential to maintain, become the advocate of a GREAT PROTESTANT LEAGUE on the basis of that Agreement.

But notwithstanding of all these hopeful signs, and the satisfaction which was generally expressed, distant murmurs began to be heard, and ultimately increased, so that CALVIN felt compelled to come forward with the admirable EXPOSITION OF THE ARTICLES OF AGREEMENT which form the next Tract in our Series.

In the Dedication of this Treatise to his friends at Zurich, and the other ministers throughout Switzerland, CALVIN expresses the greatest reluctance to be again drawn into controversy. He speaks with just commendation of the leading divines of the Lutheran Communion who had either approved of The Agreement, or, by maintaining silence, had at least proved their unwillingness to disturb the peace. On the other hand, he cannot dissemble the mingled feelings of contempt and detestation produced in his mind by individuals, equally deficient in intellect and Christian temper, who were going about as if they had "lighted a Furies' torch," and were determined to be satisfied with nothing short of a Religious War. So reluctant, however, is he to perpetuate the strife, that though he feels compelled to take special notice of the violence and absurdity of one of these

individuals, he withholds his name, that he may thus leave
him an opportunity of retracing his steps, and retiring from
a contest in which, though he may be able to do mischief,
he can only reap disgrace.

The individual thus referred to, but not named, and who
afterwards obtained an unenviable notoriety, was JOACHIM
WESTPHAL, one of the Ministers of Hamburg. He appears to
have been one of those who, determined at all events to obtain
a name, have no scruple as to the means, provided they can
secure the end. Instead of taking CALVIN's advice in good
part, and retiring from a contest to which he was unequal,
and for engaging in which he certainly could not plead any
particular call, he again came forward with a virulence and
scurrility which perhaps ought to have convinced CALVIN
that it was scarcely consistent with the respect which he
owed to himself to take any farther notice of him.

As if all Agreement were sinful in its own nature, he
takes offence at the very name, and with strange inconsistency attacks CALVIN at one time for abandoning opinions
to which he stood pledged, and at another for not abandoning but only hypocritically pretending to abandon them !
Ridiculous charges like these, which only affected CALVIN as
an individual, he could easily have disregarded, but WEST-
PHAL had been connected with certain atrocious proceedings
which had stung CALVIN to the quick ; and there cannot be
a doubt, that in the repeated castigations which CALVIN now
inflicted, he meant WESTPHAL to understand that he was
paying part of the penalty due for his share in these proceedings.

On MARY's accession to the Throne of England, a Reformed Congregation in London, under the ministry of JOHN
A LASCO, was immediately dispersed. A LASCO, who was a
personal friend of CALVIN, and stood very high in his esteem,
embarked in a vessel with 175 individuals. A storm arising, the vessel, in distress, ran into Elsinore ; but so vindic-
tive was the Lutheran feeling there that the Exiles were
immediately ordered to quit the coast. On their arrival at
Hamburg, the same abominable treatment was repeated.

WESTPHAL appears to have been personally implicated in

these proceedings ; and so far from showing any compunc-
tion, glories in the deed. Not satisfied with his own atrocious inhospitality, he calls upon the other towns of Germany to imitate it ; and, as if he had been possessed by the
spirit of a fiend, exults in the Persecutions of The Bloody
Mary, as a just judgment on The Church of England for
not holding Lutheran views on The Sacraments.

The mixed feeling of pity for the poor Exiles, and indignation at the conduct of their persecutors, occasions some of
the finest bursts which is to be found in any of Calvin's
Writings, while throughout the whole of this Sacramentarian
Controversy we every now and then meet with private allu-
sions and digressions of an interesting nature. There is,
moreover, a great amount of Patristic learning, Calvin
labouring, and with great success, to show that his views on
The Sacrament are in strict accordance with those of the
best and earliest of The Fathers.

This unhappy revival of the controversy not only opened
up the old questions which are accordingly exhibited in all
the points of view in which Westphal and his coadjutors
were able to place them, but also incidentally brought various
other matters under discussion.

The dogma of a bodily presence in the Supper naturally
leads to a consideration of the possible ubiquity of our Saviour's body. Westphal and his party, in maintaining the
affirmative, not only do not pretend to explain how one and
the same body can be in numerous different places at the
same time, but discountenance the very idea of being able
to give any explanation. Assuming the fact that such an
ubiquity is clearly taught, they complain loudly of the introduction of what they call physical arguments into religion,
and descant at large on the omnipotence of God.

In considering these arguments, Calvin is led to make
many important observations on the interpretation of Scripture, and the distinct provinces assigned to Reason and
Revelation. When God speaks, men must listen implicitly ;
and if what he says is mysterious, it is thereby the fitter for
the exercise of an humble faith. But it is an abuse of the language of piety to declaim about the omnipotence of God when

the question considered is not what God can do, but what he has told us he will do. In addressing us at all, he treats us as rational beings, capable of understanding the meaning of language ; and when, instead of attempting to pass judgment on what he has said, or to pry presumptuously into matters which he has chosen to conceal, we anxiously endeavour to ascertain the meaning which his words bear, there cannot be doubt, that in so doing we employ our reason for the very purpose for which it has been bestowed.

Another point incidentally brought forward is the great principle of Toleration, and the power of the civil magistrate in matters of religion.

WESTPHAL repeatedly denounces the views of his opponents as heretical, and calls for their extermination by the sword. He even denies their title to be heard, on the simple ground that they have been already condemned by general consent. The absurdity of any Protestant body putting forward a claim to general consent for any one of its peculiar tenets is very obvious, and is well exposed by CALVIN, who reminds WESTPHAL, that if general consent, or rather, majority of consents, is to give the law in religious controversy, they must both quit the field, and make way for another party possessing a claim with which theirs cannot stand in competition. If consent is to be WESTPHAL's law, a very slight change will bring him, perhaps, to the only place where he is fit to be—the camp of the Pope.

In regard to Toleration, it must be confessed that CALVIN's views are not much more enlightened than those of his opponent. They both agree that error is a proper subject of cognizance by the civil magistrate, and ought, if necessary, to be put down by the sword ; and the only apparent difference is, that while WESTPHAL, listening only to the violence of passion, calls for condemnation without a hearing, CALVIN strenuously maintains that such condemnation is unjust, because it provides no security against the condemnation of truth. According to his view, therefore, a candid hearing and careful examination ought always to precede.

It is curious that a mind like CALVIN's could come thus

far, and then stop. It is not easy to see how any degree of examination could make the condemnation to be just, which would have been unjust without it. Take, for instance, any of the numerous Protestant martyrdoms which were taking place in France at this period, and of which CALVIN so often speaks in terms of just indignation. Would the murders then perpetrated, by consigning unoffending Protestants to the flames, have become justifiable, if, before sentence was pronounced, every plea which the poor victims could urge had been fully heard, and patiently considered? Unquestionably, CALVIN would have been one of the first to maintain that the proceedings were atrocious in their own nature, and could not cease to be so in consequence of any degree of strictness and regularity with which they might be conducted. It would seem, then, that the application of such a test as this might have sufficed to convince CALVIN, that if Toleration was to be defended at all, it must be on broader ground than that on which he had placed it. This, however, is a subject on which the whole world was then in error. In regard to it, CALVIN was certainly not behind his age. For many reasons, it is much to be wished that he had been in advance of it; but as he was not, nothing can be more unfair than the virulent censure with which he has been assailed for acting on principles which he honestly held, and the soundness of which, moreover, was all but universally recognised.

The harmony which all good and moderate men earnestly longed for, and which at one time seemed almost secured by The Agreement of Zurich, having been broken up by the perverse proceedings of WESTPHAL, a host of new controversialists appeared, and so uniformly fastened upon CALVIN as the object of their attacks, that in the next Tract of our volume, viz., "ON THE TRUE PARTAKING OF THE FLESH AND BLOOD OF CHRIST IN THE HOLY SUPPER," he speaks as if petulant and rabid men had from all quarters entered into a conspiracy against him. In this work, while he proves himself still able and willing to defend the truth, he gives free and affecting utterance to his earnest longings for repose. He was suffering much from disease, and perhaps had

a presentiment that his course on earth was soon to termi-
nate. How desirable, then, that he could retire from the
storm, and spend the evening of his days in peace!

To no man, perhaps, was CALVIN's heart more closely knit
than to MELANCTHON. They were perfectly at one on the
great controversy by which the Protestant bodies was so
unhappily divided; and though MELANCTHON had not come
forward and avowed his sentiments so openly as might have
been expected, still CALVIN had hoped much from the high
estimation in which he was held by all, and the great and
well-earned influence which he possessed among his own
countrymen. But MELANCTHON was now dead; and CALVIN,
in giving utterance to his feelings on the event, seems almost
to say that he wishes he had died along with him. There
are few passages more impressive in CALVIN's writings than
that in which he here apostrophizes his departed friend:
" O Philip Melancthon! For I appeal to thee, who art now
living with God in Christ, and art there waiting for me, till
I may be united with thee in beatific rest." It were out of
place to quote farther; but the passage may safely be appealed to against those who, while admitting the great intellect of CALVIN, represent him as having steeled his heart
against all the softer and more amiable qualities of our
nature.

On many accounts, therefore, and not merely as able discussions of the subject to which they more immediately refer,
the TREATISES, which form the concluding part of the present Volume, constitute an important branch of CALVIN's
Writings, and could not be excluded from any Collection of
his Works. The only subject of regret is, that from the endless variety of forms in which the different parties, whom
WESTPHAL induced to take up his quarrel, stated their objections, the answers are necessarily repeated almost to weariness; and still more, that CALVIN, in dealing out the chas-
tisement which WESTPHAL undoubtedly deserved, has too
often let fall expressions, to which such a pen as his ought
never to have stooped. These, however, are comparatively
trivial blemishes, which the candid reader can easily over-

look, while he dwells with admiration on the excellencies with which the Work abounds.

In the conclusion, CALVIN again returns to his favourite topic, and in a few brief propositions, points out THE BEST METHOD OF OBTAINING CONCORD. This subject again occupies the Public mind, and nowhere are the principles on which it ought to be attempted, or the means by which it is to be carried into effect, more ably stated than in these TREATISES OF CALVIN.

H. B.

EDINBURGH, *December* 1849.

CATECHISM

OF

THE CHURCH OF GENEVA,

BEING A

FORM OF INSTRUCTION FOR CHILDREN

IN

THE DOCTRINE OF CHRIST.

DEDICATION.

JOHN CALVIN TO THE FAITHFUL MINISTERS OF CHRIST
THROUGHOUT EAST FRIESLAND, WHO PREACH THE
PURE DOCTRINE OF THE GOSPEL.

Seeing it becomes us to endeavour by all means that unity of
faith, which is so highly commended by Paul, shine forth among
us, to this end chiefly ought the formal profession of faith which
accompanies our common baptism to have reference. Hence it
were to be wished, not only that a perpetual consent in the doctrine
of piety should appear among all, but also that one CATECHISM
were common to all the Churches. But as, from many causes, it
will scarcely ever obtain otherwise than that each Church shall
have its own Catechism, we should not strive too keenly to
prevent this; provided, however, that the variety in the mode of
teaching is such, that we are all directed to one Christ, in whose
truth being united together, we may grow up into one body and
one spirit, and with the same mouth also proclaim whatever belongs to the sum of faith. Catechists not intent on this end, besides
fatally injuring the Church, by sowing the materials of dissension
in religion, also introduce an impious profanation of baptism. For
where can any longer be the utility of baptism unless this remain
as its foundation—that we all agree in one faith?

Wherefore, those who publish Catechisms ought to be the more
carefully on their guard, lest, by producing anything rashly, they
may not for the present only, but in regard to posterity also, do
grievous harm to piety, and inflict a deadly wound on the Church.

This much I wished to premise, as a declaration to my readers,
that I myself too, as became me, have made it my anxious care
not to deliver any thing in this Catechism of mine that is not
agreeable to the doctrine received among all the pious. This de-

claration will not be found vain by those who will read with candour and sound judgment. I trust I have succeeded at least so far that my labour, though it should not satisfy, will be acceptable to all good men, as being in their opinion useful.

In writing it in Latin, though some perhaps will not approve of the design, I have been influenced by many reasons, all of which it is of no use to detail at present. I shall only select such as seem to me sufficient to obviate censure.

First, In this confused and divided state of Christendom, I judge it useful that there should be public testimonies, whereby churches which, though widely separated by space, agree in the doctrine of Christ, may mutually recognise each other. For besides that this tends not a little to mutual confirmation, what is more to be desired than that mutual congratulations should pass between them, and that they should devoutly commend each other to the Lord? With this view, bishops were wont in old time, when as yet consent in faith existed and flourished among all, to send Synodal Epistles beyond sea, by which, as a kind of badges, they might maintain sacred communion among the churches. How much more necessary is it now, in this fearful devastation of the Christian world, that the few churches which duly worship God, and they too scattered and hedged round on all sides by the profane synagogues of Antichrist, should mutually give and receive this token of holy union, that they may thereby be incited to that fraternal embrace of which I have spoken?

But if this is so necessary in the present day, what shall our feelings be concerning posterity, about which I am so anxious, that I scarcely dare to think? Unless God miraculously send help from heaven, I cannot avoid seeing that the world is threatened with the extremity of barbarism. I wish our children may not shortly feel, that this has been rather a true prophecy than a conjecture. The more, therefore, must we labour to gather together, by our writings, whatever remains of the Church shall continue, or even emerge, after our death. Writings of a different class will show what were our views on all subjects in religion, but the agreement which our churches had in doctrine cannot be seen with clearer evidence than from catechisms. For therein will appear, not only what one man or other once taught, but with what rudiments learned and unlearned alike amongst us, were constantly imbued from childhood, all the faithful holding them as their formal symbol of Christian communion. This was indeed my principal reason for publishing this Catechism.

A second reason, which had no little weight with me, was, because I heard that it was desired by very many who hoped it would not be unworthy of perusal. Whether they are right or wrong in so judging is not mine to decide, but it became me to yield to their wish. Nay, necessity was almost laid upon me, and I could not with impunity decline it. For having seven years before published a brief summary of religion, under the name of a Catechism, I feared that if I did not bring forward this one, I should cause (a thing I wished not) that the former should on the other hand be excluded. Therefore if I wished to consult the public good, it behoved me to take care that this one which I preferred should occupy the ground.

Besides, I deem it of good example to testify to the world, that we who aim at the restitution of the Church, are everywhere faithfully exerting ourselves, in order that, at least, the use of the Catechism which was abolished some centuries ago under the Papacy, may now resume its lost rights. For neither can this holy custom be sufficiently commended for its utility, nor can the Papists be sufficiently condemned for the flagrant corruption, by which they not only set it aside, by converting it into puerile trifles, but also basely abuse it to purposes of impure and impious superstition. That spurious Confirmation, which they have substituted in its stead, they deck out like a harlot, with great splendour of ceremonies, and gorgeous shows without number ; nay, in their wish to adorn it, they speak of it in terms of execrable blasphemy, when they give out that it is a sacrament of greater dignity than baptism, and call those only half Christians who have not been besmeared with their oil. Meanwhile, the whole proceeding consists of nothing but theatrical gesticulations, or rather the wanton sporting of apes, without any skill in imitation.

To you, my very dear brethren in the Lord, I have chosen to inscribe this work, because some of your body, besides informing me that you love me, and that the most of you take delight in my writings, also expressly requested me by letter to undertake this labour for their sake. Independently of this, it would have been reason sufficient, that what I learned of you long ago, from the statement of grave and pious men, had bound me to you with my whole soul. I now ask what I am confident you will of your own accord do— have the goodness to consult for the utility of this token of my goodwill towards you ! Farewell. May the Lord increase you more and more in the spirit of wisdom, prudence, zeal, and fortitude, to the edification of his Church.

GENEVA, 2d *December*, 1545.

TO THE READER.

It has ever been the practice of the Church, and one carefully attended to, to see that children should be duly instructed in the Christian religion. That this might be done more conveniently, not only were schools opened in old time, and individuals enjoined properly to teach their families, but it was a received public custom and practice, to question children in the churches on each of the heads, which should be common and well known to all Christians. To secure this being done in order, there was written out a formula, which was called a Catechism or Institute. Thereafter the devil miserably rending the Church of God, and bringing upon it fearful ruin, (of which the marks are still too visible in the greater part of the world,) overthrew this sacred policy, and left nothing behind but certain trifles, which only beget superstition, without any fruit of edification. Of this description is that confirmation, as they call it, full of gesticulations which, worse than ridiculous, are fitted only for apes, and have no foundation to rest upon. What we now bring forward, therefore, is nothing else than the use of things which from ancient times were observed by Christians, and the true worshippers of God, and which never were laid aside until the Church was wholly corrupted.

Catechism of the Church of Geneva.

OF FAITH.

Master.—What is the chief end of human life?

Scholar.—To know God by whom men were created.

M. What reason have you for saying so?

S. Because he created us and placed us in this world to be glorified in us. And it is indeed right that our life, of which himself is the beginning, should be devoted to his glory.

M. What is the highest good of man?

S. The very same thing.

M. Why do you hold that to be the highest good ?

S. Because without it our condition is worse than that of the brutes.

M. Hence, then, we clearly see that nothing worse can happen to a man than not to live to God.

S. It is so.

M. What is the true and right knowledge of God ?

S. When he is so known that due honour is paid to him.

M. What is the method of honouring him duly ?

S. To place our whole confidence in him ; to study to serve him during our whole life by obeying his will ; to call upon him in all our necessities, seeking salvation and every good thing that can be desired in him ; lastly, to acknowledge him both with heart and lips, as the sole Author of all blessings.

M. To consider these points in their order, and explain them more fully—What is the first head in this division of yours ?

S. To place our whole confidence in God.

M. How shall we do so ?

S. When we know him to be Almighty and perfectly good.

M. Is this enough ?

S. Far from it.

M. Wherefore ?

S. Because we are unworthy that he should exert his power in helping us, and show how good he is by saving us.

M. What more then is needful ?

S. That each of us should set it down in his mind that God loves him, and is willing to be a Father, and the author of salvation to him.

M. But whence will this appear ?

S. From his word, in which he explains his mercy to us in Christ, and testifies of his love towards us.

M. Then the foundation and beginning of confidence in God is to know him in Christ ?

S. Entirely so.

M. I should now wish you to tell me in a few words, what the sum of this knowledge is ?

S. It is contained in the Confession of Faith, or rather

Formula of Confession, which all Christians have in common. It is commonly called the Apostles' Creed, because from the beginning of the Church it was ever received among all the pious, and because it either fell from the lips of the Apostles, or was faithfully gathered out of their writings.

M. Repeat it.

S. I believe in God the Father Almighty, maker of heaven and earth; and in Jesus Christ, his only Son, our Lord, who was conceived by the Holy Ghost, born of the Virgin Mary, suffered under Pontius Pilate, was crucified, dead, and buried: he descended into hell; the third day he arose again from the dead; he ascended into heaven, and sitteth on the right hand of God the Father Almighty, from thence he shall come to judge the quick and the dead. I believe in the Holy Ghost; the holy Catholick Church; the communion of saints; the forgiveness of sins; the resurrection of the body; and the life everlasting. Amen.

M. To understand each point more thoroughly, into how many parts shall we divide this confession?

S. Into four leading ones.

M. Mention them to me.

S. The first relates to God the Father; the second to his Son Jesus Christ, which also embraces the whole sum of man's redemption; the third to the Holy Spirit; the fourth to the Church, and the Divine blessings conferred upon her.

M. Since there is no God but one, why do you here mention three, the Father, Son, and Holy Spirit?

S. Because in the one essence of God, it behoves us to look on God the Father as the beginning and origin, and the first cause of all things; next the Son, who is his eternal Wisdom; and, lastly, the Holy Spirit, as his energy diffused indeed over all things, but still perpetually resident in himself.

M. You mean then that there is no absurdity in holding that these three persons are in one Godhead, and God is not therefore divided?

S. Just so.

M. Now repeat the first part.

S. " I believe in God the Father Almighty, maker of heaven and earth."

M. Why do you call him Father ?

S. Primarily with reference to Christ who is his eternal Wisdom, begotten of him before all time, and being sent into this world was declared to be his Son. We infer, however, that as God is the Father of Jesus Christ, he is our Father also.

M. In what sense do you give him the name of Almighty?

S. Not as having a power which he does not exercise, but as having all things under his power and hand ; governing the world by his Providence, determining all things by his will, ruling all creatures as seems to him good.

M. You do not then suppose an indolent power in God, but consider it such that his hand is always engaged in working, so that nothing is done except through Him, and by his decree.

S. It is so.

M. Why do you add " Creator of heaven and earth ?"

S. As he has manifested himself to us by works, (Rom. i. 20,) in these too we ought to seek him. Our mind cannot take in his essence. The world itself is, therefore, a kind of mirror in which we may view him in so far as it concerns us to know.

M. Do you not understand by " heaven and earth" all creatures whatever that exist ?

S. Yes, verily ; under these two names all are included, because they are either heavenly or earthly.

M. But why do you call God a Creator merely, while it is much more excellent to defend and preserve creatures in their state, than to have once made them ?

S. This term does not imply that God created his works at once, and then threw off the care of them. It should rather be understood, that as the world was once made by God, so it is now preserved by him, and that the earth and all other things endure just in as far as they are sustained by his energy, and as it were his hand. Besides, seeing that he has all things under his hand, it follows, that he is the chief ruler and Lord of all. Therefore, by his being " Creator of heaven and earth," we must understand that it is he alone who by wisdom, goodness, and power, guides the whole course and order of nature: who at once sends rain and drought, hail and other storms, as well as calm, who of his kindness fertilizes the earth, and on the contrary, by withholding his hand, makes it barren: from whom come health and disease; to whose power all things are subject, and whose nod they obey.

M. But what shall we say of wicked men and devils? Shall we say that they too are under him?

S. Although he does not govern them by his Spirit, he however curbs them by his power as a bridle, so that they cannot even move unless in so far as he permits them. Nay, he even makes them the ministers of his will, so that unwilling and against their own intention, they are forced to execute what to him seems good.

M. What good redounds to you from the knowledge of this fact?

S. Very much. It would go ill with us could devils and wicked men do any thing without the will of God, and our minds could never be very tranquil while thinking we were exposed to their caprice. Then only do we rest safely when we know that they are curbed by the will of God, and as it were kept in confinement, so that they cannot do any thing unless by his permission: the more especially that God has engaged to be our guardian, and the prince of our salvation.

M. Let us now come to the second part.

S. It is that we believe "in Jesus Christ his only Son our Lord."

M. What does it chiefly comprehend?

S. That the Son of God is our Saviour, and it at the same time explains the method by which he has redeemed us from death, and purchased life.

M. What is the meaning of the name Jesus which you give to him?

S. It has the same meaning as the Greek word Σωτηρ, (*Soter.*) The Latins have no proper name by which its force may be well expressed. Hence the term Saviour (*Salvator*) was commonly received. Moreover, the angel gave this

appellation to the Son of God, by the order of God himself.
(Matt. i. 21.)

M. Is this more than if men had given it?

S. Certainly. For since God wills that he be called so, he
must absolutely be so.

M. What, next, is the force of the name Christ?

S. By this epithet, his office is still better expressed—for
it signifies that he was anointed by the Father to be a King,
Priest, and Prophet.

M. How do you know that?

S. First, Because Scripture applies anointing to these
three uses; *secondly,* Because it often attributes the three
things which we have mentioned to Christ.

M. But with what kind of oil was he anointed?

S. Not with visible oil as was used in consecrating ancient
kings, priests, and prophets, but one more excellent, namely,
the grace of the Holy Spirit, which is the thing meant by
that outward anointing.

M. But what is the nature of this kingdom of his which
you mention?

S. Spiritual, contained in the word and Spirit of God,
which carry with them righteousness and life.

M. What of the priesthood?

S. It is the office and prerogative of appearing in the presence of God to obtain grace, and of appeasing his wrath by
the offering of a sacrifice which is acceptable to him.

M. In what sense do you call Christ a Prophet?

S. Because on coming into the world he declared himself
an ambassador to men, and an interpreter, and that for the
purpose of putting an end to all revelations and prophecies
by giving a full exposition of his Father's will.

M. But do you derive any benefit from this?

S. Nay, all these things have no end but our good. For the
Father hath bestowed them on Christ that he may communicate them to us, and all of us thus receive out of his fulness.

M. State this to me somewhat more fully.

S. He was filled with the Holy Spirit, and loaded with a
perfect abundance of all his gifts, that he may impart
them to us,—that is, to each according to the measure which

the Father knows to be suited to us. Thus from him, as the only fountain, we draw whatever spiritual blessings we possess.

M. What does his kingdom bestow upon us ?

S. By means of it, obtaining liberty of conscience to live piously and holily, and, being provided with his spiritual riches, we are also armed with power sufficient to overcome the perpetual enemies of our souls—sin, the world, the devil, and the flesh.

M. To what is the office of priest conducive ?

S. First, by means of it he is the mediator who reconciles us to the Father ; and, secondly, access is given us to the Father, so that we too can come with boldness into his presence, and offer him the sacrifice of ourselves, and our all. In this way he makes us, as it were, his colleagues in the priesthood.

M. There is still prophecy.

S. As it is an office of teaching bestowed on the Son of God in regard to his own servants, the end is that he may enlighten them by the true knowledge of the Father, instruct them in truth, and make them household disciples of God.

M. All that you have said then comes to this, that the name of Christ comprehends three offices which the Father hath bestowed on the Son, that he may transfuse the virtue and fruit of them into his people ?

S. It is so.

M. Why do you call him the only Son of God, seeing that God designs to bestow this appellation upon us all ?

S. That we are the sons of God we have not from nature, but from adoption and grace only, in other words, because God puts us in that place, (John i. 1;) but the Lord Jesus who was begotten of the substance of the Father, and is of one essence with the Father, (Eph. i. 3,) is by the best title called the only Son of God, because he alone is his Son by nature, (Heb. i. 1.)

M. You mean then, that this honour is proper to him, as being due to him by right of nature, whereas it is communicated to us by gratuitous favour, as being his members ?

S. Exactly. Hence with a view to this communication he is called the First-born among many brethren. (Rom. viii. 29.)

M. In what sense do you understand him to be " our Lord ?"

S. Inasmuch as he was appointed by the Father to have us under his power, to administer the kingdom of God in heaven and on earth, and to be the Head of men and angels. (Col. i. 15, 18.)

M. What is meant by what follows ?

S. It shows the manner in which the Son was anointed by the Father to be our Saviour—namely, that having assumed our nature, he performed all things necessary to our salvation as here enumerated.

M. What mean you by the two sentences—" Conceived of the Holy Ghost, born of the Virgin Mary ?"

S. That he was formed in the womb of the virgin, of her substance, to be the true seed of David, as had been foretold by the Prophets, and that this was effected by the miraculous and secret agency of the Spirit without human connection. (Ps. cxxxii. 11 ; Matt. i. 1 ; Luke i. 32.)

M. Was it of consequence then that he should assume our nature ?

S. Very much so ; because it was necessary that the disobedience committed by man against God should be expiated also in human nature. Nor could he in any other way be our Mediator to make reconciliation between God and man. (Rom. iii. 24 ; 1 Tim. ii. 5 ; Heb. iv. 15 ; v. 7.)

M. You say that Christ behoved to become man, that he might, as it were, in our person accomplish the work of salvation ?

S. So I think. For we must borrow of him whatever is wanting in ourselves : and this cannot be done in any other way.

M. But why was that effected by the Holy Spirit, and not by the common and usual form of generation ?

S. As the seed of man is entirely corrupt, it was necessary that the operation of the Holy Spirit should interfere in the generation of the Son of God, that he might not be affected by this contagion, but endued with the most perfect purity.

M. Hence then we learn that he who sanctifies us is free from every stain, and was possessed of purity, so to speak, from the original womb, so that he was wholly sacred to God, being unpolluted by any taint of the human race?

S. That is my understanding.

M. How is he our Lord?

S. He was appointed by the Father to rule us, and having obtained the empire and dominion of God both in heaven and on earth, to be recognised as the head of angels and good men. (Eph. i. 21 ; Col. i. 18.)

M. Why do you leap at once from his birth to his death, passing over the whole history of his life?

S. Because nothing is treated of here but what so properly belongs to our salvation, as in a manner to contain the substance of it.

M. Why do you not say in one word simply "was dead," (died,) but also add the name of the governor under whom he suffered?

S. That has respect not only to the credit of the statement, but also to let us know that his death was connected with condemnation.

M. Explain this more clearly.

S. He died to discharge the penalty due by us, and in this way exempt us from it. But as we all being sinners were obnoxious to the judgment of God, he, that he might act as our substitute, was pleased to be sisted in presence of an earthly judge, and condemned by his mouth, that we might be acquitted before the celestial tribunal of God.

M. But Pilate pronounces him innocent, and therefore does not condemn him as a malefactor. (Matt. xxvii. 24.)

S. It is necessary to attend to both things. The judge bears testimony to his innocence, to prove that he suffered not for his own misdeeds but ours, and he is formally condemned by the sentence of the same judge, to make it plain that he endured the sentence which he deserved as our surety, that thus he might free us from guilt.

M. Well answered. Were he a sinner he would not be a

fit surety to pay the penalty of another's sin ; and yet that his condemnation might obtain our acquittal, he behoved to be classed among transgressors ?

S. I understand so.

M. Is there any greater importance in his having been crucified than if he had suffered any other kind of death ?

S. Very much greater, as Paul also reminds us, (Gal. iii. 13,) when he says, that he hung upon a tree to take our curse upon himself and free us from it. For that kind of death was doomed to execration. (Deut. xxi. 23.)

M. What ? Is not an affront put upon the Son of God when it is said that even before God he was subjected to the curse ?

S. By no means ; since by undergoing he abolished it, and yet meanwhile he ceased not to be blessed in order that he might visit us with his blessing.

M. Go on.

S. Since death was the punishment imposed on man because of sin, the Son of God endured it, and by enduring overcame it. But to make it more manifest that he underwent a real death, he chose to be placed in the tomb like other men.

M. But nothing seems to be derived to us from this victory, since we still die ?

S. That is no obstacle. Nor to believers is death now any thing else than a passage to a better life.

M. Hence it follows that death is no longer to be dreaded as if it were a fearful thing, but we should with intrepid mind follow Christ our leader, who as he did not perish in death, will not suffer us to perish ?

S. Thus should we act.

M. It is immediately added, "he descended into hell." What does this mean ?

S. That he not only endured common death, which is the separation of the soul from the body, but also the pains of death, as Peter calls them. (Acts ii. 24.) By this expression I understand the fearful agonies by which his soul was pierced.

M. Give me the cause and the manner of this.

S. As in order to satisfy for sinners he sisted himself before the tribunal of God, it was necessary that he should suffer excruciating agony of conscience, as if he had been forsaken of God, nay as it were, had God hostile to him. He was in this agony when he exclaimed, "My God, my God, why hast thou forsaken me?" (Matt. xxvii. 46.)

M. Was his Father then offended with him?

S. By no means. But he exercised this severity against him in fulfilment of what had been foretold by Isaiah, that "he was smitten by the hand of God for our sins and wounded for our transgressions." (Is. liii. 4, 5.)

M. But seeing he is God, how could he be seized with any such dread, as if he were forsaken of God?

S. We must hold that it was in respect to the feelings of his human nature that he was reduced to this necessity: and that this might be, his divinity for a little while was concealed, that is, did not put forth its might.

M. How, on the other hand, is it possible that Christ, who is the salvation of the world, should have been subjected to this doom?

S. He did not endure it so as to remain under it. For though he was seized with the terrors I have mentioned, he was not overwhelmed. Rather wrestling with the power of hell he subdued and crushed it.

M. Hence we infer that the torture of conscience which he bore differs from that which excruciates sinners when pursued by the hands of an angry God. For what was temporary in him is perpetual in them, and what was in him only the prick of a sting, is in them a mortal sword, which, so to speak, wounds the heart.

S. It is so. The Son of God when beset by this anguish, ceased not to hope in the Father. But sinners condemned by the justice of God, rush into despair, murmur against him, and even break forth into open blasphemies.

M. May we hence infer what benefit believers receive from the death of Christ?

S. Easily. And, first, we see that it is a sacrifice by which he expiated our sins before God, and so having appeased the wrath of God, restored us to his favour. Secondly,

That his blood is a laver by which our souls are cleansed from all stains. Lastly, That the remembrance of our sins was effaced so as never to come into the view of God, and that thus the handwriting which established our guilt was blotted out and cancelled.

M. Does it not gain us any other advantage besides ?

S. Yes, indeed. For by its benefit, if we are members of Christ, our old man is crucified, and the body of sin is destroyed, so that the lusts of a depraved flesh no longer reign in us.

M. Proceed with the other articles.

S. The next is, " On the third day he rose again from the dead." By this he declared himself the conqueror of sin and death. By his resurrection he swallowed up death, broke the fetters of the devil, and annihilated all his power.

M. How manifold are the benefits resulting to us from the resurrection ?

S. Threefold. For by it righteousness was acquired for us ; it is also a sure pledge to us of our immortality ; and even now by virtue of it we are raised to newness of life, that by living purely and holily we may obey the will of God.

M. Let us follow out the rest.

S. " He ascended into heaven."

M. Did he ascend so that he is no more on the earth ?

S. He did. For after he had performed all the things which the Father had given him to do, and which were for our salvation, there was no need of his continuing longer on earth.

M. What good do we obtain from this ascension ?

S. The benefit is twofold. For inasmuch as Christ entered heaven in our name, just as he had come down to earth on our account, he also opened up an access for us, so that the door, previously shut because of sin, is now open. Secondly, he appears in the presence of God as our advocate and intercessor.

M. But did Christ in going to heaven withdraw from us, so that he has now ceased to be with us ?

S. Not at all. On the contrary, he has engaged to be with us even to the end of the world. (Matt. xxviii. 20.)

M. When we say he dwells with us, must we understand that he is bodily present ?

S. No. The case of the body which was received into heaven is one thing ; that of the virtue which is everywhere diffused is another. (Luke xxiv. 51 ; Acts i. 11.)

M. In what sense do you say that he "sitteth on the right hand of the Father ?"

S. These words mean that the Father bestowed upon him the dominion of heaven and earth, so that he governs all things. (Matt. xxviii. 18.)

M. But what is meant by "right hand," and what by "sitteth ?"

S. It is a similitude taken from princes, who are wont to place those on their right hand whom they make their vice-gerents.

M. You therefore mean nothing more than Paul says, namely, that Christ has been appointed head of the Church, and raised above all principalities, has obtained a name which is above every name. (Eph. i. 22 ; Phil. ii. 9.)

S. It is as you say.

M. Let us pass on.

S. "From thence he will come to judge the quick and the dead." The meaning of these words is, that he will come openly from heaven to judge the world, just as he was seen to ascend. (Acts i. 11.)

M. As the day of judgment is not to be before the end of the world, how do you say that some men will then be alive, seeing it is appointed unto all men once to die ? (Heb. ix. 27.)

S. Paul answers this question when he says, that those who then survive will undergo a sudden change, so that the corruption of the flesh being abolished, they will put on incorruption. (1 Cor. xv. 51 ; 1 Thess. iv. 17.)

M. You understand then that this change will be like death ; that there will be an abolition of the first nature, and the beginning of a new nature ?

S. That is my meaning.

M. Does it give any delight to our conscience that Christ will one day be the judge of the world ?

S. Indeed singular delight. For we know assuredly that he will come only for our salvation.

M. We should not then tremble at this judgment, so as to let it fill us with dismay?

S. No, indeed; since we shall only stand at the tribunal of a judge who is also our advocate, and who has taken us under his faith and protection.

M. Let us come now to the third part.

S. It relates to faith in the Holy Spirit.

M. What do we learn by it?

S. The object is to let us know that God, as he hath redeemed and saved us by his Son, will also by his Spirit make us capable of this redemption and salvation.

M. How?

S. As we have purification in the blood of Christ, so our consciences must be sprinkled by it in order to be washed. (1 Peter i. 2; 1 John i. 7.)

M. This requires a clearer explanation.

S. I mean that the Spirit of God, while he dwells in our hearts, makes us feel the virtue of Christ. (Rom. viii. 11.) For when our minds conceive the benefits of Christ, it is owing to the illumination of the Holy Spirit; to his persuasion it is owing that they are sealed in our hearts. (Eph. i. 13.) In short, he alone makes room in us for them. He regenerates us and makes us to be new creatures. Accordingly, whatever gifts are offered us in Christ, we receive by the agency of the Spirit.

M. Let us proceed.

S. Next comes the fourth part, in which we confess that we believe in one Holy Catholic Church.

M. What is the Church?

S. The body and society of believers whom God hath predestined to eternal life.

M. Is it necessary to believe this article also?

S. Yes, verily, if we would not make the death of Christ without effect, and set at nought all that has hitherto been said. For the one effect resulting from all is, that there is Church.

M. You mean then that we only treated of the cause of

salvation, and showed the foundation of it when we explained that by the merits and intercession of Christ, we are taken into favour by God, and that this grace is confirmed in us by virtue of the Spirit. Now, however, we are explaining the effect of all these things, that by facts our faith may be made more firm ?

S. It is so.

M. In what sense do you call the Church holy ?

S. All whom God has chosen he justifies, and forms to holiness and innocence of life, (Rom. viii. 30,) that his glory may be displayed in them. And this is what Paul means when he says that Christ sanctified the Church which he redeemed, that it might be a glorious Church, free from all blemish. (Eph. v. 25.)

M. What is meant by the epithet Catholic or Universal ?

S. By it we are taught, that as all believers have one head, so they must all be united into one body, that the Church diffused over the whole world may be one—not more. (Eph. iv. 15 ; 1 Cor. xii. 12.)

M. And what is the purport of what immediately follows concerning the communion of saints ?

S. That is put down to express more clearly the unity which exists among the members of the Church. It is at the same time intimated, that whatever benefits God bestows upon the Church, have a view to the common good of all ; seeing they all have communion with each other.

M. But is this holiness which you attribute to the Church already perfect ?

S. Not yet, that is as long as she has her warfare in this world. For she always labours under infirmities, and will never be entirely purged of the remains of vice, until she adheres completely to Christ her head, by whom she is sanctified.

M. Can this Church be known in any other way than when she is believed by faith ?

S. There is indeed also a visible Church of God, which he has described to us by certain signs and marks, but here we are properly speaking of the assemblage of those whom he has adopted to salvation by his secret election. This is neither at all times visible to the eye nor discernible by signs.

M. What comes next ?

S. I believe in " the forgiveness of sins."

M. What meaning do you give to the word forgiveness ?

S. That God of his free goodness forgives and pardons the sins of believers that they may not be brought to judgment, and that the penalty may not be exacted from them.

M. Hence it follows, that it is not at all by our own satisfaction we merit the pardon of sins, which we obtain from the Lord ?

S. That is true ; for Christ alone gave the satisfaction by paying the penalty.

M. Why do you subjoin forgiveness of sins to the Church ?

S. Because no man obtains. it without being previously united to the people of God, maintaining unity with the body of Christ perseveringly to the end, and thereby attesting that he is a true member of the Church.

M. In this way you conclude that out of the Church is nought but ruin and damnation ?

S. Certainly. Those who make a departure from the body of Christ, and rend its unity by faction, are cut off from all hope of salvation during the time they remain in this schism, be it however short.

M. Repeat the remainder.

S. I believe in " the resurrection of the body and the life everlasting."

M. To what end is this article set down in the Confession of Faith ?

S. To remind us that our happiness is not situated on the earth.   The utility and use of this knowledge is twofold. First, we are taught by it that we are to live in this world as foreigners, continually thinking of departure, and not allowing our hearts to be entangled by earthly thoughts. Secondly, however the fruit of the grace of Christ bestowed upon us may escape our notice, and be hidden from our eyes, we must not despond, but patiently wait for the day of revelation.

M. In what order will this resurrection take place ?

S. Those who were formerly dead will recover their bodies, the same bodies as before, but endued with a new quality, that is, no longer liable to death or corruption. (1 Cor. xv. 53.) Those who survive God will miraculously raise up by a sudden change.

M. But will this be common to the righteous and the wicked?

S. There will be one resurrection of all, but the condition will be different: some will rise to salvation and blessedness, others to death and extreme misery.

M. Why then is eternal life only here mentioned, and is there no mention of hell?

S. Because nothing is introduced here that does not tend to the consolation of pious minds; accordingly, only the rewards are enumerated which the Lord hath prepared for his servants, and nothing is added as to the doom of the wicked, whom we know to be aliens from the kingdom of God.

M. As we understand the foundation on which faith ought to rest, it will be easy to extract from it a true definition of faith.

S. It will. It may be defined—a sure and steadfast knowledge of the paternal goodwill of God toward us, as he declares in the gospel that for the sake of Christ he will be our Father and Saviour.

M. Do we conceive faith of ourselves, or do we receive it from God?

S. Scripture teaches that it is the special gift of God, and this experience confirms.

M. What experience do you mean?

S. Our mind is too rude to be able to comprehend the spiritual wisdom of God which is revealed to us by faith, and our hearts are too prone either to diffidence or to a perverse confidence in ourselves or creatures, to rest in God of their own accord. But the Holy Spirit by his illumination makes us capable of understanding those things which would otherwise far exceed our capacity, and forms us to a firm persuasion, by sealing the promises of salvation on our hearts.

M. What good accrues to us from this faith, when we have once obtained it?

S. It justifies us before God, and this justification makes us the heirs of everlasting life.

M. What! are not men justified by good works when they study to approve themselves to God, by living innocently and holily?

S. Could any one be found so perfect, he might justly be deemed righteous, but as we are all sinners, guilty before God in many ways, we must seek elsewhere for a worthiness which may reconcile us to him.

M. But are all the works of men so vile and valueless that they cannot merit favour with God?

S. First, all the works which proceed from us, so as properly to be called our own, are vicious, and therefore they can do nothing but displease God, and be rejected by him.

M. You say then that before we are born again and formed anew by the Spirit of God, we can do nothing but sin, just as a bad tree can only produce bad fruit? (Matt. vii. 18.)

S. Altogether so. For whatever semblance works may have in the eyes of men, they are nevertheless evil, as long as the heart to which God chiefly looks is depraved.

M. Hence you conclude, that we cannot by any merits anticipate God or call forth his beneficence; or rather that all the works which we try or engage in, subject us to his anger and condemnation?

S. I understand so; and therefore mere mercy, without any respect to works, (Titus iii. 5,) embraces and accepts us freely in Christ, by attributing his righteousness to us as if it were our own, and not imputing our sins to us.

M. In what way, then, do you say that we are justified by faith?

S. Because, while we embrace the promises of the gospel with sure heartfelt confidence, we in a manner obtain possession of the righteousness of which I speak.

M. This then is your meaning—that as righteousness is offered to us by the gospel, so we receive it by faith?

S. It is so.

M. But after we have once been embraced by God, are not

the works which we do under the direction of his Holy Spirit accepted by him ?

S. They please him, not however in virtue of their own worthiness, but as he liberally honours them with his favour.

M. But seeing they proceed from the Holy Spirit, do they not merit favour ?

S. They are always mixed up with some defilement from the weakness of the flesh, and thereby vitiated.

M. Whence then or how can it be that they please God ?

S. It is faith alone which procures favour for them, as we rest with assured confidence on this—that God wills not to try them by his strict rule, but covering their defects and impurities as buried in the purity of Christ, he regards them in the same light as if they were absolutely perfect.

M. But can we infer from this that a Christian man is justified by works after he has been called by God, or that by the merit of works he makes himself loved by God, whose love is eternal life to us ?

S. By no means. We rather hold what is written—that no man can be justified in his sight, and we therefore pray, " Enter not into judgment with us." (Ps. cxliii. 2.)

M. We are not therefore to think that the good works of believers are useless ?

S. Certainly not. For not in vain does God promise them reward both in this life and in the future. But this reward springs from the free love of God as its source ; for he first embraces us as sons, and then burying the remembrance of the vices which proceed from us, he visits us with his favour.

M. But can this righteousness be separated from good works, so that he who has it may be void of them ?

S. That cannot be. For when by faith we receive Christ as he is offered to us, he not only promises us deliverance from death and reconciliation with God, but also the gift of the Holy Spirit, by which we are regenerated to newness of life ; these things must necessarily be conjoined so as not to divide Christ from himself.

M. Hence it follows that faith is the root from which all good works spring, so far is it from taking us off from the study of them ?

S. So indeed it is ; and hence the whole doctrine of the gospel is comprehended under the two branches, faith and repentance.

M. What is repentance?

S. Dissatisfaction with and a hatred of sin and a love of righteousness, proceeding from the fear of God, which things lead to self-denial and mortification of the flesh, so that we give ourselves up to the guidance of the Spirit of God, and frame all the actions of our life to the obedience of the Divine will.

M. But this second branch was in the division which was set down at first when you showed the method of duly worshipping God.

S. True ; and it was at the same time added, that the true and legitimate rule for worshipping God is to obey his will.

M. Why so ?

S. Because the only worship which he approves is not that which it may please us to devise, but that which he hath of his own authority prescribed.

OF THE LAW, THAT IS, THE TEN COMMANDMENTS OF GOD.

M. What is the rule of life which he has given us ?

S. His law.

M. What does it contain ?

S. It consists of two parts ; the former of which contains four commandments, the latter six. Thus the whole law consists of ten commandments in all.

M. Who is the author of this division ?

S. God himself, who delivered it to Moses written on two tables, and afterwards declared that it was reduced into ten sentences. (Exod. xxiv. 12 ; xxxii. 15 ; xxxiv. 1 ; Deut. iv. 13 ; x. 4.)

M. What is the subject of the first table ?

S. The offices of piety towards God.

M. Of the second ?

S. How we are to act towards men, and what we owe them.

M. Repeat the first commandment or head.

S. Hear, O Israel, I am Jehovah thy God, who brought thee out of the land of Egypt, out of the house of bondage: thou shalt have no other gods before me.

M. Now explain the meaning of the words.

S. At first he makes a kind of preface to the whole law. For when he calls himself Jehovah, he claims right and authority to command. Then in order to procure favour for his law, he adds, that he is our God. These words have the same force as if he had called himself our Preserver. Now as he bestows this favour upon us, it is meet that we should in our turn show ourselves to be an obedient people.

M. But does not what he immediately subjoins, as to deliverance and breaking the yoke of Egyptian bondage, apply specially to the people of Israel, and to them alone?

S. I admit this as to the act itself, but there is another kind of deliverance which applies equally to all men. For he has delivered us all from the spiritual bondage of sin, and the tyranny of the devil.

M. Why does he mention that matter in a preface to his law?

S. To remind us that we will be guilty of the greatest ingratitude if we do not devote ourselves entirely to obedience to him.

M. And what does he require under this first head?

S. That we maintain his honour entire and for himself alone, not transferring any part of it elsewhere.

M. What is the honour peculiar to him which it is unlawful to transfer elsewhere?

S. To adore him, to put our confidence in him, to call upon him, in short to pay him all the deference suitable to his majesty.

M. Why is the clause added, " Before my face?"

S. As nothing is so hidden as to escape him, and he is the discerner and judge of secret thoughts, it means that he requires not the honour of outward affection merely, but true heartfelt piety.

M. Let us pass to the second head.

S. Thou shalt not sculpture to thyself the image, or form any of those things which are either in heaven above or on the earth beneath, or in the waters under the earth. Thou shalt not adore nor serve them.

M. Does it entirely prohibit us from sculpturing or painting any resemblance?

S. No; it only forbids us to make any resemblances for the sake of representing or worshipping God.

M. Why is it unlawful to represent God by a visible shape?

S. Because there is no resemblance between him who is an eternal Spirit and incomprehensible, and a corporeal, corruptible, and lifeless figure. (Deut. iv. 15; Acts xvii. 29; Rom. i. 23.)

M. You think then that an insult is offered to his majesty when he is represented in this way?

S. Such is my belief.

M. What kind of worship is here condemned?

S. When we turn to a statue or image intending to pray, we prostrate ourselves before it: when we pay honour to it by the bending of our knees, or other signs, as if God were there representing himself to us.

M. We are not to understand then that simply any kind of picture or sculpture is condemned by these words. We are only prohibited from making images for the purpose of seeking or worshipping God in them, or which is the same thing, for the purpose of worshipping them in honour of God, or abusing them in any way to superstition and idolatry.

S. True.

M. Now to what end shall we refer this head?

S. As under the former .head he declared that he alone should be worshipped and served, so he now shows what is the correct form of worship, that he may call us off from all superstition, and other vicious and carnal fictions.

M. Let us proceed.

S. He adds the sanction that he is Jehovah our God, a strong and jealous God, who avengeth the iniquity of the fathers upon the children of them who hate him, even to the third and fourth generation.

M. Why does he make mention of his strength ?

S. He thereby intimates that he has power enough to vindicate his glory.

M. What does he intimate by the term jealousy ?

S. That he cannot bear an equal or associate. For as he has given himself to us out of his infinite goodness, so he would have us to be wholly his. And the chastity of our souls consists in being dedicated to him, and wholly cleaving to him, as on the other hand they are said to be polluted with idolatry, when they turn aside from him to superstition.

M. In what sense is it said that he avengeth the iniquity of fathers on children ?

S. To strike the more terror into us, he not only threatens to inflict punishment on those who offend him, but that their offspring also will be cursed.

M. But is it consistent with the justice of God to punish any one for another's fault ?

S. If we consider what the condition of mankind is, the question is answered. For by nature we are all liable to the curse, and we have nothing to complain of in God when he leaves us in this condition. Then as he demonstrates his love for the righteous, by blessing their posterity, so he executes his vengeance against the wicked, by depriving their children of this blessing.

M. Go on.

S. To allure us by attractive mildness, he promises that he will take pity on all who love him and observe his commands, to a thousand generations.

M. Does he mean that the innocence of a pious man will be the salvation of all his posterity, however wicked ?

S. Not at all, but that he will exercise his benignity to believers to such a degree, that for their sakes he will show himself benign also to their children, by not only giving them prosperity in regard to the present life, but also sanctifying their souls, so as to give them a place among his flock.

M. But this does not always appear.

S. I admit it. For as he reserves to himself liberty to show mercy when he pleases to the children of the ungodly, so he has not so astricted his favour to the children of believers as not to repudiate at pleasure those of them whom he will. (Rom. ix.) This, however, he so tempers as to show that his promise is not vain or fallacious.

M. But why does he here say a thousand generations, whereas, in the case of punishment, he mentions only three or four ?

S. To intimate that he is more inclined to kindness and beneficence than to severity. This he also declares, when he says that he is ready to pardon, but slow to wrath. (Ex. xxxiv. 6 ; Ps. ciii. 8 ; cxlv. 8.)

M. Now for the third commandment.

S. Thou shalt not take the name of Jehovah thy God in vain.

M. What is the meaning ?

S. He forbids us to abuse the name of God, not only by perjury, but by swearing without necessity.

M. Can the name of God be lawfully used in making oath ?

S. It may indeed, when used on a fit cause : first, in asserting the truth ; and secondly, when the business is of such importance as to make it meet to swear, in maintaining mutual love and concord among men.

M. But does it not go farther than to restrain oaths, by which the name of God is profaned, or his honour impaired ?

S. The mention of one species admonishes us in general, never to utter the name of God unless with fear and reverence, and for the purpose of honouring it. For while it is thrice holy, we ought to guard, by all means, against seeming to hold it in contempt, or giving others occasion to contemn.

M. How is this to be done ?

S. By never speaking or thinking of God and his works without honour.

M. What follows ?

S. A sanction, by which he declares that he shall not be guiltless who taketh his name in vain.

M. As he, in another place, declares that he will punish the transgressors of his law, what more is contained here ?

S. He hereby meant to intimate how much he values the glory of his name, and to make us more careful of it, when we see that vengeance is ready for any who may profane it.

M. Let us come to the fourth commandment.

S. Remember the Sabbath day, to keep it holy. Six days shalt thou labour, and do all thy work : But the seventh is the Sabbath of the Lord thy God : in it thou shalt not do any work, thou, nor thy son, nor thy daughter, thy man-servant, nor thy maid-servant, nor thy cattle, nor thy stranger that is within thy gates : For in six days the Lord made heaven and earth, the sea, and all that in them is, and rested the seventh day : wherefore the Lord blessed the Sabbath day, and hallowed it.

M. Does he order us to labour on six days, that we may rest on the seventh ?

S. Not absolutely ; but allowing man six days for labour, he excepts the seventh, that it may be devoted to rest.

M. Does he interdict us from all kind of labour ?

S. This commandment has a separate and peculiar reason. As the observance of rest is part of the old ceremonies, it was abolished by the advent of Christ.

M. Do you mean that this commandment properly refers to the Jews, and was therefore merely temporary ?

S. I do, in as far as it is ceremonial.

M. What then ? Is there any thing under it beyond ceremony ?

S. It was given for three reasons.

M. State them to me.

S. To figure spiritual rest ; for the preservation of ecclesiastical polity ; and for the relief of slaves.

M. What do you mean by spiritual rest ?

S. When we keep holiday from our own works, that God may perform his own works in us.

M. What, moreover, is the method of thus keeping holiday ?

S. By crucifying our flesh,—that is, renouncing our own inclination, that we may be governed by the Spirit of God.

M. Is it sufficient to do so on the seventh day ?

S. Nay, continually. After we have once begun, we must continue during the whole course of life.

M. Why, then, is a certain day appointed to figure it ?

S. There is no necessity that the reality should agree with the figure in every respect, provided it be suitable in so far as is required for the purpose of figuring.

M. But why is the seventh day prescribed rather than any other day ?

S. In Scripture the number seven implies perfection. It is, therefore, apt for denoting perpetuity. It, at the same time, indicates that this spiritual rest is only begun in this life, and will not be perfect until we depart from this world.

M. But what is meant when the Lord exhorts us to rest by his own example ?

S. Having finished the creation of the world in six days, he dedicated the seventh to the contemplation of his works. The more strongly to stimulate us to this, he set before us his own example. For nothing is more desirable than to be formed after his image.

M. But ought meditation on the works of God to be continual, or is it sufficient that one day out of seven be devoted to it ?

S. It becomes us to be daily exercised in it, but because of our weakness, one day is specially appointed. And this is the polity which I mentioned.

M. What order, then, is to be observed on that day ?

S. That the people meet to hear the doctrine of Christ, to engage in public prayer, and make profession of their faith.

M. Now explain what you meant by saying that the Lord intended by this commandment to provide also for the relief of slaves.

S. That some relaxation might be given to those under the power of others. Nay, this, too, tends to maintain a common polity. For when one day is devoted to rest, every one accustoms himself to labour during the other days.

M. Let us now see how far this command has reference to us.

S. In regard to the ceremony, I hold that it was abolished, as the reality existed in Christ. (Col. ii. 17.)

M. How ?

S. Because, by virtue of his death, our old man is crucified, and we are raised up to newness of life. (Rom. vi. 6.)

M. What of the commandment then remains for us ?

S. Not to neglect the holy ordinances which contribute to the spiritual polity of the Church; especially to frequent sacred assemblies, to hear the word of God, to celebrate the sacraments, and engage in the regular prayers, as enjoined.

M. But does the figure give us nothing more ?

S. Yes, indeed. We must give heed to the thing meant by it; namely, that being engrafted into the body of Christ, and made his members, we cease from our own works, and so resign ourselves to the government of God.

M. Let us pass to the second table.

S. It begins, " Honour thy father and thy mother."

M. What meaning do you give to the word " honour ?"

S. That children be, with modesty and humility, respectful and obedient to parents, serving them reverentially, helping them in necessity, and exerting their labour for them. For in these three branches is included the honour which is due to parents.

M. Proceed.

S. To the commandment the promise is added, " That thy days may be prolonged on the land which the Lord thy God will give thee."

M. What is the meaning ?

S. That, by the blessing of God, long life will be given to those who pay due honour to parents.

M. Seeing this life is so full of troubles, why does God promise the long continuance of it as a blessing ?

S. How great soever the miseries to which it is liable, yet there is a blessing from God upon believers, when he nourishes and preserves them here, were it only for this one reason, that it is a proof of his paternal favour.

M. Does it follow conversely, that he who is snatched away from the world quickly, and before mature age, is cursed of God ?

S. By no means. Nay, rather it sometimes happens that the more a man is loved by God the more quickly is he removed out of this life.

M. But in so acting, how does he fulfil his promise ?

S. Whatever earthly good God promises we must receive under this condition, viz., in so far as is expedient for the good and salvation of our soul. For the arrangement would be very absurd if the care of the soul did not always take precedence.

M. What of those who are contumacious to parents ?

S. They shall not only be punished at the last judgment, but here also God will take vengeance on their bodies, either by taking them hence in the middle of their days, or bringing them to an ignominious end, or in other manners.

M. But does not the promise speak expressly of the land of Canaan ?

S. It does so in as far as regards the Israelites, but the term ought to have a wider and more extensive meaning to us. For seeing that the whole earth is the Lord's, whatever be the region we inhabit he assigns it to us for a possession. (Ps. xxiv. 1 ; lxxxv. 5 ; cxv. 16.)

M. Is there nothing more of the commandment remaining ?

S. Though father and mother only are expressed, we must understand all who are over us, as the reason is the same.

M. What is the reason ?

S. That the Lord has raised them to a high degree of honour ; for there is no authority whether of parents, or princes, or rulers of any description, no power, no honour, but by the decree of God, because it so pleases him to order the world.

M. Repeat the sixth commandment.

S. Thou shalt not kill.

M. Does it forbid nothing but the perpetration of murder ?

S. Yes, indeed. For seeing it is God who speaks, he here gives law not only to outward works, but also to the affections of the mind, and indeed to them chiefly.

M. You seem to insinuate that there is some kind of secret murder from which God here recalls us.

S. I do. For anger, and hatred, and any desire to hurt, is murder in the sight of God.

M. Is it enough if we do not hate any one ?

S. By no means. Since the Lord, by condemning hatred and restraining us from any harm by which our neighbour may be injured, shows at the same time that he requires us to love all men from the heart, and study faithfully to defend and preserve them.

M. Now for the seventh commandment.

S. Thou shalt not commit adultery.

M. Explain what the substance of it is.

S. That all kinds of fornication are cursed in the sight of God, and therefore as we would not provoke the anger of God against us we must carefully abstain from it.

M. Does it require nothing besides?

S. Respect must always be had to the nature of the Lawgiver, who, we have said, not only regards the outward act, but looks more to the affections of the mind.

M. What more then does it comprehend?

S. Inasmuch as both our bodies and our souls are temples of the Holy Spirit, (1 Cor. iii. 16 ; vi. 19,) we must observe a chaste purity with both, and accordingly be chaste not only by abstaining from outward flagitiousness, but also in heart, speech, bodily gesture, and action, (2 Cor. vi. 16 ;) in short, our body must be free from all lasciviousness, our mind from all lust, and no part of us be polluted by the defilements of unchastity.

M. Let us come to the eighth commandment.

S. Thou shalt not steal.

M. Does it only prohibit the thefts which are punished by human laws, or does it go farther?

S. Under the name of theft, it comprehends all kinds of wicked acts of defrauding and circumventing by which we hunt after other men's goods. Here, therefore, we are forbidden either to seize upon our neighbour's goods by violence, or lay hands upon them by trick and cunning, or get possession of them by any other indirect means whatever.

M. Is it enough to withhold your hand from the evil act, or is covetousness also here condemned?

S. We must ever return to this—that the law given, being spiritual, intends to check not only outward thefts, but all counsels and wishes which incommode others in any way ; and especially covetousness itself, that we may not long to enrich ourselves at the expense of our brethren.

M. What then must be done to obey this commandment?

S. We must endeavour to let every man have his own in safety.

M. What is the ninth commandment?

S. Thou shalt not bear false witness against thy neighbour.

M. Does it prohibit perjury in court only, or any kind of lying against our neighbours?

S. Under one species the general doctrine is comprehended, that we are not to charge our neighbour falsely, nor by our evil speaking and detraction hurt his good name, or harm him in his goods.

M. But why does it expressly mention public perjury?

S. That it may inspire us with a greater abhorrence of this vice. For it insinuates that if a man accustom himself to evil speaking and calumny, the descent to perjury is rapid if an opportunity is given to defame his neighbour.

M. Does it mean to keep us from evil speaking only, or also from false suspicion and unjust and uncharitable judgment?

S. It here condemns both, according to the view already stated. For whatever it is wrong to do before men, it is wrong to wish before God.

M. Explain then what it means in substance.

S. It enjoins us not to think ill of our neighbours, or be prone to defame them, but in the spirit of kindness and impartiality to think well of them as far as the truth will permit, and study to preserve their reputation entire.

M. Repeat the last commandment.

S. Thou shalt not covet thy neighbour's house, thou shalt not covet thy neighbour's wife, nor his man-servant, nor his maid-servant, nor his ox, nor his ass, nor any thing that is thy neighbour's.

M. Seeing that the whole law is spiritual, as you have so often said before, and the above commandments are set down not only to curb outward acts, but also correct the affections of the mind, what more is added here?

S. The Lord meant to regulate and govern the will and affections by the other commandments, but here he imposes a law even on thoughts which carry some degree of covetousness along with them, and yet come not the length of a fixed purpose.

M. Do you say that the least degrees of covetousness which creep in upon believers and enter their minds are sins, even though they resist rather than assent?

S. It is certainly clear that all vitious thoughts, even though consent is not added, proceed from the pravity of our nature. But I only say this—that this commandment condemns vicious desires which tickle and solicit the heart of man, without however drawing him on to a firm and deliberate act of will.

M. You understand then that the evil affections in which men acquiesce, and by which they allow themselves to be overcome, were prohibited before, but that the thing now required of us is such strict integrity that our hearts are not to admit any perverse desire by which they may be stimulated to sin?

S. Exactly so.

M. Can we now frame a short compendium of the whole law?

S. Very easily, since we can reduce it to two heads. The former is to love God with all our heart, and soul, and strength—the latter, to love our neighbours as ourselves.

M. What is comprehended under the love of God?

S. To love him as God should be loved—that is, recognising him as at once our Lord, and Father, and Preserver. Accordingly, to the love of God is joined reverence for him, a willingness to obey him, trust to be placed in him.

M. What do you understand by the whole heart, the whole soul, and the whole strength?

S. Such vehemence of zeal, that there be no place at all in us for any thoughts, desires, or pursuits, adverse to this love.

M. What is the meaning of the second head?

S. As we are by nature so prone to love ourselves, that this feeling overcomes all others, so love to our neighbour ought to have such ascendency in us as to govern us in every respect, and be the rule of all our purposes and actions.

M. What do you understand by the term neighbour?

S. Not only kindred and friends, or those connected with us by any necessary tie, but also those who are unknown to us, and even enemies.

M. But what connection have they with us?

S. They are connected by that tie by which God bound the whole human race together. This tie is sacred and inviolable, and no man's depravity can abolish it.

M. You say, then, that if any man hate us, the blame is his own, and yet he is nevertheless our neighbour, and as such is to be regarded by us, because the divine arrangement by which this connection between us was ratified stands inviolable?

S. It is so.

M. Seeing that the law of God points out the form of duly worshipping him, must we not live according to its direction?

S. We must indeed. But we all labour under infirmity, owing to which no man fulfils, in every respect, what he ought.

M. Why then does God require a perfection which is beyond our ability?

S. He requires nothing which we are not bound to perform. But provided we strive after that form of living which is here prescribed, although we be wide of the mark, that is, of perfection, the Lord forgives us what is wanting.

M. Do you speak of all men in general, or of believers only?

S. He who is not yet regenerated by the Spirit of God, is not fit to begin the least iota of the law. Besides, even were we to grant that any one is found to obey the law in any respect, we do not think that he has performed his part before God. For the law pronounces all cursed who have not fulfilled all the things contained in it. (Deut. xxvii. 26; Gal. iii. 10.)

M. Hence we must conclude, that as there are two classes of men, so the office of the law is twofold?

S. Exactly. For among unbelievers it does nothing more than shut them out from all excuse before God. And this

is what Paul means when he calls it the ministry of death
and condemnation.   In regard to believers it has a very
different use.   (Rom. i. 32 ; 2 Cor. iii. 6.)

M. What ?

S. First, while they learn from it that they cannot obtain
righteousness by works, they are trained to humility, which
is the true preparation for seeking salvation in Christ.
Secondly, inasmuch as it requires of them much more than
they are able to perform, it urges them to seek strength from
the Lord, and at the same time reminds them of their perpetual guilt, that they may not presume to be proud.   Lastly,
it is a kind of curb, by which they are kept in the fear of
the Lord.   (Rom. iii. 20 ; Gal. ii. 16 ; iii. 11 ; iv. 5.)

M. Therefore, although in this earthly pilgrimage we never
satisfy the law, we cannot judge that it is superfluous to require this strict perfection from us.   For it shows the mark
at which we ought to aim, the goal towards which we ought
to press, that each of us, according to the measure of grace
bestowed upon him, may endeavour to frame his life according to the highest rectitude, and, by constant study, continually advance more and more.

S. That is my view.

M. Have we not a perfect rule of righteousness in the law ?

S. So much so, that God wishes nothing else from us than
to follow it ; and, on the other hand, repudiates and holds
void whatever we undertake beyond its prescription.   For
the only sacrifice which he accepts is obedience.   (1 Sam.
xv. 22.)

M. To what end, then, the many admonitions, precepts,
exhortations, which both Prophets and Apostles are continually employing ?   (Jer. vii. 12.)

S. They are nothing but mere expositions of the law,
which lead us by the hand to the obedience of the law, rather
than lead us away from it.

M. But he gives no command concerning the private case
of each individual ?

S. When he orders us to render to every one his due, it is
obvious to infer what the private part of each is in his own
order and condition of life, and expositions of particular pre-

cepts, as has been said, lie scattered throughout Scripture.
For what the Lord has summarily comprised here in a few
words, is given with more fulness and detail elsewhere.

OF PRAYER.

M. As the second part of Divine Worship, which consists
in service and obedience, has been sufficiently discussed, let
us now proceed to the third part.

S. We said it was invocation, by which we flee to God in
any necessity.

M. Do you think that he alone is to be invoked?

S. Certainly; for he requires this as the proper worship
of his Divinity.

M. If it is so, how can we beseech men to assist us?

S. There is a great difference between the two things.
For when we invoke God, we testify that we expect no good
from any other quarter, and that we place our whole defence
in no other, and yet we ask the assistance of men, as far as
he permits, and has bestowed on them the power of giving it.

M. You say, then, that in having recourse to the faith
and help of men, there is nothing that interferes with our
invocation of God, seeing that our reliance is not fixed on
them, and we beseech them on no other ground, than just
because God, by furnishing them with the means of well-
doing, has in a manner destined them to be the ministers of
his beneficence, and is pleased by their hands to assist us,
and draw out, on our account, the resources which he has
deposited with them?

S. Such is my view. And, accordingly, whatever benefits
we receive from them, we should regard as coming from
God, as in truth it is he alone who bestows all these things
upon us by their instrumentality.

M. But are we not to feel grateful to men whenever they
have conferred any kindness upon us. This the mere equity
of nature and law of humanity dictates?

S. Certainly we are; and were it only for the reason that
God honours them by sending to us, through their hands,
as rivulets, the blessings which flow from the inexhaustible

fountain of his liberality. In this way he lays us under obligation to them, and wishes us to acknowledge it. He, therefore, who does not show himself grateful to them by so doing, betrays his ingratitude to God.

M. Are we hence at liberty to infer, that it is wrong to invoke angels and holy servants of the Lord who have departed this life?

S. We are not at liberty; for God does not assign to saints the office of assisting us. And in regard to angels, though he uses their labour for our salvation, he does not wish us to ask them for it.

M. You say, then, that whatever does not aptly and fitly square with the order instituted by God, is repugnant to his will?

S. I do. For it is a sure sign of unbelief not to be contented with the things which God gives to us. Then if we throw ourselves on the protection of angels or saints, when God calls us to himself alone, and transfer to them the confidence which ought wholly to be fixed upon God, we fall into idolatry, seeing we share with them that which God claimed entirely for himself.

M. Let us now consider the manner of prayer. Is it sufficient to pray with the tongue, or does prayer require also the mind and heart?

S. The tongue, indeed, is not always necessary, but true prayer can never be without understanding and affection.

M. By what argument will you prove this to me?

S. Since God is a Spirit, he requires men to give him the heart in all cases, and more especially in prayer, by which they hold communion with him. Wherefore he promises to be near to those only who call upon him in truth: on the other hand, he abominates and curses all who pray to him deceitfully, and not sincerely. (Psalm cxlv. 18; Isaiah xxix. 13.)

M. All prayers, then, conceived only by the tongue, will be vain and worthless?

S. Not only so, but will be most displeasing to God.

M. What kind of feeling does God require in prayer?

S. First, that we feel our want and misery, and that this

feeling beget sorrow and anxiety in our minds. Secondly, that we be inflamed with an earnest and vehement desire to obtain grace from God. These things will also kindle in us an ardent longing to pray.

M. Does this feeling flow from the temper natural to man, or does it proceed from the grace of God?

S. Here God must come to our aid. For we are altogether stupid in regard to both. (Rom. viii. 25.) It is the Spirit of God who excites in us groanings which cannot be uttered, and frames our minds to the desires which are requisite in prayer, as Paul says. (Gal. iv. 6.)

M. Is it the meaning of this doctrine, that we are to sit still, and, in a kind of vacillating state, wait for the motions of the Spirit, and not that each one is to urge himself to pray?

S. By no means. The meaning rather is, that when believers feel themselves cold or sluggish, and somewhat indisposed to pray, they should forthwith flee to God, and beseech him to inflame them by the fiery darts of his Spirit, that they may be rendered fit to pray.

M. You do not, however, mean that there is to be no use of the tongue in prayer?

S. Not at all. For it often helps to sustain the mind, and keep it from being so easily drawn off from God. Besides, as it, more than other members, was created to display the glory of God, it is right that it be employed to this purpose, to the whole extent of its capacity. Moreover, vehemence of desire occasionally impels a man to break forth into utterance with the tongue without intending it.

M. If so, what profit have those who pray in a foreign tongue not understood by them?

S. It is nothing else than to sport with God. Christians, therefore, should have nothing to do with this hypocrisy. (1 Cor. xiv. 15.)

M. But when we pray do we do it fortuitously, uncertain of success, or ought we to feel assured that the Lord will hear us?

S. The foundation of our prayer should always be, that the Lord will hear us, and that we shall obtain whatever we ask, in so far as is for our good. For this reason Paul tells us, that true prayer flows from faith. (Rom. x. 14.) For no man will ever duly call upon him, without previously resting with firm reliance on his goodness.

M. What then will become of those who pray in doubt, and without fixing in their minds what profit they are to gain by praying, nay, are uncertain whether or not their prayers will be heard by God?

S. Their prayers are vain and void, not being supported by any promise. For we are ordered to ask with sure faith, and the promise is added, that whatever we shall ask, believing, we shall receive. (Matt. xxi. 22; Mark xi. 24; James i. 6.)

M. It remains to be seen wherein we have such great confidence, that while unworthy, on so many accounts, of appearing in the presence of God, we however dare to sist ourselves before him.

S. First, we have promises by which we must simply abide, without making any reference to our own worthiness. Secondly, if we are sons, God animates and instigates us by his Spirit, so that we doubt not to betake ourselves to him in a familiar manner, as to a father. As we are like worms, and are oppressed by the consciousness of our sins, God, in order that we may not tremble at his glorious majesty, sets forth Christ as a Mediator, through whom we obtain access, and have no doubt at all of obtaining favour. (Psalm iv. 15; xci. 15; cxlv. 18; Isaiah xxx. 19; lxv. 1; Jer. xxix. 12; Joel ii. 32; Rom. viii. 25; x. 13.)

M. Do you understand that we are to pray to God only in the name of Christ?

S. I so understand. For it is both so enjoined in distinct terms, and the promise is added, that he will by his intercession obtain what we ask. (1 Tim. ii. 5; 1 John ii. 1.)

M. He is not then to be accused of rashness or presumption, who, trusting to this Advocate, makes a familiar approach to God, and holds forth to God and to himself Christ as the only one through whom he is to be heard? (Heb. iv. 14.)

S. By no means: For he who thus prays conceives his

prayers as it were at the lips of Christ, seeing he knows, that by the intercession of Christ, his prayer is assisted and recommended. (Rom. viii. 15.)

M. Let us now consider what the prayers of believers ought to contain. Is it lawful to ask of God whatever comes into our mind, or is a certain rule to be observed ?

S. It were a very preposterous method of prayer to indulge our own desires and the judgment of the flesh. We are too ignorant to be able to judge what is expedient for us, and we labour under an intemperance of desire, to which it is necessary that a bridle be applied.

M. What then requires to be done ?

S. The only thing remaining is for God himself to prescribe a proper form of prayer, that we may follow him while he leads us by the hand, and as it were sets words before us.

M. What rule has he prescribed ?

S. The doctrine on this subject is amply and copiously delivered in the Scriptures. But to give us a surer aim, he framed, and, as it were, dictated a form in which he has briefly comprehended and digested under a few heads whatever it is lawful, and for our interest to ask.

M. Repeat it.

S. Our Lord Jesus Christ being asked by his disciples in what way they ought to pray, answered, when ye would pray, say ye, (Matt. vi. 9 ; Luke xi. 2,) " Our Father, which art in heaven, hallowed be thy name. Thy kingdom come. Thy will be done in earth, as it is in heaven. Give us this day our daily bread. And forgive us our debts, as we forgive our debtors. And lead us not into temptation; but deliver us from evil: For thine is the kingdom, and the power, and the glory, for ever. Amen."

M. That we may the better understand what it contains, let us divide it into heads.

S. It contains six parts, of which the three first respect the glory of God alone as their proper end, without any reference to us: the other three relate to us and our interest.

M. Are we then to ask God for any thing from which no benefit redounds to us ?

S. He indeed of his infinite goodness so arranges all things that nothing tends to his glory without being also salutary to us. Therefore when his name is sanctified, he causes it to turn to our sanctification also; nor does his kingdom come without our being in a manner sharers in it. But in asking all these things, we ought to look only to his glory without thinking of advantage to ourselves.

M. According to this view, three of these requests have a connection with our own good, and yet their only aim ought to be, that the name of God may be glorified.

S. It is so; and thus the glory of God ought also to be considered in the other three, though they are properly intended to express desire for things which belong to our good and salvation.

M. Let us now proceed to an explanation of the words; and, first, Why is the name of Father, rather than any other, here given to God?

S. As security of conscience is one of the most essential requisites for praying aright, God assumes this name, which suggests only the idea of pure kindness, that having thus banished all anxiety from our minds, he may invite us to make a familiar approach to him.

M. Shall we then dare to go to him directly without hesitation as children to parents?

S. Wholly so: nay, with much surer confidence of obtaining what we ask. For as our Master reminds us, (Matt. vii. 11,) If we being evil cannot however refuse good things to our children, nor bear to send them empty away, nor give them poison for bread, how much greater kindness is to be expected from our heavenly Father, who is not only supremely good, but goodness itself?

M. May we not from this name also draw the inference which we mentioned at the outset, viz., that to be approved, all our prayers should be founded on the intercession of Christ? (John xv. 7; Rom. viii. 15.)

S. And indeed a most valid inference. For God regards us as sons, only in so far as we are members of Christ.

M. Why do you call God "our Father" in common, rather than "my Father" in particular?

S. Each believer may indeed call him his own Father, but the Lord used the common epithet that he might accustom us to exercise charity in our prayers, and that we might not neglect others, by each caring only for himself.

M. What is meant by the additional clause, that God is in heaven?

S. It is just the same as if I were to call him exalted, mighty, incomprehensible.

M. To what end this, and for what reason?

S. In this way we are taught when we pray to him to raise our minds aloft, and not have any carnal or earthly thoughts of him, nor measure him by our own little standard, lest thinking too meanly of him, we should wish to bring him into subjection to our will, instead of learning to look up with fear and reverence to his glorious Majesty. It tends to excite and confirm our confidence in him, when he is proclaimed to be the Lord and Governor of heaven, ruling all things at his pleasure.

M. Repeat to me the substance of the first petition.

S. By the name of God, Scripture denotes the knowledge and fame with which he is celebrated among men. We pray then that his glory may be promoted everywhere, and in all.

M. But can any thing be added to his glory, or taken from it?

S. In itself it neither increases nor is diminished. But we pray as is meet, that it may be illustrious among men— that in whatever God does, all his works may appear, as they are, glorious, that he himself may by all means be glorified.

M. What understand you by the kingdom of God in the second petition?

S. It consists chiefly of two branches—that he would govern the elect by his Spirit—that he would prostrate and destroy the reprobate who refuse to give themselves up to his service, thus making it manifest that nothing is able to resist his might.

M. In what sense do you pray that this kingdom may come?

S. That the Lord would daily increase the numbers of the faithful—that he would ever and anon load them with new gifts of his Spirit, until he fill them completely : moreover, that he would render his truth more clear and conspicuous by dispelling the darkness of Satan, that he would abolish all iniquity, by advancing his own righteousness.

M. Are not all these things done every day ?

S. They are done so far, that the kingdom of God may be said to be commenced. We pray, therefore, that it may constantly increase and be carried forward, until it attain its greatest height, which we only hope to take place on the last day on which God alone, after reducing all creatures to order, will be exalted and pre-eminent, and so be all in all. (1 Cor. xv. 28.)

M. What mean you by asking that the will of God may be done ?

S. That all creatures may be subdued into obedience to him, and so depend on his nod, that nothing may be done except at his pleasure.

M. Do you think then that any thing can be done against his will ?

S. We not only pray that what he has decreed with himself may come to pass, but also that all contumacy being tamed and subjugated, he would subject all wills to his own, and frame them in obedience to it.

M. Do we not by thus praying surrender our own wills ?

S. Entirely : nor do we only pray that he would make void whatever desires of ours are at variance with his own will, but also that he would form in us new minds and new hearts, so that we may wish nothing of ourselves, but rather that his Spirit may preside over our wishes, and bring them into perfect unison with God.

M. Why do you pray that this may be done on earth as it is in heaven ?

S. As the holy angels, who are his celestial creatures, have it as their only object to obey him in all things, to be always obedient to his word, and prepared voluntarily to do him service, we pray for such prompt obedience in men, that each may give himself up entirely to him in voluntary subjection.

M. Let us now come to the second part. What mean you by the " daily" bread you ask for ?

S. In general every thing that tends to the preservation of the present life, not only food or clothing, but also all other helps by which the wants of outward life are sustained; that we may eat our bread in quiet, so far as the Lord knows it to be expedient.

M. But why do you ask God to give what he orders us to provide by our own labour ?

S. Though we are to labour, and even sweat in providing food, we are not nourished either by our own labour, or our own industry, or our own diligence, but by the blessing of God by which the labour of our hands, that would otherwise be in vain, prospers. Moreover we should understand, that even when abundance of food is supplied to our hand, and we eat it, we are not nourished by its substance, but by the virtue of God alone. It has not any inherent efficacy in its own nature, but God supplies it from heaven as the instrument of his own beneficence. (Deut. viii. 3 ; Matt. iv. 4.)

M. But by what right do you call it your bread when you ask God to give it ?

S. Because by the kindness of God it becomes ours, though it is by no means due to us. We are also reminded by this term to refrain from coveting the bread of others, and to be contented with that which has come to us in a legitimate manner as from the hand of God.

M. Why do you add both " daily" and " this day ?"

S. By these two terms we are taught moderation and temperance, that our wishes may not exceed the measure of necessity.

M. As this prayer ought to be common to all, how can the rich, who have abundance at home, and have provision laid up for a long period, ask it to be given them for a day ?

S. The rich, equally with the poor, should remember that none of the things which they have will do them good, unless God grant them the use of them, and by his grace make the use fruitful and efficacious. Wherefore while possessing all things, we have nothing except in so far as we every hour receive from the hand of God what is necessary and sufficient for us.

M. What does the fifth petition contain?

S. That the Lord would pardon our sins.

M. Can no mortal be found so righteous as not to require this pardon?

S. Not one. When Christ gave this form of prayer, he designed it for the whole Church. Wherefore he who would exempt himself from this necessity, must leave the society of the faithful. And we have the testimony of Scripture, namely, that he who would contend before God to clear himself in one thing, will be found guilty in a thousand. (Job ix. 3.) The only refuge left for all is in his mercy.

M. How do you think that sins are forgiven us?

S. As the words of Christ express, namely, that they are debts which make us liable to eternal death, until God of his mere liberality deliver us.

M. You say then that it is by the free mercy of God that we obtain the pardon of sins?

S. Entirely so. For were the punishment of only one sin, and that the least, to be ransomed, we could not satisfy it. All then must be freely overlooked and forgiven.

M. What advantage accrues to us from this forgiveness?

S. We are accepted, just as if we were righteous and innocent, and at the same time our consciences are confirmed in a full reliance on his paternal favour, assuring us of salvation.

M. Does the appended condition, viz., that he would forgive us as we forgive our debtors, mean that we merit pardon from God by pardoning men who have in any way offended us?

S. By no means. For in this way forgiveness would not be free nor founded alone on the satisfaction which Christ made for us on the cross. But as by forgetting the injuries done to ourselves, we, while imitating his goodness and clemency, demonstrate that we are in fact his children, God wishes us to confirm it by this pledge; and at the same time shows us, on the other hand, that if we do not show ourselves easy and ready to pardon, nothing else is to be expected of him than the highest inexorable rigour of severity.

M. Do you say then that all who cannot from the heart forgive offences are discarded by God and expunged from his list of children, so that they cannot hope for any place of pardon in heaven ?

S. So I think, in accordance with the words, " With what measure ye mete it shall be measured to you again."

M. What comes next ?

S. " Lead us not into temptation, but deliver us from evil."

M. Do you include all this in one petition ?

S. It is only one petition ; for the latter clause is an explanation of the former.

M. What does it contain in substance ?

S. That the Lord would not permit us to rush or fall into sin—that he would not leave us to be overcome by the devil and the desires of our flesh, which wage constant war with us—that he would rather furnish us with his strength to resist, sustain us by his hand, cover and fortify us by his protection, so that under his guardianship and tutelage we may dwell safely.

M. How is this done ?

S. When governed by his Spirit we are imbued with such a love and desire of righteousness, as to overcome the flesh, sin, and Satan ; and, on the other hand, with such a hatred of sin as may keep us separated from the world in pure holiness. For our victory consists in the power of the Spirit.

M. Have we need of this assistance ?

S. Who can dispense with it ? The devil is perpetually hovering over us, and going about as a roaring lion seeking whom he may devour. (1 Pet. v. 8.) And let us consider what our weakness is. Nay, all would be over with us every single moment did not God equip us for battle with his own weapons, and strengthen us with his own hand.

M. What do you mean by the term *Temptation* ?

S. The tricks and fallacies of Satan, by which he is constantly attacking us, and would forthwith easily circumvent us, were we not aided by the help of God. For both our mind, from its native vanity, is liable to his wiles, and our will, which is always prone to evil, would immediately yield to him.

M. But why do you pray God not to lead you into temptation, which seems to be the proper act of Satan, not of God ?

S. As God defends believers by his protection, that they may neither be oppressed by the wiles of Satan, nor overcome by sin, so those whom he means to punish he not only leaves destitute of his grace, but also delivers to the tyranny of Satan, strikes with blindness, and gives over to a reprobate mind, so that they are completely enslaved to sin and exposed to all the assaults of temptation.

M. What is meant by the clause which is added, " For thine is the kingdom, and the power, and the glory, for ever ?"

S. We are here again reminded that our prayers must lean more on the power and goodness of God than on any confidence in ourselves. Besides, we are taught to close all our prayers with praise.

M. Is it not lawful to ask any thing of God that is not comprehended in this form ?

S. Although we are free to pray in other words, and in another manner, we ought, however, to hold that no prayer can please God which is not referable to this as the only rule of right Prayer.

OF THE WORD OF GOD.

M. The order already adopted by us requires that we now consider the fourth part of divine worship.

S. We said that this consists in acknowledging God as the author of all good, and in extolling his goodness, justice, wisdom, and power with praise and thanksgiving, that thus the glory of all good may remain entirely with him.

M. Has he prescribed no rule as to this part ?

S. All the praises extant in Scripture ought to be our rule.

M. Has the Lord's Prayer nothing which applies here?

S. Yes. When we pray that his name may be hallowed, we pray that he may be duly glorified in his works—that he may be regarded, whether in pardoning sinners, as merciful; or in exercising vengeance, as just; or in performing his promises, as true: in short, that whatever of his works we see may excite us to glorify him. This is indeed to ascribe to him the praise of all that is good.

M. What shall we infer from these heads which have hitherto been considered by us?

S. What truth itself teaches, and was stated at the outset, viz., that this is eternal life to know one true God the Father, and Jesus Christ whom he hath sent, (John xvii. 3,)—to know him, I say, in order that we may pay due honour and worship to him, that he may be not only our Lord but also our Father and Saviour, and we be in turn his children and servants, and accordingly devote our lives to the illustration of his glory.

M. How can we attain to such blessedness?

S. For this end God has left us his holy word; for spiritual doctrine is a kind of door by which we enter his heavenly kingdom.

M. Where are we to seek for this word?

S. In the Holy Scriptures, in which it is contained.

M. How are you to use it in order to profit by it?

S. By embracing it with entire heartfelt persuasion, as certain truth come down from heaven—by being docile, and subjecting our minds and wills in obedience to it—by loving it sincerely—by having it once for all engraven on our hearts, and there rooted so as to produce fruit in our life—finally, by being formed after its rule. Then shall it turn to our salvation, as it was intended.

M. Are all these things put in our own power?

S. None of them at all; but every thing which I have mentioned it belongs to God only to effect in us by the gift of his Spirit.

M. But are we not to use diligence, and zealously strive to profit in it by reading, hearing, and meditating?

S. Yea, verily: seeing that every one ought to exercise

himself in the daily reading of it, and all should be especially careful to attend the sermons when the doctrine of salvation is expounded in the assembly of the faithful.

M. You affirm then that it is not enough for each to read privately at home, and that all ought to meet in common to hear the same doctrine?

S. They must meet when they can—that is, when an opportunity is given.

M. Are you able to prove this to me?

S. The will of God alone ought to be amply sufficient for proof; and the order which he hath recommended to his church is not what two or three only might observe, but all should obey in common. Moreover, he declares this to be the only method of edifying as well as preserving. This, then, should be a sacred and inviolable rule to us, and no one should think himself entitled to be wise above his Master.

M. Is it necessary, then, that pastors should preside over churches?

S. Nay; it is necessary to hear them, and listen with fear and reverence to the doctrine of Christ as propounded from their lips.

M. But is it enough for a Christian man to have been instructed by his pastor once, or ought he to observe this course during life?

S. It is little to have begun, unless you persevere. We must be the disciples of Christ to the end, or rather without end. But he has committed to the ministers of the Church the office of teaching in his name and stead.

OF THE SACRAMENTS.

M. Is there no other medium, as it is called, than the Word by which God may communicate himself to us?

S. To the preaching of the Word he has added the Sacraments.

M. What is a Sacrament?

S. An outward attestation of the divine benevolence towards us, which, by a visible sign, figures spiritual grace, to seal the promises of God on our hearts, and thereby better confirm their truth to us.

M. Is there such virtue in a visible sign that it can establish our consciences in a full assurance of salvation ?

S. This virtue it has not of itself, but by the will of God, because it was instituted for this end.

M. Seeing it is the proper office of the Holy Spirit to seal the promises of God on our minds, how do you attribute this to the sacraments ?

S. There is a wide difference between him and them. To move and affect the heart, to enlighten the mind, to render the conscience sure and tranquil, truly belongs to the Spirit alone ; so that it ought to be regarded as wholly his work, and be ascribed to him alone, that no other may have the praise ; but this does not at all prevent God from employing the sacraments as secondary instruments, and applying them to what use he deems proper, without derogating in any respect from the agency of the Spirit.

M. You think, then, that the power and efficacy of a sacrament is not contained in the outward element, but flows entirely from the Spirit of God ?

S. I think so ; viz., that the Lord hath been pleased to exert his energy by his instruments, this being the purpose to which he destined them : this he does without detracting in any respect from the virtue of his Spirit.

M. Can you give me a reason why he so acts ?

S. In this way he consults our weakness. If we were wholly spiritual, we might, like the angels, spiritually behold both him and his grace ; but as we are surrounded with this body of clay, we need figures or mirrors to exhibit a view of spiritual and heavenly things in a kind of earthly manner ; for we could not otherwise attain to them. At the same time, it is our interest to have all our senses exercised in the promises of God, that they may be the better confirmed to us.

M. If it is true that the sacraments were instituted by God to be helps to our necessity, is it not arrogance for any one to hold that he can dispense with them as unnecessary ?

S. It certainly is ; and hence, if any one of his own accord abstains from the use of them, as if he had no need of them, he contemns Christ, spurns his grace, and quenches the Spirit.

M. But what confidence can there be in the sacraments as a means of establishing the conscience, and what certain security can be conceived from things which the good and bad use indiscriminately?

S. Although the wicked, so to speak, annihilate the gifts of God offered in the sacraments in so far as regards themselves, they do not thereby deprive the sacraments of their nature and virtue.

M. How, then, and when does the effect follow the use of the sacraments ?

S. When we receive them in faith, seeking Christ alone and his grace in them.

M. Why do you say that Christ is to be sought in them ?

S. I mean that we are not to cleave to the visible signs so as to seek salvation from them, or imagine that the power of conferring grace is either fixed or included in them, but rather that the sign is to be used as a help, by which, when seeking salvation and complete felicity, we are pointed directly to Christ.

M. Seeing that faith is requisite for the use of them, how do you say that they are given us to confirm our faith, to make us more certain of the promises of God?

S. It is by no means sufficient that faith is once begun in us. It must be nourished continually, and increase more and more every day. To nourish, strengthen, and advance it, the Lord instituted the sacraments. This indeed Paul intimates, when he says that they have the effect of sealing the promises of God. (Rom. iv. 11.)

M. But is it not an indication of unbelief not to have entire faith in the promises of God until they are confirmed to us from another source ?

S. It certainly argues a weakness of faith under which the children of God labour. They do not, however, cease to be believers, though the faith with which they are endued is still small and imperfect ; for as long as we continue in this world remains of distrust cleave to our flesh, and these there is no other way of shaking off than by making continual progress even unto the end. It is therefore always necessary to be going forward.

M. How many are the sacraments of the Christian Church ?

S. There are only two, whose use is common among all believers.

M. What are they ?

S. Baptism and the Holy Supper.

M. What likeness or difference is there between them ?

S. Baptism is a kind of entrance into the Church ; for we have in it a testimony that we who are otherwise strangers and aliens, are received into the family of God, so as to be counted of his household ; on the other hand, the Supper attests that God exhibits himself to us by nourishing our souls.

M. That the meaning of both may be more clear to us, let us treat of them separately. First, what is the meaning of Baptism ?

S. It consists of two parts. For, *first*, Forgiveness of sins ; and, *secondly*, Spiritual regeneration, is figured by it. (Eph. v. 26 ; Rom. vi. 4.)

M. What resemblance has water with these things, so as to represent them ?

S. Forgiveness of sins is a kind of washing, by which our souls are cleansed from their defilements, just as bodily stains are washed away by water.

M. What do you say of Regeneration ?

S. Since the mortification of our nature is its beginning, and our becoming new creatures its end, a figure of death is set before us when the water is poured upon the head, and the figure of a new life when instead of remaining immersed under water, we only enter it for a moment as a kind of grave, out of which we instantly emerge.

M. Do you think that the water is a washing of the soul?

S. By no means ; for it were impious to snatch away this honour from the blood of Christ, which was shed in order to wipe away all our stains, and render us pure and unpolluted in the sight of God. (1 Pet. i. 19 ; 1 John i. 7.) And we receive the fruit of this cleansing when the Holy Spirit sprinkles our consciences with that sacred blood. Of this we have a seal in the Sacrament.

M. But do you attribute nothing more to the water than that it is a figure of ablution ?

S. I understand it to be a figure, but still so that the reality is annexed to it ; for God does not disappoint us when he promises us his gifts. Accordingly, it is certain that both pardon of sins and newness of life are offered to us in baptism, and received by us.

M. Is this grace bestowed on all indiscriminately ?

S. Many precluding its entrance by their depravity, make it void to themselves. Hence the benefit extends to believers only, and yet the Sacrament loses nothing of its nature.

M. Whence is Regeneration derived ?

S. From the Death and Resurrection of Christ taken together. His death hath this efficacy, that by means of it our old man is crucified, and the vitiosity of our nature in a manner buried, so as no more to be in vigour in us. Our reformation to a new life, so as to obey the righteousness of God, is the result of the resurrection.

M. How are these blessings bestowed upon us by Baptism ?

S. If we do not render the promises there offered unfruitful by rejecting them, we are clothed with Christ, and presented with his Spirit.

M. What must we do in order to use Baptism duly ?

S. The right use of Baptism consists in faith and repentance ; that is, we must first hold with a firm heartfelt reliance that, being purified from all stains by the blood of Christ, we are pleasing to God : secondly, we must feel his Spirit dwelling in us, and declare this to others by our actions, and we must constantly exercise ourselves in aiming at the mortification of our flesh, and obedience to the righteousness of God.

M. If these things are requisite to the legitimate use of Baptism, how comes it that we baptize Infants ?

S. It is not necessary that faith and repentance should always precede baptism. They are only required from those whose age makes them capable of both. It will be sufficient, then, if, after infants have grown up, they exhibit the power of their baptism.

M. Can you demonstrate by reason that there is nothing absurd in this ?

S. Yes ; if it be conceded to me that our Lord instituted nothing at variance with reason.   For while Moses and all the Prophets teach that circumcision was a sign of repentance, and was even as Paul declares the sacrament of faith, we see that infants were not excluded from it.   (Deut. xxx. 6 ; Jer. iv. 4 ; Rom. iv. 11.)

M. But are they now admitted to Baptism for the same reason that was valid in circumcision ?

S. The very same, seeing that the promises which God anciently gave to the people of Israel are now published through the whole world.

M. But do you infer from thence that the sign also is to be used ?

S. He who will duly ponder all things in both ordinances, will perceive this to follow.   Christ in making us partakers of his grace, which had been formerly bestowed on Israel, did not condition, that it should either be more obscure or in some respect less abundant.   Nay, rather he shed it upon us both more clearly and more abundantly.

M. Do you think that if infants are denied baptism, some thing is thereby deducted from the grace of God, and it must be said to have been diminished by the coming of Christ?

S. That indeed is evident ; for the sign being taken away, which tends very much to testify the mercy of God and confirm the promises, we should want an admirable consolation which those of ancient times enjoyed.

M. Your view then is, that since God, under the Old Testament, in order to show himself the Father of infants, was pleased that the promise of salvation should be engraven on their bodies by a visible sign, it were unbecoming to suppose that, since the advent of Christ, believers have less to confirm them, God having intended to give us in the present day the same promise which was anciently given to the Fathers, and exhibited in Christ a clearer specimen of his goodness ?

S. That is my view. Besides, while it is sufficiently clear that the force, and so to speak, the substance of Baptism are common to children, to deny them the sign, which is inferior to the substance, were manifest injustice.

M. On what terms then are children to be baptized?

S. To attest that they are heirs of the blessing promised to the seed of believers, and enable them to receive and produce the fruit of their Baptism, on acknowledging its reality after they have grown up.

M. Let us now pass to the Supper. And, first, I should like to know from you what its meaning is.

S. It was instituted by Christ in order that by the communication of his body and blood, he might teach and assure us that our souls are being trained in the hope of eternal life.

M. But why is the body of our Lord figured by bread, and his blood by wine?

S. We are hence taught that such virtue as bread has in nourishing our bodies to sustain the present life, the same has the body of our Lord spiritually to nourish our souls. As by wine the hearts of men are gladdened, their strength recruited, and the whole man strengthened, so by the blood of our Lord the same benefits are received by our souls.

M. Do we therefore eat the body and blood of the Lord?

S. I understand so. For as our whole reliance for salvation depends on him, in order that the obedience which he yielded to the Father may be imputed to us just as if it were ours, it is necessary that he be possessed by us; for the only way in which he communicates his blessings to us is by making himself ours.

M. But did he not give himself when he exposed himself to death, that he might redeem us from the sentence of death, and reconcile us to God?

S. That is indeed true; but it is not enough for us unless we now receive him, that thus the efficacy and fruit of his death may reach us.

M. Does not the manner of receiving consist in faith?

S. I admit it does. But I at the same time add, that

this is done when we not only believe that he died in order to free us from death, and was raised up that he might purchase life for us, but recognise that he dwells in us, and that we are united to him by a union the same in kind as that which unites the members to the head, that by virtue of this union we may become partakers of all his blessings.

M. Do we obtain this communion by the Supper alone?

S. No, indeed. For by the gospel also, as Paul declares, Christ is communicated to us. And Paul justly declares this, seeing we are there told that we are flesh of his flesh and bones of his bones—that he is the living bread which came down from heaven to nourish our souls—that we are one with him as he is one with the Father, &c. (1 Cor. i. 6; Eph. v. 30; John vi. 51; John xvii. 21.)

M. What more do we obtain from the sacrament, or what other benefit does it confer upon us?

S. The communion of which I spoke is thereby confirmed and increased; for although Christ is exhibited to us both in baptism and in the gospel, we do not however receive him entire, but in part only.

M. What then have we in the symbol of bread?

S. As the body of Christ was once sacrificed for us to reconcile us to God, so now also is it given to us, that we may certainly know that reconciliation belongs to us.

M. What in the symbol of wine?

S. That as Christ once shed his blood for the satisfaction of our sins, and as the price of our redemption, so he now also gives it to us to drink, that we may feel the benefit which should thence accrue to us.

M. According to these two answers, the holy Supper of the Lord refers us to his death, that we may communicate in its virtue?

S. Wholly so; for then the one perpetual sacrifice, sufficient for our salvation, was performed. Hence nothing more remains for us but to enjoy it.

M. The Supper then was not instituted in order to offer up to God the body of his Son?

S. By no means. He himself alone, as priest for ever, has

this privilege; and so his words express when he says, "Take, eat." He there commands us not to offer his body, but only to eat it. (Heb. v. 10 ; Matt. xxvi. 26.)

M. Why do we use two signs?

S. Therein the Lord consulted our weakness, teaching us in a more familiar manner that he is not only food to our souls, but drink also, so that we are not to seek any part of spiritual life anywhere else than in him alone.

M. Ought all without exception to use both alike?

S. So the commandment of Christ bears : and to derogate from it in any way, by attempting anything contrary to it, is wicked.

M. Have we in the Supper only a figure of the benefits which you have mentioned, or are they there exhibited to us in reality?

S. Seeing that our Lord Jesus Christ is truth itself, there cannot be a doubt that he at the same time fulfils the promises which he there gives us, and adds the reality to the figures. Wherefore I doubt not that as he testifies by words and signs, so he also makes us partakers of his substance, that thus we may have one life with him.

M. But how can this be, when the body of Christ is in heaven, and we are still pilgrims on the earth?

S. This he accomplishes by the secret and miraculous agency of his Spirit, to whom it is not difficult to unite things otherwise disjoined by a distant space.

M. You do not imagine then, either that the body is inclosed in the bread or the blood in the wine?

S. Neither is inclosed. My understanding rather is, that in order to obtain the reality of the signs, our minds must be raised to heaven, where Christ is, and from whence we expect him as Judge and Redeemer, and that it is improper and vain to seek him in these earthly elements.

M. To collect the substance of what you have said—You maintain that there are two things in the Supper, viz., bread and wine, which are seen by the eyes, handled by the hands, and perceived by the taste, and Christ by whom our souls are inwardly fed as with their own proper aliment?

S. True ; and so much so that the resurrection of the body also is there confirmed to us by a kind of pledge, since the body also shares in the symbol of life.

M. What is the right and legitimate use of this Sacrament ?

S. That which Paul points out, "Let a man examine himself," before he approach to it.   (1 Cor. xi. 28.)

M. Into what is he to inquire in this examination ?

S. Whether he be a true member of Christ.

M. By what evidence may he come to know this ?

S. If he is endued with faith and repentance, if he entertains sincere love for his neighbour, if he has his mind pure from all hatred and malice.

M. Do you require that a man's faith and charity should both be perfect ?

S. Both should be entire and free from all hypocrisy, but it were vain to demand an absolute perfection to which nothing should be wanting, seeing that none such will ever be found in man.

M. Then the imperfection under which we still labour does not forbid our approach ?

S. On the contrary, were we perfect, the Supper would no longer be of any use to us.   It should be a help to aid our weakness, and a support to our imperfection.

M. Is no other end besides proposed by these two Sacraments ?

S. They are also marks and as it were badges of our profession.   For by the use of them we profess our faith before men, and testify our consent in the religion of Christ.

M. Were any one to despise the use of them, in what light should it be regarded ?

S. As an indirect denial of Christ.   Assuredly such a person, inasmuch as he deigns not to confess himself a Christian, deserves not to be classed among Christians.

M. Is it enough to receive both once in a lifetime ?

S. It is enough so to receive baptism, which may not be repeated.   It is different with the Supper.

M. What is the difference ?

S. By baptism the Lord adopts us and brings us into his Church, so as thereafter to regard us as part of his household. After he has admitted us among the number of his people, he testifies by the Supper that he takes a continual interest in nourishing us.

M. Does the administration both of baptism and of the Supper belong indiscriminately to all?

S. By no means. It is confined to those to whom the office of teaching has been committed. For the two things, viz., to feed the Church with the doctrine of piety and administer the sacrament, are united together by an indissoluble tie.

M. Can you prove this to me by the testimony of Scripture?

S. Christ gave special commandment to the Apostles to baptize. In the celebration of the Supper he ordered us to follow his example. And the Evangelists relate that he himself in dispensing it, performed the office of a public minister. (Matt. xxviii. 19 ; Luke xxii. 19.)

M. But ought pastors, to whom the dispensing of it has been committed, to admit all indiscriminately without selection?

S. In regard to baptism, as it is now bestowed only on infants, there is no room for discrimination ; but in the Supper the minister ought to take heed not to give it to any one who is clearly unworthy of receiving it.

M. Why so?

S. Because it cannot be done without insulting and profaning the Sacrament.

M. But did not Christ admit Judas, impious though he was, to the Communion?

S. I admit it ; as his impiety was still secret. For though it was not unknown to Christ, it had not come to light or the knowledge of men. (Matt. xxvi. 25.)

M. What then can be done with hypocrites?

S. The pastor cannot keep them back as unworthy, but must wait till such time as God shall reveal their iniquity, and make it manifest to all.

M. But if he knows or has been warned that an individual is unworthy?

S. Even that would not be sufficient to keep him back

from communicating, unless in addition to it there was a legitimate investigation and decision of the Church.

M. It is of importance, then, that there should be a certain order of government established in churches ?

S. It is : they cannot otherwise be well managed or duly constituted.   The method is for elders to be chosen to preside as censors of manners, to guard watchfully against offences, and exclude from communion all whom they recognise to be unfit for it, and who could not be admitted without profaning the Sacrament.

SEVERAL GODLY PRAYERS.

My God, my Father and Preserver, who of thy goodness hast watched over me during the past night, and brought me to this day, grant also that I may spend it wholly in the worship and service of thy most holy deity. Let me not think, or say, or do a single thing which tends not to thy service and submission to thy will, that thus all my actions may aim at thy glory and the salvation of my brethren, while they are taught by my example to serve thee. And as thou art giving light to this world for the purposes of external life by the rays of the sun, so enlighten my mind by the effulgence of thy Spirit, that he may guide me in the way of thy righteousness. To whatever purpose I apply my mind, may the end which I ever propose to myself be thy honour and service. May I expect all happiness from thy grace and goodness only. Let me not attempt any thing whatever that is not pleasing to thee.

Grant also, that while I labour for the maintenance of this life, and care for the things which pertain to food and raiment, I may raise my mind above them to the blessed and heavenly life which thou hast promised to thy children. Be pleased also, in manifesting thyself to me as the protector of my soul as well as my body, to strengthen and fortify me against all the assaults of the devil, and deliver me from all the dangers which continually beset us in this life. But seeing it is a small thing to have begun, unless I also persevere, I therefore entreat of thee, O Lord, not only to be my guide and director for this day, but to keep me under thy protection to the very end of life, that thus my whole course may be performed under thy superintendence. As I ought

to make progress, do thou add daily more and more to the
gifts of thy grace until I wholly adhere to thy Son Jesus
Christ, whom we justly regard as the true Sun, shining constantly in our minds.   In order to my obtaining of thee
these great and manifold blessings, forget, and out of thy
infinite mercy, forgive my offences, as thou hast promised
that thou wilt do to those who call upon thee in sincerity.

(Ps. cxliii. 8.)—Grant that I may hear thy voice in the
morning since I have hoped in thee.   Show me the way in
which I should walk, since I have lifted up my soul unto
thee.   Deliver me from my enemies, O Lord, I have fled
unto thee.   Teach me to do thy will, for thou art my God.
Let thy good Spirit conduct me to the land of uprightness.

PRAYER ON PREPARING TO GO TO SCHOOL.

> Ps. cxix. 9.   Wherein shall a young man establish his way?
> If he wisely conduct himself according to thy word.   With
> my heart have I sought thee, allow me not to err from thy
> precepts.

O LORD, who art the fountain of all wisdom and learning,
since thou of thy special goodness hast granted that my youth
is instructed in good arts which may assist me to honest and
holy living, grant also, by enlightening my mind, which
otherwise labours under blindness, that I may be fit to
acquire knowledge ; strengthen my memory faithfully to
retain what I may have learned : and govern my heart, that
I may be willing and even eager to profit, lest the opportunity which thou now givest me be lost through my sluggishness.   Be pleased therefore to infuse thy Spirit into me,
the Spirit of understanding, of truth, judgment, and prudence, lest my study be without success, and the labour of
my teacher be in vain.

In whatever kind of study I engage, enable me to remember to keep its proper end in view, namely, to know thee in
Christ Jesus thy Son ; and may every thing that I learn
assist me to observe the right rule of godliness.   And seeing
thou promisest that thou wilt bestow wisdom on babes, and

such as are humble, and the knowledge of thyself on the
upright in heart, while thou declarest that thou wilt cast
down the wicked and the proud, so that they will fade away
in their ways, I entreat that thou wouldst be pleased to
turn me to true humility, that thus I may show myself
teachable and obedient first of all to thyself, and then to
those also who by thy authority are placed over me. Be
pleased at the same time to root out all vicious desires from
my heart, and inspire it with an earnest desire of seeking
thee. Finally, let the only end at which I aim be so to
qualify myself in early life, that when I grow up I may
serve thee in whatever station thou mayest assign me.
AMEN.

> The secret of the Lord is with them that fear him ; and he
> will make known his covenant unto them. (Ps. xxv. 14.)

BLESSING AT TABLE.

> All look unto thee, O Lord ; and thou givest them their meat
> in due season ; that thou givest them they gather : thou
> openest thine hand, and they are filled with all things in
> abundance. (Ps. civ. 27.)

O LORD, in whom is the source and inexhaustible fountain of all good things, pour out thy blessing upon us, and
sanctify to our use the meat and drink which are the gifts
of thy kindness towards us, that we, using them soberly and
frugally as thou enjoinest, may eat with a pure conscience.
Grant, also, that we may always both with true heartfelt
gratitude acknowledge, and with our lips proclaim thee our
Father and the giver of all good, and, while enjoying bodily
nourishment, aspire with special longing of heart after the
bread of thy doctrine, by which our souls may be nourished
in the hope of eternal life, through Christ Jesus our Lord.
AMEN.

> Man liveth not by bread alone, but by every word which pro-
> ceedeth from the mouth of God. (Deut. viii. 3.)

THANKSGIVING AFTER MEAT.

Let all nations praise the Lord : let all the people sing praises to God. (Ps. cxvii. 1.)

WE give thanks, O God and Father, for the many mercies which thou of thy infinite goodness art constantly bestowing upon us ; both in that by supplying all the helps which we need to sustain the present life, thou showest that thou hast a care even of our bodies, and more especially in that thou hast deigned to beget us again to the hope of the better life which thou hast revealed to us by thy holy gospel. And we beseech thee not to allow our minds to be chained down to earthly thoughts and cares, as if they were buried in our bodies. Rather cause that we may stand with eyes upraised in expectation of thy Son Jesus Christ, till he appear from heaven for our redemption and salvation. AMEN.

PRAYER AT NIGHT ON GOING TO SLEEP.

O LORD GOD, who hast given man the night for rest, as thou hast created the day in which he may employ himself in labour, grant, I pray, that my body may so rest during this night that my mind cease not to be awake to thee, nor my heart faint or be overcome with torpor, preventing it from adhering steadfastly to the love of thee. While laying aside my cares to relax and relieve my mind, may I not, in the meanwhile, forget thee, nor may the remembrance of thy goodness and grace, which ought always to be deeply engraven on my mind, escape my memory. In like manner, also, as the body rests may my conscience enjoy rest. Grant, moreover, that in taking sleep I may not give indulgence to the flesh, but only allow myself as much as the weakness of this natural state requires, to my being enabled thereafter to be more alert in thy service. Be pleased to keep me so chaste and unpolluted, not less in mind than in body, and safe from all dangers, that my sleep itself may turn to the glory of thy name. But since this day has not passed away without my having in many ways offended thee through my proneness to evil, in like manner as all things are now covered by the darkness of the night, so let every thing that is sinful in me lie buried in thy mercy. Hear me, O God, Father and Preserver, through Jesus Christ thy Son. AMEN.

FORMS OF PRAYER FOR THE CHURCH.

On ordinary Meetings the Minister leads the devotions of the people in whatever words seem to him suitable, adapting his address to the time and the subject of the Discourse which he is to deliver, but the following Form is generally used on the Morning of the LORD'S DAY.

OUR help is in the name of the Lord, who made heaven and earth. AMEN.

Brethren, Let each one of us sist himself before the Lord, and confess his sins, and follow me with his mind, while I go before with these words :

O LORD GOD, eternal and almighty Father, we acknowledge and sincerely confess before thy Holy Majesty that we are miserable sinners, conceived and born in guilt and sin, prone to iniquity, and incapable of any good work, and that in our depravity we make no end of transgressing thy commandments. We thus call down destruction upon ourselves from thy just judgment. Nevertheless, O Lord, we anxiously lament that we have offended thee, and we condemn ourselves and our faults with true repentance, asking thee to succour our wretchedness by thy grace.

Deign, then, O most gracious and most merciful God and Father, to bestow thy mercy upon us in the name of Jesus Christ thy Son our Lord. Effacing our faults, and washing away all our pollutions, daily increase to us the gifts of thy Holy Spirit, that we from our inmost hearts acknowledging our iniquity, may be more and more displeasing to ourselves, and so stimulated to true repentance, and that he mortifying us with all our sins, may produce in us the fruits of righteousness and holiness pleasing to thee, through Jesus Christ our Lord. AMEN.

*After this a Psalm is sung by the whole Congregation;
then the Minister again engages in Prayer, in which he
begs God to grant the gift of the Holy Spirit, in order
that his Word may be faithfully expounded to the glory
of his name and the edification of the Church, and be received with becoming submission and obedience of mind.
The Form of Prayer suitable for this the Minister selects
for himself at pleasure. Having finished the Sermon,
he exhorts the people to pray, and begins thus :*

ALMIGHTY GOD, heavenly Father, thou hast promised us
that thou wilt listen to the prayers which we pour forth to
thee in the name of thy beloved Son, Jesus Christ our Lord;
and we have been taught by him and by his apostles to as-
semble ourselves together in one place in his name, with
the promise that he will be present with us to intercede for
us with thee, and obtain for us whatever we shall, with one
consent, ask of thee on the earth.

Thou enjoinest us to pray first for those whom thou hast
appointed to be our rulers and governors, and next to draw
near and supplicate thee for all things which are necessary
for thy people, and so for all men. Therefore trusting to thy
holy commands and promises, now that we come into thy
presence, having assembled in the name of thy Son our Lord
Jesus Christ, we humbly and earnestly beg of thee, O God,
our most gracious Father, in the name of him who is our
only Saviour and Mediator, that of thy boundless mercy thou
wouldst be pleased to pardon our sins, and so draw our
thoughts to thyself, that we may be able to invoke thee
from our inmost heart, framing our desires in accordance
with thy will, which alone is agreeable to reason.

We therefore pour out our prayers before thee, O heavenly
Father, in behalf of all rulers and magistrates, whose service
thou employest in governing us, and especially for the magistrates of this city, that thou wouldst be pleased to impart to
them more and more every day of thy Spirit, who alone is
good, and truly the chief good, so that feeling fully convinced
that Jesus Christ thy Son, our Lord, is King of kings and Lord
of lords, like as thou hast given him all power in heaven and

on earth, so they too may in their office have an eye above all
to his worship and the extension of his kingdom, governing
those under them (who are the work of thy hands and the
sheep of thy pasture) according to thy will, so that we, enjoying stable peace both here and in every other part of the
world, may serve thee with all holiness and purity, and
freed from the fear of our enemies, have ground to celebrate
thy praise during the whole period of our lives.

Next, O faithful Father and Saviour, we commend to thee
in our prayers all whom thou hast appointed pastors over
thy faithful, and to whose guidance thou hast committed our
souls; whom, in fine, thou hast been pleased to make the dispensers of thy holy gospel; that thou wouldst guide them by
thy Holy Spirit, and so make them honest and faithful
ministers of thy glory, making it all their study, and directing all their endeavours to gather together all the wretched
sheep which are still wandering astray, and bring them back
to Jesus Christ the chief Shepherd and Prince of bishops;
and that they may increase in righteousness and holiness
every day; that in the meanwhile thou wouldst be pleased
to rescue all thy churches from the jaws of ravening wolves
and all hirelings, who are led only by a love of fame or
lucre, and plainly care not for the manifestation of thy glory,
and the salvation of thy flock.

Moreover, we offer up our prayers unto thee, O most gracious God and most merciful Father, for all men in general,
that as thou art pleased to be acknowledged the Saviour of
the whole human race by the redemption accomplished by
Jesus Christ thy Son, so those who are still strangers to the
knowledge of him, and immersed in darkness, and held captive by ignorance and error, may, by thy Holy Spirit shining upon them, and by thy gospel sounding in their ears, be
brought back to the right way of salvation, which consists
in knowing thee the true God and Jesus Christ whom thou
hast sent. We beg that those on whom thou hast deigned
already to bestow the favour of thy grace, and whose minds
thou hast enlightened by the knowledge of thy word, may
daily profit more and more, being enriched with thy spiritual
blessings, so that we may all together, with one heart and

mouth, worship thee, and pay due honour, and yield just
service to thy Christ, our Lord, and King, and Lawgiver.

Furthermore, O Author of all consolation, we commend to
thee all of thy people whom thou chastisest in various ways :
those afflicted by pestilence, famine, or war ; individuals also
pressed by poverty, or imprisonment, or disease, or exile, or
any other suffering in body or mind, that wisely considering
that the end which thou hast in view is to bring them back
into the right path by thy rod, they may be imbued with
the sense of thy paternal love, and repent with sincere purpose of heart, so as to turn unto thee with their whole mind,
and being turned, receive full consolation, and be delivered
from all their evils.

In a particular manner, we commend unto thee our unhappy brethren who live dispersed under the tyranny of
Antichrist, and deprived of the liberty of openly calling upon
thy name, and who have either been cast into prison or are
oppressed by the enemies of the gospel in any other way,
that thou wouldst deign, O most indulgent Father, to support them by the strength of thy Spirit, so that they may
never despond, but constantly persevere in thy holy calling :
that thou mayest be pleased to stretch out thy hand to them,
as thou knowest to be best for them, to console them in
their adversity, and taking them under thy protection,
defend them from the ravening of wolves ; in fine, load them
with all the gifts of thy Spirit, that their life and death
may alike tend to thy glory.

Lastly, O God and Father, allow thyself to be entreated
of us, who have here assembled in the name of thy Son
Jesus, for the sake of his word, (*only when the Supper is dispensed add* "and of His Holy Supper,") that we, truly conscious of our lost original, may at the same time reflect how
greatly we deserve condemnation, and how much we add to
our guilt every day by impure and wicked lives ; that when
we recognise that we are devoid of all good, and that our
flesh and blood are plainly averse to discern the inheritance
of thy kingdom, we may with full purpose of heart and firm
confidence devote ourselves to thy beloved Son, Jesus Christ,
our Lord and only Saviour and Redeemer ; that he, dwelling

in us, may extinguish our old Adam and renovate and invigorate us for a better life ; that thus (*the remainder is a paraphrase of the Lord's Prayer—Hallowed be thy name*) thy name, as it excels in holiness and dignity, may be extolled in every region and in every place ; that at the same time (*thy kingdom come*) thou mayest obtain right and authority over us, and we learn more and more every day to submit to thy authority, so that thou mayest everywhere reign supreme, governing thy people by the sceptre of thy word and the power of thy Spirit, and by the strength of thy truth and righteousness crushing all the attempts of thy enemies. Thus may all power and every high thing that opposes itself to thy glory be daily effaced and destroyed, until thy kingdom is made complete in all its parts, and its perfection thoroughly established, as it will be when thou shalt appear as judge in the person of thy Son. May we with all creatures (*thy will be done*) yield thee true and full obedience, as thy heavenly angels feel wholly intent on executing thy commands. May thy will thus prevail, none opposing it ; and may all study to obey and serve thee, renouncing their own will and all the desires of the flesh. And be pleased, (*give us this day our daily bread,*) while we retain the love and fear of thee in all the actions of our lives, to nourish us of thy goodness, and supply us with all things necessary for eating our bread in peace and quietness ; that thus seeing the care which thou takest of us, we may the better recognise thee as our Father, and expect all blessings at thy hand, no longer placing hope and confidence in any creature, but entirely in thy goodness. And since in this mortal life we are miserable sinners, (*forgive us our debts,*) labouring under such infirmity that we constantly give way and deviate from the right path, be pleased to pardon all the sins of which we are guilty in thy sight, and by this pardon free us from the liability to eternal death which lies upon us : let not our iniquity be imputed to us, just as we ourselves, obeying thy command, forget the injuries done to us ; and so far from wishing to take vengeance on our enemies, study to promote their good. In time to come (*lead us not into temptation*) be pleased to support us by thy power, and not allow us to fall under the weakness of our flesh ; and seeing that our strength is so feeble that we cannot stand for a single moment—while at the same time so many enemies beset and attack us, while the devil, the world, sin, and our flesh make no end of assailing us—do thou strengthen us with thy Holy Spirit, and arm us with the gifts of thy grace, that we may be able firmly to resist all temptations and sustain this spiritual contest, till, having gained the complete victory, we may at length triumph in thy kingdom, with our Prince and Protector, Jesus Christ our Lord. AMEN.

[Thereafter the Apostle's Creed is repeated.]

When the Lord's Supper is dispensed, there is added to the above :

AND as our Lord Jesus Christ, not content with having once offered his body and blood upon the cross for the forgiveness of our sins, has also destined them to us as nourishment for eternal life, so grant us of thy goodness, that we may receive this great blessing with true sincerity of heart and ardent desire, and endued with sure faith, enjoy together his body and blood, or rather himself entire, just as he himself, while he is true God and man, is truly the holy bread of heaven that gives us life, that we may no longer live in ourselves, and after our own will, which is altogether depraved, but he may live in us, and conduct us to a holy, happy, and ever-during life, thus making us truly partakers of the new and eternal covenant, even the covenant of grace ; and in feeling fully persuaded that thou art pleased to be for ever a propitious Father to us, by not imputing to us our offences, and to furnish us, as dear children and heirs, with all things necessary as well for the soul as the body, we may pay thee endless praise and thanks, and render thy name glorious both by words and deeds. Fit us, then, on this day thus to celebrate the happy remembrance of thy Son : grant also that we may exercise ourselves therein, and proclaim the benefits of his death, that thus receiving new increase and strength for faith and every other good work, we may with greater confidence profess ourselves thy children, and glory in thee our Father.

After the dispensation of the Supper the following Thanksgiving, or one similar to it, is used :

WE offer thee immortal praise and thanks, O heavenly Father, for the great blessing which thou hast conferred upon us miserable sinners, in bringing us to partake of thy Son Jesus Christ, whom thou didst suffer to be delivered to death for us, and now impartest to us as the food of everlasting life. And now in continuance of thy goodness towards us, never allow us to become forgetful of these things, but grant rather, that carrying them about engraven on our hearts, we may profit and increase in a faith which may be effectual unto every good work. Hence, too, may we dedicate the remainder of our life to the advancement of thy glory and the edification of our neighbours, through the same Jesus Christ thy Son, who, in the unity of the Holy Spirit, liveth with thee and reigneth for ever. AMEN.

THE BLESSING *which the Minister asks for the People, when about to depart, according to the injunction of the Divine Law :*

THE LORD bless you and keep you safe. The Lord cause his countenance to shine upon you, and be gracious to you. The Lord turn his face toward you, and bestow upon you all prosperity. AMEN.

As the Scriptures teach us that Pestilence, War, and other calamities of this kind are chastisements of God, which he inflicts on our sins, so when we see these take place we ought to acknowledge the anger of God against us ; and then if we are truly believers, it behoves us to call our sins to remembrance, that we may be ashamed and grieved at our conduct, and turning to the Lord with unfeigned repentance and a better life, suppliantly and submissively beg pardon of him. Therefore, if at any time we see God threatening us, that we may not tempt his patience, but rather turn away his judgment, (which we then see to be otherwise impending over us,) it is proper that there should be a day every week on which to admonish the people specially of these things, and pray and supplicate God as the occasion may require. The Form following is intended for that purpose. At the beginning of the service the Minister uses the General Confession used on The Lord's Day, as given above. But at the end of the Service, after warning the people that God is now exercising his vengeance against men, because of the iniquities which prevail over the whole world, and because of the iniquity to which all have everywhere abandoned themselves; after exhorting them to turn and amend their lives, and pray God for pardon, he employs the following Form :

ALMIGHTY GOD, heavenly Father, we acknowledge and humbly confess, as is indeed true, that we are unworthy to lift up our eyes unto heaven and appear in thy presence, and that we ought not to presume to hope that thou wilt listen to our prayers if thou takest account of the things which we lay before thee; for we are accused by our own consciences, and our sins bear witness against us, while we know thee to be a just Judge, who justifiest not sinners and wicked men, but inflictest punishment on those who have broken thy commands. Hence it is, O Lord, that when we reflect on the state of our whole life, we are ashamed of ourselves, and can do nothing but despond, just as if we were plunged into the abyss of death.

And yet, O Lord, since thou hast deigned, of thy boundless mercy, to command us to call upon thee, and that from the lowest hell, and the more devoid of strength we see ourselves to be to flee the more to thy supreme goodness; since, moreover, thou hast promised that thou wilt listen to our prayers in the name of the Lord Jesus Christ, (whom thou hast appointed to be our advocate and intercessor,) and for his merit, without looking to what we have deserved, we here, renouncing all human confidence, and trusting solely to thy goodness, hesitate not to come into thy sight, and call upon thy holy name, in order to obtain mercy.

First, O Lord, besides the innumerable blessings which thou art constantly bestowing on all men whatever that live upon the earth, thou hast specially imparted to us so many gifts of thy grace that we cannot count them—nay, we cannot even embrace them in our thoughts. And there is this, in particular, that thou hast deigned to call us to the knowledge of thy holy gospel, shaking off the miserable yoke of bondage by which the devil oppressed us, and, after delivering us from the execrable idolatry and vain superstitions in which we were immersed, hast brought us to the light of thy truth. Nevertheless, (such is our ingratitude,) forgetting the blessings which thy hand has bestowed upon us, we have declined from the right way, and, forsaking thee, have followed the desires of our own flesh : nay, even thy holy word have we defrauded of due reverence and obedience, and we have not duly heralded thy praise. And though the faithful admonitions of thy word have constantly sounded in our ears, we have, however, neglected them.

Thus, O Lord, have we sinned and offended thee, and therefore we are covered with shame, acknowledging that, in the eye of thy justice, we are guilty of grievous iniquities, so that wert thou to inflict condign punishment upon us, we could expect nothing but death and damnation ; for if we would excuse ourselves, our own consciences accuse us, and our iniquity lies open before thy sight to our condemnation. And surely, O Lord, from the very chastisements which thou hast inflicted upon us, we know that for the justest causes thy wrath is kindled against us ; for, seeing thou art a just Judge, thou afflictest not thy people when not offending. Therefore, beaten with thy stripes, we acknowledge that we have provoked thy anger against us : and even now we see thy hand stretched forth for our punishment. The swords which thou art wont to use in inflicting vengeance are now drawn, and those with which thou threatenest sinners and wicked men we see ready to smite.

But though thou mightest take much severer punishment upon us than before, and thus inflict blows an hundredfold more numerous, and though disasters only less dreadful than those with which thou didst formerly chastise the sins of thy people of Israel, should overtake us, we confess that we are worthy of them, and have merited them by our crimes. But, Lord, thou art our Father, and we nothing else than earth and clay: thou art our Creator, we are the workmanship of thy hands: thou art our Shepherd, we are thy fold: thou art our Redeemer, we the people redeemed by thee: thou art our God, we thy inheritance. Be not so angry with us, therefore, as to chastise us in thy fury: remember not our iniquity to punish it, but of thy mercy chasten us leniently. Thy wrath is indeed kindled against us because of the sins which we have committed, but remember that we are called by thy name, and that we bear thy banner. Rather preserve the work which thy grace has begun in us, that the whole world may acknowledge thee to be our God and Saviour. Thou certainly knowest that the dead in hell, and those whom thou hast destroyed and driven away utterly, will never praise thee; but that the sad, and those devoid of all consolation, contrite hearts, consciences oppressed by a sense of guilt, and thirsting for the favour of thy grace, will pay thee glory and honour.

Thy people of Israel often provoked thee to anger by their iniquities, and thou in thy just judgment didst afflict them; but as often as they turned unto thee, they had ever access to thy mercy, and however grievous their sins were, yet on account of the covenant which thou hadst made with thy servants Abraham, Isaac, and Jacob, thou didst turn away thy rod and the disasters which impended over them, so that their prayers never suffered a repulse from thee. Us thou hast honoured with a more excellent covenant on which we can lean, that covenant which thou didst establish in the right hand of Jesus Christ our Saviour, and which thou wast pleased should be written in his blood and sealed with his death. Wherefore, O Lord, renouncing ourselves and abandoning all other hope, we flee to this precious covenant by which our Lord Jesus Christ, offering his own body to thee in sacrifice, has reconciled us to thee. Look, therefore, O Lord, not on us but on the face of Christ, that by his intercession thy anger may be appeased, and thy face may shine forth upon us for our joy and salvation, and receive us to be henceforth guided and governed by thy Holy Spirit, who may regenerate us to a better life, by which

Hallowed be thy name. Thy kingdom come. Thy will be done in earth, as it is in heaven. Give us this day our daily bread. And forgive us our debts, as we forgive our debtors. And lead us not into temptation, but deliver us from evil: For thine is the kingdom, and the power, and the glory, for ever. Amen.

But though we are unworthy to open our mouths for ourselves and call upon thee in adversity, yet as thou hast commanded us to pray one for another, we pour out our prayers for all our brethren, members of the same body, whom thou now chastisest with thy scourge, and beseech thee to turn away thine anger from them; in particular, we pray for *N.* and *N.* Remember, Lord, that they are thy children as well as we; and therefore though they have offended thee, interrupt not the course of thy goodness and mercy toward them, which thou hast promised will endure for ever towards all thy children.

Deign then to look upon all thy churches with an eye of pity, and on all the nations whom thou now smitest with pestilence, or war, or any other kind of scourge, and on all the individuals who are receiving thy stripes ; on all who are bound in prison or afflicted with disease or poverty, and bringing consolation to all, as thou knowest them to require it, and rendering thy chastisements useful for the reformation of their lives ; deign to furnish them with patience, to moderate thy severity, and by at length delivering them, to give them full cause to exult in thy goodness, and bless thy holy name.

In particular, be pleased to turn thine eyes upon those who contend for thy truth both in public and in private, that thou mayest strengthen them with invincible constancy ; defend and everywhere assist them, rendering all the wiles and engines of thine and their enemies of no avail, curbing their fury, dooming all their attempts to ignominy. Permit not Christendom to be altogether laid waste, lest thou allow the remembrance of thy name to be utterly banished from the earth, lest thou suffer those whom thou hast permitted to be called by thy name, to be overwhelmed by a lamentable destruction, lest Turks, heathens, barbarians, and Papists, and other infidels, insult thy name with blasphemy.

We therefore pour out our prayers before thee, O heavenly Father, in behalf of all rulers and magistrates, whose service thou employest in governing us ; and especially for the magistrates of this city, that thou wouldst be pleased to impart to them more and more every day of thy Spirit, who alone is good and truly the chief good, so that feeling fully convinced that Jesus Christ thy Son, our Lord, is King of kings and Lord of lords, like as thou hast given him all power in heaven and on earth, so they too may in their office have an eye above all to his worship and the extension of his kingdom, governing those under them (who are the work of thy hands and the sheep of thy pasture) according to thy will, so that we, enjoying stable peace both here and in every other part of the world, may serve thee with all holiness and purity, and freed from the fear of our enemies, have ground to celebrate thy praise during the whole period of our lives.

Next, O faithful Father and Saviour, we commend to thee in our prayers all whom thou hast appointed pastors over thy faithful, and to whose guidance thou hast committed our souls ; whom, in fine, thou hast been pleased to make the dispensers of thy holy gospel ; that thou wouldst guide them by thy Holy Spirit, and so make them honest and faithful ministers of thy glory, making it all their study, and directing all their endeavours to gather together all the wretched sheep which are still wandering astray, and bring them back to Jesus Christ the chief Shepherd and Prince of bishops ; and that they may increase in righteousness and holiness every day ; that in the meanwhile thou wouldst be pleased to rescue all thy churches from the jaws of ravening wolves and all hirelings, who are led only by a love of fame or lucre, and plainly care not for the manifestation of thy glory, and the salvation of thy flock.

Moreover, we offer up our prayers unto thee, O most

gracious God and most merciful Father, for all men in general, that as thou art pleased to be acknowledged the Saviour of the whole human race by the redemption accomplished by Jesus Christ thy Son, so those who are still strangers to the knowledge of him, and immersed in darkness, and held captive by ignorance and error, may by thy Holy Spirit shining upon them, and by thy gospel sounding in their ears, be brought back to the right way of salvation, which consists in knowing thee the true God and Jesus Christ whom thou hast sent. We beg that those on whom thou hast deigned already to bestow the favour of thy grace, and whose minds thou hast enlightened by the knowledge of thy word, may daily profit more and more, being enriched with thy spiritual blessings, so that we may all together, with one heart and mouth, worship thee, and pay due honour and yield just service to thy Christ, our Lord, and King, and Lawgiver. AMEN.

FORM OF ADMINISTERING THE SACRAMENTS.

COMPOSED FOR THE USE OF THE CHURCH OF GENEVA.

FORM OF ADMINISTERING BAPTISM.[1]

It is particularly necessary to know that infants are to be brought for baptism either on the Lord's Day, at the time of catechising, or at public service on other days, that as baptism is a kind of formal adoption into the Church, so it may be performed in the presence and under the eyes of the whole Congregation.

OUR help is in the Lord who made heaven and earth. AMEN.

Do you offer this infant for baptism?

Answer. We do indeed.

Minister. Our Lord demonstrates in what poverty and wretchedness we are all born, by telling us that we must be born again. For if our nature requires to be renewed in order to gain admission to the kingdom of God, it is a sign that it is altogether perverted and cursed. By this then he admonishes us to humble ourselves and be displeasing to ourselves, and in this way he disposes us to desire and seek for his grace, by which all the perverseness and malediction of our first nature may be abolished. For we are not capable of receiving grace unless we be first divested of all trust in our own virtue, wisdom, and righteousness, so as to condemn everything we possess.

---

[1] The French being here the only original, the translation of the remaining forms are made from it. The Amsterdam edition, however, contains the whole in Latin.

But when he has demonstrated our wretchedness, he in like manner consoles us by his mercy, promising to regenerate us by his Holy Spirit to a new life, which forms a kind of entrance into his kingdom. This regeneration consists of two parts. First, we renounce ourselves, not following our own reason, our own pleasure, and our own will, but bringing our understanding and our heart into captivity to the wisdom and justice of God, we mortify every thing belonging to us and to our flesh; and, secondly, we thereafter follow the light of God, seeking to be agreeable to him, and obey his good pleasure as he manifests it by his word, and conducts us to it by his Holy Spirit. The accomplishment of both of these is in our Lord Jesus Christ, whose death and passion have such virtue, that in participating in it we are as it were buried to sin, in order that our carnal lusts may be mortified. In like manner, by virtue of his resurrection, we rise again to a new life which is of God, inasmuch as his Spirit conducts and governs us, to produce in us works which are agreeable to him. However, the first and principal point of our salvation is, that by his mercy he forgives us all our offences, not imputing them to us, but effacing the remembrance of them, that they may no longer come against us in judgment.

All these graces are bestowed upon us when he is pleased to incorporate us into his Church by baptism; for in this sacrament he attests the remission of our sins. And he has ordained the symbol of water to figure to us, that as by this element bodily defilements are cleansed, so he is pleased to wash and purify our souls. Moreover, he employs it to represent our renovation, which consists, as has been said, in the mortification of our flesh, and in the spiritual life which it produces in us.

Thus we receive a twofold grace and benefit from our God in baptism, provided we do not annihilate the virtue of the sacrament by our ingratitude. We have in it sure evidence, first, that God is willing to be propitious to us, not imputing to us our faults and offences; and, secondly, that he will assist us by his Holy Spirit, in order that we may be able to war against the devil, sin, and the lusts of our flesh, and gain the victory over them, so as to live in the liberty of his kingdom, which is the kingdom of righteousness.

Seeing then that these two things are accomplished in us by the grace of Jesus Christ, it follows, that the virtue and substance of baptism is included in him. And, in fact, we have no other laver than his blood, and no other renovation than his death and resurrection. But as he communicates his riches and blessings to us by his word, so he distributes them to us by his sacraments.

Now our gracious God, not contenting himself with having adopted us for his children, and received us into the communion of his Church, has been pleased to extend his goodness still farther to us, by promising to be our God and the God of our seed to a thousand generations. Hence though the children of believers are of the corrupt race of Adam, he nevertheless accepts them in virtue of this covenant, and adopts them into his family. For this reason he was pleased from the first, (Gen. xvii. 12,) that in his Church children should receive the sign of circumcision, by which he then represented all that is now signified to us by baptism. And as he gave commandment that they should be circumcised, so he adopted them for his children, and called himself their God, as well as the God of their fathers.

Now then since the Lord Jesus Christ came down to earth, not to diminish the grace of God his Father, but to extend the covenant of salvation over all the world, instead of confining it as formerly to the Jews, there is no doubt that our children are heirs of the life which he has promised to us. And hence St. Paul says, (2 Cor. vii. 14,) that God sanctifies them from their mothers' womb, to distinguish them from the children of Pagans and unbelievers. For this reason our Lord Jesus Christ received the children that were brought to him, as is written in the nineteenth chapter of St. Matthew, " Then were brought unto him little children, that he might put his hands on them, and pray. But the disciples rebuked them. And Jesus said unto them, Suffer the little children to come unto me, and forbid them not ; for of such is the kingdom of heaven."

By declaring that the kingdom of heaven belongs to them,

laying hands on them, and recommending them to God his Father, he clearly teaches that we must not exclude them from his Church. Following this rule then, we will receive this child into his Church, in order that it may become a partaker of the blessings which God has promised to believers. And, first, we will present it to him in prayer, all saying with the heart humbly,—

O Lord God, eternal and omnipotent Father, since it hath pleased thee of thy infinite mercy to promise us that thou wilt be our God, and the God of our children, we pray that it may please thee to confirm this grace in the child before thee, born of parents whom thou hast called into thy Church ; and as it is offered and consecrated to thee by us, do thou deign to receive it under thy holy protection, declaring thyself to be its God and Saviour, by forgiving it the original sin of which all the race of Adam are guilty, and thereafter sanctifying it by thy Spirit, in order that when it shall arrive at the years of discretion it may recognise and adore thee as its only God, glorifying thee during its whole life, so as always to obtain of thee the forgiveness of its sins. And in order to its obtaining such graces, be pleased to incorporate it into the communion of our Lord Jesus Christ, that it may partake of all his blessings as one of the members of his body. Hear us, O merciful Father, in order that the baptism, which we communicate to it according to thy ordinance, may produce its fruit and virtue, as declared to us by the gospel.

Our Father, which art in heaven, hallowed be thy name. Thy kingdom come. Thy will be done in earth, as it is in heaven. Give us this day our daily bread. And forgive us our debts, as we forgive our debtors. And lead us not into temptation ; but deliver us from evil : For thine is the kingdom, and the power, and the glory, for ever. Amen.

As the object is to receive this child into the fellowship of the Christian Church, you promise, when it shall come to the years of discretion, to instruct it in the doctrine which is received by the people of God, as it is summarily comprehended in the Confession of Faith, which we all have, viz. :

I believe in God the Father Almighty, maker of heaven

and earth ; and in Jesus Christ, his only Son, our Lord, who
was conceived by the Holy Ghost, born of the Virgin Mary,
suffered under Pontius Pilate, was crucified, dead, and buried :
he descended into hell ; the third day he arose again from the
dead ; he ascended into heaven, and sitteth on the right
hand of God the Father Almighty, from thence he shall
come to judge the quick and the dead. I believe in the
Holy Ghost ; the holy Catholick Church ; the communion
of saints ; the forgiveness of sins ; the resurrection of the
body ; and the life everlasting. Amen.

You promise then to be careful to instruct it in all this
doctrine, and generally in all that is contained in the Holy
Scriptures of the Old and New Testaments, in order that it
may receive them as the sure word of God coming from
heaven. Likewise you will exhort it to live according to
the rule which our Lord has laid down in his law, which is
contained summarily in two points—to love God with all
our heart and mind and strength, and our neighbour as ourselves : in like manner, to live according to the admonitions
which God has given by his prophets and apostles, in order
that renouncing itself and its own lusts, it may dedicate and
consecrate itself to glorify the name of God and Jesus Christ,
and edify its neighbour.

*After the promise made the name is given to the child, and
the minister baptizes it, saying :*

N., I Baptize thee in the name of the Father, and of the
Son, and of the Holy Spirit.

*The whole is said aloud, and in the common tongue, in
order that the people who are present may be witnesses
to what is done, (for which purpose it is necessary that
they understand it,) and in order that all may be edified by recognising and calling to mind the fruit and
use of their own Baptism.*

*We know that elsewhere there are many other ceremonies
which we deny not to be very ancient, but because they have
been invented at pleasure, or at least on grounds which, be
these what they may, must be trivial, since they have been*

devised without authority from the word of God, and because, on the other hand, so many superstitions have sprung from them, we have felt no hesitation in abolishing them, in order that there might be nothing to prevent the people from going directly to Jesus Christ. First, whatever is not commanded, we are not free to choose. Secondly, nothing which does not tend to edification ought to be received into the Church. If any thing of the kind has been introduced, it ought to be taken away, and by much stronger reason, whatever serves only to cause scandal, and is, as it were, an instrument of idolatry and false opinion, ought on no account to be tolerated.

Now it is certain that chrism, tapers, and other pomposities are not of the ordination of God, but have been added by men, and have at length gone so far that people have dwelt more on them, and held them in higher estimation, than the proper institution of Jesus Christ. At all events, we have a form of baptism such as Jesus Christ instituted, the Apostles kept and followed, and the Church put in practice; and there is nothing for which we can be blamed, unless it be for not being wiser than God himself.

THE MANNER

CELEBRATING THE LORD'S SUPPER.

It is proper to observe, that the Sunday before the Supper is dispensed it is intimated to the people : first, in order that each may prepare and dispose himself to receive it worthily and with becoming reverence ; secondly, that young people may not be brought forward unless they are well instructed, and have made a profession of their faith in the Church ; thirdly, in order that if there are strangers who are still rude and ignorant, they may come and present themselves for instruction in private. On the day of communion the minister adverts to it at the end of his sermon, or indeed, if he sees cause, makes it the sole subject of sermon, in order to expound to the people what our Lord means to teach and signify by this ordinance, and in what way it behoves us to receive it.

After Prayer and The Confession of Faith, to testify in the name of the people that all wish to live and die in the doctrine of Christ, he says aloud :

Let us listen to the institution of the Holy Supper by Jesus Christ, as narrated by St. Paul in the eleventh chapter of the First Epistle to the Corinthians :

For I have received of the Lord that which also I delivered unto you, That the Lord Jesus, the same night in which he was betrayed, took bread : And, when he had given thanks, he brake it, and said, Take, eat ; this is my body, which is broken for you : this do in remembrance of me. After the same manner also he took the cup, when he had supped, saying, This cup is the new testament in my blood : this do ye, as oft as ye drink it, in remembrance of me. For as often as ye eat this bread, and drink this cup, ye do shew the Lord's death till he come. Wherefore, whosoever shall eat this bread, and drink this cup of the

Lord, unworthily, shall be guilty of the body and blood of the Lord. But let a man examine himself, and so let him eat of that bread, and drink of that cup. For he that eateth and drinketh unworthily, eateth and drinketh damnation to himself, not discerning the Lord's body.

We have heard, brethren, how our Lord makes his Supper among his disciples, and thereby shows us that strangers— in other words, those who are not of the company of the faithful—ought not to be admitted. Wherefore, in accordance with this rule, in the name and by the authority of the Lord Jesus Christ, I excommunicate all idolaters, blasphemers, despisers of God, heretics, and all who form sects apart to break the unity of the Church, all perjurers, all who are rebellious to parents and to their superiors, all who are seditious, mutinous, quarrelsome, injurious, all adulterers, fornicators, thieves, misers, ravishers, drunkards, gluttons, and all who lead a scandalous life ; declaring to them that they must abstain from this holy table, for fear of polluting and contaminating the sacred viands which our Lord Jesus Christ gives only to his household and believers.

Therefore, according to the exhortation of St. Paul, let each prove and examine his conscience, to see whether he has truly repented of his faults, and is dissatisfied with himself, desiring to live henceforth holily and according to God ; above all, whether he puts his trust in the mercy of God, and seeks his salvation entirely in Jesus Christ, and whether, renouncing all enmity and rancour, he truly intends and resolves to live in concord and brotherly charity with his neighbours.

If we have this testimony in our hearts before God, let us have no doubt at all that he adopts us for his children, and that the Lord Jesus addresses his word to us to invite us to his table, and present us with this holy sacrament which he communicated to his disciples.

And although we feel within ourselves much frailty and misery from not having perfect faith, but being inclined to unbelief and distrust, as well as from not being devoted to the service of God so entirely and with such zeal as we ought, and from having to war daily against the lusts of our flesh, nevertheless, since our Lord has graciously deigned to have his gospel imprinted on our hearts, in order to withstand all unbelief, and has given us this desire and affection to renounce our own desires, to follow righteousness and his holy commandments, let us all be assured that the vices and imperfections which are in us will not prevent his receiving us, and making us worthy of taking part at this spiritual table; for we do not come to declare that we are perfect or righteous in ourselves; but, on the contrary, by seeking our life in Christ, we confess that we are in death. Let us understand that this sacrament is a medicine for the poor spiritual sick, and that all the worthiness which our Saviour requires in us is to know ourselves, so as to be dissatisfied with our vices, and have all our pleasure, joy, and contentment in him alone.

First, then, let us believe in these promises which Jesus Christ, who is infallible truth, has pronounced with his own lips, viz., that he is indeed willing to make us partakers of his own body and blood, in order that we may possess him entirely in such a manner that he may live in us, and we in him. And although we see only bread and wine, yet let us not doubt that he accomplishes spiritually in our souls all that he shows us externally by these visible signs; in other words, that he is heavenly bread, to feed and nourish us unto life eternal.

Next, let us not be ungrateful to the infinite goodness of our Saviour, who displays all his riches and blessings at this table, in order to dispense them to us; for, in giving himself to us, he bears testimony to us that all which he has is ours. Moreover, let us receive this sacrament as a pledge that the virtue of his death and passion is imputed to us for righteousness, just as if we had suffered it in our own persons. Let us not be so perverse as to keep back when Jesus Christ invites us so gently by his word; but while reflecting on the dignity of the precious gift which he gives us, let us present ourselves to him with ardent zeal, in order that he may make us capable of receiving him.

With this view, let us raise our hearts and minds on high, where Jesus Christ is, in the glory of his Father, and from whence we look for him at our redemption. And let us not amuse ourselves with these earthly and corruptible elements which we see with the eye, and touch with the hand, in order to seek him there, as if he were enclosed in the bread or wine. Then only will our souls be disposed to be nourished and vivified with his substance, when they are thus raised above all terrestrial objects, and carried as high as heaven, to enter the kingdom of God where he dwells. Let us be contented, then, to have the bread and wine as signs and evidences, spiritually seeking the reality where the word of God promises that we shall find it.

This done, the Ministers distribute the bread and cup to the people, having warned them to come forward with reverence and in order. Meanwhile some Psalms are sung, or some passage of Scripture read, suitable to what is signified by the Sacrament.

At the end thanks are given, as has been said.

We are well aware what occasion of scandal some have taken from the change made in this matter. Because the mass has been long in such esteem, that the poor people seemed disposed to think that it was the principal part of Christianity, it has been thought very strange in us to have abolished it. And for this cause those who are not duly informed think that we have destroyed the Sacrament. But when they have well considered our practice, they will find that we have restored it to its integrity. Let them consider what conformity there is between the mass and the institution of Jesus Christ. It is clear that there is just as much as there is between day and night. Although it is not our intention here to treat this subject at length, yet to satisfy those who through simplicity might be scandalized at us, it seemed advisable to touch upon it in passing. Seeing then that the Sacrament of our Lord has been corrupted by the many adulterations and horrible abuses which have been introduced, we have been constrained to apply a remedy, and change many things which had been improperly introduced, or at least turned to a bad use. Now, in order to do so, we have found no means better or more proper than to return to the pure institution of Jesus Christ, which we follow simply, as is apparent. Such is the reformation which St. Paul points out.

FORM AND MANNER

OF

CELEBRATING MARRIAGE.

It is necessary to observe that in celebrating marriage it is published in the Church on three Sundays, that any one knowing of any hinderance may timeously announce it, or any one having interest may oppose it.

This done the parties come forward at the commencement of the Sermon, when the Minister says :

Our help be in the Lord who made heaven and earth. Amen.

God, our Father, after creating heaven and earth, and all that therein is, created and formed man after his own image and likeness, to have dominion and lordship over the beasts of the earth, the fish of the sea, and the birds of the air, saying, after he had created man, It is not good that the man be alone, let us make him a help meet for him. (Gen. i. 26 ; ii. 18, 21, 22.) And our Lord caused a deep sleep to fall upon Adam, and while Adam slept God took one of his ribs, and of it formed Eve, giving us to understand that the man and the woman are only one body, one flesh, and one blood. (Matt. xix. 6.) Wherefore the man leaves father and mother and cleaves to his wife, whom he ought to love just as Jesus loves the Church, or, in other words, the true believers and Christians for whom he died. (Eph. v. 25.) And likewise the woman ought to serve and obey her husband in all holiness and honesty, (1 Tim. ii. 11 ;) for she is subject to and in the power of the husband so long as she lives with him. (1 Pet. iii. 5.)

And this holy marriage, ordained of God, is of such force, that in virtue of it the husband has not power over his body, but the woman : nor the woman power over her body, but the husband. (1 Cor. vii. 4.) Wherefore being joined together of God they can no more be separated, except for a time by mutual consent to have leisure for fasting and prayer, taking good heed not to be tempted of Satan through incontinence. (Matt. xix. 6 ; 1 Cor. vii. 5.)

And they ought to return to each other. For in order to avoid fornication each one ought to have his wife, (1 Cor. vii. 2,) and each woman her husband, so that all who have not the gift of continence are obliged by the command of God to marry, in order that the holy temple of God, in other words, our bodies, be not violated and corrupted. (1 Cor. iii. 9 ; vi. 15, 16.) For seeing that our bodies are members of Jesus Christ, it would be a gross outrage to make them the members of a harlot. (1 Cor. vi. 16.) Wherefore we ought to preserve them in all holiness. For whoso pollutes the temple of God, him will God destroy.

You then, *N.* and *N.*, (*naming the bridegroom and bride,*) knowing that God has so ordained it, do you wish to live in this holy state of marriage which God has so highly honoured ; have you such a purpose as you manifest here before his holy assembly, asking that it be approved ?

They answer.

Yes.

The Minister.

I take you all who are here present as witnesses, praying you to keep it in remembrance : however, if there is any one who knows of any impediment, or that either of them is connected by marriage with another, let him say so.

If nobody opposes, the Minister says :

Since there is nobody who opposes, and there is no impediment, our Lord God confirms your holy purpose which he has given you, and let your commencement be in the name of God, who has made heaven and earth. Amen.

The Minister, addressing the Bridegroom, says :

Do you, N., confess here, before God and his holy congregation, that you have taken, and take *N.*, here present, for your wife and spouse, whom you promise to keep, loving and maintaining her faithfully, as is the duty of a true and faithful husband to his wife, living holily with her, observing

faith and lealty to her in all things, according to the word
of God and his holy gospel ?

Answer,

Yes.

Then addressing the Bride, he says :

You, *N.*, confess here, before God and his holy assembly,
that you have taken, and take, *N.* for your lawful husband,
whom you promise to obey, serving and being subject to him,
living holily, observing faith and lealty to him in all things
as a faithful and loyal spouse owes to her husband, according
to the word of God and his holy gospel ?

Answer,

Yes.

Then the Minister says :

The Father of all mercy, who of his grace has called you to
this holy state for the love of Jesus Christ his Son, who, by
his holy presence, sanctified marriage, there performing his
first miracle before the Apostles, anoint you with his Holy
Spirit to serve and honour him together with one common
accord. Amen.

Listen to the Gospel how our Lord intends that holy marriage should be kept, and how firm and indissoluble it is,
according as it is written in St. Matthew, at the nineteenth
chapter:

The Pharisees also came unto him, tempting him, and
saying unto him, Is it lawful for a man to put away his
wife for every cause ? And he answered and said unto
them, Have ye not read, that he which made them at the
beginning, made them male and female ; And said, For this
cause shall a man leave father and mother, and shall cleave
to his wife : and they twain shall be one flesh ? Wherefore
they are no more twain, but one flesh. What therefore God
hath joined together, let not man put asunder.

Believe in these holy words which our Lord uttered, as
the gospel narrates them, and be assured that our Lord God
has joined you in holy marriage: wherefore live holily together in good love, peace, and union, keeping true charity,
faith, and loyalty to each other, according to the word of
God.

Let us all with one heart pray to our Father.

GOD, all mighty, all good, and all wise, who from the beginning didst foresee that it was not good for man to be alone, and therefore didst create him a help meet for him, and hast ordained that two should be one, we beg of thee, and humbly request, that since it has pleased thee to call these persons to the holy state of marriage, thou wouldst deign, of thy grace and goodness to give and send them thy Holy Spirit, in order that they may live holily in true and firm faith, according to thy good will, surmounting all bad affections, edifying each other in all honesty and chastity, giving thy blessing to them as thou didst to thy faithful servants Abraham, Isaac, and Jacob, that having holy lineage they may praise and serve thee, teaching them, and bringing them up to thy praise and glory, and the good of their neighbour, through the advancement and exaltation of thy holy gospel. Hear us, Father of Mercy, through our Lord Jesus Christ, thy very dear Son.   AMEN.

Our Lord fill you with all graces, and anoint you with all good, to live together long and holily.

VISITATION OF THE SICK.

THE office of a true and faithful minister is not only publicly to teach the people over whom he is ordained pastor,
but, so far as may be, to admonish, exhort, rebuke, and
console each one in particular. Now, the greatest need
which a man ever has of the spiritual doctrine of our Lord
is when His hand visits him with afflictions, whether of
disease or other evils, and specially at the hour of death, for
then he feels more strongly than ever in his life before
pressed in conscience, both by the judgment of God, to
which he sees himself about to be called, and the assaults of
the devil, who then uses all his efforts to beat down the poor
person, and plunge and overwhelm him in confusion. And
therefore the duty of a minister is to visit the sick, and console them by the word of the Lord, showing them that all
which they suffer and endure comes from the hand of God,
and from his good providence, who sends nothing to believers
except for their good and salvation. He will quote passages
of Scripture suitable to this view.

Moreover, if he sees the sickness to be dangerous, he will
give them consolation, which reaches farther, according as
he sees them touched by their affliction ; that is to say, if
he sees them overwhelmed with the fear of death, he will
show them that it is no cause of dismay to believers, who
having Jesus Christ for their guide and protector, will, by
their affliction, be conducted to the life on which he has
entered. By similar considerations he will remove the fear
and terror which they may have of the judgment of God.

If he does not see them sufficiently oppressed and agonized
by a conviction of their sins, he will declare to them the

justice of God, before which they cannot stand, save through his mercy embracing Jesus Christ for their salvation. On the contrary, seeing them afflicted in their consciences, and troubled for their offences, he will exhibit Jesus Christ to the life, and show how in him all poor sinners who, distrusting themselves, repose in his goodness, find solace and refuge. Moreover, a good and faithful minister will duly consider all means which it may be proper to take to console the distressed, according as he sees them affected : being guided in the whole by the word of the Lord. Furthermore, if the minister has anything whereby he can console and give bodily relief to the afflicted poor, let him not spare, but show to all a true example of charity.

BRIEF FORM

OF A

CONFESSION OF FAITH,

FOR THE USE OF THOSE WHO DESIRE TO HAVE A COMPENDIUM
OF THE CHRISTIAN RELIGION ALWAYS AT HAND.

BRIEF CONFESSION OF FAITH.

I CONFESS that there is one God, in whom we ought to rest, worshipping and serving him, and placing all our hope in him alone. And although he is of one essence, he is nevertheless distinguished into three persons. Wherefore, I detest all heresies condemned by the first Council of Nice, and likewise those of Ephesus and Chalcedon, along with all the errors revived by Servetus and his followers. For I acquiesce in the simple view, that in the one essence of God is the Father, who from eternity begat his own Word, and ever had in himself his own Spirit, and that each of these persons has his own peculiar properties, yet so that the Godhead always remains entire.

I likewise confess, that God created not only this visible world, (that is, heaven and earth, and whatever is contained in them,) but also invisible spirits, some of whom have continued obedient to God, while others, by their own wickedness, have been precipitated into destruction. That the former have persevered, I acknowledge, to be due to the free election of God, who hastened to love them, and embrace them with his goodness, by bestowing upon them the power of remaining firm and steadfast. And I accordingly abominate the heresy of the Manichees, who imagined that the devil is wicked by nature, and derives origin and beginning from himself.

I confess that God once created the world to be its perpetual Governor, but in such manner that nothing can be done or happen without his counsel and providence. And though Satan and the reprobate plot the confusion of all things, and even believers themselves pervert right order by their sins, yet I acknowledge that the Lord, as the Sovereign Prince and ruler of all, brings good out of evil; in short, directs all things as by a kind of secret reins, and overrules them by a certain admirable method, which it becomes us to adore with all submissiveness of mind, since we cannot embrace it in thought.

I confess that man was created in the image of God, *i.e.*, endued with full integrity of spirit, will, and all parts of the soul, faculties and senses; and that all our corruption, and the vices under which we labour, proceeded from this, viz., that Adam, the common father of all men, by his rebellion, alienated himself from God, and forsaking the fountain of life and of every blessing, made himself liable to all miseries. Hence it is that each of us is born infected with original sin, and cursed and condemned by God from his mother's womb, not on account of another's fault merely, but on account of the depravity which is within us, even when it does not appear.

I confess that in original sin are included blindness of mind and perverseness of heart, so that we are utterly spoiled and destitute of those things which relate to eternal life, and even all natural gifts in us are tainted and depraved. Hence it is that we are not at all moved by any consideration to act aright. I therefore protest against those who attribute to us some degree of free-will, by which we can prepare ourselves for receiving the grace of God, or as it were of ourselves co-operate with the power which is given us by the Holy Spirit.

I confess that by the infinite goodness of God, Jesus Christ has been given to us, that by this means we may be recalled from death to life, and recover whatever was lost to us in Adam; and that accordingly he who is the Eternal Wisdom of God the Father, and of one essence with him, assumed our flesh, so as to be God and man in one person. Therefore I detest all heresies contrary to this principle, as those of Marcion, Manes, Nestorius, Eutyches, and the like, together with the deliriums which Servetus and Schuencfeldius wished to revive.

In regard to the method of obtaining salvation, I confess

that Jesus Christ by his death and resurrection, most completely performed whatever was required to wipe off our offences, that he might reconcile us to God the Father, and overcame death and Satan, that we might obtain the fruit of the victory; in fine, received the Holy Spirit without measure, that out of it such measure as he pleases may be bestowed on each of his followers.

I therefore confess that all our righteousness, by which we are acceptable to God, and in which alone we ought wholly to rest, consists in the remission of sins which he purchased for us, by washing us in his own blood, and through that one sacrifice by which he appeased the wrath of God that had been provoked against us. And I hold the pride of those intolerable who attribute to themselves one particle of merit, in which one particle of the hope of salvation can reside.

Meanwhile, however, I acknowledge that Jesus Christ not only justifies us by covering all our faults and sins, but also sanctifies us by his Spirit, so that the two things (the free forgiveness of sins and reformation to a holy life) cannot be dissevered and separated from each other. Yet since until such time as we quit the world, much impurity, and very many vices remain in us, (to which it is owing that whatever good works we perform by the agency of the Holy Spirit, have some taint adhering to them,) we must always betake ourselves to that free righteousness, flowing from the obedience which Jesus Christ performed in our name, seeing that it is in his name we are accepted, and God does not impute our sins to us.

I confess that we are made partakers of Jesus Christ, and of all his blessings, by the faith which we have in the gospel, that is, when we are truly and surely persuaded that the promises comprehended in it belong to us. But since this altogether surpasses our capacity, I acknowledge that faith is obtained by us, only through the Spirit of God, and so is a peculiar gift which is given to the elect alone, whom God, before the foundation of the world, without regard to any worthiness or virtue in them, freely predestinated to the inheritance of salvation.

I confess that we are justified by faith, inasmuch as by it

we apprehend Jesus Christ the Mediator given us by the Father, and lean on the promises of the gospel, by which God declares that we are regarded as righteous, and free from every stain, because our sins have been washed away by the blood of his Son. Wherefore I detest the ravings of those who endeavour to persuade us that the essential righteousness of God exists in us, and are not satisfied with the free imputation in which alone Scripture orders us to acquiesce.

I confess that faith gives us access to God in prayer, (we ought to pray with firm reliance that he will hear us as he has promised,) and that to it alone belongs the honour of being the primary sacrifice, by which we declare that we ascribe all we receive to him. And though we are obviously unworthy to sist ourselves before his Majesty, yet if we have Jesus Christ as our Mediator and Advocate, nothing more is required of us. Hence I abominate the superstition which some have devised of applying to saints, male and female, as a kind of advocates for us with God.

I confess that both the whole rule of right living, and also instruction in faith, are most fully delivered in the sacred Scriptures, to which nothing can, without criminality, be added, from which nothing can be taken away. I therefore detest all of men's imagining which they would obtrude upon us as articles of faith, and bind upon our consciences by laws and statutes. And thus I repudiate in general whatever has been introduced into the worship of God without authority from the word of God. Of this kind are all the Popish ceremonies. In short, I detest the tyrannical yoke by which miserable consciences have been oppressed—as the law of auricular confession, celibacy, and others of the same description.

I confess that the Church should be governed by pastors, to whom has been committed the office of preaching the word of God and administering the sacraments; and that, in order to avoid confusion, it is not lawful for any one to usurp this office at pleasure without lawful election. And if any called to this office do not show due fidelity in discharging it, they ought to be deposed. All their power con-

sists in ruling the people committed to them according to
the word of God, so that Jesus Christ may ever remain supreme Pastor and sole Lord of his Church, and alone be
listened to. Wherefore, what is called the Popish hierarchy
I execrate as diabolical confusion, established for the very
purpose of making God himself to be despised, and of exposing the Christian religion to mockery and scorn.

I confess that our weakness requires that sacraments be
added to the preaching of the word, as seals by which the
promises of God are sealed on our hearts, and that two such
sacraments were ordained by Christ, viz., Baptism and the
Lord's Supper—the former to give us an entrance into the
Church of God—the latter to keep us in it. The five sacraments imagined by the Papists, and first coined in their own
brain, I repudiate.

But although the sacraments are an earnest by which
we may be rendered secure of the promises of God, I however acknowledge that they would be useless to us did not
the Holy Spirit render them efficacious as instruments, lest
our confidence, being fixed on the creature, should be withdrawn from God. Nay, I even confess that the sacraments
are vitiated and perverted when it is not regarded as their
only aim to make us look to Christ for every thing requisite
to our salvation, and whenever they are employed for any
other purpose than that of fixing our faith wholly in him.
Moreover, since the promise of adoption reaches even to the
posterity of believers, I acknowledge that the infants of believers ought to be received into the Church by baptism;
and in this matter I detest the ravings of the Anabaptists.

In regard to the Lord's Supper, I confess that it is an
evidence of our union with Christ, since he not only died
once and rose again for us, but also truly feeds and nourishes
us by his own flesh and blood, so that we are one with him,
and his life is common to us. For though he is in heaven
for a short while till he come to judge the world, I believe
that he, through the secret and incomprehensible agency of
his Spirit, gives life to our souls by the substance of his body
and blood.

In general, I confess that, as well in the supper as in

baptism, God gives in reality and effectually whatever he figures in them, but that to the receiving of this great boon we require to join the word with the signs. In which matter I detest the abuse and perversion of the Papists, who have deprived the sacraments of their principal part, viz., the doctrine which teaches the true use and benefit flowing therefrom, and have changed them into magical impostures.

I likewise confess that water, though it is a fading element, truly testifies to us in baptism the true presence of the blood of Jesus Christ, and of his Spirit; and that in the Lord's Supper the bread and wine are to us true and by no means fallacious pledges that we are spiritually nourished by the body and blood of Christ. And thus I join with the signs the very possession and fruition of that which is therein offered to us.

Likewise, seeing that the sacred supper as instituted by Jesus Christ is to us a sacred treasure of infinite value, I detest as intolerable sacrilege the execrable abomination of the Mass, useful for no one purpose but to overturn whatever Christ has left us, both in that it is said to be a sacrifice for the living and the dead, and also in all the other things which are diametrically opposed to the purity of the sacrament of the Lord's Supper.

I confess that God would have the world to be governed by laws and polity, so that reins should not be wanting to curb the unbridled movements of men, and that for that purpose he has established kingdoms, princedoms, and dominations, and whatever relates to civil jurisdiction; of which things he wills to be regarded as the Author; that not only should their authority be submitted to for his sake, but we should also revere and honour rulers as the vicegerents of God and ministers appointed by him to discharge a legitimate and sacred function. And therefore I also acknowledge that it is right to obey their laws and statutes, pay tribute and taxes, and other things of the same nature; in short, bear the yoke of subjection ultroneously and willingly; with the exception, however, that the authority of God, the Sovereign Prince, must always remain entire and unimpaired.

CONFESSION OF FAITH

IN NAME OF

THE REFORMED CHURCHES OF FRANCE:

DRAWN UP DURING THE WAR,

FOR PRESENTATION TO

THE EMPEROR, PRINCES, AND STATES OF GERMANY,
AT THE DIET OF FRANKFORT;

BUT WHICH COULD NOT REACH THEM, THE PASSES BEING CLOSED.

NOW PUBLISHED

FOR THE ADVANTAGES WHICH MAY ACCRUE FROM IT, AND EVEN
BECAUSE NECESSITY REQUIRES IT.

ANNO M.D.LXII.

TO THE READER.

BECAUSE during the troubles of war which have happened in France, to the great regret of the Princes and Lords who were even constrained to take up arms, many false charges were disseminated against them to render the truth odious in their persons, they were constrained at the time to publish certain declarations in defence of their integrity. Now that it has pleased God to regard France in pity and give her peace, and that the conduct of those who had been defamed has been approved by his Majesty and his Council, so that there is no need to make any apology for them, the evil, which lasted only too long, may well be allowed to remain as it were buried, and wo to those who would in any way disturb the public tranquillity. However, as several ignorant persons, from being ill informed on the doctrine against which they have fought, have always persisted in holding it in horror and detestation, it has seemed more than useful to bring forward this Confession of Faith, which was sent on the occasion above mentioned to be presented to the Emperor and States of the Empire met at the diet of Frankfort, but could not reach them, as all the passes were closed. True, indeed, it may seem as if the time were past; but when everything is well considered, it is still in the present day as seasonable as ever, as by the grace of God the result will show. Be this as it may, it were a pity that any thing so valuable should remain as it were effaced, seeing that it may be serviceable in many ways.

CONFESSION OF FAITH,

IN NAME OF THE REFORMED CHURCHES OF FRANCE.*

1. JUST DEFENCE OF THE CHURCHES OF FRANCE.

SIRE, we doubt not that since those troubles which have been stirred up in the kingdom of France to our great regret, some have endeavoured by all means to render our cause odious to your Majesty, and that you also, illustrious Princes, have heard many sinister reports to animate you against us. But we have always hoped, and hope more than ever, that having obtained audience to make our apology, it will be received so soon as you shall have ascertained the facts of the case.

2. DIFFERENT DECLARATIONS OF THE CHURCHES.

Now the truth is, that we have already, on former occasions, published many declarations, by which all Christendom must be sufficiently advertised of our innocence and integrity, and that so far are we from having wished to excite any sedition against the King, our sole Sovereign Prince and Lord under God, that on the contrary we expose our lives and our goods in this war to maintain the superiority which is due to him, and the authority of his edicts, as in fact his Majesty has no more loyal, obedient, and peaceful subjects than we are and wish to be to the end. Wherefore without stopping at those things which have been amply enough explained heretofore, it will be sufficient to show at present what the religion is, for the exercise of which, as authorized

* Translated from the French.

by the edicts of the King our Sovereign Lord, we have been constrained to defend ourselves by arms. For we understand that the malevolent, who have nothing else to gainsay in us, falsely and tortiously throw blame before your Majesty, and before you, illustrious Princes, on the religion which we follow, and make you believe several things in order to disgust you with it, so that if we were not allowed our defence our cause would be altogether oppressed by such calumnies.

3. THEIR CONFESSION OF FAITH.

True it is that the Confession of Faith of the Churches of France, to which we adhere, might so far remedy the evil, for since it has been twice solemnly presented to the King our Sovereign Lord, it may be clearly seen from it what is the summary of our faith. And but for this we would not have waited so long to clear ourselves from the false detractions which have been uttered against us. Not that the mouth of evil speakers ever can be closed, but inasmuch as it is our duty to use all pains and diligence in order that our integrity may be known, and our persons not lie under scandal, so by much stronger reason should the pure simplicity of our faith be known, in order that the malignant may not with open mouth blaspheme the truth of the gospel   Wherefore we have thought it advisable, to address this brief summary to your Majesty, and to your Excellencies, most illustrious Princes, in order that the faith which we hold may be attested by our own subscriptions. And as we desire to be in good reputation with you, Sire, for the reverence which we bear your Majesty, and also you, most illustrious Princes, we humbly supplicate and pray that this Confession may have access to be heard and graciously listened to.

4. OF GOD AND THE THREE PERSONS.

In the first place, we protest that on all the articles which have been decided by ancient Councils, touching the infinite spiritual essence of God, and the distinction of the three

persons, and the union of the two natures in our Lord Jesus
Christ, we receive and agree in all that was therein resolved,
as being drawn from the Holy Scriptures, on which alone
our faith should be founded, as there is no other witness
proper and competent to decide what the majesty of God is
but God himself.

5. OF THE HOLY SCRIPTURES AND THE TWO NATURES IN CHRIST.

But as we hold the Old and New Testaments as the only
rule of our faith, so we receive all that is conformable to
them : such as believing that there are three distinct persons in the one essence of God, and that our Lord Jesus
Christ, being very God and very man, has so united the two
natures in himself that they are not confounded.   Wherefore we detest all the heresies which were of old condemned,
such as those of the Arians, Sabellians, Eunomians, and the
like, as well as the Nestorians and Eutychians.   God forbid
that we should be infected with those reveries which troubled
the Catholic Church at the time when it was in its purity.

6. SUMMARY OF THE DIFFERENCES.

Wherefore all our differences relate to the following points:
on what our confidence of salvation should rest, how we ought
to invoke God, and what is the method of well and duly
serving him.   And there are points depending on these, viz.,
what is the true polity of the Church, the office of prelates
and pastors, the nature, virtue, and use of the Sacraments.

7. OF ADAM'S FALL.

To know well wherein consists the true salvation of men,
it is necessary to know what is their state and condition.
Now we hold what Scripture teaches, that the whole human
race was so corrupted by the fall of Adam, that by nature

we are all condemned and lost, not only by another's guilt, but because we are sinners from the womb, and God can justly condemn us, although there be no outward act by which we have deserved condemnation.

8. OF ORIGINAL SIN.

Moreover, we hold that original sin is a corruption spread over our senses and affections, so that right understanding and reason is perverted in us, and we are like poor blind persons in darkness, and the will is subject to all wicked desires, full of rebellion, and given up to evil; in short, that we are poor captives held under the tyranny of sin; not that in doing evil we are not pushed by our own will in such a way that we cannot throw our sins upon another, but because sprung of the cursed race of Adam, we have not one particle of strength to do well, and all our faculties are vicious.

9. OF THE SOURCE OF OUR SALVATION.

Hence we conclude, that the source and origin of our salvation is the pure mercy of God; for he cannot find in us any worthiness to induce him to love us. We also being bad trees cannot bear any good fruit, and therefore cannot prevent God, so as to acquire or merit grace from him; but he looks upon us in pity, to show mercy to us, and has no other cause for displaying his mercy in us but our misery. We likewise hold that the goodness which he displays towards us proceeds from his having elected us before the creation of the world, not seeking the cause of so doing out of himself and his good pleasure. And here is our first fundamental principle, viz., that we are pleasing to God, inasmuch as he has been pleased to adopt us as his children before we were born, and has by this means delivered us by special privilege from the general curse under which all men have fallen.

10. OF FAITH IN JESUS CHRIST.

But because the counsel of God is incomprehensible, we confess that in order to obtain salvation it is necessary to have recourse to the means which God has ordained ; for we are not of the number of fanatics who, under colour of the eternal predestination of God, have no regard to arrive by the right path at the life which is promised to us; but rather we hold, that in order to be adopted children of God, and to have a proper certainty of it, we must believe in Jesus Christ, inasmuch as it is in him alone that we must seek the whole grounds of our salvation.

11. OF OUR RECONCILIATION WITH GOD.

And first we believe that his death was the one perpetual sacrifice to reconcile us to God, and that in it we have full satisfaction for all our offences ; by his blood we are washed from all our pollutions, and we therefore place all our confidence in the forgiveness of sins which he has purchased for us, and that not only for once, but for the whole period of our life : for which reason also he is called our righteousness. (1 Cor. i. 30.) And so far are we from presuming on our merit, that we confess in all humility that if God look to what is in us he will find only ground to condemn us. Thus to be assured of his grace we have no other resource than his pure mercy, inasmuch as he receives us in the name of his well-beloved Son.

12. OF GOOD WORKS.

But as our sins are not pardoned to give us license to do wickedly, but rather as it is said in the psalm, (Ps. cxxx. 4,) God is propitious to us, in order that we may be induced to fear and reverence him, we also hold that the grace which has appeared to us in Jesus Christ ought to have reference to the end which St. Paul mentions, (Tit. ii. 12,) that renouncing all ungodliness and worldly lusts, we should walk in holiness of life, aspiring to the hope of the kingdom of heaven.   Wherefore the blood of Jesus Christ is not our laver, in order to make us wallow in pollution, but rather to draw us to true purity.   In one word, being the children of God we must be regenerated by his Spirit.   And this is the reason why it is said, (1 John iii. 8,) that our Lord Jesus Christ came to destroy the kingdom of the devil, which is the kingdom of iniquity, inasmuch as he has been given us as Mediator, not only in order to obtain pardon of our sins, but also to sanctify us, which is equivalent to saying that it was, as it were, to dedicate us to the service of God, by withdrawing us from the pollutions of this world.   Hence we cannot be Christians without being new creatures, (Eph. ii. 2,) formed unto good works, which God has prepared, in order that we should walk in them, seeing that of ourselves we would not be so disposed.   But the will and execution are given us by God, and all our sufficiency is of him, (Phil. ii. 13 ;) and for this purpose our Lord Jesus Christ has received all fulness of grace, that we may draw from him, (2 Cor. iii. 5.) Thus we presume not on our free-will or virtue and ability, but rather confess that our good works are pure gifts of God.

13. HOW WE PARTAKE OF JESUS CHRIST AND HIS BENEFITS.—OF FAITH.

Now we understand that we are made partakers of all his blessings by means of faith ; for this it is which brings us into communication with Christ, in order that he may dwell in us, that we may be ingrafted into him as our root, that we may be members of his body, that we may live in him, and he in us, and possess him, with all his benefits.   And that it may not be thought strange that we attribute such virtue to faith, we do not take it for a fleeting opinion, but for a certainty which we have of the promises of God, in which all these blessings are contained, and by which we embrace our Lord Jesus Christ as the surety of all our salvation, and apply to our own use what he has received of God his Father to impart unto us.   This faith we likewise know that we cannot have if it be not given us from above, and as Scripture declares, (Eph. ii. 9 ; i. 18,) till the Holy Spirit enlightens us to comprehend what is beyond all human sense, and seals in our hearts what we ought to believe.

14. OF THE IMPERFECTION AND PERFECTION OF BELIEVERS.

Now, although being called to do good works, we produce the fruits of our calling, as it is said, (Luke i. 75,) that we have been redeemed in order to serve God in holiness and righteousness, we are however always encompassed with many infirmities while we live in this world. What is more, all our thoughts and affections are so stained with impurity that no work can proceed from us which is worthy of the acceptance of God. Thus so far are we, in striving to do well, from being able to merit anything, that we always continue debtors. For God will always have just cause to blame us in whatever we do, and reward is promised to none but those who fulfil the law ; which we are very far from doing. (Deut. xviii. 5 ; Ezek. xx. 11 ; Rom. x. 5 ; Gal. iii. 12.) See then how we hold that all our merits are suppressed. It is not only that we fail in the perfect fulfilment of the law, but that also in every act there is some evil vicious taint. We are well aware that the instruction commonly given is to repair the faults we commit by satisfactions ; but as the Scripture teaches us that our Lord Jesus Christ has satisfied for us, we cannot repose in any thing else than the sacrifice of his death, by which the wrath of God is appeased, wrath which no creatures could sustain. (Gal. iii. 13 ; iv. 5 ; Tit. ii. 14 ; 1 Pet. i. 18, 19.) And the reason why we hold that we are justified by faith alone is because it is necessary for us to borrow elsewhere, namely, from our Lord Jesus Christ, that righteousness which is wanting to us, not in part but wholly.

15. OF INVOCATION.

It is this which gives us boldness to call upon God, for without this we should have no access, Scripture teaching that we never shall be heard while in doubt and disquietude. (Heb. xi. 6 ; James i. 6, 7.) Therefore we hold that our sovereign good and repose consists in being assured of the forgiveness of sins, by the faith which we have in Jesus Christ, seeing that this is the key which opens the gate that leads us to God. (Rom. iv. 6 ; James i. 32.) Now it is said that whosoever will call on the name of the Lord will be saved. Still, according as Scripture teaches us, we address our prayers to God in the name of our Lord Jesus Christ, who has become our Advocate, because without him we should not be worthy of obtaining access. (Eph. iii. 12 ; Heb. iv. 16.) That we do not pray to holy men and women in common fashion, should not be imputed to us as a fault: for since in all our actions we are required to have our conscience decided, we cannot observe too great sobriety in prayer. We accordingly follow the rule which has been given us, viz., that without having known him, and that his word has been preached to us in testimony of his will, we cannot call upon him. Now in regard to prayer, the whole of Scripture refers us to him only. What is more, he regards our prayers as the chief and supreme sacrifice by which we do homage to his Majesty, as he declares in the fiftieth Psalm, and hence to address our prayers to creatures, and go gadding about to this quarter and to that, is a thing which we may not do, if we would not be guilty of sacrilege. To seek other patrons or advocates than our Lord Jesus Christ, we hold not to be in our choice or liberty. True it is that we ought to pray one for another, while we are conversant here below, but as to having recourse to the dead, since Scripture does not tell us to do so, we will not attempt it, for fear of being guilty of presumption. Even the enormous abuses which have been and still are in vogue, warn us to confine ourselves within such simplicity, as a limit which God has set to check all curiosity and boldness. For many prayers have been forged full of horrible blasphemies, such as those which request the Virgin Mary to command her Son, and exert her authority over him—and which style her the haven of salvation, the life and hope of those who trust in her.

16. OF PRAYERS FOR THE DEAD.

We refuse to pray for the dead, not only for this reason, but also because the practice implies a great deal more, viz., presupposes that there is a purgatory in which souls are punished for the faults which they have committed. Now, on this view, the redemption made by Jesus Christ cannot be complete, and we must detract from the death which he suffered, as if it had only procured a partial acquittal—a thing which cannot be said without blasphemy. Thus believing that the poor people have been imposed upon in this respect, we are unwilling to devise any thing against the principles of our Christian faith. We deem it sufficient to hold by the pure doctrine of Holy Scripture, which makes no mention of all this. Be this as it may, we hold that it is a superstition devised by the fancy of men, and besides, as we are not permitted to pray to God at hap-hazard, we would not be so presumptuous as to usurp the office of our Lord Jesus Christ, who has fully acquitted us of all our offences.

17. OF THE SERVICE OF GOD.

The second principal point in which we differ from the custom and opinion received in the world, is the manner of serving God. Now on our part, in accordance with his declaration, that obedience is better than sacrifice, (1 Sam. xv. 22,) and with his uniform injunction to listen to what he commands, if we would render a well regulated and acceptable sacrifice, we hold that it is not for us to invent what to us seems good, or to follow what may have been devised in the brain of other men, but to confine ourselves simply to the purity of Scripture. Wherefore we believe that anything which is not derived from it, but has only been commanded by the authority of men, ought not to be regarded as the service of God. And in this we have two articles as a kind of axioms. The one is, that men cannot bind the conscience under pain of mortal sin: for not in vain does God insist on being re-

garded as the only lawgiver, saying, (James iv. 12,) that it
is for him to condemn and acquit, nor in vain does he so
often reiterate, that we are not to add to his ordinances.
This indeed cannot be done without taxing him with not
having known all that was useful, (Deut. iv. 2 ; xii. 32,) or
with having forgotten this thing or that through inadvertence.
The second axiom is, that when we presume to serve God at
our own hand, he repudiates it as corruption.   And this is
the reason why he exclaims by his prophet Isaiah, (Is. xxix.
13,) that all true religion has been perverted by keeping the
commandments of men.   And our Lord Jesus Christ confirms the same by saying, (Matt. xv. 9,) that in vain would
we know God by human tradition.   It is with good reason,
therefore, that his spiritual supremacy over our souls remains
inviolable, and that at the very least his will as a bridle
should regulate our devotions.

18. OF HUMAN TRADITION.

We have in this matter such notable warnings from common experience, that we are the more confirmed in not passing the limits of Scripture.   For since men began to make
laws to regulate the service of God, and subject the conscience, there has been neither end nor measure, while, on
the other hand, God has punished such temerity, blinding
men with delusions which may make one shudder.   When
we look nearer to see what human traditions are, we find
that they are an abyss, and that their number is endless.
And yet there are abuses so absurd and enormous, that it is
wonderful how men could have been so stupid, were it not
that God has executed the vengeance which he announced
by his prophet Isaiah, (Is. xxix. 14,) blinding and infatuat-
ing the wise who would honour him by observing the commandments of men.

19. OF IDOLATROUS INTENTIONS.

Since men have turned aside from pure and holy obedience
to God, they have discovered that good intention was sufficient to approve everything.   This was to open a door to

all superstitions. It has been the origin of the worship of images, the purchase of masses, the filling of churches with pomp and parade, the running about on pilgrimages, the making of vows by each at his own hand. But the abyss here is so profound that it is enough for us to have touched on some examples. So far is it from being permitted to honour God by human inventions, that there would be no firmness nor certainty, neither bottom nor shore in religion : every thing would go to wreck, and Christianity differ in nothing from the idolatries of the heathen.

20. OF THE TYRANNICAL ORDINANCES OF THE POPE.

There is another evil which we have alleged in the tyranny by which poor souls are oppressed. When men are commanded to confess their sins once a year to a priest, it is just to throw the whole world into despair. For if a man cannot keep count of the faults of a single day, who can be able to collect them at the end of a year? And yet the decree declares that pardon cannot otherwise be obtained. This is to close the gate of paradise against all mankind. Moreover, though the observance of human laws were not impossible, there is always sacrilege in encroaching on the jurisdiction of God, as when it is said that sins will not be pardoned unless they are confessed in the ear of a priest. This is to append a condition to the promise of God, so as to render it false or vain. The same may be said of the prohibition to eat flesh on certain days under pain of mortal sin. We confess, indeed, that fasting and abstinence is a laudable virtue, but such a prohibition trenches on the authority of God. The prohibition of marriage to priests, as well as monks and nuns, contains in itself two vices. First, it belonged not to mortal men to prohibit what God has permitted, and secondly, to constrain those who have not the gift of continence to refrain from the remedy, is as it were to plunge them into an abyss. And, in fact, we see the fruits which have been produced by it, and have no need to say what we are even shamed to think.

21. OF THE AUTHORITY AND GOVERNMENT OF THE CHURCH.·

We intend not, however, to annihilate the authority of the Church, or of prelates and pastors, to whom the superintendence of its government has been given. We admit that bishops and pastors ought to be listened to with reverence, in so far as they discharge the office of preaching the word of God, and moreover, that all churches, and each one in particular, have powers to make laws and statutes for the common guidance, (1 Cor. xiv. 40,) as it is necessary that every thing be done decently and in order. Such statutes ought to be obeyed, provided they do not restrict consciences nor establish superstition, and we hold those to be fanatical and contumacious who will not conform to them. But we desemble not that it is necessary to distinguish true and legitimate pastors from those who have only a frivolous title. For in fact it is but too notorious that those who call themselves prelates and would be acknowledged as such, do not even make a semblance of discharging their duty. But the worst is, that, under colour of their state and dignity, they lead poor souls to perdition, turning them aside from the truth of God to their lies. And hence, though they were to be tolerated in other respects, yet when they would feed us on false doctrines and errors, we must put in practice St. Peter's answer, " We must obey God rather than man." (Acts v. 29.)

22. OF THE PRIMACY OF THE POPE.

Moreover, we hold that the primacy which the Pope attributes to himself is an enormous usurpation. For were we to admit the expediency of having some head in the Church, (this, however, is completely repugnant to the word of God, Eph. i. 22; iv. 15; v. 23 ; Col. i. 18,) still it is extravagantly absurd that he who is to be head over bishops should not be a bishop himself. And when we examine all that they say of their hierarchy, we find that it bears no resemblance to what our Lord Jesus and his apostles taught us, or

rather that it is a corruption fitted to overturn the government of the Church.   We touch not on all the dissoluteness
and scandals which are only too notorious, but we say that
all Christians, in order not to be rebels against God, ought
to reject what they know to be contrary to the purity of his
service.   For when there is a question as to the spiritual
jurisdiction which God reserves to himself, all human supremacy must give way.   The laws of earthly princes, however
grievous and harsh they should be, nay, even should they be
felt to be unjust, are nevertheless valid, and it is not lawful to despise them : for the goods and bodies of this world
are not so precious as that the authority which God has
given to all kings, princes, and rulers, should not take precedence of them.   But it is a very different case to subject
our souls to tyrannical or strange and bastard laws, which
are to turn us aside from subjection to God.   Meanwhile we
confess, that it is not for private persons to correct such
abuses, in order to remove them entirely ; it is enough that
all Christians abstain from them, keeping themselves pure
and entire for the service of God.

23. OF THE DUTY OF PASTORS AND FLOCK IN THE CHURCH.

As to all pastors who acquit themselves faithfully of their
charge, we hold that they ought to be received as representing the person of him who has ordained them ; and that all
Christians ought to array themselves under the common
order of the faithful to hear the doctrine of salvation, to
make confession of their faith, to keep themselves in union
with the Church, to submit peacefully to censure and correction, and assist in preventing any schism or disturbance from
taking place.   Hence we hold as schismatics all who stir up
trouble and confusion, tending to rend the Church, which
cannot retain its proper state without being governed by its
pastors, since it has so pleased God, and he has commanded
all, from the greatest to the least, to conform in subjection
to it ; so that all who separate and voluntarily cut them-

selves off from the company of the faithful also banish themselves from the kingdom of heaven. At the same time, those who would be listened to in the name of Christ must take heed to deliver the doctrine which has been committed to them.

24. OF THE SACRAMENTS.

It remains to declare what is our faith touching the Sacraments. We hold them to be at once an attestation to the grace of God to ratify it in us, and external signs, by which we declare our Christianity before men. True it is that the word of God should suffice to assure us of our salvation ; but seeing that God has been pleased, because of our ignorance and frailty, to add such helps, it is very reasonable that we accept of them, and apply them to our profit. Thus the sacraments are, as it were, seals to seal the grace of God in our hearts, and render it more authentic, for which reason they may be termed visible doctrine. Now we believe that all which is there figured and demonstrated is accomplished in us. For they are not vain or elusory figures, since God, who is infallible truth, gives them to us for confirmation of our faith. Moreover, we believe that whatever unworthiness there may be in the minister, the sacrament fails not to be good and available. For the truth of God does not change or vary according to the wickedness of men, as it is not their office to give virtue or effect to what God has appointed.

Hence we believe, that though the sacraments should be administered by wicked and unworthy persons, they always retain their nature, so as to bring and communicate truly to the receivers the thing signified by them. We hold, however, that they are useful only when God gives effect to them, and displays the power of his Spirit, using them as instruments. Hence the Spirit of God must act to make us feel their efficacy for our salvation. We also confess that the use of them is necessary, and that all those who make no account of them declare themselves despisers of the grace of God, and are blinded by devilish pride, not knowing their infirmity which God has been pleased to sustain by such means and remedy.   Moreover, since God has placed the sacraments as a sacred deposit in his Church, we believe that individuals are not to use them apart, but that the use of them ought to be common to the assembly of the faithful, and that they ought to be administered by the pastors to whom the charge and dispensation of them has been committed.

25. TO WHOM IT APPERTAINS TO INSTITUTE SACRAMENTS.—THE NUMBER OF THEM.

From this we infer that it belongs to God only to ordain sacraments, seeing that he alone can bear witness to his will, seal the promises, represent his spiritual gifts, and make earthly elements to be, as it were, earnests of our salvation. Hence the ceremonies which have been introduced by men cannot, and ought not to be, held as sacraments.   To attribute to them this title and quality is only to deceive. Wherefore we confess that the number of seven sacraments, which they are commonly held to be, is not received by us, seeing they are not sanctioned by the word of God.   Still, though we do not avow marriage to be a sacrament, it is not because we despise it.   Neither do we mean to lessen the dignity of the temporary sacraments which were used in the days of miracles, although we say that they are not now in use, *e.g.*, the anointing of the sick.   At all events, it is very reasonable that the ordinances which have proceeded from God should be distinguished from those which have been introduced by men.

26. OF BAPTISM.

As there are two sacraments for the common use of the whole Church, viz., Baptism and the Holy Supper, we will make a brief confession of our faith in regard to both.   We hold, then, that baptism being a spiritual washing and sign of our regeneration, serves as an evidence that God introduces us into his Church to make us, as it were, his children and heirs ; and thus ought we to apply it during the whole period of our life, in order to confirm us in the promises

which have been given us, as well of the forgiveness of our
sins as of the guidance and assistance of the Holy Spirit.
And because the two graces which are there signified to
us are given us in Jesus Christ, and cannot be found elsewhere, we believe, that in order to enjoy the fruit of our
baptism it is necessary to refer it to its proper end, that is,
to hold that we are washed by the shedding of the blood of
Jesus Christ, and in virtue of his death and resurrection, die
in ourselves and rise again to newness of life ; and because
Jesus Christ is the substance, the Scripture says that we
are properly baptized in his name. (Acts ii. 38 ; x. 48 ; xix.
5.) Moreover, we believe, that since baptism is a treasure
which God has placed in his Church, all the members
ought to partake of it. Now we doubt not that little children born of Christians are of this number, since God has
adopted them, as he declares. Indeed we should defraud
them of their right were we to exclude them from the sign
which only ratifies the thing contained in the promise :
considering, moreover, that children ought no more in the
present day to be deprived of the sacrament of their salvation than the children of the Jews were in ancient times,
seeing that now the manifestation must be larger and clearer
than it was under the law. Wherefore we reprobate all fanatics who will not allow little children to be baptized.

27. OF THE SUPPER.—OF THE MASS.

To make clear our belief in the Supper, we are constrained
to show how it differs from the Mass. For we cannot conceal that there is nothing common or conformable between
them, or even approaching to resemblance. We are not ignorant that this acknowledgment is odious to many persons,
in respect that the Mass is in high reverence and esteem,
and, in fact, we were no less devoted to it than others until
we were shown its abuses : but we hope, that when our
reasons have been patiently heard and understood, nothing
strange will be found in what we hold respecting it.

It is true, the term Sacrifice was long ago applied to the
Supper, but the ancient doctors were very far from using it in

the sense which has been given to it since, viz., as being a meritorious oblation to obtain pardon and grace as well to the dead as the living. Now, though there are in the present day a kind of middle-men, who, to colour the general error which has prevailed in the world, make a pretence of receiving the doctrine of the ancient fathers, use and practice, however, demonstrate that the things are quite contrary, and at least as distant as heaven is from earth. It is notorious, that in the ancient Church there were no private masses, no foundations, and that the Sacrament was used for communicating, whereas in the present day masses are purchased as satisfactions, to obtain acquittal with God, and each individual has them apart at will. Such merchandise cannot cloak itself under the ancient practice of the Church. Another profanation is, that whereas the Holy Supper ought only to bear the name of Jesus Christ, they forge masses at will, of Christopher, or Barbara, or any other saint of the calendar, as it is called—fashions which agree no more with the nature of the Sacrament than fire agrees with water.

28. OF THE AUTHOR OF THE SUPPER.

Moreover, though we honour antiquity, and do not willingly reject what was approved by holy fathers, yet it seems to us very reasonable, that the institutions of our Lord Jesus Christ should be preferred to all that men have devised. All human authority must cease when it is a question of obeying him to whom all power has been given. Our Lord Jesus Christ, none but he, is the author of the Supper. Therefore what he has ordained is the inviolable rule which ought to be observed without contradiction. Now he distributed the bread and wine, saying, Take, eat, drink: this is my body and my blood. (Matt. xxvi. 26 ; Matt. xiv. 22 ; 1 Cor. ii. 24.) Hence to offer instead of receiving is to contravene the ordinance of the Son of God. Whatever excuses men may pretend, in introducing a kind of sacrifice, they have metamorphosed the sacrament, and converted it into an entirely different form. This is the reason why we cannot consent to the use of any mode of sacrificing in the Supper :

for it is not lawful for us to deviate from what our Lord Jesus Christ has commanded, seeing the heavenly Father has published his decree, "Hear ye him." (Matt. xvii. 5.) And in fact, St. Paul, when wishing to reform some abuse which had already sprung up in the Church of Corinth, leads back the faithful to the observance of what they had received from our Lord Jesus Christ. (1 Cor. xi. 23.) Hence we see that there is no firm footing anywhere else.

29. OF THE SACRIFICE OF THE MASS.

We hold, then, that since Scripture teaches that our Lord Jesus Christ, by one only sacrifice, purchased perpetual redemption for us, and that it was only once for all he offered his body as the price and satisfaction of our sins, it is unlawful to reiterate such a sacrifice ; and since the Father, by ordaining him sole and perpetual Priest after the order of Melchisedec, has confirmed this by solemn oath, we hold also that for others to offer is blasphemously to derogate from his dignity. We believe, moreover, that it is an abuse and intolerable corruption to have masses in which none communicate, seeing that the Supper is nothing else than a sacrament in which all Christians partake together of the body and blood of Jesus Christ.

30. OTHER CORRUPTIONS OF THE MASS.

We also reprobate another abuse which is common throughout the world. It is that the people communicate only in the half of the Supper, while one solitary priest receives the whole sacrament. It is distinctly said—Drink all of this cup. (Matth. xxvi. 27.) What God has joined men may not put asunder. Even the usage of the primitive Church was conformable to the institution of our Lord Jesus Christ, and this separation, which takes away the cup from the people, was recently introduced. Nor can we consent to another abuse, viz., that of celebrating the ordinance in an unknown tongue. For our Lord wished to be understood by his disciples when he said—Take. eat, this is my body, &c. ;

and these words are addressed to the Church.   It is therefore a mockery of the sacrament when the priest mutters
over the bread and over the cup, and no one understands
what he is about.

31. WHY THE HOLY SUPPER WAS INSTITUTED.

In regard to the Supper of our Lord we have to say, in the
first place, for what end it was instituted : for from this it
will be seen what its use is, and what benefit accrues to us
from it.   The end, then, to which it ought to be referred is to
continue in us the grace which we received in baptism.   For
as by baptism God regenerates us to be his children, and by
such spiritual birth introduces us into his Church, to make
us, as it were, of his household ; so in the Supper he declares
to us that he wishes not to leave us unprovided, but rather
to maintain us in the heavenly life till such time as we shall
have attained to the perfection of it.   Now, inasmuch as there
is no other food for our souls than Jesus Christ, it is in him
alone that we must seek life.   But because of our weakness
and ignorance, the Supper is to us a visible and external
sign to testify to us, that in partaking of the body and blood
of Jesus Christ we live spiritually in him.   For as he does
not present himself to us empty, so we receive him with all
his benefits and gifts in such manner, that while possessing
him we have in him all that appertains to our salvation.

In saying that the Supper is a sign, we mean not that it is
a simple figure or remembrance, but confess that the thing
signified by it is verily accomplished in us in fact.   For seeing that God is infallible truth, it is certain that he means not
to amuse us with some vain appearance, but that the substance of what the sacraments signify is conjoined with them.

32. OF THE REAL RECEIVING OF THE BODY AND BLOOD OF THE LORD.

Wherefore we hold that this doctrine of our Lord Jesus
Christ, viz., that his body is truly meat, and his blood truly
drink, (John vi.) is not only represented and ratified in the

Supper, but also accomplished in fact. For there under the symbols of bread and wine our Lord presents us with his body and blood, and we are spiritually fed upon them, provided we do not preclude entrance to his grace by our unbelief. For as a vessel, though it be empty, cannot receive any liquor while it is closed and corked, so also must faith give an opening to make us capable of receiving the blessings which God offers us, as it is said in the Psalm, (Ps. lxxxi. 11,) Open thy mouth and I will fill it. Not that our unbelief can destroy the truth of God, or that our depravity can hinder the sacraments from retaining their virtue; for let us be what we may, God is ever like himself, and the virtue of the sacraments depends not on our faith, as if by our ingratitude we could derogate from their nature or quality.

33. THE UNWORTHY COMMUNICATE ONLY IN THE SIGNS.

Wherefore the supper is a certain attestation, which is addressed to the bad as well as the good, in order to offer Christ to all indiscriminately; but this is not to say that all receive him when he is offered to them. And in fact it were grossly absurd to hold that Jesus Christ is received by those who are entire strangers to him, and that the wicked eat his body and drink his blood while destitute of his Spirit. For in this way he would be dead, being despoiled of his virtue and yielding nothing.

34. REASON OF THIS.

Though it is said that the wicked are guilty of the body and blood of Christ when they partake unworthily of the Supper, this does not prove that they receive any more than the sign. For it is not said by St. Paul that they are condemned for having received the body and the blood, but for not having discerned between them and profane things. Their offence then is that they rejected Christ when he was presented to them. For such contempt carries with it detestable sacrilege. We confess indeed that speaking sacramentally, as it is called, the wicked receive the body and blood of Jesus Christ, and the ancient fathers sometimes used this language, but they explained themselves by adding that it was not really and in fact, but in so far as the sacrament implies it. Indeed we can have no part in Jesus Christ except by faith, and he has no connection with us if we are not his members.

35. OF TRANSUBSTANTIATION.

It remains to see the way and manner in which our Lord Jesus communicates himself to us in the Supper. In regard to this, several questions and disputes have been raised in our time. Now, in the first place, we reject not only the common reverie in regard to what is called transubstantiation, but also what was decided at the Council of Tours, viz., that we chew with our teeth and swallow the body of Christ. For to say that the bread is changed and becomes no more than a form without substance, is repugnant to the nature of the sacrament, in which it is shown that as we are supported on bread and wine, so our souls are nourished with the flesh and blood of Jesus Christ. Now it is necessary that there be a correspondence between the spiritual reality and the external symbol. If then there was only the figure of bread, there would also be a figure only in regard to the body and blood of Christ. We conclude, then, without doubt, that the bread and the wine remain as the sign and the pledge to testify to us that the flesh of Jesus Christ is our heavenly bread and his blood our true drink. In the second place, to imagine that we swallow the body of Jesus Christ, and that it passes into us as material bread, is a thing which cannot be received by Christians, and is altogether at variance with the reverence with which we ought to regard the sacred union which we have with the Son of God.

36. OF CONSUBSTANTIATION.

Still we confess that we are truly united with our Lord Jesus, so that he invigorates us by the proper substance of his body. Our meaning is not that he descends here below or has an infinite body to fill heaven and earth, but that this grace of uniting us with him and living on his substance is everywhere diffused by the virtue of his Spirit. We are aware indeed that some say that in so high and deep a mystery it is not lawful to inquire into the mode ; but after they have thus spoken, they determine that the body of Jesus Christ is under the bread, just as wine may be contained in a pot. Thus under colour of sobriety they take license to say what they please. On our part we confess that the mode of communicating with Jesus Christ is miraculous and transcends our conceptions, and we are not ashamed to exclaim with St. Paul, (Eph. v. 32,) that it is a great mystery, which ought to fill us with amazement, but this hinders us not from rejecting all absurdities contrary to Holy Scripture, and to the articles of our faith.

37. OF UBIQUITY.

Now we hold for certain and infallible, that though the human nature of our Lord Jesus is conjoined with his divinity, so as to establish in him a true unity of person, still his human nature retains its quality and condition, and every thing which is proper to it. In like manner then as our Lord Jesus took a body capable of suffering, this body had its magnitude and measure and was not infinite. We confess indeed that when it was glorified it changed its condition, so as to be no longer subject to any infirmity. It however retained its substance ; otherwise the promise given us by the mouth of St. Paul (Phil. iii. 21) would fail, that the corruptible and fading bodies which we now have will be rendered conformable to the body of Jesus Christ. At all events, we cannot be blamed for seeking Jesus Christ on high as we are admonished to do, even in terms of the preamble which has at all times been used in celebrating this ordinance—Raise your hearts on high.

38. OF THE POWER OF GOD.

Those who accuse us of wishing to derogate from the power of God, do us great wrong. For the question is not what God can do? but, what his word bears? beyond which we ought not to speculate in order to guess at this thing or that. And in fact, we enter not into the dispute whether or not God can make the body of Jesus Christ to be everywhere, but with all modesty we remain within the doctrine of Scripture (Phil. i. 5) as our proper limit. It bears that our Lord Jesus assumed a body like ours in every respect, that he sojourned here below in the world, and ascended to heaven in order to descend and appear from thence on the last day, as it is distinctly stated that the heavens must receive him until he appears. (Acts i. 11.) And what the angel said to the disciples ought to be well considered—Jesus, who has been taken from you into heaven, will come in like manner as you have seen him ascend. Still we magnify the power of God more than those do who would defame us by such reproaches ; for we confess that however great the distance of space between Jesus Christ and us, he fails not to give us life in himself, to dwell in us, to provide for us and make us partakers of the substance of his body and his blood, by the incomprehensible virtue of his Spirit. From this it appears that the blame which some cast upon us is only calumny. They charge us with measuring the power of God by our own capacity, after the fashion of philosophers, whereas our philosophy is to receive in simplicity what the Scripture shows us.

39. OF THE TRUTH OF GOD.

Those also who represent that we give no credit to the words of our Lord Jesus Christ—This is my body, this is my blood—ought to be ashamed of injuring us so falsely. God forbid it should ever come into our thought to reply against him who is immutable truth. So far are we from being so abandoned as to wish to vent such blasphemy, that we implicitly receive what our Lord Jesus Christ pronounced; only we require that the natural sense of the words be well understood.

Now we do not seek the exposition of them in our own brains, but derive it from the constant usage of Scripture, and the common style of the Holy Spirit. Did we bring forward any novelty, it might be odious or suspicious ; but when we wish to abide by the property common to all sacraments, it seems to us well entitled to be received. To be brief, we protest that we neither think nor speak otherwise than St. Augustine has expressed word for word, (Ep. 23, ad Bonif.,) viz., that if the sacraments had not some resemblance to the things which they signify, they would not be sacraments at all, and that hence they take the names of the things themselves ; and thus, properly speaking, the sacrament of the body of Jesus Christ is the body of Jesus Christ, and the sacrament of his blood is his blood. Still we always conjoin the reality with the figure in such manner that this sacrament is not illusory.

Now, SIRE, your Majesty, and your Excellences, most illustrious Princes, have a declaration of our faith, in which there is nothing either coloured or disguised, and by which we desire that our cause be judged and decided. Meanwhile, we most humbly supplicate your Majesty and your Excellences, most illustrious Princes, that as we have with all reverence proceeded to declare what we believe, so it would please you attentively to consider the contents of this statement with such benignity that reason and equity alone may rule, laying aside all human opinions, so as not to prejudge the truth.

SHORT TREATISE

ON

THE SUPPER OF OUR LORD,

IN WHICH IS SHOWN

ITS TRUE INSTITUTION, BENEFIT, AND UTILITY.

AN. M.D.XL.

SHORT TREATISE

ON

THE HOLY SUPPER OF OUR LORD JESUS CHRIST.[1]

1. REASON WHY MANY WEAK CONSCIENCES REMAIN IN SUSPENSE AS TO THE TRUE DOCTRINE OF THE SUPPER.

As the holy sacrament of the Supper of our Lord Jesus Christ has long been the subject of several important errors, and in these past years been anew enveloped in diverse opinions and contentious disputes, it is no wonder if many weak consciences cannot fairly resolve what view they ought to take of it, but remain in doubt and perplexity, waiting till all contention being laid aside, the servants of God come to some agreement upon it. However, as it is a very perilous thing to have no certainty on an ordinance, the understanding of which is so requisite for our salvation, I have thought it might be a very useful labour to treat briefly and, nevertheless, clearly deduce a summary of what is necessary to be known of it. I may add that I have been requested to do so by some worthy persons, whom I could not refuse without neglecting my duty. In order to rid ourselves of all difficulty, it is expedient to attend to the order which I have determined to follow.

2. THE ORDER TO BE OBSERVED IN THIS TREATISE.

First, then, we will explain to what end and for what reason our Lord instituted this holy sacrament.

Secondly, What fruit and utility we receive from it, when it will likewise be shown how the body of Jesus Christ is given to us.

[1] From the French.

Thirdly, What is the legitimate use of it.

Fourthly, We will detail the errors and superstitions with which it has been contaminated, when it will be shown how the servants of God ought to differ from the Papists.

Lastly, We will mention what has been the source of the discussion which has been so keenly carried on, even among those who have, in our time, brought back the light of the gospel, and employed themselves in rightly edifying the Church in sound doctrine.

3. AT BAPTISM GOD RECEIVES US INTO HIS CHURCH AS MEMBERS OF HIS FAMILY.

In regard to the first article—Since it has pleased our good God to receive us by baptism into his Church, which is his house, which he desires to maintain and govern, and since he has received us to keep us not merely as domestics, but as his own children, it remains that, in order to do the office of a good father, he nourish and provide us with every thing necessary for our life. In regard to corporal nourishment, as it is common to all, and the bad share in it as well as the good, it is not peculiar to his family. It is very true that we have an evidence of his paternal goodness in maintaining our bodies, seeing that we partake in all the good things which he gives us with his blessing. But as the life into which he has begotten us again is spiritual, so must the food, in order to preserve and strengthen us, be spiritual also. For we should understand, that not only has he called us one day to possess his heavenly inheritance, but that by hope he has already in some measure installed us in possession; that not only has he promised us life, but already transported us into it, delivering us from death, when by adopting us as his children, he begot us again by immortal seed, namely, his word imprinted on our hearts by the Holy Spirit.

4. THE VIRTUE AND OFFICE OF THE WORD OF GOD IN REGARD TO OUR SOULS.

To maintain us in this spiritual life, the thing requisite is

not to feed our bodies with fading and corruptible food, but
to nourish our souls on the best and most precious diet. Now
all Scripture tells us, that the spiritual food by which our
souls are maintained is that same word by which the Lord
has regenerated us ; but it frequently adds the reason, viz.,
that in it Jesus Christ, our only life, is given and administered to us.   For we must not imagine that there is life any
where than in God.   But just as God has placed all fulness of
life in Jesus, in order to communicate it to us by his means,
so he ordained his word as the instrument by which Jesus
Christ, with all his graces, is dispensed to us.   Still it always
remains true, that our souls have no other pasture than Jesus
Christ.   Our heavenly Father, therefore, in his care to nourish us, gives us no other, but rather recommends us to take
our fill there, as a refreshment amply sufficient, with which
we cannot dispense, and beyond which no other can be found.

5. JESUS CHRIST THE ONLY SPIRITUAL NOURISHMENT OF OUR SOULS.

We have already seen that Jesus Christ is the only food by
which our souls are nourished ; but as it is distributed to us
by the word of the Lord, which he has appointed an instrument for that pupose, that word is also called bread and
water.   Now what is said of the word applies as well to the
sacrament of the Supper, by means of which the Lord leads
us to communion with Jesus Christ.   For seeing we are so
weak that we cannot receive him with true heartfelt trust,
when he is presented to us by simple doctrine and preaching, the Father of mercy, disdaining not to condescend in
this matter to our infirmity, has been pleased to add to his
word a visible sign, by which he might represent the substance of his promises, to confirm and fortify us by delivering
us from all doubt and uncertainty.   Since, then, there is
something so mysterious and incomprehensible in saying
that we have communion with the body and the blood of
Jesus Christ, and we on our part are so rude and gross that
we cannot understand the least things of God, it was of im-

portance that we should be given to understand it as far as our capacity could admit.

6. THE CAUSE WHY OUR LORD INSTITUTED THE SUPPER.

Our Lord, therefore, instituted the Supper, first, in order to sign and seal in our consciences the promises contained in his gospel concerning our being made partakers of his body and blood, and to give us certainty and assurance that therein lies our true spiritual nourishment, and that having such an earnest, we may entertain a right reliance on salvation. Secondly, in order to exercise us in recognising his great goodness toward us, and thus lead us to laud and magnify him more fully.   Thirdly, in order to exhort us to all holiness and innocence, inasmuch as we are members of Jesus Christ; and specially to exhort us to union and brotherly charity, as we are expressly commanded.   When we shall have well considered these three reasons, to which the Lord had respect in ordaining his Supper, we shall be able to understand, both what benefit accrues to us from it, and what is our duty in order to use it properly.

7. THE MEANS OF KNOWING THE GREAT BENEFIT OF THE SUPPER.

It is now time to come to the second point, viz., to show how the Lord's Supper is profitable to us, provided we use it profitably.   Now we shall know its utility by reflecting on the indigence which it is meant to succour.   We must necessarily be under great trouble and torment of conscience, when we consider who we are, and examine what is in us. For not one of us can find one particle of righteousness in himself, but on the contrary we are all full of sins and iniquities, so much so that no other party is required to accuse us than our own conscience, no other judge to condemn us. It follows that the wrath of God is kindled against us, and that none can escape eternal death.   If we are not asleep and stupified, this horrible thought must be a kind of perpetual hell to vex and torment us.   For the judgment of

God cannot come into our remembrance without letting us see that our condemnation follows as a consequence.

8. THE MISERY OF MAN.

We are then already in the gulf, if God does not in mercy draw us out of it.   Moreover, what hope of resurrection can we have while considering our flesh, which is only rottenness and corruption ?   Thus in regard to the soul, as well as the body, we are more than miserable if we remain within ourselves, and this misery cannot but produce great sadness and anguish of soul.   Now our heavenly Father, to succour us in this, gives us the Supper as a mirror, in which we may contemplate our Lord Jesus Christ, crucified to take away our faults and offences, and raised again to deliver us from corruption and death, restoring us to a celestial immortality.

9. THE SUPPER INVITES US TO THE PROMISES OF SALVATION.

Here, then, is the singular consolation which we derive from the Supper.   It directs and leads us to the cross of Jesus Christ and to his resurrection, to certify us that whatever iniquity there may be in us, the Lord nevertheless recognises and accepts us as righteous—whatever materials of death may be in us, he nevertheless gives us life— whatever misery may be in us, he nevertheless fills us witn all felicity.   Or to explain the matter more simply—as in ourselves we are devoid of all good, and have not one particle of what might help to procure salvation, the Supper is an attestation that, having been made partakers of the death and passion of Jesus Christ, we have every thing that is useful and salutary to us.

10. ALL THE TREASURES OF SPIRITUAL GRACE PRESENTED IN THE SUPPER.

We can therefore say, that in it the Lord displays to us all the treasures of his spiritual grace, inasmuch as he associates

us in all the blessings and riches of our Lord Jesus.   Let us
recollect, then, that the Supper is given us as a mirror in
which we may contemplate Jesus Christ crucified in order
to deliver us from condemnation, and raised again in order
to procure for us righteousness and eternal life.   It is indeed
true that this same grace is offered us by the gospel, yet as
in the Supper we have more ample certainty, and fuller enjoyment of it, with good cause do we recognise this fruit as
coming from it.

11. JESUS CHRIST IS THE SUBSTANCE OF THE SACRAMENTS.

But as the blessings of Jesus Christ do not belong to us
at all, unless he be previously ours, it is necessary, first of
all, that he be given us in the Supper, in order that the
things which we have mentioned may be truly accomplished
in us.   For this reason I am wont to say, that the substance
of the sacraments is the Lord Jesus, and the efficacy of them
the graces and blessings which we have by his means.   Now
the efficacy of the Supper is to confirm to us the reconciliation which we have with God through our Saviour's death
and passion ; the washing of our souls which we have in the
shedding of his blood ; the righteousness which we have in
his obedience ; in short, the hope of salvation which we have
in all that he has done for us.   It is necessary, then, that
the substance should be conjoined with these, otherwise nothing would be firm or certain.   Hence we conclude that
two things are presented to us in the Supper, viz., Jesus
Christ as the source and substance of all good ; and, secondly,
the fruit and efficacy of his death and passion.   This is implied in the words which were used.   For after command-
ing us to eat his body and drink his blood, he adds that his
body was delivered for us, and his blood shed for the remission of our sins.   Hereby he intimates, first, that we ought
not simply to communicate in his body and blood, without
any other consideration, but in order to receive the fruit
derived to us from his death and passion ; secondly, that we

can attain the enjoyment of such fruit only by participating
in his body and blood, from which it is derived.

12. HOW THE BREAD IS CALLED THE BODY, AND THE WINE THE BLOOD OF CHRIST.

We begin now to enter on the question so much debated,
both anciently and at the present time—how we are to understand the words in which the bread is called the body of
Christ, and the wine his blood. This may be disposed of
without much difficulty, if we carefully observe the principle
which I lately laid down, viz., that all the benefit which we
should seek in the Supper is annihilated if Jesus Christ be
not there given to us as the substance and foundation of all.
That being fixed, we will confess, without doubt, that to
deny that a true communication of Jesus Christ is presented
to us in the Supper, is to render this holy sacrament frivolous and useless—an execrable blasphemy unfit to be listened to.

13. WHAT IS REQUISITE IN ORDER TO LIVE IN JESUS CHRIST.

Moreover, if the reason for communicating with Jesus
Christ is to have part and portion in all the graces which
he purchased for us by his death, the thing requisite must
be not only to be partakers of his Spirit, but also to participate in his humanity, in which he rendered all obedience to
God his Father, in order to satisfy our debts, although, properly speaking, the one cannot be without the other ; for
when he gives himself to us, it is in order that we may possess him entirely.   Hence, as it is said that his Spirit is our
life, so he himself, with his own lips, declares that his flesh
is meat indeed, and his blood drink indeed.   (John vi. 55.)
If these words are not to go for nothing, it follows that in
order to have our life in Christ our souls must feed on his
body and blood as their proper food. This, then, is expressly
attested in the Supper, when of the bread it is said to us
that we are to take it and eat it, and that it is his body, and

of the cup that we are to drink it, and that it is his blood. This is expressly spoken of the body and blood, in order that we may learn to seek there the substance of our spiritual life.

14. HOW THE BREAD AND WINE ARE THE BODY OF JESUS CHRIST.

Now, if it be asked whether the bread is the body of Christ and the wine his blood, we answer, that the bread and the wine are visible signs, which represent to us the body and blood, but that this name and title of body and blood is given to them because they are as it were instruments by which the Lord distributes them to us. This form and manner of speaking is very appropriate. For as the communion which we have with the body of Christ is a thing incomprehensible, not only to the eye but to our natural sense, it is there visibly demonstrated to us. Of this we have a striking example in an analogous case. Our Lord, wishing to give a visible appearance to his Spirit at the baptism of Christ, presented him under the form of a dove. St. John the Baptist, narrating the fact, says, that he saw the Spirit of God descending. If we look more closely, we shall find that he saw nothing but the dove, in respect that the Holy Spirit is in his essence invisible. Still, knowing that this vision was not an empty phantom, but a sure sign of the presence of the Holy Spirit, he doubts not to say that he saw it, (John i. 32,) because it was represented to him according to his capacity.

15. THE SACRAMENT IS REPRESENTED BY VISIBLE SIGNS.

Thus it is with the communion which we have in the body and blood of the Lord Jesus. It is a spiritual mystery which can neither be seen by the eye nor comprehended by the human understanding. It is therefore figured to us by visible signs, according as our weakness requires, in such manner, nevertheless, that it is not a bare figure but is combined with the reality and substance. It is with good reason then that the bread is called the body, since it not only represents but also presents it to us. Hence we indeed infer that the name of the body of Jesus Christ is transferred to the bread, inasmuch as it is the sacrament and figure of it. But we likewise add, that the sacraments of the Lord should not and cannot be at all separated from their reality and substance. To distinguish, in order to guard against confounding them, is not only good and reasonable, but altogether necessary ; but to divide them, so as to make the one exist without the other, is absurd.

16. THE PROPER BODY AND BLOOD OF JESUS CHRIST RECEIVED ONLY BY FAITH.

Hence when we see the visible sign we must consider what it represents, and by whom it has been given us. The bread is given us to figure the body of Jesus Christ, with command to eat it, and it is given us of God, who is certain and immutable truth. If God cannot deceive or lie, it follows that it accomplishes all which it signifies. We must then truly receive in the Supper the body and blood of Jesus Christ, since the Lord there represents to us the communion of both. Were it otherwise, what could be meant by saying, that we eat the bread and drink the wine as a sign that his body is our meat and his blood our drink ? If he gave us only bread and wine, leaving the spiritual reality behind, would it not be under false colours that this ordinance had been instituted ?

17. THE INTERNAL SUBSTANCE IS CONJOINED WITH THE VISIBLE SIGNS.

We must confess, then, that if the representation which God gives us in the Supper is true, the internal substance of the sacrament is conjoined with the visible signs ; and as the bread is distributed to us by the hand, so the body of Christ is communicated to us in order that we may be made partakers of it. Though there should be nothing more, we have good cause to be satisfied, when we understand that Jesus Christ gives us in the Supper the proper substance of his body and blood, in order that we may possess it fully, and possessing it have part in all his blessings. For seeing we have him, all the riches of God which are comprehended in him are exhibited to us, in order that they may be ours. Thus, as a brief definition of this utility of the Supper, we may say, that Jesus Christ is there offered to us in order that we may possess him, and in him all the fulness of grace which we can desire, and that herein we have a good aid to confirm our consciences in the faith which we ought to have in him.

18. IN THE SUPPER WE ARE REMINDED OF OUR DUTY TOWARDS GOD.

The second benefit of the Supper is, that it admonishes and incites us more strongly to recognise the blessings which we have received, and receive daily from the Lord Jesus, in order that we may ascribe to him the praise which is due. For in ourselves we are so negligent that we rarely think of the goodness of God, if he do not arouse us from our indolence, and urge us to our duty. Now there cannot be a spur which can pierce us more to the quick than when he makes us, so to speak, see with the eye, touch with the hand, and distinctly perceive this inestimable blessing of feeding on his own substance. This he means to intimate when he commands us to show forth his death till he come. (1 Cor. xi. 26.) If it is then so essential to salvation not to overlook the gifts which God has given us, but diligently to keep them in mind, and extol them to others for mutual edification ; we see another singular advantage of the Supper in this, that it draws us off from ingratitude, and allows us not to forget the benefit which our Lord Jesus bestowed upon us in dying for us, but induces us to render him thanks, and, as it were, publicly protest how much we are indebted to him.

19. THE SACRAMENT A STRONG INDUCEMENT TO HOLY LIVING AND BROTHERLY LOVE.

The third advantage of the Sacrament consists in furnishing a most powerful incitement to live holily, and especially

observe charity and brotherly love toward all. For seeing
we have been made members of Jesus Christ, being incor-
porated into him, and united with him as our head, it is
most reasonable that we should become conformable to him
in purity and innocence, and especially that we should cultivate charity and concord together as becomes members of
the same body. But to understand this advantage properly,
we must not suppose that our Lord warns, incites, and
inflames our hearts by the external sign merely; for the
principal point is, that he operates in us inwardly by his
Holy Spirit, in order to give efficacy to his ordinance, which
he has destined for that purpose, as an instrument by which
he wishes to do his work in us. Wherefore, inasmuch as the
virtue of the Holy Spirit is conjoined with the sacraments
when we duly receive them, we have reason to hope they
will prove a good mean and aid to make us grow and advance in holiness of life, and specially in charity.

20. WHAT IT IS TO POLLUTE THE HOLY SUPPER.—THE GREAT GUILT OF SO DOING.

Let us come to the third point which we proposed at the
commencement of this treatise, viz., the legitimate use,
which consists in reverently observing our Lord's institution.
Whoever approaches the sacrament with contempt or indif-
ference, not caring much about following when the Lord
calls him, perversely abuses, and in abusing pollutes it.
Now to pollute and contaminate what God has so highly
sanctified, is intolerable blasphemy. Not without cause then
does St. Paul denounce such heavy condemnation on all who
take it unworthily. (1 Cor. xi. 29.) For if there is nothing
in heaven nor on earth of greater price and dignity than the
body and blood of the Lord, it is no slight fault to take it
inconsiderately and without being well prepared. Hence he
exhorts us to examine ourselves carefully, in order to make
the proper use of it. When we understand what this examination should be, we shall know the use after which we are
inquiring.

21. THE MANNER OF EXAMINING OURSELVES.

Here it is necessary to be well on our guard. For as we cannot be too diligent in examining ourselves as the Lord enjoins, so, on the other hand, sophistical doctors have brought poor consciences into perilous perplexity, or rather into a horrible Gehenna, requiring I know not what examination, which it is not possible for any man to make. To rid ourselves of all these perplexities, we must reduce the whole, as I have already said, to the ordinance of the Lord, as the rule which, if we follow it, will not allow us to err. In following it, we have to examine whether we have true repentance in ourselves, and true faith in our Lord Jesus Christ. These two things are so conjoined, that the one cannot subsist without the other.

22. TO PARTICIPATE IN THE BLESSINGS OF CHRIST, WE MUST RENOUNCE ALL THAT IS OUR OWN.

If we consider our life to be placed in Christ, we must acknowledge that we are dead in ourselves. If we seek our strength in him, we must understand that in ourselves we are weak. If we think that all our felicity is in his grace, we must understand how miserable we are without it. If we have our rest in him, we must feel within ourselves only disquietude and torment. Now such feelings cannot exist without producing, first, dissatisfaction with our whole life ; secondly, anxiety and fear ; lastly, a desire and love of righteousness. For he who knows the turpitude of his sin and the wretchedness of his state and condition while alienated from God, is so ashamed that he is constrained to be dissatisfied with himself, to condemn himself, to sigh and groan in great sadness. Moreover, the justice of God immediately presents itself and oppresses the wretched conscience with keen anguish, from not seeing any means of escape, or having any thing to answer in defence. When under such a conviction of our misery we get a taste of the goodness of God, it is then we would wish to regulate our conduct by his will, and renounce all our bygone life, in order to be made new creatures in him.

23. THE REQUISITES OF WORTHY COMMUNION.

Hence if we would worthily communicate in the Lord's Supper, we must with firm heart-felt reliance regard the Lord Jesus as our only righteousness, life, and salvation, receiving and accepting the promises which are given us by him as sure and certain, and renouncing all other confidence, so that distrusting ourselves and all creatures, we may rest fully in him, and be contented with his grace alone. Now as that cannot be until we know how necessary it is that he come to our aid, it is of importance to have a deep-seated conviction of our own misery, which will make us hunger and thirst after him. And, in fact, what mockery would it be to go in search of food when we have no appetite ? Now to have a good appetite it is not enough that the stomach be empty, it must also be in good order and capable of receiving its food. Hence it follows that our souls must be pressed with famine and have a desire and ardent longing to be fed, in order to find their proper nourishment in the Lord's Supper.

24. SELF-DENIAL NECESSARY.

Moreover, it is to be observed that we cannot desire Jesus Christ without aspiring to the righteousness of God, which consists in renouncing ourselves and obeying his will. For it is preposterous to pretend that we are of the body of Christ, while abandoning ourselves to all licentiousness, and leading a dissolute life. Since in Christ is nought but chastity, benignity, sobriety, truth, humility, and such like virtues, if we would be his members, all uncleanness, intemperance, falsehood, pride, and similar vices must be put from us. For we cannot intermingle these things with him without offering him great dishonour and insult. We ought always to remember that there is no more agreement between him and iniquity than between light and darkness. If we would come then to true repentance, we must endeavour to make our whole life conformable to the example of Jesus Christ.

25. CHARITY ESPECIALLY NECESSARY.

And while this must be general in every part of our life, it must be specially so in respect of charity, which is, above all other virtues, recommended to us in this sacrament : for which reason it is called the bond of charity. For as the bread which is there sanctified for the common use of all is composed of several grains so mixed together that they cannot be distinguished from each other, so ought we to be united together in indissoluble friendship. Moreover, we all receive there one body of Christ. If then we have strife and discord among ourselves, it is not owing to us that Christ Jesus is not rent in pieces, and we are therefore guilty of sacrilege, as if we had done it. We must not, then, on any account, presume to approach if we bear hatred or rancour against any man living, and especially any Christian who is in the unity of the Church. In order fully to comply with our Lord's injunction, there is another disposition which we must bring. It is to confess with the mouth and testify how much we are indebted to our Saviour, and return him thanks, not only that his name may be glorified in us, but also to edify others, and instruct them, by our example, what they ought to do.

26. ALL MEN IMPERFECT AND BLAMEWORTHY.

But as not a man will be found upon the earth who has made such progress in faith and holiness, as not to be still very defective in both, there might be a danger that several good consciences might be troubled by what has been said, did we not obviate it by tempering the injunctions which we have given in regard both to faith and repentance. It is a perilous mode of teaching which some adopt, when they require perfect reliance of heart and perfect penitence, and exclude all who have them not. For in so doing they exclude all without excepting one. Where is the man who can boast that he is not stained by some spot of distrust ? that he is not subject to some vice or infirmity ? Assuredly the faith which the children of God have is such that they have

ever occasion to pray,—Lord, help our unbelief. For it is a
malady so rooted in our nature, that we are never completely
cured until we are delivered from the prison of the body.
Moreover, the purity of life in which they walk is only such
that they have occasion daily to pray, as well for remission
of sins as for grace to make greater progress. Although
some are more and others less imperfect, still there is none
who does not fail in many respects. Hence the Supper
would be not only useless, but pernicious to all, if it were
necessary to bring a faith or integrity, as to which there
would be nothing to gainsay. This would be contrary to
the intention of our Lord, as there is nothing which he has
given to his Church that is more salutary.

27. IMPERFECTION MUST NOT MAKE US CEASE TO HOPE FOR SALVATION.

Therefore, although we feel our faith to be imperfect, and
our conscience not so pure that it does not accuse us of
many vices, that ought not to hinder us from presenting
ourselves at the Lord's holy table, provided that amid this
infirmity we feel in our heart that without hypocrisy and
dissimulation we hope for salvation in Christ, and desire to
live according to the rule of the gospel. I say expressly,
provided there be no hypocrisy. For there are many who
deceive themselves by vain flattery, making themselves believe that it is enough if they condemn their vices, though
they continue to persist in them, or rather, if they give them
up for a time, to return to them immediately after. True
repentance is firm and constant, and makes us war with the
evil that is in us, not for a day or a week, but without end
and without intermission.

28. THE IMPERFECTIONS OF BELIEVERS SHOULD RATHER INCLINE THEM TO USE THE SUPPER.

When we feel within ourselves a strong dislike and hatred
of all sin, proceeding from the fear of God, and a desire to
live well in order to please our Lord, we are fit to partake

of the Supper, notwithstanding of the remains of infirmity which we carry in our flesh. Nay, if we were not weak, subject to distrust and an imperfect life, the sacrament would be of no use to us, and it would have been superfluous to institute it. Seeing, then, it is a remedy which God has given us to help our weakness, to strengthen our faith, increase our charity, and advance us in all holiness of life, the use becomes the more necessary the more we feel pressed by the disease; so far ought that to be from making us abstain. For if we allege as an excuse for not coming to the Supper, that we are still weak in faith or integrity of life, it is as if a man were to excuse himself from taking medicine because he was sick. See then how the weakness of faith which we feel in our heart, and the imperfections which are in our life, should admonish us to come to the Supper, as a special remedy to correct them. Only let us not come devoid of faith and repentance. The former is hidden in the heart, and therefore conscience must be its witness before God. The latter is manifested by works, and must therefore be apparent in our life.

29. TIMES OF USING THE SUPPER.—PROPRIETY OF FREQUENT COMMUNION.

As to the time of using it, no certain rule can be prescribed for all. For there are sometimes special circumstances which excuse a man for abstaining; and, moreover, we have no express command to constrain all Christians to use a specified day. However, if we duly consider the end which our Lord has in view, we shall perceive that the use should be more frequent than many make it : for the more infirmity presses, the more necessary is it frequently to have recourse to what may and will serve to confirm our faith, and advance us in purity of life ; and, therefore, the practice of all well ordered churches should be to celebrate the Supper frequently, so far as the capacity of the people will admit. And each individual in his own place should prepare himself to receive whenever it is administered in the holy assembly, provided there is not some great impediment

which constrains him to abstain. Although we have no express commandment specifying the time and the day, it
should suffice us to know the intention of our Lord to be,
that we should use it often, if we would fully experience the
benefit which accrues from it.

30. IMPROPRIETY OF ABSTAINING ON FRIVOLOUS GROUNDS.—PRETENDED UNWORTHINESS IN OURSELVES.

The excuses alleged are very frivolous. Some say that
they do not feel themselves to be worthy, and under this
pretext, abstain for a whole year. Others, not contented
with looking to their own unworthiness, pretend that they
cannot communicate with persons whom they see coming
without being duly prepared. Some also think that it is
superfluous to use it frequently, because if we have once received Jesus Christ, there is no occasion to return so often
after to receive him. I ask the first who make a cloak of
their unworthiness, how their conscience can allow them to
remain more than a year in so poor a state, that they dare
not invoke God directly? They will acknowledge that it is
presumption to invoke God as our Father, if we are not
members of Jesus Christ. This we cannot be, without having
the reality and substance of the Supper accomplished in us.
Now, if we have the reality, we are by stronger reason
capable of receiving the sign. We see then that he who
would exempt himself from receiving the Supper on account
of unworthiness, must hold himself unfit to pray to God.
I mean not to force consciences which are tormented with
certain scruples which suggest themselves, they scarcely
know how, but counsel them to wait till the Lord deliver
them. Likewise, if there is a legitimate cause of hindrance,
I deny not that it is lawful to delay. Only I wish to show
that no one ought long to rest satisfied with abstaining on
the ground of unworthiness, seeing that in so doing he deprives himself of the communion of the Church, in which all
our wellbeing consists. Let him rather contend against all
the impediments which the devil throws in his way, and not

be excluded from so great a benefit, and from all the graces consequent thereupon.

31. ABSTAINING BECAUSE OF PRETENDED UNWORTHINESS IN OTHERS.

The second class have some plausibility. The argument they use is, that it is not lawful to eat common bread with those who call themselves brethren, and lead a dissolute life— *a fortiori*, we must abstain from communicating with them in the Lord's bread, which is sanctified in order to represent and dispense to us the body of Christ. But the answer is not very difficult. It is not the office of each individual to judge and discern, to admit or debar whom he pleases ; seeing that this prerogative belongs to all the Church in general, or rather to the pastor, with the elders, whom he ought to have to assist him in the government of the Church. St. Paul does not command us to examine others, but each to examine himself. It is very true that it is our duty to admonish those whom we see walking disorderly, and if they will not listen to us, to give notice to the pastor, in order that he may proceed by ecclesiastical authority. But the proper method of withdrawing from the company of the wicked, is not to quit the communion of the Church. Moreever, it will most frequently happen, that sins are not so notorious as to justify proceeding to excommunication ; for though the pastor may in his heart judge some man to be unworthy, he has not the power of pronouncing him such, and interdicting him from the Supper, if he cannot prove the unworthiness by an ecclesiastical judgment. In such case we have no other remedy than to pray God that he would more and more deliver his Church from all scandals, and wait for the last day, when the chaff will be completely separated from the good grain.

32. EXCUSE, THAT HAVING ALREADY RECEIVED CHRIST, IT IS UNNECESSARY TO RETURN OFTEN TO RECEIVE HIM.

The third class have no semblance of plausibility. The spiritual bread is not given us to eat our fill of it all at once, but rather, that having had some taste of its sweetness, we may long for it the more, and use it when it is offered to us. This we explained above. So long as we remain in this mortal life, Jesus Christ is never communicated in such a way as to satiate our souls, but wills to be our constant nourishment.

33. FOURTH GENERAL DIVISION.—ERRORS ON THE SUPPER.

We come to the fourth principal point. The devil knowing that our Lord has left nothing to his Church more useful than the holy sacrament, has after his usual manner laboured from the beginning to contaminate it by errors and superstitions, in order to corrupt and destroy the benefit of it, and has never ceased to pursue this course, until he has as it were completely reversed the ordinance of the Lord, and converted it into falsehood and vanity. My intention is not to point out at what time each abuse took its rise and at what time it was augmented; it will be sufficient to notice articulately the errors which the devil has introduced, and against which we must guard if we would have the Lord's Supper in its integrity.

34. FIRST ERROR.

The first error is this—While the Lord gave us the Supper that it might be distributed amongst us to testify to us that in communicating in his body we have part in the sacrifice which he offered on the cross to God his Father, for the expiation and satisfaction of our sins—men have out of their own head invented, on the contrary, that it is a sacrifice by which we obtain the forgiveness of our sins before God. This is a blasphemy which it is impossible to bear. For if we do not recognise the death of the Lord Jesus, and regard it as our only sacrifice by which he has reconciled us to the Father, effacing all the faults for which we were accountable to his justice, we destroy its virtue. If we do not acknowledge Jesus Christ to be the only sacrifice, or, as we commonly call it, priest, by whose intercession we are restored to the Father's favour, we rob him of his honour and do him high injustice.

35. THE SACRAMENT NOT A SACRIFICE.

The opinion that the Supper is a sacrifice derogates from that of Christ, and must therefore be condemned as devilish. That it does so derogate is notorious. For how can we reconcile the two things, that Jesus Christ in dying offered a sacrifice to his Father by which he has once for all purchased forgiveness and pardon for all our faults, and that it is every day necessary to sacrifice in order to obtain that which we ought to seek in his death only? This error was not at first so extreme, but increased by little and little, until it came to what it now is. It appears that the ancient fathers called the Supper a sacrifice; but the reason they give is, because the death of Christ is represented in it. Hence their view comes to this—that this name is given it merely because it is a memorial of the one sacrifice, at which we ought entirely to stop. And yet I cannot altogether excuse the custom of the early Church. By gestures and modes of acting they figured a species of sacrifice, with a ceremony resembling that which existed under the Old Testament, excepting that instead of a beast they used bread as the host. As that approaches too near to Judaism, and does not correspond to our Lord's institution, I approve it not. For under the Old Testament, during the time of figures, the Lord ordained such ceremonies, until the sacrifice should be made in the person of his well-beloved Son, which was the fulfilment of them. Since it was finished, it now only remains for us to receive the communication of it. It is superfluous, therefore, to exhibit it any longer under figure.

36. THE BREAD IN THE SUPPER ORDAINED TO BE EATEN, NOT SACRIFICED.—ERRORS OF THE MASS.

And such is the import of the injunction which Jesus Christ has left. It is not that we are to offer or immolate, but to take and eat what has been offered and immolated. However, though there was some weakness in such observance,

there was not such impiety as afterwards supervened. For
to the Mass has been wholly transferred what was proper to
the death of Christ, viz., to satisfy God for our sins, and so
reconcile us to him. Moreover, the office of Christ has been
transferred to those whom they name priests, viz., persons to
sacrifice to God, and in sacrificing, intercede to obtain for
us grace, and the pardon of our offences.

37. ATTEMPTED DEFENCE OF THE SACRIFICE OF THE MASS.

I wish not to keep back the explanations which the enemies of the truth here offer. They say that the Mass is not
a new sacrifice, but only an application of the sacrifice
of which we have spoken. Although they colour their
abomination somewhat by so saying, still it is a mere
quibble. For it is not merely said that the sacrifice of
Christ is one, but that it is not to be repeated, because its
efficacy endures for ever. It is not said that Christ once
offered himself to the Father, in order that others might
afterwards make the same oblation, and so apply to us the
virtue of his intercession. As to applying to us the merit of
his death, that we may perceive the benefit of it, that is done
not in the way in which the Popish Church has supposed,
but when we receive the message of the gospel, according as
it is testified to us by the ministers whom God has appointed
as his ambassadors, and is sealed by the sacraments.

38. ERRORS CONNECTED WITH THE ABOMINATION OF THE MASS.

The common opinion approved by all their doctors and
prelates is, that by hearing Mass, and causing it to be said,
they perform a service meriting grace and righteousness before God. We say, that to derive benefit from the Supper,
it is not necessary to bring any thing of our own in order
to merit what we ask. We have only to receive in faith the
grace which is there presented to us, and which resides not
in the sacrament, but refers us to the cross of Jesus Christ
as proceeding therefrom. Hence there is nothing more con-

trary to the true meaning of the Supper, than to make a sacrifice of it. The effect of so doing is to lead us off from recognising the death of Christ as the only sacrifice, whose virtue endures for ever. This being well understood, it will be apparent that all masses in which there is no such communion as the Lord enjoined, are only an abomination. The Lord did not order that a single priest, after making his sacrifice, should keep himself apart, but that the sacrament should be distributed in the assembly after the manner of the first Supper, which he made with his apostles. But after this cursed opinion was forged, out of it, as an abyss, came forth the unhappy custom by which the people, contenting themselves with being present to partake in the merit of what is done, abstain from communicating, because the priest gives out that he offers his host for all, and specially for those present. I speak not of abuses, which are so absurd, that they deserve not to be noticed, such as giving each saint his mass, and transferring what is said of the Lord's Supper to St. William and St. Walter, and making an ordinary fair of masses, buying and selling them with the other abominations which the word sacrifice has engendered.

39. TRANSUBSTANTIATION.

The second error which the devil has sown to corrupt this holy ordinance, is in forging and inventing that after the words are pronounced with an intention to consecrate, the bread is transubstantiated into the body of Christ, and the wine into his blood. First of all, this falsehood has no foundation in Scripture, and no countenance from the Primitive Church, and what is more, cannot be reconciled or consist with the word of God. When Jesus Christ, pointing to the bread, calls it his body, is it not a very forced construction to say, that the substance of the bread is annihilated, and the body of Christ substituted in its stead? But there is no cause to discuss the thing as a doubtful matter, seeing the truth is sufficiently clear to refute the absurdity. I leave out innumerable passages of Scripture and quotations from the Fathers, in which the sacrament is called bread. I only say

that the nature of the sacrament requires, that the material
bread remain as a visible sign of the body.

40. FROM THE NATURE OF A SACRAMENT THE SUBSTANCE OF THE VISIBLE SIGN MUST REMAIN.

It is a general rule in all sacraments that the signs which
we see must have some correspondence with the spiritual
thing which is figured. Thus, as in baptism, we are assured
of the internal washing of our souls when water is given us
as an attestation, its property being to cleanse corporal pollution ; so in the Supper, there must be material bread to
testify to us that the body of Christ is our food. For otherwise how could the mere colour of white give us such a
figure ? We thus clearly see how the whole representation,
which the Lord was pleased to give us in condescension to
our weakness, would be lost if the bread did not truly remain. The words which our Lord uses imply as much as if
he had said: Just as man is supported and maintained in
his body by eating bread, so my flesh is the spiritual nourishment by which souls are vivified. Moreover, what would
become of the other similitude which St. Paul employs ?
As several grains of corn are mixed together to form one
bread, so must we together be one, because we partake of
one bread. If there were whiteness only without the substance, would it not be mockery to speak thus ? Therefore
we conclude, without doubt, that this transubstantiation is
an invention forged by the devil to corrupt the true nature
of the Supper.

41. FALSE OPINION OF THE BODILY PRESENCE OF CHRIST IN THE SUPPER.

Out of this fantasy several other follies have sprung.
Would to God they were only follies, and not gross abominations. They have imagined I know not what local presence
and thought, that Jesus Christ in his divinity and humanity
was attached to this whiteness, without paying regard to all
the absurdities which follow from it. Although the old
doctors of Sorbonne dispute more subtilely how the body and

blood are conjoined with the signs, still it cannot be denied that this opinion has been received by great and small in the Popish Church, and that it is cruelly maintained in the present day by fire and sword, that Jesus Christ is contained under these signs, and that there we must seek him. Now to maintain that, it must be confessed either that the body of Christ is without limit, or that it may be in different places. In saying this we are brought at last to the point, that it is a mere phantom. To wish then to establish such a presence as is to enclose the body within the sign, or to be joined to it locally, is not only a reverie, but a damnable error, derogatory to the glory of Christ, and destructive of what we ought to hold in regard to his human nature. For Scripture everywhere teaches us, that as the Lord on earth took our humanity, so he has exalted it to heaven, withdrawing it from mortal condition, but not changing its nature.

42. THE BODY OF OUR SAVIOUR IN HEAVEN THE SAME AS THAT WHICH HE HAD ON EARTH.

We have two things to consider when we speak of our Lord's humanity. We must neither destroy the reality of the nature, nor derogate in any respect from his state of glory. To do so we must always raise our thoughts on high, and there seek our Redeemer. For if we would place him under the corruptible elements of this world, besides subverting what Scripture tells us in regard to his human nature, we annihilate the glory of his ascension. As several others have treated this subject at large, I refrain from going farther. I only wished to observe, in passing, that to fancy Jesus Christ enclosed under the bread and wine, or so to conjoin him with it as to amuse our understanding there without looking up to heaven, is a diabolical reverie. We will touch on this in another place.

43. OTHER ABUSES ARISING OUT OF AN IMAGINARY BODILY PRESENCE.

This perverse opinion, after it was once received, engendered numerous other superstitions. First of all comes that carnal adoration which is mere idolatry. For to prostrate ourselves before the bread of the Supper, and worship Jesus Christ as if he were contained in it, is to make an idol of it rather than a sacrament. The command given us is not to adore, but to take and eat. That, therefore, ought not to have been presumptuously attempted. Moreover, the practice always observed by the early Church, when about to celebrate the Supper, was solemnly to exhort the people to raise their hearts on high, to intimate, that if we would adore Christ aright, we must not stop at the visible sign. But there is no need to contend long on this point when the presence and conjunction of the reality with the sign (of which we have spoken, and will again speak) is well understood. From the same source have proceeded other superstitious practices, as carrying the sacrament in procession through the streets once a-year ; at another time making a tabernacle for it, and keeping it to the year's end in a cupboard to amuse the people with it, as if it were a god. As all that has not only been invented without authority from the word of God, but is also directly opposed to the institution of the Supper, it ought to be rejected by Christians.

44. REASON WHY THE PAPISTS COMMUNICATE ONLY ONCE A-YEAR.

We have shown the origin of the calamity which befell the Popish Church—I mean that of abstaining from communicating in the Supper for the whole period of a year. It is because they regard the Supper as a sacrifice which is offered by one in the name of all. But even while thus used only once a year, it is sadly wasted and as it were torn to pieces. For instead of distributing the sacrament of blood to the people, as our Lord's command bears, they are made to believe that they ought to be contented with the other half. Thus poor believers are defrauded of the gift which the Lord Jesus had given them. For if it is no small benefit to have communion in the blood of the Lord as our nourishment, it is great cruelty to rob those of it to whom it belongs. In this we may see with what boldness and audacity the

Pope has tyrannized over the Church after he had once usurped domination.

45. THE POPE HAS MADE EXCEPTIONS TO THE GENERAL RULES LAID DOWN BY OUR LORD.

Our Lord having commanded his disciples to eat the bread sanctified in his body, when he comes to the cup, does not say simply, "drink," but he adds expressly, that all are to drink. Would we have any thing clearer than this? He says that we are to eat the bread without using an universal term. He says that we are *all* to drink of the cup. Whence this difference, but just that he was pleased by anticipation to meet this wickedness of the devil? And yet such is the pride of the Pope that he dares to say, Let not all drink. And to show that he is wiser than God, he alleges it to be very reasonable that the priest should have some privilege beyond the people, in honour of the sacerdotal dignity; as if our Lord had not duly considered what distinction should be made between them. Moreover, he objects dangers which might happen if the cup were given in common to all. Some drop of it might occasionally be spilt; as if our Lord had not foreseen that. Is not this to accuse God quite openly of having confounded the order which he ought to have observed, and exposed his people to danger without cause?

46. FRIVOLOUS REASONS FOR WITHHOLDING THE CUP.

To show that there is no great inconvenience in this change, they argue, that under one species the whole is comprised, inasmuch as the body cannot be separated from the blood: as if our Lord had without reason distinguished the one from the other. For if we can leave one of the parts behind as superfluous, what folly must it have been to recommend them separately. Some of his supporters, seeing that it was impudence to maintain this abomination, have wished to give it a different colour, viz., that Jesus Christ, in instituting, spoke only to his apostles whom he had raised to the sacerdotal order. But how will they answer what St. Paul

said, when he delivered to all the people what he had received of the Lord—that each should eat of this bread and
drink of this cup?   Besides, who told them that our Lord
gave the Supper to his apostles as priests ?   The words import
the opposite, when he commands them to do after his example.   (Luke xxii. 19.)   Therefore he delivers the rule
which he wishes to be always observed in his Church ; and
so it was anciently observed until Antichrist, having gained
the upper hand, openly raised his horns against God and
his truth to destroy it totally.   We see then that it is an
intolerable perversion thus to divide and rend the sacrament,
separating the parts which God has joined.

47. THE BUFFOONERY OF THE POPE IN REGARD TO THE SUPPER.

To get to an end, we shall embrace under one head what
might otherwise have been considered separately.   This
head is, that the devil has introduced the fashion of celebrating the Supper without any doctrine, and for doctrine
has substituted ceremonies partly inept and of no utility,
and partly dangerous, having proved the cause of much mischief.   To such an extent has this been done, that the Mass,
which in the Popish Church is held to be the Supper, is, when
well explained, nothing but pure apishness and buffoonery.
I call it apishness, because they there counterfeit the Lord's
Supper without reason, just as an ape at random and without
discernment imitates what he sees done.

48. THE WORD OUGHT ALWAYS TO ACCOMPANY THE SACRAMENTS.

The principal thing recommended by our Lord is to celebrate the ordinance with true understanding.   From this it
follows that the essential part lies in the doctrine.   This being
taken away, it is only a frigid unavailing ceremony.   This is
not only shown by Scripture, but attested by the canons of
the Pope, (Can. Detrahe. i. 4, 1,) in a passage quoted from St.
Augustine, (Tract 80, in Joan.) in which he asks—" What is

the water of baptism without the word but just a corruptible element? The word (he immediately adds) not as pronounced, but as understood." By this he means, that the sacraments derive their virtue from the word when it is preached intelligibly. Without this they deserve not the name of sacraments. Now so far is there from being any intelligible doctrine in the Mass, that, on the contrary, the whole mystery is considered spoiled if every thing be not said and done in whispers, so that nothing is understood. Hence their consecration is only a species of sorcery, seeing that by muttering and gesticulating like sorcerers, they think to constrain Jesus to come down into their hands. We thus see how the Mass, being thus arranged, is an evident profanation of the Supper of Christ, rather than an observance of it, as the proper and principal substance of the Supper is wanting, viz., full explanation of the ordinance and clear statement of the promises, instead of the priest standing apart and muttering to himself without sense or reason. I call it buffoonery, also, because of mimicry and gestures, better adapted to a farce than to such an ordinance as the sacred Supper of our Lord.

49. THE CEREMONIES OF THE ANCIENT LAW, WHY APPOINTED.—THOSE OF THE PAPISTS CENSURABLE.

It is true, indeed, that the sacrifices under the Old Testament were performed with many ornaments and ceremonies, but because there was a good meaning under them, and the whole was proper to instruct and exercise the people in piety, they are very far from being like those which are now used, and serve no purpose but to amuse the people without doing them any good. As these gentry allege the example of the Old Testament in defence of their ceremonies, we have to observe what difference there is between what they do, and what God commanded the people of Israel. Were there only this single point, that what was then observed was founded on the commandment of the Lord, whereas all those frivolities have no foundation, even then the difference would be large. But we have much more to censure in them.

50. THE JEWISH CEREMONIES HAVING SERVED THEIR PURPOSE, THE IMITATION OF THEM ABSURD.

With good cause our Lord ordained the Jewish form for a time, intending that it should one day come to an end and be abrogated. Not having then given such clearness of doctrine, he was pleased that the people should be more exercised in figures to compensate for the defect. But since Jesus Christ has been manifested in the flesh, doctrine having been much more clearly delivered, ceremonies have diminished. As we have now the body, we should leave off shadows. To return to the ceremonies which are abolished, is to repair the vail of the temple which Jesus Christ rent by his death, and so far obscure the brightness of his gospel. Hence we see, that such a multitude of ceremonies in the Mass is a form of Judaism quite contrary to Christianity. I mean not to condemn the ceremonies which are subservient to decency and public order, and increase the reverence for the sacrament, provided they are sober and suitable. But such an abyss without end or limit is not at all tolerable, seeing that it has engendered a thousand superstitions, and has in a manner stupified the people without yielding any edification.

51. THE DEATH AND PASSION OF OUR LORD THE PERFECT AND ONLY SACRIFICE.

Hence also we see how those to whom God has given the knowledge of his truth should differ from the Papists. First, they cannot doubt that it is abominable blasphemy to regard the Mass as a sacrifice by which the forgiveness of sins is purchased for us; or rather, that the priest is a kind of mediator to apply the merit of Christ's passion and death to those who purchase his mass, or are present at it, or feel devotion for it. On the contrary, they must hold decidedly that the death and suffering of the Lord is the only sacrifice by which the anger of God has been satisfied, and eternal righteousness procured for us; and, likewise, that the Lord Jesus has entered into the heavenly sanctuary in order to appear there for us, and intercede in virtue of his sacrifice. Moreover, they will readily grant, that the benefit of his death is communicated to us in the Supper, not by the merit of the act, but because of the promises which are given us, provided we receive them in faith. Secondly, they should on no account grant that the bread is transubstantiated into the body of Jesus Christ, nor the wine into his blood, but should persist in holding that the visible signs retain their true substance, in order to represent the spiritual reality of which we have spoken. Thirdly, they ought also to hold for certain, that the Lord gives us in the Supper that which he signifies by it, and, consequently, that we truly receive the body and blood of Jesus Christ. Nevertheless they will not seek him as if he were enclosed under the bread, or attached locally to the visible sign. So far from adoring the sacrament, they will rather raise their understandings and their hearts on high, as well to receive Jesus Christ, as to adore him.

52. VIEW OF ENLIGHTENED CHRISTIANS IN REGARD TO THE SUPPER.

Hence they will despise and condemn as idolatrous all those superstitious practices of carrying about the sacrament in pomp and procession, and building tabernacles in which to adore it. For the promises of our Lord extend only to the uses which he has authorized. Next, they will hold that to deprive the people of one of the parts of the sacrament, viz., the cup, is to violate and corrupt the ordinance of the Lord, and that to observe it properly it must be administered in all its integrity. Lastly, they will regard it as a superfluity, not only useless but dangerous, and not at all suitable to Christianity, to use so many ceremonies taken from the Jews contrary to the simplicity which the Apostles left us, and that it is still more perverse to celebrate the Supper with mimicry and buffoonery, while no doctrine is stated, or rather all doctrine is buried, as if the Supper were a kind of magical trick.

53. LAST DIVISION.—RECENT DISPUTES ON THE SUPPER.

To have done, it is necessary to come to the last principal point, viz., the contention which has arisen in our time in regard to this matter.   Now, as it is an unhappy business— the devil, no doubt, having stirred it up to impede, nay altogether to interrupt the course of the gospel—so far am I from taking pleasure in referring to it, that I could wish the remembrance of it were altogether abolished.   Nevertheless, as I see many good consciences troubled, because they do not know to what side to turn, I shall only say as much as may seem necessary to show them how they ought to decide.

54. GOD SOMETIMES ALLOWS HIS OWN PEOPLE TO FALL INTO ERROR.

First, I beseech all believers, in the name of God, not to be too much scandalized at the great difference which has arisen among those who ought to be a kind of leaders in bringing back the light of truth.   For it is no new thing for the Lord to leave his servants in some degree of ignorance, and suffer them to have debate among themselves—not to leave them for ever, but only for a time to humble them. And indeed had every thing till now turned out to a wish without any disturbance, men might possibly have forgotten themselves, or the grace of God might have been less known than it ought.   Thus the Lord has been pleased to take away all ground of glorying from men, in order that he might alone be glorified.   Moreover, if we consider in what an abyss of darkness the world was when those who have shared this controversy began to bring back the truth, we shall not wonder that they did not know every thing at the beginning.   The wonder rather is, that our Lord in so short a time enlightened them that they were themselves able to escape and draw others out of that sink of error in which they had been so long immersed.   But no better course can be taken than to show how matters have proceeded, because this will make it appear that people have not so much cause to be scandalized at it as is commonly supposed.

55. HISTORY OF THE CONTROVERSY ON THIS SUBJECT AMONG THE REFORMERS.—LUTHER.

When Luther began to teach, he took a view of the subject which seemed to imply, that in regard to the corporal presence in the Supper he was willing to leave the generally received opinion untouched ; for while condemning transubstantiation, he said that the bread was the body of Christ, inasmuch as it was united with him. Besides, he added similitudes which were somewhat harsh and rude ; but he was in a manner compelled to do so, as he could not otherwise explain his meaning. For it is difficult to give an explanation of so high a matter without using some impropriety of speech.

56. VIEWS OF ZUINGLIUS AND ŒCOLOMPADIUS.

On the other hand arose Zuinglius and Œcolompadius, who, considering the abuse and deceit which the devil had employed in establishing such a carnal presence of Christ as had been taught and held for more than six hundred years, thought it unlawful to disguise their sentiments, since that view implied an execrable idolatry, in that Jesus Christ was worshipped as enclosed in the bread. Now, as it was very difficult to remove this opinion, which had been so long rooted in the hearts of men, they applied all their talents to bring it into discredit, showing how gross an error it was not to recognise what is so clearly declared in Scripture touching the ascension of Jesus Christ, that he has been received in his humanity into heaven, and will remain there until he descend to judge the world. Meantime, while engrossed with this point, they forgot to show what presence of Jesus Christ ought to be believed in the Supper, and what communion of his body and blood is there received.

57. LUTHER IMPUGNS THEIR VIEWS.

Luther thought that they meant to leave nothing but the bare signs without their spiritual substance. Accordingly he began to resist them to the face, and call them heretics.

After the contention was once begun it got more inflamed by time, and has thus continued too bitterly for the space of fifteen years or so without the parties ever listening to each other in a peaceful temper. For though they once had a conference, there was such alienation that they parted without any agreement. Instead of meeting on some good ground, they have always receded more and more, looking to nothing else than to defend their own view and refute the opposite.

58. ATTEMPTED RECONCILIATION.—CAUSE OF FAILURE.

We thus see wherein Luther failed on his side, and Zuinglius and Œcolompadius on theirs. It was Luther's duty first to have given notice that it was not his intention to establish such a local presence as the Papist's dream ; secondly, to protest that he did not mean to have the sacrament adored instead of God ; and lastly, to abstain from those similitudes so harsh and difficult to be conceived, or have used them with moderation, interpreting them so that they could not give rise to any scandal. After the debate was moved, he exceeded bounds as well in declaring his opinion, as in blaming others with too much sharpness of speech. For instead of explaining himself in such a way as to make it possible to receive his view, he, with his accustomed vehemence in assailing those who contradicted him, used hyperbolical forms of speech very difficult to be borne by those who otherwise were not much disposed to believe at his nod. The other party also offended, in being so bent on declaiming against the superstitious and fanatical opinion of the Papists, touching the local presence of Jesus Christ within the sacrament, and the perverse adoration consequent upon it, that they laboured more to pull down what was evil than to build up what was good ; for though they did not deny the truth, they did not teach it so clearly as they ought to have done. I mean that in their too great anxiety to maintain that the bread and wine are called the body of Christ, because they are signs of them, they did not attend to add, that though they are signs, the reality is conjoined

with them, and thus protest, that they had no intention
whatever to obscure the true communion which the Lord
gives us in his body and blood by this sacrament.

59. DUTY OF THE SERVANTS OF GOD IN REGARD TO THE ADVANCEMENT OF TRUTH.

Both parties failed in not having the patience to listen to
each other in order to follow the truth without passion,
when it would have been found. Nevertheless, let us not
lose sight of our duty, which is not to forget the gifts which
the Lord bestowed upon them, and the blessings which he
has distributed to us by their hands and means. For if we
are not ungrateful and forgetful of what we owe them, we
shall be well able to pardon that and much more, without
blaming or defaming them. In short, since we see that they
were, and still are, distinguished for holiness of life, excellent
knowledge, and ardent zeal to edify the Church, we ought
always to judge and speak of them with modesty, and even
with reverence ; since at last God, after having thus humbled
them, has in mercy been pleased to put an end to this unhappy disputation, or at least to calm it preparatory to its
final settlement. I speak thus, because no formulary has
yet been published in which concord is fixed, as is most expedient. But this will be when God will be pleased to as-
semble those who are to frame it in one place.

60. FRATERNAL CONCORD AMONG THE CHURCHES.

Meanwhile it should satisfy us, that there is fraternity and
communion among the churches, and that all agree in so
far as is necessary for meeting together, according to the
commandment of God. We all then confess with one mouth,
that on receiving the sacrament in faith, according to the
ordinance of the Lord, we are truly made partakers of the
proper substance of the body and blood of Jesus Christ.
How that is done some may deduce better, and explain more
clearly than others. Be this as it may, on the one hand, in
order to exclude all carnal fancies, we must raise our hearts
upwards to heaven, not thinking that our Lord Jesus is so

debased as to be enclosed under some corruptible elements; and, on the other hand, not to impair the efficacy of this holy ordinance, we must hold that it is made effectual by the secret and miraculous power of God, and that the Spirit of God is the bond of participation, this being the reason why it is called spiritual.

MUTUAL CONSENT

IN REGARD TO

THE SACRAMENTS;

BETWEEN

THE MINISTERS OF THE CHURCH OF ZURICH

AND

JOHN CALVIN, MINISTER OF THE CHURCH OF GENEVA.

NOW PUBLISHED

BY THOSE WHO FRAMED IT.

M.D.LIV.

JOHN CALVIN

TO THE MOST EXCELLENT MEN AND FAITHFUL SERVANTS OF CHRIST,

THE PASTORS AND DOCTORS OF THE CHURCH OF ZURICH,

HIS VERY DEAR COLLEAGUES AND RESPECTED BRETHREN.

ALTHOUGH I speak with you repeatedly on the same subject, I do not think there is any reason to fear that you will think me irksome. As we agree in judgment, you cannot but approve what I do. In regard to the keenness with which I urge the matter, I am stimulated by the constant entreaties of worthy individuals. I have already sometimes mentioned that, for a slight cause, and yet not without some apparent ground, very many are offended because my doctrine seems in some respect, I scarcely know what, to differ from yours. They highly revere your Church, which is adorned by many noble gifts: they also defer somewhat to our Church, and perhaps to myself as an individual. They are desirous in learning the doctrine of piety to be assisted by my writings, but would not have any appearance of disagreement to retard their progress. Thinking no means better fitted to remove this offence than a friendly conference, in which we might together adopt means to testify our agreement, I for this purpose paid you a visit, my venerable colleague William Farel, (indefatigable soldier of Christ as he is,) who had suggested and advised the visit, not declining to accompany me. That we are agreed, we can indeed on both sides truly and faithfully declare; but as I cannot persuade all of the fact as it really stands, it very much grieves me that some remain in anxiety and suspense, for whose peace of mind I am desirous to consult. Hence, as I observed before, I think that I am not acting out of season in urging that there should be some public testimony of the agreement existing between us.

The leading articles on which we conferred I have deemed it of consequence briefly to collect and digest, in order that, if my purpose shall be approved by you, it may be in the power of any one to have, as it were, a tabular view of what was done and transacted between us. That in every thing I set down I give a faithful record of the conference, I am confident that you will bear me witness. That we (I mean Farel and myself) have, with like zeal as your own, studied sincere perspicuity, free from all gloss and cunning, pious readers will, I hope, perceive. I wish it however to be understood that nothing is here contained which our colleagues also, as many as serve Christ under the jurisdiction of the city of Geneva or in the Canton of Neufchatel, have not approved by their subscription. Farewell, most excellent men and brethren, whom I truly love in my heart. May the Lord always guide you by His Spirit, and bless your labours for the edification of His Church.

GENEVA, 1st *August* 1549.

LETTER FROM THE PASTORS OF ZURICH TO CALVIN.

THE PASTORS, DOCTORS, AND MINISTERS OF THE CHURCH OF ZURICH TO THEIR VERY DEAR BROTHER, JOHN CALVIN, FAITHFUL PASTOR OF THE CHURCH OF GENEVA.

CALVIN, most respected brother in the Lord, your ardent zeal and sedulous labours in endeavouring, from day to day, to illustrate the doctrine of the Sacraments, and remove from amid the Church offences which seem to have arisen from some rather obscure exposition of these ordinances, are so far from being irksome to us, that we think them not only worthy of being proclaimed with applause, but also assisted and imitated by us to the best of our ability. For while the sacred laws of our Prince, Jesus Christ, refer all actions to the cultivation of charity, and zeal to assist each other, there is nothing they more strictly prohibit than for any one to throw an obstacle in another's way so as to prevent him from judging rightly and truly concerning things, the knowledge of which is necessary, or at least useful and salutary to men, or from properly performing the duty which he owes both to God and his neighbour. With the same strictness they enjoin us to remove, as far as may be, the offences at which men are wont to stumble.

Wherefore the cause of the visit which you and our venerable brother, the Rev. William Farel, paid us seemed to us most honourable and specially worthy of men holding office in the Church. The object was, first, that we should, by friendly conference, mutually and in the simplest terms possible, explain our views on the Sacraments, especially on those articles on which some controversy had hitherto existed among those who in regard to other articles delivered the purer doctrine of the gospel with great uniformity ; and, secondly, that we should testify our consent by a published document. We see no more convenient way and method of ending religious controversy or suppressing vague suspicions where no discrepancy exists, or, in fine, of removing offences which sometimes arise in the Church of God from contrariety of opinion in the teachers, than by mutually explaining their mind with the greatest openness both by speech and writing.

But it were little that the truth thus investigated and discovered should be retained by them if it is not made patent to other men also, by expounding to them more fully what had been more sparingly indicated, and enunciating what was more obscurely expressed in more familiar terms, and making any thing formerly ambiguous clear by words certain, appropriate, and significant. This method was ever approved by the Fathers of the Church, and was very often employed, never without advantage to the Church, in settling religious controversies. In short, it was approved by the sovereign example of the apostles of Jesus Christ our Lord and our God. For just in this manner and way, as we read in the fifteenth chapter of the Acts, was a very great dissension quelled, when the Apostles and their genuine disciples taught that hearts were purified by faith in the name of Christ, and men saved wholly by his grace ; while some persons contended that they behoved to be circumcised, and keep the law of Moses.

Wherefore, dear brother Calvin, we cannot but entirely approve of your holy efforts, and those of all pious men, who study by fit means to remove offences, and renew the tottering peace and tranquillity of the Church, endeavouring, by simple and accurate explanation, to render Christian doctrine more and more plain and clear to men, and rid their minds of vague causes of discord, and endeavouring, moreover, to bring back those who have somewhat differed in word and opinion to true, entire, and holy concord. That the public document in which we wished clearly to testify our agreement, alike to the pious and to the enemies of the truth, will have the beneficial effect which you augur in your letter, we are induced to hope, after having made the trial. We transmitted the formula of our mutual consent to some brethren, and have exhibited it to some persons here who love Christ and truth, and are not unskilled in sacred things. They have not only recognised that we agree even in those articles in which it was hitherto supposed by many that we differed, but have also given thanks to Christ our Saviour on perceiving that we agree in God and in truth, and entertain great hopes of larger fruit in the Church.

Some, however, have desired a more copious treatment of this subject, because of certain minds, who, on hearing of our purpose, are not easily satisfied. But of what use was it to explain more fully that God is the author of the sacraments, and instituted them for the legitimate sons of the Church, or to tell how many sacraments were delivered by Christ to the Church, or what have been devised by men— what the parts of sacraments, at what place, at what time, by what sacred instrumentality the ordinances are to be performed? That in these, and some other articles of the same class, there was no semblance or shade of difference between us, is sufficiently proved by published treatises, which either our preceptors, of pious and blessed memory, or we ourselves, have written on the sacraments. Of the bodily presence of Christ our Lord, of the genuine meaning of the formal words, of the eating of the body of Christ, of the end, use, and effect of the sacraments, (articles on which many hitherto suppose that our opinions, or at least our words, were conflicting,) we have spoken so copiously, so plainly and simply, as to hope that men studious both of brotherly concord and clear truth, will not feel in our document any want of either copiousness or clearness. Nor are we diffident that the ministers of other churches in Switzerland will readily acknowledge that the doctrine we have expressed on the sacraments is the very same that has for many years been commonly received among the Christian people, and that they are the very last to differ from us. This, too, we promise ourselves, not without strong reasons, from all the pious in other nations.

Should any one, however, produce a clearer explanation of the sacraments, we would rather use it with all the pious, than urge one individual to subscribe an Agreement in which we have used the words of Holy Scripture, and aptly expressed in what sense we understand them, and hold it perfectly clear that we agree with the Catholic Church. Even though this document should not have removed the offences of all whom any semblance of disagreement among us has impeded in the ways of the Lord, we still think, however, that it has admirably fulfilled its office in having attested to all clearly, and without equivocation, that we, whom God has enabled to think and speak the same thing on the doctrines of religion, do not at all differ in the exposition of its ordinances. Farewell, dearest Brother.

ZURICH, 30th *August* 1549.

JOHN CALVIN

To the Pastors of the Town and Territory of Zurich, of Berne, Basle, Schaffhonsen, Coire, and all the Country of the Grisons, of St. Gall, Bienne, Milhausen, and Neufchatel, his well-beloved Brethren and Servants of Jesus Christ.[1]

My Dear and Honoured Brethren,

FOUR years ago we caused to be printed a brief statement of our agreement in doctrine touching the sacraments, which

---

[1] From the French.

we thought well fitted to stifle the troublesome disputes which had too long been carried on between learned and God-fearing people. And certainly we had inserted enough in that little summary to appease and satisfy all well disposed minds, as in fact many learned and honourable persons have not only approved our measure, but also declared that our doctrine therein pleased them exceedingly. If some from being somewhat obstinate in their fancy, or rather, as happens after great disturbances, from having some remains of suspicion rooted in their heart, have not been able to come so soon to a full agreement with us, still by keeping silence, they have shown that they considered nothing better than to cherish peace and friendship. Still, however, some ignorant and wrong-headed persons give themselves such license in disturbing the matters set at rest, that if we do not come forward to repress them, there is reason to fear that they will kindle a new war.

It is true, indeed, that as they are few in number, and are possessed of no quality which can give them authority or credit, while moreover they by their foolish babble expose themselves to universal hatred and derision, we might with good reason despise them, were it not that by making a show of advocating the public cause, they under such pretext, vain though it be, abuse the weak who are not sufficiently on their guard. Wherefore seeing that their audacity does great harm, and that the more patient we are the more it increases and breaks bounds, we cannot do better than resist it, necessity constraining us thereto.

I can indeed declare, that although their books fly up and down, vexing the good, disturbing the weak, and arming the wicked with slander, it is with great regret, and as it were in spite of myself, that I have engaged in putting a stop to their foolishness. But because I would have thought it cruel if, on discovering their fallacies, I had not delivered many worthy simple persons from error, I have not hesitated to oppose myself frankly to these rioters who only seek to throw every thing into confusion.

I have had in view also to remind persons of weight and learning, whose names these brainless fellows pretend to use, that it is a shame in them to give loose reins to evil by their silence. For while all Christians ought to endeavour to extinguish the fire which Satan is endeavouring to kindle up by such bellows, the persons referred to, whom these disturbers bring into their quarrel, have more interest in this than we have, and therefore ought to strive doubly to repress their unseasonable intermeddling, which redounds to the common dishonour of many churches.

For the hot-headed men to whom I refer, stirring up the contention which formerly existed in regard to the Sacraments, pretend to maintain the doctrine which is preached in Saxony and Lower Germany. Now when that is heard and believed, some are troubled because of the respect which they bear to those churches, others make a mock of all the teachers in that quarter, seeing they make use of such creatures to plead their cause, while several knowing well that the sounder part give them no countenance, inveigh against their excessive patience. Meanwhile the declared enemies of Jesus Christ are delighted at seeing us fighting together as if it were a kind of cock-fight. Now since it is perverse and unworthy dissimulation to give loose reins to evil, persons of letters and renown in those countries should consider well, in discharging their duty, whether it be possible to repress the impetuous rage of those who trouble the Church without cause.

As I am desirous to bring back to the good way all who are in any degree fit to be dealt with and have not yet exceeded all bounds, that they may have it in their power to return peacefully, I shall here refer to only one individual, and that without naming him.

This foolish man, after boasting loudly of his great zeal for the Catholic faith, prays on the learned and renowned (persons whom I love and honour, he calls his masters) to join in assisting him. The high honour which he pays them, is to arm them against us. These excellent doctors are to follow the rash course of their scholar as archers do a man-at-arms. But on whom does he wish war to be made? He answers in a single word, on the " Sacramentarians." But when he is pleased to explain, he declares that all his talk is against those who leave nothing to the sacrament of the Supper but bare and empty signs. If so, he had as well rest himself, and leave the office to more competent persons. There are famous churches in the country of Switzerland and the Grisons, among which our own may well be classed. Surely far better captains will be found among us to maintain the dignity and virtue of the sacraments than such a gendarme as he. Moreover, there are an infinite number of persons who will make a better defence of this cause, and be faithfully enough disposed to it. For who is there amongst us who labours not to show that the Sacraments are conjoined with their reality and effect?

But when this venerable doctor, after so fine a preface, puts into his list several worthy persons who are as distant from this crime as heaven is from earth, and not only so, but expressly refers to our Agreement, as if we had therein consented to the error of which he speaks, instead of having expressly condemned it, is not the assertion too impudent and the absurdity too gross? It is not necessary to go far for arguments in our defence, seeing that this foolish man shortly afterwards quotes our own words, in which we openly acknowledge that the body of Jesus Christ is truly communicated to believers in the Supper. I pray you, do we leave nothing but empty signs when we affirm that what is figured is at the same time given, and that the effect takes place? To cover himself, he has recourse to a subterfuge the most meagre and frivolous imaginable. He says, that we speak of a spiritual manner of eating. How then? Would he have the flesh of the Christ to be eaten like the beeves of his country? But he adds, he does not think that we speak of the true body: as if we imagined the body of Christ to be a phantom. We leave this reverie to him and his fellows.

Holding it as a settled point, that Jesus Christ has only a true and natural body, we say that as he was once offered on the cross to reconcile us to God, he is also daily offered in the Supper. For the Lord Jesus, to communicate the gift of salvation which he has purchased for us, must first be made ours, and his flesh be our meat and nourishment, see-

ing that it is from it that we derive life. Such are the words
which we clearly use in our Agreement.

But this worthy corrector, bringing forward what suits his
purpose, like a traitor and falsifier, keeps out this article,
though it is the chief. As he had professed to quote our
sentences word for word, by what right or title does he
separate, not to say dissever, members which are joined together, so that our meaning is not given ? Is not this to act
like a mad dog who bites straightforward at all the stones
in his way ? And yet, shortly after, he cannot refrain
from producing our testimonies to the reality of the Sacraments, which he would falsely make it to be believed that
we deny. But here this disturber charges us with finesse
and cunning, because he says, that by talking at large of
receiving Christ in a spiritual manner we impose on the
simple. As if we could spiritually communicate with Jesus
Christ without having him dwelling in us by means of faith,
and being united to his body so as to live in him. This cannot
be, unless Jesus Christ, inasmuch as he was once offered in
sacrifice for us, give himself to us in order that we may enjoy
him. Hence it follows, that his flesh gives us life.

After this fine preface, this great defender of the faith, in
order to specify the error against which he is combating,
strives to show that there is great diversity of opinion
amongst us, that he may by this means throw obloquy upon
us. He takes it for an axiom, that the characteristic of
heretics is to disagree. Though I should grant what he
asks, I maintain that it does not touch us. He says, that
we differ, inasmuch as, according to some, the bread signifies
the body ; according to others, is a mark or model of the
body ; to others, its sign ; to others, its figure ; to others, a
memorial ; to others, a representation ; to others, an evidence
or seal of the communion which we have with Christ ; to
others, a remembrance of the body which was delivered for
us ; to others, an assurance to testify to us his spiritual grace ;
to others, the communion which we have in the body of
Christ. Who, pray, would not think on hearing him speak
thus, that he is a mere dissembler who has an understanding
with us ? For it is impossible better to commend and prove

a good agreement and full conformity than by collecting all these forms of speech which he opposes to each other as quite contrary, while every one sees that they all come to the same thing. Moreover, to play his part with more finesse, he is not contented with giving a simple narrative, but has framed a table so as it were to exhibit the thing to the eye. Meanwhile, seeing that, as far as the words go, St. Matthew is less conformable to St. Paul, and St. Mark to St. Luke, than a dozen of expositors whom he produces as discordant with each other, to get quit of this difficulty he says that we not only differ in words but disagree in meaning. Let us then make a comparison of the whole, to judge if it is so.

What St. Matthew and St. Mark call blood, Luke and St. Paul call covenant in the blood. Here is great diversity. On our part what does he find? Surely the words sign, signification, figure, earnest, memorial, representation, do not give a contrary meaning, seeing they are so closely connected together that any one draws the others after it. You see what the reasons are which have moved this wrongheaded man to forge in his closet fiery darts to set all Europe in flames if he could.

But what does he say for himself and his companions? In one place he affirms that the words of Christ, when he says that the bread is his body, are sufficiently clear of themselves and need no explanation. Soon after he denies not that there is some figure. It is unnecessary for us to inquire farther against whom he means to strike, since we see that in his frenzy he breaks down of himself. Still, at all events, let him name this figure which, he says, does not prevent the bread from being properly the body of Christ. For whatever the figure be, the effect of it is to make the sense to be neither simple nor literal. Thus he is caught as in a trap. For when in bringing forward his opinion, he agrees not with those whom he calls heretics, it follows from his argument, that he himself is of the number, unless he can show that his figure, which he conceals, is by universal consent so holy and sacred, that it is not lawful to think any ill of it. In concealing it he uses finesse to prevent judgment being passed upon it.

But more than this, he confesses that some of us use the very words which he holds to be good and Catholic, though he says that their meaning is not so. In that case what will become of the great contrariety of expressions which alone, according to him, make heretics even of those who are constrained to be different from others, in order not to give consent to error. It is certainly very distressing to see an impetuosity so blind that it would be unpardonable in a youth, thus transporting a poor old man and exposing him to the derision of children.

I mean not to disguise that he rakes together some passages from certain expositors, which apparently do not accord with each other, although in truth they may be reconciled. But the evil is that, in the first place, he maliciously lays hold of what is touched upon as it were by the by, and turns in this way and in that, as if it were to give a full determination of the whole matter; and secondly, it is rather too tyrannical and barbarous in him to lay down a law compelling all to speak in the same style and language, without one syllable of difference, seeing that each has his own peculiar mode of expressing himself, and ought to have liberty to do so. One has said that the mystical body of Christ is here figured. What then? Has not Augustine said the like? not to mention St. Paul, when he says that we are all one bread. Another has said that the Supper is a solemn memorial of the redemption which has been purchased for us. What? Does not this correspond very well with that which is taught us not only by St. Paul but our Sovereign Master, viz., that this sacrament has been ordained in order that his death may be shown forth? There was no occasion to make so much noise or excite any disturbance, far less is there any excuse for a man who calls himself a minister of peace, and in fact bears the message of reconciliation between God and men, when he raises such unseasonable alarm.

But assume that there was formerly some discordance, because the thing could not be fully cleared up at the first glance and disposed of, what humanity is there in reopening a sore which was closed up and cured? In order that the faithful might not be distracted by disputes which have only too much prevailed, we proposed to them our Agreement by which they could hold. This good zealot saw clearly that all whom he styles Sacramentarians have one same faith and confess it as with one same mouth, and even if the two excellent doctors, Zuinglius and Œcolompadius, who were known to be faithful servants of Jesus Christ, were still alive, they would not change one word in our doctrine. For our good brother of blessed memory, Martin Bucer, after seeing our Agreement, wrote me that it was an inestimable blessing for the whole Church. Wherefore there is the more malice in this new corrector thus stirring up odium on account of it. On my part, not to pay him back in kind, but to repel the foolish calumny with which he has been pleased to assail us, I will reply in three sentences—first, it is characteristic of the devil to be a calumniator, as it is his name ; secondly, it is also his characteristic to obscure what is clear, to stir up noise and discord by disturbing the peace ; and, finally, it is his characteristic to break and destroy the unity of the faith. Since all these three meet in this man, I have no need to pronounce him a son of the devil, since the thing shows to great and small what he is.

On the whole, my dear and honoured brethren, as we ought to take at least as much pains in maintaining the truth and cherishing concord as Satan in striving to ruin both, I have wished to do what was in my power, and also try if, peradventure, those who have hitherto been of too obstinate a temper might be tamed ; if not, that those who are of sound judgment should be furnished with the defence of our cause, so as to be the better able to stop their mouths. Now the method which I have here adopted, of giving a fuller explanation of our meaning, has seemed to me the most proper. For the too great brevity of our first writing lays it open to much cavilling, and does not remove scruples which are deeply rooted. I have therefore dilated the summary which was formerly printed, and made the same confession at greater length, to render it more clear.

This blockhead, of whom I am sorry to speak so often, reproaches us with having such an abyss of opinions that no one understands what his companion would say. Now, methinks, I know so well what you believe and hold, that I am confident of having here written down what each of you would write in the same place.   For I have not usurped the office of dictating what you are to confess after me, but rather refer the whole to your discretion.   I have, however, proceeded boldly to compose this short treatise, because by former experience I had learned how agreeable my labour had been to you, and that you had also sufficiently declared it to be so.   Brethren, I commend you to God, praying him to guide you by his Spirit, and bless the pains which you take to edify his Church.   My colleagues, ministers of the word, salute you.

GENEVA, 28th November 1554.

HEADS OF AGREEMENT.

1. THE WHOLE SPIRITUAL GOVERNMENT OF THE CHURCH LEADS US TO CHRIST.

Seeing that Christ is the end of the law, and the knowledge of him comprehends in itself the whole sum of the gospel, there is no doubt that the object of the whole spiritual government of the Church is to lead us to Christ, as it is by him alone we come to God, who is the final end of a happy life.   Whosoever deviates from this in the slightest degree, can never speak duly or appositely of any ordinances of God.

2. A TRUE KNOWLEDGE OF THE SACRAMENTS FROM THE KNOWLEDGE OF CHRIST.

As the sacraments are appendages of the gospel, he only can discourse aptly and usefully of their nature, virtue, office, and benefit, who begins with Christ: and that not by adverting cursorily to the name of Christ, but by truly holding for what end he was given us by the Father, and what blessings he has conferred upon us.

3. NATURE OF THE KNOWLEDGE OF CHRIST.

We must hold therefore that Christ, being the eternal Son of God, and of the same essence and glory with the Father, assumed our flesh, to communicate to us by right of adoption that which he possessed by nature, namely, to make us sons of God. This is done when ingrafted by faith into the body of Christ, and that by the agency of the Holy Spirit we are first counted righteous by a free imputation of righteousness, and then regenerated to a new life : whereby being formed again in the image of our heavenly Father, we renounce the old man.

4. CHRIST A PRIEST AND KING.

Thus Christ, in his human nature, is to be considered as our priest, who expiated our sins by the one sacrifice of his death, put away all our transgressions by his obedience, provided a perfect righteousness for us, and now intercedes for us, that we may have access to God. He is to be considered as a repairer, who, by the agency of his Spirit, reforms whatever is vicious in us, that we may cease to live to the world and the flesh, and God himself may live in us. He is to be considered as a king, who enriches us with all kinds of blessings, governs and defends us by his power, provides us with spiritual weapons, delivers us from all harm, and rules and guides us by the sceptre of his mouth. And he is to be so considered, that he may raise us to himself, the true God, and to the Father, until the fulfilment of what is finally to take place, viz., God be all in all.

5. HOW CHRIST COMMUNICATES HIMSELF TO US.

Moreover, that Christ may thus exhibit himself to us and produce these effects in us, he must be made one with us, and we must be ingrafted into his body. He does not infuse his life into us unless he is our head, and from him the whole body, fitly joined together through every joint of supply, according to his working, maketh increase of the body in the proportion of each member.

6. SPIRITUAL COMMUNION.—INSTITUTION OF THE SACRAMENTS.

The spiritual communion which we have with the Son of God takes place when he, dwelling in us by his Spirit, makes all who believe capable of all the blessings which reside in him.   In order to testify this, both the preaching of the gospel was appointed, and the use of the sacraments committed to us, namely, the sacraments of holy Baptism and the holy Supper.

7. THE ENDS OF THE SACRAMENTS.

The ends of the sacraments are to be marks and badges of Christian profession and fellowship or fraternity, to be incitements to gratitude and exercises of faith and a godly life ; in short, to be contracts binding us to this.   But among other ends the principal one is, that God may, by means of them, testify, represent, and seal his grace to us. For although they signify nothing else than is announced to us by the word itself, yet it is a great matter, *first*, that there is submitted to our eye a kind of living images which make a deeper impression on the senses, by bringing the object in a manner directly before them, while they bring the death of Christ and all his benefits to our remembrance, that faith may be the better exercised ; and, *secondly*, that what the mouth of God had announced is, as it were, con-firmed and ratified by seals.

8. GRATITUDE.

Now, seeing that these things which the Lord has given as testimonies and seals of his grace are true, he undoubtedly truly performs inwardly by his Spirit that which the sacraments figure to our eyes and other senses ; in other words, we obtain possession of Christ as the fountain of all blessings, both in order that we may be reconciled to God by means of his death, be renewed by his Spirit to holiness of life, in short, obtain righteousness and salvation ; and also in order that we may give thanks for the blessings which were once exhibited on the cross, and which we daily receive by faith.

9. THE SIGNS AND THE THINGS SIGNIFIED NOT DISJOINED BUT DISTINCT.

Wherefore, though we distinguish, as we ought, between the signs and the things signified, yet we do not disjoin the reality from the signs, but acknowledge that all who in faith embrace the promises there offered receive Christ spiritually, with his spiritual gifts, while those who had long been made partakers of Christ continue and renew that communion.

10. THE PROMISE PRINCIPALLY TO BE LOOKED TO IN THE SACRAMENTS.

And it is proper to look not to the bare signs, but rather to the promise thereto annexed. As far, therefore, as our faith in the promise there offered prevails, so far will that virtue and efficacy of which we speak display itself. Thus the substance of water, bread, and wine, by no means offers Christ to us, nor makes us capable of his spiritual gifts. The promise rather is to be looked to, whose office it is to lead us to Christ by the direct way of faith—faith which makes us partakers of Christ.

11. WE ARE NOT TO STAND GAZING ON THE ELEMENTS.

This refutes the error of those who stand gazing on the elements, and attach their confidence of salvation to them ; seeing that the sacraments separated from Christ are but empty shows, and a voice is distinctly heard throughout proclaiming that we must adhere to none but Christ alone, and seek the gift of salvation from none but him.

12. THE SACRAMENTS EFFECT NOTHING BY THEMSELVES.

Besides, if any good is conferred upon us by the sacraments, it is not owing to any proper virtue in them, even though in this you should include the promise by which they are distinguished. For it is God alone who acts by his Spirit. When he uses the instrumentality of the sacraments, he neither infuses his own virtue into them nor derogates in any respect from the effectual working of his Spirit, but, in adaptation to our weakness, uses them as helps ; in such manner, however, that the whole power of acting remains with him alone.

13. GOD USES THE INSTRUMENT, BUT ALL THE VIRTUE IS HIS.

Wherefore, as Paul reminds us, that neither he that planteth nor he that watereth is any thing, but God alone that giveth the increase ; so also it is to be said of the sacraments that they are nothing, because they will profit nothing, unless God in all things make them effectual. They are indeed instruments by which God acts efficaciously when he pleases, yet so that the whole work of our salvation must be ascribed to him alone.

14. THE WHOLE ACCOMPLISHED BY CHRIST.

We conclude, then, that it is Christ alone who in truth baptizes inwardly, who in the Supper makes us partakers of himself, who, in short, fulfils what the sacraments figure, and uses their aid in such manner that the whole effect resides in his Spirit.

15. HOW THE SACRAMENTS CONFIRM.

Thus the sacraments are sometimes called seals, and are said to nourish, confirm, and advance faith, and yet the Spirit alone is properly the seal, and also the beginner and finisher of faith. For all these attributes of the sacraments sink down to a lower place, so that not even the smallest portion of our salvation is transferred to creatures or elements.

16. ALL WHO PARTAKE OF THE SACRAMENTS DO NOT PARTAKE OF THE REALITY.

Besides, we carefully teach that God does not exert his power indiscriminately in all who receive the sacraments, but only in the elect. For as he enlightens unto faith none but those whom he hath foreordained to life, so by the secret agency of his Spirit he makes the elect receive what the sacraments offer.

17. THE SACRAMENTS DO NOT CONFER GRACE.

By this doctrine is overthrown that fiction of the sophists which teaches that the sacraments confer grace on all who do not interpose the obstacle of mortal sin. For besides that in the sacraments nothing is received except by faith, we must also hold that the grace of God is by no means so annexed to them that whoso receives the sign also gains possession of the thing. For the signs are administered alike to reprobate and elect, but the reality reaches the latter only.

18. THE GIFTS OFFERED TO ALL, BUT RECEIVED BY BELIEVERS ONLY.

It is true indeed that Christ with his gifts is offered to all in common, and that the unbelief of man not overthrowing the truth of God, the sacraments always retain their efficacy ; but all are not capable of receiving Christ and his gifts. Wherefore nothing is changed on the part of God, but in regard to man each receives according to the measure of his faith.

19. BELIEVERS BEFORE, AND WITHOUT THE USE OF THE SACRAMENTS, COMMUNICATE WITH CHRIST.

As the use of the sacraments will confer nothing more on unbelievers than if they had abstained from it, nay, is only destructive to them, so without their use believers receive the reality which is there figured. Thus the sins of Paul were washed away by baptism, though they had been previously washed away. So likewise baptism was the laver of regeneration to Cornelius, though he had already received the Holy Spirit. So in the Supper Christ communicates himself to us, though he had previously imparted himself, and perpetually remains in us. For seeing that each is enjoined to examine himself, it follows that faith is required of each before coming to the sacrament. Faith is not without Christ; but inasmuch as faith is confirmed and increased by the sacraments, the gifts of God are confirmed in us, and thus Christ in a manner grows in us and we in him.

20. THE BENEFIT NOT ALWAYS RECEIVED IN THE ACT OF COMMUNICATING.

The advantage which we receive from the sacraments ought by no means to be restricted to the time at which they are administered to us, just as if the visible sign, at the moment when it is brought forward, brought the grace of God along with it. For those who were baptized when mere infants, God regenerates in childhood or adolescence, occasionally even in old age. Thus the utility of baptism is open to the whole period of life, because the promise contained in it is perpetually in force. And it may sometimes happen that the use of the holy Supper, which, from thoughtlessness or slowness of heart does little good at the time, afterwards bears its fruit.

21. NO LOCAL PRESENCE MUST BE IMAGINED.

We must guard particularly against the idea of any local presence. For while the signs are present in this world, are seen by the eyes and handled by the hands, Christ, regarded as man, must be sought nowhere else than in heaven, and not otherwise than with the mind and eye of faith. Wherefore it is a perverse and impious superstition to inclose him under the elements of this world.

22. EXPLANATION OF THE WORDS—"THIS IS MY BODY."

Those who insist that the formal words of the Supper— "This is my body; this is my blood," are to be taken in what they call the precisely literal sense, we repudiate as preposterous interpreters. For we hold it out of controversy that they are to be taken figuratively—the bread and wine receiving the name of that which they signify. Nor should it be thought a new or unwonted thing to transfer the name of things figured by metonomy to the sign, as similar modes of expression occur throughout the Scriptures, and we by so saying assert nothing but what is found in the most ancient and most approved writers of the Church.

23. OF THE EATING OF THE BODY.

When it is said that Christ, by our eating of his flesh and drinking of his blood, which are here figured, feeds our souls through faith by the agency of the Holy Spirit, we are not to understand it as if any mingling or transfusion of substance took place, but that we draw life from the flesh once offered in sacrifice and the blood shed in expiation.

24. TRANSUBSTANTIATION AND OTHER FOLLIES.

In this way are refuted not only the fiction of the Papists concerning transubstantiation, but all the gross figments and futile quibbles which either derogate from his celestial glory or are in some degree repugnant to the reality of his human nature. For we deem it no less absurd to place Christ under the bread or couple him with the bread, than to transubstantiate the bread into his body.

25. THE BODY OF CHRIST LOCALLY IN HEAVEN.

And that no ambiguity may remain when we say that Christ is to be sought in heaven, the expression implies and is understood by us to intimate distance of place. For though philosophically speaking there is no place above the skies, yet as the body of Christ, bearing the nature and mode of a human body, is finite and is contained in heaven as its place, it is necessarily as distant from us in point of space as heaven is from earth.

26. CHRIST NOT TO BE ADORED IN THE BREAD.

If it is not lawful to affix Christ in our imagination to the bread and the wine, much less is it lawful to worship him in the bread. For although the bread is held forth to us as a symbol and pledge of the communion which we have with Christ, yet as it is a sign and not the thing itself, and has not the thing either included in it or fixed to it, those who turn their minds towards it, with the view of worshipping Christ, make an idol of it.

EXPOSITION OF THE HEADS OF AGREEMENT.

ALL pious men, and men of sense and sound judgment, feeling disgust and annoyance at the contention which had arisen in our age concerning the Sacraments, and by which they saw that the prosperous course of the gospel was unhappily retarded, not only always wished for some convenient method of burying or settling it, but some of them made no small exertion for this very purpose. If the success was not immediately what might have been wished, a sad proof was given how difficult it is to put out fire once kindled by the artifice of Satan. This much indeed was gained, that both parties, calming their fervour somewhat, became more intent on teaching than fighting. But as sparks were ever and anon starting forth from the smouldering coals, and gave some cause to fear a new conflagration, we, the Pastors of the Churches of Zurich and Geneva, with the assistance of our most excellent brother Farel, attempted what we thought the best remedy, so that no material might remain for future discord. We published a brief compendium, which attests our doctrine on the sacraments, and contains the common consent of the other pastors who preach a pure gospel in Switzerland and the Grisons. We felt persuaded that by the publication of this testimony satisfaction was given to moderate men, and we certainly thought that no person would be so rigidly scrupulous as not to rest appeased ; for, as we shall afterwards see, it contains a lucid definition of all the points which were formerly debated, and leaves no room for any uncharitable suspicion. And by the special goodness of God, it has in a great measure succeeded to a wish.

. But, lo ! while all was quiet, some wrong-headed men have started up, and as if their food were discord, call again to arms. They cannot excuse their intemperance by pretending holy zeal. We are all agreed that peace is not to be purchased by the sacrifice of truth: and hence I acknowledge that better were heaven confounded with earth, than that the defence of sound doctrine should be abandoned. Whosoever heartily and strenuously opposes sophistical quibbles, which conciliate by giving a gloss to erroneous doctrine, I blame not : nay, rather, I claim for myself this praise, that there is scarcely an individual who can take more pleasure than I do in a candid confession of the truth. Wherefore let them have done with the empty pretence, that oftentimes disturbance must be raised, if the truth is not to lie undefended. For I will show, first, that in this matter nothing has been stated by us obscurely or enigmatically, nothing craftily concealed, in short, nothing essential omitted ; and, secondly, that the last thing proposed by us was to interrupt the free course of truth. Nay, rather, our greatest care was how that which is useful to be known in this matter might be both delivered and read calmly, and without offence. But not to bandy words upon this, all I ask of my readers is, to receive what I shall place before their eyes, and prove by solid and clear arguments.

In the first place, then, in treating of the sacraments, it cannot be denied that the chief thing to be considered is, the ordinance of our Lord and its object. In this way both the virtue and use of the sacraments is best ascertained, so that whosoever turns his mind in this direction, to which our Lord himself invites us, cannot err. That the end for which the sacraments were instituted has been rightly taught by us, even those who have the least fairness will be forced to confess. The end, we say, is to bring us to communion with Christ. I will speak more confidently, and say, that none of our detractors ever brought forward any thing which more distinctly expressed what is intended. If it is on the dignity of the sacraments that their heart is set, what better fitted to display it than to call them helps and means by which we are either ingrafted into the body of

Christ, or being ingrafted, are drawn closer and closer, until he makes us altogether one with himself in the heavenly life ? If their desire is, that our salvation may be assisted by the sacraments, what more apt can be imagined, than that being conducted to the very fountain of life, we draw life from the Son of God ? Therefore, whether our own advantage is looked to, or the dignity and reverence which ought to be attributed to the sacraments, we have clearly explained the end and cause of their institution. Certainly the objection which Paul makes to vain teachers, who puff men up with idle speculations instead of edifying, that they do not hold the head, is by no means applicable to us, who refer all things to Christ, gather all together in him, and arrange all under him, and maintain that the whole virtue of the sacraments flows from him. Now let these rigid censors prescribe a better method of teaching than was delivered by Paul, if they are dissatisfied with the adaptation of the sacraments to that symmetry between the head and the members, which St. Paul applauds so highly, and by which he estimates the entire perfection of doctrine.

It is well, then, that when about to speak of the sacraments, we used the best and most apposite exordium, and assigned them an end which all fair and moderate readers will, without controversy, approve. Then in regard to the legitimate use, two faults are to be avoided. For if their dignity is too highly extolled, superstition easily creeps in ; and, on the other hand, if we discourse frigidly, or in less elevated terms of their virtue and fruit, profane contempt immediately breaks forth. If a middle course has been observed by us, who will not call those obstinate enemies of the truth, who choose rather to carp maliciously at a holy consent, than either civilly embrace, or at least silently approve it ?

We do not ask them to swear to our words, but only to be quiet, and not stone those who are speaking correctly. They pretend indeed to make it their ground of quarrel, that we do not give the sacraments their due virtue. But when we come to the point, some produce nothing but bad names and blind tumult, while others, with a toss of disdain, condemn, in a word, what they never read. That they quarrel without consideration, the case itself shows.

With what vehemence this cause was pleaded by Luther, whose imitators they would fain be thought, is too well known to all. I am aware how many hyperbolical things fell from him in debate; but whenever he wished to make his cause appear most plausible to pious and upright judges, what did he profess to be the ground of controversy? First, that he could not bear that the sacraments should be regarded merely as external marks of profession, and not also as badges and symbols of divine grace; and, secondly, that he held it an indignity to compare them to void and empty figures, while God truly testifies in them what he figures, and, at the same time, by his secret agency, performs and fulfils what he testifies. Whether he was right or wrong in flaming out so much, I do not at present discuss. It is enough for me, that though he was by no means remiss in pleading this cause, yet when it was necessary to act seriously, he found no resting-place for his foot but the pretext that the whole controversy lay here.

Without making further mention of a man whose memory I revere, and whose honour I am desirous to consult, let me declare my opinion simply. Taking this pretext out of the way, those who would raise a quarrel with us cannot but excite the disgust of all honest and sound-headed men by their rigidity. The pretext I mentioned is ever and anon on their lips. If they use it candidly, and not merely to tickle the ears of the simple, surely when they hear us confess on the one hand, that the sacraments are neither empty figures nor mere external badges of piety, but seals of the divine promises, testimonies of spiritual grace to cherish and confirm faith, and, on the other, that they are instruments by which God acts effectually in his elect; that, therefore, although they are signs distinct from the things signified, they are neither disjoined nor separated from them; that they are given to ratify and confirm what God has promised by his word, and especially to seal the secret communion which we have with Christ;—there certainly remains no reason why they should rank us in their list of enemies.

While, as I lately mentioned, they are constantly exclaiming that they have no other purpose than to maintain the doctrine that God uses the sacraments as helps to foster and increase faith, that the promises of eternal salvation are engraven on them to offer them to our consciences, and that the signs are not devoid of the things, as God conjoins the effectual working of his Spirit with them ; then all this being granted, what, I ask, prevents them from freely giving us their hand ? And to make it unnecessary to turn up and examine the private writings of each, readers will find in our Agreement every thing contained in the Confession published at Ratisbon, and called the Confession of Augsburg, provided only that it be not interpreted as having been composed under fear of torture, to gain favour with the Papists. The words are—" In the holy Supper, the body and blood of Christ are truly given with the bread and wine." Far be it from us either to take away the reality from the sacred symbol of the Supper, or to deprive pious souls of so great a benefit. We say, that lest the bread and wine should deceive our senses, the true effect is conjoined with the external figure, so that believers receive the body and blood of Christ. Nay, as it was our design to leave pious readers in no doubt, we have attempted to explain more clearly and fully what that Confession only glanced at.

It is asked, what is the efficacy of the sacraments ? what their use ? what their office ? Our document answers, that as the whole safety of believers depends on the communion which they have with the Son of God, in order to attest it the use as well of the gospel as of the sacraments was commanded. Let the reader observe that the sacraments are conjoined with the gospel, as conferring the same advantage upon us in the matter of salvation. Hence it follows, that what Paul says of the gospel (Rom. i. ; 2 Cor. vii.) we are at liberty to apply to them. Wherefore we deny not that they are part of that power which God exerts for our salvation, and that the ministry of our reconciliation with God is also contained in them. For seeing we always willingly professed to assent to the words of Augustine, that " a sacrament is a kind of visible word," we undoubtedly acknowledge that our salvation is promoted in like manner by both means.

Now if it is asked what the nature of that communion is, by the description of it given by us a little before, it cannot be said to be fictitious and shadowy, viz., (and this, too, is the proper and perpetual office of faith,) that we must coalesce with the body of Christ, in order to his fulfilling in us the effects of his grace. There is no other way of infusing his life into us than by being our head, from which the whole body, joined together and connected by every joint of supply, according to his operation in the measure of every part, maketh increase of the body.

Next follows the clearer explanation to which I lately adverted, that although the sacraments are marks and badges of Christian profession or fellowship, and likewise incitements to gratitude, in short, exercises of piety, and mutual contracts obliging us to the worship of God, they have, however, this principal end amongst others, viz., to testify, represent, and seal the grace which the Lord bestows upon us: moreover, that they are not mere shows presented to our eyes, but that therein are represented the spiritual graces, the effect of which believing souls receive. The words are—" Seeing they are true testimonies and seals which God has given us of his grace, he undoubtedly performs inwardly by his Spirit whatever the sacraments figure; in other words, we obtain possession of Christ, the fountain of all blessings, are reconciled to God by means of his death, are renewed by his Spirit to holiness of life, in short, obtain righteousness and salvation." To this we immediately after add, that by distinguishing between the signs and the things signified, we disjoin not the reality from the signs, but confess that all who by faith embrace the promises there offered receive Christ spiritually, with all his gifts.

Were I dealing with Papists I would collect passages of Scripture and ancient writers, and show more accurately that nothing has either proceeded from God, or ever been believed by the Church concerning the sacraments, that we have not briefly included. But it is strange that men, whose formal practice it is daily to cry, "the word of the Lord, the word of the Lord," are not ashamed any longer to stir up strife about this matter. For while nothing is more absurd than to extol the sacraments above the word, whose appendages and seals they are, they will find nothing applicable to the word that we do not also give to the sacraments. In short, if they acknowledge God as the only author of our salvation, how do they ask more to be given to the sacraments than to be means and instruments of his secret grace, adapted to our weakness? To vindicate them completely from contempt this one fact should suffice—that they are not only badges of all the blessings which God once exhibited to us in Christ, and which we receive every day, but that the efficacy of the Spirit is conjoined with their outward representation, lest they should be empty pictures.

On the other hand, how carefully we ought to guard against superstition, not only does the experience of all ages teach, but every individual may be convinced by his own weakness. For as our mind is prone to earth, external elements have too much influence in drawing us to themselves without being extravagantly adorned. When immoderate commendation is added, scarcely one in a hundred refrains from carrying his reverence to a depraved and vicious excess. In this matter the pertinacity of our detractors is more than blind. For being forced to vociferate against the Papists, they dare not explain the matter clearly, lest they may be thought to subscribe to our view; nay, lest they should descend to true moderation, they purposely entangle themselves, and leave their readers in suspense.

That I may not seem to complain without cause, I will now make it plain by a brief explanation that there is nothing in our Agreement deserving of censure. To guard against superstition, we said, in the first place, that those act foolishly who look only to the bare signs, and not rather to the promises annexed to them. By these words we meant nothing more than what, with universal consent, Augustine truly and wisely teaches, (Homil. in Joan. 80,) that the elements become sacraments only when the word is added, not because it is pronounced, but because it is believed. And the

reason why our Saviour pronounces the apostles clean is because of the word which they had heard from him, not because
of the baptism with which they had been washed. For if the
visible figures which are introduced as sacraments without
the word are not only jejune and lifeless elements but noxious
impostures, what else is gazing upon a sacrament without
waiting for the promise but mere illusion? Certainly if a man
only brings his eyes and shuts his ears, they will differ in
no respect from the profane rites of the heathen. For though
we confess that of the ancient rites of the heathen very
many had their origin from the holy patriarchs, yet, as being
devoid of doctrine, they retained nothing of pure faith, we
justly say that they were degenerate and corrupt.

The matter stands truly thus. If the sign be not seasoned
with the promise, being insipid in itself, it will be of no
avail. For what can a man of mortality and earth do by
pouring water on the heads of those whom he baptizes, if
Christ does not pronounce from above that he washes their
souls by his blood, and renews them by his Spirit? What
will the whole company of the faithful gain by tasting a
little bread and wine, if the voice does not echo from heaven
that the flesh of Christ is spiritual food and his blood is truly
drink? We therefore truly conclude, that it is not at all by
the material of water, and bread and wine that we obtain
possession of Christ and his spiritual gifts, but that we are
conducted to him by the promise, so that he makes himself
ours, and, dwelling in us by faith, fulfils whatever is promised and offered by the signs. What any man should disapprove in this, I see not, unless perhaps he thinks it an
honour to the sacred signs, to be regarded as illusory forms
without faith.

On this occasion we again properly lead back pious minds
to Christ, not allowing them to seek or hope elsewhere for
the blessings of which a badge and pledge is held forth to
them in the signs. And in this way we follow the rule
which the Lord prescribed to Moses, namely, to make all
things after the model which he had shown him in the
mount. For this passage is not without reason referred to
by Stephen in the Acts, and the Apostle in the Epistle to

the Hebrews. But as anciently the best method of correct-
ing gross error among the Jews was not to let them stop
at the visible tabernacle and the sacrifices of beasts, but to
set Christ before their eyes and make them look up to him,
so in the present day we should be intent on that spiritual
archetype, and not delude ourselves with empty shows. And,
certainly, our Lord in instituting the sacraments by no means
surrounded us with impediments to confine us to the world.
He rather set up ladders by which we might scale upwards
to the heavens; for nowhere else is Christ to be sought, and
nowhere are we to rest than in him alone. What? did
Christ, I would ask, die and rise again that he might cease
to be the cause and groundwork of our salvation? Nay, he
has furnished us with aids to seek him, while he remains in
his own place.

We next proceed to correct a more common but not less
ruinous superstition, when we teach that if any thing is bestowed on us through the sacraments, it is not owing to any
proper virtue in them, but inasmuch as the Lord is pleased
in them to exert the agency of his Spirit. For the human
mind is unable to refrain from either enclosing the power
of God in signs, or substituting signs in the place of God :
hence it is that God himself is robbed of the praise of his
virtue, men attributing to lifeless creatures that which is
peculiarly his. The sum of our doctrine, which we declare
in lucid and by no means ambiguous terms, is, that God
alone performs whatever we obtain by the sacraments, and
that by his secret and, as it is called, intrinsic virtue. But
lest any one should object, that the signs too have their
office, and were not given in vain, we hasten to meet the
objection by saying, that God uses their instrumentality, and
yet in such manner that he neither infuses his virtue into
them, nor derogates in any respect from the efficacy of his
Spirit.

What would these worthy men here have? Would they
have God to act by the sacraments? We teach so. Would
they have our faith to be exercised, cherished, aided, confirmed by them? This, too, we assert. Would they have
the power of the Holy Spirit to be exerted in them, and

make them available for the salvation of God's elect ?   We
concede this also.   The question turns upon this—should we
ascribe all the parts of our salvation entirely to God alone,
or does he himself by using the sacraments transfer part of
his praise to them ?   Who but one devoid of all modesty
dares maintain so ?   And as a witness to our doctrine we
cite Paul, who declares that ministers are nothing, and in
planting and watering do nothing at all apart from God, who
alone giveth the increase.   Hence it is easy for any one to see,
that, provided God is not to be robbed of his own, we detract
nothing from the sacraments.   It is well known how highly
Paul, in another passage, extols the preaching of the word.
How comes it then that he here reduces it to almost nothing,
unless it be that when it comes into contrast with God he
alone must be acknowledged as the author of all blessings,
while he uses the creatures thus freely, and at his own will
acts by means of them so far as he pleases ?   No injury is
done to earthly elements in not decking them with the spoils
of God.

What we subjoin from Augustine, viz., that it is Christ
alone who baptizes inwardly, and that it is he alone who
makes us partakers of himself in the Supper, strongly displays the excellence of both ordinances.   For we hence
infer, that acts of which the Son of God is the author, over
which he presides, in which, as with outstretched hand from
heaven, he displays his virtue, are no acts of man.   Then
nothing is more useful than to withdraw our sense from
gazing on mortal man and an earthly element, that our faith
may behold Christ as if actually present : though this indeed
is intended to claim for Christ his own right, and not allow
it to be supposed that in committing the external ministry to
men, he resigns to them the merit of the spiritual effect.   In
this sense Augustine at great length maintains, (Hom. 5, 6,
in Joann.,) that the power and efficacy of baptism are competent to none but Christ.   And what need is there of
human testimony while the words which fell clear from the
lips of the Baptist ought to be continually sounding in our
ears, " He it is who baptizeth with the Spirit," (John i.)   It
is clear that this title distinguished him from all ministers,

and acquaints us that he alone does inwardly what men attest by visible sign.

This Augustine well explains in these words, (Quaest. Vet. Test., lib. iii. c. 84,) " How then does Moses and how does our Lord sanctify ? Moses does not sanctify in place of the Lord, but by visible sacraments through his ministry; whereas the Lord sanctifies by invisible grace through the Holy Spirit, wherein lies the whole fruit even of visible sacraments." For without that sanctification of invisible grace, what can visible sacraments avail ? Nor in any other way can we reconcile passages of Scripture in which there is an apparent discrepancy. Of this class are those which we have there referred to, viz., that the Holy Spirit is a seal by which faith in the future inheritance is ratified to us, and that the sacraments are also seals. For there is no more consistency in placing these in the same rank than in transferring to signs what is competent to none but the Spirit. The only solution, therefore, is in the common axiom, that there is no repugnance between superior and subaltern. For were any one to contend that our salvation is not sealed by lifeless signs, this being the proper office of the Holy Spirit, I ask what answer these censors whom our argument does not please would give ? Just what we maintain—that though God uses inferior means, it does not at all imply that he does not begin and perfect our faith solely by the agency of his Spirit.

When we say, that the signs are not available to all indiscriminately, but to the elect only, to whom the inward and effectual working of the Spirit is applied, the thing is too clear to require any lengthened statement. If any one would make the effect common to all, he is not only refuted by the testimony of Scripture but by experience. As the outward voice of man by itself cannot at all penetrate the heart, but out of many hearers those alone come to Christ who are inwardly drawn by the Father, (according to the words of Isaiah, that none believed his preaching save those to whom the word of the Lord was revealed,) so it is in the free and sovereign determination of God to give the profitable use of signs to whom he pleases.

When we thus speak, we do not understand that any thing is changed in the nature of the sacraments, so as to make them less entire. Nor does Augustine, (Tract in Joann. 26,) when he confines the effect of the holy Supper to the body of the Church, consisting in the predestinate, who have already been justified in part, and are still justified, and will one day be glorified, make void or impair its force considered in itself in regard to the reprobate. He only affirms that the benefit is not alike common to all. But seeing that in the reprobate the only obstacle to their possession of Christ is their own unbelief, the whole blame resides in themselves. In short, the exhibition of the sign disappoints no man but him who malignantly and spontaneously defrauds himself. For it is most true, that every one receives from the sign just as much benefit as his vessel of faith can contain.

And we justly repudiate the fiction of Sorbonne, that the sacraments of the new law are available to all who do not interpose the obstacle of mortal sin. For to ascribe to them a virtue which the external use merely, as a kind of channel, infuses into souls, is plainly a senseless superstition. But if faith must intervene, no man of sense will deny that the same God who helps our infirmity by these aids, also gives faith, which, elevated by proper ladders, may climb to Christ and obtain his grace. And it ought to be beyond controversy, that as it would not be enough for the sun to shine, and send down its rays from the sky, were not eyes previously given us to enjoy its light, so it were in vain for the Lord to give us the light of external signs, if he did not make us capable of discerning them. Nay, just as the light of the sun, while it invigorates a living and animated body, produces effluvia in a carcase; so it is certain that the sacraments where the Spirit of faith is not present, breathes mortiferous rather than vital odour.

But lest any should suppose from this that any thing is lost to the virtue of the sacraments, or that by the unbelief and wickedness of man the truth of God is impaired, I think we carefully put them on their guard when we say, that the signs nevertheless remain entire, and offer divine grace to the unworthy, and that the effect of the promises does not fail, though unbelievers receive not what is offered. We are not here speaking of the ministers as to whom it was at one time foolishly doubted, whether their perfidy, or any other unworthiness, vitiated the sacraments. We hold the ordinance of God to be too sacred to depend for its efficacy on man. Be it then that Judas, or any other epicurean contemner of every thing sacred, is the administrator of baptism or the Lord's Supper, we hold that both the washing of regeneration, and the spiritual nourishment of the body and blood of Christ, are conferred through his hand, just as if he were an angel come down from heaven.

Not that it becomes the Church at large, by carelessness or connivance, to foster vicious ministers, or those who pollute the holy place by impure lives. She ought rather to exert herself both in public and in private, to cleanse the sanctuary of God as far as may be of such defilements. But if it happens that men altogether ungodly surreptitiously obtain the honour, or the ambitious favour of certain persons prevents the dissolute from being brought to order, or as was most desirable, forthwith discarded, how detestable soever their unworthiness may be, it detracts nothing from the sacraments, since that which Christ then bestows he takes from himself, and does not draw or derive from ministers. We have no doubt, therefore, that the Popish requisite of intention in the officiating minister, is a perverse and pernicious figment. But as the Lord is always ready to perform what he figures, as well by ungodly as by faithful ministers, we acknowledge that what is offered is received only by faith, while we hold that unbelievers are sent empty away.

We deny, therefore, that the Lord withholds his hand. On the contrary, we maintain, that in order to be perpetually consistent with himself, and in infinite goodness strive with the wickedness of men, he truly offers what they reject. But there is a wide difference between the two things—that the Lord is faithful in performing what he shows by a sign, and that man, in order to enjoy the proffered grace, makes way for the promise. Before any one can receive what is given, he must have the capacity, as it is written, " Open thy mouth wide and I will fill it." It is mere ignorance, therefore, that makes some cry out, that the figure of the holy Supper is made empty and void, if the ungodly do not receive as much in it as believers. If they hold that the same thing is given to both indiscriminately, I could easily subscribe to their inference, but that Christ is received without faith is no less monstrous than that a seed should germinate in the fire. By what right do they allow themselves to dissever Christ from his Spirit? This we account nefarious sacrilege. They insist that Christ is received by the wicked, to whom they do not concede one particle of the Spirit of Christ. What else is this than to shut him up in a tomb as if he were dead?

But it will be said, that Paul would not charge those who eat unworthily with being guilty of the body and blood of the Lord, were they not also made partakers of Christ. Nay, I should rather say, that if access was given them to Christ, it would exempt them from all guilt. But now as they foully trample upon the pledge of sacred communion, which they ought to receive with reverence, it is not strange that they are counted guilty of his body and blood.

Ignorant men absurdly imagine that they would not be guilty, did they not handle with their hands, and chew with their teeth, and swallow the body of Christ. Then, according to them, what kind of receiving will this be? Paul declares faith to be the mode by which Christ dwells in us. Wherefore, if faith is wanting, he can only be received for a moment, and then vanish. How much more rightly does Augustine, as became a man well versed in the Scriptures, say, (Hom. in Joan. 62,) that the bread of the Lord was given to Jesus to make him a slave of the devil, just as a messenger of Satan was given to Paul to perfect him in Christ. He had previously said, (Hom. 59,) that the other disciples ate the Lord the bread, whereas Judas ate the bread of the Lord against the Lord. In another place also, (Hom. 26,) he wisely expounds the celebrated saying of Christ, that those who eat him shall never die, meaning, he says, that the virtue of the sacrament is not only the visible sacrament, that it is within, not without, in those who eat with the heart, not press with the teeth. Whence he at length concludes, that a sacrament of the thing is held forth at the Lord's table, and is taken by some unto destruction, by others unto life, but that the thing itself, of which the Supper is a sign, yields life to all, destruction to none who partake of it.

That there may be no doubt as to the mind of this writer, it will not be disagreeable to go a little deeper into his views. After saying that the hunger of the inner man seeks for this bread, he subjoins, Moses and Aaron and Phinehas, and many others, who pleased the Lord and did not die, ate of the manna. Why? Because they understood the visible food spiritually; they hungered spiritually; they tasted spiritually; they were filled spiritually. For we, too, of the present day, have received visible food; but the sacrament is one thing, the virtue of the sacrament is another. A little after he says—" And by this he who abides not in Christ, and in whom Christ abides not, doubtless neither spiritually eats his flesh nor drinks his blood, though he carnally and visibly press the sign of the body and blood with his teeth, but he rather eats and drinks the sacrament of this great thing to his condemnation, because, though unclean, he has presumed to approach the sacraments of Christ."

You see how he concedes to the profane and impure nothing but a visible taking of the sign. I admit, he says elsewhere, (Lib. 5, de Bapt. contra Donatist.,) that the bread of the Supper was the body of Christ to those to whom Paul said, " Whoso eateth unworthily, eateth and drinketh judgment to himself, not discerning the Lord's body," and that they received nothing, just because they received badly. But in what sense he wished this to be understood, he explains more fully in another place, (Lib. de Civ. Dei. 21, c. 25.) For undertaking professedly to explain how the wicked and abandoned, who profess the Catholic faith with their lips, eat the body of Christ, and this in opposition to the opinion of some who pretended that they ate not only of the sacrament but of the reality, he goes on, " Neither can those be said to eat the body of Christ, since they are not to be accounted among the members of Christ. For not to mention other grounds, they cannot be the members of Christ and the members of a harlot." In short, our Saviour himself, when he says, " Whoso eateth my flesh and drinketh my blood remaineth in me and I in him," shows what it is not to eat of the sacrament merely, but really of the body of Christ. For one to abide in Christ, means that Christ abides in him. It was just as if he had said—Let not him who does not abide in me, and in whom I do not abide, say or think that he eats my body or drinks my blood. Let ignorant men cease to contend for Judas, if they would not seem to desire a Christ without Christ.

We next proceed to say, that the effect of the spiritual blessings which the sacraments figure, is given to believers without the use of the sacraments. As this is daily experienced to be true, and is proved by passages of Scripture, it is strange if any are displeased with it. When martyrs shut up in prison cannot take the external sign, shall we say that those in whom Christ is triumphantly magnified are without Christ ? Nor can any one altogether devoid of Christ make a due approach to the Supper. The reality of baptism was not wanting to Cornelius, who, previous to the washing of water, had been sprinkled with the Holy Spirit, just as Moses was not devoid of the divine unction, of which he communicated the sign to others, though he himself never received it.

By thus teaching, we by no means intend that we are to lay aside the use of signs, and be contented with secret inspirations. Although the Lord occasionally, to prove that his virtue is not tied to any means, performs without sign what he represents by sign, it does not follow that we are to cast away any thing which he ordained for our salvation, as if it were superfluous. Far less will this be lawful for us, whose faith ought to be intent on his word and seals. For it has been truly said by Augustine, (Lib. Quaest. Vet. Test. 3,) that although God sanctifies whom he pleases without the visible sign, yet whoso contemns the sign is justly deprived of invisible sanctification.

Akin to this article is that which we next add, viz., that the advantage received from the sacraments ought not to be restricted to the time of external taking, as if they carried the grace of God along with them at the very moment.

Herein if any one dissents from us he must of necessity both accelerate the gift of regeneration in many, and fabricate innumerable baptisms for the remainder of life. We see the effect of baptism, which for a time was null, appear at last. Many are dipt with water from their mother's womb, who, as they advance in life, are so far from showing that they were inwardly baptized that they rather make void their baptism by doing what in them lies to quench the Spirit of God. Part of these God calls back to himself. He, therefore, who would include newness of life in the sign as a capsule, so far from doing honour to the sign, dishonours God.

Then, seeing that repentance and advancement in it ought to be our constant study even until death, who sees not that baptism is impiously mutilated if its virtue and fruit, which embraces the whole course of life, is not extended beyond the outward administration ? Nay, no greater affront to the sacred symbols can be imagined than to hold that their reality is in force only at the time of actual exhibition. My meaning is, that though the visible figure immediately passes away, the grace which it testifies still remains, and does not vanish in a moment with the spectacle exhibited to the eye. I have no intention to countenance the superstition of those who absurdly preserve the elements of bread and water in their churches, as if after the present use to which they were destined the effect of consecration still adhered to them. This it was necessary distinctly to declare, lest any one should affix the hope of salvation, which is liable to no change of times, to temporary signs, and faith apprehend no more than the eye perceives.

I come now to the question out of which such violent and bitter conflicts have arisen,—of what nature is the communion of our Lord's body and blood in the holy Supper ? We have not given a definition of it before refuting the figment of a local presence, and explaining the meaning of the words of Christ, as to which there has heretofore been too much contention. But as our purpose is to meet the objections of captious and unlearned men, who are borne headlong by a blind impulse to slander, or to pacify the honest and simple whom they have imbued with their deleterious speeches, I will now begin with that third article.

First, then, we acknowledge that Christ truly performs what he figures by the symbols of bread and wine, nourishing our souls with the eating of his flesh and the drinking of his blood. Away, then, with the vile calumny, that it would be theatrical show if the Lord did not perform in truth what he shows by the sign; as if we said that any thing is shown which is not truly given. The Lord bids us take bread and wine. At the same time he declares that he gives the spiritual nourishment of his flesh and blood. We say that no fallacious figure of this is set before our eyes, but that a pledge is given us, with which the substance and reality are conjoined; in other words, that our souls are fed with the flesh and blood of Christ. The term faith is thus used by us not to denote some imaginary thing, as if believers received what is promised only in thought or memory, but only to prevent any one from thinking that Christ is so far prostituted that unbelievers enjoy him.

When Paul teaches that Christ dwells in our hearts by faith, he does not substitute an imaginary for true habitation, but reminds us in what way we may ascertain the possession of so great a blessing. We acknowledge, then, without any equivocation, that the flesh of Christ gives life, not only because we once obtained salvation by it, but because now, while we are made one with Christ by a sacred union, the same flesh breathes life into us, or, to express it more briefly, because ingrafted into the body of Christ by the secret agency of the Spirit, we have life in common with him. For from the hidden fountain of the Godhead life was miraculously infused into the body of Christ, that it might flow from thence to us.

But here again, as the minds of men always conceive grossly of the heavenly mysteries of God, it was necessary to obviate delirious dreams. With this view we laid down the definition, that what we say of the partaking of Christ's flesh must not be understood as if any commingling or transfusion of substance took place, but that we draw life from the flesh once offered in sacrifice. If any one is dis-

pleased with this explanation, I say, first, that he has some
fiction of his own brain which is nowhere taught in Scripture, and by no means accords with the analogy of faith;
and I say, secondly, that it is too presumptuous, after taking
up a meaning at random, to lay down the law to others.
If they insist that the substance of the flesh of Christ is
commingled with the soul of man, in how many absurdities
will they involve themselves?

They say it is not lawful to bring down this sublime
mystery to secular reasoning, or to gauge its immense magnitude by the little measure of our capacity. To this I
readily assent. But is the modesty of faith to be made to
consist in disfiguring religion all over with horrid monsters?
In this way every thing that is most absurd would be most
accordant with Christ and his doctrine. We acknowledge
that the sacred union which we have with Christ is incomprehensible to carnal sense. His joining us with him so as
not only to instil his life into us, but to make us one with
himself, we grant to be a mystery too sublime for our comprehension, except in so far as his words reveal it. But are
we therefore to dream that his substance is transferred into
us so that he is defiled by our impurities? Their boast, that
they shut their eyes and inquire not too curiously into what
the Lord has concealed, is proved to be most vain from this,
that they do not allow themselves to be taught by the word
of God. Sobriety of faith is not only to acquiesce in the
decision of God, and apprehend no more than his sacred lips
have revealed, but also to attend diligently to the spirit of
prophecy, and embrace a sound interpretation with meek
docility. It is presumptuous petulance either not to confine
yourself within due limits, or to fastidiously reject the light
of sound understanding.

None of us denies that the body and blood of Christ are
communicated to us. But the question is, what is the nature
of this communication of our Lord's body and blood? I
wonder how these men dare to assert simply and openly that
it is carnal. When we say that it is spiritual, they roar out
as if by this term we were making it not to be what they
commonly call real. If they will use *real* for true, and op-

pose it to *fallacious* or *imaginary,* we will rather speak barbarously than afford material for strife. We are aware how little strivings about words become the servants of Christ, but as nothing is gained by making concessions to men who are in all ways implacable, I wish to declare to peaceful and moderate men, that according to us the spiritual mode of communion is such that we enjoy Christ in reality. Let us be contented with this reason, against which no man, unless he is very quarrelsome, will rebel, that the flesh of Christ gives us life, inasmuch as Christ by it instils spiritual life into our souls, and that it is also eaten by us when by faith we grow up into one body with Christ, that he being ours imparts to us all that is his.

In regard to local presence, I wonder that our censors are not ashamed to raise a quarrel. As they deny that the body of Christ is circumscribed by local space, they hold it to be immense. What do we hold? That we are to seek it in heaven, which, as Scripture declares, has received him till he appear to judgment. There is no ground, however, for any individual to charge us with holding that he is absent from us, and thus separating the head from the members. Certainly if Paul could say, that so long as we are in the world we are absent as pilgrims from the Lord, we may say, on the same ground, that we are separated from him by a certain species of absence, inasmuch as we are now distant from his heavenly dwelling. Christ then is absent from us in respect of his body, but dwelling in us by his Spirit he raises us to heaven to himself, transfusing into us the vivifying vigour of his flesh, just as the rays of the sun invigorate us by his vital warmth. Their common saying, that he is with us invisible, is equivalent to saying, that though his form is treasured up in heaven, the substance of his flesh is on the earth. But a sense of piety clearly dictates that he infuses life into us from his flesh, in no other way than by descending into us by his energy, while, in respect of his body, he still continues in heaven.

The same view must be taken of what we immediately add, viz., that in this way we not only refute the Popish fiction of transubstantiation, but all the gross figments, as

well as futile sophistry, which derogate either from the
heavenly glory of Christ, or are repugnant to the reality of
his human nature.   It is unnecessary to dwell more on this
explanation, which was not added without consideration.

Some who would make the body of Christ immense deprive it of the nature of a body, others enclose his Deity
under a lifeless element.   If the one party has erred through
ignorance, and the other, carried away in the heat of contention, has rashly uttered an absurdity, let it remain
buried.   I do not attack or inveigh against the persons of
men.   We have not attacked any one in our writing, but
have held it sufficient to cut off all handle for error.   Who
can be offended when we wish Christ to remain complete
and entire in regard to both natures, and the Mediator who
joins us to God not to be torn to pieces?   The immensity
which they imagine the flesh of Christ to possess, is a monstrous phantom, which overturns the hope of a resurrection.
To all the absurdities they advance concerning the heavenly
life, I will always oppose the words of St. Paul, that we wait
for Christ from heaven, who will transform our poor body
and make it conformable to his own glorious body.   Need
we say how absurd it were to fill the whole world with the
single body of each believer?

Let those men, then, allow us modestly to profess what is
sound and right, and not force us by their intemperance to
uncover their disgrace, which is better hid.   Let them not
fiercely assail us, because sparing names, as I have said, we
have been contented with a bare refutation of errors.   They
think it intolerable in us to deny that Christ is placed
under the bread, or coupled with the bread.   What then?
Will they pull him down from his throne, that he may lie
enclosed in a little bit of bread?   Should any one say that
the body of Christ is offered to us under the bread, as an
earnest, we will not quarrel with him on that account, any
more than when in disposing of the carnal or local coupling
we endeavoured to make a divorce between the sign and its
reality.   Let believers then receive the body of Christ under
the symbol of bread; for he is true who speaks, and it is not
at all in accordance with his character to deceive us by

holding forth an empty badge ; only let there be no local enclosing or carnal infusing.

All that now remains is the exposition of our Lord's words. If in it there is any offence, let them impute it to their own perverseness in being determined to involve what is clear in itself in darkness by clamour and tumult. Christ having called the bread his body, they insist on the precise words, and refuse to admit any figure. But if the bread is properly the body of Christ, it will follow that Christ himself is just as much bread as he is man. We may add, that if the expression is not figurative, they themselves act perversely in saying that the same body is under the bread, with the bread, and in the bread. If they assume such gross liberty of interpretation, why will they not allow us to open our mouth ? When in searching for the meaning of the words we consider in what manner Scripture usually speaks of the sacraments, they refuse to listen because it was once said, This is my body. What ? was it not also said that Christ was a Rock ? And in what sense, but just that he was the same spiritual drink with him whom we now drink in the cup ? That they might not be forced to yield to plain reason, they madly dissever things sacredly joined.

To be silent as to this, and let it pass, I would ask, by what right they allow themselves to resolve this sentence of theirs, on which they insist so much, into different forms of speech ? After insisting that the bread is Christ, why do they afterwards fly off to their own fictions, and say, that he is with the bread, in the bread, and under the bread ? Who gave them this authority to sport futile fictions, not less remote from usage than self-contradictory, and debar others from sound understanding ? If the bread must be regarded as the body, because it is so called, just as much must it on the authority of Paul be regarded as the communion of the body. Nay, if I should say that Paul in this passage expounds more clearly what was rather obscurely expressed by Christ, what sober man will gainsay me ? The Lord declares that the bread is his body. The disciple follows, certainly not intending to throw darkness on the light, and explains that the bread is the communion of the body.

Here, if they give us their consent, the dispute is at an end, for we also declare that in the breaking of bread the body of Christ is communicated to believers.

They insist on retaining the word. Very well. Since Christ, according to Luke and Paul, calls the cup the *covenant* in his blood, whenever they cry that the bread is the body and the wine the blood, I, in my turn, will on the best authority rejoin, that they are *covenants* in the body and blood. Let unlearned men then cease from that pertinacity by which, not to use harsher terms, they must ever and anon find themselves perplexed and ensnared.

It is not worth while to enter into a full discussion at present, but this much I take for granted. After saying that the bread is the body, they are forced at the same time to confess that it is a sign of the body. How can they know this but just from the words of Christ? Therefore the very term sign, for the use of which they so invidiously quarrel with us, they stealthily extract from the very passage which they insist on being only literally interpreted. We, again, while in deference both to common sense and piety, we candidly acknowledge that the mode of expression is figurative, have no recourse either to allegories or parables; but we assume an axiom received by all pious men without controversy, that whenever the sacraments are treated of, it is usual to transfer the name of the thing signified by metonymy to the sign. Examples occur too frequently in Scripture for any opponents, however keen, to venture to deny that this mode of speech must be regarded as the general rule. Hence as the manna of old was spiritual food, as the water was Christ, as the Holy Spirit was a dove, as baptism was the laver of regeneration, so the bread is called the body and the wine the blood of Christ. If they choose to call it synecdoche rather than metonymy, and thus reduce it to a quarrel about a word, we shall leave grammarians to settle it. What, however, will they gain but just to expose themselves to derision for their ignorance, even boys being judges?

To pass over this, whosoever is disposed to strive about words proves that he is by no means a servant of Christ.

While we are entirely agreed as to things, what can be more preposterous than to rend Churches and stir up fierce tumults because some hold that the bread is called body, inasmuch as the body is exhibited under it and with it, whereas others hold that it is a symbol—not an empty illusory symbol, but one to which its own reality is annexed, so that all who receive the sign with their mouth and the promise by faith become truly partakers of Christ. But if they have determined to make no end of their evil speaking, I am confident that no man not engaged in the contention will be so unjust as not to acknowledge that we teach correctly, and practise sincerity, and are lovers of peace. I do not think there is any reason to fear that any person, if he be not smitten with the mad fury of those men, will countenance their importunate clamour.

SECOND DEFENCE

OF THE

PIOUS AND ORTHODOX FAITH CONCERNING THE SACRAMENTS,

IN ANSWER TO

THE CALUMNIES OF JOACHIM WESTPHAL.

M.D.LVI.

AND SINCERE WORSHIPPERS OF GOD, WHO OBSERVE AND FOLLOW THE PURE
DOCTRINE OF THE GOSPEL IN

THE CHURCHES OF SAXONY AND LOWER GERMANY,

JOHN CALVIN,

WITH BROTHERLY AFFECTION, WISHES INCREASE OF GRACE FROM GOD THE
FATHER AND OUR LORD JESUS CHRIST.

ALTHOUGH I am perfectly conscious to myself that the cause
which I have undertaken to defend in this book is right and just,
and that I have acted faithfully in pleading it, yet, as the full conviction of my own mind does not satisfy me unless I study to
approve my conduct to all the children of God, I have thought it
of importance, venerable and beloved brethren, to protest to you
at the outset that this book has been extorted from me if I were
not by my silence to betray the truth of Christ, in oppressing
which certain ferocious men exceed the barbarism of the Papacy.

A dispute unhappily carried on among the learned for more than
twenty years on the subject of THE SACRAMENTS having been somewhat calmed, and men's minds disposed to moderation, nothing
seemed so likely to lead to a full settlement as to give an attested
statement in few and simple terms of the doctrine which THE
CHURCHES OF SWITZERLAND follow. For as long as the contest
raged, and the minds of both parties were exasperated, it is probable that the subject was not expounded with sufficient clearness,
nor the words employed duly weighed. Most of you are well
aware of the short description which we published five years ago
under the name of AGREEMENT, and in which, without attacking
any one, and without any asperity of language, we not only
arranged the substance of the whole controversy under distinct
heads, but also endeavoured, in so far as a candid confession of
the truth allowed, entirely to remove all offences. It ought also
to have had the effect of appeasing the minds of any who were less
disposed to take an equitable view that we offered, in case any

were not satisfied, to exert ourselves in adding an explanation. We also promised that we would be open to instruction and obedient to better counsels should any one show that the matter had not been properly handled.

About two years after arose one Joachim Westphal, who, so far from being softened to concord by that temperate simplicity of doctrine, seized upon the name of Agreement as a kind of Furies' torch to rekindle the flame. For he avowedly collected from all quarters opinions which he would have to be thought adverse to each other, that he might thus destroy our Agreement; and showed himself to be inflamed with such a hatred of peace, that he vented his peculiar venom against us, for no other reason but because he was annoyed by our thinking and speaking the same thing. He writes that my books were highly esteemed and relished by the men of his sect, at the time when they thought that I differed from the teachers of the Church of Zurich. Whence the sudden alienation now? Is it because I have abandoned my opinion? Even he himself does not disguise, nay, he has written on the margin of his book, that every thing which our Agreement contains occurs throughout my writings. Who now sees not that the hatred which this man bears to those against whom he has once declared war is so implacable, that he assails the very doctrine which he formerly favoured, in order that he may have nothing in common with them?

His apology is, that he is the enemy of nothing but a dissembled concord. But how comes it that the doctrine which formerly pleased him in my writings, excites his deep aversion now that it has come from the Zurichers? However he may hide the sore, assuredly nothing has impelled him but a wish to furnish a new defence to the inflexible pertinacity of some persons in not yielding to the plain truth.

The perverse attack of this man I was forced to repel in a short treatise. He, as if an inexpiable crime had been committed, has flamed forth with much greater impetuosity. It has now become necessary for me to repress his insolence. Should I inveigh rather vehemently against him, be pleased of your prudence and equity to consider what provocation I have had. Heresies and heretics, diabolical blasphemies, impious denial of Scripture, subversion of all that is sacred, and similar opprobrious epithets, are the words ever in his mouth. In short, his book has no other apparent object than to precipitate us by the thunderbolts of anathemas to the lower regions. What was left for me but to apply a hard wedge to a bad knot, and not allow him to have too much complacency in his savage temper? Were there any hope of mollifying those men, I would not refuse to humble myself, and by supplicating them, purchase the peace of the Church. But to what lengths they are borne by their violence is notorious to all. Therefore my austerity in rebuking their hard-heartedness has the sanction of God himself, who not only declares (Ps. xviii.) that to the froward he will show himself without mercy, but will treat them frowardly. But though it was my most earnest wish to proceed directly to the point, and digress as little as possible from the discussion of it, yet as my opponent, leaping from this topic to that, according to his humour, has not allowed me to proceed in regular order, it will be proper briefly to glance at the substance of the whole matter in dispute.

That I have written reverently of the legitimate use, dignity, and efficacy of the sacraments, even he himself does not deny. How skilfully or learnedly in his judgment I care not, since it is enough to be commended for piety by an enemy. The contest remaining with him embraces three articles: First, he insists that the bread of the Supper is substantially the body of Christ. Secondly, in order that Christ may exhibit himself present to believers, he insists that his body is immense, and exists everywhere without place. Thirdly, he insists that no figure is to be admitted in the words of Christ, whatever agreement there may be as to the thing. Of such importance does he deem it to stick doggedly to the words, that he would sooner see the whole globe convulsed than admit any exposition. We maintain that the body and blood of Christ are truly offered to us in the Supper in order to give life to our souls, and we explain, without ambiguity, that our souls are invigorated by this spiritual aliment which is offered us in the Supper, just as our bodies are nourished by earthly bread. Therefore we hold, that in the Supper there is a true partaking of the flesh and blood of Christ. Should any one raise a dispute as to the word substance, we assert that Christ, from the substance of his flesh, breathes life into our souls; nay, infuses his own life into us, provided always that no transfusion of substance be imagined.

The cause of the implacable wrath of Westphal is this. While we confess that the flesh of Christ gives life, and that we are truly made partakers of it in the Supper, he, not contented with this simplicity, urges and contends that the bread is substantially the body. From this springs the other dogma, that the body and blood of Jesus Christ are taken into the mouth of a wicked man in the very same way as bread and wine. For how comes he to affirm so pertinaciously that the body of Christ was taken by Judas no less than by Peter, unless it be because the substance of the sign is not changed by man's unbelief? He, moreover, imagines a substance which is by no means agreeable to the word of God, viz., that Christ affixes his own flesh substantially to the bread.

The pretext, that it is absurd to make the truth of the divine promise depend on man's faith, is easily disposed of. We distinctly declare that no unbelief prevents the sacred ordinance of Christ from retaining its force and nature; prevents his flesh from being offered and given to all as spiritual food, and his blood as spiritual drink; prevents the bread from being a true symbol of flesh, and the wine of blood; prevents that which Christ pronounces from heaven to be firm and sure, viz., that the body which he once offered to the Father in sacrifice he now offers as food to men. If the wicked defraud themselves of this benefit, and their unbelief causes that the fruition does not reach them, we deny that any thing is lost to the sacrament on this account, inasmuch as it remains entire.

The second question has no other source than the mode of communion, which Westphal supposes to be necessarily conjoined with the immensity of Christ's body. He holds that if the body of Christ be not actually placed before us, there is no real communion. We, on the contrary, maintain that no extent of space interferes with the boundless energy of the Spirit, which transfuses life into us from the flesh of Christ. And here we detest the dishonesty of those who invidiously disseminate among the people that we take away the presence of Christ from the Supper, and measure the power of God by our own sense. As if the sublimity of this mystery, viz., that Christ, though remaining in heaven as to the locality of his body, yet descends to us by the secret agency of his Spirit, so as to unite us with him and make us partakers of his life—did not transcend the reach of human intellect, or as if the power of God were less magnificently extolled by him who teaches that life flows into us from the flesh of Christ, than by him who brings his flesh out of heaven to enable it to give us life. These points I now merely allude to, as you will find them more fully and copiously expounded in their proper place.

Not to detain you longer from the perusal of the work, I will now advert to the third article. He thinks it unlawful to inquire into what Jesus Christ meant when he said, that the bread is his body, the clearness of the terms precluding all exposition. We again appeal to the familiar and well known usage of Scripture, which, whenever the sacraments are treated of, transfers the name of the thing signified to the sign. Examples of this occur not once or twice, but among those skilled in Scripture its frequency makes it to be regarded as the common rule. Still, we do not feed the eyes of believers with an empty figure, since we distinctly declare that what the Lord testifies he really performs. We only insist on the distinction, that an analogy is drawn between the sign and the visible action and the spiritual reality. For to what end does Christ hold forth a pledge of his flesh and blood under earthly elements unless it be to raise us upwards? If they are helps to our weakness, no man will ever attain to the reality, but he who thus assisted shall climb, as it were, step by step from earth to heaven. Those, therefore, who deny that the body of Christ is represented to us under the symbol of bread, not only pervert the whole order of Christ, but deprive the Spirit of God of his wonted mode of speech. Westphal attributes the name of body to the bread. But where is the modesty of being so extravagant in doing this, as to keep crying that interpretation must be regarded as the height of sacrilege?

We thought it right thus to point, as with the finger, to the sources of the whole controversy, to make it plain that a dissension which ought to have been extinct is again kindled, more from proud disdain in the opposite party than from any just cause. If you fear a lamentable and fatal result, (and there is certainly ground to fear it,) I beseech you by the sacred name of Christ and the bond of our unity in him, that you earnestly endeavour to find a remedy. Whatever be the method of conciliation offered, I declare that I will not only be disposed but eager to embrace it.

On your part, also, it may be expected from your piety and humanity that you will rather assist one whom you know to bestow all his studies and labours for the edification of the Church in the best faith, and with results not to be repented of, than allow him to be trampled upon by the insolent caprice of an intractable individual. But why do I speak of myself personally? You must rather take into account the holy union of so many Churches which that man is labouring to destroy. Whatever he may babble to the contrary, it is certain that this concert in faith, after the miserable scattering of the Papacy, was not of man's devising.

In regard to the one God and his true and legitimate worship, the corruption of human nature, free salvation, the mode of obtaining justification, the office and power of Christ, repentance and its exercises, faith which, relying on the promises of the gospel, gives us assurance of salvation, prayer to God, and other leading articles, the same doctrine is preached by both. We call on one God the Father, trusting to the same Mediator; the same Spirit of adoption is the earnest of our future inheritance. Christ has reconciled us all by the same sacrifice. In that righteousness which he has purchased for us, our minds are at peace, and we glory in the same head. It is strange if Christ, whom we preach as our peace, and who, removing the ground of disagreement, appeased to us our Father in heaven, do not also cause us mutually to cultivate brotherly peace on earth. What shall I say of our having to fight daily under the same banner against Antichrist and his tyranny, against the foul corruptions of the Christian religion, against impious superstitions, and the profanation of all that is sacred. To disregard these many pledges of sacred unity, and this concert which has visibly been sanctioned by heaven, and plot disunion among those who are fighting in the same service, is a not less cruel than impious laceration of the members of Christ. This it were most unjust in you to favour or countenance in any way. Farewell, respected brethren. May the Lord defend you and govern you by his Spirit, and bless you more and more.

GENEVA, 5th *January* 1556.

SECOND DEFENCE

OF THE

PIOUS AND ORTHODOX FAITH CONCERNING THE SACRAMENTS,

IN ANSWER TO

THE CALUMNIES OF JOACHIM WESTPHAL.

How unwillingly I am again dragged into this contest, which from the first till now I endeavoured to shun, I deem it unnecessary to declare in many words. For all who have read my writings must be aware of my moderation in handling a subject which in our day had excited bitter contests among pious and learned men. In this respect at least I cannot have given serious offence. For though I have not framed my method of teaching with a view to the favour of men, yet as I have always candidly and sincerely made profession according to the genuine convictions of my mind, it was of a kind which ought to have had the effect rather of appeasing men's minds than of increasing strife. The fervour of contention to which I have alluded had in some measure calmed down, and writings composed in a placid spirit were beginning to give a purer exposition of the subject. I feel proud to think that while the disputants were thus drawing nearer to each other, their consent, though not yet full and complete, was considerably helped forward by me.

For when on beginning to emerge from the darkness of Papacy, and after receiving a slight taste of sound doctrine, I read in Luther that Zuinglius and Œcolompadius left nothing in the sacraments but bare and empty figures, I confess I took such a dislike for their writings that I long refrained from reading them. Moreover, before I engaged in writing, the ministers of Marpurg having held a conference together, had laid aside somewhat of their former vehemence, so that if the atmosphere was not altogether clear, the denser mists had to a considerable extent disappeared. What I justly claim for myself is, that I never by employing an ambiguous mode of expression captiously brought forward any thing different from my real sentiment. After I thus made my appearance without disguise, none of the dissentients then in highest fame and authority gave any sign of offence. For I was afterwards brought into familiar intercourse with the leading advocates and keenest defenders of Luther's opinions, and they all vied in showing me friendship. Nay, what opinion Luther himself formed of me, after he had inspected my writings, can be proved by competent witnesses. One will serve me for many—Philip Melancthon.

It happened afterwards unfortunately that Luther, kindled by the very bellows by which the quiet of the Church is now disturbed, was in private again flaming against the Zurichers. For although the vehemence of his nature sometimes carried him farther than was meet, he never would have hurried spontaneously into the old strife had not excessive ardour been supplied by pestiferous torches. To myself, as to very many other worshippers of God and ministers of Christ, it gave no little grief that the wounds were thus opened afresh. I did, however, the only thing that was left for me, I lamented in my own breast in silence. Meanwhile, lest any semblance of dissension might rend the churches in these quarters, or a suspicion might arise that diverse opinions were here and there entertained, and as some were muttering that there was not a proper agreement between myself and the excellent men and faithful ministers of Christ, the teachers of the Church of Zurich, it was thought well on both sides that a testimony of our mutual agreement should be published. We accordingly drew up a brief summary of the doctrine in controversy, to remain as a simple and perspicuous confession of our faith.

Who can call this fuel for a new conflagration? One Joachim Westphal started up, and as if it were an intolerable

crime to efface all remembrance of offences, in order that
there might be no hidden rancour among brethren, shouting
to arms, threw every thing into confusion. Let his farrago
be read, and the reader will find that the thing purposed by
him was not so much to impugn the doctrine comprehended in
our formula of Agreement as agreement itself.   Is the name
of peace so odious to a preacher of the gospel that he cannot bear to see a remedy for abolishing discord attempted?
While he touches slightly on doctrine, the main thing urged
by him is, that agreement shall not be entertained. Accordingly where any repugnance in doctrine had formerly appeared, he drags it out of darkness and turbulently holds it
up to view.   If from error or oversight contradictory opinions
(as occasionally happens) had escaped from different writers,
why should they not be permitted on better consideration to
express their meaning more appropriately ?   How malicious
is it not to be quiet on any other condition than that innumerable dissensions shall everywhere prevail ?   And what
insane fury is it to force into unwilling conflict those who
not only agree among themselves but speak the same thing ?
    Granting that in the heat of discussion a temperate mode
of expression was not always observed, it is now desired
that those in whom there was some diversity, should adopt
the same method of teaching.   If the reason is asked, it is
because we wish to guard against troubling the ignorant and
weak, by presenting them with any semblance of contradiction. Will you, Westphal, as your passion leads you in a
different direction, force us to fight against our will to the
public ruin ?   But in the books formerly published, something discordant is detected. This will afterwards be considered in its own place ; but now what envy or malice instigates you to call for thunder from all quarters to rend
agreement ? You say you must fight strenuously against
any conspiracy to establish an impious dogma. I admit,
that if any cover were used to cloak imposture, there would
be good cause for reclaiming. I would also readily admit,
that all means ought to be employed, to prevent any congeries
of errors from shrouding themselves under the pretext of concord. But when our simple and perspicuous Confession is

brought forward, if it contains any thing false, it can be impugned with less trouble.

In every debate, nothing is more desired by honest and ingenuous men, than to be able to confine themselves within
certain limits, to keep without ambiguity to one subject, and
be able in treating that one, to know, as it were, where to
fix their foot.   Why such a state of matters is displeasing
to Westphal, I see not, unless, that distrustful of his cause,
he has sought for plausibility in equivocation.

If the doctrine which we profess is false, let him, after
furnishing himself with the oracles of Scripture, strong argument, and the consent of the Church, come forward as its
enemy and overthrow it.   But now, declining fair fight, he
rides up and down in a tortuous course, crying that the heretics are at variance among themselves.   Were he persuaded
that he has a sufficient defence in the truth itself, how much
better would it be to come to close quarters at once, than to
continue his winding circuits?   I again repeat, that our
Confession, if it contains any error, is naked and open: why
does not Westphal make a direct attack upon it, but just in
order to obscure the clear light by smoke?

I wished to call the reader's attention to this, to let every
one see how strong a necessity has compelled me to the defence of our Agreement, which this hot-headed zealot, without any just cause to induce him, has attempted to overthrow.
And yet the excuse he now makes is, that he is undertaking the defence of himself and a good cause against my accusation.   Nay, to give his tract currency among the ill-in-
formed, he has inserted this in the title.   What if I rejoin,
(it is easy for me to do so, and the fact shows without my
saying it,) that my tract (which he absurdly slanders under
the name of an accusation) had no other aim than to dissipate his calumnies.   He indeed complains vehemently, and
not without great obloquy to me, if there were any colour
for it, of my evil speaking; but the only thing necessary to
refute this, is for the reader to judge from his intemperance
how mercifully I spared him.

Into my tract I confess that I put a sprinkling of salt.   I
did so, because it grieved me that one who calls himself a

preacher of the gospel was so savourless. I now see that I
lost my labour in attempting to cure an incurable disease.
But where does he find my bitter and wanton invective ?
He is not ashamed falsely to assert, that all imaginable vitu-
peration has been heaped by me into a few pages, when the
fact is, that I have there inserted without any contention
much more pure doctrine than he and those like him give
in large volumes. His reply is, at least, thrice as long as
my tract. How skilfully or learnedly he discourses in it, I
do not now say ; only let the reader collect all the calm doctrine he can find, and it will scarcely amount to a tenth of
what is contained in my very brief compendium. With the
same modesty, one of his companions lately sporting in the
character of a dreamer, ventured to give out, among other follies, that my Commentary on Genesis is filled with fierce invectives against Luther, though there, from respect to him, I
refrained more than a hundred times from mentioning his
name ; and if anywhere I do allude to him, there is so far
from any thing like contumely in my censure, that I am
confident all sound and pious readers will give me credit for
having treated him with no less honour than was due to an
illustrious servant of Christ.

The first charge by which Westphal endeavours to bring
me into odium is, that I have vented my rage against him
in all kinds of invective. I only ask my readers, first, to
consider what he deserved, and how much more severely it
was easy to have handled him, and then conclude how very
moderate I have been. But because he was, perhaps, afraid
lest if he himself only was hurt, he should find few to con-
dole with a private grievance, he incites all his countrymen
to a common fight, as if I had brought a general charge of
drunkenness against all Germans. Were it so, I would not
even pardon myself. But attend to the proof which he immediately after gives. He says, I bring this charge against
him once and again, as if he were given to drink, and could
not get drunk without boon companions. That he may not
here annoy himself for nothing, let him know that I made
no war on his cups ; let him know that I spoke of another
kind of drunkenness, namely, that which the prophet Isaiah

says is not from wine. I wish, however, that he would not
plunge himself so deep into the mire, or rush headlong with
such violent impetus, as to make his jejune ebriety too notorious to all.

With no less absurdity does he digress into the commonplace, that he has the same lot with Christ and his apostles,
in being loaded, without cause, with falsehoods and reproaches. His writings testify that his lungs are as large
and strong in venting these, as his complaints declare that
his stomach is delicate in bearing and digesting them.
What has most grievously wounded him, it is not difficult to
perceive. I had reminded him, that if he were conscious of
his own ignorance, he would not behave so confidently. Nothing, certainly, was farther from my intention than to inflict
so sharp a wound. Now, by ever and anon repeating in a rage
that he is held to be unlearned, he betrays where the sore lies.

To let you understand, Westphal, that I did not previously
make it my endeavour to find out something that might sting
you, and that even now I have no pleasure in your pain, I
shall cease henceforth to call you unlearned; only do you
in your turn show yourself to be a candid and upright man.
But though you should, after your fashion, give full vent to
your unbridled license of evil speaking, I will not contend with
you in reproaches. Were it true, however, that I chid you
harshly, in order to repress your audacity, you are wrong in
thinking or pretending that I employed the cunning artifice
of trying to overwhelm you by my invectives, and compel
you to be quiet : as if I did not know what a fine rhetorician
you are, as far as evil speaking goes, and what copiousness
of such material flows in upon you.

But while by your mode of dealing, if I glance at you
in a single word, I am a scold, and you lay yourself under
no restraint as to lacerating me, how shall I be able to
manage my pen ? The best and shortest course to follow
will be to speak simply of the subject. The prudent reader
will observe, that whenever I was compelled to address you
in strong language, I never went beyond grave and serious
admonition. You, inflated by what spirit I know not, seem,
until you have sent forth your foam from full cheeks, to

have your stomach charged with some kind of oppressive load. The more strange it is, that you, with the greatest confidence, repudiate a vice which notoriously exists in you, in its ugliest form, as if you were perfectly free from it.

But that there may be no suspicion of my making a fictitious charge, I must again briefly remind the reader, how ingenuous you are in accusing me of petulance. You produce, as a memorable specimen of it, that I employed the sharpness of my tongue against the name of Luther. In what does this sharpness consist? You answer, that I charged him with being fickle, vehement, and contentious. Why in two of these epithets you choose to lie, I know not; I never called him fickle and contentious. If you take it ill that his vehemence in this cause was remarked, contend that at mid-day the sun does not shine.

How eagerly Westphal runs away from his subject into commonplaces, and as musty rhetoricians do wander away into declamation, is sufficiently clear from this, that in order not to seem to trust in numbers, he invents the empty fiction, that I boast of immense hosts which I threaten to lead forth from all corners. He accordingly adds, that I, trusting to this great force, despise his unwarlike crowd. Were Eck or Cochlæus to vent such silliness, I would with less regret hold it up to the derision of boys; but now when a professor of the gospel prostitutes himself so flagitiously, my readers must pardon me, if I am moderate in my refutation, because the disgraceful spectacle both shames and pains me. I see, however, what it is. Having nothing like Athanasius but the fewness of his adherents, he has seized on this mark of resemblance to make himself orthodox.

I had said that while the learned and right-hearted were quiet, a few unlearned individuals were disturbing the Church by their clamour. I hoped that thus admonished, they would cease from their turbulence; their fewness being an indication of their folly. Here, indeed, we do not simply contend about number. But while I show that many whom he boasts to be of his opinion, though in every way much more competent and better instructed, yet remain silent and cultivate peace with us, if there was a grain of modesty in

Westphal, he would throw away the spear, leave off conflict, and return to his post.

Again, I had added, that if he was so desirous to maintain the proper nature of the sacraments, that was no reason why he should make a rush at us, because the sacraments are not only mentioned by us in the most honourable terms, but should any one say that they are empty figures, many of us are prepared strenuously to refute his error. Let the reader look at my words, and it will appear how sillily the declaimer here seeks for adventitious colouring. That he may not be thought inferior in numbers, he hesitates not to drag into his faction those persons in France and Italy who have embraced the pure doctrine of the gospel, but are withheld by fear alone from freely professing it.

Here, though I fain would, I cannot be silent, lest by per-fidious dissimulation I should seem, knowingly and willingly, to suppress the confession made by Christ's holy martyrs. Since you are so stupid, Westphal, as to count for nothing that sacred blood by which the truth of our profession has been sealed, know that when about fifteen years ago one hundred or even more in France offered themselves to the most terrific death with no less alacrity than you sit spout-ing at your ease, there was not one who did not subscribe with us. Go now and set a higher price on your ink than on their blood.

More than two years ago, five persons were burnt at Lyons on one day, and that nothing might be wanting to the cruelty of the torture, they were consumed by a slow fire. Shortly after these, others followed in the same city, and two in neighbouring towns. Four months have not yet elapsed since at Chambery (a city not one day's journey from this) five were burnt together on one day. How skilfully they acquitted themselves in discussion is attested by documents written by their own hand, and I doubt not of equal authen-ticity with public records. Undoubtedly any one who reads them will not only acknowledge that they talked moderately and wisely of the leading articles of the faith, but also ad-mire their erudition, that none may say they were misled by ignorance or the fervour of rash zeal: and so intrepid

was the constancy which shone forth in their serene looks
till their last breath, that even the wretched Papists were
amazed. Their confession declared what all the godly under
the tyranny of Antichrist everywhere believe. Henceforth,
therefore, never pretend that they are your supporters.
They all with one consent repudiate your doctrine, and with
silent wishes abominate the intemperance of yourself and
your companions. This hot-headed man forces me to go
farther than I would. I take heaven and earth to witness
that I speak of a fact well ascertained. Where cruelty has
hitherto raged against numerous martyrs of Christ, the fire
in which they were consumed was heated as it were by blasts
from the mouths of those men whose greatest piety consists
in vociferating against the Sacramentarians.

As Westphal was debating with a Frenchman, he has
produced one of my countrymen to cover me with odium.
He says that we have revived the heresy of Berengarius.
If you hold him to be a heretic, why do you not take up your
banner and go over to the camp of the Pope? It is not indeed of much consequence where you settle, as you insinuate
yourself among the band of Antichrist. An hundred and
fourteen horned bishops, with Pope Nicolas for president, force
Berengarius to recant. You, without hesitation, give your
assent to their tyranny, as if they had justly condemned a
heresy. And what was the confession extorted from the
unhappy man? (De Conse. Distinct. 2 cap. Ego Berengarius.)
That after consecration, the true body and blood of Christ
is sensibly and in truth handled and broken by the hands
of the priests, and chewed by the teeth of the faithful. Such,
verbatim, are the terms of the form of recantation dictated
by the Council.

If Westphal cannot be appeased unless we confess that
Christ is sensibly chewed by the teeth, were not an hundred
deaths to be chosen sooner than implicate ourselves in such
monstrous sacrilege? The Canonists themselves were so
much ashamed of it, that they confessed there was a greater
heresy in the words, unless they referred to the species of
bread and wine, than in saying that the bread and wine are
bare signs. See why our Westphal behoved to borrow the

name of Berengarius to fill us with dismay. It is not strange that the new satellites of the Pope, who are ever and anon venting mere anathemas at us, lay hold at hazard of weapons from his tyrannical forge. This, no doubt, is the humanity with which these good fellow-soldiers hold me up to view, while I daily stand in the line of battle exposed to the first strokes of the enemy. It is not enough for Joachim to whet their rage against me by virulent calumnies. Trampling me under foot, because I presume freely to rebuke him, he brings a charge against me of extreme petulance, while regardless of the bad words which he sends forth, he acquits himself of the same charge—no doubt because any thing is lawful against a heretic. But as the only ground of his rage is, that the truth of my doctrine and faith is proof against his teeth, what weight does he hope to give to such a futile calumny?

If under this pretext he is so eager to obtain full license for his talk, let him openly symbolize with the Papists, with whom heretic is only another name for enemy of the Roman See. As to his declaring so disdainfully that we have been condemned by the Churches, when looked to more closely it comes, like his other sayings, to nothing; unless indeed he is to arm himself with the Council of Trent as a shield of Ajax, or confine the Churches of Christ to his companions who boil with the same impetuosity. For I always except grave and right-hearted teachers who, mingled with them, not only keep themselves calm, but though differing somewhat with us, decline not brotherly fellowship; because agreeing with us in the main, they willingly cherish and cultivate peace with us, and are most anxious for reconcilement among the Churches. Of their wish in this respect, should an occasion offer, I think they will give no obscure proof. Westphal, with all his importunity, will not prevail so far as to gain either their suffrage or assent to the accursed schism at which he aims, so far are they from giving their sanction to his wicked league to vex us by hostility. Nay, while he opposes to us all who subscribe the Confession of Augsburg, readers cannot soon fail to discover that this is mere pretence. Put the question to whoever may be the ablest defender of that Confession, and I doubt not he will answer that the peace is disturbed under evil auspices. This desire to maintain peace is not disguised by persons who deserve to have somewhat more authority in Saxony than an hundred Westphals.

When he enumerates the reasons which induced him to write, he says he was very anxious to defend his good name, lest the ministry he discharges should fall into contempt, and the credit of his writings be diminished. If a good name is dear to you, what evil genius impelled you to prostitute it, when by your silence you might have kept it safe and entire ? You have brought infamy upon yourself, which will not be so easily effaced, and you will increase it until you desist from your hateful love of quarrelling. I repeat, you could not have consulted better for yourself at first, and cannot even now, than by holding your peace. As to your anxiety lest the credit of your writing be lost, estimate from your feeling with regard to one, how much more grievously all the pious must be tortured when they see you making violent efforts to impair the credit of the valuable writings of so many great and excellent men.

Hold that I am not one of those whose credit you have attempted to impair. But while all see it to be your purpose completely to destroy the reputation of Œcolompadius, Zuinglius, Bucer, Peter Martyr, Bullinger, John a Lascus, do you think there is any pious and impartial man in the world who does not feel indignant at your malicious detraction ? What flattering applause your books receive from your own herd, I know not ; what do you yourself think of them ? You will not say that injustice is done you if I give the preference over you to every one of those whom I have mentioned. And yet if your foolish self-love so blinds you, that you are desirous to be higher in honour than those whom you follow far behind in learning, we who are not bound to you by any law, must pay greater regard to the public good.

The mention of books which you repeatedly introduce, implies that you scribble sometimes. Whatever it be, were it to perish the loss of the Church would be less than that of any one of the many books, all of which it was in your mind to destroy. Hence, even on your own showing, I have a good defence for interposing my credit and labour to prevent you from robbing the Church of her noble riches.

He divides his book into four chapters. First, he under-takes to refute my assertion, that we were wickedly and ignorantly traduced by him as contradicting each other in our writings ; secondly, he undertakes to refute my assertion, that we were unjustly censured by him, as leaving nothing but empty symbols in the Lord's Supper ; thirdly, he as-sumes that he is not exciting discord while opposing the authors of disturbance ; fourthly, he promises to reply to the charges made against him.

In the outset of the first part he charges me with proving our agreement from certain synonymous terms, as figure, sign, symbol: and he wonders that I do not gather as much out of the syllables. But what if here children can detect him in manifest falsehood. It never came into my mind to bring forward this affinity of words in proof of our agree-ment. But as he himself had calumniously attacked those words, nay, had said that we had proved ourselves to be heretics by this mark of contradiction, I simply laughed at the man's folly as it deserved. Now, however, as if he had escaped, he boasts that he makes a much more liberal con-cession, viz., that we agree not only in a few vocables, but in things and sentences. And to appear facetious, he says, that as they agree among themselves, he dignifies them all with the common name of Sacramentarians. His quibble is too gross to escape under this frivolous jactation.

He, with great asperity of language, traduced us as heretics for differing among ourselves. The demonstration seemed to him the very best. One calling the bread a symbol of the Supper, another calling it a figure, another a sign, made our disagreement most palpable; and to give his sophistry a more showy appearance, he exhibited it in a table. What could I do ? Was I to omit what is obvious to all before a word is said, viz., that our agreement could not have been better proved ? I will go farther, and say, that when at any time I would throw light on my doctrine, I will seek an explana-tion in these words. Will he pretend that I speak contra-dictions, or am contrary to myself, because I study to inter-pret one thing more conveniently by several methods ?

Coming to close quarters, I will press him harder. All

who expound the words of Christ otherwise than according
to the letter, as it is called, he hesitates not to style Sacramentarians. I am pleased with the terms: for in this way
Augustine is brought into our ranks. He wrote, in answer
to Faustus, that our Lord said, " This is my body," when
he was giving a sign of his body. Seeing he expounds the
words of Christ figuratively, he will no doubt be regarded as
a Sacramentarian. He elsewhere says, that on account of
their resemblance to the thing signified, the sacrament of
the body and blood are called the body and blood. Is not
this, according to Westphal, an abominable rending of the
words of Christ? He elsewhere writes, that our Lord, in
the Supper, committed and delivered the figure of his body
and blood to the disciples. Will he find two of us who differ
more from each other than Augustine does from himself?
It is vain, therefore, for Westphal to deny that he played
the fool when he held up an example of dreadful dissension
in the use of terms almost synonymous.

He denies the soundness of an argument drawn *a par-
ticulari,* as if we were agreed in every thing, because we
think and speak alike in some things. I deny that I ever
so argued : as it was sufficient to have simply refuted his
absurd delirium, that we were proved manifest heretics by a
single mark of disagreement, viz., one using the term figure,
another sign, another symbol. If he produce nothing more,
I conclude that there is no disagreement. As if he were
afraid that his impudence might not be visible enough, he
pursues the same idea at greater length, introducing me
as speaking thus : " I write mutual agreements with the
Zurichers ; our opinion is one ; we give our mutual labour :
at no time, therefore, was there ever any discrepancy among
the Sacramentarians." The whole of this, while it is a
naughty fiction, immediately involves him in another falsehood, viz., that he neither indicates persons nor time, but
speaks indefinitely of our differences. Trifler, where, then,
is that farrago extracted from our books, with the name of
each writer designated ?

He utters a fouler falsehood against us, which it is right
should fall back on its author's pate. Mixing us up with the

Anabaptists, Davidians, and almost all other fanatics,he forms them into one sect, like a hydra, because they all profess the dogma of Zuinglius. I will not say, what is amply attested by public documents, that none have been more strenuous than we in opposing sects, whether those he names, or any others that have sprung up in our age. But by what bands does he bind us all up into one bundle? Is it enough to say, in one word, that all are involved in one and the same error? Need I call angels to witness, when the very devils expose the dishonesty of Westphal? If sectaries be inquired after, it will be found that they approach nearer to himself. Servetus, who was both an Anabaptist and the worst of heretics, agreed entirely with Westphal; and on this article of doctrine annoyed Œcolompadius and Zuinglius with his writings, just as if he had hired himself out to Westphal.

The former method not having succeeded, he attempts to show our contradictions by another: and he premises, that as the same thing was attempted by Luther, it is lawful also for him. But whatever be the example under which he cloaks himself, we must look at the thing. The attempt to throw darkness on the subject by an imagination of Carlostadt, as it is evidently far-fetched, I labour not to refute. Although I know not whence he took his other interpretations, nothing can be more vile than such calumnies as these, that the context and the order of our Saviour's words are unbecomingly and violently wrested, because some one understands that the body of Christ is spiritual food, and another transposes it thus—This, which is delivered for you, is my body. What absurdity is there, pray, in a spiritual feast preceding, in order, a sacrifice of death?

But as these frivolous reasons also fail him, he has recourse, after his fashion, to fables, and relates that a preacher of approved faith wrote to him, that in Friesland the words of Christ are mutilated; for when the bread is held forth, the minister supplies these words: "Eat, believe, and call to mind that the body of our Lord, offered on the cross, is a true sacrifice for your sins." A great crime, no doubt, to celebrate the memory of Christ's death in the holy Supper. If the minister, in the very act of distribution, calls upon

the people to meditate on the benefit of Christ's death, is
the ordinance of Christ therefore passed by ? Nay, since
Westphal elsewhere contends that two things are distinctly
enjoined us—to eat the body, and cultivate the memory of
the death of Christ—why does he lash our brethren of Friesland merely for obeying the divine command ?

He next proceeds to say that this scheme originated with
Suenckfeldius, who ordered the words, " This is my body," to
be kept out of sight : as if we had any thing in common with
Suenckfeldius, or had to pay the penalty of his raving. Nay,
where is the fairness, that after we, while these little fathers
were asleep, diligently exerted ourselves in opposing the
errors of Suenckfeldius, they, who bore no part in the labour,
should suddenly awake and hurl at us every thing odious
which they find in our adversary ? Of the same nature is
his subsequent remark—that feeling offended because our
deceptions are put to shame by the clear words of Christ,
we throw them aside with contempt, and murmur that we
are objected to for only three words once spoken. Should
I here complain that odium is wickedly thrown upon me
by an invented slander, he will forthwith rejoin that he
speaks indefinitely. But where is the candour of bringing a
charge of blasphemy against an indefinite number of persons
without mentioning one of them as its author ? We do not
pay so little reverence to the words of our heavenly Master
as not to regard it as sufficient authority that any thing has
been once spoken by him. And to make it more apparent
that we have no need of such quibbles, I retort, that the
Ark of the Covenant is more than forty times called the presence of God, and yet in no other sense than that in which the
bread is called the body. You see, that so far from shunning
the light, we hesitate not to throw ourselves right in your way,
with this for our shield—that in Scripture the name of God
is everywhere transferred to the visible symbol of the presence of God. On this subject we have to treat more fully.

The contradictions against which he thundered being not yet
apparent, he begins to weave his web anew, saying, that the
words are violently wrested to different meanings, which are
not at all consistent with each other. And he again invidiously

brings forward the gloss of Carlostadt, which all of us long ago distinctly repudiated.   Afterwards, to deceive the eyes of the simple by a semblance of repugnance, he says that this absurd fiction is rejected by me: as if it were a tragical crime to throw off obloquy falsely cast upon us.   What would you have, you quarrelsome man ?   I have said that Carlostadt improperly interpreted the words of Christ.   In this you agree with me.   How, then, can you concoct a charge out of a repugnance which is common to me with yourself ?

He next attacks our venerable brother, John a Lascus, for saying that the whole action is denoted by the demonstrative pronoun : as if it were not easy to defend this by the suffrage of Luther.   According to Luther, the bread, exclusive of its use in the Supper, is nothing but bread, and, therefore, the pointing out of the material is included within the limits of the action.   Shall the same doctrine, then, be regarded as an oracle in the mouth of Luther, and be stigmatized as heresy if it come from any other quarter ?

In the fourth place, he inveighs against Œcolompadius, who understands the pronoun *which*, in the words of Christ, not relatively but causally: as if it were unlawful for an interpreter to explain in a simpler manner what otherwise gives unnecessary trouble.   Œcolompadius said that the body of Christ is not offered to believers to be eaten, inasmuch as it was once offered to expiate sins ; in other words, to acquaint us that the previous parts are attributed to the sacrifice.   Westphal now asks what will become of Matthew and Mark, by whom the relative pronoun is not added, as if that brevity was to take away the principal thing in the use of the Supper.

Paul, before exhorting us to feast, tells us that Christ our passover is sacrificed.   I confess, indeed, that in that passage he is not treating of the Supper ; but as the reason is the same, why should Westphal fall foul of a holy man for having wisely remarked this quality, without which the utility of the Supper is lost to us ?   This, forsooth, is the reason why, with inflated lungs, he exclaims—" In what colour will the Sacramentarians paint, with what gloss will they cover the manifest repugnance ?" I answer, that no man is so blind as not to see through your dreams.

As he sees that he has not yet gained what he wished, or at least not performed what he had professed, he heaps together certain mutilated expressions, and says—that the bread of the Supper is at one time called by us flesh ; at another time, the figure of the body ; at another, the passion ; at another, the death ; at another, the memorial of the passion ; at another, faith ; at another, the vigour ; at another, the virtue of Christ ; at another, the merits ; at another, the quality of the body ; at another, the action and form of the Supper : that it is likewise called the fellowship of the Church ; the right of partaking the body of Christ ; the festival ; and many other things besides. What can you make of this man, who, given over to a reprobate mind, sees not that he is venting things which render his malice universally detestable ? The brief and simple answer to all this is, that by different modes of speech, without any repugnance, a description is given of the end for which the bread is called body.

I agree with him, that the question chiefly relates to the meaning of the words of Christ—this is my body. I also agree with him, that in this controversy the thing asked is not what this or that man dreams, and that consciences are not satisfied by the fictions of men, but by showing them the clear and indubitable truth. When he requires some certain definition explaining wherein faith consists, I object not. Let this then be shown to us by these strict or rather morose censors, who disdain all interpretation.

They urge the literal sense, that the bread is truly and naturally the body of Christ. But when they in their turn are urged to say whether the body is properly bread, they temper their previous inflexible rigidity, and say that the body is given under the bread or with the bread. And certainly did they not concede this, the cup, of whatever material fabricated, would be the blood of Christ. Therefore, while they allow themselves to say that the body of Christ is contained by the bread as wine by a goblet, how comes it that a desire to discover a convenient interpreta--

tion so stirs up their bile ? When he says that in the words
a uniform style is observed by Paul, what can he gain by
the puerile falsehood ?   It is superfluous to observe how
much wider the difference is between *blood* and *covenant in
blood*, than between *sign* and *symbol*. But Westphal, who
is delighted with uniformity in *blood* and *covenant in blood*,
shows what a peculiar taste he has, by nauseating the disagreement between *sign* and *symbol*. Now, however, he begins to speak more cautiously, affirming that he blames difference not in words, but things and opinions. I, however,
feeling confident that readers of sense see clearly how he
distorts, mutilates, and obscures various modes of expression, which tend to demonstrate the use and end of the
Supper, no longer dwell upon it.

He adds, that overcome by the clear truth, I acknowledge
a contrariety in the things. But in what terms ? Just because I said, that one party, while they discuss an obscure
and intricate question, although they do not differ in fact,
present an appearance of difference.   Here is candour
worthy of a divine—candour which among profane rhetoricians would not escape being stigmatized as vile and frigid
quibbling. When he afterwards says, jestingly, that each of
them was inspired by a prophetical spirit when they first
entered on this subject, I leave him to enjoy his pertness
sooner than take up my time in refuting it.   When he next
asserts, that I look about for another evasion when I bring
forward what was only observed in passing, and seize upon
it as if it were a full explanation, it is obvious that he does
not quote, simply because he is aware that he would make
himself doubly ridiculous.   Is there any evasion, when, if
you believe him, I have imprudently submitted the thing to
the view of all ? Who does not see his malignity in mutilat-
ing sentences ? To omit the examples to which I lately referred, whom can he persuade that what was said of the
fellowship of the Church was intended for a full definition,
as if there were no other fellowship (κοινωνια) of the body
of Christ ? And yet in the tangled forest of our discord he
finds nothing more plausible than that κοινωνια is interpreted by some, the right of fellowship which has been given

us in the body of Christ, and by others, the mystical fellowship of the Church. Were I to carp in this way at the expressions of ancient writers, a far more serious difference
would be found among them. But my mind has no love for
it, and my will abhors to make ill-natured and illiberal attacks on every one whom he drags into his party.

Meanwhile, how dexterously and honestly he amplifies
the charge, thinking it would be productive of odium,
the reader must be briefly informed. His words are: As
often as they take up the passage in Paul, the Sacramentarians make the utmost efforts to corrupt his words. And he
inserts on the margin to draw attention, What, according
to Sacramentarians, is the κοινωνια of the body of Christ.
What ? Ought he not at least to have excepted those who
speak differently? Let him turn over my Commentaries, where
he will find not an intricate but a genuine interpretation,
which, let him do his utmost to the contrary, he will be forced
to receive. Nor do I affirm this of myself alone, for well-
informed readers are not ignorant that this passage has
been lucidly and fully handled by others whom he defames,
making it plain, that under an insatiable lust for quarrelling,
he is too eager in his hunt after endless materials for strife.
Certainly, when calling upon me by name, he ought not to
have forgotten what I have written on that passage.

My words are: It is true that believers are associated by
the blood of Christ so as to become one body ; it is true,
also, that this kind of unity is properly called κοινωνια. I
say the same thing of the bread. I hear also what Paul
adds, as if by way of explanation, that we who communicate
in the same bread are all made one body. And whence, I
ask, is that κοινωνια between us, but just that we are together made one with Christ, under the condition that we are
flesh of his flesh and bones of his bones ? For to be incor-
porated, so to speak, in Christ, we must first be made one
amongst ourselves. Add that Paul is now discoursing not
only of mutual communion among men, but of the spiritual
union of Christ and believers, in order thence to infer that
it is intolerable sacrilege for them to be mingled with idols.
From the whole connection of the passage, therefore, we may

infer that κοινωνια of the blood is the fellowship which we
have with the blood of Christ when he ingrafts us altogether
into his body, that he may live in us and we in him. I
admit that the mode of expression is figurative, provided
only that the reality of the figure be not taken away ; in
other words, provided the thing itself also be present, and
the soul receive the communion of the blood not less than
the mouth receives the wine.

After raging at will, he at length, in a short clause, admits
that the definition given by our people is not bad, when they
call it a distinguished memorial of purchased redemption,
but says that it explains only the half of it, not the whole :
as if heaven and earth were to be confounded whenever a
complete definition is not given. He allows us to use the
expression, that the unity of the Church is represented by
symbols ; but if ever he observes that any of our people has
so spoken, he gets into a passion, as if the body of Christ
were according to us nothing but the fellowship of the
Church, although they all with one consent declare that the
whole body is joined together by the head ; in other words,
that believers are formed into one body in no other way
than by being united with Christ. When he denies absolutely that the name *body* can be applied to the mystical
body of the Church, let him settle the matter with Paul, who
has ventured so to apply it.

From my having charged Westphal with senselessness for
having first condemned all tropes, and then found it impossible to disentangle himself without a trope, he beseeches
all his readers to attend and see what a grievous fault I have
committed. And not contented with simple objurgation, he
asks at himself, What fury drives me on to presume to launch
such a calumny at him ? Let the reader then attend and
see with what dexterity he wards off my javeline. I said,
I admit that there was as much consistency in the deliriums
of a frantic person, as in the two things, viz., saying that
the words of Christ are clear and need no interpretation,
and then admitting a trope, which, however, does not prevent the bread from being properly the body of Christ. He
answers, that he has indefinitely opposed a true trope, which

the nature of the passage rendered necessary to a false trope. As if I had lain in wait to catch him at fault in a single word, and had not rather made his gross error palpable.

He keeps ever crying that all are heretics who, in attempting to explain the words of Christ, differ from each other. He cannot get off without giving his own exposition, and yet he differs from us. What then follows, but just that he must be classed among heretics? If the body of Christ is given in the bread, and through the bread, and is received with the bread, it is clear that the bread is figuratively called the body, as containing the body in it, but is not naturally and properly that which it is said to be. I am aware how doggedly he sometimes insists on the words, maintaining that a clearer sentence is not to be found in Scripture. But when he comes to the point, he, along with his masters, admits of this exposition—that the body of Christ is contained under the bread, is held forth in the bread, and is received with the bread. For what could be more monstrous than to deny that the bread is a symbol of the body, and not distinguish the earthly sign from its heavenly mystery? The words cannot be taken in an absolutely literal sense without holding that the bread is converted into the body, so that the visible bread is the invisible body; without holding, in short, that the two propositions are equally literal—Christ is the beloved Son of God, and the bread is the body of Christ.

But there is no need to discuss the matter as if there were any doubt about it, when nothing is more common or more generally received among them than that the body of Christ is given under the bread. The Papists could better evade the necessity of a trope by their transubstantiation. How can he, who acknowledges that the bread and the body are different things, get rid of a figure in the words, This is my body? What? When the cup is called blood, are they not forward to explain that the thing containing is taken from the thing contained? I am not therefore playing the heroics in trifles when I say, I care not with whom it is that this frantic man, who so beautifully mauls himself, contends. This it was absolutely necessary to say, if I would not knowingly betray the cause. Let him learn henceforth not to trifle so in a serious matter.

I again freely repeat, that unless he can show that his trope is sanctioned by public consent, he, out of his own mouth, stands condemned of heresy, having boldly pronounced all without exception to be heretics who, in explaining the words of Christ, admit a figure. He artfully gets off by upbraiding me with wishing to appear facetious. See, Joachim, which of the two is fonder of facetiousness—I who, without any affectation, used that expression which was naturally suggested by the circumstances, or you who, without any wit, go far to seek your frigid buffoonery? But your triumph, that your trope was sanctioned by Christ and his Apostles, is not chanted by you before victory; for you cease not to applaud yourself for having already vanquished me and laid me prostrate. Your boast is, that you agree with Christ—a sure and invincible argument, if the fact is conceded to you. But on what principle do you assume it to be more in accordance with the words of Christ, to hold that the bread is called the body, because the body is given with it, than because it is a visible symbol of the body, and a symbol conjoined with its reality?

As you allege that Scripture is not tied down to the laws of logicians or grammarians, which we willingly grant you, I will ask, with what conscience, or even with what face, you, in the same page, charge us with contradiction, because in the words of Christ some of us say there is a synecdoche, others a metaphor, others a metonymy; for if all these figures are alike respectful, every man should be left to his freedom. But as Joachim concludes, that though our people agree in defending their doctrine, and there is some consonance in their words, they yet write contradictorily, I, in my turn, am at liberty to conclude from clear demonstration, that he acts neither honestly nor ingenuously, when, from an insatiable love of contention, he, for the purpose of making out a difference, fastens upon things which could very easily be reconciled, wrests much in a calumnious spirit from its true meaning, and converts every slight variation into a serious disagreement: that in endeavouring as far as he can

to darken and mystify our Agreement, in which all differences are buried, he is the enemy of peace and concord:
and that it is mere impudence which makes him bring into
the arena of conflict men who have explained this article of
doctrine in the same words with greater consent than has
hitherto been done by any out of the herd of those whom
he opposes to us as enemies.

I come now to the second part, in which he endeavours
to clear himself from the charge of having uttered a calumny, in saying that we leave nothing in the sacraments
but empty signs. Here there is an opportunity of seeing
how stupidly obstinate he is. We uniformly testify in our
writings, that the sacraments which the Lord has left us as
seals and testimonies of his grace, differ widely from empty
figures. Our Agreement distinctly declares, that the Lord,
who is true, performs inwardly by his Spirit that which the
sacraments figure to the eye, and that when we distinguish
between the signs and the thing signified, we do not disjoin
the reality from the signs. This view is followed out more
clearly and fully in my Defence.

The substance, however, is, that Christ is truly offered to
us by the sacraments, in order that being made partakers of
him, we may obtain possession of all his blessings ; in short,
in order that he may live in us and we in him. Does not
he who, on the other hand, keeps crying out that we convert them into empty signs, plainly reduce Christ and all
his virtue to nothing ? For if Christ is any thing, and any
value is set on his spiritual riches, the pledge by which he
communicates himself to us must not be called empty and
void. Should I now rejoin, as I am perfectly entitled to
do, that Christ is nothing at all to Westphal, he would complain of grievous injustice being done him. And not to
waste more words in debate, let him simply tell me, if he
contends that signs which carry with them the true fruition
of Christ are empty, what value he puts upon Christ ? If a
complete fulness of spiritual blessings does not make the
signs to contain something real and solid, is not the virtue
of the Holy Spirit, according to him, evanescent ? What
impostures can he employ so as to prevent this execrable

blasphemy from becoming instantly apparent ?   His attempt
to obscure the light, by covering it over, is mere childishness.

He says that tropes have been discovered even in the word
is and the term *body*, in order to prove the absence of Christ.
But according to us, the bread means body in such a sense,
that it effectually and in reality invites us to communion
with Christ. For we say that the reality which the promise
contains is there exhibited, and that the effect is annexed
to the external symbol. The trope, therefore, by no means
makes void the sign, but rather shows how it is not void.
No more does the absence of a local body make void the
sign, because Christ ceases not to offer himself to be enjoyed by his faithful followers, though he descend not to the
earth.

In vain does he endeavour to find a subterfuge in my acknowledgment, that Œcolompadius and Zuinglius, at the
commencement of the dispute, from being too intent on refuting superstition, did not speak of the sacraments in sufficiently honourable terms, and discourse of their effect, and
that the churches were now to be distinctly informed how
far, and in what things agreement has been made. We
stated the matter articulately, in order that no part of the
controversy might be omitted. A clearer and fuller exposition was added afterwards. What else then is this but to
remain blind in light, which even the blind may see ? Will
he here again tell me that I have a two-edged sword ;
that if he produces clear passages, I accuse him of uttering
contradictions ; and if he omits them, charge him with
perfidy ? I was perfectly entitled to charge him with perfidy, for having laid hold of mutilated passages, to make
them the ground of a calumnious charge ; and I showed at
the same time, that his absurdity could not be better established than by the passages which he had quoted, and
which would remove every ground of suspicion.

In one place he takes away the half of a sentence, and
picks a quarrel with us as to the other half. I refer my
readers to the book ; an inspection of it detects and proves
the malice of Joachim. While the passages produced by
him clear us from his calumnies, why should I disguise that

in other passages he is at war with himself? There is
no reason, therefore, why he should upbraid me with having
a two-edged sword, seeing he cuts his wretched self in two,
and furnishes me with two swords whose edge he would fain
have taken off by his blunt dilemma. Assuredly though no
blow should be struck by me, he is proved to have been every
way a calumniator, when seeking to bring groundless obloquy
upon us, he alleged that we left nothing in the sacraments
but bare and empty signs.

If he has any thing in common with Luther, he thinks he
has in his authority a complete exculpation from the charge.
He says then, that Luther wrote that all who refuse to believe that the true and natural body of Christ is in the
sacred Supper, are ranked by him in the same place. Luther
was too imperious in this, not deigning to distinguish between opinions most remote from each other, and confounding them contrary to their nature. This passage amply
proves that I did not speak rashly in saying that Luther,
inflamed by false informers, pleaded this matter too vehemently. Who does not see that he would have laid more
restraint upon himself had he not been urged to this extravagance by a foreign impulse? Westphal certainly pays little
honour to Luther, and would have others pay little, by denying him the slight degree of judgment necessary to distinguish between an empty and imaginary phantom, and a
spiritual partaking of Christ. We assert that in the sacred
Supper we are truly made partakers of Christ, so that by the
sacred agency of the Spirit, he instils life into our souls from
his flesh. Thus the bread is not the empty picture of an absent
thing, but a true and faithful pledge of our union with Christ.

Some one will say, that the symbol of bread does not
shadow forth the body of Christ any otherwise than a lifeless statue represents Hercules or Mercury. This fiction is
certainly not less remote from our doctrine than profane is
from sacred. Does not he, then, who, pulling us from our
place, precipitates us into the same condemnation, destroy
the distinctions of things, as if by shutting his eyes he could
pluck the sun from the sky?

Though I said that we comprehended in our Agreement

what the Confession of Augsburg contains, there is no ground for charging me with deceit ; for I subscribe to the words which I there quoted. As to their meaning, since Westphal is no competent judge, to whom can I better appeal than to the author himself? If he declares that I deviate in the smallest from his idea, I will immediately submit. The case is different with Luther. I have always candidly declared what I felt wanting in his words, so far am I from having bound myself to them. I care not for the great delicacy of Westphal, who seems to think it an intolerable affront to Luther to say, that in the dispute he was carried beyond just bounds. He asks, Do you call the servant of God contentious ? I do not ; but as it happens even to the most moderate men to exceed the proper limit in debate, if I deplore this in Luther, whose vehemence is known to all, there is nothing strange in it. Westphal is sorry without cause, that I attempted a fallacious reconciliation between Luther and Zuinglius, when I wished to bury their un-happy conflicts. Granting that their views were repugnant, what forbids us, warned by their example, both to weigh the matter in calm temper and deliver the sound doctrine in a more temperate style? Westphal, who will not hear of this, only gives readers of sense a proof of his sour rigidity.

He infers that if I still continue in the belief which I professed about twenty years ago, there is nothing I less believe than that the body of Christ is given substantially in the Supper. Though I confess that our souls are truly fed by the substance of Christ's flesh, I certainly do this day, not less than formerly, repudiate the substantial pre-sence which Westphal imagines : for though the flesh of Christ gives us life, it does not follow that his substance must be transferred into us. This fiction of transfusion being taken out of the way, it never came into my mind to raise a debate about the term substance. Nor will I ever hesitate to acknowledge that, by the secret virtue of the Holy Spirit, life is infused into us from the substance of his flesh, which not without reason is called heavenly food.

In constantly affirming this, my simplicity was always too great for your calumnies to have the least effect in obscur-

ing its light or destroying its credit. I said that the body
of Christ is exhibited in the Supper effectually, not naturally,
—in respect of virtue, not in respect of substance. In this
last term I referred to a local infusion of substance. At the
same time, however, I said that Christ does not communicate
his blessings to us except in so far as he is himself ours.
In this doctrine I still persist, and therefore Westphal is no
less ignorant than unjust in comparing me to an eel. What
does he find dubious or equivocating in the doctrine, that the
body of Christ is truly spiritual food, by whose substance
our souls are fed and live, and that this is fulfilled to us in
the Supper not less really than it is figured by the external
symbols ? Only let no one falsely imagine that the body is
as it were brought down from heaven and inclosed in the
bread. This exception offends Westphal, and he exclaims
that I am an eel which cannot be held by the tail.

He says that I was more guarded in my Commentaries,
and tempered my colours so that some, though not stupid
or obtuse, could scarcely divine what I meant. As to my
desire, this much I sacredly declare, that while I most religiously endeavoured to deliver divine truth purely and
sincerely, it was no less my care to express myself in a manner distinguished by its simplicity and perspicuity. What
I gained by my diligence is declared by the books themselves, which he pretends to have been more acceptable from
my seeming to be of the same sentiments with his party ;
whereas now since the Agreement has brought me forth
from my lurking-places into the light, they have fallen into
disrepute. What favour my Commentaries acquired with
Westphal and his fellows, and what the Agreement has cost
them, I know not. But what if it can be properly shown
that every article which he censures in the Agreement was
taken from my Commentaries, or stands there in almost as
many words ? Whence this new alienation ? What he aims
at no man is so dull as not to scent. Indeed, in another
place he does not disguise that he is aiming with his fellows
to exterminate my books in all quarters. With what fairness, let themselves see ; since it is not probable that they
were acceptable to pious readers without being fit and useful

for the edification of the Church.   I believe that honest men, and men of sound judgment who have experienced this, will not be so fastidious, as for one article to deprive themselves of the benefit of manifold instruction.

How beautifully consistent he is, let the reader judge from two of his sentences.   He says, that in writing my Defence I had again recourse to subterfuges, that I might walk about incognito, covered by a cloud ; while, in the next page, he declares it unnecessary to furnish proofs to convict me of holding different sentiments, because the Defence alone supplies them in abundance.   Where, then, is the cloud in which I wished to be shrouded ?   He says, that I am not so concealed by my disguises as not to betray myself. Had I been attempting any thing fraudulent, a slight degree of caution might have enabled me to be on my guard. But the reader will find that nothing has been my greater care than, in absence of all ambiguity, to deliver distinctly what I daily profess and teach in the Church, and what God is my best witness and judge that I sincerely believe.   Westphal having divided whatever he deemed deserving of censure, or at least wished to carp at, into nine heads, I will follow the same order.

FIRST, Because I say, that Christ dwelling in us raises us to himself, and transfuses the life-giving vigour of his flesh into us, just as we are invigorated by the vital warmth of the rays of the sun ; and again, that Christ, while remaining in heaven, descends to us by his virtue, he charges me with overturning the faith of the Church, as if I were denying that Christ gives us his body.   But when I say that Christ descends to us by his virtue, I deny that I am substituting something different, which is to have the effect of abolishing the gift of the body, for I am simply explaining the mode in which it is given.   He rejoins, that I am deceiving by using the term body in an ambiguous sense.   But I thought I had sufficiently obviated such cavils by so often repeating, that it was the true and natural body which was offered on the cross.   From what forge the fiction of a twofold body proceeded, I know not : this I know, that I hold it detestable impiety to imagine Christ with two bodies.   I know, indeed, that the mortal body which Christ once assumed is now endued with new qualities of celestial glory, which, however, do not prevent it from being in substance the same body. I say, then, that by that body which hung on the cross our souls are invigorated with spiritual life, just as our bodies are nourished by earthly bread. But as distance of place seems to be an obstacle, preventing the virtue of Christ's flesh from reaching us, I explain the difficulty by saying, that Christ, without changing place, descends to us by his virtue. Is it to use subterfuge, when I simply define the mode of that eating which others mystify by a perplexed mode of teaching it ?

Westphal insists that the body of Christ is given in the Supper to be eaten, and thinks it impious to inquire into the mode. Should any one object that, according to Peter, Christ is contained in heaven until he appear to judge the world, he does not admit the clear evidence of Scripture. I again, leaving Christ in his heavenly seat, am contented to be fed with his flesh by the secret influence of his Spirit. Which of the two is it that sports in tortuous courses ? But when I inculcate that the reality is conjoined with the signs, I mean the virtue of the sacrament, not the substance of the flesh. Granting it to be so, still it will not be a bare sign if it is not devoid of virtue and effect. But from what does he infer, that I take away the substance of the flesh ? Just because I say, that so far as spiritual effect goes, we become partakers of the body of Christ not less truly than we eat bread. For he infers that I manifestly deny the presence of the substance of the body, if the body is only exhibited, inasmuch as its spiritual virtue is exerted on believers.

If he is contending for a local presence, I assuredly confess that I abhor that gross fiction. For I hold that Christ is not present in the Supper in any other way than this—because the minds of believers (this being an heavenly act) are raised by faith above the world, and Christ, by the agency of his Spirit, removing the obstacle which distance of space might occasion, conjoins us with his members. Westphal objects that the merits or benefits of Christ are not his body.

But why does he maliciously extenuate the force of an expression by which I highly extol our communion with Christ? For I not only say that his merits are applied, but that our souls receive nourishment from the very body of Christ in the same way as the body eats earthly bread. In adding the proviso, "as far as spiritual effect goes," my object is to prevent any one from dreaming that Christ cannot be offered to us in the Supper without being locally enclosed. He is offended at my opposing a real to an imaginary communion. What more, then, does he ask? That I should oppose it to one in figure. This I might easily grant, provided he would not deny what ought to be known to all pious men as one of the first elements of the faith—that the bread is a sign or figure of the body. Provided there is agreement as to this, I now again confirm what I have hitherto professed, that as the thing itself is present, a bare figure is not to be imagined. That Bucer, of blessed memory, took the same view, I can easily prove by clear evidence.

Though I have classed among opinions to be rejected the idea that the body of Christ is really and substantially present in the Supper, this is not at all repugnant to a true and real communion, which consists in our ascent to heaven, and requires no other descent in Christ than that of spiritual grace. It is not necessary for him to move his body from its place in order to infuse his vivifying virtue into us. Wishing to point out the difference between the two modes of presence, he calls the former *physical*, and stammers as to the other, merely saying that the presence of the body is asserted by his party. But a division is vicious when the members coincide with each other. Westphal insists on the presence of the flesh of Christ in the Supper: we do not deny it, provided he will rise upwards with us by faith. But if he means, that Christ is placed there in a corporeal manner, let him seek other supporters.

We do not shelter ourselves under the ambiguity of the term *physical*, for we object no less decidedly to a fictitious ubiquity than to a mathematical circumscription under the bread. Westphal will deny that he imagines a physical presence of Christ, because he does not include the body

lineally under the bread. I rejoin, that he does no less erroneously when assigning an immense body to Christ, he contends that it is present wherever the Supper is celebrated.
For to say that the body which the Son of God once assumed, and which, after being once crucified, he raised to
heavenly glory, is ατοπος, (without place,) is indeed very
ατοπος, (absurd.) What he afterwards triflingly says about
a spiritual body, he falsely and without colour applies to
us. Let him with his band dream as they will of a spiritual
body, which has no affinity with a real body, I deem it unlawful to think or speak of any other body than that which
was offered on the cross to expiate the sins of the world, and
has been received into heaven. If Westphal cannot, without
indignation, hear of that body as spiritual nourishment, who
can labour to appease him? He says, that it is fallaciously
opposed to the presence and reception of a true body. I
rejoin, that if he is not craftily glossing the matter, he is
under a gross delusion, as the controversy with us is not as
to reception, but only the mode of reception.

He conceives that there is no bodily presence if the body
lurk not everywhere diffused under the bread; and if believers do not swallow the body, he thinks that they are denied the eating of it. We teach that Christ is to be sought
by faith, that he may manifest his presence; and the mode
of eating which we hold is, that by the gift of his Spirit he
transfuses into us the vivifying influence of his flesh. This
is not to bring down the mysteries of faith to carnal sense, or
measure them by natural reason, as Westphal falsely pretends,
but is to make the sacred ordinance of the Supper conformable to the rule of faith. Westphal objects, that whatever is
done according to the word of God and faith is done spiritually,
without considering that the word of God itself prescribes to
us how we are to behave in regard to spiritual ordinances.

Of old the fathers were commanded to prostrate themselves before the ark of the covenant, and there worship God.
I ask, if it would have been sufficient to fasten upon the
mere word, and pay no regard to the kind of worship. Gross
and brutish men, as a pretext for superstition, might easily
have alleged, that as they were obeying the precept of the

law, they were worshipping God spiritually. But the servants of God were prepared with the answer, that they, by blindly and absurdly wresting the word of God, were feeling and acting carnally. Wherefore if Westphal would prove himself spiritual, let him cease to insist on his own sense, with which, when a man is fascinated, he will never come to the proper end. Whom can he persuade that we treat the holy Supper carnally, by wresting the Scriptures contrary to the word and to faith ? I confess, if it were conceded to him that the bread is the body of Christ, but not a symbol, all err from the faith who say that the body is represented under the symbol of bread. But in order to wrest the word from us, he wildly tears up the first elements of piety. He says, that all we preach about spiritual eating, goes to aggravate our crime, because, according to him, it shamefully sports with Christ's little ones. Our exposition is, that the flesh of Christ is spiritually eaten by us, because he vivifies our souls in the very manner in which our bodies are invigorated by food : only we exclude a transfusion of substance. According to Westphal, the flesh of Christ is not vivifying unless its substance is devoured. Our crime then is, that we do not open our arms to the embrace of such a monster.

His SECOND HEAD is, That the presence and taking of the body and blood, is made by me to consist in the spiritual fruition of Christ, so that eating the flesh and drinking the blood is nothing else than believing in Christ. And yet my writings everywhere proclaim, that eating differs from faith, inasmuch as it is an effect of faith. I did not begin only three days ago, to say that we eat Christ by believing, because being made truly partakers of him, we grow up into one body, and have a common life with him. Years have now elapsed since I began, and have never ceased to repeat this. How base then was it in Westphal, while my words distinctly declare that eating is something else than believing, impudently to obtrude, what I strenuously deny, upon his readers, as if it had been actually uttered by me ? The reason, no doubt, is, that in his eagerness to misrepresent me, he would rather be detected in falsehood than not do something to excite prejudice against me. This vile fiction he cloaks by saying, that according to me the body of Christ is eaten by us in the present day in no other manner than it anciently was by the Fathers, as all communicate with Christ and enjoy him. Therefore, according to me, to eat the flesh of Christ is nothing else than to believe. Perhaps he thinks that fruition and communion are to go for nothing.

Desiring to throw obloquy upon me, he now, with the same sincerity, substitutes looking in the room of fruition, as if I taught that Christ is eaten in no other way than when faith looks to him as having died for us. Why should I now attempt to refute this calumny, from which an hundred passages in my books are my vindicators? But since Westphal more than acquits me in the same page, I will not go farther for my defence: for he quotes my words, that the spiritual mode of communion consists in our really enjoying Christ; that the bread is a symbol of Christ's body; so that those who receive the sign by the mouth, and the promise by faith, are truly made partakers of Christ. Does he, by these words, prove it to be my doctrine, that the fruition of Christ is nothing else than the look of faith? Here, then, the reader perceives by what glosses he obscures my doctrine, or rather, how he manifests his own impurity, and employs it in foully bespattering the clearest truth.

Of the same nature is his next assertion, that if my words are taken, to eat the body of Christ is equivalent to receiving the promise by faith. But how dare he so prostitute himself? Taking himself as witness, I distinctly affirm, that those who receive the promise by faith, become truly partakers of Christ, and are fed by his flesh. Therefore, the eating of Christ is something else than the receiving of the promise, if indeed he admits that the cause differs from its effect. For who will not infer from my words, that it is the incomparable fruit of faith to make the flesh of Christ spiritual aliment to us? Lest any one should think that the promise by which the body of Christ is offered to us is without efficacy, I deny that any who receive the promise by faith go away from the Supper empty and void, for they truly enjoy Christ who was once offered. How will he invert the thing, so as to make readers who have eyes believe that I

deny what I distinctly affirm?   When he imputes it to me
as a crime, that I teach that nothing is received by the
mouth but the sign, I am so far from refusing to take it so,
that I am willing that the whole controversy shall be decided on these terms.   The ground of Westphal's quarrel
with me is revealed and laid open by this one word ; for he
acknowledges none as brethren but those who come with
mouth and stomach to devour Christ.   I deny not, indeed,
that those who exclude the substance of vivifying flesh and
blood from the communion, defraud themselves of the use of
the Supper.   I only object, that things devised by Westphal's
own brain are made a ground of charge against us.   For although we bring not down the substance of Christ's body
from heaven to give us life, yet we are far from excluding
it from the Supper, as we testify that from it life flows
into us.

His THIRD HEAD is, That I deny the true presence of the
body and blood when I infer the absence of Christ in respect
of body.   My readers will pardon me for being forced to go over
the same ground so often in refuting the prattle of this man.
How distance of place does not prevent Christ from being
present with his people in the Supper, I formerly considered.
The principle I always hold is, that in order to gain possession
of Christ, he must be sought in heaven, not only that we
may not have any earthly imagination concerning him, but
because the body in which the Redeemer appeared to the
world, and which he once offered in sacrifice, must now be
contained in heaven, as Peter declares.   I acknowledge,
however, that by the virtue of his Spirit and his own divine
essence, he not only fills heaven and earth, but also miraculously unites us with himself in one body, so that that flesh,
although it remain in heaven, is our food.   Thus I teach
that Christ, though absent in body, is nevertheless not only
present with us by his divine energy, which is everywhere
diffused, but also makes his flesh give life to us.   For seeing he penetrates to us by the secret influence of his Spirit,
it is not necessary, as we have elsewhere said, that he should
descend bodily.

Westphal here exclaims that I am opposing the presence

of the Spirit to the presence of the flesh ; but any one not
blinded by malevolence sees that the same passage makes it
clearly evident how far I do so.   For I do not simply teach
that Christ dwells in us by his Spirit, but that he so raises
us to himself as to transfuse the vivifying vigour of his flesh
into us.   Does not this assert a species of presence, viz., that
our souls draw life from the flesh of Christ, although, in
regard to space, it is far distant from us ?   Westphal cannot
bear to hear it said that Christ, while wholly remaining in
heaven, descends to us by his virtue.   His reason is, that
the Church believes that wherever the Supper is celebrated
his body is present.   Provided he hold the mode of presence
which I explained, I object not to this view.   But if he insists on bringing Christ down from heaven, as Numa Pom-
pilius did his Jupiter, he is the Church to himself.   When
he admits that Christ is not now conversant on the earth as
he was in the time of his public ministry, what does it imply
but just that he supposes him still to dwell on earth, though
invisibly ?   When Scripture speaks of the ascension of Christ,
it declares, at the same time, that he will come again.   If
he now occupies the whole world in respect of his body, what
else was his ascension, and what will his descent be, but a
fallacious and empty show ?   If he is so near us in respect
of body, was it not absurd that the heavens should be opened
to let Stephen see him sitting in his glory ?

I know how they are wont to quibble, that by the term
heaven nothing more is meant than his boundless glory.
But if he was expressly taken up from the earth, and a cloud
was interposed, in order that pious minds might rise upwards, it is absurd to introduce an invisible habitation,
which, preventing the ascent of faith, causes us to rest on
the earth.   Westphal must therefore have done with his pretended judgment of the Church, making it a deviation from
sound faith not to admit that Christ is bodily present in the
Supper.   No man will place such an one as he on the throne
of judgment, and thereby eject Augustine from the Church.
For Augustine clearly affirms with us, (in Joann. Tract. 50,)
that " Christ, in respect of the presence of his majesty, is
always present with believers, but that in respect of the

presence of his flesh, it was rightly said to the disciples, 'Me ye have not always.'" And lest the term flesh should be captiously laid hold of as a subterfuge, he more fully explains it to be his meaning that Christ has taken his crucified body to heaven, and therefore it does not continue with us. Westphal, on the other hand, objects that we separate the Church, the Word, and the Sacraments, from the Spirit of Christ dwelling in us. Let him then quit the Church, whose faith he professes in my words. He has said, more than an hundred times, that the Supper is the sacred bond of our union with Christ. In defending our Agreement, I openly maintain that Christ effectually uses this instrument, in order to dwell in us. While Westphal borrows my words to expound the faith of the Church, he at least gives me some place in the Church. What new asylum, then, will he seek for himself? For who will consent to his fiction in regard to a gross partaking of the body? We, too, admit as well as he, that Christ denies his Spirit to all who reject the participation of his flesh. The only question between us here is, whether or not the partaking of the Spirit is carnal?

In the FOURTH HEAD, Westphal plainly lets out that he acknowledges none but a carnal presence of the flesh. Let him have done, then, with those bad names which he employs to darken the cause. At the outset I am called a Sacramentarian. I am said to defame those who hold that the true flesh of Christ is distributed in the Supper: as if I did not uniformly declare, in distinct terms, that nourishment from the true flesh of Christ is set before us in the Supper. What, then, does he gain by employing the mists of lies to darken the light which clearly removes all difficulty from the case? If any sincerely and distinctly teach that the flesh of Christ is set before us to be eaten by us, I, too, am of the number: I only explain the manner, viz., that Christ overcomes the distance of space by employing the agency of his Spirit to inspire life into us from his flesh. Which of the two speaks and thinks more honourably of Christ—I, who surmount all impediments by faith, or Westphal, to whom the flesh of Christ gives no life, if it be not

introduced into his mouth and stomach ? There is nothing
to perplex in my statement. If he insists that the flesh
of Christ is distributed, I assent ; and when the question
relates to the mode, I set it before the eye, while he involves
it in ambiguity. If my readers bear this in mind, Westphal
will henceforth gain nothing by falsely pretending that our
quarrel is about the partaking of the flesh of Christ. He
could not say this through ignorance, after being so carefully
warned by me. Merely to make the ignorant think he was
gaining a victory, he, without any reverence or modesty, has
tried to darken what is clear as day.

Equally paltry is the figment he subjoins, that we do not
think the real body can be given to us unless we see and handle
the flesh and the bones. Nay, rather, instead of dragging
the body down from heaven, we believe that it is given to
us so as to nourish and invigorate our souls unto spiritual
life. Thus, when he introduces his objection, that we, in
explaining the mode, measure the mystery of the Supper by
geometrical reasons, it is obvious and easy to answer, that it
is clear, on his own showing, that we rather hang on the lips
of Christ, since he is perpetually crying that we wrest our
Saviour's words, Handle and see : a Spirit has not flesh
and bones. What are we to think of the body of Christ, but
just what he himself says of it ? We do not call in the aid of
Euclid to assist us, but acquiesce in the declaration of the
Son of God, from whom we can best learn what the nature
of his body is. Westphal, feeling it impossible to twist this
in any way, has recourse to a most perverse fiction, viz., that
Christ spoke thus to prove the truth of his resurrection, but
that the object of the Supper is different. My answer is,
that though the Lord instituted the Supper for a different
purpose, yet his declaration concerning the nature of his
body always remains true.

To take off the apparent absurdity of teaching that the
body is everywhere invisibly present—the very body which
we know to have been enclosed in the Virgin's womb, suspended on the cross, and laid in the sepulchre—they tell us,
that the immensity of which they speak is competent to a
heavenly and glorious body. Our answer is obvious, that

the body was glorious at the time when our Saviour gave it
to the disciples to be felt and seen. This answer is certainly
relevant, and there is therefore no ground for what Westphal
trumpets forth with regard to a conflict between theology
and philosophy. For it is not philosophy that dictates to us
either that human flesh is endued with spiritual virtue, so
as to give life to our souls, or that this life breathes from
heaven, or that we gain effectual possession of the same life
under the external symbol of bread. Nothing of this kind
lies within the reach of common sense, or can come forth
from schools of philosophy. Hence it appears how careful
we are to extol the mystery of the Supper, as transcending
the reach of human intellect.

But Westphal introduces the Author of nature as speaking on the opposite side. And what does he say? That he
gives his body. Let our antagonist himself then come forth
and overturn the belief of this promise which we reverently
embrace. For although our eyes see nothing but bread and
wine, yet by faith we apprehend the life which, emanating
from the flesh and blood of Christ, penetrates even to our
souls. He orders us by the mouth of Christ to answer,
whether credit is to be given to carnal reason or to the Son
of God? I would rather perish an hundred times than put
one little word of Christ into the balance, and counterweigh
it by the whole body of philosophy, as Westphal demands.
We hold the authority of Christ not only sacred and complete in itself, (αυτοπιστος,) but amply sufficient to subdue
all the wisdom of the world. The question to be decided is
very different. It is, whether credit is to be given to the
heavenly oracles which declare that we are to hope for a
resurrection which shall make our mean and corruptible body
like unto the glorious body of Christ—that the Son of man
shall come on the clouds of heaven to judge the world—that
Jesus of Nazareth, after ascending to heaven, will come in
like manner as he was seen to ascend?

Let Westphal say whether he thinks that anybody will be
immense at the last day. For when Paul asks us to form an
estimate of the power of Christ from the fact of his trans-
forming our bodies into the same glory, either that power is

reduced to nothing, or we must believe that the body of Christ is not more immense now than ours will then be. Our inference drawn from what Scripture says concerning the ascent of Christ to heaven and his second advent, Westphal confidently derides, as if the body of Christ, which was taken up to heaven in visible shape, for the sake of proving the resurrection, had afterwards laid aside its form and dimension. But the angels speak of its remaining in the same state from its ascension until the last day.

He ultimately tries to evade us by a silly quibble. He says that our physical notion is at variance with Paul's, when he declares that Christ ascended above all heavens. What? Do we place Christ midway among the spheres? or do we build a cottage for him among the planets? Heaven we regard as the magnificent palace of God, far outstripping all this world's fabric. Westphal makes a great talk about our making Christ dwell without having any locality: as if we had not taken care to obviate this quibble. Our reason for denying that Christ is concealed under the bread is, not because he is not properly inclosed by place, but because superior to all elements he dwells beyond the world. He rejoins, that it is not more contradictory of physical ideas to hold that the body is in several places, than that it is contained by no place. I again repeat that we have no dispute about physical ideas, but only contend for the reality of the body as asserted by Scripture. Though the body carried above the heavens is exempt from the common order of nature, it does not however cease to be a true body : though deprived of earthly qualities, it still retains its proper substance. Unjustly, therefore, does Westphal charge us with leaning more on the dictates of philosophy than on the word of God. I in my turn admonish him to lay aside his petulance, and allow himself to be instructed in the genuine meaning of the word of God. If he will not, I must leave him and the phantom which he absurdly discovers in the words of Christ.

The FIFTH HEAD relates to the transfusion of substance, where, after his manner, he begins with stating that I regard the faith of the Church as a dream. I wonder why he had

not at least learned from Luther, whom he always pretends
to be his master, to use the name of the Church more sparingly and modestly; for I have never yet seen any Papist
use it more wantonly and with more unbridled audacity.
I ask, not indignantly but on the strongest reason, whether
we ought to dream that the substance of Christ is transfused
into us and thereby defiled by our impurities? This rare
orator, who without any colour talks of my rage, flames out
as if I were imputing my own dreams to him. I have no
wish to throw such grave suspicion either on him individually
or on his party; my purpose being rather to dispose of the
suspicion implied in his vague words. And I will now show
by my example how much better it is civilly to embrace
what is rightly said, than, as he is wont, to reject it disdainfully and in the slump.

Laying aside contention, then, I willingly take what he
grants me, viz., that the flesh of Christ is neither transfused
into us, nor placed in the bread, nor conjoined with the
bread. As far as I am concerned, he shall hear no more of
those forms of expression, which he complains to have been
falsely devised by us to distort the contrary dogma. I wish
that the modesty and sobriety which he pretends were apparent in their books, in which nothing else is thought of than
the urging of their fiction, that the body of Christ is in the
bread. However, I make it perfectly free for Westphal to
give utterance to his convictions in whatever terms he
pleases. He says, it is enough for him that the wisdom of
the Eternal Father declares, that the body is given, that the
body is actually present in the Supper; but as to the mode
of presence, seeing it is incomprehensible, he does not inquire. My sure and simple defence is, that to the giving of
the body, its presence is not at all requisite: for as I have
already explained, the obstacle arising from distance of space
is surmounted by the boundless energy of the Spirit. We
both acknowledge that the body is given; but I hold that a
bodily presence is thence erroneously inferred. Still I deny
not that there is a mystery, surpassing human comprehension, in the fact, that Christ in heaven feeds us on earth
with his flesh, provided he refuse not to obviate the absur-

dities which he carelessly passes by with his eyes shut
What can be more tyrannical than to urge the presence in
a single word, and then make it unlawful to inquire into it
farther; to send forth monosyllables as edicts, and then en-
slave every mind, as well as stop every mouth?

Westphal says, that our talk about the mixture of Christ's
substance with our own is supposititious. Let him, therefore,
explain how the bread which is eaten by the mouth is the
body of Christ. He refuses, nay, pronounces wo on those
who presume to inquire. Such is his magisterial theology.
With the same imperiousness, he declares it to be my custom to hold all as dreamers who believe that the true body
of Christ is given. If he allow us to discuss the matter ra-
tionally with him, how will he prove the existence of a custom which is nowhere to be found in my writings? In another place, though he mentions my assertion, that the bread
of the Supper is not a bare figure, but is conjoined with its
reality and substance, he still contends that I deny all substance in the Supper. In what sense he here uses the
term substance, I know not, and do not much care. Let
it suffice to remind my readers, that Christ is uniformly
called by me the substance of baptism and of the Supper.
And that there may be no room for misconception, I say
that two things are offered to us, viz., Christ and the gifts
which we receive from him. Thus, as the sacred Supper
consists of the earthly symbols of bread and wine, so Christ I
hold to be, as it were, the spiritual material which corresponds
to the symbols. But when we have grown into sacred union
with Christ, the fruit and utility of spiritual gifts flows from
this, that his blood washes us, the sacrifice of his death reconciles us to God, his obedience produces righteousness and
all the benefits which the heavenly Father bestows by his
hands.

While this distinction is clearly expressed in the Agreement, Westphal pretends that I transfer the name of substance to the use and virtue of the flesh of Christ, abstract-
ing the substance itself. There is little modesty in this, unless he can persuade others that that to which I assign the
first place is reduced to nothing. Still I disguise not that

my doctrine differs widely from his fiction of the present substance of the body. It is one thing to say that the substance of Christ is present in the bread to give life to us, and another to say, that the flesh of Christ gives us life, because life flows from its substance into our souls.

Under the SIXTH HEAD he assails me for making the bread and wine to be the body and blood of Christ in the same sense that to the fathers of old the manna was spiritual food, and the rock was Christ. But why is he angry at me rather than at the Apostle? Surely I was entitled to quote his words. But he says the manna and the water were only figures. Let him settle the matter with St. Paul as he will: it is enough for me to be wise according to the rule of the Holy Spirit. Here, at least, he will not object a physical meaning. In regard to the ordinance of the Supper, I dare not form any conception that is not dictated from heaven. Paul, comparing the Jews with us, says, that they ate of the same spiritual meat, and drank of the same spiritual drink. Let Westphal now cry out that there is no obscurity in the words, This is my body. The interpretation of the Apostle is far clearer in my support: for it does not tell us simply that the manna was spiritual food to the fathers, but the same as that which is given us in the Supper.

It cannot be denied that St. Paul there compares the two sacraments. Unless Westphal holds Paul not to be a competent interpreter, he must admit that the comparison I have made is fairly drawn from it. But then the Son of God had not yet become incarnate. Had he any candour he would not conceal that this difficulty has been solved by me in my Commentary, where I say that the mode in which the fathers ate differed from ours in this, that the eating is now substantial, and could not be so then: Christ now feeding us with the flesh sacrificed for us, that we may draw life from its substance. As the Lamb is said to have been slain from the foundation of the world, so must the fathers under the law have sought spiritual food from the flesh and blood which, in the present day, we enjoy more abundantly not only from the larger measure of revelation, but also because the flesh once offered in sacrifice is daily set before us to be enjoyed.

Therefore, when Westphal concludes that we make the figure equal to the reality, he only exposes the extent of his malice, as he is perfectly aware of the different degrees having been observed by me.

How it came into his mind, that I leave nothing to the ancient fathers but a shadow, I cannot conjecture. For although we acknowledge that the whole of the administration of the law was shadowy, yet it is neither lawful nor right to deny the fathers the reality of the signs which they used. How much better does Augustine, who, distinguishing the species of one symbol from the species of another, places Christ in the middle, as common to both. But if the comparison of things dissimilar shows that we, neglecting the nature of Christ's ordinance and words, as Westphal alleges, imagine a Supper that is devoid of his flesh and blood, the same charge will fall upon the head of Paul, from whom we derived the view. Westphal tells us it was not said of the manna, This is the body of Christ that is to come, nor of the water, This is the blood of the new covenant. But the answer is easy ; for he must either deny that there was the same spiritual food under both signs, or admit that what is said of the bread and cup is applicable in its own measure to that legal sacrament. For although Christ, by the substance of the flesh in which he has been manifested, vivifies us more fully than he did the fathers under the law, yet this disparity does not prevent their being partakers in common with us.

Let us see then what cause he has for here exulting so proudly. As these inexorable masters fix us down so closely to words, I said that the bread is called the body and the wine the blood, just as the manna is called Christ and a dove is called the Spirit. We have a dispute as to the expression, our adversaries seizing upon the letter and holding it fast. I produce similar expressions which are the same in effect. If Westphal now objects, that it was said of the bread, This is my body, why may not I in my turn object, that it was said of the old sacrament, (the rock,) This is Christ, and of the dove, This is the Holy Spirit ? Until he proves that the rule of grammar is applicable to one passage only, and not to all others, he will not convince sound judges of more than this, that the bread is the body, just as the dove is stiled the Holy Spirit.

Under the SEVENTH HEAD he resumes the web which he began to weave under the fourth. The repetition will not be disagreeable to me, as it will make more manifest to the reader what the point is for which he is contending. He alleges that I exhibit a Supper devoid of Christ, because I shut up Christ in heaven, just as Zuinglius did, who insisted that he was to be sought in heaven, and taught that he is received into heaven until he shall appear in judgment. Our good censor perceives not that the words he is lashing, as if they had proceeded from Zuinglius, were uttered by the Apostle Peter. I omit, that because Zuinglius in explaining his sentiment wrote, *Nos volumus*, the expression is taken up and criticised, as if that faithful and strenuous teacher of the Church were thereby subjecting Christ to his authority. Trifler, if you know not that the word which Latin writers use, simply to express their meaning, and that without any feeling akin to haughtiness, is *volo*, where is your erudition which you are so tortured with anxiety to maintain, as is visible from your book? If you know, where is your integrity and candour?

But to come to the point. If Westphal insists that Christ is not to be sought in heaven, let him explain how, according to Peter, it is necessary that the heavens should receive him. Shutting his eyes to the testimony of Peter, he diverges into a commonplace, that he is not to be sought where men wish, but where he has promised that he will be present : as if we were fighting him with our own or any human decisions, and not with the oracles of heaven. But Christ exhibits himself in the word and sacraments. This we deny not : only let the nature of the exhibition be explained. As Westphal here points to the promises, he must necessarily admit that the presence of Christ is manifested without the use of the Supper as well as in the Supper. The promise of Christ is, "I am with you always, even to the end of the world ;" and again, "Where two or three are met together in my name, there am I in the midst of them." He will say

that there is no mention of flesh and blood. What ? Is not
the whole and entire Christ, God manifest in the flesh ? I
hold, therefore, that there also Christ is in a certain sense
to be sought.

If we transfer the same thing to the Supper, Westphal
puts on his buskins, and getting into the heroics, exclaims,
that credit is refused to the words of Christ. Let us have
no doubt, says he, that the heaven and earth of God are in
the Sacraments, and that Christ is there certainly found.
As if it were not an expression of very frequent occurrence,
God sitteth between the cherubim. Hence it follows that
the holy fathers of old ought there also to have sought him.
And indeed when David exhorts them to seek his face, he
brings forward the ark of the covenant with the altar and
whole sanctuary. Nor in the present day, when bidding
pious minds rise up to heaven, do we turn them away from
Baptism and the holy Supper. Nay, rather, we carefully admonish them to take heed that they do not rush upon a
precipice, or lose themselves in vague speculations, if they
fail to climb up to heaven by those ladders which were not
without cause set up for us by God. We teach, therefore,
that if believers would find Christ in heaven, they must begin
with the word and sacraments. We turn their view to Baptism and the Supper, that in this way they may rise to the
full height of celestial glory. Thus Jacob called Bethel the
gate of heaven, because aided by vision he did not fix down
his mind upon the earth, but learned to penetrate by faith to
heaven.

Let Westphal, then, cease to exclaim that it is a total
mistake to seek God in any other way than he has revealed.
This we teach with greater lustre than he can attain to.
Let him rather consider with himself what as yet he has not
at all apprehended, viz., that God from the first manifested
himself by visible symbols that he might gradually raise believers to himself, and conduct them by earthly rudiments to
spiritual knowledge. He is far wrong in thinking himself
free from all blame, because he preaches that Christ is present where his word and promise are. When the Jews,
abusing the word of God, sought him superstitiously in the

temple, Scripture rebuked them as severely as if they had gone beyond the limits of the word.   It is true, indeed, that Christ is present wherever his promise appears, (it being his living image,) provided we follow where it leads.   But Westphal urges us beyond this, to fancy that Christ is present in the Supper in another way than he has expressed in his word ; because we deny that he is present with his body and blood, and are dissatisfied with a corporeal presence. Hence also he infers that we have abandoned the true and retain only a void and empty Supper.

It was easy for Westphal with his usual audacity to blurt out something of this kind ; but who will give him any credit until he has explained how Christ holds forth the bread in the Supper, and yet invites believers upwards, in order to receive his body?   This we assert, not trusting to any philosophical speculation, or to the fallacious pretext of any single word, but to the whole doctrine of Scripture.   Let this acknowledgment of ours be tested by the analogy of faith, and I have no fear that it will be found to vary from it.   If a corporeal presence, the product of a source by no means legitimate, displeases us, does it follow that we do not subscribe to the express words of Christ ?   The Son of God promises to give his body, and we at once give full credit to his word. And though carnal sense murmurs, and nature receives not a sublime mystery, wonderful even to angels, yet we firmly believe that he, by his celestial energy, accomplishes what the visible symbol figures.   While we are thus perfectly at one with our Master, Westphal comes between and raises a disturbance, and, as if we were abolishing the holy Supper by refusing to acknowledge that the bread is substantially the body, declares that, on our view, he gives nothing, and we receive nothing but bread.   What ?   If Christ grants his body to unbelievers, whence this new austerity which denies it to us ?   He contends, that Christ is accused of falsehood if Judas does not receive his flesh and blood equally as much as Peter.   Assume that we, from the small measure of our faith, do not yet understand the miracle which these doctors allege, what so great crime do we commit that they thrust us farther away than Judas ?   Such, forsooth, is their reverence

for Christ that his sacred ordinance has no value for them,
unless it rest on their decision. If any filthy fornicator, per-
jurer, poisoner, robber, any one guilty of atrocious wickedness, any half heathen, comes to the holy Supper, let him
bring to it his defilements of iniquity or superstition, these
men prostitute Christ's sacred body to him. To us, because
we do not consent to their mode of receiving, they leave nothing but bread and wine.

Westphal also declares, with open mouth, that it can do
us no good to talk of spiritual eating, as if the single article
about the presence of the flesh were of more consequence
than a full and solid faith. In regard to the nature, virtue,
and all the benefits of Christ ; in regard to the two-fold
nature of Christ, his function and office, the efficacy both of
his death and resurrection, and his spiritual kingdom, he is
forced to admit that my faith is orthodox. He also denies
not that the end and use of the Supper is rightly explained
by me. All this he values not a straw, because of one little
doubt—our refusal to believe that the substance of the flesh
is swallowed by the mouth. He says that, as the two things
—Do this in remembrance of me, This is my body—are conjoined, we must believe both: it is of no use to believe the
one and disbelieve the other. To what end is this wordy
denunciation, while the only thing discussed is not the
authority of Christ, but only the meaning of the words ? I
long ago taught with sufficient copiousness that the command and the promise are inseparable. Why then does this
declaimer perversely insist, that the form of expression in
the words of Christ is not sacramental, and does not at all
agree with the other passages of Scripture which treat of the
sacraments, and betray his absurdity and heartlessness by
calling us unbelievers ?

Under the EIGHTH HEAD he maintains, from the absurdities with which I charge the carnal presence, that it is perfectly plain I have no belief at all in any real distribution of
the flesh of Christ in the Supper. My answer is, that it is
one thing to believe that the body of Christ is truly given
to us, and another, that his substance is placed under
the earthly elements. This assertion, therefore, as to true

partaking, will not prevent me from showing the folly of those who hold that they cannot be the members of Christ in any other way than by having the body of Christ substantially under the bread. But our Westphal, no doubt to show how acute and provident a man he is, takes a short method of saving himself from all the annoyance of discussion, by declaring it unlawful to touch on any absurdity in his idea. His pretence is the clearness of the words, This is my body. Are they clearer than innumerable passages which attribute feet, hands, eyes, and ears to God? Let some anthropomorphite now come forward, and perversely assert that God is corporeal; let him vociferate that there is nothing ambiguous in the words—The eyes of the Lord have seen, The Lord has lifted up his hand, The cry has gone up to the ears of the Lord of hosts: must we be overwhelmed by this series of passages, hold our peace, and allow fanatics to convert spirit into body? It is surely just as tolerable to clothe God with a body as to divest the body of Christ of its proper nature; and just as plausible to support that view by numerous passages of Scripture. There is nothing more in the verbose declaration of Westphal on this part of the subject than there would be in the assertion of an anthropomorphite, that all who deny God to be corporeal are disbelievers in Scripture.

He scolds us roundly for presuming to inquire how we are to reconcile the passages of Scripture which declare that Christ, by his ascension into heaven, has withdrawn his bodily presence, so as no longer to dwell on the earth, and that yet his body is truly offered to believers in the Supper. To any one who gives due attention, and does not exclude the entrance of true knowledge by obstinacy or morose rigidity, the mode of reconciling the passages at once occurs, viz., that Christ, by the incomprehensible agency of his Spirit, perfectly unites things disjoined by space, and thus feeds our souls with his flesh, though his flesh does not leave heaven, and we keep creeping on the earth. Here Westphal, seized by some kind of whirlwind, inveighs against us, denying that we have faith in Christ if we allow ourselves to inquire whether Christ is to be brought down from his heavenly throne to be inclosed in a little bit of bread, or if we object that the bread is not properly the body unless Christ be made bread, just as much as he was made man. I admit it to be impious curiously to scrutinize the mysteries of God, which lie beyond the reach of our own reason; but we must prudently distinguish between different kinds of questions. For in what labyrinth shall we not be involved if, without taking care to avoid absurdity, we seize at random on every thing that is said. All are aware of the allegory which the ancient Fathers drew from its being required in clean beasts that they should cleave the hoof. They said, that in the same way, if discretion did not guide our faith, we should, under a show of humility, allow ourselves to give foolish and easy credence to the most monstrous dreams.

It remains, therefore, for the reader to examine what the questions are which Westphal so bitterly denounces. At the same time, I would have him observe how tyrannically silence is imposed on us by men who stigmatize an investigation which is absolutely necessary, calling it curiosity, the parent of blasphemy. When he says that we have taken up a wrong beginning, in refusing to believe the words of Christ, he only betrays his excessive stupidity; our diligence in inquiry being rather the proper offspring of faith. When the people of Capernaum regarded the words which fell from the lips of Christ as fabulous, they asked, in scorn, how he could give them his flesh to eat? It was not more unbelief than a gross imagination that impelled them thus to murmur. A thing which their sense does not comprehend they judge to be impossible. Why so? Just because they foolishly imagine that the flesh of Christ will not be food to them without being eaten in the ordinary way. We, because we reverently embrace the words of Christ, and are firmly persuaded that Christ does not deceive us when he calls the bread which he holds forth to us in the Supper his body, inquire after a mode which may not be at variance with the rule of faith. Westphal, therefore, in inveighing against curious questions, cannot fix any stigma on us, who are evidently compelled clearly to explain what the nature of our participation in the flesh and blood of Christ is, if we would not, under the influence of a brutish stupor, confound heaven with earth. When he says that the Arians fell into horrid blasphemy by philosophically investigating the generation of the Son of God, what resemblance has it, I ask, to any thing we do? Having resolved avowedly to detract from the eternal essence of Christ, they endeavoured, by various cavils, to evade whatever favoured an opposite view. We, without any craft and without gloss, acknowledge that Christ performs in the Supper what he figures, and explain that the words contain a metonymy which occurs uniformly in all the passages of Scripture which relate to the sacraments. We say that the sacramental mode of expression is to transfer the name of the thing signified to the sign. We make this plain, not by one passage or two, but prove, from the uniform usage of Scripture, that all who are moderately versant in it must regard this as a common axiom.

Were I disposed to amass heresies with that rashness with which Westphal, who makes stupidity the director of our faith, has introduced them, how much more copiously might I be supplied? But not to go farther, I hurl back his Arians at him, and tell him, that the error by which they overthrew the majesty of Christ was the same as that by which he rends his body, by extending it over heaven and earth. Why did the Arians regard Christ as inferior to the Father, but just because they disdainfully rejected the distinction between the divine and the human nature? Arming themselves with the expression, "My Father is greater than I," they maintained that blasphemous injustice was done to the Supreme God by admitting Christ to an equality of rank. The reason assigned by holy Fathers would have satisfied them if they would only have listened to the fact that Christ was speaking in his character of Mediator. In as far as the mere expression went, they had the advantage; but it was an expression which they had no right to misinterpret and pervert to a vile purpose. If Westphal does not yet recognise himself, the readers, at least, have a mirror in which they can see his living image. We neither imagine monstrosities, when we point out the method by which pious minds may free themselves from difficulty, nor impute to others the offspring of our own house, when we obviate the absurdities which Westphal holds forth for us to swallow without judgment. Far less do we pave the way for the prostitution of religion, while we act so as to place undoubted faith in our Saviour's words, and exhibit the heavenly mystery in its full splendour, yet rejecting all vicious fancies, and maintaining within ourselves, in full vigour, that spiritual communion which comprehends the whole efficacy and fruit of the holy Supper.

Under the NINTH HEAD, Westphal pugnaciously contends that I make void the Supper, because I send unbelievers empty away. He boasts that this is a clear argument, not an uncertain conjecture ; for he infers from my words, that I speak only of the virtue and effect of the sacrament whenever I assert that the reality is combined with the sign. To confirm the thing, he adds, that I teach, that though the Lord offers his grace to all, it is received by believers only. I presume, that to the mind of no man, however acute, would this ingenious ratiocination of Westphal have occurred. And who could have guessed that, in using the term grace, I was abolishing the primary head and source of all grace ? In speaking of the free mercies of God, I am always accustomed to begin with Christ, and justly ; for, until he become ours, we must necessarily be devoid of all the graces, the fulness of which is contained in himself. How far I am from desiring to escape by a sophism, let the passage itself declare.

I have there said, generally, that whatever free gifts God offers us for eternal salvation are received only by faith. Hence it follows, that believers alone are partakers of Christ and his spiritual blessings. Westphal's clear argument finds what no man would have suspected to be contained in my words. Beginning thus shrewdly, he calumniously misrepresents my doctrine to be, that if a wicked man approaches the table, virtue is no longer connected with the signs, though I have never said any thing of the kind. When he asks, what, then, will become of the word of the Lord which sets the same sacrament before all, whether good or bad, the same page contains an answer, which any man who has eyes may see, nay, which even the blind may feel. Besides, in the

Agreement it is distinctly stated that the unbelief of men does not overthrow the faith of God, because the sacraments always retain their virtue ; that thus, on the part of God, nothing is changed, whereas, in regard to men, every one receives according to the measure of his faith.   How careful I am to guard against any idea that the truth of God depends on men, let the reader, after perusal, determine.

The substance of what I say is, that there is a wide difference between the two propositions, that the faithfulness of God consists in performing what he demonstrates by a sign, and that man, in order to enjoy the offered grace, makes room for the promise.   I think it is now evident to all, that in our doctrine the authority of the word is as stable as the ordinance of the sacrament is firm and efficacious.   But Westphal insists that the sacrament remains the same to both as regards the substance of the flesh, but not as regards the effect.   What ? Does this mean that unbelievers eat the dead body of Christ ?   Not at all, he says; for though he who does not use the sacrament duly receives no gift from the Spirit, still he enjoys the flesh and blood of Christ.   Who sees not that Christ is rendered lifeless and is dissevered by sacrilegious divorce from his Spirit and all his virtue ?

He pretends that the sacrament is made by the word, not by our faith.   Were I to grant this, it does not enable him to prove that Christ is prostituted indiscriminately to dogs and swine that they may eat his flesh.   God ceases not to send rain from heaven, though the moisture is not received by stones and rocks.   There is here a strange stupidity.   He himself denies the effect of the Supper to unbelievers, without once considering that what he claims for them is the first part of the effect ; unless indeed he holds that communion with Christ has nothing to do with the effect of the Supper.

It is worth while here to observe his wondrous shrewdness.   He says, that in the Supper, when the word of Christ is added to the bread, the bread becomes a sacrament.   Be it so ; provided he would not add the presence of the flesh. But I willingly allow that the sacrament of flesh and blood is constituted by the words of Christ.   Does it therefore follow that the body of Christ is received by unbelievers? Nay; we are always brought back to the same point, that there is a wide difference between offering and receiving.

Westphal adds, that when faith is added to the word, the fruit of the sacrament is received, because we enjoy the benefits of Christ. What is this but to say that we gain possession of Christ without faith, and yet by faith become partakers of his blessings, thus making Christ inferior to his gifts? He says, that though unbelievers defraud themselves of the benefit, the bread does not however cease to be to them an entire sacrament. Thus the integrity of the sacrament, according to Westphal, consists only in a lifeless Christ. His words are, that in regard to the integrity of the sacrament, the unworthy receive in the very same way as the worthy. Wherein then will the integrity of baptism consist, if the washing and regeneration are not taken into account?

When Augustine teaches that by the addition of the word the element becomes a sacrament, he is expressly treating of baptism. His words are, Wherefore Christ says not, ye are clean because of the baptism wherewith ye have been washed, but because of the word which I have spoken unto you. The context clearly shows his meaning to be, that by the word the element becomes a sacrament, so that its virtue or effect may reach us. Westphal, excluding the effect, wrests the meaning, and applies it to some strange figment of substance. Augustine adds, Whence such virtue in water to touch the body and clean the heart, but just from the operation of the word? Such is Augustine's idea of the integrity of a sacrament, viz., that it is an effectual instrument of grace to us. Westphal imagines this operation of the word to take place without grace. But his disgraceful forging of a false meaning is exposed by the clause which Augustine immediately subjoins, viz., This is done by the word, not because it is said, but because it is believed; whereas Westphal contends that the efficacy there spoken of is effectual without faith, and feigns a word with which faith has nothing to do. And yet, after all this, he dares to lay claim to the support of Augustine: for he asserts, that in several passages free from all ambiguity he says that Judas

ate the real body of Christ. He might at least have produced one, or let him even now produce it. It is more than
vain to pretend that I have intentionally omitted it. Can
any one wonder at my producing him as a witness in support
of my opinion, when he comes forward of his own accord,
and not only gives us his support, but as it were leads the
way?

Westphal concludes that no alleged absurdities can induce
him to depart from the words of Christ and Paul, and the
firm consent of the Church: as if this were not the trite
and common excuse for all errors. If it is to be received, I
should like to know what answer he will make to the Anabaptists, whose regular custom it is to hold it forth as a
shield, and carry it aloft as a banner—that baptism cannot
be lawfully conferred on infants, because it is a symbol of
faith and repentance. What then can we infer from his
words, but just that he and his band remain fixed in error,
being prevented by mere obstinacy from yielding obedience
to the truth? And yet by way of attempt to rid himself of
some of his many absurdities, he says that there cannot be
a falser accusation than that which charges his doctrine with
dissevering Christ from his Spirit. It were better to have
been silent, than to have exposed his wretched nakedness
by so shabby a refutation. For what is his answer? That
the same baptism is received by unbelievers, though they do
not obtain the virtue of baptism, nor partake of the Spirit
of Christ: and yet he upbraids others with a dissimulation
which has no existence, while he is plainly evading the question, and substituting a stone for a tree.

The matter now controverted between us, viz., Whether unbelievers receive the substance of the flesh of Christ without
his Spirit, is peculiarly applicable to the Supper. It has no
resemblance in this respect with baptism. Westphal, indeed,
would fain steal away from the Supper, but feeling that his
craft is detected, he, at once, without hesitation, leaps off to
baptism. But we, too, maintain that baptism always remains
the same, be the minister or receiver who he may. The
hinge of the whole controversy is simply this,—Do unbe-

lievers become substantially partakers of the flesh of Christ?
To this let Westphal reply, if he would not, by his silence,
stand convicted of prevarication. If he acknowledges it in
regard to the substance of the flesh, he debates about nothing. I have openly declared, that the body of Christ is
offered and given to unbelievers as well as to believers, and
that the obstacle which prevents enjoyment is in themselves.
Westphal rests not, but insists that the real flesh of Christ
is eaten by unbelievers, though they taste not a particle of
his Spirit. Is not this to deprive Christ of his Spirit, and
make him the prey of unbelievers? He feels that he is
giving way in the middle of the act, and therefore drawing
up the curtain, he presents his readers with another play,
promising them some little book or other. How dexterously
he there acquits himself I neither know nor care, but as he
here shamefully turns his back, all can see that he is absolutely without an answer.

He then passes over to another subject, and says it is
now clear how beautifully I agree with the Confession of
Augsburg, and how cunningly I changed the subject of controversy, when I pretended that the only thing for which
Luther contended was to show that the sacred and divinely
ordained signs were not vain or empty figures. As to the former point, I repeat what it was sufficient to have once adverted
to, that in the Confession, as published at Ratisbon, there is
not a word contrary to our doctrine. If any ambiguity occurs in the meaning, there is no fitter interpreter than the
author of it; and this honour, as due to his merit, all pious
and learned men will readily confer upon him. While I
thus boldly appeal to him, what becomes of Westphal's im-
pertinent garrulity? As to the latter point, I again answer,
that if Luther had any other end than that which I have
said was chiefly contemplated by him, it will be difficult to
keep him free from stigma. There is nothing which he more
frequently inculcates in all his writings, than that he is
fighting for the sacraments, to prevent their being stripped
of all their effect, and reduced to frigid and empty figures.
If he pretended, what was not really the case, only to throw
odium on his opponents, who will approve of such a proceed-

ing? Moreover, I did not affirm absolutely that he went no farther with his hyperboles. I simply stated in his own words why it was that he took up the matter so keenly, and, therefore, there is the less excuse for Westphal, who, coming forward under the name of scholar, throws no little contumely on his teacher. That Luther disagreed with us in regard to substantial eating, and also when carried by the heat of debate beyond the limits of just moderation, uttered several things from which I dissent, it was never my intention to deny. Why, indeed, should I wish to deny what I have freely declared? We are speaking only of the principal point in dispute, which Westphal places in a substantial presence, thus making only an unimportant accessory of the other point, viz., that the sacraments are not empty figures, but true pledges of spiritual grace, and living organs of the Holy Spirit.

He labours in vain to prove the same thing by the words of Œcolompadius. That holy man wisely and appropriately urged against his opponents, when they would not admit the bread to be a sign of the body, the inevitable consequence, that the bread is substantially the body, that he might horrify them at the gross absurdity, and thus bring them to a sounder mind. But this remark does not do away with the many earnest declarations in which Luther and his followers state the great cause of their zeal to be, that they cannot permit the sacraments to be reduced to nothing, and made to differ in no respect from profane theatrical shows. What aid does Westphal find in my words? Before quoting them he inserts a preface, to serve as a kind of cloak to conceal his fallacy. I had said, that Œcolompadius and Zuinglius were induced by the best of reasons, nay, compelled by urgent necessity, to refute a gross error which had long before become inveterate and was connected with impious idolatry, but that while intent on this one object, they, as often happens in debate, lost sight of another. This passage Westphal endeavours to blacken, as if I had said, that they contended for the empty symbols, without thinking that the reality was combined with them. This is the reason why he asks pardon for using my own testimony against me.

I say nothing as to his insisting so strongly that Luther was alike the enemy of all who denied the substantial presence of Christ in the Supper. This will do me little prejudice, as all know the excessive heat which Luther showed in pleading this cause. And yet in private so far was he from wishing to be my enemy, that though not ignorant of my opinion, he declined not to address me in his own hand in terms of respect, (*reverenter*.) The dishonesty of Westphal makes so much a fool of me, that I state the very term which he used. As I wish his honour safe, it certainly grieves me to see his good faith so rashly traduced by Westphal. He affirms, that after a reconciliation had been half effected at Marpurg, he left the meeting with the same feeling which he had before against Œcolompadius and Zuinglius, though he had then solemnly promised that he would in future regard them as brethren. Both parties having there agreed that they would cultivate mutual peace, either Luther must have been softened, or he entered into a paction at variance with his real sentiments ; a paction, too, which was reduced to a regular deed.

As if my evidence had served Westphal's purpose, (so he boasts,) he proceeds to quote several passages from the different writings of Zuinglius, and from these at last infers, that if our doctrine prevail the holy Supper is made void. He premises that in order that the thing may be established in the mouth of two witnesses, he gives me Zuinglius as a companion, and one too who is by no means to be despised. But although the defence of Zuinglius would be just, and not difficult, I must make my readers aware of the malice with which he attempts to bring me into this arena. Fifteen years ago I publicly stated wherein I was dissatisfied with the pleadings of both parties. I added, that nothing was more desired by all good and pious men than that this unhappy dispute were buried in perpetual oblivion. Should I now appear as the defender of Zuinglius, before I proceed to plead, Westphal will ask me, with what conscience, nay, with what face, I dare to defend what I do not approve? He will object that I am reviving that which I formerly devoted to eternal darkness : in short, he will overwhelm me with reproaches.

Being thus brought into a doubtful and slippery place, not by the hidden craft, but the open effrontery of my enemy, in whatever direction I move I shall be exposed to his male-diction. The truth, however, opens up a way in which I can walk secure from his invective.

He thinks he has gained some very great point when he finds Zuinglius declaring, that the Swiss Churches do not agree with those of Saxony in expounding the passage, " This is my body." As if the dispute were not perfectly notorious, which so long occupied such great and celebrated men, whose books proclaim the dissension in such a way as to show that when Satan saw the gospel revived or restored to its ancient rights, he, in order to retard its course, not only hired professed enemies, but by an old artifice stirred up intestine strife among the very servants of Christ. Nay, another thing is to be observed, which Westphal labours to suppress : How came it that to other dogmas Satan only opposed the Papists, but on this article engaged Luther in a quarrel with excellent men and right-hearted teachers, who, but for this, would have been his faithful coadjutors, unless because he saw that every extremity was to be tried to pre-vent the world from returning from mad superstition ? I confess that under the Papacy men were miserably infatuated in innumerable ways, but the most fearful and monstrous fascination was that of stupidly adoring the bread in place of God. When Westphal invidiously says, that Zuinglius left nothing in respect of substance but bread and wine, it is easy to answer, that he was only contending against a carnal presence, which we are determined to oppose with our last breath.

I am not to be so deterred by the silly reproach of West-phal, as to desert the defence of the truth, when he charges Zuinglius with blasphemy, for having called the substantial union of the bread and the flesh a fiction. He might have more correctly and not less truly have called it a dream. The eating which has been revealed by the Son, who was in the bosom of the Father, we holily and reverently observe, though our faith has no resemblance to the Scythian bar-barity of Westphal. He is not less wrong in pretending that we insist on adhering to common sense. We have not profited so little in the school of Christ as not to have learned to bring all our thoughts into the obedience of the faith. Nay, our doctrine, as I have already observed, and any one may easily perceive, is as far removed from carnal sense as Westphal and his party are from the sense of the Holy Spirit, when they produce monstrous fictions to establish their error.

Is it common sense that tells us to seek the immortal life of the soul from human flesh? Is it natural reason which declares that the living virtue of Christ's flesh penetrates from heaven to earth, and is in a wondrous manner infused into our souls? Is it in accordance with philosophical speculation, that a lifeless earthly element should be the effectual organ of the Holy Spirit? Is it from natural principles we learn that whatever the minister pronounces with his lips according to the word of God and figures by a sign, Christ inwardly performs? Certainly did we not regard the holy Supper as a heavenly mystery, we should not attribute to it effects so distinguished and incredible to carnal reason. Wherefore, as far as we are concerned, we are willing to have done with that common sense which Westphal repudiates, though he still perversely insists on having us for his antagonists. Who will seek the nourishment of his soul from the flesh of Christ, and persuade himself that he has a true and certain pledge of it in the bread, if he has not previously brought down his own feelings to the foolishness of the cross? Any one may see how absurdly Westphal wanders about and deals in commonplace whenever he charges us with measuring the power of God by our carnal reason. But though I have good reason for wishing to bury in silence the things which long ago fell in dispute from Zuinglius and Luther, as it is rare and difficult to regulate one's words in the heat of conflict, still on a fair and civil interpretation of what Joachim so bitterly assails, the substance will be found to be, that the body of Christ neither lies hid under the bread, nor is held forth by the minister, nor, in short, is present in its substance when the Supper is celebrated.

Thus far Westphal thinks, or at least in word boasts, that

he has proved that we distort the words of the Supper, and differ in opinion amongst ourselves. In one thing he contends that we are of the same mind, though from varying in word we would not have it seem so, and that thing is in denying the substance of present flesh and blood in the communion of the Supper. As to our variance with each other, we leave sound and impartial readers to judge. The presence of the substance of flesh, as he imagines it, I have no reason to disguise that I deny, seeing this is what I uniformly teach, and am not ashamed of having hitherto from the beginning constantly professed. Was the immensity of Christ's flesh ever repudiated by me in an obscure manner? Did I not openly testify that Marcion was brought up from the lower regions, if in the first Supper the body of Christ, mortal, visible, and circumscribed by space, stood in one place, and was at the same time stretched forth by his hand, invisible, glorious, and immense? Were not believers always distinctly enjoined to rise to heaven, in order to feed on the flesh and blood of Christ? The sincerity of our faith here certainly needs no disguise. Nor meanwhile does Christ cease to be ours, though he is not placed in our hand any more than the true communion of his flesh ceases to be offered to us under the bread, that he may invigorate our souls by his substance, though the bread be not substantially body.

Westphal, as if his part here were now well performed, says, that he must descend to deal with a different kind of grievance, namely, to repel charges, in which, if he is to be believed, I exhibit a canine eloquence. Although I long not for the praise of eloquence, I am not so devoid of the gift of speaking as to be obliged to be eloquent by barking. Westphal ought either to change his mode of writing, or take back the epithet which properly describes it. From the withered flowers which he sheds over his discourse, it is plain how very jejune a rhetorician he is, while his intemperance sounds more of the Cyclops than any thing human. One thing I deny not: I am not less alert in pursuing the sacrilegious, than the faithful dog in hunting off thieves.

In the *first* place, he endeavours to get rid of the charge of disturbing the peace, by saying that the contention did not begin with him : as if I had said, that disturbance had now, for the first time, only commenced. I rather distinctly complained that, when, by the special goodness of God, it had been calmed for a time, it was now kindled anew by those restless men. I did not charge Westphal, in absolute terms, with having excited commotion, lest he should retort, as he does, that many had used our doctrine as an occasion for tumult. I certainly admit, nay, I glory before angels, in having said, that as soon as that gross error about the impanation of Christ began to be discussed, Satan had risen to throw every thing into confusion, and prevent the truth from shining forth. And the numerous martyrdoms of holy men in the present day attest the height of madness and fury to which that doctrine impells all unbelievers. But while Westphal and his fellows keep throwing oil on the fire, after they have armed the rage of Papists against us, it is exceedingly unjust to give us the blame of the disturbance. If the first origin of the strife be inquired into, Luther, when opposing transubstantiation, so to speak, blew the trumpet. Here I am, so far from blaming him, that, among his many virtues deserving of the highest praise, I give not the lowest place to the magnanimity with which, undismayed by commotions, he proceeded boldly to root up that preposterous fiction. Therefore, whenever disturbances arise, the point to be determined is, which of the parties has justice on his side.

My complaint as to the revival of disturbance Westphal chooses to take up and, without cause, apply in a different sense. While, among the Churches which have embraced a purer doctrine, and serve under the one banner of Christ against the Papacy, there was reason to lament that the flame of an unhappy dissension which was sopited had again suddenly burst forth, I said, justly, that it was excited under bad auspices by the instigation of the devil. On this Westphal absurdly asks, " If the devil, twenty-five years ago, brought the tragedy on board, with what face can I charge him with being the mover of discord ?" I spoke not of the first assault, but only of the renewal of the war, and of that

he, after the devil, bears the blame. Why should I have
accused Thomas Muntzer, Melchior Pelletier, and Nicolas
Pelagius, men whom I do not know, and who had long ago
lost the power of doing mischief ?   When I am squeezed in
a crowd, it were foolish to expostulate with any but those
who are squeezing me.   He wittily compares me to an incendiary, who not only secretly supplies materials, but openly,
by throwing brands, sets houses on fire, and prevents those
who come running up from extinguishing the flames.   Is
this now to be my reward, for having ever exerted myself in
favour of sound and pious conciliation ?   What new thing
has lately proceeded from me ? 'Nay, my agreement with
the brethren of Zurich ought rather to have softened the
exasperated minds of the opposite party, as I can show, by
a letter of Vitus Theodorus, that it was a thing he more
wished than hoped for.

I had advised him not to taint the works of Luther with
any mention of that unhappy contest. He answered, that
provided I could prevail with my friends to give effect to the
doctrine contained in our Agreement, he would have a good
reason for keeping quiet.   Gasper Cruciger subscribed with
me in sentiment, and privately declared it as much as those
who openly gave their names.   I speak only of the dead,
lest, if I should mention the living, Westphal should make
a more furious onset on them.   And yet judging from the
tempers of many others, I hoped, when our Agreement was
published, that many who had previously been rather keen
would become pacified, and be more friendly with us.   This
hope, if Westphal has disappointed, impartial and moderate
men will bear me witness that I had not conceived it on
slight grounds.

It was not, as he babbles, a conspiracy to establish error,
but a candid declaration of our sentiment, which seemed admirably fitted to remove offences.   Pious men were long
tortured with thinking, that the sacred signs in which God
offers his favour, were put on a footing with the profane in-
signia of earthly warfare, and with theatrical shows.   A
suspicion, no less grave, as to making void the efficacy, was
removed.   If any thing in this testimony displeases West-

phal, we make him perfectly free to show it. But when he lays aside the office of censuring, and turns to inveigh against our Agreement, who can pardon his malice? Our preface bears ample evidence that we had no intention to bind any one to our words. Let Westphal only do what we then modestly requested. Nay, he makes it a ground of charge, that while candidly declaring our sentiment, we promise to be docile, if any one produces what is better, and to comply with the request of all who may desire fuller explanation. If he did not deem it right to subscribe to our doctrine, he was at liberty openly to show what it was he disapproved. All we asked was, that he would not deal roughly with a newly cured sore.

Let him have done, then, with his unseasonable declamation, that peace purchased at the expense of truth is cursed. We desire no other peace than one, of which the pure truth of Christ may be the sacred bond. I had taken away all handle for censure, had not Westphal been determined, by wandering up and down, to draw off the reader's attention from the cause. Moreover, with regard to the discussions which have taken place in England, I would rather leave it to Peter Martyr, a faithful teacher of the church of Strasburg, to give the answer, which, I trust, he is now preparing. Here I must only, in a few words, call attention to the no less cruel and barbarous than sacrilegious insults of our censor.

He grins ferociously at all the worshippers of God, who had promised themselves that the state of the church in England would prove lasting. Who can now pity you, should it ever be your lot to be reduced to the last extremity? It is not enough for you to sit at ease, while all pious men are in mourning, but you must turn your insolent invectives against the Church, while undergoing a miserable and mournful wasting. Did not the sacred blood of so many martyrs calm your fury—blood which, with its sweetest odour, breathes strength and vigour into faithful souls in the remotest regions of the earth, as it delights God himself and the angels in heaven? A king, of the highest promise, being suddenly cut off, the edifice of piety which had begun to rise, is overthrown; Satan and his adherents are triumphing over the extinguished

light of pious doctrine; the most fearful cruelty rages against
the children of God; distinguished men, dragged to the flames,
seal the truth with the invincible constancy with which they
had embraced it: Joachim not only puts out his tongue in
scorn against the afflicted daughter of Zion, but savagely
derides the hope which had been entertained of a happier
issue. This one specimen will, I hope, suffice to give the
reader a full idea of the man's temper.

But he says he has good cause to be indignant while our
books are everywhere flying about. Let him attack them,
then, if he finds any thing in them deserving of censure:
we will reply, and the Church will judge. He does not disguise that these conditions do not suit him, as it seems a
shorter method to put all the books into the fire, and so
prevent them from giving further trouble. For nothing
could be more odious to him than our offer to discuss, or to
subject to discussion, a doctrine to which he insists that all
shall be bound to submit without controversy. Where is
now the generous and indefatigable soldier of Christ, who
elsewhere is so loud in heralding his combats? We come
down prepared to render an account of our doctrine, and we
humbly beg to be heard. The sum of our wishes is, that
judgment be given according to the word of the Lord. Not
only are we excluded, but Westphal barbarously upbraids us,
telling us that nothing is more unjust than to discuss a doctrine so generally received. Is it more generally received
than transubstantiation, the sacrifice of the Mass, and the
withholding of the cup? If Westphal's censure is to hold
good, Luther must have been guilty of sacrilegious audacity
when he dared to root up those figments which had received
the suffrages of almost the whole world. That the bread is
substantially the body of Christ, is a recent decision, formerly never heard of. For Westphal trifles when he boasts
the consent of the Catholic Church. But while some of his
companions have thought that this ought to be maintained
to the last, he thinks it sufficient not to admit of discussion.
This is truly ridiculous, until he has gone with his herd, and
made a surrender of themselves to the Pope. If consent is
to be gloried in, which of the two, I ask, has the greater

plausibility—the Pope, who holds a great part of Europe so astricted that no man dare mutter against him, or Westphal, who holds up a little parasol to keep off the light?

Here I appeal to all the children of God, whom Scripture declares to be endowed with the spirit of meekness and obedience. We beg audience both of Westphal and of the Pope. Both refuse on the ground that having already obtained possession by general consent, they are unwilling to yield it up. This is no idea of mine: it is Westphal's naked defence. But if the thing is to depend on numbers, why should not a place be also given to us? Westphal pronounces us heretics, of whom no account is to be taken. Let us now hear the Pope, who has the largest number of votes. What will he decide with regard to him as well as us? We, however, can rejoin that we stand always ready for discussion. Such too has been the conduct hitherto pursued by the advocates of the Confession of Augsburg, whose name I wonder that Joachim so boldly uses, while he is so far from imitating them.

The German princes who had undertaken to defend the gospel thought they had duly performed their duty when, so far as depended on them, they were willing that due investigation should be made, and they always complained that this was denied them. This too was our method of acting whenever we were called to plead the cause of religion, and no diets of the empire were held in which our people did not call for discussion. At some of them I was personally present. What they were wont to do formally appears from the public records. To go farther, both in this city and elsewhere, I have repeatedly had to discuss doctrine with turbulent men, and also with heretics. So far from refusing to discuss, I have been the first spontaneously to offer it. The goodness of the cause gave me confidence, and made me have no fear of coming to the light. Whence then this new fastidiousness on the part of Westphal, who not only refuses all investigation to heretics, but obstinately denies evidence to pious worshippers of God, to whom has been given more skill than to such as he to illustrate the glory of the gospel, and who by beneficial labours have not deserved ill of the Church?

Were the sacred majesty of the word of God to be called in question, such license, I admit, ought to be withstood; but here, Westphal, it is not Scripture, but an opinion of your own that is brought under discussion.   The question is not whether Christ truly and correctly called the bread his body, but what he meant to say, and what his words, which we reverently embrace, signify.   You contend that they are too clear to need exposition.   We assert the same thing as to their clearness, provided you refuse not to open your eyes. When you pretend that all men will deride our Agreement as futile, it is not worth my while to refute you harshly, while the anxiety with which you labour to discredit my writings only betrays your malignity and envy too clearly to require any lengthened demonstration.   This much, indeed, I hold. Were he not distrustful of his cause, being in other respects more than pugnacious enough, he would not be so ready to take flight.

For the same reason he digresses from the subject, and gathers together rhapsodies of calumny, that he may bring us into discredit with the simple.   And the first charge which he brings against us is, that we make every thing new in our Churches, and abolish customs that are not without use.   I wish he had mentioned particulars, or at least instanced one or two, not to leave readers in suspense.   We can, however, easily remove any doubt.   We celebrate the sacred Supper without histrionic robes; we do not light tapers at mid-day; we do not by sound of bell invite the populace to worship the bread when, in the manner prescribed by the law of Moses, it is lifted up like a sacrifice. Other things, which he afterwards enumerates, I purposely omit until the proper time comes.

What is it, Westphal?   For what rites, pray, are you so zealous, but just for those which are in use with you?   But what presumption is it for any man to insist that his custom shall everywhere be regarded as a law?   It grieves you that we omit what you observe: as if we had not the same ground for expostulation.   For why are we not angry at your neglect of our ceremonies, while you would imperiously bind us to the observance of yours, unless it be that from fraternal meekness, we tolerate faults which cannot be corrected, while you and yours cannot lie still in the mud without dragging others in along with you?

Who sees not that the tapers savour of Judaism? We may add, that no man inveighed more harshly against those follies than Luther, though he retained them because of the weakness of the times. Why did he censure them so severely, but just because he saw that they were the offspring of absurd superstition, and noxious from abuse ; and not only so, but that the world was so infatuated that the error could not easily be rooted out of their minds? The use of such vehemence is laudable when necessity so demands. His not immediately removing them we pardon ; you, not contented with such equity, hold us criminal for having allowed them to fall into desuetude.

Not to be tedious, let the reader consider that the contest which we have with Joachim and his friends at the present day is the same which Paul once had with the semi-Jews, who, coming down from Jerusalem, and wishing to admit nothing different from received custom, attempted to impose their yoke on the Gentiles. While they magnified the Apostles, in whose school, and as it were lap, they boasted of having been brought up, they invidiously assailed Paul for pursuing a different course. In short, they regarded him as all but an apostate, who had presumed to abolish Apostolic customs among the Gentiles. Joachim, as if he were trumpeting with their mouth, says, that by our change of customs we have separated from Churches which agreement in Catholic doctrine and the manifold graces of the Holy Spirit declare to be Churches of Christ. Shall Wittemberg then, or Hamburg, be of more consequence in the present day than at the first preaching of the gospel was Jerusalem, from which, as from a fountain, salvation was diffused over the whole world? For what was the objection which some of the Galatians took to Paul, but just that he did not observe the ceremonies retained by the first ministers of Christ? Whence the vitious emulation which made them obtrude the same custom everywhere, but just from proud disdain? Those who contumeliously spurn the custom of others can-

not but be excessively addicted to their own. The more
insolently Westphal conducts himself, the better right have
we to put down his vile boasting.

He boasts that the Churches, whose rites we do not observe, are adorned with manifold gifts of the Spirit : as if
our Churches were devoid of such gifts. For here not merely
Switzerland and the Grisons are concerned, but all Upper
Germany is condemned by one vote : and yet, heralding his
own modesty, he tells us that no man is farther removed
from Thrasonic boasting than he who thus, from his quiet
corner, insults so many distinguished Churches. Strasburg,
Augsburg, Frankfort, and several other cities, are reduced
to nothing by one blast from his mouth. O Ishmael, thy
hand is against every man, and every man's hand against
thee. The more praise Luther deserves for magnanimity,
in not hesitating, single-handed, to attack the whole Papacy, the more detestable is thy moroseness in seeking
materials for dissension among the people of God in very
trifles.

It is here worth while to touch, in passing, on the particular things at which he expressly carps. The *first* is, that
we sometimes allow children to die unbaptized. What is
the fault he finds here, but just that we do not resign the
office of baptizing to silly women ? Assuredly, if any one
neglects to present his children early to baptism, he is
severely rebuked for his negligence. The church is open
every day. If any man's child die without baptism, because
he did not embrace the opportunity, he is censured. The
only thing wanting to us is, that women do not, without any
command from Christ, seize upon the solemn office of pastors. Joachim holds the necessity for baptism to be so absolute, that he would sooner have it profaned by illicit usurpation, than omitted when the lawful use is denied. The
thing that offends him he immediately after discloses. It
is because we give hopes that infants may obtain salvation without baptism, because we hold, that baptism, instead
of regenerating or saving them, only seals the salvation of
which they were previously partakers.

As I have elsewhere refuted these gross errors at full

length, I shall here be brief with my answer. If the salvation of infants is included in the element of water, then the covenant, by which the Lord adopts them, is made void. Let Joachim say, in one word, what weight he attaches to the promise,—I will be thy God, and the God of thy seed. If God do not ingraft into the body of his people those on whom he bestows this high privilege, not only is injury done to his word, but infants ought to be denied the external sign. Let an Anabaptist come forward and maintain that the symbol of regeneration is improperly conferred on the cursed children of Adam whom the Lord has not yet called to the fellowship of his grace. Either Westphal must remain dumb, or the only defence that can avail him is, that the grace which was offered in the person of their parents is common to them. Hence it follows, that they are not absolutely regenerated by baptism, from which they ought to be debarred, did not God rank them among the members of his Son. With what face can he deny infants the title of *holy*, by which Paul distinguishes them? If the reader will look at this passage as it is explained in our Catechism, they will pronounce, while I am silent, that our children trained in such rudiments, have much sounder views than this veteran theologian has derived from his speculations.

His *second* objection is, that the Lord's Supper is not given to the sick at their homes. I wish that they had gone before us in this with a purer example. Had they been careful to adapt their practice to the genuine rule of Christ, we would willingly have followed them. But since nothing is less accordant with the doctrine of our heavenly Master than that the bread should be carried about in procession like cakes in a fair, and then that one individual should receive in private and eat apart, disregarding the law of communicating, pious and learned men were from the very first much averse to private dispensations of the Supper. Nothing, therefore, can be more absurd than Westphal's calumny, that owing to the crafty counsel of Satan, poor souls are deprived of consolation. For we carefully recall to the remembrance of the sick the pledge of life which was once deposited with us, that they may thence confirm their faith, and borrow weapons for the spiritual combat. In short, we herein profit so far that the Supper received in the public assembly, according to the ordinance of Christ, supports them with present consolation not less effectually than if they were to enjoy it privately without communion.

He goes on to add (*thirdly*) that we admit to the Supper without previous examination, and without private absolution. I deny not that we everywhere do wrong from excessive facility. The rule is, that the young do not come forward to the sacred table till they have given an account of their faith. Elder persons are examined, if they are not of known and ascertained piety. I admit, however, that we gain less by this discipline than I could wish, though it is most false to say that we knowingly and willingly offer the Supper indiscriminately to strangers and persons not approved. This, however, is not the thing with which Westphal finds fault: it is because we omit private absolution. If he can find an origin for this practice anywhere else than in the fetid lagoons of the Pope, I will readily acknowledge the fault.

The utility of private absolution it is not my purpose to deny. But as in several passages of my writings I commend the use of it, provided it is optional, and free from superstition, so it is neither lawful, nor even expedient, to bind it upon consciences by a law. Let Westphal show, that at a time when the Church flourished, and pure religion prospered, private absolution was sanctioned by any law. But if it is perfectly notorious that it was made imperative by a device of the devil at the time when the whole state of the Church was corrupted, nay, piety completely overthrown, there is no ground for pretending that the abrogation of it was a crime. Westphal is wrong, too, in inferring, that because we do not absolve every individual in private, we admit to the Supper without previous examination: as if there were an inseparable connection between trial of faith and private absolution; the former of which was always maintained in holy vigour among believers, whereas the latter, in regard to its being made a law, crept in among degenerate rites after things had gone to confusion.

His *fourth* head of accusation is, that in order to defend the image-war of Carlostadt, we divide the first commandment into two. I wish that the heat of his frenzy would not drive him headlong to expose his own disgrace and that of his party, which, for us, would remain buried. That the ten commandments are rightly and regularly divided by us, we have shown by solid and clear arguments : we have also the support of antiquity. Westphal and his party, to keep the commandment which distinctly prohibits idolatry in the shade, improperly make two commandments of the tenth : and yet on this occasion he hesitates not to throw the blame of schism upon us. Hence it is easy to infer what the terms of peace are which these implacable masters would impose. Let him rather see, or, if blindness prevents him, let the reader observe whether it was not by a fatal artifice of Satan that the second commandment of the law was removed from its place and hidden, in order that the people of God might not have idolatry in so much horror and detestation. The less excuse is to be made for Westphal, who, in an error equally gross and noxious, not only contumaciously plumes himself, but stigmatizes all who dissent from him.

I come to his *fifth* charge, which is the abrogation of feast-days, and also of the divisions of the Gospel and Epistles, which were in common use. He says, that the distinction of feast-days is alike ancient and useful. But I should like this good antiquary to point out the period when feast-days first began to be dedicated in honour of the Virgin Mary and the Saints. I am not unaware that the memory of the Martyrs has been celebrated for more than thirteen hundred years, the object being to give a greater stimulus to the faithful to imitate them. Among other corruptions which afterwards followed, we ought justly to class this one of instituting holidays and feast-days. And yet to Joachim Christianity is gone, brotherly communion destroyed, and a nefarious schism introduced, if the observance of days is not looked out in the calendar of Hamburg. Surely Augustine, who deplores that the liberty of the Church was oppressed in his day by the excessive number of rites, plainly testifies that very few feast-days were handed down from his fore-fathers. This makes it apparent, that in the correction which we have made, nothing more was attended to than to renew that pure antiquity.

In regard to the division of the Gospels and Epistles, it is evident from all the Homilies of Ancient Writers that the Books of Scripture were expounded to the people in one uninterrupted series. A custom gradually prevailed of ex-tracting from the Gospels and Epistles passages for read-ing suitable to the season. Hence arose those divisions for which Westphal contends, as if it were for altars and hearths; though a perusal shows that they were made in-eptly and without any judgment. Certainly if portions were to be selected to be read each Lord's day, a very different selection should have been made. Lest any one suppose that Westphal is flaming for nothing, I must inform the reader that it is about the Postils he is anxious; for how could a great part of those whom he is courting get on with-out the Postils?

LUTHER, who, while matters were yet unsettled, accom-modated himself to the common custom, must be pardoned. Nay, in adopting this compendious method of disseminating the Gospels, his care and diligence are to be praised. But it is very absurd in Westphal, who, determined always to stick in the same mire, makes the rudiments of Luther the pretext; just as if one, after entering on the right path, no sooner sees the person who had shown it to him turn back, than he obstinately takes up his station and refuses to ad-vance another step. Let Westphal, then, celebrating the Martinalia with the Papists, join them in singing out the Gospel and Epistles according to the form prescribed in the Mass, provided we be at liberty to arrange the doctrine of the Gospel as the Apostles delivered it to us for the use of our people. Our censor does not permit this; but, getting into heroics, exclaims, that no doubt this is done by us at the suggestion of the devil, in order that no good may be got out of the Gospel! as if the Gospel were lost by not being cut into pieces. Can any one doubt that this man has got too little to do in his retirement, and has therefore set about

giving trouble for nothing to those who are busily employed ?

Perhaps his excuse is, that he is busy in the sense in which
Cataline threatened to be so—that he is employing fire to put
fire out. As I had said that the torch of discord was now
kindled by him under evil auspices, the only kind of defence
he is able to make, is to give the name of torches and furies
to all who do not decorate their churches with idols, who
regard baptism as an appendage of the promise, and a means
of confirming grace, but not a cause of salvation, who do
not whisper a form of absolution into every ear, nor keep
holiday in honour of saints, nor follow the Missal in breaking down Scripture into lessons. Such is his reason for
saying that he was obliged to make a wound and prevent
hidden putridity from lurking within: as if he could not
cherish and practise holy peace with us unless we slavishly
defile ourselves with other men's impurities. Of those apes
who take such delight in preposterous imitation, Horace
truly exclaims, O imitators, servile herd ! When I said
that the fire was smothered, I acknowledge I was deceived
by attributing too much sense to those who are now raving
without measure. Since the hope of peace has been destroyed by their unseasonable rage, may God quell these
furies and retort on their own heads the reproaches which
they vent against us with no less insolence than injustice.

As if he had admirably disposed of the charge of having
disturbed the peace, he now attempts to assert his erudition. But, to prove that he is modest, he premises that my
impudence has forced him to exceed the bounds of modesty.
How can he prove me to be impudent but just for having
said that he is unlearned ? But he is welcome for me to
enjoy his titles of Master and Doctor, provided he aspire not
too eagerly to a place among the learned to the common
injury of the Church. I pass his insipid irony, in which he
jeers at me for thinking of him less honourably than he
wished. If any gift has been given me, I study to employ
it usefully, without show or ostentation, for the edification
of the Church ; and my books are clear evidence, that so
far from striving for the palm of talent or learning, I avoid

nothing more carefully than display. Nor was there any
reason why he should drag me into comparison, as without
any mention of myself I only advised him to give place to
more competent defenders of his cause, and not incur the
disgrace of presumption.   Let him now compare himself
with the men of his own party, and claim the first place for
himself, if he is desirous to refute me.   To this he comes at
last, when he boasts that he yields to no pillars, and not
even to heavenly angels.   O Luther! how few imitators of
your excellence have you left, how many apes of your holy
boasting!   It is not wonderful that this expression was ever
and anon in the mouth of him who could not fight boldly for
Christ without despising all the powers of the world.   Now,
when the same sound comes from drones, who are only disturbing the hive, it is absolutely insufferable.

I wish he would show these pillars to which he says he
would not yield.   Paul might speak thus when certain
vagrants endeavoured to overwhelm him with the splendid
names of Peter and others.   We have lately seen how contumeliously he has discarded all churches in which he finds
any thing in the least degree at variance with his rules.   Let
him take heed, then, that he do not, when raising himself
against pillars, stumble against a stone of offence.   For whom
does he expect to give him credit for power bestowed by God
unless he produce his diploma?   He no more approaches to
Paul, whose character he ridiculously borrows, than a player
to a king.   I wish he would prove himself an apostle of
Christ by true testimonials.   Of what use is it for a man,
filled with wind or folly, to boast himself a defender of
the faith as if he had come from heaven?   If we are to believe Westphal, it was necessary for him to put to his shoul-
der that the integrity of the faith might not fail.   This is
true, if we grant that faith stands supported by the absurd
fictions by which he deludes himself and others.

In the same way we dispose of his boast, that he has not
made so little progress as not to discern the voice of the
shepherd from the howling of wolves.   Why then does he
with his howling tumultuously disturb the Church, and prevent the voice of Christ from being calmly heard?   And

whom will he persuade of our howling, while it is well known
that night and day we do and aim at nothing else than to
see the scattered sheep gathered together by the voice of the
heavenly shepherd ?   How faithfully I labour to make the
whole world hang on the lips of Christ alone, I may not only
take my writings and sermons to witness, but all who
see me in my daily occupations will bear a sure testimony.
The Lord seals my labours with his blessing too clearly to
allow the benefit derived from them to be contemptible to
ten Westphals.   This commendation of my calling I have
in common with Paul.   Where will he seek for his, while
heralding his own companions only, he calls for reciprocal
heralding from them ?   He seems to himself a fit discerner
of spirits; but while all hiss him, is the opinion which he has
inwardly conceived of himself to operate as a previous judgment in his favour ?

He tells us, that he not unsuccessfully devotes to sacred
literature good hours which others waste in play or trifling.
Whom he means to upbraid, I see not, unless it be that he
wished to frighten me by a display of his studies.   At Wittemberg and elsewhere he was a hearer of faithful teachers,
but just as those had been disciples of Peter and the Apostles, who endeavoured by their mists to obscure the Gospel
when far and widely spread.   Nor does he omit to mention
among his praises, that in his own country he holds the
office of Doctor ; and he thinks he has found a plausible
ground for exulting over me that I am an exile from my
country.   It is strange he does not also direct his jeers
against Paul, for not having been bishop of Tarsus.   So far
am I from being ashamed of voluntary exile, that I by no
means envy those delicate apostles the quiet of their nest.
In short, whoever will attend closely to his narrative will,
without my saying a word, clearly perceive in it the living
image of a false apostle, as pourtrayed by Paul in both Epistles to the Corinthians.   Although he set out with humbly
declaring that he was conscious of his own weakness, and
left the praise of his talents and learning to others, shortly
after, forgetting this feigned modesty, he is forced to discover how much sour leaven his stomach contains.

" Unlearned !" he exclaims, " I should like to know what idea that man has of learned." As if it were necessary to have recourse to Platonic ideas, when any learned man, besides Westphal, is looked for in the world. That you may not trouble yourself to no purpose with long speculation, I declare that at Leipsic and Wittemberg, and places adjacent, are many who, in my judgment, deserve a place in a catalogue of the learned. You have no pretext for charging me with holding none to be learned who have not been taught in the school of Zuinglius. Though Luther differed from us, did we ever contemn his erudition ? Nay, what is the whole drift of my language, which Westphal is now assailing, but just that he has been rash in pushing himself forward, while learned and grave men keep back ? When he sees me applying the epithets of learned and grave to men of his party, how shamefully is his charge at variance with fact ? The reason no doubt is, that he allows none to be called learned, if he be not of the number. Accordingly, he thinks that no blemish of ignorance can be discovered in him, unless it be that he does not measure the body of Christ geometrically. Perhaps he thinks of himself so highly, that he does not see any thing deserving of contempt. But if he supposes that all the learned will be provoked by one little expression, to declare war on me, he is greatly mistaken. His silly talk about geometrical measurement, I have already shown to be mere calumny. That the body of Christ, which has been received into the heavens, is absent from the earth, we did not learn in the school of Archimedes, but believe as it is delivered in the clear oracles of Scripture. From what philosophy he drew, that, in the first celebration of the Supper, Christ had a twofold body, the one mortal, visible, occupying its own place, the other invisible, immortal, and immense, I, in my ignorance, am unable to divine.

When decking himself in illustrious titles, he contends, that he deserves a place in the album of the learned, because out of the Scriptures he produces things new and old, observes the leading scope of Scripture, and with simple faith assents to the word of God, he certainly adduces nothing which is not common to myself. I wish he would show by

fact that he possesses this skill and dexterity. He is ridiculous in this also, though it is just his way, that after professing to be contented with the lowest place, he immediately
raises himself to the summit, applying to himself the words,
" I am wise above all my teachers." What place will be assigned to Luther, if he who occupies the lowest is above him?
At last he says, that there is no cause to fear that he would
retain the title of Doctor, if he were not learned. Little is
wanting to extort from him a confession of the desire by
which he is strangely tortured. He asks, why do I labour
to prevent an unlearned man from disturbing Europe, a
danger which could come from none but able and literary men endued with authority and eloquence? As if no
harm were to be dreaded or guarded against from the foolish
and insane. He says there is good ground for the common
proverb, The unlearned make no heresies. What then did
the Anabaptists do? What Muntzer? What the Libertines?
Nay, in the whole crew, of whom Irenæus, Epiphanius, and
Augustine speak, how many more were involved in error by
gross ignorance than by erudition? More correctly and
wisely does Augustine say, that the mother of all heresies is
pride, by which we often see that the most ignorant are
most highly swollen.

Westphal next makes me a deceiver, because I professed
it to be my care not to deceive the simple ; and he compares
me to the Jews, who said the same thing of Christ before
Pilate. Let him, then, show himself to be like Christ, if he
wishes to thrust me among that crew. That there is no
deception in the word of God, I confess no less sincerely
and from the heart, than Westphal does windily with the
tongue. But where is the expression for which he has so
reproachfully assailed me ? Just as if he were some comic
Jupiter carrying a Minerva in his skull, he boldly masks
all his fictions with the word of God. Had it not of old
been the ordinary practice for false prophets to make louder
pretence of the name of God the more they were estranged
from him, he might perhaps gain something by his airs; but
now, when devoid of all evidence, he argues as if it were
after proof, who is to be moved by his futile trifling ? The

word of God he has constantly in his mouth, but it is only in word, just as Marcion, when assigning a heavenly body to Christ, denounced all as enemies of the word who believed that he was born of the seed of Abraham, because it is written, The second Adam is heavenly from heaven. But since, on better evidence than Westphal can produce from his party, we have been enabled to testify the reverence which we feel for the word of God ; since even our books furnish clear proof that we are faithful and honest interpreters, Westphal will be a wondrous juggler if he can impose upon the eye of the reader, so as to convert obvious reality into an empty phantom.

Let him have done, then, with his unseasonable garrulity, from which it is apparent that the only thing he is hunting after is to delude the unskilful, and prevent them from knowing the fact. Of what use is it to charge us with folly, as if we did not believe Moses and the prophets ? If we interpret the words of Christ as the common usage of Scripture demands, we are not, on that account, to be forthwith regarded as unbelievers. Did we not feel astricted to the truth of Christ ; did not religion bind us, why should we stand continually in the line of battle ? We know, indeed, what it is to be foolish in our own eyes, so as soberly, and in the spirit of meekness, to embrace what God teaches to babes ; and we trust we understand the wisdom which, as Paul declares, comprehends heaven and earth in its breadth and length, its depth and height. But to Westphal there is nothing in the inestimable love wherewith God has embraced us in his only-begotten Son—nothing in the whole mystery of redemption, the boundless virtue of Christ, and his glorious resurrection, if the bread be not substantially the body. To him, too, there is nothing in our doctrine that Christ, by his Spirit, infuses into us the vivifying virtue of his flesh and blood, that in a wonderful manner he performs within what the bread figures to the eye, so that we are united to his life, and our souls are invigorated by the substance of his flesh. Wherefore let him be a monitor to himself rather than to others, and not deceive himself by thinking he is somewhat when he is nothing. Were he not intoxicated with inconceivable pride, he would not, in comparison with himself, despise all others who do not humbly yield to his obstinacy.

The same pride dictates his querulous assertion, that to charge him with insanity is to blaspheme God. If it is so, it is clear that he is not animated by any zeal for the glory of God, as he shows no desire to return to sanity; but until he be joined to God by a more sacred tie, there is no reason at all to fear that any thing deservedly said of him can offer contumely to God. The Apostles were derided on the day of Pentecost as being intoxicated. This Westphal transfers to himself with no better right than sibyls and bacchanalians might. He certainly could not offer a greater affront to the Apostles than by introducing himself into their order; until imbued with a new spirit, and transformed to other manners, he has ceased to be like himself. As it was sacrilegious scorn to regard the inspiration of the Spirit as drunkenness, so to use the name of God as a pretext for intemperate raving is a worse evil than drunkenness. But although sober and impartial men desiderate moderation in the vehemence of Luther, Westphal is too far distant from him to be able to hide his disgrace under Luther's shade. We grant that in Scripture the corrupt in the faith are condemned as insane; but when he infers from this that therefore we will not be sane before we detest our error, I wonder where he gets his *therefore*. When he here inserts, as if by stealth, that in the celebration of the Supper some, struck with Satanic fury, omit the words of Christ, "This is my body," we must just take it as if some abandoned person were to go about giving bad names at hazard to everybody he should chance to meet.

The charge of arrogance he disposes of by denying it in word, and then proving, by solid evidence, that he is a very Thraso. He thinks he is doing nothing inconsistent with his profession while he professes himself a defender of the orthodox faith. First, what does he mean by saying he professes nothing inconsistent with his profession? Assuredly I deny not that by professing he professes: only I wish he would do it truly. Nay, if the fact corresponded to the word, he would get us all to subscribe, instead of being forced, as we now are, publicly to oppose his false fictions. But where is that stammering simplicity for which he commends himself? Nothing like simplicity will be found throughout his book, and for stammerers to be so loquacious is against nature. When he alleges that he is doing the work of the Church, he would have spoken more truly had he said that he is undoing it, his whole object being to give annoyance to the children of God.

He would have it thought that he might, in another way, consult better for his own quiet: as if it would not also suit me better to desist from writing if this restless man would not force me to it, and drag me away from other useful studies. I may indeed truly declare, that as I might remain silent without being hurt, and the weapons of Westphal cannot wound me individually, the good of the Church is the only motive that induces me to write. What place he would hold among his people, did he not make a name for himself by exciting disturbance, I leave all men to judge. He raises his notes louder, and says, that were he to declare that he is contending not only for the Churches of Saxony, but others, however remote, it would be no vain boast. And yet a little after, as if he had forgotten himself, he adds, very inconsiderately, that I cannot produce a page in which he gives out that he is fighting for Saxony. I have no need to turn over each of his pages. Let the book itself be brought forth, and display its author's vanity. And I know not what modesty it is that prevents one who embraces the whole globe from professing himself the defender of Saxony. For, as if he alone were sustaining the whole weight, he says, that he writes in Latin with a view to foreign countries. In the common name of all, I affirm that there is not a man of sound brain who will not most willingly free him of his labour. If he continues to go on, he will gain nothing for his pains but malediction from all whose favour he is courting.

If he is to be believed, he is from nature and habit a great lover of modesty and bashfulness, so much so that these virtues from his youth up have always been his chosen attendants. Would that they had rather been his guides, and

not as we see remained behind to punish his contempt.
The blush of shame (*verecundia*) must certainly be a common
attendant of the Westphals; for it cannot but be that God
will cast down in disgrace those who exalt themselves so
highly. He so transfigures himself as to make it difficult to
select the proper point of attack. Modesty and liberty are,
I admit, most becoming in the servants of Christ; but two
things remain for Westphal to prove—first, that the cause
he pleads is the cause of Christ; and secondly, that the
frantic impetus with which he is carried and hurried along,
differs in no respect from the spirit of liberty with which the
sons of God are endowed. For what can he gain by a prolix
commendation of his office, unless the fact be distinctly ascertained? He says that he has been forced into this warfare
by a heavenly guide, whereas we, under no legitimate auspices, fight against God, take up arms against Christ sitting
on the right hand of the Father, and bear hostile standards
against his soldiers. In other words, a stolid braggart arrogates every thing to himself; an impure calumniator vents
at hazard invectives which fall of their own accord before
they reach us; a profane man shamefully and licentiously
abuses passages of Scripture, just as sorcerers distort sound
words in impious incantations. And yet he quarrels with
me for rebuking him, for combating instead of encouraging
him; for I cannot give any other meaning to his words,
that good leaders are wont to encourage their soldiers by
praises and promises, not to rebuke them for fighting.

I wish he would conduct himself so that one might feel at
liberty to encourage him as one of the soldiers of Christ.
As I admonished him to retire from a war improperly begun,
he vainly tries to wrest my words, and make me mean that
I despise common soldiers, and seek to raise a noble trophy
to some great leader. Have I challenged any one? Do I
not rather study to offer myself as a coadjutor, that we may
with one mind extend the kingdom of Christ? It is worth
while to attend to his next remark, that it were a kind of
Thrasonic boasting to undertake to contend with the leaders.
This is completely proved by Westphal's example. How
numerous and how distinguished are the individuals whom he

has presumed to engage at once!   Throwing them all, living
and dead, into one bundle, he has attempted to put them all
to route by one little book.   Meanwhile, his honour, as to
which he is on other occasions more than duly anxious, he lays
too low when he charges me with being unwilling to fight
with him, because I regard him as too insignificant an opponent.   He then passes to another subject, and says, that we
did not yield to the chief men.   If it was wrong not to do so,
with what face did he, without any provocation, presume to
rise against the chief men ?   It is less excusable audacity
voluntarily to make war on those who are quiet and silent,
than to defend ourselves against those who assail us.   But
to spare him, now that he flees to his common asylum, (the
regular custom of those men being to take shelter under the
name of Luther, and hold it up as the shield of Ajax,) how
shall he excuse the unbridled impudence which he blurts
forth against us ?

He assigns us for patrons Carolstadt, Suinckfeldius, and
others of like stamp, whom he calls satellites of Satan.
What I long ago wrote concerning Suinckfeldius he is not ignorant, and the whole world is my witness.   In speaking of
profane men who make void the sacraments, I have set him
down as the standard-bearer.   (Commentary, 1 Cor. x.)   See
the spiritual power with which Westphal has been armed to lie
by any one rather than by Christ.   Let the reader now judge
whether I did him injustice when I said that he sported at
his ease, seeing it is evident that, for the sake of beguiling
the time, he and his fellows not only licentiously talk what
they please against us, but also introduce it into published
writings.   He says he is not exempted from the common
lot of all who bear the pastoral office.   Certainly if he contrasts my cares with his seat, he may justly hold himself to
be a Cathedral bishop.   In this I do not envy him : only I
would not have him to pursue hostility to us for his mere
gratification.   Were he to employ his vehemence to some
useful purpose, I would rather stimulate his holy zeal by applause and congratulation than check it by rebuke.

Why does he now complain that his calumnies have met
with their just reward ?   His boast of zeal for the house of

God must be classed among the other boasts by which he foully profanes all that is sacred. When he says that he sometimes feels keenly against obstinate men, but by employing moderation takes care that his fervour does not become a fault, you would say that Cato the Censor is speaking, and the stern gravity of that sage would produce a kind of terror did not the long ears immediately appear and show it to be only Westphal. There is great truth in the words he quotes from Nanzianzen, that the soldiers of Christ, though meek in other things, must be pugnacious for the faith. But not only common experience, but this man's intemperance, shows it to be equally true that the servants of the devil are more than pugnacious against the faith. Therefore if he would escape the charge of perverse violence, let him not deck himself in another's feathers, but begin to show himself the servant of God, instead of continuing as hitherto to be too strenuous a soldier of the father of discord. When he bids me compare my letter with all his writings, and holds his violence excused by the comparison, I refuse not the offer, only let the reader judge from his farrago which I discussed, how much he deserved, and how far I am from having done him injustice by my sharpness. Moreover, in order that he may not bear the whole burden of obloquy, he throws part of it on tale-bearers. But lest any one should suppose that these words go to my exculpation, he immediately after adds, that there is little difference between the fault of those who hurt the reputation of others by their tales, and those who, lending too ready an ear, bring charges against the persons thus defamed, because God forbids us no less to receive false evidence than to give it. Why then does he in each of his pages lie so licentiously against an unoffending multitude, and tear me so atrociously?

He dares to cite me before the bar of God. Had he any thought of divine judgment, he would either spare a man who has deserved well of the Church of God, or at least treat him more humanely. But why do I ask any regard to be paid to me, when I see such indignity and invective against illustrious servants of God, who either spent their whole life in maintaining his glory and promoting the kingdom of

Christ, or still surviving, hold on the same course? His truculence appears in strong colours when he inveighs against fugitives. He deems it not sufficient to have denied them hospitality and driven them away amidst the rigour of a most severe winter, when they wished to breathe a little, unless he also endeavours, by all the means in his power, to exterminate them from the face of the earth. Although just indignation was then wrung from me by the pity with which, if I am not of iron, I behoved to be touched at the sad calamities of my brethren, still I now see and confess that I was deceived. I thought that Westphal and his fellows had had some cause or other for being more than ordinarily exasperated. Now I see that to exercise unbounded severity against all of us indiscriminately, it is enough for them that we do not subscribe at their dictation. With such virulent hatred do they inveigh against us, that they would sooner make peace with the Turks, and fraternize with Papists, than keep truce with us. If this indignity stirs my bile, no man need wonder. If I have exceeded bounds, the goodness of the cause will, I trust, procure my pardon with equitable judges.

But Westphal does not leave me this excuse; for he says, first, that the cause I plead is not good; and secondly, that I have given loose reins to my passions in order that I might obscure the light of truth. As to the cause, I presume that all pious men are satisfied. I think I have defended it by strong arguments, as well as discussed it in a regular manner; for to call in the aid of invective is a thing which the case did not require, and which my mind never thought of. While he harangues rhetorically that any cause, be it what it may, is rendered suspicious by mingling invective with it, why does he not exercise some self-restraint? How comes it that he is ever and anon calling out heresy and blasphemy? How comes it, in short, that he never abstains from any kind of insolence? And yet, as if it were sufficient to wipe his mouth, he pretends that the only purpose he had was to repel my assault. See why he charges me with having adorned a bad cause with declamation, as a kind of adventitious colouring, though it is plain that, after taking a firm grasp of the subject, I have said nothing that was not relevant to it, while he, touching it sparingly and meagerly, keeps wandering and winding about in commonplace. Assuredly he will never be so eloquent a rhetorician as to persuade others that I am a declaimer. My concise brevity in writing, and the firm stand I take in handling argument, are known to all.

Westphal has made the conclusion of his book consist of certain cavils, by which he has endeavoured to excite suspicion, and detract from the credit of what was correctly stated. At the outset, indeed, he does not dare openly to censure, but pretends to call for the examination of the Church; at length, collecting courage, he ventures to condemn. It is something, indeed, that by his confession I pay more honour to the sacraments, and speak of their virtue, use, and dignity with more reverence than most others. If it is so, why did this moderation of mine not soften him? So far from having had any effect in soothing his anger, it would seem rather to have exasperated him. If by my doctrine, which he declares to be moderate, his moroseness could not be entirely appeased nor his asperity softened, what cause was there for assaulting me so violently? For although mixing me up with a crowd of others he did not select a single enemy, yet he has conceived more bitterness from our Agreement than from all other writings whatever. Let us proceed, however, to his censures.

He acknowledges with me that the sacraments were instituted to lead us to the communion of Christ, and be helps by which we may be ingrafted into the body of Christ, or, being ingrafted, be united more and more. He asks why I say that infants begotten of believers are holy and members of the Church before they are baptized? I answer, that they may grow up the more into communion with Christ. He thinks he is arguing acutely in denying that they are ingrafted into the Church before baptism, if they are ingrafted by baptism. I easily retort the objection. For if I am right as to the effect of the sacraments, viz., that it makes those who are already ingrafted into the body of Christ to be united to him more and more, what forbids the application of this to baptism? I do not, however, insist on this answer.

I admit that the proper office of baptism is to ingraft us into the body of Christ, not that those who are baptized should be altogether aliens from him, but because God attests that he thus receives them. There is a well-known saying of Augustine, that there are many sheep of Christ without the Church, just as there are many wolves dwelling within; in other words, those whom God invites to himself by the Spirit of adoption, were known to him before they knew him by faith. Therefore, although God acknowledges as in his Church persons who seem to be strangers, and are so in so far as they themselves are concerned, he is justly said to ingraft them into his Church when he enlightens them unto faith, which is their first entrance into the hope of eternal life.

I admit that the difficulty of the question is not yet solved. I only adverted to these principles to let Westphal see there is no absurdity in saying, that persons who were formerly members of the Church are afterwards ingrafted into the Church. Before I give my answer with regard to children and infants, I should like to have his as to the four thousand men whom Peter gained over to Christ by his first sermon : also as to Cornelius and others. If he denies that they were members of the Church before baptism, then, according to him, faith and repentance have no effect. If those whom God has regenerated by his word—whom he has formed again after his image—whom he has honoured with the celestial light of faith—whom he has enriched with the gifts of his Spirit, belong not to the body of the Church, by what marks can the children of God be distinguished from the rest of the world ? What, then, remains but for Westphal to concede, that in some measure, or *secundum quid,* (in some respect,) as it is called, there were members of the Church who were afterwards initiated into its society by baptism ? Thus the sins of Paul were washed away in baptism, though he had previously obtained pardon of them by faith.

There is nothing to prevent our applying this to infants, whose case is not unlike ; for either the covenant by which God adopts them is vain, and the promise void, or those whom God declares to be of his flock are not wholly strangers.

God gives the name of sons to those to whom the inheritance of salvation has been promised in the person of their
parents. By what title can he be their Father if they in
no way belong to the Church ? There is nothing, however,
to prevent his sealing this grace, and confirming anew the
same thing that he had given before. It is strange that
Westphal denies this right to infants, though without it he
could not properly admit them to baptism. But while I
acknowledge that we become members of the Church by
baptism, I deny that any are duly baptized if they do not
belong to the body of the Church. It is not ours to confer
the sacraments on all and sundry ; but we must dispense
them according to the rule prescribed by God. Who authorized you, Westphal, to bestow the pledge of eternal life, the
symbol of righteousness and renovation, on a profane person
lying under curse ? Were an Anabaptist to debate with you,
I presume your only valid defence would be, that baptism is
rightly administered to those whom God adopted before they
were born, and to whom he has promised that he will be a
Father. Did not God transmit his grace from parents to
children, to admit new-born infants into the Church would
be a mere profanation of baptism. But if the promise of
God under the law caused holy branches to proceed from a
holy root, will you restrict the grace of God under the gospel, or diminish its efficacy by withholding the testimony of
adoption by which God distinguishes infants ?

The law ordered infants to be circumcised on the eighth
day. I ask, whether that was a legitimate ingrafting into
the Church of God ? Who dares deny that it was ? But
Scripture declares them to have been holy from the womb,
as being the offspring of a holy race ; in other words, for the
reason for which Paul teaches, that the children of believers
are now holy. Westphal argues as if God were not at liberty
gradually to perfect the faith of his people. I again say,
that they are in some respect ingrafted into the Church,
though in a different respect they were previously ingrafted.
The promise of God must not be deemed of no moment, as
if it were insufficient for the salvation of those whom he
calls sons and heirs. Confiding in it, I hold that those whom

God has already set apart for himself are rightly brought for baptism. We are not now speaking of secret election, but of an adoption manifested by the word, which sanctifies infants not yet born. But as baptism is a solemn recognition by which God introduces his children into the possession of life, a true and effectual sealing of the promise, a pledge of sacred union with Christ, it is justly said to be the entrance and reception into the Church. And as the instruments of the Holy Spirit are not dead, God truly performs and effects by baptism what he figures.

If Westphal do not admit this rule, the Apostles waited foolishly, and against reason, till those whom they were afterwards to admit to baptism should be made sons of God. According to his dogma, they ought to have baptized first, lest the Church, by receiving them into her bosom as already holy, should render baptism superfluous : unless, indeed, with the same equity with which he denied hospitality to the pious exiles of Christ, he expunge those who are regenerated by the Spirit from the kingdom of heaven. Cornelius, before he was baptized with his household, having received the Holy Spirit, being adorned with the badges of saints, justly held some place among the children of God. The baptism which was afterwards added Westphal must hold to be pre-posterous, if he insists that none are to be admitted to it but strangers.

It is a frivolous cavil to say that I am sporting with an ambiguous expression, as if the reception which is given by baptism were nothing else than an external distinction be-fore men, since I plainly affirm, that in baptism we have to do with God, who, not only by testifying his paternal love, pledges his faith to us, so as to give us a sure persuasion of our salvation, but also inwardly ratifies by his divine agency that which he figures by the hand of his minister.

This disposes of another calumny, where he says, that some of us, while holding that infants, who, before eternal ages, had been adopted as sons, are afterwards visibly in-grafted into the body of Christ, introduce paradoxes which are repugnant to the words of Christ, " Whoso believeth and is baptized shall be saved ;" and again, " Unless ye be born of water and of the Spirit," &c.   No one, I believe, ever proposed to dissever the sanction of grace from baptism, that the covenant might be ratified which God made by his word. Here the reader sees how little he cares to defile the Scripture with unwashen hands.   The question between us turns on infants.   He contends, that by baptism they become members of Christ and heirs of life.   By what passage does he confirm this view?   Just by one, by which infants would be cut off from the hope of salvation, were it not clear that it is to be understood as only referring to adults, who from age are already fit to believe.   When fanatical men impugn Pædobaptism, they argue from this passage, not without plausibility, that the order appointed by Christ is overthrown if faith do not precede baptism.   Their error is properly refuted, by observing, that Christ there treats expressly of the preaching of the gospel, which is addressed to none but adults.   Westphal breaks forth, and extracts from it, like oil from stone, that salvation is given to infants by baptism. The other passage, when he has more carefully examined it, he will cease improperly to apply to baptism.

Again, he asks, if the sacraments are instruments by which God acts efficaciously, and testifies and seals his grace to us, why do we deny, that by the washing of baptism men are born again?   As if our alleged denial were not a fiction of his own.   Having distinctly asserted, that men are regenerated by baptism, just as they are by the word, I early obviated the impudence of the man, and left nothing for his invective to strike at but his own shadow.   When he expostulates with me for having charged him and his companions with blindness, because they erroneously affix their confidence of salvation to the sacraments, and transfer to them what properly belongs to God alone, he either is actuated by strange eagerness for quarrelling, or he has determined for once to carry all the superstitions in the world into his own stye.

We know how gross the errors on the sacraments are which prevail in the Papacy, how the minds of all, being fascinated by a kind of magical enchantments, pass by Christ, and fix their confidence of salvation on the elements.   We know, that so far from applying the sacraments to their proper end, they rather make them the cause of grace. Nothing of all this does Westphal allow to be touched, without crying out that he is hurt: as if to please him, so many vile corruptions were to be fostered; whereas, had he one particle of true piety in his mind, he would use his utmost endeavour to purge them away. But it is obvious, that under the influence of some incredible perversity, he would sooner immerse himself in the deepest pools of the Papacy than make any approach to us. He denies that he transfers any part of salvation to creatures, because the question is concerning the presence of God working by means which he has appointed. I assent. What he afterwards adds, being borrowed from us almost verbatim, why should I repudiate? Nay, I am rather obliged to him for agreeing and subscribing to my words so far, until, in accordance with his nature, he falls back again upon his calumnies.

He infers, I know not from what principles, that I in ignorance partly destroy the effect of baptism, partly bring it into doubt. How do I destroy it? He answers, Because I deny that the benefit derived from the sacraments is confined to the time at which they are administered. What says he to the contrary? He confesses with me that the virtue of baptism extends to the whole of life, and that infants who have been washed at the sacred font often show no benefit from it after some progress of years. But he rejoins, that their baptism was not therefore void and without effect. By these words he thinks he solves the difficulty. He certainly frees me: only he adds shortly after, that they are always truly regenerated and sanctified in baptism, though afterwards, from want of due training, they relapse into the defilements of sin. In these words he insinuates something too gross to be tolerated by the ordinance of God.

I ask, if Simon Magus was truly sanctified at the same moment when he was washed with the water? It is not likely that the hypocrisy for which he is so severely rebuked by Peter was ever eradicated from his mind: hence it followed, that the effect of baptism did not immediately appear. But had he repented at Peter's admonition, would not the

grace of baptism have resumed its place?   And how many
daily approach the holy table who by negligence and luke-
warmness are deprived of present benefit, and yet, when
afterwards aroused, begin to receive it?   Who dare say that
none partake of Christ but those who receive him in the
very act of the Supper?   Westphal's rejoinder, that this
does not imply that the sacraments do no good when they
are administered, is easily answered.   They do good just as
a seed when thrown into the ground, though it may not take
root and germinate at the very moment, is not without its
use.   Had it not been sown in this manner it would not in
process of time have sent forth its shoot.   Baptism becomes
at last effectual, though it does not work effectually at the
same moment at which it is performed.   Westphal objects,
that its virtue is not to be put off to distant years, as if God
did not regenerate infants when they are baptized.   Granting this, he has still to prove that they are always regenerated.   For as I do not hold it to be a universal rule, so the
exception which I adduce is manifest, that the nature of
baptism or the Supper must not be tied down to an instant
of time.   God, whenever he sees meet, fulfils and exhibits
in immediate effect that which he figures in the sacrament.
But no necessity must be imagined so as to prevent his
grace from sometimes preceding, sometimes following, the
use of the sign.   The dispensation of it, its Author so
tempers as not to separate the virtue of his Spirit from the
sacred symbol.

It is easy to show how groundlessly he presses a passage
of Augustine into his service.   Augustine is arguing against
the Manichees, that perfection is not to be looked for in the
very commencement of regeneration, because renovation begun by the sacred laver is perfected by progress, sooner in
some, later in others.   What can any one infer from this but
just that the ordinary method in which God accomplishes
our salvation is by beginning it in baptism and carrying it
gradually forward during the whole course of life?   Thus he
shows, (De Trinit. Cont. Cath. et Donat. 14,) that full and
entire regeneration is not conferred at the same instant when
entire forgiveness of sins is received.   Hence it follows, that

it is not always received at the very moment when it is offered. For though there can be no doubt that on the part of God, (to use a common expression,) this is the perpetual virtue and utility of baptism, and this, too, the ordinary method of dispensing grace, it is erroneous to infer that the free course of Divine grace is tied down to instants of time.

I come now to the second branch of the calumny. He says, that the effect of baptism is brought into doubt by me, because I suspend it on predestination, whereas Scripture directs us to the word and sacraments, and leads by this way to the certainty of predestination and salvation. But had he not here introduced a fiction of his own, which never came into my mind, there was no occasion for dispute. I have written much, and the Lord has employed me in various kinds of discussion. If out of my lucubrations he can produce a syllable in which I teach that we ought to begin with predestination in seeking assurance of salvation, I am ready to remain dumb. That secret election was mentioned by me in passing, I admit. But to what end? Was it either to lead pious minds away from hearing the promise or looking at the signs? There was nothing of which I was more careful than to confine them entirely within the word. What? While I so often inculcate that grace is offered by the sacraments, do I not invite them there to seek the seal of their salvation? I only said that the Spirit of God does not work indiscriminately in all, but as he enlightens the elect only unto faith, so he also provides that they do not use the sacraments in vain. Should I say that the promises are common to all, and that eternal salvation is offered in common to all, but that the ratification of them is the special gift of the Spirit, who seals the offered grace in the elect, would Westphal say that the word is removed from its place? And what does he himself daily declare to the people from the pulpit, but just that faith comes by hearing, and yet that those only obey to whom the arm of the Lord is revealed? The reason is, that while God invites all by the word, he inwardly gives an effectual call to those whom he has chosen. Let him cease then to cavil and pretend that I render the

effect of baptism doubtful when I show that election is the
source from which the profit found in the sacraments flows
to those to whom it has been specially given. For while,
according to the common proverb, things standing to each
other in the relation of superior and inferior are not contradictory, an inferior sealing of grace by the sacraments is not
denied, while the Spirit is called the prior and more internal
seal; and the cause is at the same time stated, viz., because
God has elected those whom he honours with the badge of
adoption.

Not less unworthy is his last cavil, by which he distorts a
sentiment that is most true, and not more true than useful.
I said that those act foolishly who look only to the bare
signs and not also to the promises annexed to them. He
admits that it was rightly said, and he freely gives it his
support. Shortly after, as if some new wasp had stung him,
he murmurs that caution must be used, otherwise the promise may be dissevered from the sacraments. What? Was
not the promise distinctly admitted when I joined it to them
by an indissoluble tie? I observed that a sacrilegious divorce
was made if any one should insist on having the bare sign,
and that dissevered from the promise. Westphal cries out
that we must beware of separating the promise from the
signs, just as if he were to keep scolding and calling to the
builder of a cistern, who was carefully stopping up the chinks,
to take care that the water did not escape through them.

What am I endeavouring to do, but just to make those
who desire benefit from the sacraments confine themselves
within the word? Westphal comes upon me while so employed, and finds fault with me, as if I were maintaining
that baptism is nothing but water, and that in the Supper
there is nothing but bread and wine. Why then did I
quote the testimony of Augustine—that without the word
the water is nothing but an element, and that with the word
it begins to become a sacrament—but just to show that the
sacraments derive their value from the word with which they
are so closely connected, that on being dissevered from it
they lose their nature? Westphal's motive, no doubt, was
this. He did not think that his hostility to us would seem

fierce enough if he did not out of mere spite attack the plainest truth, seize upon the minutest particles as materials for strife, and infect honey itself with his bitter.   He chose to publish his disgrace before the whole world sooner than not prove to the little brothers who kept soothing and flattering him, that he is our declared enemy out and out.

LAST ADMONITION OF JOHN CALVIN

TO

JOACHIM WESTPHAL,

WHO, IF HE HEEDS IT NOT, MUST HENCEFORTH BE TREATED IN THE WAY
WHICH PAUL PRESCRIBES FOR OBSTINATE HERETICS ;

HEREIN ALSO ARE REFUTED THE CENSURES BY WHICH THOSE OF
MAGDEBURG AND ELSEWHERE HAVE TRIED TO
OVERTURN HEAVEN AND EARTH.

JOACHIM WESTPHAL has published a letter, written to
one of his friends, whose name shame makes him conceal.
Having there promised that he is going to answer the charges
of John Calvin, he mournfully deplores that I have treated
him more harshly than the Anabaptists, Libertines, and
Papists. Were I to grant this, (though he here shamefully
exposes his vanity,) why does he not sit down calmly and
consider with himself, what he has deserved both by his atrocious attacks on sound doctrine, and his barbarous cruelty
towards pious and unoffending individuals ? He asks if he
deserves no mercy, while others are more mildly treated, as
if one who has violated all the rights of humanity, and been
seen, of set purpose, making war on equity and modesty,
had not precluded himself from all title to expostulate.
Why does he not rather attend to the declaration of our
heavenly Master, " With what measure ye mete, it shall be
measured to you again ?" As if he had been brought up in
the Roman court during his whole life, and learned nothing
but anathema, he surpasses all the scribes and clerks of the
Pope, by fulminating against us in almost every sentence.
When argument fails him, he overwhelms the best cause, by
damnatory sentences and reproaches. Nay, as in comedies
wicked slaves, driven to despair, throw every thing into confusion, so he by his clamour mingles light and darkness.

Why should I not give this insanity its proper name? Nay, as I had to do with a hard and stubborn head, why should I not be permitted to use a hard wedge for a bad knot? Unless, indeed, he can show that he is protected by some new privilege, which entitles him petulantly to employ his bad tongue on others, without hearing a harsh word in reply.

This, no doubt, is the reason why both those censors pronounce my book full of sting and virulence. I am not surprised at the former epithet, nor am I sorry that men so stupid have, at least, felt some pricks. As to virulence, they will find more of it in themselves than in the book. Still, whatever contumely Westphal may deserve, I ought not, it seems, to toss him about so violently. Accordingly, he exclaims, that all covering, gloss, and pretext are removed, and my temper stands disclosed by this one book: nay, he pretends that I have hitherto gone about personating a different character from my own. The character which God gave me, I, by his grace, so bear, that the sincerity of my faith is abundantly manifest. I wish the integrity of Westphal and his fellows were half as well proved by similar fruit. I do not envy others, though they should surpass me an hundredfold, but it is intolerable to hear lazy drones crying down the industry which they cannot imitate.

To prove that I am devoid of all fear of God, modesty, humility, patience—that, in short, I have nothing becoming a servant of Christ, he alleges, that unmoved by the dreadful denunciation of Christ, " Whoso shall say to his brother, Thou fool, shall be liable to hell fire," I have filled numerous sheets with more than six hundred reproaches. One would say, that we have here Julian the apostate, while he cruelly rages against the whole Christian name, discoursing in mockery about bearing the cross. He who has hitherto allowed himself a thousand times to vociferate, without measure or restraint, against the faithful servants of Christ, ever and anon calling them heretical, impious, blasphemous, crafty, forgers, plagues, and devils, cannot bear to have one word of condemnation uttered against his presumption. If, in rebuking the Galatians for fickleness and thoughtlessness

in being too easy and credulous, Paul did not hesitate to
employ the term madness, with what vehemence should not
the presumption of one who, with phrenzied impetus, attacks
the doctrine of Christ and his true worshippers, be repressed?
The only wish I have is, that the rebuke had so touched the
mind of Joachim as not to leave him guilty before that
heavenly tribunal, the terror of which he holds out to others.

But the precept of Christ is, to love our enemies, and bless
those that curse us. Why, then, has he of his own accord
made a hostile assault on his friends, and those who were
desirous to cultivate fraternal goodwill with him? Why did
he pronounce maledictions on those who were quiet, and had
never harmed him by a single word? He denies both charges.
Let his writings be read, that one especially in which he
attacks our Agreement. Till that time I had never touched
him or one of his faction, but had rather humbly begged,
that if any thing in our doctrine did not please, it might
not be deemed too troublesome to correct it by placid admonition. And, indeed, as experience afterwards showed, some
then justly derided me for being so simple as to hope that
those who had previously forgotten the rights of humanity,
and vehemently flamed out against us, would be calmed
down. Why did Joachim, when so mildly requested, choose
to cry out heresy, rather than to point out the error, if any
there was? Thus unworthily treated, not in the heat of
passion, as he falsely imagines, but to curb the excessive
ferocity in which he was indulging, I applied the remedy
somewhat more sharply than I could desire. I wish the
pain had stung him to repentance. But since he is so much
exasperated, and has, in no degree, laid aside his perverse
conduct, I console myself with another good result, viz., that
others will understand how insipidly he has defended his
error against the clear light of sound doctrine. Meanwhile,
if from blind hatred he is unable to perceive my intention,
Christ the common Judge recognises it, and, in his own time,
will make it manifest that I am not so given to avenge private injuries, as not to be ready, when any hope of cure appears, to lay aside all remembrance of them, and try all
methods of brotherly pacification.

When he says in another place that I have anxiously la-
poured not to omit any kind of insult, how much he is mistaken will best appear from the fact. Many can bear me
witness that the book was hastily written. What the case
required, and occurred spontaneously at the time, I dictated
without any lengthened meditation, and with a feeling so
remote from gall, (with which, he says, I am thoroughly infected,) that I afterwards wondered how harsher terms had
fallen from me while I had no bitterness in my heart. But,
perhaps, the unworthy conduct of the man, while indulging
his proud moroseness, required that he should be made to
feel that the defenders of the truth were not without sharp
weapons. It is easy for Joachim to attribute to me the
black salt of absurd scurrility and sycophantish mendacity;
but it is equally easy for me in one word to dispose of the
calumny, by defying him to find any thing that can justify
his hateful charge. Though I should be silent, the candid
reader will alike detest his impudence and deride his folly.
With the same modesty he alleges, that I hunt in words and
syllables for absurd and insipid squibs, while it is plain that
so far from being on the watch for bitter terms, I have purposely omitted those which spontaneously presented themselves. In short, if the reader will consider to what derision
Westphal has exposed himself, and how much subject for
irony his stupidity affords, none will be so unjust or preju-
diced as not to say, that in this matter I have spared him
and used restraint. If I am a dealer in reproaches, because
I have held up the mirror to Joachim, who was winking too
much at his faults, and made him at last begin to feel
ashamed of his conduct, he must also bestow the same epithet
on the Prophets, and the Apostles, and Christ himself, whose
practice it was to administer severe reproof to the enemies
of sound doctrine, those of them especially whom they saw to
be proud and obstinate. Nay, laying hold of commonplace,
without modification and selection, as if it were unlawful to
charge the wicked defenders of error as they deserve, he
avowedly undertakes the defence of all false prophets, seeking to augment their licentiousness by impunity.

Westphal's complaint that I have treated him more unmercifully than Papists, Libertines, and Anabaptists, the reader will perceive from my writings to be most false. To render their pernicious errors by which all religion is corrupted detestable to all the pious, I depict them in their true colours. In this matter, Westphal does not disapprove of my severity by censuring it; but as soon as he himself is touched, he cries out that all charity is disregarded. That bitter reproaches and scurrilous witticisms are unbecoming in Christians, both sides agree. But as the Prophets did not refrain from derision, and our Saviour himself speaks in cutting terms of perverse and deceitful teachers, and the Holy Spirit everywhere inveighs with full freedom against this class of men, it is thoughtless and foolish to raise the question, whether it be lawful gravely and sternly to rebuke those who expose themselves to shame and disgrace ; for this is to bring a charge against the servants of God, whom holy zeal often impelled to harsh and bitter speeches. No doubt every individual is always bound to look well to the cause for which he either takes fire or speaks keenly.

After our Agreement was published, and Westphal had full liberty to correct any thing that was faulty, calumniously searching in all quarters for an appearance of repugnance, he in savage mood lashed the living and the dead. I, in repelling this savage attack, refrained from giving his name, in order that if he was of a temper that admitted of cure his ignominy might be buried. Repudiating this by a violent, not to say cyclopical production, he attempted not only to confound heaven and earth, but to stir up Acheron. Considering that this obstinate intemperance was not to be cured by gentle remedies, I took the liberty to sharpen my pen. What could I do? I must either by silence betray the truth, or by soft and placid pleading, give signs of timidity and diffidence. As if he had wrested all the thunder out of the hand of God to hurl it fearfully at our heads, he endeavoured by the sound of words to strike us with dismay. A graver refutation having dissipated the terrors of his ridiculous anathemas, he has vented all his petulance and fury against us, pretending it to be very sweetness, and then alleges that I have forgotten all humanity and modesty. Since his ferocity has proved intractable, it is easy to see the frivolousness and puerility of all his declamation. As if lions and bears, after rushing madly at every one in their way, should complain that they do not meet with soothing treatment, this delicate little man, after atrociously attacking the doctrine of Christ and his ministers, regards it as a great crime that he is not treated like a brother.

The whole question turns upon this—Did I attempt to avenge a private injury, or was it in the defence of a public cause that I strenuously opposed Westphal? Any private injury he did me I was bound patiently to bear. But if the whole aim of my vehemence was to prevent a good cause, even the sacred truth of Christ, from being overwhelmed by the loud clamours of Westphal, why should it be imputed to me as a fault? I wish this perverse censor could have any slight idea of what is meant by the words, " The zeal of thy house hath eaten me up; and the reproaches of them that reproached thee fell upon me." Had he any such idea, he would not so preposterously, as if in mockery, wrest the holy admonition of Peter to his own purpose. Peter exhorts us, by the example of Christ, to submit calmly to all kinds of contumely and reproach. Westphal therefore insists that such silence as Christ kept when unjustly accused, should be observed by his ministers whenever the truth is assailed : as if instead of the injunction to all to cry aloud, the Apostle were there imposing a law of perfidious tolerance on the preachers of the gospel. Wherefore, until Westphal show that I retaliated private wrongs, and was more devoted to my own cause than to the defence of doctrine, the reader will understand that it is the veriest trifling for him to talk of patience and silence.

He also accuses me of not having studied to gain my enemy. At first I followed the method best fitted to remove offences, and now if he wishes reconciliation, though he has so often injured me, I decline not. I appeal to Christ as Judge, and call all angels to witness, that the moment Westphal shall turn from his perverseness there will be no delay in me in maintaining brotherly good-will with him. Nay, if he can now put on the mind of a brother, I in my turn am prepared to embrace him as a brother. But the iniquitous condition is imposed, that I shall renounce the confession of true and holy doctrine—a price for which I would not purchase the peace even of the whole world. And not to go on debating to weariness and without any profit, let the reader attend to one leading point on which the whole controversy turns. Joachim insists that any thing is lawful to him against us, because, as he says, he is defending true doctrine against impious error. When once he shall have proved this, I acknowledge that we must be quiet. But if I teach and show that what he falsely arrogates to himself truly belongs to me—that I am the faithful defender of pure and holy doctrine, and faithfully exert myself not only in refuting impious error, but in wiping off atrocious calumnies, why should not I have the same liberty he claims? Let judgment then be first given on the cause, that neither he nor I may keep beating the air. What prevents the reader from drawing a sure distinction between holy zeal and licentious invective, but just the attempt of Westphal to darken the clear light, by clamouring that my book is stuffed with bitter words?

Here it is worth while in passing to notice the combined stupidity and impudence of the man. In my former writings, wishing to bring him back to a moderate discussion of the subject, I said it was base and absurd to attack us with so much pride and petulance. He fiercely replied, that it was necessary to fight with the utmost keenness against heretics, and that, therefore, a composed or sedate style was not to be used—that the more ardour any man felt in such a contest the better he proved himself a zealous soldier of Christ. In short, he used all the colouring he could to excuse not only the vehemence but the fury of passion. What does he now do? Paul, he says, wished not that the disobedient should be regarded as enemies, but be corrected as brethren. He also quotes recommendations of meekness from Ambrose and Gregory Nazianzen. Whoever will compare these two passages together, will not only say that this man, who so varies and differs from himself, has lost his memory and his senses, but will easily see that possessing no ingenuousness, he sophistically catches now at this defence, now at that, and endeavours by empty froth to convert virtues into vices.

Tell me, Joachim, if you ever were in earnest when you said that severity was by no means to be spared in condemning error, or whether by now singing a disgraceful palinode, you would condemn the rigour which you lauded as holy zeal, in order to be able to throw obloquy on me? Meanwhile, this worthy assertor and teacher of charity, who denies that it is to be violated by the smallest word, cries out that all persons whatsoever who are found to favour us ought to be driven from the face of the earth, boasts of having written that we ought to be refuted by the sword of the magistrate rather than by the pen, and advises the magistrates to pronounce interdict from fire and water, not only against the professors but even the approvers of our doctrine. Westphal's definition of charity therefore is, that he is to rage at will with fire and sword against us, and then to pronounce that we have fallen from Christianity, if we use any freedom in speaking of him. To omit other things, what gave him this great confidence, this atrocious censorship, worthy of Phalaris, to be ever and anon styling us heretics, a name which starts up not only in every page but almost in every sentence, but just our refraining hitherto to use invective in reply? Assuredly, it was nothing but our mildness that added so much to his ferocity. What say you to this, good teacher of modesty? While it is perfectly clear that you abuse our patience in venting your anathemas, what ground can you have for charging us with treating you with harshness and austerity?

He again entangles himself, by denying that he was warned. After he had raged like a bacchanalian against the living and the dead, and not hesitated to form a catalogue of heretics out of our names, and I, suppressing his name, had showed my indignation, so little did I succeed, that he proceeded much more violently to fulminate at us with all kinds of curses and execrations. And yet the worthy man thinks that the time had not yet arrived for severe rebuke. When he again returns to his vulgar song,

that he was not yet convicted of error, whereas he had, by
solid reasons and arguments drawn from sacred Scripture,
proved our heresy to be damnable, of what use is it to pollute our sheets with the odour of such falsehoods ? To remove
all ambiguity, let my book be brought forward and vindicate
itself from the haughty charge. Assuredly, if I get it to
be read, it will soon appear how he upbraids me with being
more a buffoon than a divine, and how far from candour he
is in asserting that it is filled with nothing but empty invective. I would not object here to give a short summary
of it did not its brevity spare both the reader and myself
this trouble. Westphal has produced no argument which
was not there solidly refuted. I also adduced arguments
which neither he nor his whole band, do what they may,
will ever be able to shake off. This, too, I venture to assert,
that all endued with any moderate degree of impartiality
will at once, on reading the book, admit that a doctrine
so tolerable could not without the greatest injustice be so
invidiously traduced.

But however some may embrace the doctrine of my
book, and others at least think it deserving of excuse, it
would seem I am not to gain any thing by it. For Westphal has fallen upon a witty device to elude me, and sit
quiet while he calls in others to bear the brunt of the
battle. In order to prove that we overturn the Confession
of Augsburg, he introduces as our opponent Philip Melancthon, its most distinguished author—a man alike admirable
for piety and learning. In another writing he brings us
into controversy with the ancient Church under the name of
Augustine. And lastly, he draws a dense phalanx from
different places in the neighbourhood of Saxony. By this
splendid array he hopes to dazzle the eyes of the simple.
As I have to deal with a man of no modesty, but of the
greatest loquacity, I must ask my readers, first, to put aside
all circumlocution, and look at the bare facts ; and secondly,
to use prudence and impartiality in judging.

As the Confession of Augsburg has obtained favour with
the pious, Joachim, with his faction, began long ago to do
as is common with men destitute of argument, to obtrude it

upon us as a shield of authority. If he could show that we are opposed to the general consent given to it, he thought that he would in a manner becloud the sky, or at least bring a thick mist over the eyes of the simple, so as to prevent one ray of light from appearing even at noon-day. To free ourselves from the prejudice thus craftily sought to be excited, I appealed, I admit, to the author of the Confession, and I do not repent having done so. What does Westphal do? With his gross barbarism he represents me as making the victory to depend upon Philip's subscribing to us. Let not my readers wait till he himself becomes ashamed of this falsehood; there is too much brass in his brow: let them only judge what such vile talk deserves.

My words are: in regard to the Confession of Augsburg my answer is, that (as it was published at Ratisbon) it does not contain a word contrary to our doctrine. If there is any ambiguity in its meaning, there cannot be a more competent interpreter than its author, to whom, as his due, all pious and learned men will readily pay this honour. To him I boldly appeal; and thus Westphal with his vile garrulity lies prostrate.

Let him extract from these words, if he can, that I made the victory to depend on the subscription of any single man. No less sordid is the vanity which makes him wonder exceedingly that such a stigma was fastened on his master, though, from Philip's answer, he has learned the fact of our agreement more clearly than I ventured to declare it. But what need is there of words? If Joachim wishes once for all to rid himself of all trouble and put an end to the controversy, let him extract one word in his favour from Philip's lips. The means of access are open, and the journey is not so very laborious, to visit one whose consent he boasts so loftily, and with whom he may thus have familiar intercourse. If I shall be found to have used Philip's name rashly, there is no stamp of ignominy to which I am not willing to submit.

The passage which Westphal quotes it is not mine to refute, nor do I regard what, during the first conflict, before the matter was clearly and lucidly explained, the importunity of some may have extorted from one who was then too backward in giving a denial. It were too harsh to lay it down as a law on literary men, that after they have given a specimen of their talent and learning, they are never after to go beyond it in the course of their lives. Assuredly, whosoever shall say that Philip has added nothing by the labour of forty years, does great wrong to him individually, and to the whole Church. The only thing I said, and, if need be, a hundred times repeat, is, that in this matter Philip can no more be torn from me than he can from his own bowels. But although fearing the thunder which threatened to burst from violent men, (those who know the boisterous blasts of Luther understand what I mean,) he did not always speak out so openly as I could have wished, there is no reason why Westphal, while pretending differently, should indirectly charge him with having begun to incline to us only after Luther was dead. For when more than seventeen years ago we conferred together on this point of doctrine, at our first meeting not a syllable required to be changed. Nor should I omit to mention Gaspar Cruciger, who, from his excellent talents and learning, stood next after Philip highest in Luther's estimation, and far beyond all others. He so cordially embraced what Westphal now impugns, that nothing can be imagined more perfectly accordant than our opinions. But if there is still any doubt as to Philip, do I not make a sufficient offer when I wait silent and confident for his answer, assured that it will make manifest the dishonesty which has falsely sheltered itself under the venerable name of that most excellent man ?

I come to Augustine, whom, though all his writings proclaim him to be wholly ours, Westphal, not content with wresting from us, obtrudes as an adversary, not hesitating to claim him for himself with the same audacity with which he uniformly turns light into darkness. What view James Bording, to whom he dedicates his farrago, now takes, I know not; certainly if he has not greatly changed his mind, he would rather that an office fraught with dishonour had not been conferred on him. At the time when I knew him he was distinguished not less by ingenuous modesty than by learning. It is now only worth while briefly to advert to

what the Letter contains, not that I am going to expose all
its loquacity, but to enable my readers to form an estimate
of the temper of the man, as it will be easy to do from a few
heads. First, he maintains, that to prevent the contagion
from spreading, sectaries and heretics are to be banished
or otherwise subjected to punishment. As we are both
agreed on that matter, all he had to do was to subscribe to
us. It would certainly have been more honest to have
quoted our books, from which he borrows any arguments he
adduces, than, while pretending to make war upon us, to
fight with our own weapons. In this way he would not have
given a disgraceful specimen of stupidity, which the man's
unreasonable conduct compels me to notice.

As in the twenty-fourth Psalm, the Vulgate Version has
improperly rendered, " Lift up your doors, ye Princes," instead of " Lift up your heads, O ye doors," a certain learned
man, who has deserved well of the Church, from lapse of
memory, as often happens, wishing to exhort princes to
defend piety, had used this passage. The error might be
tolerated. Westphal, quoting exactly " Lift up your heads,
O ye doors," says, the passage enjoins magistrates to open
the doors to the Lord, and shut them against false prophets.
From this the reader may infer what reverence these men
show in handling Scripture, which they so impurely and
presumptuously lacerate. Yet the worthy man, in his eagerness to throw obloquy on me, was not ashamed to insert in
the farrago, to which he gives the name of Confessions, the
letter of some follower of SERVETUS, in which I am called
an incendiary for having taught that heretics are justly
punished. Let the letter be read. It brings no other charge
against me than that I teach that rulers are armed with the
sword not less to punish impiety than other crimes. The
only difference between me and Westphal is, that I say there
is no room for severity unless the case has been previously
discussed. Nay, as it is usual with the Papists in the present day to inflict cruelties on the innocent without any
investigation, I justly condemn the barbarity, and recommend that no severe measure be ever adopted until after
due cognizance ; and I carefully warn them against being

too credulous, lest they may defile their hands by indiscriminate slaughter.

I then complain and lament that the world has been reduced to such slavery that no discussion takes place, and those who domineer under the name of prelates will not hear a word at variance with their decrees ; nay, will not even allow doubt or inquiry. I say that it is barbarity not to be tolerated, when without cognizance mere possession, unsupported by right or reason, is maintained by the sword. Certainly as, according to an ancient saying, ignorance is audacious, so in this preposterous zeal cruelty is added to audacity. I therefore enjoin the true worshippers of God to take heed not rashly to undertake the defence of an unknown cause, nor be hurried by intemperance into severity ; for as, in earthly causes, a judge who, himself in ignorance of the whole matter, lazily passes sentence on the opinion of others, is justly condemned ; so, how much more deserving are judges of condemnation when, in the cause of piety, they, from disdain, omit to investigate ?

And I have not taught in word any thing that I have not confirmed by act. For when Servetus was, by nefarious blasphemies, overthrowing whatever piety exists in the world, I, nevertheless, called him to discussion ; and not only came prepared to give an account of my own doctrine, but chose rather to swallow the reproaches of that vilest of men, than furnish a bad example, by enabling any one afterwards to object that he was crushed without being heard. Westphal deems it enough for magistrates to oppose the sword in place of discussion ; and it is no wonder that a man, whose only hope of victory is placed in darkness, should tyrannically rage while suppressing the light of truth.

He is not ashamed to employ the name of AUGUSTINE, as if he had any thing in common with that mild spirit. It is strange, however, that while he professes in his book to speak almost in the very words of Augustine, he so securely differs from him at the very outset, both in words and meaning. Augustine's words, in the forty-eighth Letter to Vincentius, are, "If they are frightened, and not taught, it will seem wicked tyranny." And yet he is speaking of heretics, who, impelled only by proud moroseness, had made a schism from the Church. He therefore wishes, in order to make the fear useful, that salutary doctrine be added. Again, he says, (*Epist. ad Fest.* 167,) " Perverseness in heretics ought not to be driven out by terror merely, but their mind and intellect should be instructed by the authority of the word of God. And, indeed, as the Church seeks the confession of her faith at the mouth of God, so, in order not to act preposterously, she tempers her zeal according to the same rule." Westphal, however, that he might not seem to have nothing to say, shuts us out from all access to a lawful judgment, by declaring that we have been convicted! Very differently does Augustine, who was always prepared to refute error, before calling in the aid of the magistrate. When any one rose against the purity of the faith, he did not call him to the bar of the judge without a previous fair investigation before the people. Accordingly, his recorded discussions testify, that he never acted more willingly than when he entered the field of contest armed with the sword of the word. Nor was he ever so tired out by conflict as not to be ready to refute all the most pestilential heretics, while the Church stood witness and judge.

What does Westphal do? To shake himself free of all annoyance by a single word, he puts a black mark on any of his colleagues that he chooses, and forthwith contends that they are to be driven into exile. If they request to be heard, he says, that the unseasonable application is not to be listened to, because they are already more than convicted. If he did not distrust his cause, would not some sense of shame force him even against his will into discussion? For however specious he deems it to pretend that we have been convicted, it is a miserable and shabby cowardice to admit no investigation. But how, pray, does he prove that we were convicted? The consent of many churches ought, he says, to suffice for condemnation. Why, then, does not he in his turn acquiesce in the judgment of our churches, by which he is condemned? Is it because he is near to the frozen ocean, and while he beholds its shore, considers it the utmost limit of the globe, that he regards all other churches wherever dispersed as nonentities? Let him learn, if he would not make himself ridiculous, to give a place to churches of some note, whose suffrages approve our doctrine.

He adds, that a council was held at Smalcald, in which we were condemned. What was done at Smalcald I dispute not, nor do I think that Westphal knows. The only thing certain is, that a convention of princes was there held for the purpose of entering into a League, and that nothing was decreed on the subject of Religion, unless that all who then professed the Confession of Augsburg bound themselves to mutual defence. A few learned men were present, among others, BUCER, whom, though dead, Westphal assigns to our party. If these men had the chief authority, as Westphal declares, certainly he among them, who was ours to the day of his death, did not pass a censure upon us. MELANCTHON, second to none, still survives, and will not acknowledge that he passed so grave a sentence against us. Nor will Westphal by all his furious uproar cause the Church of Wittemberg to pronounce against us so harshly. Meanwhile, I wonder that the Synod of Marpurg is passed over, in which LUTHER and the opposite party did not hesitate to acknowledge us as brethren, though the controversy was not so fully and lucidly explained as in the present day. When Westphal knows this, and conceals it, what can he gain with prudent and sober readers by babbling about fictitious synods?

But he is driven much further by his desperate impudence, when he is not ashamed to invite the patronage of Nicolas II. and Gregory VII. Though I should not say one word as to this, I cannot doubt that all good men would detest his blind rage. So far am I from being annoyed, that in a Roman Council, over which Nicolas II. presided, and in that of Vercelli, which was assembled under the auspices of Gregory VII., the doctrine which I follow was condemned, that I consider it a ground of the highest congratulation, as showing that our doctrine was always hated by the manifest enemies of God and by Antichrists. Certainly, in my eyes, their approbation would throw some suspicion on it. But who is not horrified at the monstrous blindness of Westphal, who seeks a colour for his doctrine from suffrages which might rather cover the sun with darkness? Since he has chosen this vile pig-stye for his school, let him regale himself on the husks which are fit for him : only let the reader remember the proof he gives of his shameful poverty when he is forced to bring his judges from the lowest dregs of the Papacy.

As to the Council of Ephesus, the answer is not very difficult. Let Westphal produce from its decrees one sentence which is in the least degree adverse to us. If he cannot, let him cease to take out of it indirect charges, which he absurdly hurls at us. The confession there inserted, when duly and impartially weighed, so far from bearing hard upon us, rather discloses the untameable perverseness of Westphal, who, in his malignant temper, fabricates dissensions out of nothing. But as Paul orders us to hear all prophets who are endued with the gift of the Spirit, and patiently examine whatever any of them may have produced, Westphal, to wrest this testimony from us, first strips us of all gifts of the Spirit, and then restricts the liberty which Paul claims for the prophets to the Doctors of Saxony. As it will here be easy for any reader, however little versed in Scripture, to detect the wild raving of the man, I feel at liberty to contemn it. Westphal, forsooth, by whom not one iota of a letter of Scripture was ever properly illustrated, will be deemed a prophet, and we, whose labours are well known to have at least yielded fruit to the Church, shall not be permitted to occupy the lowest seat. Surely, if faith and religious reverence in the interpretation of Scripture, if learning, and judgment, and dexterity show that a man has been divinely called, let not Westphal arrogate to himself an ounce of the prophetical spirit, but leave it in full tale to his betters. When he says that we speak to destruction and not to edification, whether it be so or not, let those who are competent judge.

After this dexterous and happy preface, he begins to draw AUGUSTINE to his party ; and that he may obtrude his lies more securely, and with more impunity, he, with much bluster, heralds his ancient lore. Undoubtedly, unskilful or less cautious readers would think that he not only has all that

Augustine ever wrote in his memory, but that, by long and familiar use, he has almost imbibed his mind, and all his hidden meanings. For he declares, contemptuously, that most of us either never saw the writings of Augustine, or have only looked at them slightly, and from a distance, as he expresses it. There is no reason for his doleful complaint, that I had presumed to address him as an unlearned man, now that he has completely wiped away the suspicion ; for who will dare to think a man unlearned to whom the whole theology of Augustine is as well known as his own fingers? Whether or not I have looked from a distance at the writings of this holy teacher, I presume I have given evidence to all. If Westphal is in doubt, let him ask his master, PHILIP MELANCTHON, who assuredly will scarcely refrain from giving a crushing reproof to his petulance. But why do I spend time in superfluous matters? Let the passages which Westphal hurls at us from Augustine be brought forward.

Augustine refutes the gross error of those who took offence at our Saviour's discourse in Capernaum, because they imagined that his flesh was to be eaten and his blood drunk in an earthly manner. Westphal contends that this passage condemns us because we are like the Capernaumites. But there is a well-known refutation by Augustine, " Why do you prepare your teeth and your stomach ? Believe, and you have eaten." This passage clearly teaches that Augustine's Capernaumites were those who pretend that the body of Christ is chewed by the teeth, and swallowed by the stomach. How can Westphal deny that he is of this class while he regards the decree of a Roman Council under Nicolas as a kind of oracle ? A little ago he insisted, on the authority of that Council, that we were convicted of heresy ! That worthy prelate of Westphal's, in the recantation which Berengarius was forced to read, gave vent to this decree, " I consent to the Holy Roman Church and the Apostolic See ; and I profess that I hold the same faith which my Lord and venerable Pope Nicolas, and this Holy Synod, has affirmed to me, viz., that the Bread and Wine, which are placed on the altar, are, after consecration, not only a Sacrament, but also the true

Body and Blood of our Lord ; and that sensibly, not only a Sacrament, but the reality is handled and broken by the priests, and chewed by the teeth of the faithful."—Let Westphal, according to whom the glorified body of Christ is broken, sensibly handled, and chewed by the teeth, now see how he is to disengage himself from the Capernaumites.

He next accumulates all the passages in which the bread of the sacred Supper is called the body of Christ. Any one endued with moderate judgment will not only laugh at the silly garrulity of the man, but also feel indignant that such a show is made out of nothing. So far am I from having to think how to make my escape, that I have rather to fear I may rouse the reader's indignation by occupying him with a matter so frivolous. Augustine writes, that the victim which was offered for us, viz., the body of Christ, is dispensed, and his blood is exhibited to us in the holy Supper : as if similar modes of expression were not in use amongst ourselves. And yet Westphal acts inconsiderately in huddling together those passages in which Augustine indiscriminately calls the holy bread, at one time the body of Christ, at another, the Eucharist or Sacrament. I ask what he means by triumphing over us, because in one passage the body of Christ is said to be distributed, and in another, the sacrament of the body and blood to be given ?

If Westphal puts his confidence in a single expression, how much greater will the authority of Christ be than that of Augustine ? And beyond all controversy, our Lord himself declared of the bread, " This is my body." The only question is, Whether he means that the bread is his body properly and without figure, or whether he transfers the name of the thing signified to the symbol? Westphal, interposing the opinion of Augustine with a view to end the dispute, produces nothing more than that the body of Christ is communicated to us in the Supper. Founding on this, he hesitates not to exclaim, that all are heretical who hold that the bread is called the body, because it is a figure of the body. What does Augustine himself say ? " Had not the sacraments," he says, (*Ad Bonif. epist.* 23,) " some resemblance to the things of which they are sacraments, they should not be

sacraments at all. From this resemblance they generally take
the names of the things themselves. As then, after a certain
manner, the sacrament of the body of Christ is the body of
Christ, and the sacrament of the blood is his blood, so the
sacrament of faith is faith." What does Westphal understand
in this passage by *a certain manner?* What is the resemblance of the sign to the thing signified, because of which the
name is transferred? Now, though the name of body should
occur an hundred times in Augustine, we understand what
the holy man meant by the form of expression. He will assuredly always acknowledge the metonymy which he once
asserted, and which he shows to be in daily use in the
Church. (Cont. Adimanth. Manich. c. 12.) And it is not
strange that this rule is laid down by him, as he distinctly
affirms, that when Christ gave the sign of his body, he expressly called it his body.

But Augustine distinctly says, that the body of Christ
falls to the earth and enters the mouth. Yes, but in the same
sense in which he affirms that it is consumed. Will Westphal acknowledge, that after the celebration of the ordinance is over, the body of Christ is consumed? It is from
thoughtlessness he quotes these words from Augustine. I
add what immediately follows in the same place. (Lib. 3,
de Trinit. c. 10.) After saying, that after the ordinance is
over bread is consumed, he adds, Because these things are
known to men, because they are done by men, they may receive honour as being religious, they cannot produce astonishment as being miraculous. If we admit Westphal's
fiction, that the body of Christ lies hid, and is enclosed under
a little bit of bread, who can deny the existence of a miracle
fit to excite astonishment? Let him cease then to dazzle
the eyes of the simple, by collecting the ancient passages
which say, that Christ is received by the mouth, just as he
is believed by the heart, it being sufficiently evident that
though they were accustomed to the sacramental mode of expression, they still knew wherein the reality differed from the
sign. We are not displeased at the magnificent terms in which
the ordinance is extolled, though Westphal, after his usual
fashion, charges us with speaking of it contemptuously.

The passage which he quotes from the thirty-third Psalm, (his book gives a wrong number, but we presume it is an error of the printer,) is easily disposed of. Augustine says, that when Christ instituted the sacred Supper, he was carried in his own hands. Does Westphal think there is no importance in the correction, which he immediately subjoins, when he inserts the word *quodammodo*, (in a manner,) which means that the expression is not strictly proper? But just as the hungry dog catches at the shadow instead of the flesh, so Westphal feeds on his own imagination. Let him not attempt to carry readers of sense along with him in his deception. Christ then, in a manner, carried himself in his own hands, because on holding out the bread, he offered his own body and blood in a mystery or spiritually. And that candid readers may the more thoroughly scorn his vile impudence, let them observe, that Westphal, to draw attention to this sentence, prints it twice over in capital letters, and yet omits the word *quodammodo*, which removes all ambiguity. For who, on hearing that a figure or similitude is distinctly expressed, can doubt what the writer means?

To pass to another point, I should like Westphal to tell me whether the term *oblation*, which occurs in Augustine a thousand times, admits of no satisfactory interpretation? or, whether, when the Papists allege that the Mass is truly and properly a sacrifice, a full solution is not given by the passage in which Augustine says, that the only sacrifice of which we now celebrate the remembrance was shown by the old sacraments? (Cont. Faust. Manich. l. 6, c. 9.) How much akin to this expression that which follows is, let the reader judge: Of this sacrifice, he says, the flesh and blood, before the advent of Christ, was promised by typical victims; in the passion of Christ, was exhibited by the reality; since the ascension, is celebrated by a sacrament of remembrance. Let Joachim see how he is to reconcile these words with his dogma, that the body which was once exhibited in reality on the cross, is celebrated by itself (*nudum*) by a sacrament of remembrance. And to omit this testimony, who sees not that every thing which he has attempted to produce is more than frivolous, and that Augus-

tine, though no body should force him out of his hands, slips
from him of his own accord ? I may add, that in repeatedly
giving out that he was only making a selection, he frees me
from all further trouble. For seeing he is so continually
versant in his writings, and holds his whole doctrine to a
tittle, it is not to be believed that he has omitted any
thing.

The substance of the whole passage is, that Christ is given
in the Supper. But if an expression is contended for, I rejoin that it is repeatedly called the sacrament of the body :
hence it follows, that all Westphal's proof comes to nothing.
For when he replies, that it is not less called the body in
some passages, than the sacrament of the body in others, I
leave children to judge how sillily he argues. Meanwhile, let
the reader remember that there is nothing in these words at
variance with our doctrine, that the body of Christ is truly
exhibited to us in the holy Supper, as the whole dispute
relates to the mode.

Thus we refute over and over the silly talk in which
Westphal endeavours to throw odium on us by drawing false
contrasts, and representing us as holding that the sacred
Supper is destitute of its reality. He says that the Supper
of the Lord was held in high honour and estimation, and regarded with great reverence, and hence it was that they went
to it fasting, some every day, others more seldom, and that
great anxiety was shown to prevent the body of the Lord from
falling to the ground. As if we were withheld by no reverence from prostituting the Supper ; as if we did not study
to maintain it in the highest splendour ; as if, previous to
the celebration of it, we did not employ serious and anxious
exhortation to raise the minds of the pious to heaven ; as if
we did not hold forth the dreadful crime of sacrilege, in
order to debar any from approaching rashly ; as if, in short,
we did not publicly testify that such persons are guilty of
the body and blood of the Lord, communion in which is
here held forth to us. The following words, assuredly not
Westphal's, I willingly borrow from Chrysostom—Christ in
laying this table, does not feed us from any other source,
but gives himself for food. I think it is now sufficiently

plain, that if the mode of communion be properly explained, we agree perfectly with the holy Fathers, but that their words, when adapted to the gross dream of Westphal, are in a manner torn to tatters.

On another ground, Westphal thinks he has a plausible cause, viz., from its being said by Augustine, that the body of Christ is given alike to good and bad. Hence he infers, that the holy teacher makes no distinction between the two, in regard to the thing itself, but places the whole difference in the end, or use, or effect. How true this is, the reader must judge from Augustine's own words, as it is not safe to trust to the quotations of a man whose shameless audacity makes him capable of any fiction. That the body of Christ is given indiscriminately to the good and bad, I uniformly teach, because the liberality or faithfulness of Christ depends not on the worthiness of man, but is founded in himself. Whatever, therefore, be the character of him who approaches, because Christ always remains like himself, he truly invites him to partake of his body and blood, he truly fulfils what he figures, he truly exhibits what he promises. The only controversy is as to the receiving, which, if Augustine seems anywhere to assert, let him be his own interpreter, and it will soon appear that he speaks metonymically.

A candid and impartial judge will be freed from all doubt by a single passage, in which he declares that the good and the bad communicate in the signs. (Cont. Faust. l. 13, c. 16.) If the unworthy received the thing, he would not have omitted altogether to mention what was more appropriate to the subject. In another passage he speaks much more clearly, (De Verbis Apostoli, sec. 33,) Prepare not your palate, but your heart: for that was the Supper recommended. Lo! we believe in Christ when we receive him by faith ; in receiving we know what we think : we receive a little, and our heart is filled. It is not therefore what is seen but what is believed that feeds. According to Westphal unbelief also receives, and yet is not fed; whereas Augustine teaches that there is no receiving except by faith. This is the reason why, in numerous passages, as if explaining himself, he says that the sacraments are common to the good and the bad.

He was not unaware that many who are not members of the body of Christ intrude themselves unworthily at the sacred table, nor was he of such perverted intellect as to imagine that those who belong in no way to the body of Christ are partakers of his body. Westphal restricts this to the effect, but how frivolously is manifest from other passages.

Augustine distinguishes between a sacrament and its virtue. (In Joann. Tract. 26.) If the distinction consisted of three members Westphal might sing his pæans with full throat. His fiction implies that in the holy Supper there is a visible element; there is the body of Christ without fruit; there is the body combined with its use and end. But as Augustine confines himself to two members only, our doctrine needs no other defence. The Fathers, he says, did not die who understood the visible food spiritually, hungered spiritually, tasted spiritually, that they might be spiritually filled. We see how, opposing the intelligence of faith to the external sign, he says, that nothing but the bare sign is taken by unbelievers. If Westphal objects that he is speaking of the manna, this quibble is easily disposed of by the context, for he immediately subjoins, that these sacraments were different in the signs, but alike in the thing signified; and immediately after, repeating what he had said of the virtue of the sacrament and the visible sacrament, he teaches, that believers alone do not die who eat inwardly, not outwardly, who eat with the heart, not chew with the teeth. If nothing is left to unbelievers but the visible sacrament, where is Westphal's hidden and celestial body?

We therefore rightly infer, that when Augustine says that unbelievers receive the body of Christ, it ought to be no otherwise understood than as he himself explains, namely, only as a sacrament. That there may be no doubt as to this, it should be known, Westphal himself being witness, that the two things—the body of Christ, and the vivifying food—are synonymous. For in order to prove that the body lurks enclosed under the bread, Westphal adduces the latter expression, arguing, that if the bread were not the body of Christ, it would not be vivifying food. Let him now say whether the bread of the Supper vivifies the wicked. If it does not bestow life, I will immediately infer that they have not the body of Christ.

When among other passages he quotes one from *De Civitate Dei*, lib. xix. c. 20, I would willingly set it down as an error of the press, did not the wicked cunning of the man betray itself. He quotes the twentieth chapter of the twenty-first book, where Augustine is giving the view of others, not his own. The twenty-fifth chapter, where Augustine answers the objection, he passes in silence. In the words which he has produced, there is so far from any thing adverse to us, that we need go no farther for a sure and clear proof of our doctrine. For what is meant by saying that those who are in the very body of Christ, take the body of Christ not only by sacrament but in reality, unless it be that which plainly appears, that the body of Christ is taken in two ways—sacramentally and in reality. If the reality is taken away, certainly nothing remains but the sign. From this too, we without doubt infer that the wicked do not eat the body of Christ in any other way than in respect of the sign, because they are deprived of the reality.

The explanation which follows in the twenty-fifth chapter is much more clear, where he strenuously maintains that those who are not to be classed among the members of Christ do not eat his body, because they cannot be at the same time the members of Christ and the members of a harlot. And immediately after, Christ himself saying, " Whoso eateth my flesh and drinketh my blood abideth in me and I in him," he shows what it is to eat the body of Christ and drink his blood not sacramentally but in reality ; for this is to dwell in Christ that Christ also may dwell in him. For it is as if he had said, Let not him who dwelleth not in me, and in whom I dwell not, say or think that he eats my body or drinks my blood. If this does not sting Westphal to the quick, he is more impervious than the cattle of his fields.

Out of the first book, against the Letters of Petilian, he quotes a sentence in which we are enjoined to distinguish the visible sacrament from the invisible unction of charity.

Augustine is there discussing Baptism. If Christ baptizes
not with the Spirit all who are dipt in water, will it immediately follow that Judas ate the body of Christ? But if
the discourse were about the Supper, I would say that it gives
the strongest support to us, because nothing is conceded to
the wicked but the visible sacrament, which Westphal, according to his phantasm, will certainly admit to differ from
the invisible flesh of Christ. The passage from the first
book against Cresconius Grammaticus (the place is erroneously given, the twenty-third chapter being set down for the
twenty-fifth) goes no farther than to say that the wicked
corrupt the use of God's gifts by abusing them. Nay, the
whole drift of Augustine in writing against the Donatists, is
to show that things which are good do not change their
nature by the fault of those who use them improperly, and
that therefore baptism is not to be considered null because
unbelievers from abusing get no benefit from it. In this way
it is not strange for Augustine to say that Judas was a partaker of the body of Christ, provided you restrict this to the
visible sign. This he elsewhere states to be his view. Nor
can we in any other way understand his distinction, (Tract.
in Joann. 59,) that others took the bread the Lord, Judas
nothing but the bread of the Lord. Nay, Westphal himself,
as if he were changing sides, assists us by mentioning that
Peter and Judas ate of the same bread.

Proceeding now as if he had made good his claim to
Augustine, he attempts to dispose of the passages, which he
says that we have quoted in a perfidious and garbled manner. But I should like to know where is the perfidy or
garbling. Is it that any change is made on the words, and
so, as Westphal is constantly doing, one thing is substituted
for another? Is it that our people, by wresting those passages to their own purpose improperly, give them a meaning different from the true one? Westphal will perhaps
say, that a syllable has been falsely produced by them. In
that respect, therefore, it follows that things which Augustine wished to be understood differently, are improperly and
irrelevantly quoted. But should any one not very appositely
adduce Augustine as a witness in his favour, is he to be re-

garded of course as a perfidious garbler? So, indeed, West-phal chooses to say. This law, however hard it be, I refuse not. Let us bear the charge of perfidy, then, while he only alleges our want of skill.

In this part of the subject the good man uses tergiversa-tion. For what could he do? As a shorter method of dis-entangling himself, he says, that we overturn the local pre-sence of Christ in the Supper in three ways—either by feigning a figure, or by pretending that the eating is spiri-tual, or by denying that the body of Christ is immense. We having undertaken to prove these three articles out of Au-gustine, let us see by what artifice Westphal refutes them. Talking of the figure, he denies that Augustine ever inter-preted the words of Christ, This is my body, so as to show that the bread signified body. Is it in this way he is to convict us of perfidy, when we ingenuously come forward provided with expressions that are not in the least degree obscure? Augustine's words are: The Lord hesitated not to say, This is my body, when he was giving the sign of his body. And with what view does he say so? To prove that Scripture often speaks figuratively. He elsewhere says, that Christ admitted Judas to the first feast, in which he commended and delivered the figure of his body to the dis-ciples. He also says that the bread is in a manner the body of Christ, because it is a sacrament of the body. Producing a passage from the Third Book on Christian Doctrine, how dexterously does he escape? He says, Augustine is in a general way admonishing believers not to fasten upon signs, but rather to attend to the things signified. Although I deny not that this was the holy man's purpose, I would yet have it carefully considered how it may be said to be carnal bondage or servile weakness to take the signs for the thing. If it were not preposterous to confound the signs with the things, there would be no ground for condemning it as superstition. When Westphal rejoins, that still the reality ought not to be disjoined from the signs, he says nothing that is at all ad-verse to us. He indeed pretends the contrary, but with little modesty, as it is perfectly notorious that we call the bread a sign of the body of Christ, inasmuch as it is a badge of the communion, and truly exhibits the spiritual food which it figures.

This much remains fixed, that in the words of Christ the mode of speaking is sacramental, and the sign must be distinguished from the reality, if we would not continue servilely grovelling on the earth. Hence, too, it is clearly inferred that Augustine gives his full sanction to that interpretation which Westphal so bitterly assails. As neither the substance nor the principal effects of the Supper are taken away by the word *signifying*, let Westphal seek some new colour for his quarrel. But by no means contented with this, he clings with desperation to the word *essential*, maintaining that the bread is truly and properly called the body of Christ. I say that in this he abandons the view of Augustine. He maintains that he does not. But how does he evade the passages ? Because the words of Christ, This is my body, are not quoted for the express purpose. What matters it, so long as we have Augustine's authority for the mode of expression, viz., that Christ said, This is my body, when he was giving a sign of his body ? Then when Augustine teaches generally that the name of the thing signified is transferred to the sign, whenever the names of flesh and blood are applied to the external symbols of the Supper, who can hesitate to follow that rule in seeking for the sense In the epistle to Evodius, when Augustine says, that in the sacraments there is a frequent and trite metonymy, Westphal seeks a frivolous subterfuge, by saying that the Supper is not mentioned, because he could not argue in this way from the genus to the species. Why should the observation of Augustine as to all the signs not be applied to the Supper ? A dove is called the Holy Spirit. Augustine tells us that this ought to be understood metonymically, for it is not new or unusual for signs to take the name of the thing signified. The case of the Supper is exactly the same. Westphal will on no account allow it to be touched. But it is not strange that he cavils so frigidly about that matter, as he is not ashamed with more pertness to elude the words of St. Paul.

St. Paul says that the rock which accompanied the people

in the wilderness was Christ. Westphal admits no interpretation, because Christ was truly and properly a spiritual rock. But it is clear, nay palpable to the very blind, that Paul is there speaking of an external sign, no less than Christ is when he says of the bread, This is my body. No other view would be consistent with the context, in which Paul compares our Baptism and Supper to the ancient signs, so that it is out of Westphal's power to deny that the rock is called Christ in the same sense in which the bread is called his body. Here at least he must make room for the term *signifying*. I do not ask him to make the holy Supper void of its reality. This is the falsehood by which he so iniquitously attempts to bring us into odium with the simple. I would only have the distinction to be carefully drawn between the thing and the sign, so that a transition may be made from the earthly element to heaven. The bread is put into our hands. We know that Christ is true, and will in reality exhibit what he testifies, viz., his body, but only if we rise by faith above the world. As this cannot take place without the help of a figure or sign, what right Westphal has to object I leave sober and candid readers to judge. Though he should protest a hundred times over, we certainly have the support of Augustine in regard to the term *signifying*. I may add, that if in the discourse of Christ, where he says that we must eat his flesh and drink his blood, the expression is figurative, as Westphal is forced to admit, the same thing must be said of the holy Supper. Nay, a term of significance will be much more adapted to a sacrament than to simple doctrine. Were I to go over his absurdities in detail, there would be no end : nor is there any occasion for it, unless indeed there be so much weight in his words that the reader, after being taught and convinced by so many arguments, should still believe that there is no figure in the expression, This is my body, merely because Westphal so declares.

Spiritual eating is held by us in such a manner as by no means excludes sacramental eating, provided always that Westphal do not by his vague dream dissever things that are conjoined. But the reader ought to understand what the sacramental eating of this good theologian is, namely, that

unbelievers without faith, without any sense of piety, gulp
down the body of Christ. He dreams that Christ is spiritually eaten when the stomach not only swallows his body,
but the soul also receives the secret gift of the Spirit. We
maintain that in the sacrament Christ is eaten in no way
but spiritually, because that gross gulping down which the
Papists devised, and Westphal too greedily drinks in from
them, is abhorrent to our sense of piety. The substance of
our doctrine is, that the flesh of Christ is vivifying bread,
because when we are united to it by faith, it nourishes and
feeds our souls. We teach that this is done in a spiritual
manner, only because the bond of this sacred union is the
secret and incomprehensible virtue of the Holy Spirit. In
this way, we say, that our souls are assisted by the sacred
symbol of the Supper, to receive nourishment from the flesh
of Christ. We even add, that therein is fulfilled and exhibited all that Christ declares in the sixth chapter of John.
But although believers have spiritual communion with Christ
without the use of the sacrament, still we distinctly declare
that Christ, who instituted the Supper, works effectually by
its means.

Westphal confines spiritual eating to the fruit merely, regarding it a means by which the salvation obtained by the
death of Christ is applied to us, while his sacramental eating,
as I have observed, is nothing more than a gulping down of
Christ's flesh. What does Augustine say ? He teaches that
the body of Christ is eaten sacramentally only when it is
not eaten in reality. In two passages this antithesis is distinctly expressed by him. Hence we surely gather that the
sacramental is equivalent merely to the visible or external
use, when unbelief precludes access to the reality. Westphal, therefore, acts calumniously in charging our spiritual
eating as a fallacious pretext for destroying the true communion which takes place in the Supper. For if spiritual is
to be separated from sacramental eating, what are we to
make of the following passage of Augustine ? (In Psal. 98.)
You are not about to eat the body which you see and to
drink the blood which those who are to crucify me will shed.
I have committed a sacrament to you: when spiritually

understood, it will give you life. Now, if it is clear that in the Supper, when the body is not spiritually eaten, nothing is left but a void and empty sign, and we infer from the words of Christ that spiritual eating takes place when faith corresponds to the mystical and spiritual doctrine, there is no ground for Westphal's attempt to dissever things which cannot be divided. I admit it to be certain that the same body which Christ offered on the cross is eaten, because we do not imagine that Christ has two bodies, nor is aliment for spiritual life to be sought anywhere else than in that victim. How does Augustine deny it to be the same body, but just in respect that having been received into heaven it inspires life into us by the secret virtue of the Spirit? Therefore a different mode of eating is denoted, viz., that though the body remains entire in heaven, it quickens us by its miraculous and heavenly virtue. In short, Augustine's only reason for denying that the body on which the disciples were looking is given in the Supper, was to let us know that the mode of communion is not at all carnal, that we become partakers of flesh and blood in a mystery, our teeth not consuming that grace, as he elsewhere expresses it. Thus Westphal gains nothing by his quibbling. He is also detected in a manifest calumny, when he charges us with wresting this passage to mean that the Supper gives us nothing but an empty figure.

But how does Westphal excuse the term *spiritually*? By reason of faith, he says. If so, how does he pretend that there is an eating without faith? For to prove that there is nothing carnal in his gross fiction, he denies that Christ is carnally eaten, unless he is cut into pieces like a carcass, and palpably chewed by the teeth; and he says, that while the body is offered to be taken invisibly, it is spiritually eaten, because it is received by faith. The more he attempts to get out of this dilemma the faster it will hold him—the dilemma that profane men, endued only with carnal sense, when they rashly and unworthily intrude themselves at the Lord's table, eat spiritually without faith, and yet there is no such eating except in respect of faith.

I do not however admit what he stammers out on no

authority but his own, viz., that when the flesh of Christ is consumed in the bread the mode of eating is spiritual, because it is invisible. The exception is too weak, that, according to the definition of Augustine, those only taste carnally who think that the body of Christ is to be torn as in the shambles. Although gross men imagine that Christ intends to prepare a supper of the Cyclops out of his flesh, we must adopt another definition, viz., that he is *spiritually* eaten, though not taken into the stomach, because he quickens us by the secret virtue of the Spirit. Nor can Westphal make his escape by the term faith, for our Saviour not only distinctly requires faith to be given to his words, but, recalling us to their force and nature, declares them to be spiritual. These two things, it is apparent, are not less distant from each other than heaven is from earth.

Westphal contends that the body of Christ is truly and properly eaten, because we must believe the plain and literal expression, This is my body, which admits no figure, and thus the Spirit, which Christ distinctly places in his own words, he places only in faith. With the same license he afterwards fabricates a twofold spiritual eating, one of substance, another of fruit, as if the latter could be separated from the former. He pretends that Augustine, when he treats of spiritual eating, at one time joins the two together, at another points to each of them separately. He says, that we eat the body of Christ spiritually in regard to the fruit, when the forgiveness of sins obtained by his death is received by us by faith unto salvation ; and yet that this kind of eating does not prevent our spiritually swallowing the invisible substance of the flesh in the Supper. Hence he infers that we act sophistically when under pretext of the fruit we take away the substance : as if we said that any are partakers of the blessings of Christ who do not partake of his flesh and blood. We hold that every thing which the death and resurrection of Christ confer on us flows from this source—that he is truly ours, and that his flesh is spiritual meat. Still we admit not any gross mode of swallowing, nor dissever what our Lord has expressly joined. He did not order us to receive any body but that which was offered on the cross for our reconciliation, nor to drink any blood but that which was shed for the remission of sins.

It is clear that this connection of substance and fruit is perversely and barbarously dissevered, when the wicked, without faith, are said to receive the lifeless body of Christ. Nay, why does Augustine (Tract. in Joann. 26) oppose visible appearance to spiritual virtue in the Supper, if, when this virtue is wanting, the body of Christ is still truly and substantially eaten? He certainly explains the matter very differently when he says a little farther on: A sacrament of this thing, I mean of the union of the body and blood of Christ, is in some places daily, in others at certain intervals, prepared on the Lord's table, and taken from the Lord's table by some unto life, by others unto destruction, whereas the thing itself of which there is a sacrament, is taken by those who partake of it, unto life by all, unto destruction by none. Certainly when the reality of the sign is considered, no man of sound mind will exclude secret communion in the body and blood of Christ. Augustine holds, that this is not common to unbelievers, and hence it follows, that as they reject it when offered, nothing is left them but the bare sign. To make this clearer, I disguise not that those who simply explain, that we eat the flesh of Christ and drink his blood, when we believe that our sins have been expiated by his death, speak too narrowly and stringently. This faith flows from a higher principle. If Christ is our head, and dwells in us, he communicates to us his life; and we have nothing to hope from him until we are united to his body. The whole reality of the sacred Supper consists in this—Christ, by ingrafting us into his body, not only makes us partakers of his body and blood, but infuses into us the life whose fulness resides in himself: for his flesh is not eaten for any other end than to give us life.

This doctrine Satan will in vain endeavour to pluck up by a thousand Westphals. For when Augustine says, that none truly and in reality eat the flesh of Christ but those who abide in him, to refer the terms *truly* and *in reality*, not to the reality of the body, but the reality of communion, as Westphal contends, is nugatory. As Augustine distinctly

denies that any eat the flesh of Christ but those who, endued with living faith, abide in him, what is meant by
saying, that not the reality of the body, but only real
communion is denied? The only account of the matter
doubtless is, that monstrous things bring monstrous terms
along with them. Westphal holds, that persons who do truly
swallow the body of Christ, have no communion with him.
For according to him, the reality of the body is nothing else
than substantial swallowing. Now communion is enjoyment of the spiritual gifts which come to us from Christ. I
should like then to know to what end Christ invites us to
partake of his flesh and blood in the Supper, if it be not
that he may feed our souls. Should the body of Christ cease
to be food, of what avail would the swallowing of it be?

With similar artifice he cuts a knot which he could not
untie, evading the passage in which Augustine teaches, that
Judas ate the bread of the Lord, while others ate the bread
the Lord. He says, that a twofold eating is there implied.
That indeed is clear. But when he says that Judas ate
Christ substantially, I desire to know how he reconciles it
with Augustine's words. If Judas is distinguished from the
other disciples by this mark, that he did not eat the bread
the Lord, it follows that he received nothing but the naked
symbol. I wish that Westphal had an ounce of sound brain
to weigh the words which he quotes from Augustine. He
asserts that the twofold communion is nowhere more clearly
distinguished than in this sentence, (Serm. 2, de Verb. Apost.,)
" Then will the body and blood of Christ be life to every
one, if that which is taken visibly in the sacrament is eaten
spiritually in the reality." So willingly do I embrace this
passage, that I am contented with it alone to refute Westphal's absurdity.

Spiritual eating is so despised by Westphal, that he deems
it an execrable heresy to insist on it alone. For why does
he inveigh so fiercely against us, and keep crying that we
ought to be corrected by the sword rather than the pen, but
just because we rest satisfied with spiritual eating? Let
us now see what the other kind of eating is, without which,
according to those censors, no man in heaven or earth can

be saved. Augustine says that it is visible. With what eyes did Westphal ever behold his imaginary swallowing of the substance of Christ? Augustine teaches, that every thing which is received in the sacrament beyond spiritual eating is taken visibly. Let Westphal then open his eyes, and at length recognise what is meant by sacramental eating. But he objects that the sacrament would not be entire if the body of Christ were not eaten. Just as if the body of Christ were less real, because unbelievers reject what he offers. We admit that he offers his body at the same time to the worthy and the unworthy, and that no depravity of man hinders the bread from being a true and, as it is called, exhibitory pledge of his flesh; but it is absurd and fatuous to infer that it is received promiscuously by all.

Equally absurd is the following syllogism of Westphal: Those things which the Lord by his word declares to be, truly are—therefore the body of Christ must be taken by the wicked under the bread. Who knows not that the doctrine of Christ was fatal to the apostates to whom it seemed a hard saying? Yet he, with his own lips, declared, "The words I speak unto you are Spirit and life." But not to detain the reader longer, let it be sufficient to advert to Westphal's famous conclusion of this head, in which he says, that the matter of the sacrament, in Augustine's sense, is not the body and blood of the Lord, but the reality, grace, and fruit. These are his very words. If so, he is certainly contending about nothing, and seeking some imagination of his own away from the subject. If the body and blood are not the reality of the sacrament, why does he everywhere style us falsifiers, especially while he is forced to confess that we detract in no way from this reality of the sacrament?

The third head which he has undertaken to refute is, That we communicate in the flesh and blood of Christ, but in such manner, that the reality of his human nature remains entire. Our people, after showing, from numerous passages of Scripture, that God has taught them this doctrine, have also proved that it is held by Augustine. Westphal, purposing to deprive us of this support, but feeling it somewhat more troublesome than he could wish, goes beating about, and saying, that in the mysteries of the faith we are not to depend on human reason or physical arguments. Granting all this, I say that our argument is derived not from philosophy, but from the heavenly oracles of God. Scripture uniformly teaches that we are to wait for Christ from heaven, from whence he will come as our Redeemer. And there is no obscurity in the doctrine of Paul, that the image and model of future redemption is displayed in the person of Christ, who will transform our poor body, so as to be like his own glorious body. Have done, then, with the futile evasion, that philosophy should not be the mistress of our faith, since we hold nothing in regard to the reality of our flesh that was not delivered by Christ himself, the highest and the only teacher.

But as it properly belongs to this place, let the reader hear how finely Westphal forces Augustine away from us. That holy teacher says, that against nature Christ came in to the disciples when the doors were shut, just as against nature he walked on the water, because with God all things are possible. If Christ, by his divine energy, miraculously opened the doors when they were shut, does it therefore follow that his body is immense? But Augustine forbids the reason to be asked here, where faith ought to reign : in other words, we must surely believe what the Evangelist has testified, that the Son of God was not prevented by any obstacles from giving that astonishing display of his power. Therefore Westphal stolidly exults, calling it a theological demonstration of what he and his party falsely pretend as to the omnipotence of God. God is not subject to our fictions, to fulfil whatever we imagine ; but his power must be conjoined with his good pleasure, as the Prophet also reminds us,—Our God in heaven hath done whatever he hath pleased.

His will, says Westphal, has been sufficiently manifested in the ordinance of the Supper. But this is a begging of the question. For who told him that Christ, in holding forth the sacred bread, changed the nature of his body, and made it immense ; nay, that at the same moment he made the same body double, so that it was visible in one place, and invisible in another ; immense, and yet of limited dimensions ? At the first Supper Christ is seen incarnate ; he retains the condition of human nature : then, however, if we are to believe Westphal, he carried in his hands the same body, invisible and immense. If Augustine saw this miracle of divine power in the Supper, why did he nowhere mention, in a single word, that against nature the body of Christ lurked invisible in the bread, filled heaven and earth, and was a thousand times entire in a thousand places, because nothing is impossible with God ? His remark, therefore, that in miracles which transcend the reach of the human mind, Augustine is wont to bring forward the power of God, I retort upon him ; for had that holy man imagined such a presence as Westphal fabricates, he could never have had a fitter opportunity to proclaim the power of God ; and therefore we may infer from his silence, that he had no knowledge of the fiction which the devil afterwards suggested under the Papacy.

And not to dwell on a superfluous matter, if the omnipotence of God may be turned hither and thither, the fanatics who deny the resurrection of the body will have a specious colour for their delirious dream. They produce the words of Peter, that we are called to be partakers of the Divine nature, and infer that the restitution of the human race will be of such a sort that the spiritual essence of God will absorb the corporeal nature. Why may they not, when any one objects, follow the example of Westphal, and exclaim that the power of God is not to be pent up in a corner ? As there is thus no use in asserting that God can do it, while it does not appear that he will, all Westphal's loquacity on this head falls to the ground, unless he can prove that Christ has deprived his flesh of the common nature of flesh.

When Westphal comes, as he pretends, to dispose of the passages which our party have employed, his affected talk is puerile and shameful in the extreme. Tell us, Joachim, what use there was to fill several pages with buffoonery, but just to lead the minds of the simple to wander away with you from the subject ? The simple argument of our party is, that Augustine plainly asserts that our Saviour, in respect of his human nature, is in heaven, whence he will come at the last day ; that in respect of human nature, he is not everywhere diffused, because though he gave immortality to his flesh, he did not take away its nature ; that therefore we must beware of raising the divinity of the man so as to destroy the reality of the body ; that if we take away locality from bodies they will be situated nowhere, and consequently not exist ; that Christ is everywhere present as God, but in respect of the nature of a real body occupies some place in heaven.

After Westphal has amused himself to satiety with his wanderings, lest he should seem to have nothing to say, he at first tells his readers that when Augustine thus speaks he was not treating professedly of the Lord's Supper. What ? When you lately quoted his words in celebration of the power of God, did you remember that then, too, he was not treating of the Supper ? I there showed that you were presumptuously involving Augustine in your own errors. Here, however, the case is very different. Augustine clearly declares that the nature of Christ's body does not admit of its being everywhere diffused, and that therefore it is contained in heaven. If so, how will he subscribe to you when you say that it is immense ? You are just doing like the Papists, who tell us that nothing which we produce from Scripture against their fictitious worship and tyrannical laws has any application to them, because nothing of theirs is denounced by the Spirit in express terms. Thus when we quote the words of Christ, In vain do they worship me with the commandments of men, &c., they disentangle themselves without any trouble—Christ was then directing his speech against the Pharisees. With what face have you dared to obtrude such absurdity on the world, making it obvious that you, with the proudest disdain, despise all men's judgments ? Had you thought that the readers of your farrago were possessed of common sense, you must have seen they would certainly argue either that what Augustine says is false, or that the body of Christ does not, as you dream, lie everywhere diffused. I will again repeat, that if what Augustine says

holds invariably true, there will be no body of Christ without a local habitation, and therefore in respect of its nature
as body it is contained in heaven. It certainly cannot
occupy a thousand places on the earth, far less be everywhere without being circumscribed by space. What then
will become of that integrity which you confidently assert?

Joachim afterwards adds, that Augustine had no other
intention than to teach that the body of Christ is in heaven,
and we have no other than to deny that he is in the Eucharist. How brazen-faced this dishonesty that would get rid
of so clear a matter by a manifest falsehood? Augustine
teaches clearly, that Christ is nowhere else than in heaven,
in as far as he is man, and is falsely supposed to be everywhere diffused in respect of his flesh, which he did not deprive of its properties. When we teach the same thing in
as many words and syllables, who can say that we have a
different end in view? Westphal says, that Augustine's object is to prevent the reality of the human nature from being
destroyed. Just because he never could have thought that out
of such presence of the flesh as the sophists have imagined,
such a monster would arise, and, being contented with the
true and genuine meaning of the words of Christ, he did not
advert to those fatuous speculations. When Joachim subjoins, that the reality of human nature is not destroyed if
the body of Christ is distributed in the Supper, his assertion
is most absurd. The reality, Augustine being witness, consists in the body being contained by some place in heaven.
Westphal is too oblivious. After expressing his utter detestation of this physical argument, he now pretends to
embrace it. Were he to hear from me the very thing which
he has been forced to quote from Augustine, he would cry
out sacrilege. Now, as he has determined to drag Augustine into his party in whatever manner, provided he can
avoid the semblance of self-contradiction, there is no shape
which he is not willing to assume.

But abandoning all circuitous paths, we must now determine once for all, whether the true nature of the flesh is destroyed if it is believed to be in several places at the same
time, nay, to occupy no place. Westphal confidently takes

the negative. What Augustine holds, it is unnecessary to weary the reader with repeating. We may add, that this man who catches at everything, now changing his style, pretends that the human nature of Christ is not wholly taken away, that is, destroyed, because it remains entire and unharmed in heaven. Just as when it is immerged in profane stomachs, he pretends that it is everywhere unharmed on the earth. Westphal cannot help himself by the promise of perpetual presence which Christ made to the Church. We believe that he is always present with his people, and ever dwells in them, not merely in respect of his being God, as Westphal perversely misrepresents, but as the members must always be united to their head, so we hold that the Mediator who assumed our nature is present with believers: For he sits at the Father's right hand for the very purpose of holding and exercising universal empire. If the mode of his presence is asked, we hold that it must be attributed to his grace and virtue.

Though Westphal uses the same terms, he immediately falls back on the flesh, because he reckons grace as nothing if the body of Christ be not substantially before him in the celebration of the Supper. It is a strange metamorphosis to convert what was said of the boundless virtue of the Holy Spirit into a finite substance of flesh. Let the reader remember the state of the question to be, Whether or not Christ exhibits himself present by his grace in any other way than by having his body present on the earth and everywhere? Our view is, that though Christ in respect of his human nature is in heaven, yet distance of place does not prevent him from communicating himself to us—that he not only sustains and governs us by his Spirit, but renders that flesh in which he fulfilled our righteousness vivifying to us. Without any change of place, his virtue penetrates to us by the secret operation of his Spirit, so that our souls obtain spiritual life from his substance. Nothing suffices Westphal but to exclude the body of Christ from any particular locality and extend it over all space.

It is worth while to see how very consistent he is when he insists that the presence of grace is corporeal, and yet

understands it to be referred to in the law, in these words,
Wherever I shall make record of my name, there will I come
to you. (Ex. xx. 24.) I ask, whether he thinks that the
essence of God then dwelt between the cherubim in the
same manner in which the body of Christ is now supposed to
lie hid under the bread? To the same effect, according to him,
is the promise,—I and my Father will come unto him, and
make our abode with him. Does he think then that the
essence of the Godhead descends to us in the same way as
he affirms of the flesh of Christ, that it enters under the consecrated bread to be there devoured? How has he so soon
fallen away from what he had quoted from Augustine in the
same page, that God is everywhere by the presence of his
essence, not everywhere by indwelling grace ; where this holy
teacher distinctly opposes the essence of God, in regard to
the nature of its presence, to grace! But if such a descent
as Westphal inculcates in respect to the flesh of Christ is
not at all applicable to the essence of the Father, let him
loose a knot of his own tying.

Having a little before repeatedly declared that he acknowledges with Augustine that Christ, in respect of the
nature of his flesh, is in heaven, at last, as if he had forgotten himself, he says that the two natures are inseparably
conjoined, so that the Son of God is nowhere without flesh.
Where then is the nature of the flesh, if the divinity of Christ
extends it in proportion to his own immensity? I confess,
indeed, that we may not conceive of the Son of God in any
other way than as clothed with flesh. But this did not prevent him, while filling heaven and earth with his divine
essence, from wearing his flesh in the womb of his mother,
on the cross, in the sepulchre. Though then the Son of God,
he was, nevertheless, man in heaven as well as on earth.
Should any one infer from this that his flesh was then in
heaven, he will confound every thing by arguing absurdly,
and be brought at last to rob Christ of his human nature,
and divest him of his office of Redeemer. Nay, if the flesh
of Christ is so conjoined to the Godhead that there is no
distinction between the immensity of the one and the finite
mode of existence of the other, why does Westphal contend

that Christ is present by his grace in any other way than by
his Deity? If it is not lawful to separate the flesh from the
divine essence, as soon as it is conceded that Christ in respect of Deity is everywhere, the same will also hold true
in regard to the flesh. But if this is conceded, the mouth of
the profane will be opened, and they may freely assert that
Christ, by his habitation on the earth, and, in like manner,
by his ascent into heaven, passed off a mere imposture. See
what it is to defend a bad cause obstinately and without any
conscience!

Shortly after he gives a new colouring to what he had
previously said, alleging that the body of Christ is defined by a visible form in heaven, but lies invisible under
the bread, and that in this way should be understood what
Augustine teaches in his Epistle to Dardanus, as well as
numerous other places. But by what mechanism is he to
adapt to his fiction Augustine's doctrine, that there would
be no body if local space were taken away, and that the
nature of the flesh requires that it occupy some locality in
heaven? If the body can exist invisible without place,
Augustine's argument, that unless it be bounded by its cir-
cumference it no longer exists, is unsound. Unsound also
would be the general proposition, that the nature of a true
body requires that it occupy some locality in heaven. In
short, throughout the whole of that discussion, Augustine
would have omitted the principal point, that Christ is in an
invisible manner diffused through heaven and earth in respect of his flesh, although he is visible in one place.

The question is concerning the divine presence. Augustine answers, that the divine nature is everywhere, that the
human nature is confined to a certain place. How careless
would it have been, supposing the body to fill all things in the
same manner as the Godhead, that is, invisibly, to say nothing
about it? Westphal contends, that the doctrine of Scripture
is perfectly true: but how does he prove it? When Christ
says that he is going to his Father, and will no more be in the
world; when Luke relates that he was taken up in a cloud;
when the angels say, that he will come in like manner as he
was seen to ascend, he restricts it all to the visible form.

This I, too, admit, provided he would at the same time add, that wherever the body of Christ is, it is, according to its nature, visible. When he comes to the invisible mode, he repeats the passages which he had formerly produced concerning the presence of grace : as if it followed, that when Christ comes to us with the Father he is placed bodily on the earth, whereas all Scripture proclaims, that he penetrates to us by the virtue of his Spirit. The flesh of Christ, which we see not with the eye, we experience to be vivifying in us by the discernment of faith. If no operation of the Spirit were here interposed, Westphal might justly boast that he is victor; but if it is evidently owing to the secret agency of the Spirit that our souls are fed by the flesh of Christ, the inference is certain, that in no other way than a celestial mode of presence can his flesh descend to us. These few observations expose the poverty of Westphal, who cannot produce a single syllable out of Scripture in support of his error.

What shall we say of the contrast which Augustine draws between the word and the flesh, when he is treating of the absence and presence of Christ? What, but just that it utterly excludes Westphal's fiction? Augustine says, that Christ is to be heard, as if he were bodily present, because although his body must be in one place, his real presence is everywhere diffused. Certainly if the Lord, through his word, exhibited himself present in the flesh in an invisible manner, Augustine would be in error in saying, that he is absent in the flesh, while he is present with us in his word ; and he would be in error, when in distinguishing between presence and absence, he opposed the body to the word. Whatever mists Westphal may here employ, the thing is too clear for the reader to be mystified by his trifling. When he is held perplexed, he says, facetiously, that the common exposition of Augustine's sentiment, in regard to the Eucharist, is that he held that the real presence of Christ is everywhere diffused, as if any man, not frantic, could wrest his words to any thing else than the doctrine of the gospel, to which Augustine there avowedly pays reverence. He pretends, that in a like sense in another passage, the sacrifice

of the body of Christ is said to be diffused over the whole
world, as if, because Christ invites the nations everywhere to
partake in the benefit of his cross, it follows that his body is
immense. And though the term *diffusing* should apply to
the celebration of the Supper, whom can he persuade, as he
intends, that the body of Christ is wherever the Supper is
celebrated? What Augustine distinctly declares concerning
the benefit of his death, Westphal contends to be said of the
Supper: and when this holy doctor teaches that the sacrifice
which Christ performed is celebrated everywhere, alluding
to the Church diffused over the whole world, is it not absurd
to apply this which is said of the body of the faithful to
their head ?

Westphal, after long turning, comes at last to this, that
violence is done to the words of Augustine, if we are deprived of the bodily presence of Christ which he elsewhere
asserts. But though he has hitherto laboured to prove this,
it has only been at a snail's speed. It accordingly stands
fixed, that the Son of God, though present with his word, is
above with his body. Still, however, he persists, and says
that Augustine (Tract. in Joann. 50) distinctly affirms the
invisible presence. The presence of flesh or of power? If
of flesh, let the passage be produced, and I retire vanquished;
but if the flesh is expressly distinguished from grace and
virtue, what can be imagined more impudent than Westphal,
who assigns that invisible mode of presence properly to the
flesh ? I may add, that Augustine makes Christ present
not less in the sign of the cross than in the celebration of
the Supper ; but if he thinks fit to apply this to the essence
of the flesh, then the moment that any one makes a cross
with his finger the body of Christ will be formed.

The passage from Sermon cxl., as to time, answers for itself, without my saying a word. " The Lord was unwilling to
be acknowledged except in the breaking of bread, on account
of us who were not to see him in the flesh, and yet were to
eat his flesh." For the method of eating, as the writer himself
elsewhere explains it, will, when it is known, remove all question. But here Westphal acts too liberally in supplying us
with shields to ward off his attacks. For he tells us out of

Augustine how we may possess Christ though absent, viz., because while he has introduced his body into heaven, he has not withdrawn his majesty from the world ; and again, that while he said in regard to the presence of his body, Me ye shall not always have, he said in respect of his majesty, in respect of his providence, in respect of his ineffable and invisible grace, I am with you even to the end of the world. We see how Augustine, in speaking of the invisible presence, always excludes the body, and shows without ambiguity that it is to be looked for only in heaven.

Similar in meaning is the passage from the forty-seventh Psalm, that Christ is felt to be present by his hidden mercy. Were there any obscurity in this passage, another from Tract. in Joann. 92, is more luminous, viz., that Christ left his disciples in corporeal presence, but will always be with his people in spiritual presence ; unless indeed the epithet corporeal is to be held equivalent to visible. Westphal would like this, but nothing is clearer than that the essence of the flesh is distinguished from the virtue of the Spirit. And yet, as if he had gained the victory, he exclaims that the spiritual is opposed to the visible presence. In this he betrays no less folly than impudence, as Augustine uniformly asserts that Christ is absent in the flesh. If to Westphal the expression— that provided faith be present, he whom we see not is with us—is clear, why does he throw darkness on the light ? And yet he gains nothing by it ; for Augustine admirably explains himself by saying that we are to send up to heaven not our hands but faith, in order to possess Christ ; because although Christ has taken his body to heaven, he has not deserted us ; his majesty remains in the world.

Though these words do not awaken Westphal, it is no wonder, as he has no shame. After quoting the words of Augustine : In respect of the flesh which the Son of God assumed, in respect of his being born of a virgin, in respect of his being apprehended by the Jews, he is no longer with us,—he raises a shout of triumph, as if he had proved by this that Christ remains with us invisible. But Augustine declares that Christ, in respect of the flesh which he once assumed, is absent from us. If he deludes himself with the fallacious principle that Christ as God and man is wholly everywhere, let him at least spare Augustine, whose view is more correct. He will not allow this, but pretends that he clearly delivers the same doctrine. In what words? Why, that the same Christ was in respect of unity of person in heaven when he spake on earth. The Son of Man was in heaven as the Son of God was on earth, in his assumed flesh Son of Man, in heaven by oneness of person. I wish Westphal's ears were not so very long, as to make him when he quotes only hear himself. So far is Augustine from saying that God and man was entire in heaven at the time when he sojourned on earth, that he distinctly affirms that he was then in respect of his flesh nowhere else than on the earth, and that it was in respect of oneness of person it was said, The Son of Man who is in heaven. Hence, too, we infer that whenever he says he will be present, it is by a proper attribute of Godhead. For although he adheres to his body as Mediator, yet the Spirit is the bond of sacred union, who, raising our souls upwards by faith, infuses life into us from the heavenly head. Were any one to go over the whole of Augustine, he would find nothing else than that though Christ, in respect of oneness of person, was in heaven as Son of Man, while he also dwelt as Son of God on earth, still he was nowhere but on the earth in respect of his flesh.

As it is by the resemblance between our flesh and that of Christ that we are wont to refute the fiction of ubiquity, Westphal assails this argument at great length and with much fierceness. At first he exclaims that it is detestable blasphemy to make the flesh of Christ wholly like our own. It would be easy to appease the man were his rage sincere, but when he maliciously stirs up fictitious disturbance about nothing, what kind of treatment does he deserve? He says that the contamination of sin is excepted. Which of us does not say so? He says that the flesh of Christ has this special privilege, that it was the temple of divinity, and the victim to expiate the sins of the world. What has this to do with the property of essence? When from the resemblance we infer that the body of Christ is finite, and has its dimensions just like our own, we have no intention to annihilate the excellent endowments with which it was adorned: we only show that the hope of future resurrection is overthrown, if a model of it is not exhibited in the flesh of Christ. For it has no other foundation than the fellowship of the members with their head. Here we introduce nothing of our own: we only ask due weight to be given to the doctrine of Paul in the fifteenth chapter of first Corinthians. We also appeal to the unambiguous declaration in the second chapter of the Philippians, that we look for Christ our Redeemer from heaven, who will transform our vile body, and make it like his own glorious body. If Westphal detect any blasphemy in this comparison, he may impose upon himself, but the imposture will not harm any other person. Moreover, unless he hold that after the resurrection we shall be everywhere, the flesh of Christ, as Paul testifies, cannot now possess any immensity.

As we quote a passage from Augustine, in which he declares that the sacraments under the law, though differing from ours in signs, were the same in reality, Westphal thought it would gain applause for the concluding act of his play, if he could deprive us of this support, and he accordingly makes his refutation the conclusion of his book. But what does he accomplish? He says that we craftily produce maimed and garbled passages. And yet the only way in which he corrects our fault is by quoting *verbatim* what our writings contain. Surely the whole controversy lies in these few words: The Fathers ate the same spiritual food in the manna that is now offered to us in the Supper; for the sacraments are different in the signs, alike in the thing: they differ in visible form, are the same in spiritual virtue. Westphal quibbles that Augustine is speaking of the spiritual mode of eating. But nothing is clearer than that describing the nature of the signs, as ascertained from the ordinance, he holds that while the signs are different the thing is one. What avails it then to apply to man what is thus delivered in explaining the force and efficacy of the signs?

The question is, What is the Supper to us now, or what its effect? Augustine answers, That in it we enjoy the same spiritual food which the Fathers anciently received from the manna. This certainly is not to discuss how either the fathers used the symbol of the law, or we now use ours; but what the Lord anciently instituted under the law, and what Christ afterwards instituted in the gospel. But as the substance, efficacy, and reality of the signs depend on the word, we certainly infer that the promises given are the same, as according to the word we have the fruition of Christ in both. But as it was not safe for Westphal to take his stand on the meaning of Augustine, he wanders and winds about, and yet all his windings only bring him back to this, that we argue vitiously from the genus to the species. But such mode of arguing is allowed by logicians. For what prevents us from applying to the Supper that which is truly said of all the sacraments? He afterwards, however, explains himself a little more exactly, perversely objecting that we confound things that are different, or omit to mention wherein the species differ from each other, or employ not proper but only accidental differences. How unjust this charge is may easily be made palpable from our books.

First, from want of skill or from malice, he represents it as our general proposition, that sacraments, which are different in the signs, are alike in the thing, whereas in that passage the manna only is compared with our Supper. It is needless, therefore, to talk of sacrifices and other ceremonies. He asks, Must we equal the ancient sacrifices to the sacraments instituted by Christ, merely because it appears that they were signs? As if we were deriving an argument from the term signs, when we say that Augustine makes out this resemblance between the manna and the Supper—that under different signs they contain one thing or the same spiritual virtue. Here, indeed, he brings a most pernicious error into the very elements of piety; when wishing to show the difference, he denies that the ancient sacraments, with the sole exception of circumcision, contained any promise of the forgiveness of sins. How dares he to call himself a theologian, while he knows not or sets at nought a statement which Moses makes a hundred times, viz., that by the offering of sacrifice iniquity will be expiated? Meanwhile, let the reader observe how malignantly he perverts the equality which we assert out of Augustine: because in assuming the principle, that while our Supper differs from the manna in visible form, the thing and spiritual reality is the same, we do not assert that the mode of communication is altogether equal. Nay, on the contrary, I uniformly declare that the same Christ who was held forth under the law is now exhibited to us more fully and richly. I also add, that we are now substantially fed on the flesh of Christ, which in the case of the fathers only exerted its virtue before it actually existed. This more clearly establishes Westphal's dishonesty in charging us with confounding degrees, which, as we justly ought, we carefully distinguish.

But that inequality does not at all prevent the same Christ, who now communicates himself to us, from having communicated himself to the fathers under the signs of the law. This makes Westphal's impiety more intolerable in maintaining that the manna and the rock were figures, whereas the reality is the body of Christ given us in the Supper. I omit to say, how injurious he is to the fathers in robbing them of the communion of Christ. Is it not sacrilegious audacity to make void the effect of a sacrament ordained by God? And to treat him with more leniency, it is preposterous to talk so frigidly and jejunely of a sacrament which Paul adorns with the noblest title. The words of Paul are, that the same spiritual food which we receive in the Supper was given to the fathers. Westphal mutters, that they ate and drank in a figure, many of them even without faith: as if this latter remark were not applicable also to the Supper, or as if the context of Paul would admit that when a comparison of parts is made, the substance and reality is placed in one, and the figure remains in another. Westphal tells us, it was not said of the manna or the water, This is my body, This is my blood: as if there were not the same force in Paul's declaration that the rock was Christ. This, let Westphal do what he will, must be understood of the external sign. For it were altogether inconsistent with the exhortation not to bring on ourselves by abusing the gifts of God the same destruction which befell them, should we confine to believers alone that which Paul expressly applies to unbelievers.

The substance of what he says is, that as the communication of Christ was formerly offered to the whole ancient people under the manna and water, and yet many of them did not please God, we must not now plume ourselves too highly on the invitation which Christ gives us to partake of the same, but must endeavour to make a due and pious use of the inestimable gift. Any differences which Westphal produces out of Augustine tend only to show that the spiritual gifts which the fathers tasted under the law, or possessed only according to the measure of that time, are fully exhibited in the gospel. The two distinctly teach, that our sacraments and those of the fathers differ in respect of the degrees of more or less, because though Christ is the substance of both, he is not equally manifested in both. This again overthrows the impiety, as the words which he quotes from Augustine prove the impudence of Westphal, in maintaining that they were the same in meaning not in reality, the figure being then but the truth now; as if either Paul were opposing the figure to the reality when he makes us common partakers of the same spiritual grace under similar signs, or as if Augustine were placing the dissimilarity anywhere else than in the mode of signifying. When he says, that if it may be denied that the body of Christ is received in the Supper, because the ancients had Christ present in figure, it may equally be denied that the Apostles saw Christ in the Supper, because he was present to the fathers by faith, he proves himself to be just as acute a logician as he had previously proved himself to be an honest and faithful divine. For since it is clear that under the figure of bread the same Christ is offered to us who was formerly given under the figure of manna, the nature of the difference is as great as that between ocular inspection and faith.

It is of no use to go farther in pursuit of the follies of this man, which vanish of their own accord. He occupies six pages in enumerating the differences in degree between the sacraments of the law and those of the gospel, as observed

by Augustine, and at length concludes that they are the same
in respect of the things signified, but not in respect of the exhibition of the things, as if significance without effect were any
thing more than a mere fallacy. After twisting himself about
with the tortuosity of a snake, he endeavours to cloak his
absurdity; but any one who attends to the scope will see
that there is not less difference between his fiction and the
doctrine of Augustine, than there is between that holy
teacher and Scotus, or any other of the band of the Sophists.
I will therefore leave all his vain boastings, because they
disappear with the same idle wind which brought them.

I come now to THE CONFESSIONS OF THE SAXONS, either
elicited by the flattery or extorted by the importunity of
Westphal, as appears, I do not say from his own statement,
but from letters which he could not keep to himself. I
would only have the reader to observe how servilely he
fawns on his acquaintance when supplicating their suffrage,
and how harshly he insults others. I say nothing as to his
scamperings up or down, the rumour of which has reached
even as far as this. Certainly as he has chosen to leave
none ignorant of the means by which he has drawn his party
into subscription, or impelled them to speak evil of the opposite view, we are at liberty to infer what degree of credit
is due to their testimony; and yet this good man is brazen-
faced enough to write, that for four years I have been seeking suffrages in support of my error, in Germany as well as
Switzerland: as if this labour were necessary among the
Swiss, none of whom conceal that they hold the doctrine
which I have defended in common with me. No doubt
those who to a man were ready to lend me their aid, had to
be humbly entreated not to spurn what I offered! As to the
Germans, I wait calmly for the witnesses by whom he is to
prove my importunity. Meanwhile his beggary is notorious
to all. As to the men whom he has found to declare with
long ears that they are my enemies, he makes a loud boast
that nothing now remains for me but to sing dumb, because

all Saxony is against me. But while I have learned modestly to cultivate connection with the pious and faithful servants of Christ, I do not depend on their decisions. Being persuaded that there are not a few learned and right-hearted men, and men of sound judgment in Saxony, among whom truth and reason would have some effect, I offered my book to the inspection of all. Westphal proudly upbraids me with having been repulsed ; as if I were responsible for the continuance of our mutual civility.

Since Westphal makes such a boast of the number of his supporters, as to imagine that my tongue is tied, I may be permitted to answer in a few words, that I had no occasion, in order to obtain favour to my cause, to pay a high price for the purchase of any man's stolidity. I have hitherto thought, according to what is everywhere believed, that Wittenberg and Leipsic are the two eyes of Saxony. Westphal will not deny that he tried these churches. Nay, the fawning letters to N. and N., which he has published, proclaim more loudly than his distinct acknowledgment could have done that he met with a repulse. Now that, after having plucked out the eyes of a remainder, consisting perhaps of the tenth part of Saxony, he is not ashamed to give them the name of the whole, I am confident that no man is so stupid as not to feel disgust at his trifling. I may add, that distrusting his own strength, and feeling a want of better support, he has been compelled to insert the letter of some follower of Servetus, as if he had been building up a wall with dirt collected from all quarters. It is probable, indeed, that any sprinkling of praise which was formerly bestowed on a man who was famishing for it, has been raked together by him to take off the stigma of ignorance.

There is one letter, the purpose of which it is not easy to conjecture. Westphal himself proclaims, that it was sent him from *La Babylone*, as if it were not apparent, without interposing the Italian article, that the author is a Babylonian. Accordingly, some acute persons guess that it comes from a Piedmontese lawyer, who, in many places, has plainly acknowledged that he is an advocate of the impious and execrable dogmas of Servetus. If this conjecture is true, he has put an amusing hoax on Westphal, as it is certain that nothing gives him greater pleasure than to look on while we fight. Be this as it may, I make the subscribers to Westphal welcome to enjoy this associate, since by publishing their shame, they have not refused to submit to this ignominy, which I wish it had been in my power to hide: only I am not sorry that their blind impetus has thus been rewarded from above. In their writings I also observe the perfect truth of an observation made to me in a letter from a friend of distinguished learning and eloquence, that in that maritime district some men are so wondrously wise, that if the Sibyl of Cumae were still alive, she should be sent to them to learn to divine. For those little fathers pronounce on this cause no less confidently than the Roman Pontiff from his chair hurls thunderbolts of anathema at the whole doctrine of the gospel: and not contented with this arrogance, they assail a man on friendly terms with them with barbarous invective, as if the best method of gaining a reputation for strict gravity were to spare no contumely or reproach. But as this is not to speak but to spit, it is better to contemn their ridiculous censures than to take the spittle with which they have defiled none but themselves and throw it back into their face.

But as those of Magdeburg seem not to attach such sovereign authority to their opinion as not to fight with argument also, and observe some method in their doctrine, I must discuss their confession, which, if overthrown, will easily involve all the others in its downfal. But to leave them no ground for the smallest self-complacency, I hope soon to make it manifest to all that it is a compound of futile quibbles. The truculence of the style, which might at first give some fear to the simple, afterwards degenerates into mere scurrility, and therefore does not greatly move me. It might, however, have been decent, in remembrance of their own calamity, to deal a little more mercifully with the many churches by which, as God is witness, anxious and earnest prayers were during three whole years constantly offered for their deliverance. The severity of my defence against Westphal displeased them, and they pronounce his rage to be necessary zeal. It is enough for me to appeal from their unjust and savage intemperance to the tribunal of God. Meanwhile, though I were silent all see that it is perverse hatred to Philip (Melancthon) which makes them humbly, not to say sordidly, flatter Westphal. Matthias of Illyria seemed to act modestly in withdrawing his name, but has consulted ill for his reputation by again subscribing. However he may now put a black mark upon me, it is not very long since in his own hand he deigned to address me with respect. The same is to be said of Erasmus Sarcerius, who, after addressing me by letter as his ever to be respected preceptor, places me by his censure among detestable heretics. I freely forgive him the title of preceptor, but I regret a want of constancy of faith in the cultivation of brotherly good-will to which nothing should put an end but change of doctrine, which cannot be said of me. Henceforth, not to seem too much occupied with my own case, I shall advert only to the doctrine.

When they say that Christ is the author of his own Supper, and thence infer that he is its efficient cause, they mention what is not the subject of any controversy. When they enumerate two material causes, viz., the outward elements of bread and wine, and also the body and blood of Christ, in this also I assent to them. For to say that we utterly remove the true and natural body of Christ from the Supper, is false and calumnious. Their petulance is less tolerable when they charge us with making types, shadows, phantasms, and deceptions of the body of Christ. Perhaps they suppose that by a futile falsehood they can obliterate what I long ago declared in my Institutes, as well as repeatedly elsewhere, not only that Christ was from the first the matter of all the sacraments in general, but was especially so in the holy Supper. Nor have I passed this in silence in my reply to Westphal. How the body and blood of Christ are the matter of the Supper, we shall afterwards explain more fully. This only I must now say, that the men of Magdeburg, in throwing obloquy upon us, maliciously darken the cause at the very threshold.

In regard to the formal cause, there is no wonder if I

differ from them. They say that there is a coupling of the bread and wine, first with the flesh and blood of Christ ; and secondly, with the promise of salvation and the command which enjoins all to take the sacrament. I willingly embrace the sentiment of Augustine, that the element becomes a sacrament as soon as the word is added; but the Magdeburgians confusedly and erroneously confound the effect or fruit of the Supper with the matter itself. But it is perfectly clear from the context that they fall from their distinction : for wishing shortly after to mark the distinction between themselves and us, they say that we take away part of the matter. In this they betray their want of thought. How dexterously they infer, that according to us figures only and symbols are held forth, will appear more fitly in its own place. At present, let the reader only observe that these methodical doctors understand not what it is they are speaking of, nor attend to a distinction which they themselves had laid down three sentences before. When they add that we differ from their sentiment, inasmuch as we insist that faith has reference to the promise and to the corporeal presence of Christ, they say something and yet do not say the whole. The promise to which we direct the faithful, does not exclude the communion of the flesh and blood of Christ which it offers ; but as the exhibition of what is promised depends on it, we bid them keep their minds fixed on it. In this way we acknowledge that the promises in the sacraments are not naked but clothed with the exhibition of the things, seeing they make us truly partakers of Christ. The miracle which the Magdeburgians pretend is well enough known to be foreign from our doctrine,—I mean that the Lord places his body under the bread and his blood under the wine; but it is equally well known that we hold the mode of communication to be miraculous and supernatural. But as the whole of this belongs to the second head, and is irrelevantly introduced here, I will not follow it farther.

When they add, that not only is the audible word to be attended to, but the visible signs also, which for this reason Augustine terms visible words, there is nothing in it opposed to us in the least, as we uniformly teach that the signs are appendages and seals of the word. The formal cause may, therefore, be more simply and correctly defined to be the command (with the addition of the promise) by which Christ invites us to partake of the sacred symbol. In the final cause the perplexity caused by their introduction of various things is repugnant to their proposed method. Their titles promise a beautiful and harmonious arrangement of topics, but what follows is an indigested mass. But as my purpose is not to attack the method in which they deliver their doctrine, it will be sufficient briefly to dispose of the calumnies by which we are unjustly assailed.

They wish it to be carefully observed, that the promise of grace is not given to the eating of bread alone, but to the body of Christ, in order to teach contrary to us, that the forgiveness of sins is not applied by symbols merely. But the world is witness, that many years before they thus spoke I had written that as we do not communicate in the blessings of Christ till he himself is ours, those who would receive due fruit from the Supper should begin with Christ himself, that being ingrafted into his body they may be reconciled to God by his sacrifice. The calumny goes the further length of declaring that we deny the application of the forgiveness of sins in the Supper, as if I did not use the term application in its proper and genuine meaning. They represent us as reasoning thus : We are justified by faith alone, therefore not by the sacraments. But we are not so raw as not to know that the sacraments, inasmuch as they are the helps of faith, also offer us righteousness in Christ. Nay, as we are perfectly agreed that the sacraments are to be ranked in the same place as the word, so while the gospel is called the power of God unto salvation to every one that believeth, we hesitate not to transfer the same title to the sacraments. Therefore did not a lust for carping and biting impel them to attack us in any way, there was no reason for their here putting themselves into so great a passion. I care not for their evil speaking, provided I make it manifest to the reader that we are loaded undeservedly with alien and fictitious charges. Seeing we everywhere teach, as the true end of the Supper, that being reconciled to God by the sacrifice of Christ we may obtain salvation, it cannot be doubtful or obscure to any one how unworthily they deny us the elements of piety.

Before I proceed farther, I must again remind the reader, in a few words, that as the Magdeburgians in various ways obscure or explain away our doctrine, they must not take it on their statement. Whether it be from error or malice, I know not; and yet as the tendency of their account is to throw obloquy upon us, it is probable that being more intent on fighting than on teaching, they have not dealt with us sincerely or faithfully. Wherefore, lest the eye of the reader should be blinded either by their tortuous sophistry, or by the odious sentiments which they ascribe to us, I would here declare that in separating the external symbols from Christ's flesh and blood, we still hold that he truly and in reality performs and fulfils what he figures under the bread and wine, namely, that his flesh is meat to us and his blood is drink. We accordingly teach, that believers have true communion with Christ in the holy Supper, and receive the spiritual food which is there offered. Away, then, with the vile calumny that we leave nothing but an empty phantom, as we have hitherto candidly declared, that the truth is so conjoined with the signs, that our souls are fed with spiritual food not less than our tongues taste bread and wine. The difference is only in the mode, we holding that the visible bread is held forth on the earth, in order that believers may climb upwards by faith and be united with Christ their head, by the secret agency of the Spirit.

But although Christ infuses life into us from his flesh and blood, we deny that there is any mingling of substance, because, while we receive life from the substance of the flesh and blood, still the entire man Christ remains in heaven. In this way we repudiate the bodily immensity which others feign. In order that Christ may feed and invigorate us by his flesh, it is not necessary that it should be inclosed under the bread and swallowed by us. Meanwhile we teach that nothing else than the true and natural body is there held forth, so that here too it plainly appears that our enemies act disingenuously, while they so much contend that the same body which hung on the cross is communicated to us : as if we pretended that Christ has two bodies, instead of testifying by our writings, that life is to be sought from the same flesh which was once offered in sacrifice.

The whole question turns on this—Are we fed by the flesh and blood of Christ, when by them he infuses life into us ; or is it necessary that the substance of his flesh should be swallowed up by us in order to be meat, and that the blood should be substantially quaffed in order to be drink ? The other head of controversy relates to promiscuous eating, we asserting that the blood and flesh of Christ are offered to all, and yet that believers alone enjoy the inestimable treasure. Yet though unbelief precludes the entrance of Christ, and deprives those who approach the Supper impurely of any benefit from it, we deny that any thing is lost to the nature of the Sacrament, inasmuch as the bread is always a true pledge of the flesh of Christ, and the wine of his blood, and there is always a true exhibition of both on the part of God. Our opponents so include the body and blood under the bread and wine, as to hold that they are swallowed by the wicked without any faith. It is not now my purpose to establish our faith on its own grounds, but I wished to make this declaration, in order that if at any time the reader should see us invidiously assailed by the false cavils of the Magdeburgians, he may always carry back his eyes to this mirror. What I shall afterwards add will not only tend to clear explanation, but suffice for solid confirmation, and prevent the fumes of calumny which the Magdeburgians have sent abroad from casting a shade on the noonday sun.

As the Magdeburgians contend that we must abide by the literal sense of the words of Christ, they insist that the bread is without figure substantially the body ; and to prove this opinion they collect twenty-eight reasons, which they call foundations. So they would have them thought ; but their readers discover that what at the outset they count three are in fact only one. I ask what they are to gain by this show of multiplying their number ? The sum of all they say is, that a sincere, proper, and certain understanding of this controversy, and a plain and firm decision must be sought from the *ipsissima verba* of Christ, from their clear and native meaning, not from the will or gloss of man; and as the natural man receiveth not the things which are of God, and carnal reason is blind, being involved in darkness, that which Christ asserts in distinct and perspicuous terms must be apprehended by faith; for though an owl cannot see the sun's rays, the sun does not therefore cease to shine. We must therefore hold the thing simply implied in the words, This is my body.

That the whole of this is not less frivolous than they deemed it plausible, will readily appear in three sentences. We are perfectly agreed that we must acquiesce in the words of Christ: the only question is as to their genuine meaning. But when it is inquired into, our masters of the letter admit of no interpretation. Away, then, with all this cunning, and leave us at liberty to ask what our Saviour meant. Let the *ipsissima verba* remain, only let them not be fastened on without judgment, just as if one crying out that in Scripture he finds eyes, ears, hands, and feet attributed to God, should insist that God is corporeal. We do not fasten extraneous glosses on the word of God, but only wish to ascertain from the common and received usage of Scripture what is meant by the sentence, This is my body. Nor do we measure the recondite mystery of the Supper by our sense, but with modesty and pious docility we desire to learn what Christ promises to us. In the meantime, if we adapt the sacramental mode of expression to the analogy of faith, surely the sun does not therefore cease to shine.

While I admit the *fourth* reason adduced to be true, I deny its relevancy. Christ does not make a parable of his ordinance. Who ever said so? But neither does Paul make a parable when he says that the rock was Christ; and in all the passages which treat of sacraments, we say not that parables are delivered, but that there are sacramental modes of speaking, by which an analogy is expressed between the thing and the sign. When they add, that Christ does the very thing which he shows, and ratifies what he does, I willingly admit it; but from this it is erroneously inferred that there is no mystery to which the sacramental mode of expression applies. Though our Lord did not speak in parables when he told his disciples of his ascension to heaven, it does not follow that the bread is not a symbol of the body.

In the *fifth* reason they inculcate what they had said before, that they found on the simple words and oppose them to the wisdom not only of men but of angels, because we are enjoined by the heavenly oracle to hear the Son of God. With equal malice and dishonesty do they object to us the authority of Christ, as if it were our purpose to deviate one iota from pure and genuine doctrine, whereas we have shown not less strongly by facts than they pretend by words that we receive with reverence every thing that fell from the sacred lips of our Lord. Therefore let the Son of God be, without controversy, our supreme, perfect, only Master, in whose doctrine it is not lawful to change one word or syllable. But the obedience of faith does not hinder us from giving attention to the sound meaning of his words. How many of his expressions are on record, the harsh sound of which cannot be softened in any other way than by skilful and appropriate interpretation? Nay, if we are to be bound by a law to receive the simple sound of the words, there is no kind of absurdity for which profane men may not defame and scoff at his doctrine. The Magdeburgians then have no ground for making it their boast to the unskilful that they hear Christ according to the command of God. So far are we from desiring to be wise above his teaching, that in ingenuously defending it many of our brethren daily meet death. We, too, stand daily in the field while arrows fly around.

Their *sixth* objection, that we are forced without any necessity to feign a trope, will be sustained, when they shall have disposed of all the arguments by which we have shown a hundred times, that this passage cannot be duly expounded without admitting a trope. Nay, if we grant them all they ask or imperiously demand, the bread will not be properly called the body. Therefore, let them twist themselves and the words of Christ as they may, they will never logically conjoin the body of Christ to the bread, as the predicate to the subject: and hence they cannot avoid the metonymy by which it is strange they are so much offended, seeing the body of Christ cannot be in the Supper, unless it be given under the symbol of bread. The words, they say, are clear, and are not an image of the sun, but the sun himself. Why they speak of an image of the sun, I know not. The clearness of the words, did not their obstinacy interpose a cloud, would be manifest to us by itself; but if they choose to wink in the light, why do they insult sound and candid interpreters?

How solid their *seventh* reason is, let the reader determine for himself. They say that the ordinance of the Supper is new, having been ordained by Christ only in the New Testament, and that there is nowhere else any mode of expression similar to this, Eat, this is my body: as if Paul, after premising that not similar, but the same spiritual food was given to the fathers, and immediately adding, That rock was Christ, had not used an expression admirably accordant with it. When in another passage Paul calls baptism the laver of regeneration, is there no resemblance in the words? But if baptism washes us, how is the blood of Christ elsewhere termed our ablution? If they answer that baptism instrumentally cleanses our defilements, I, in my turn, rejoin, that the bread is sacramentally the body of Christ. However incensed they may be, they cannot deprive us of the weapons furnished by the Spirit of God.

The *eighth* reason is, that it is contrary to the usage of all languages to make the demonstrative pronoun in this passage point out any thing but that which is held forth. I never could have thought there was such audacity outside the cloisters of monks. For why, pray, should it be lawful in other passages to expound the demonstrative pronoun otherwise than is lawful here? And even were this granted, how will they prove the restriction from the common use of all languages? It is a trite and common usage in the languages of all nations, to denote absent things by the demonstrative pronoun. If they deny this, let them go to boys to learn their first rudiments, nay, let them recall to mind what they learned from their nurses, provided they were nursed on mothers' milk. If this is generally true,

why in one passage only shall all languages lose their force
and nature ?   Still we deny not, that under the symbol of
bread we are called to partake of the flesh of Christ : I only
show how disgracefully absurd it is to insist, that the pronoun *this* refers entirely to the body.   It signifies no more
in respect of the bread, than the fuller expression in the
other part of the Supper, This cup.   For what else does
This cup mean, but just This ?   As, therefore, the term cup
means the cup which is held forth, so it is plain that the
pronoun, This, is affirmed of the bread which is offered with
the hand ; unless, indeed, they make out that we have two
grammars in the one Supper of Christ.

The *ninth* reason is, that Christ used the substantive verb.
How long are we to have the same thing ?   Just as the rustic host made many dishes out of the same pig, when he
wished to hide his poverty ; so those men, while they only
insist on one reason, compound their heap out of various
colours.   Moreover, if this is the nature and property of the
substantive verb, why should it not take effect in all the other
words of Christ ?   He certainly used the substantive verb in
all his parables.   If they object that parables are to be kept
by themselves, yet Christ everywhere uses them.   The words,
" I am the true vine, ye are the branches, my Father is the
husbandman," fell from the lips of Christ, not less than those
for which they contend so rigidly.   What if I should also
urge the words of John, " As yet the Holy Spirit was not,
for Christ was not yet glorified."   The substantive verb is
there used, and ought to have the same force in denying as
in affirming.   Had the essence of the Holy Spirit then its
first origin in the resurrection of Christ ?   They will say
that the words are used of the manifestation of the Spirit.
Let them cease, then, to obtrude the substantive verb upon
us in a different sense, as admitting of no interpretation.

They say that Christ, who was the eternal Word (Λογος)
of God, might have spoken differently if he choose, *e.g.*, This
figures, symbolises, shadows forth my body.   As if to catch
favour it were sufficient to play the buffoon, they invent
monstrous terms.   To bear us down, they without any shame
put forth what must produce shame in candid and right-

hearted readers. That Christ meant to speak most clearly, I deny not, nor do I see why the Magdeburgians should extort from him the grossest expression, unless it be that under the shadow of it their gross delirium may find a lurking place. And though Christ were adapting himself to our capacity in these words, I deny that in the sacramental mode of expression there was any great danger. They complain that they are led into a pernicious error, if Christ does not give his body. I answer, that although Christ gives what he promises, and performs in reality what he figures, his words are not to be astricted to the grossness of those who insist, that the bread differs in no respect from the body. My last remark with regard to the substantive verb will be this, Christ is in the New Testament called the Church, just as much as the bread is called the body. Paul's words are, " As the members of our body being many, are one body, so also is Christ." If this is a new expression, to which none similar is found, let them show me a difference preventing me from maintaining, that we all are truly and properly Christ, on the very ground on which they maintain that the bread is his body. Paul declares, that Christ is such as is the connection of one body with its different members. Is Christ found such in himself? Unless they would form a confused chaos, and plunge themselves into a fearful labyrinth, they must become somewhat more moderate in regard to the admission of tropes.

The *tenth* reason is, that Christ did not call it a figure of the body. Nor did Moses say that the lamb was a figure of the passover, and yet unless any one chooses voluntarily to betray his own madness, it is clear, by the consent of all men, that the lamb which is called the passover is a figure. Whenever it is said of the old sacraments, This will be an expiation, none will presume to deny that the expression is to be understood figuratively. The Evangelist hesitates not to call a dove the Holy Spirit, evidently on the same ground on which the name of body is transferred to the bread. Still more insipid is their next observation, that Christ, when he discourses of his body, does not call it a figure; as if such a monstrous expression ever fell from any one, as that the body is a figure of the body. Had the Lord pointed to his own body, there would have been no dispute ; but when, in pointing to the bread, he uses the name of body, we must doubtless look for an analogy between the thing and the thing signified.

On the *eleventh* head, repeating the same thing, they perhaps think, I know not how, that they are doing some good to their cause. He said, My body, not the figure of a body which will be elsewhere : I, says he, exhibit myself present to you, this body which I have ! As I have already declared that no other body of Christ is offered in the Supper than that which was once offered on the cross, let them have done with the calumny which they are so eager to concoct out of the term figure. But as the figure does not exclude the thing signified, so neither does the reality repudiate the figure. What is to prevent the Son of God, while he invites us to partake of his flesh and blood, from consulting at the same time for our weakness, by holding forth the external symbol ? We, holding that the Lord does not deal deceitfully with us, certainly infer that the body is given to us when he exhibits a figure of it before our eyes. Let them explain how the Lord gave to his disciples, under the bread, the same body which was visibly before them. If they insist that he was substantially swallowed under the bread, his nature was double. In one place it was visible and mortal ; and it was elsewhere, or nowhere, and yet at the same time lurked everywhere, hidden and endued with celestial glory. Meanwhile, we hold a different mode of presence from that of which the Magdeburgians dream ; for, in order to our gaining possession of the flesh and blood of the Lord, it is not necessary to imagine that both descend to us, the secret agency of the Spirit sufficing to form the connection.

The *twelfth* foundation totters miserably. Their words are : " In the other part of this Supper he does not vary in the words, but again lucidly and distinctly repeats the same, This is my blood. Here at least our Saviour would have figured somewhat had he not delivered the very things of which he speaks. He is ordaining a matter of the utmost importance : he accordingly speaks seriously, not feignedly ;

openly, not in parables. We neither attribute dissimulation to the Son of God, when we willingly acknowledge that this mystery is accomplished by the incomprehensible agency of the Holy Spirit, nor do we make any pretence of parables : and hence, without our saying a word, it is very obvious that those who prate thus are mere buffoons. But with what face do they dare to affirm that there is no variation of expression in holding forth the cup. Luke and Paul, as if from the lips of Christ, narrate, This cup is the new covenant in my blood. Had the Magdeburgians been contented with their *somewhat,* so clear a difference would not have affected them. The ordinance of the Supper is expounded by four witnesses sent down from heaven under the guidance and teaching of the same Spirit. Two of them call the cup the blood of the new covenant ; the other two call it the covenant in the blood. If these words differ nothing in meaning, why do we not immediately give up our debate. If the Magdeburgians insist that the meaning is different, there will be a variation in the thing, not to say in the words. I might wonder at their being so oblivious, did not their supine security always carry them to the same license. But as all the evangelists delivered the same thing in the same words, we justly hold it as confest that the body of Christ is not given in the Supper in any other way than the nature of the new covenant admits, namely, that he is our head, and we are his members. Not to expatiate longer, no other communion of the flesh and blood must be sought in the Supper than that which is described in the sixth chapter of John—a communion very different from the carnal eating of which these gross doctors dream.

The *thirteenth* objection proves them to be nothing better than falsifiers and wicked calumniators. As Christ says that the body which he gives is no other than that which was shortly after to be sacrificed on the cross, they infer that it is not a spiritual body, in other words, not the Church ; as if we took the mystical body in the Supper for the Church. Whether they will or not, this principle is certainly common to us both, that by the words of Christ is designated the true body, whose immolation has reconciled us to God. The only question is how it is designated. The Magdeburgians say, that it retains its native signification. That is, it lets us know that that body on which our souls are spiritually fed is the same which hung on the cross, but not that the bread becomes body, or that the body lies hid under the bread. What need was there to represent Christ as prudent and explicit, in order to guard against trans- ferring his words to another new body? They say that by prudence and a learned tongue he took care that no falsifier should be able to say that shadows only, types, figures, masks, or magical impostures were given. This is the reason why I said that their falsity is here made manifest. For as we are the last to teach that naked or empty figures are given, so there is nothing to prevent the true exhibition of the thing from having the figure annexed. The Supper of Christ without type or figure would not be a sacrament. Magical impostures we leave to those who are not ashamed to make a bi-corporeal Christ, who, while exhibiting his body present before their eyes, gave it to each of them invisible under the bread.

On the *fourteenth* head I cannot make out their meaning. They say that the natural, not spiritual blood of Christ was shed on the cross, and is therefore given in the Supper; as if we imagined any other blood of Christ than that which he assumed on becoming man. Only, when wishing to express the manner of drinking, seeing it is not drunk in a human manner, we call it spiritual drink. Thus pious and sound teachers have always spoken, and in this the Magdeburgians, however much they may murmur, will not find any thing absurd. Nay, Irenæus says, that whatever is given in the Supper besides bread and wine is spiritual. In the same way I interpret the expression of Jerome—(In Cap. 1. ad Ephes.)—"The flesh of Christ is understood in a twofold sense, the one spiritual and divine, of which he says, my flesh is meat indeed, and that which was crucified; not that he makes it twofold in reality, but because the mode of partici- pation raises us above heaven." Not unlike is the passage which we have elsewhere quoted from Augustine, (in Ps. xcviii.,) that the body given to the disciples was not that which hung upon the cross. As he in another place teaches, that the Jews when converted drank the blood which they had shed, how comes it that he now denies it to be the same, but just because the spiritual communion could not otherwise be expressed ?

In the *fifteenth* foundation, they infer that the proper body and blood of Christ are undoubtedly communicated in the Supper, because he meant to institute a thing difficult, miraculous, and new, like nothing previously in the world, and that purposely, and no doubt with the counsel of the Father and the Spirit, in order that there might be a most evident and most transparent and most certain application of his love and merits in so precious and arduous a pledge. Were I to concede all this, the doctrine which they impugn would still remain entire. For we deny not that the flesh and blood of Christ are communicated to us. We only explain the mode, lest carnal eating should either derogate in any respect from the heavenly glory of Christ, or overthrow the reality of his human nature. But these men are not to be satisfied, unless that which is received only by virtue of faith be devoured by the mouth. The real aim of this *miraculous* and *arduous*, I know not what, is not to leave a place for faith or the secret operation of the Spirit.

The magniloquence which bursts from them on the *sixteenth* head, easily falls and vanishes of itself. They premise that the Evangelists and Apostles are most worthy of belief, and have a testimony that they spoke by the Holy Spirit, and do not err. What, pray, do they produce after this long breath ? They all say, This is my body. They point to the bread and the cup, and use the substantive verb. But there is no controversy as to this. The only thing is to see whether, as Christ instituted a sacrament, we are not at liberty to say, by way of interpretation, that the bread is the body sacramentally. It is indeed certain that Christ is called the Son of God in another and different sense from that in which the bread is called the body. For after all the thunder of their clamour, they are forced to confess that the bread is a symbol of the thing which it figures. Moreover, how much they are fascinated by their fiction appears from this, that to them the covenant in the blood is equivalent to the blood inclosed in the cup.

The same argument is repeated in the *seventeenth* head. They oppose to us great and approved witnesses; as if our interpretation were detracting one iota from their authority. They ask, If the bread and wine were shadows, symbols, and figures of absent things, would not the Evangelists have made out of one *Is* one *Signifies?* Would not the Holy Spirit, the guide of hearts and tongues, have somehow suggested one vocable of symbol or figure? Since he was to suggest all things that Christ taught, I answer that they act rigidly and presumptuously in daring to dictate words to the Holy Spirit. A mode of expression uniformly employed in treating of the sacraments, is to give the sign the name of the thing signified. It was anciently said that God dwelt between the cherubim; and Moses declared that God was present in the sanctuary, that the lamb was the passover, that circumcision was a covenant, that the sacrifices were expiations for sins, just as much as it was said that the bread and the cup are the body and blood of Christ. In all these modes of expression there is no obscurity or harshness, would not the Magdeburgians disdainfully reject every thing that is not said according to their rule. It is repeatedly said of circumcision, This is my covenant, as it is said of the bread, This is my body. While in the old sacraments, the name of the thing signified is metonymically transferred to the sign, the substantive verb occurs an hundred times; the word symbol or figure not once. Why should the Holy Spirit not now have the same freedom? Is he to be forced to change his language at the dictation of men of Magdeburg?

They proceed still further in the *eighteenth* head, and subject the Apostles to their laws. They say, If the Apostles did not dare to mutilate any thing in the narration itself, on the ground that witnesses may not take away or add any thing, they ought at least in some other place to have explained the true view. But what if the truth has been sufficiently explained to the teachable in the words? For who can doubt that in all the sacraments we are to rise from the ex-

ternal and earthly sign to the heavenly reality? I hear a
dove called the Holy Spirit. I do not quarrel with the
Evangelists for not expressly telling me it was a figure, because on attending to the analogy between the sign and the
thing signified, all ambiguity is removed. Thus in the words
of Christ, on attending to what the nature of a sacrament
requires, though I hold it certain that that which the words
imply is truly fulfilled, yet I reject not the figure by which
Christ has been pleased to help the weakness of my faith.
Thus, too, a proper transition is made from the bread and
the cup to the flesh and the blood. Nor in this way is the
doctrine of Christ concealed—a doctrine which, if the Magdeburgians were so desirous to illustrate as they pretend, they
would not so preposterously involve and confound things
which, when kept distinct, throw full light upon it. They
insist that the bread is substantially the body: we teach
that it is a symbol to which the true exhibition of the thing
is annexed, because the Lord does not fallaciously figure
that his flesh is meat to us, but shows to the eye what he
truly performs within by the energy of his Spirit. This simple doctrine the Magdeburgians in vain endeavour to distort
by monstrous terms, when, like silly buffoons, they attribute
to us the spurious word *figurizing*. They ought rather,
while they relate that Paul speaks as well of the elements as
of the body and blood of the Lord, to consider more attentively what place the elements hold. For unless they are
regarded as symbols, and figures, and signs, and types, of
spiritual things, the action will be not only ludicrous but
absurd.

The *nineteenth* foundation will for me remain untouched.
For who can deny that the true body of Christ is celebrated
by Paul, just as I hold, that not a fallacious, or imaginary, or
shadowy body is given us in the Supper, but that natural
body, by the sacrifice of which on the cross sins were expiated? If ubiquity is no more applicable to it than opaque
density or earthly ponderousness to the sun, it follows, that
by the fiction of the Magdeburgians, we are drawn away
from the true body of Christ to some indescribable phantom.
For in vain do they exclaim that it is the true body of Christ,

while they make it a false body. Because Paul charges those with sacrilege who eat the bread of Christ unworthily, not discerning the Lord's body, they coolly and absurdly infer that the substance of the flesh lies hid under the bread. Though it is not given to be chewed by the teeth, this does not excuse the impious profanation of those who contemn what is spiritually offered.

The passage which they quote in the *twentieth* head plainly supports us. Paul says, that the bread which we break is the fellowship (κοινωνια) of the Lord's body. They interpret this to mean dispensing, as if it could be said that fellowship is any thing but distribution. The meaning of κοινωνια is made perfectly clear from the context, when he says, that those who sacrifice are partakers (κοινωνοι) of the altar, and forbids believers to become κοινωνοι with devils. If κοινωνια of the altar and with devils means dispensation, the meaning will be the same in regard to the body of Christ. But if all agree, that fellowship is denoted, why do the men of Magdeburg carry their heads so high? They contend that nothing more significant or expressive can be said of the material cause of the Supper. Verily so be it. Nay, I assist them, for I teach that no term could better explain the mode in which the body of Christ is given to us, than the term *communion*, implying that we become one with him, and being ingrafted into him, truly enjoy his life. It is clear and certain, that this is done not naturally, but by the secret agency of the Spirit. I hold that the spiritual matter of the Supper is the body and blood of Christ, just as the earthly matter is the bread and wine. The only question is, whether the body of Christ becomes ours by our devouring it? Paul points out a different mode, by directing us to the fellowship by which we are made one with him. They object that Paul does not term the elements of bread and wine figures or symbols. But if they are bare elements and not signs of spiritual things, the Supper will cease to be a sacrament.

Such is the result of the material theology to which they remain so fixed, that from hatred to signs, they take away all significancy from the sacraments. In order to make an impression on the unskilful, they say that Paul, with full and clear voice, declares that the bread is κοινωνια, not a shadow or type. And of what thing? Not of the bread, but of the body; as if it had been possible to call the bread the communion of the bread. When, pray, is this trifling to end? Did it require such a wide mouth to declare that we communicate with Christ in the Supper? I should like to know whether, according to them, this communion belongs indiscriminately to unbelievers as well as to believers. This they assert with their usual confidence. How admirably are those said to communicate with Christ who are alto-gether aliens from him! That the body of Christ is devoured by the wicked, monstrous though it be, may be easily said; but no man not actually turned into a trunk can believe that he who is not a member of Christ can partake of Christ.

When, on the *twenty-first* head, they say that the final cause ought not to be confounded with the matter, I grant it. There was no need of calling in Jerome as a witness to a point sufficiently agreed between us, unless, perhaps, they imagine that they are the only custodiers of logic, and none but themselves know how to distinguish between the end and the matter.

On the *twenty-second* head they again exaggerate, saying, that as the Supper of Christ is a testament, it cannot law-fully be violated or corrupted by a different meaning. Which of the two pays more respect to the testament, I leave the impartial to judge. The Magdeburgians expose the body of Christ to the wicked and sacrilegious without faith, without the Spirit; as if the Son of God had by testament appointed the profane despisers of his grace the lords of his body and blood. Our doctrine is, that whosoever receives the promise of the Supper in faith truly becomes a partaker of the body and blood of Christ, because he never meant to deceive when he plainly declared that it was his body. What violation can be discovered here? Surely, while contented with external signs and earthly pledges, we firmly believe that the body of Christ is vivifying bread to us, and that every thing which the sign represents to the eye is truly performed, we by no means rescind the testimony of Christ. The charge which they falsely bring against us I retort on their own head, viz., that the sacrament is abolished and extinguished, if the spiritual truth is not figured by external symbols.

In the *twenty-third* head they call the ancient and orthodox fathers to their support; as if it were not easy to dispose of all their glosses by a single word. Nor had Philip (Melancthon) any other intention than to prove the communion, as to which he entirely agrees with us. What Westphal has gained by his farrago I leave the reader to judge.

In the *twenty-fourth* head they excuse themselves by saying that they believe no other mode of presence than that which Christ appointed. If this were true, there would be no reason for debating. But when they add, that the body of Christ is everywhere present, before they obtain what they want, they will have to prove that this dream of their's is the heavenly oracle of Christ. How unseasonably they introduce the power of Christ, methinks I have sufficiently shown in my defence against Westphal. I admit that it is Christ who reveals hidden things to us. Why, then, do they throw darkness on his revelations? In regard to Christ, we acknowledge that the Father commands from heaven that all are to hear him. Why, then, do they make a turmoil, and pretend that no interpretation of his words is to be admitted? We acknowledge that with Christ nothing is impossible. Why, then, do they themselves not believe, that though he is in heaven, he can, notwithstanding, by the wondrous virtue of his Spirit, give us his flesh and blood for spiritual nourishment? It is certainly a proof of truly divine and incomprehensible power, that how remote soever he may be from us, he infuses life, from the substance of his flesh and blood, into our souls, so that no distance of place can impede the union of the head and members. Hence it clearly appears how vain and calumnious it is to say that we measure this mystery by human reason. But as the Magdeburgians, from the proud obstinacy of their own brain, despise the work of Christ, they pretend that all must give way who depend not on their pleasure. I wish that they themselves would stand on some solid foundation, rather than cast others down headlong by their empty thunder.

They croak the same thing in the *twenty-fifth* article. How can I otherwise describe it ? They pretend to be horrified at our theology, as savouring of nothing but what is carnal; as if it were a dictate of the flesh that the boundless virtue of Christ penetrates through heaven and earth, in order to feed us with his flesh from heaven: that the flesh, which by nature was mortal, is to us the fountain of life: that every thing which he figures by the visible symbol is truly fulfilled by him: and that, therefore, the flesh of Christ in the Supper is spiritual food, just as our bodies are daily fed with bread. There is something worse, when, in order to condemn what they pretend to be our carnal sense, they quote a passage from the eighth chapter of the Romans, in which Paul says that the flesh is enmity against God. This, no doubt, is their reverence in handling Scripture; and lest any thing should be wanting to complete their fatuity, they append, as if from Paul, Likewise, he who receives with the faith of the Sacramentarians is guilty of the body and blood of Christ. But were I disposed to sport after their fashion, I could extract from their words, that there is therefore no need of carnal eating, in order to be guilty of the body and blood of Christ; for our faith excludes their carnal eating, which they, however, pretend to extract from the words of Paul.

In the *twenty-sixth* head, they most unjustly charge us with explaining away the dignity of this sacrament. Every thing belonging to the sacred Supper is set forth in the most honourable manner by us: only we do not give the body of Christ to be swallowed by Judas as well as by Peter. In order to prove their charge, they affirm that we do not distinguish between bare promises and those clothed with sacraments: as if after they have produced their best, the reader could not learn more clearly and fully from our writings, how Christ works effectually in the Supper and in baptism.

In the *twenty-seventh* head, they object that the person of Christ is dissolved by us, because we deny that he can be in his human nature wheresoever he pleases. If this is to dissolve the person, it will be necessary to rob the human nature of every thing that is most proper to it, in order to his continuing to be Mediator. What can be imagined more absurd than that the flesh of Christ was in heaven while he hung upon the cross? Yet undoubtedly the whole Christ, God and man, was then also in heaven. But those proud censors must be taught a vulgar distinction which was not unknown either to Peter Lombard (Lib. 3. Sentent. dist. 22) or the sophists who came after him, viz., that Christ, the Mediator, God and man, is whole everywhere, but not wholly, (*totus ubique, sed non totum,*) because in respect of his flesh he continued some time on earth and now dwells in heaven. It is strange how these men fly so petulantly in the face of the primitive Church. Let those who are inclined see a full and clear proof of this, by that faithful minister of Christ, our venerable brother Bullinger. They say that Christ, by these words, This is my body, intends to be present with the whole Church. Be it so, only let them not append to it this most wicked falsehood, that we upset this will and presence of Christ on philosophical principles, since it is perfectly notorious, that there is no article of Christian doctrine which we support by more numerous passages of Scripture.

No less perversely do they, *in the last place,* bring the calumnious charge against us of taking away the credit due to Christ, together with his omnipotence : as if any of us had ever before raised the question, or now disputes whether it is possible for Christ to fulfil what he promises, or whether he deludes us by fallacious phantoms. Our method of doctrine so reconciles the will of Christ with all the principles of the faith, that the presence and communion of his flesh which we enjoy is tied down to no space, and he performs what he promises in a wonderful manner, transcending the comprehension of our mind. In short, we so harmonize the analogy of the sign and the thing signified, that to the word and visible symbol are annexed not only the fruit or effect of the grace which we receive from Christ, but also the reality of secret communion with his flesh and blood.

We must now see how dexterously they dispose of our arguments which they pretend to be woven of sand, because

IRENÆUS so spoke of heretics. The first of the fifty-nine arguments which they enumerate is amply sufficient to dispose of all the objections with which they have hitherto imagined themselves to be completely fortified. On looking more closely at what they advance, the substance amounts to this, that we must reject all interpretation, and simply adhere to what the words contain. This, however, is our wall of brass—As Christ instituted a sacrament, his words ought to be expounded sacramentally according to the common usage of Scripture. For a kind of perpetual rule in regard to all the sacraments is, that the sign receives the name of the thing signified. What do the Magdeburgians say to this? They say, that this may be conceded, on the condition, that the sacrament be taken as it was ordained in clear terms by Christ, not as it is measured by human reason. I accept the condition, provided they do not obscure the clearness of the terms by their obstinacy. For if the sacramental mode of expression is admitted, the metonymy and the analogy which ought always to be maintained between the sign and the thing signified will dissipate all doubts. How then will the bread be the body? Just in the sense in which a sacrament implies, viz., our faith must rise from the earthly symbol to the celestial gift. There is no measuring by human reason when it is said, that the spiritual reality transcends the whole order of nature. We do not here imagine some kind of theatrical exhibition, but look up with reverence to the secret agency of the Spirit in effecting this mystery, inasmuch as it cannot be comprehended by our capacity. The Magdeburgians, indeed, dare not deny, that the words of Christ ought to be taken sacramentally. This being granted, they have no longer any cause to plume themselves. Their allegation, that we strenuously abuse the term sacrament, is nugatory; for, according to them, many teachers in the Church hold a sacrament to be a kind of mystical allegory. I rejoin, that there is no ambiguity in the common rule, that the sacramental form of speech ought to receive effect in the sacraments. Having thus finely explained, they say they are going to enter more particular labyrinths: as if they had disentangled themselves from the first.

Our *second* argument, to which they refer, is, That if the
expression in the words of the Supper were to be strictly
urged, the Evangelists would not have varied, nor have
themselves used any trope : But they do vary, and speak
figuratively ; for Luke and Paul, while the others use the
term blood, say, " a covenant in the blood." The Magdeburgians reply, that the major might be conceded, had the
Evangelists always, and everywhere in the same case, spoken
figuratively, but that as they do not heap up various figures
and allegories it is false. We contend, that the figure is
everywhere; for the bread is called body, and the wine blood
metonymically. As they perversely deny this, we compel
them to acknowledge a variation, at least in one part, and
thus rightly conclude that they ought not to insist rigidly on
the words. It was said of the bread, This is my body, in no
other sense than it is added of the cup, This is my blood.
Luke and Paul, who wrote after the others, interpret the
blood more fully and clearly as the covenant in the blood.
Reason requires that the same thing should be transferred
to the bread also, so as to make it a covenant in the body.
The reader will find no sophistry in this.

The reply which they make to the minor proposition is
the same, viz., that as the variation is only in the second
part, it ought not to be transferred to the first : as if there
were any difference in the reason. But they allege a rule,
that what is clear and properly expressed, must not be expounded by figurative expressions : as if the bread were
called the body properly, and without figure, or as if there
were any obscure trope in the expression, This cup is the
covenant in my blood. Hence it appears how securely they
keep chattering in their nests. We hold that the words of
Christ, because they contain a figure, need interpretation.
This is, in some measure, supplied by Luke and Paul, who,
as they wrote after the others, probably made an addition to
interpret what had been previously written. The Magdeburgians answer, that obscure and figurative expressions
ought to be explained by those which are clear and simple.
We, too, contend for this. As we have to do with hard and
obstinate heads, I leave the reader to judge which of the

two expressions is the more clear—This cup is my blood, or, This cup is the covenant in my blood. Surely as brevity always tends towards obscurity, the fuller expression naturally gives more light. Luke and Paul might justly be charged with culpable thoughtlessness, had they, after a thing was clearly expressed by their colleagues, purposely darkened it by a circumlocution.

Our *third* argument is, That the words of the Supper ought not to be separated from others, which Christ uttered almost at the same instant of time: Now, he at that time repeatedly declared, that he was leaving the world. The solution of the Magdeburgians is, that however the major might have been tolerated, nothing is said of the mystery of the Supper in that lengthened discourse from which we have made quotations concerning the departure of Christ. What then? This much, in the meanwhile, remains fixed, that as the Son of God, when about to institute the Supper, distinctly promised that he was leaving the world to go to the Father, and when the Supper was over, frequently repeated the same thing, the intermediate action ought to be understood in a sense which leads us to seek him afterwards only in heaven. We do not in this way confound all the actions and sentiments of Christ. Though he instituted the sacrament separately, it is certain that his discourse depends on it so far, that he speaks to his disciples of his departure more freely, because of the distinguished consolation he had just given them.

There is no ground for the remark, that it is all over with us if Christ has actually left us. For while we loudly proclaim the spiritual presence of Christ, which with them goes for almost nothing, they only betray their shamelessness by such silly calumnies. Accordingly we hold, that though by Christ's ascension into heaven the presence of his flesh has been taken from us, still he fills all things by his virtue and grace, and extends the vigour of his empire over the whole globe. Nor does he only defend us by present aid. He also truly dwells in us; nay, feeds our souls by his flesh and blood. In this way there is no repugnance between the expressions, "I go to the Father," and, "Take, this is my

body;" because, while we are reminded that Christ is not
to be sought on the earth, we climb by faith to heaven in
order to enjoy him. The Magdeburgians insist, that Christ
is not in the world in visible shape, but is invisibly hid under
the bread. So they say; but who will believe them? No less
absurd is their additional remark, that this departure commenced at death itself, because he then said, "I go to the
Father." I wish they were as literary as they long to be
literal. Nothing in Hebrew phraseology is more trite than
the use of the present tense for the future. They, disregarding all reason, restrict the departure of Christ to the
moment at which he said, I go. This ignorance might, perhaps, be pardoned, did it not carry with it the other impious
dream, that when Christ truly ascended to heaven, a departure was exhibited to the Apostles which had previously
taken place. As if Luke were telling of some phantom, and
making void one of the leading articles of our faith.

The *fourth* argument is, Luke makes the Supper of the
paschal lamb precede the Lord's Supper: the supper of the
paschal lamb is a mystery or figure: therefore the Lord's
Supper is mystical or figurative. Whether anybody has
argued in this way, I know not; I certainly do not think it
likely. What they have turned to suit their own purpose I
will restore thus, Christ ordained the Supper to be substituted in the place of the paschal lamb: but the nature and
end of both sacraments is alike: therefore it is not strange
if they bear a mutual affinity to each other, and also a resemblance in the words. What do the Magdeburgians now
say? They say that the argument drawn from unequals is
not good. But I neither urge their equality nor infer any
necessity that what is said of the one should be as applicable to the other. I only extort from them, whether they will
or not, that it is reasonable to expect that a comparison with
the paschal lamb will assist us in understanding the Supper.
It is a frigid quibble to say, that the passover was then abolished. Though the use of the ceremony ceased, still the
doctrine and the reality remain entire; otherwise when
baptism is considered, there would be no room to refer to circumcision. Nor are they helped by the distinction, that the

sacraments of the law designed Christ who was to come, whereas ours exhibit him present; provided the presence be referred as it ought to be to the advent of Christ, by which God fulfilled what he had promised under the law.

The *fifth* argument is, If the mode of expression in the Supper were different from that of other sacraments, as when the lamb is called the passover, the Apostles would have interrogated their Lord as they were wont to do on other occasions; this they did not; therefore they understood the Supper mystically, the expressions being such as they were used to. The Magdeburgians answer, that a consequence drawn from symptoms not necessary is not valid. Still they do not make out that it is not a probable conjecture. We know that not only were they accustomed to interrogate Christ in difficulty or perplexity, but as often as their ignorance threw them into any doubt. If, as these men pretend, something new and miraculous had then been suddenly declared concerning the invisible presence of the flesh, was there such perfection of faith in the disciples that no doubt arose in any one mind? Who, I ask, will believe that men slow of heart and doubtful in the smallest matters, on the unheard of announcement, hastened with readiness and alacrity to swallow the immense and invisible body of Christ under the bread? Wherefore we not unaptly argue from probability, that as they were accustomed to sacramental modes of expression, they raised no question on a matter that was known. I will not honour with a reply their rejoinder, viz., that Christ clearly and without tropes uttered the sentence, This is my body, and hence the Apostles being contented did not think of tropes, figures, and allegories; otherwise, from their desire to learn, they would have interrogated their Lord. First, seeing that the clearness of the words depends on the figure, in order to perceive the former it is not proper to exclude the latter. Secondly, seeing that the thing was plain, what use was there, according to the common expression, to seek a knot in a thorn? The question only arises when the bread is said to be properly and substantially the body of Christ.

In regard to the *sixth* argument, as it was only produced for a calumnious purpose, I give a brief reply. We hold, indeed, that it is not only to pervert the whole order of Christ, but to rob the Holy Spirit of freedom of utterance, to insist literally on the controverted terms, This is my body, as if it were unlawful to add a syllable in the way of interpretation. They ask whether *is* and *signifies* are always to be equivalent, and whether the Holy Spirit nowhere speaks properly? as if we were laying down an universal rule, and not rather holding, from the circumstance of place and subject, that we ought to consider what is most appropriate. In this ordinance we wish to give effect to that which those who are moderately versant in Scripture know to be common to all the sacraments. We insist on the intervention of a symbol which may enable us to make a transition to the spiritual reality. These new doctors protest that it is unlawful to deviate one hair's-breadth from the words and syllables. What is this but to rise up and imperiously forbid freedom of speech to the Holy Spirit?

They next ask more petulantly, whether the term body, is always to be held equivalent to phantasm of the body? Must we hold, then, that as the Apostle teaches that throughout the worship of the law there were figures of spiritual blessings, we are at liberty to substitute phantasms for figures? See what they gain by throwing their ugly squibs at us. No one ever said that the body is taken for the figure of the body, but that the bread is called the body symbolically, being interposed as a kind of visible pledge when Christ would make us partakers of his flesh. Let their subsequent reproaches be left to their own nostrils. Their ever and anon recurring to the same thing is a sign of weakness and poverty. They contend that the words of Christ, This is my body, are plain, because he says not symbol or spectre. As to spectre, of what use is it again to utter a disgraceful falsehood? We maintain that the analogy between the sign and the thing signified is to be observed, in order that the reality may be conjoined with the visible element. If in this way we make a spectre of the bread of the Supper, much more may the same be said of the ark of the covenant. Their question, Where will there be any religion, if it be lawful to substitute shadows and types for the realities, I retort upon them. If it be lawful to substitute realities for types and shadows, where will religion be ? No longer the blood of Christ, but corruptible water will be our ablution.

The *seventh* argument they quote is, Explanation must be sought from the words of Christ—but he declares that the flesh profiteth nothing—hence it follows that the eating delivered by him in the Supper is not carnal but spiritual. They admit the major, provided what is more obscure receives light from what is clearer. Now, in order to put an end to the controversy, if we believe them, we must abide by the very institution of the Supper. I object that when our Lord instituted the Supper, he spoke briefly, as is usually done in federal acts, whereas in the sixth chapter of John he discourses copiously and professedly of that mystery of sacred conjunction, of which he afterwards held forth a mirror in the Supper. In vain will they now keep crying that we must go to the fountain-head: just as an Anabaptist, by laying hold at random of the words, Preach and baptize, He who believeth and is baptized, would, by the same pretext, preclude all entrance to argument. Wherefore no man of sound mind can now doubt which of the two passages is fitter and more convenient to illustrate the subject. When they come to the minor, they show how much they are perplexed. At first they object that the words are clear and manifest, The bread which I will give is my flesh which I will give for the life of the world. I wish they had been less accustomed to unbridled license in lacerating Scripture. I not only admit their postulate, that the bread is truly flesh, but I go farther, and add what they injuriously and shamefully omit, that this bread is given daily, as the flesh was offered once on the cross for the salvation of the world. Nor is the repetition of the expression, *I will give,* superfluous. The bread, therefore, is truly and properly the flesh of Christ, inasmuch as he is there speaking not of a corruptible or fading but of heavenly aliment.

The Magdeburgians subjoin, that Christ speaks explicitly in these words, Unless you eat the flesh and drink the blood of the Son of Man, you have no life abiding in you. Again,

My flesh is meat indeed and my blood is drink indeed. They tell us he might as easily have said, The bread signifies my flesh; but that no one might dream of any figure, he was pleased to speak simply, and thus early obviate all fictions: as if he had then used a visible symbol instead of having spoken of his flesh as meat or bread metaphorically—there being no other way in which our souls can be nourished unto eternal life. It is just as if any contentious person, laying hold of the term water in Isaiah and Ezekiel, should deny that in baptism the external symbol of water is annexed to spiritual washing. Christ had not instituted the Supper when he thus discoursed in Capernaum. What he then said he was pleased afterwards to seal in the Supper by a visible figure. What madness is it to confound the spiritual bread with a corruptible element? The Magdeburgians proceed, that the same offence at which we stumble was objected by the people of Capernaum, because they robbed Christ of divine virtue. What limit, pray, will there be to falsehoods? Did a carnal eating of Christ ever come into our mind? If their associates, whose obstreperous unbelief is there condemned, complain, let those come forward who differ with them in one thing only, pretending that the flesh of Christ is devoured in an invisible and yet carnal manner. Our eating is just that which the words of Christ express.

It cannot be doubted that the language of Christ is metaphorical. He gives the name of bread not to that which is composed of flour; he gives the name of meat not to that which is baked in an oven or dish, but to spiritual aliment, by which our souls are fed for the heavenly life. Therefore, the eating and drinking which he mentions does not at all require the teeth, palate, throat, or stomach, but hungering of soul; for we do not, in compliance with that commandment of Christ, eat his flesh or drink his blood in any other way than by being made one with him by faith, so that he, dwelling in us, may truly give us life. Why he claims the office of nourishing for his flesh and blood is by no means obscure. It was to let us know that our life is to be sought nowhere else than in the sacrifice by which he has reconciled the Father to us. Many in their pride would willingly pass by the flesh in which the expiation was made, and climb beyond the clouds. Therefore, as Christ was humbled for us, he, in order to keep our faith humble, recommending the mystery of redemption, declares that his flesh gives us life. How, pray, can the Magdeburgians disentangle themselves, in insisting that the flesh is received carnally? They also stumble more grossly, in teaching that there is an antithesis which is of very common occurrence in St. Paul. But as it is a regular practice for them to corrupt Scripture, by quoting it inconsiderately, let their error here, so far as I am concerned, remain buried. I would only have their answer in regard to a declaration of Christ. If the quickening Spirit is nothing else than the gift of understanding, what does our Saviour mean by immediately after adding, The words which I speak unto you are spirit and life? Will they deny that the words are called spirit, because they are spiritual? This being granted, it will be easy to infer that the eating of which he speaks is of the same nature.

The *eighth* argument they produce from us is, All sacramental modes of expression have a like principle : the principle is, that the name of the thing is transferred to the sign ; therefore there is such a metonymy in the words of the Supper. The major they restrict by adding to it, When they are of the same kind and time. But they deny that the sacraments of the Old and New Testament are of the same kind, because, in the Old Testament, figures and shadows were brought forward ; whereas, in the New, the thing itself is clearly exhibited, as is expressly implied by the words, This is my body. If the dispute is as to the words, the same are read in the Old Testament also : nor is the form of expression, This is my body, more transparent than, The lamb is the passover ; Circumcision is my covenant. Let them cease then to attempt to excite a vain prejudice in their favour from the words, the sense and meaning of which forms the subject of dispute. The diversity which they pretend savours of the delirium of Servetus ; as if the holy fathers, contented with bare figures, had had no fellowship with us in spiritual gifts. I admit that the shadows of future things

were then held forth ; only let it be understood that Christ
also was held forth to them, that we may not think they
were deluded by empty figures. Surely to them the lamb
was the passover, and circumcision a covenant, in the same
way in which the bread is now body to us. Their allegation,
that ever since Christ was exhibited to the world, there is
no more room for types, not only originates in disgraceful
ignorance, but shows, that from proud contempt, they spurn
the grace of Christ. Is their faith so perfect that they can
reject the aid of types, and receive Christ present ? And to
what end did Christ institute the Supper and Baptism, but
just in accommodation to our weakness, to raise us upwards
to himself by the vehicles of types ? I confess, indeed, that
the body and substance of those things which the law shadowed forth now exist in Christ, as Paul plainly teaches ;
only let this be referred to the different modes of signifying,
and let us not be altogether deprived of the use of signs,
which experience shows to be no less necessary to us than to
the ancient fathers.

The Magdeburgians, to disentangle themselves, make a
childish play upon the term *sin*, the victim being called *sin :*
as if we did not use this passage. Why do they not rather
reply to the other points, to dispose of which no amount of
mere talk will suffice ? The blood of a beast is said to be expiation, and Christ is called circumcision. Here it will do
them no good to philosophize on guilt and punishment. But
feeling that they are still held fast, they devise what, if we
believe them, is a good interpretation, viz., that the lamb is
the passover not figuratively but in reality ; just as Christ
is called our passover, not by way of memorial, but because
he redeemed us. I thought that Christ was called the passover, because that legal sacrifice was a type of him, and represented in a mystery the redemption for which they hoped.
If so, that lamb was to the ancient people a sign and pledge
of an entire and eternal deliverance, just as the bread of the
Supper is to us now.

But if it be asked whether they admit no figure in the
Supper, they answer, Let the thing itself remain, and away
with tropes, shadows, and all darkness, as suited only to the

Old Testament. Let the reader remember that we are here treating of figure. These literal masters utterly repudiate it, and though they use invidious names, they annihilate the most essential property of a sacrament. For what is a sacrament without type or figure ? Their absurdity afterwards betrays itself more plainly. They say the things themselves being safe, that is, the material, and formal, and principal ends being exhibited, some figures may be admitted, at least soberly. When they place a twofold matter in the Supper, they insist that there are lifeless and profane elements there, as if Christ were shutting up his body in a little chest. Do they think that the body is coupled with the bread by magical incantation, so that the faithful are deprived of all doctrine ? What then will be the use of the word if there is no figure ? If the visible word be not engraven on the element, away with an empty and worthless spectacle. Whether types and figures are suitable to the Old Testament only, let the Holy Spirit answer for himself, who appeared twice in the form of a dove, and a third time in tongues of fire, unless indeed he used those external appearances without any view to teaching ; as a kind of boyish show, or something still more ridiculous and insipid. I omit the gross contumely which they offer to God, when they give the name of darkness to the exercises of piety, by which he guided the pious under the law to the Sun of Righteousness. Did they say that the persons were in darkness, the expression would be rough and harsh ; but to stigmatize the lamps which showed them the way as darkness, is altogether intolerable blasphemy. But on the decision of the Magdeburgians, what figure will remain ? The Supper will denote the union of the Church, and that it is exposed to the cross and to trials. They have therefore already forgotten what they said of the final cause. For if it was the purpose of Christ to hold forth his body under the bread to be eaten for the forgiveness of sins, this doctrine ought certainly to be taken into account. For to what end or to whom did Christ direct the words ? Was it that they might vanish uselessly away ? And what is more plain than that the bread being offered before their eyes, taught that his flesh was spiritual meat ? Let them go now and deny being so fascinated with their error, that though veteran theologians, they understand not what children learn in their catechism.

The *ninth* argument is, That since the ark of the covenant is above four hundred times called the presence of God, it is not strange if in the same way the bread be called the body. They deny the antecedent, as if by denying they did not palpably augment their disgrace. Whenever it is said in the law, Thou shalt not come into the presence of God empty ; again, When thou shalt have appeared before the face of thy God ; again, O God, that dwellest in the sanctuary ; again, God sitting between the cherubim, they must grant that the presence of God is denoted. If they are to contend for words, nothing can be found in the Supper more distinctly expressed than these. If in all the passages of the law there is a figure, why do they decline to admit it in a similar place ? They say that in strict propriety the ark is not so called, but the better thing which was added to the ark by the word of God. The solution is subtle, but it is one by which they put a rope about their own necks. On their own authority I now say that the bread is improperly called body. The thing denoted is the better thing adjoined to it by the word of God.

The *tenth* argument is taken from a comparison of the manna with the Supper. They answer, that the things are dissimilar, because the manna was not a sacrament. Paul, therefore, is mistaken in making the fathers like us in this respect, that they ate spiritual food. For how could food be spiritual without a mystery? Nay, how could it be spiritual, except in so far as it represented Christ in a mystery? They afterwards add, that the manna was food by feeding the stomach, and that the spiritual thing farther denoted by it was not the principal. It is enough for me, that inasmuch as the manna was a sacred symbol of Christ, it was spiritual food to the fathers, and the same with that which Christ now sets before us. For from this I will immediately infer, that those act perversely who imagine any other spiritual food at the sacred table of Christ, although the mode of eating be different, the condition of the fathers being inferior to ours.

In regard to the sentence which is immediately subjoined, there is need of no ordinary attention. I will not say, that Turks, Saracens, in short, the worshippers of Ceres and Bacchus, speak more honourably of their sacred rites ; but seldom did any thing so delirious and profane fall from a man in a frenzy as that which the Magdeburgians here send forth as an oracle. We deny not, they say, that the Eucharist and the other sacraments were, in a certain way, spiritual. Is it come to this, that the mysteries of our salvation, which raise us from the earth above the heavens, they are ashamed to call spiritual without inserting a modification ? One might rather expect to hear that every thing contained in them must be regarded as spiritual. Their carnal dream now so absorbs all their senses, that they are averse to the distinguishing epithet of the kingdom of Christ. In what can they say that the gospel differs from the law, except that the spiritual reality of the ancient shadows has been exhibited in Christ ? Why then are they so much afraid of this mark, without which Christ is not Christ ? This doubtless is the just reward of those who defend a bad cause with a bad conscience—their boldness undoes them. For the reader will uniformly observe, that the name of mystery, or mystical virtue, is not less frightful to them than spiritual reality is irksome.

The example which they afterwards append from baptism is wholly in our favour. Baptism is external washing, and yet is a spiritual laver. But how skilfully do they apply this to the Supper ? They say it is not corporeal aliment, though the body of Christ is taken by the external mouth. So anxious are they about the palate, throat, and stomach, that they dare not to call the Supper a spiritual mystery, lest the body of Christ should escape their teeth. They say they do not understand it to be spiritual, so as to mean only some invisible thought or phantasy, or such a spiritual eating as Abraham ate, who knew nothing of this sacrament. You would say that they are muttering something or other in Arabic, still more to stupify their stupid disciples. What is an invisible thought ? As if they could produce a visible one. We leave them the phantasy. Contented with the true and vivifying participation of Christ, we have no need of their erratic fiction, which only goes to replenish the gullet. Then what is it to eat an eating? Perhaps they mean to say, that as Abraham had not the internal sign, he was not a partaker of Christ. Than this nothing can be imagined more unbecoming or more preposterous: for though we now excel in abundance of grace, it was common to all the sacraments to ingraft all believers into Christ.

The *eleventh* argument, which either from ignorance or malice, they construct badly, we frame thus,—No conception is to be formed concerning the mystery of the Supper, except what is dictated from heaven: Paul saying that the Jews ate the same spiritual food with us, adds by way of interpretation, That rock was Christ: Therefore this divine declaration should be held to prove, that the bread and wine in the Supper are the body and blood of the Lord to feed us spiritually. The Magdeburgians wonder that we insist so incautiously on what they call gross and inconvenient foundations, after they have so often told us, that Paul is speaking of a spiritual rock. I am aware of their usual talk on the subject, but the proof is required. The rock, they say, did not accompany the Jews through the wilderness. I answer, that their own information ruins them. Paul gives the name of rock, not to the stone composing it, but to the drink flowing from it. Were it otherwise, the clauses would not correspond with each other. Then unless reference is made to the external and visible symbol, Paul's reasoning would be maimed, for this would make him speak of persons who ate a spiritual sacrament, not spiritually. They hold the expression clearly to mean, The spiritual rock was Christ. But Paul's argument does not allow any application of the rock to any thing else than the drink which he compares to our mystical cup. They add in concluding, Most of the expressions of the Old Testament differ from the words of the Lord's Supper: as if Paul, after speaking a little before of the Supper of Christ, had intended to employ a different discourse to banish the remembrance of it from the hearts of the pious.

The *twelfth* argument is, The letter of the words of the

Supper ought not to be pertinaciously retained, since, in most other passages of Scripture, great absurdity would follow from pressing the precise terms. They afterwards quote examples, as if we had produced them from our bosom,—The bread was made flesh; The Father is greater than I; He who sees me sees the Father also. Where they got the two latter examples, I know not; but as they are by no means apposite to the present cause, I prefer selecting from a countless number others that are more appropriate. It is certain, that were Scripture pressed so violently as they insist, almost as many absurdities would spring up as it contains verses. God will be a man of war; he will repent; he will come down from heaven to know the deeds of men ; he will desire revenge; he will at one time be carried away by anger, at another he will smile appeased ; at one time he will sleep, at another he will rise, as if awakened from a debauch ; at one time he will turn away his eyes, at another he will remember. Let the Magdeburgians say whether they mean to insist on all the syllables in these sentences. There is no room here for tortuous windings. For I have already said, what all perceive to be strictly true, that when they reject all interpretation, and insist simply on the expression, This is my body, they take up a cause not unlike that which the old Anthropomorphites had, when from his ears, eyes, and feet, they proved that God was corporeal. For what is more manifest than the numerous passages of Scripture which attribute nostrils, eyes, feet, and hands to God? The odour of the incense of Noah's sacrifice was grateful to God. How could he smell it without possessing nostrils? The Magdeburgians, in continuing the same strain after we have warned them of the consequence, show any thing but candour.

They afterwards add, Some passages are to be taken, not according to the letter (τὸ ῥῆτον) but the meaning, (διάνοιαν;) but they are unwilling to place the words of the Supper in this class, because it would be necessary to prove from the words themselves that they ought to be understood differently from their literal meaning. We find no difficulty in drawing the proof, as well from the common nature of sacraments. as from the ordinance of the Supper itself, and this has been shown by us too distinctly to be answered by the silly gibe, that it is too hard a nut for our tooth. As yet, they say, no sacramentarian has descended into this arena, to which Luther challenged them, viz., to show by sure and strong reasons, that the words of the Supper are to be understood figuratively: as if the reasons were not strong, which they have hitherto in vain endeavoured to overthrow. But it is well. If we have sung to the deaf, we have recovered, at least, three hundred thousand men from error. Surely when our Catechism has been subscribed by two hundred thousand, exclusive of German, Swiss, Italians, and English, it is ridiculous in men of Magdeburg to attempt to overthrow our arguments by their deafness or stupidity.

The *thirteenth* argument is drawn from the authority or consent of the primitive Church. The Magdeburgians answer that the primary antiquity is in Christ. This we willingly admit, but as we had to remove the charge of novelty which they invidiously and unjustly brought against us, it was not out of place to produce passages from pious writers to show that the doctrine which we now deliver is none else than that which was anciently received without controversy. But Christ distinctly said, This is my body. Yes, as we too distinctly say it. While we are enjoined implicitly to obey the words of Christ, we are also permitted to seek the interpretation of them. Wherein then is the clearness of this sentence, but just in its accommodation to the nature of a sacrament? Were it otherwise it would not only be puzzling but replete with absurdity. But the fathers themselves often call the bread the body of the Lord, and the wine his blood. Provided they agree as to the sense, we are perfectly pleased with this mode of expression; if it is clear that they considered the bread as symbolically the body, their authority will undoubtedly go to our support.

If we believe the Magdeburgians, the fathers never explain their mind without letting some inconsistency escape them. One would say that these censors assume so much authority that their mere breath is to dim the eyes of the whole world. What they forthwith adduce concerning allegories is wholly irrelevant. I admit that the fathers were too much addicted to allegory; but the question here is, how did they expound the words of the Supper? Then, though it is clear enough that they admirably accord with each other, the Magdeburgians, by talking to no purpose, endeavour to obscure their consent. The glossing of a few ancient passages is all they think necessary for victory. Justin says, that the bread and wine, by the word of prayer and thanksgiving, become the flesh and blood of Christ. We, too, say the same thing, provided the mode of communion, which was then known to the Church, be added. Cyril teaches, that by virtue of the mystical benediction Christ dwells in us bodily. If the mystical benediction effects this, why have they hitherto so strongly maintained that the Lord's Supper, inasmuch as his body is therein given to us, is not mystical? Why, according to them, does mystery differ from corporeal eating? Cyril says in another place, When we eat the flesh of Christ, which is vivifying by the conjunction of the word, we have life in us; why then do they maintain that unbelievers eat of it without benefit? If the flesh of Christ when it is eaten gives life, it is incongruous to say that it is promiscuously eaten by those who remain in death. Here, however, we must inform the reader, that, as Cyril was contending against the Arians, he is led into hyperbole, and teaches that believers become substantially one with Christ, just as he is one with the Father. The same was the case with Hilary, whose words, however, are so far from being contrary to our doctrine that I appositely retort them on the Magdeburgians.

That saint contends, that the real nature of flesh and blood is proved by the words, My flesh is meat indeed. And on what point have we at this day a debate with the Magdeburgians, but just that while they feign an immense phantasm instead of the flesh, we defend the reality of the human nature on which our faith is founded. Hilary adds, These received and taken make us to be in Christ and Christ to be in us. What say the Magdeburgians? That unbelievers, though eating the body of Christ and drinking his blood, remain in a state of complete alienation from him. Irenæus says, When the cup is mingled and the bread broken the word of God causes it to become the Eucharist of the flesh and blood of Christ, by which the substance of our flesh is increased and consists. What is to be gathered from the term Eucharist let the Magdeburgians show. I hold it to be equivalent to mystery. This they recoil from as if it were some dire omen. That our flesh is refreshed by that spiritual meat and drink I deny not. For we have communion with Christ in the hope of a blessed resurrection, and therefore we must be one with him not in soul only but in flesh ; just as each of us in respect of the flesh is said to be a member of Christ, and the body of each a temple of the Holy Spirit.

They quote the words of Cyprian, That this common bread being changed into flesh and blood, procures life to our bodies. This they do inconsiderately or with wicked guile, since the difference of style plainly shows that the expression is not Cyprian's. But granting that it is, why do they craftily withhold the exposition which immediately follows, That the Son alone is consubstantial with the Father, whereas our connection with him neither mingles persons nor unites substances, but associates affections and confederates wills ? Were I to speak in this way, would they not exclaim that the matter of the Supper is taken away ? Shortly after, in the same discourse, it is added, " The eating of this flesh is a kind of greediness and appetite to remain in him ; by this we so impress and melt within us the sweetness of charity that it adheres to our palate, and the savour of love is infused into our bowels, penetrating and imbuing all the recesses of soul and body. Drinking and eating are of the same nature. As by them the bodily substance is nourished and lives and continues safe, so the life of the spirit is nourished by this proper aliment. The same that eating is to the flesh is faith to the soul ; the same that food is to the body is the word to the Spirit, by its more excellent virtue performing eternally what corporeal elements do temporally." When he professedly explains the mode of eating, where is the swallowing ? Nay, in place of it he substitutes faith and spirit. This the Magdeburgians hold in the greatest detes-

tation. Theodoret quotes the words of Ambrose to Theodosius, " With what eyes will you behold the temple of our
common Lord ? With what feet will you tread his holy pave-
ment ? How will you stretch out hands from which innocent
blood is still dropping ? How with such hands will you receive the holy body of the Lord, and drink with your mouth
the cup of precious blood ?" Is it strange if the holy man, to
make his rebuke more stinging, spoke in the highest and
most splendid terms he could use of that sacred ordinance ?
But had any one asked Ambrose whether the body of Christ
was actually handled in the Supper, he undoubtedly would
have abominated the gross delirium. Therefore, when he
says that it is handled by the hands, every sober and sensible man sees the metonymy.

The communion mentioned by Augustine is not in the
least adverse to us, to whom the Supper is the true and
spiritual communion of the flesh and blood of Christ. In
the second passage, where he says, that Christ, when he
handed the Supper to his disciples, was in a manner carried
in their hands, their impudence and falsehood are detected,
inasmuch as they wickedly omit the expression, *in a manner*,
which entirely removes any difficulty. When Augustine
elsewhere says, that in the bread is received that which hung
upon the cross, and in the cup is drunk that which was shed
upon the cross, I have no objection to receive it, provided
the method of eating and drinking is explained in other
words of Augustine. Let the Magdeburgians, therefore,
cease henceforth to vend their smoke to the simple. It has
been so often dissipated, that there is no place for it in
the clear light. They substitute Westphal as a pledge or
surety in their stead, but his nakedness has lately been so
completely exposed by me that it is vain to look to him for
any help.

The *fourteenth* argument is, As our opponents admit a
trope in the words of Christ, they must also allow us to do the
same. They deny that they acknowledge a figure in the words,
This is my body, holding that they ought to be taken most
strictly. What ? When they would express their own meaning most strictly, do they not say that the body of Christ is

given under the bread or with the bread? They answer,
that when a man is said to be under his clothes there is no
figure: as if this quibble will avail them unless they can
show that a man is most strictly and without figure his
clothes. Whence do they gather that the body of Christ is
under the bread or with the bread, unless from our Lord himself having declared of the bread, This is my body? But if
this expression is to be taken so strictly, not only are they
wrong in extracting from it more than they ought, but they
are falsifiers and corrupters in introducing so far-fetched a
metamorphosis. The body with the bread is a thing of
heaven with a thing of earth: to hold that the bread is the
body is nothing else than to confound heaven and earth together.

Akin to this argument is the *fifteenth.* Our opponents
confess that the bread and the body are different things:
therefore they admit a trope. They say the consequence
does not hold. Whether it holds or not, let the reader consider. They say that the major is not good in the syllogism,
viz., Whenever the things are different, there is a trope.
What can they gain by this puerile quibbling? It is certain
that whenever the predicate does not correspond strictly
with the subject, the expression is either false or figurative.
If the proposition, The bread is the body, is taken without
a figure, it will be monstrously false: inasmuch as that will
be predicated of the essence of bread, which is altogether
different.

The *sixteenth* argument, as they give it, states feebly and
frigidly, The Papists admit no trope; therefore let those who
agree with them take up their banner and go over to their
camp. When Westphal was not ashamed to obtrude a
decree of Hildebrand, and to say that our doctrine was sufficiently condemned by the judgment of that sacrilegious miscreant, I answered that there was nothing now to hinder
him from going over to the Papists. Whether I was right
or wrong in this let the reader judge. These Magdeburgians,
therefore, have no ground for their invidious answer, that
they do not admit squibs and sarcasms to be arguments.
I ask, where was there any affectation of wit or sarcasm in

my simple remark? I wish rather they would refrain from their squibs and not make themselves ridiculous by excessive eagerness to raise a laugh. Of this nature is their absurd irony, that we are not only tropologists but tenebrists; and again, their representing us as saying that the bread is not the body, but symbolizes, umbrizes it. They boast that they employ their vigils, their cares, and labours in opposing the Pope, as if no struggles were to be borne by us, over whose necks the violence of the Papacy is specially impending. Whether I fight for worldly glory, the Son of God, under whose auspices I serve, will be my witness and judge on that day. Those to whom my condition is better known, see clearly that if I were not intent on that tribunal nothing would be more desirable for me than quiet retirement. But it was not enough for the Magdeburgians to take up the common defence of a foul error, without hastening to patronize all the wild sayings of a madman.

The *seventeenth* argument is, Circumcision was a sign, and yet the thing was at the same time offered—there is nothing therefore to prevent a visible sign in the Lord's Supper, and the spiritual reality from being at the same time annexed to it. They answer, that it is not sound to argue from things unlike. The question here is not what pleases us, but what the Son of God, the author of the Supper, has ordained. We do not pass in silence any dissimilarity which there may be in the sacraments, nor do we introduce our own decisions to abolish the faith of Christ, whose authority is not less reverently maintained, nor doctrine less faithfully expounded by us, than is proudly pretended and imagined to be skilfully achieved by the Magdeburgians. In what respect circumcision differs from the Supper the reader will fully learn from our writings. This much they certainly have in common, that a spiritual reality was conjoined with a visible symbol. God, who was pleased to give circumcision to his ancient people as a pledge of his adoption, did not deceive his children. Now, I say that there is nothing to prevent our Saviour from employing the symbols of bread and wine in the Supper to figure what he there means to testify, and truly accomplishing the reality signified by them. If the spiritual reality of

the Supper is different from that which I have attributed to
circumcision, the Magdeburgians will be entitled to insist
that the difference ought to be observed.   But there is no
controversy as to this, nor have I profited so ill in the school
of Christ as not to point out the different modes and degrees.   I hold, then, that just as by circumcision the fathers
were ingrafted as a sacred people, in order that trusting to
the paternal love of God they might be heirs of heavenly
life, so we now receive a figure, symbol, badge, and pledge
of sacred union with the Son of God.   But as Christ does
not act deceitfully with us, the symbols truly represent what
they signify, so that the flesh and blood of Christ in reality
feed and give life to us by their substance.

Nothing, therefore, can be imagined more absurd than
the conduct of the Magdeburgians, who falsely assert, that
instead of a spiritual reality we substitute a figure of the
forgiveness of sins and of divine grace : and that it is clear
from our words, that the sign of a sign only is given, and not
the things themselves ; as if I did not say a hundred times
over, that the matter of the Supper differs from the effect or
fruit, inasmuch as the graces which we receive from Christ
are preceded in order by spiritual communion with his flesh
and blood.   Nay, so shameless are they, that they clamour
against us as leaving only a sign of the forgiveness of sins.
When they at last add, that we introduce only the signs of
signs, the shadows of shadows, and nothing but mere dreams
and phantoms, it is not only sarcasm, but vile pertness
mingled with virulent mendacity, and nothing better than
the snarling of dogs.   Immediately after they betray themselves by quoting my words, viz., that the flesh of Christ, by
the secret agency of the Spirit, penetrates to us, and effectually inspires life into our souls.   Is this a mere phantasm
or the shadow of a shadow ?   Though I do not make the
mode of communication to be the same as the Magdeburgians make it, am I therefore to be subjected to the twofold calumny of not only taking away the reality but also
the sign of the reality, and leaving only the sign of a sign ?
They rejoin, that it is not what man utters, but what Christ
asserts that is to be looked to : and Christ does not say, I,

sitting in heaven, will operate in you the virtue of my flesh, but, This is my body: as if the eating of the body were to do us any good without our knowing that it is given us for spiritual food as being vivifying. What the effect, what the aim of the Supper, are things of which these dull men have no idea. The words of Christ will yield us no fruit unless they speak to our hearts thus: This bread is my body, and this cup is my blood, because my flesh is meat indeed, and my blood is drink indeed. There is no swallowing here, but the life which we receive is obtained by secret communion.

And yet the Magdeburgians hesitate not to attack us again with their falsehoods, charging us with a most violent rending of the Supper, as urging the promise alone, and even it not sincerely, or as urging the spiritual operation of Christ in us in such a manner that the Supper only signifies the forgiveness of sins, but does not apply it. They must, therefore, regard it as a kind of disgraceful thing to insist on the promises. I always supposed it the highest praise of faith and piety to rest in the promises of God. All their fulminations and vain clamour have too little effect to make me desirous for more than the promise of Christ offers me. Of the application of grace, I have elsewhere said as much as was sufficient, viz., that it is as highly celebrated by us as any ability of theirs enables them to do. Let them as they will explain away the kind of communion which I teach, their malignity will not prevent all the pious from recognising that I omit nothing which tends to the advancement of faith. Wherefore no man of sound brain will be moved in the slightest degree by their cruel calumny, that we altogether take away the earnest of the assurance of faith from the Supper, inasmuch as we take away the matter, viz., the body of Christ, and make the whole effect of the Supper depend on the secret communion of flesh and blood, to which it is owing that he infuses his own life into us and we become one with him. But what kind of earnest of assurance will the body be if all men, however wicked, may swallow it indiscriminately? They, making carnal eating their prow and anchor, care not one straw for spiritual life.

The *eighteenth* argument they state is, No interpretation

contrary to faith ought to be admitted—but this interpretation, that Christ gives his own body to be eaten substantially
and in an invisible manner, is not agreeable to the analogy of
faith—it is therefore to be rejected. Although there is no
difficulty in the major, they mutter, however, that false teachers bring forward many things for the sake of giving a colour.
Our proof of the minor is, that when he held forth the bread,
his body was visibly before his disciples, and therefore it
must, according to this view, be bicorporal. But it is absurd
and repugnant to the principles of faith to give Christ a
double body. They answer, Although human reason, dash-
ing violently against the rock of offence, makes shipwreck,
faith rests satisfied with the distinct words of Christ : as if
any thing delivered clearly in Scripture were a device of
human reason. Human reason did not dictate to us that
the Son of God, to reconcile us to the Father by the sacrifice
of his death, assumed our flesh : and in order to become our
brother, was made like unto us, sin excepted. That true
flesh, by which the sins of the world were shortly after to be
taken away, was then before the eyes of the Apostles, and
they behoved to fix their faith on the view of it, so as not
to hope for salvation anywhere else. For their minds to fly
off to some kind of invisible body, had been nothing else
than to avert their eyes from the true and only price of redemption. There is no ground for obstreperously asserting
that thus the power of Christ is diminished, and that he is
accused of falsehood. They themselves do not believe him
to be true, except by supposing that he was a sorcerer. To
us his reality is entire, while we hold that he gave the
natural body with which he was invested to be eaten in the
Supper. We must call the reader's attention to the sincerity
with which these men deal with us in falsely attributing to
us a fiction of their own. Whether there was a true and
natural body, which, subject to death, was seen by the eye
in one place, and elsewhere a celestial and invisible body
lurking at the same moment in the Supper, let not common
sense answer, but faith instructed according to the word of
God. Assuredly no pious mind can doubt that a twofold
body destroys the true nature of a single body. They con-

tend that it is the same; as if the Son of God had practised a delusion in assuming our flesh, that he might therein procure righteousness. And yet they hesitate not to asperse us with the stigma of denying that the true and natural body of Christ is given us in the Supper.

They mention as the *nineteenth* argument, As the Supper is a heavenly action, the minds of believers ought to be raised up to heaven. They object to this reasoning on the ground of ambiguity. For though the action is heavenly, as Christ is the dispenser, still we are not enjoined to perform it in the heavens. By heavenly action, we mean nothing more than must immediately occur to the mind of any man, viz., that it is a spiritual mystery, and ought, according to the nature of Christ's kingdom, to be separated from earthly actions. It is strange that these men, who pretend to be fighting for the dignity and excellence of the sacred Supper, can scarcely concede what tends especially to recommend it. In short, the term *heavenly* is understood in no other sense than is no less truly than skilfully described in the words of Augustine, viz., that it is performed on earth but in a heavenly, by man but in a divine manner. If the Magdeburgians hesitate to admit this, let them have shambles for their temple. But they object, that though the mind ought to have respect to the heavenly promises, it ought also to be directed to the present action, by which Christ, as with outstretched hand, brings us his body. I admit that any one who passes by the external sign cannot be benefited by this sacrament. But how can we reconcile the two propositions, that the sacraments are a kind of ladders by which believers climb upwards to heaven, and yet that we ought to stop at the elements themselves, or remain fixed, as if Christ were to be sought on earth? It is preposterous in them to pretend that Christ holds out his hand to us, while they overlook the end for which he does it, viz., to raise us upwards. For we must remember that our Lord descends to us, not to indulge our body, or keep our senses fixed on the world, but rather to draw us to himself, and hence the preamble of the ancient Church, Hearts upward, as Chrysostom interprets. But if the Magdeburgians repudiate him, let us be contented

with the authority of Paul, who raises us upwards, in order
that we may be conjoined with Christ. Though they tell us
a hundred times that heaven does not mean the visible con-
cave firmament, it remains certain that none duly enjoy
Christ but those who seek him above.

The *twentieth* argument is, Whatever is not in something
qualitatively or quantitively, or in place, is present not cor-
porally but spiritually—all admit that the body is not under
the bread in these modes—therefore the mode of presence is
spiritual. They answer, that an argument is not good that
is drawn *a non distributo ad distributum*, meaning by these
terms, when there is not a full enumeration of parts. Let
them, therefore, divide more subtilely, if any thing seems
imperfect. They are satisfied, however, with saying, in one
word, that more modes of existence might be produced. But
though they cut and mutilate, they can never find a fourth
member. Driven from this resource, they flee to their ordinary pretext, that God is not bound by physical principles.
I admit he is not, except in so far as he has so ordained.
They rejoin, that this order takes effect only in the common
course of nature, but not at all in theology. That is true,
unless indeed part of theology be the very order of nature,
as it is in the present case. For we do not simply assert
that Christ's body is in one place, because it is natural, but
because God was pleased to give a true body to his Son, and
one finite in its dimensions, and he himself was pleased to
sojourn for a time on earth under the tabernacle of this
body, and with the same body to ascend into heaven, from
whence he bids us look for him. Do not the words of the
angel bear, Christ is not in the sepulchre in respect of his
flesh, for he is risen? Shall we charge the angel with falsehood in openly denying immensity to the body of Christ?
They reply, that the special actions of God are to be distinguished from common and natural actions. Well, be it so;
only let not the alleged specialty be a fiction devised by a
human brain. But the expression, This is my body, is very
far from proving its immensity. For though the body retain
its quality, it will not cease to be truly offered in a mystery.
How Christ entered when the doors were shut, has been

elsewhere stated. He was able to open the doors for himself as he was to remove the stone that closed the sepulchre. It was not necessary to deprive his body of its nature in order that he might penetrate through wood or stone. Accordingly the reasoning founded on a perverse interpretation is frivolous.

When they say that sacramental actions ought not to be compared with nature, they state what is true, provided they would not use the incomparable power of God as a pretext for imagining monstrosities contrary to his word. Our faith rests in the saying, " This is my body," so far as to have no doubt that the communion of Christ is truly offered. In this way there is no need of subtle arguments as to the quantity of the body. These we are forced to use by the extravagance of those who, depriving Christ of the reality of his flesh, transform him into a phantasm. When we say that we are made partakers of Christ spiritually, we do not mean that his body is held forth to be eaten only in a figurative, symbolical, and allegorical sense. This vile falsehood, like the others, sufficiently declares that these men who thus assume a license of making anything out of anything, have not one particle of ingenuous shame. The spiritual mode we oppose to the carnal, because the Holy Spirit, who is the bond of our union with Christ, infuses life into us from the substance of his flesh and blood.

I know not where they got the *twenty-first* argument. It is, That which is perceived ineffably is not perceived corporeally. I do not believe that any of us have spoken thus. Some, perhaps, may have objected, as I confess I have done myself, that an ineffable mode is rather spiritual than carnal. Seeing, then, they found on an ineffable miracle, they are justly condemned for their perverseness, in not allowing the intervention of the secret agency of the Spirit to unite us to Christ.

The *twenty-second* argument is, It is the saying of a theologian, not a philosopher, Take away a local position from bodies, and they will be nowhere, and being nowhere, will not exist,—therefore the body of Christ cannot be present in the Supper, unless a place be assigned to it. They an-

swer, that though the sentiment was advanced by a theologian, it is, however, physical, and is ineptly applied to
divine things. They add, that the fathers often unseasonably
mixed up human with divine things, and in this way shamefully diluted theology. This, no doubt, means, that as they
dare not deprive Augustine of the name of theologian, they
think it less contumelious to charge him with a shameful
corruption, which makes it difficult to excuse him from blasphemy. Augustine is there professedly treating of the flesh
of Christ ; and he mentions, that in order to be real, it must
have its finite dimensions. The Magdeburgians answer, that
theology has been shamefully corrupted by physical arguments ; as if they had persuaded themselves that in divine
things they see much more acutely than that holy man,
than whom all antiquity has not produced one who taught
ecclesiastical doctrines with more solidity and moderation.
No wonder that those who treat Augustine pertly trample
down little men like us with magisterial superciliousness.

The *twenty-third* argument is not produced sincerely. It
will be found that none of our party ever used it. It is,
Baptism retains its efficacy, though the water is not converted into the blood of Christ ; therefore the Supper also
will retain its efficacy though the true body of Christ be not
eaten under the bread. That they may not torture themselves with a nugatory answer, we must tell them that we
compare the Supper with Baptism for a different purpose.
To baptism is attributed a property which belongs only to
the blood of Christ and the Holy Spirit ; and yet it must
not therefore be said that water is changed into blood or
Spirit. Hence there is no absurdity in transferring to bread
that which does not properly belong to it. If they object
that the cases are unlike, because the water is nowhere
called either blood or Spirit, it is enough for my purpose
that it is adorned with the proper epithets of both, as being
a symbol of both. I may add, that Paul's expression, That
we put on Christ in baptism, is not a whit more obscure
than, This is my body. Let them tell me how we put on
Christ. Is it in a corporeal manner, as they contend in
regard to the Supper ? If so, it will follow that Christ is not

less included under the water than under the bread. They will betake themselves to their asylum, that it is not said of baptism, This is ; as if he who says that we put on Christ were asserting nothing at all. This certainly disposes of their frivolous answer, that the difference between the Supper and Baptism consists in this,—that the Supper was instituted, in order that therein the body of Christ might be given us under the bread ; Baptism, that we might be washed in the name of the Father, and the Son, and the Holy Spirit. This is at variance with Paul's definition, from which it plainly appears that we no less put on Christ in baptism than eat him in the Supper.

The *twenty-fourth* argument, which they maliciously corrupt and mutilate, I thus frame,—Christ dwells in the hearts of the pious, so as to be their life, by a different method from that of carnal presence, and, therefore, it is of no use to contend so much for carnal presence. Here our censors not only charge us with presumption, but add, that we deserve something more severe for daring to reform God : as if we were denying that the body of Christ is substantially eaten, by insisting, that he can effect our salvation in a different manner by the agency of his Spirit. Our argument is, *first*, that when a thing is not necessary, it ought not to be pertinaciously contended for ; and, *secondly*, that the mode of communication must be learned from the common doctrine of Scripture. They will object, as usual, that there is something special in the Supper. Were I to admit this to be true, still we must hold that it has no other end in view than that which is elsewhere described. The perfection and crown of our felicity is, when Christ dwelling in our hearts by faith not only makes us sharers and associates in all the blessings bestowed upon him by the Father, but also infuses his own life into us, and so becomes one with us. As this is the goal beyond which we may not go, we hold that the Supper was instituted with no other intention than that by means of it we might be united to the body of Christ. Here the Magdeburgians foolishly restrict the promise of eating the flesh of Christ to the carnal mouth, because it was said, " Take, eat, this is my body ;" for although a promise was annexed

to the ordinance, we must carefully consider what the nature
of the ordinance itself implies. The external and sacramental
act was indeed annexed to the promise, but in such a manner, that nothing is more preposterous than to confound
that act with spiritual eating. When Paul was discoursing
of the perfect communion or union of believers with Christ,
had there been anything more excellent in the Supper, he
was not so oblivious as to have omitted it. On the whole,
since the special end of the holy Supper is to communicate
Christ and his life to us, we should consider in what way
Christ is our life: if there is any deviation from this mark,
there is an impious laceration of the holy ordinance.

The *twenty-fifth* argument is, The promises of the gospel
are spiritual, and as they are to be received by faith, so they
are made effectual by faith—but all the sacraments depend
on the promise—therefore, the Supper is spiritual, and is
made effectual only by faith—if so, it is not necessary that
Christ should be eaten corporeally. They answer, that either
the definition is faulty, or that the enumeration of parts is
not complete. They insist, that the major is to be understood only of bare promises, exclusive of the sacraments.
But who except themselves ever attempted to disjoin the
Spirit and faith from the sacraments? If we adopt their
view, it will be necessary to say, that the promises annexed
to the signs are carnal and efficacious without faith. Though
they should protest a hundred times, I say that the promise
of the forgiveness of sins, in the very same way as that of
eating, has been connected with the act of the Supper, since
the two things are mentioned conjointly, and are united by
an indissoluble tie, when it is said, This is the blood which
is shed for the remission of sins. How portentous the result, were God to reconcile carnal men to himself without
faith. Though they say that that is not their view, it matters not. Their perverse speculation certainly binds them
to it by a knot which they cannot untie.

Then how do they say that the enumeration is incomplete,
because the corporeal action is omitted? Can we judge of
it in any other way than from its promise? What else is
the bread and wine of the Supper than a visible word?

Therefore, if the Supper is separated from the word, it differs in no respect from a profane feast. We are right, then, in contending, that it ought not to be viewed in any other way than is implied in the promises from which all its importance is derived. But the spiritual promise and corporeal eating ought not to be dissevered! Certainly no more than faith and the word should be dissevered from the external sign, when the name of sacrament is mentioned. But corporeal eating is to be defined differently, namely, from the promise. Here we see their reason for attacking a sentiment which we have advanced, and which is not less true than useful, viz., that Christ does not impart to us the matter of bread and wine, but rather would have us to look to the promise. They object that we dissever things which are conjoined. On the contrary, we fitly explain the nature of the conjunction, when we teach, that we are not to look to the bare elements, which, in themselves, can do nothing for spiritual life, but to turn our eyes to the view of the word there engraven. Should any one, discarding the bread and wine from the Supper, (this some fanatics have done,) make the Supper allegorical, the Magdeburgians might, not without reason, insist that the sign is visible. But how does this apply to us, whose object is to show whence the utility of the signs is to be sought, in order to prevent a judgment from being formed of their virtue from their corruptible nature? Therefore, that the meaning may be true and effectual, and the reality may be exhibited, we recall the minds of the pious to the promise. To this Augustine refers, when he says, Let the word be added to the element, and it will become a sacrament. Hence it appears with what good faith the Magdeburgians charge us with guile, and how modestly and civilly they upbraid us with imperiously ordering what never came into our mind. For who sees not, that the use of signs is truly held to profit in piety, when due honour is given to the promise, without which the whole action degenerates into a kind of ludicrous show?

The *twenty-sixth* argument is, The Lord's Supper is received by faith: Faith applies to things absent: Therefore, in the Supper the body of Christ is not actually present. It might be more correctly stated thus, The Supper was instituted that we might by faith seek Christ seated in his heavenly glory ; for in this way is fulfilled the Apostle's declaration, that faith is in things absent : Christ, therefore, is locally absent in respect of his human nature. I use the term *locally*, because distance is no obstacle to such presence as faith desires. Here there is no room for the answer of the Magdeburgians, that faith is sometimes conversant with corporeal objects ; for though it apprehends Christ as born of the Virgin, and crucified, it does not draw him down from heaven and make him locally present. We acknowledge in the Supper such a presence as is accordant with faith, and confine the absence to the real human nature. In this way believers recognise, in a manner which surpasses hope, that though they are pilgrims on the earth, they have life in common with their head.

The *twenty-seventh* argument is, The human body is definite, and cannot be everywhere : Christ truly assumed a human body, and still retains it : Therefore, he cannot, in respect of his human nature, be everywhere. It appears that the Magdeburgians have played into each other's hands; and while wishing to overturn the sacred and inviolable symbol of Christ, have each brought their own symbols, as it were, to market. I wish here to forewarn my readers, that when they afterwards see that what has now been said of place is repeated even to weariness, they should infer from the confused mass that our opponents have digested nothing with judgment or reason, but, while mutually indulging themselves, have received every absurdity which each individual may have been pleased to advance. To omit other things, what is meant by inculcating the very same thing under the thirtieth head, but just that he who had first advanced it did not like to repudiate it when it was afterwards advanced by his fellow ?

I come now to their reply. They say that we argue from the special to the absolute, (*a dicto secundum quid ad dictum simpliciter.*) How do they prove it ? Because the major contains a physical principle which is understood of bodies, in which there is nothing more than the creature. They accordingly ask, Was the body in which God appeared to

Abraham infinite or not ? Had they any shame, they would here certainly be dumb, and not, by their childish talk, expose the profane ambition which they cherish among themselves. To the minor they answer, that Christ is endued not only with the human, but also with the divine nature, the two natures being united in an ineffable manner. What, pray, can they make out of this ? Certainly they cannot construct the monster which they have imagined, since unity of person neither mingles nor confounds the natures. When they cite the Church as a witness, they ought at least to have attended to the difference which there is according to ordinary usage between the terms *unity* and *union*. Unity of person in Christ is received without controversy by all the orthodox. If an unity of the divine with the human nature is affirmed, there is no pious person who will not abhor it. In the union, therefore, it is necessary that each nature retain its own properties.

When they ask how Christ passed through his tomb without breaking the seal, and how he came in to the disciples while the doors were shut, there is no need of any new explanation. How can any barriers, constructed by human art, prevent God from making a passage for himself. He who made all things of nothing may for a time annihilate whatever seems to impede the progress of his operations. And, indeed, what shall we say became of the bodies in which he clothed both himself and his angels, after his purpose was accomplished ? These bodies appeared at the command of God, and afterwards vanished ; and yet it must be confessed that they were real bodies. Here we do not pry more than we ought into the power of God, as those men accuse us of doing. I wish that they would duly reverence that power instead of using it merely as a cloak. Let them have done, then, with their glossing pretexts, that Christ raised his own body into the air : for we are not here considering what miracles Christ performed in the flesh, but what the true nature of body necessarily requires. Peter walked upon the water. Did he therefore cease to have a true body ? This would have been the case had he at the same moment sat either in the vessel or in the harbour ; for whatever had appeared, would have been a phantom and imagination. When Peter came out of prison he did not pass through doors that were shut ; and yet, as he did come out after the doors were locked and barred, we acknowledge that a miracle was performed beyond the ordinary power of nature ; but that he was in two places at the same time, we deny ; just as we would deny that he had two bodies. This explanation shows that we have no need to accuse Christ of falsehood, a charge which the Magdeburgians, with their usual insolence, bring against us. We know that our faith by which we rest in the words of Christ, is a sacrifice of sweet savour in heaven. While they throw out the hyperboles of Luther to gain favour, at one time with the populace, at another with their little brethren, contented with the applause of this popular theatre, they care little either for the judgment of God or angels. It was this which made me formerly say that Luther has had many apes, but few imitators.

As if they had put on their buskins and got into the heroics, they say, We leave it to himself to explain how it is possible for a definite body to be present wherever the Supper is celebrated : sufficient for us the sure command to hang on his lips. But Christ himself has sufficiently explained, and it is in vain for them, while spontaneously closing their eyes, to throw the blame of their ignorance upon him. When they endeavour to shelter themselves by saying, that the one person of Christ is God and man, we have elsewhere shown how inept it is. After they have said all they can say, this doctrine stands approved by the consent of the primitive Church, that Christ as Mediator is everywhere, and inasmuch as he is one person, he, as God and man, or God manifest in the flesh, fills all things, although in respect of his flesh he is in heaven. Whether they are entitled to say that we put an affront on Christ, the supreme king and high-priest, by refusing to extend his body to a fantastical immensity, we leave it to all, high and low, to judge. Their sovereign oracle is a reply of Luther, One body cannot be in different places, according to human reason, but it may according to the power of God : because whatever God says, he is able to perform, and nothing is impossible with God. This is just as if one were to prove that the world was created from eternity, because God is eternal: or that the same sun may at the same time give light and no light, because God can do all things.

In the *twenty-eighth* place, they construct an argument at their own pleasure, that they may at their own pleasure overthrow it. It would seem that they have made it their business to frame something which might catch applause under the form of a negative. They state it thus, God can only do what he wills: He only wills things whatever is accordant with the nature of things: It is not accordant with the body of Christ to be at the same time in the Supper and in heaven: Therefore, Christ cannot make his body to be received corporeally in the Supper. Such, I perceive, is the kind of prattle they have among themselves. Our mode of reasoning is different. It is, As God does whatever he wills, his power is not to be separated from his will: It is therefore foolish, irrelevant, and preposterous, to dispute about what he can do without taking his will into account: But as he has nowhere shown that he wishes to make the true and natural body of his Son immense, those are preposterous and perverse heralds of his power who insist on proving from the immense power of God, that there is an immensity of flesh in Christ. The only remaining solution left to the Magdeburgians is, that the will of God is clear, from the words of Christ, This is my body. This might perhaps be listened to were the use of prophecy and the gift of interpretation entirely abolished. Such is all their victory.

The *twenty-ninth* argument is, Christ ascending into heaven and leaving this world cannot be everywhere: But he did ascend into heaven : Therefore, he is not bodily on the earth. They answer, that the major holds in regard to mere creatures. Did the angel then say of a mere creature, He is not here ; he is risen ? When Mark speaks of his withdrawing, or when Peter declares that the heavens must receive him at the last day, are we to understand it of a new creature ? I wish these men would rather confine themselves to their rudiments, than prove by bad logic that they are very bad theologians ! They afterwards reply to the

minor, that the invisible presence of Christ is not destroyed
by his visible ascent to heaven, because there are clear passages of Scripture in favour of both. The testimony of God
in regard to the local absence of the body, I hear through
the angel: He is not here ; he is risen. Unless the logic they
have learned be better than that of angels, the argument
will hold good that the assigning of one place is the denial
of any other. The same is to be said of the words of Peter,
that the heavens must contain him. Peter is not there
speaking of a visible form, and yet he fixes the abode of
Christ in heaven, which he says must contain him. If there
were not dimensions, where were the containing? (*compre-
hensio.*) We hold, therefore, that as the body of Christ is contained it is not immense. Will they say that the doctrine of
godliness has been shamefully corrupted by Peter also ?

They seem to think they have fallen on the best evasion
when they compare the visible ascension of Christ with the
visible exhibition of the Spirit. They say, The Spirit, though
he was everywhere invisible, appeared under the form of
tongues of fire, and therefore the visible ascension of Christ
does not take away his invisible presence. This is just as
if they were to argue, God appeared in visible form in the
tabernacle, and in other places, and yet was everywhere invisibly : therefore there is nothing in the visible form of the
world to prevent the world from being invisible. They will
reply, that the same thing has not been declared of the world
that was declared of the flesh of Christ. But I am only speaking of their comparison, which vanishes without refutation.

It is no new thing for God, who is invisible by nature, to
assume whatever forms he pleases, whenever he would in
this way manifest himself to men. This preternatural manifestation makes no change on the nature of God. But how
does this apply to Christ ? A manifest repugnance appears
at once. The body of Christ, which was naturally visible,
was taken up to heaven while the Apostles beheld. The
Magdeburgians insist that contrary to its nature it remained
invisible on earth. Let them now, discarding a comparison
which does not assist them in the least, prove that though
Christ is in heaven he may in respect of his flesh be invisibly

wherever he pleases. It is easy for them to say he is, but the pious are not to be driven by empty sound out of what Scripture affirms concerning the ascension of Christ to heaven. They say that Christ ascended to heaven in a visible manner, in order to show by some external act that he was truly risen, that he had thrown open the kingdom of heaven to all believers, and would be their high-priest in the heavenly sanctuary. This is some part, but not the whole. He declared to the Apostles that his departure was expedient for them, because if he did not go away the Spirit would not come. Could the Spirit not come while he was present? The meaning is, that it was necessary that their minds should be raised upwards to receive his divine influence. Of the same import is his saying to Mary,—Touch me not, for I have not yet ascended to my Father. Why, do we suppose, was Christ unwilling that his feet should be embraced, but just that he wished henceforth to be touched by faith only? This too is the reason why a cloud received him out of their sight. Had they been persuaded that he was in the bread invisibly they would not have stood gazing up to heaven.

The *thirtieth* argument is, He who is in a place is not everywhere: Christ being received into the heavens is in a kind of place: Therefore, he is not corporeally in the Supper. They reject the major as being a physical principle; as if theology were to perish if in deference to God, the Author of nature, we refuse to violate the order which he has made. Away with the absurd cavils which flow in too large a stream from these men. For the principle which we assume is the same in effect as if we were to prove that Christ was really man, because he felt hunger, was fatigued by travelling, feared, was sorrowful, in short, because he grew up from infancy to manhood and died. If the Magdeburgians grin here and say, that these are nothing but physical principles, will their perverseness be endurable? Nature dictates that the sun is warm and bright; in short, that the sun is the sun is a natural principle. Must we, in order to be theologians, deny that it is an illustrious specimen of the admirable wisdom of God? To be in a place and everywhere is the same in effect as that a place is no place. There is nothing however which the hyperbolical faith of the Magdeburgians does not overleap, not even excepting the incomprehensible depths of divine wisdom. This is apparent from their words.

When by passages of Scripture, as well as of the fathers, we prove that Christ is in heaven as in a place, they answer in regard to the fathers, that their sayings are towers of paper. Away then with all human authority, provided these masters will concede that we make common cause with the fathers, and provided also they will refrain henceforth from fuming so indignantly against the heresy of Berengarius. They object the saying of Christ, This is my body, and tell us, that no reason, not even that of angels, can overthrow it; as if we were either Platonics, or of some other sect opposed to Christ. But what do they gain by rejecting interpretation and boasting the authority of Christ while giving his words a perverse and alien sense? That the fiction of the invisible presence of Christ was known to the father' all readers sound and foolish will believe when it is shown to have the support of Scripture. They say, it is not to be inferred that Christ is tied to heaven, how spacious soever it may be. Let us leave the tying, and content ourselves with Peter's expression, where he says that he must be contained (*comprehendi*) by heaven. What more do they desire? Let them also add the words of the angel, He is not here, he is risen; it is in vain for the Apostles to keep gazing up to heaven, for Jesus will come on the last day as he has been seen to ascend. They rejoin, that he will come in visible form; as if the angel had omitted the far more appropriate consolation, which, had he been educated in the school of Magdeburg, he would undoubtedly have given, namely, that if he lies invisible under the bread it was not necessary to go far to find him.

When they insist on our proving that Christ spoke falsely when he said, This is my body, their raving is too detestable to detain us long in refuting it. As if they were advancing something great or new they call upon their readers to observe that he did not say, This is a symbol, figure, shadow, phantasm; as if we held the body to be a phantasm such as that which they fabricate in their own forge. We acknowledge that it is a true body communion which is offered under the bread. Although the communion be mystical, the words of Christ cease not to maintain their credit and truth, did not they indirectly charge him with falsehood by trampling his ordinance under their feet, and subjecting him to their gross delirium. But as Christ has promised to be with us to the end of the world, they say that they are only believing his word ; as if he could not be present with believers by his boundless energy without including a phantastical body under the bread.

As the *thirty-first* argument is perfectly identical with the previous one and the *twenty-seventh,* I am unwilling to waste words upon it.

In the *thirty-second* place they attribute to us what I readily allow them to refute. It is, Christ sitteth on the right hand of the Father, and therefore cannot be everywhere. While they avowedly direct their whole virulence against me, of what use was it to catch at applause with the unlearned by a thing of nought ? Nor is the answer given in any other than my own words, except that they insert their own fiction regarding the ubiquity of human nature. Therefore, if their purpose is to attack me, let there be an end on both sides to this dispute about the right hand. My mode of expressing the doctrine is this : As Christ is in heaven in respect of the substance of his flesh, so he sits in his flesh on the right hand of the Father, yet filling the whole world with his power and virtue. Hence it appears that Christ the Mediator is God and man everywhere whole, not wholly, (*totus non totum,*) because his empire and the secret power of his grace are not confined within any limits.

The *thirty-third* argument is, Scripture declares, that Christ, after his resurrection, retained the body which he had formerly had, and that its nature was not changed : The same thing is taught with great uniformity by the Fathers : Therefore Christ cannot be corporeally in the Eucharist. They answer, that every thing which we assert concerning the nature of the body springs from a bad fountain : because the natural man receiveth not the things of the Spirit. But it is most false to say, that we judge by carnal sense, when we quote words which certainly proceeded from God

himself. The angels said, that Christ was not to be sought
in the tomb, when no mention was made of the Supper.
Did they not speak of the very body which the Magdeburgians inclose in a tomb, as often as they bury him under the
bread ? Christ, speaking of his flesh, uttered two expressions between which there is an apparent repugnance—the
one, Handle me and see, for a spirit hath not flesh and bones;
and the other, Take, eat, this is my body. The question is,
how are they to be reconciled ? As if the former expression
were of no moment, the Magdeburgians take desperate hold
of the second, and reject all interpretation ; as if the same
credit were not due to Christ in everything. They are unable to disentangle themselves without feigning a twofold
mode of presence, and obtruding upon us a fiction not more
repugnant to reason than to faith, viz., that the body which
Christ gave to be handled and seen, was of a different nature
from that which lies hid under the bread.

The *thirty-fourth* argument is, Scripture declares that our
bodies will be made conformable to the glorious body of
Christ ; but our bodies will not then be everywhere : Therefore, neither is the body of Christ everywhere. They answer,
that it is vicious to argue from the special to the absolute,
(*a dicto secundum quid ad dictum simpliciter.*) But let
them show where the dissimilarity is in the present case. I
admit that the degrees of glory in the head and members
will not be equal ; but in so far as pertains to the nature of
the body, there will be no conformity unless that flesh which
is the type and model of our resurrection retains its dimensions. They object, that it was not said of the flesh of Peter
or Paul, Take, this is my body. But as the point in dispute
is the sense in which these words ought to be taken, the interpretation of them must be sought from other passages.
The Magdeburgians become furious, and will not hear of
this, as if there was to be no freedom of interpretation without their permission. But when the Holy Spirit declares,
that Christ was transported to celestial glory, in order to
make our bodies conformable to his own body, who will
adopt the distinction which these new masters prescribe?
Add, that Paul celebrating the virtue of Christ, by which he

can do all things, extols the miracle which the Magdeburgians would explain away, extols it too highly for sound and pious readers to allow themselves to be driven out of so sure a doctrine by their objection of *dictum secundum quid.*

The *thirty-fifth* argument is, Among the early Christians there was no contention as to the Lord's Supper : Therefore, they all understood Christ's words figuratively. They retort, that as there was no controversy, they all unanimously embraced the literal sense. But as nothing is more silly than to sport in disposing of some jejune argument which they have themselves chosen to concoct, let the readers allow me to give them the true argument.—As some early writers taught freely that Christ said, This is my body, when he was giving a sign of his body, and also, that the bread is the body of Christ, because a sacrament is regarded as in a manner the thing itself; as others taught, that the body of which a sign was given in the Supper was the true body of Christ, while others called the bread a type, of which the body was the antitype, there is no probability that the error of a corporeal presence under the bread prevailed at that time, as in that case the controversy must have immediately arisen. Here there is no reason why they should compare us to the Philistines, unless, according to the practice often adopted in plays, they would suddenly break off the pleading by the crashing sound of broken benches, and thus disappoint the readers.

The *thirty-sixth* argument relates to novelty, which ought justly to be suspected of error, and states as a good ground for condemning the figment of a corporeal presence, that it originated at no ancient date among the gross corruptions of ignorance and superstition. They answer, that it is a regular practice with the advocates of bad causes to lay hold of some kindred subject on which they may declaim plausibly, and make great tragic display ; that in this way we transfer to the corporeal presence what applies only to transubstantiation, which they themselves strenuously condemn. So they say. But, *first*, I deny that we vociferate tragically in this matter, when we simply say, that the fiction which they venerate as a heavenly oracle, was fabricated by sophists, who knew nothing of a purer theology ; and, *secondly*,

I deny that we court applause by fastening on a kindred subject. How strenuously they oppose transubstantiation, appears from the writings of Westphal, who hesitates not to rank Councils held under Nicolas and Gregory VII., as orthodox. But let us have done with transubstantiation. We accuse them of feeling and speaking more grossly of the corporeal presence than the Papists. There is no reason why they should get into the heroics, and exult so furiously on producing the words, This is my body. We deny not that these are the words of Christ, though this they, with little modesty, make a ground of charge against us. Neither can they deny the following to be the words of God, The earth is my footstool, though from them, if we adopt their method of judging, it will follow, that the feet of God rest upon the earth, and support his body. The novelty is not in the words, but in insisting on their being understood strictly according to the letter.

In the *thirty-seventh* place, they mention as an argument adduced by us, that as ancient writers were accustomed to use both modes of expression—to say that the bread and wine are the body and blood of Christ, and also that they are signs, and symbols, and sacraments of the body and blood, it may hence be inferred that the words were not understood by them without a figure. Here they exult over us, for having lately contended that the ancients were ignorant of the corporeal presence, and now distinctly admitting that they call the bread the body: as if it were not common to us both so to call it. But here we are considering the meaning. No man objects to use a form of expression of which the Son of God, our heavenly Master, is the author. We only maintain, that as often as the fathers call the bread and wine signs, symbols, and sacraments of the body and blood, they sufficiently explain their meaning, as this implies that clear distinction between the sign and the thing signified for which we contend. Nay, a distinct reason is given why the terms flesh and blood are applied to the bread and the wine. Here the Magdeburgians pertinaciously insist, that it is enough for them, that, according to the ancients, the bread is the body: as if the other expression, as being fuller and more explicit, were not to be added by way of interpretation. Paul says in one passage, that he supplies what is lacking in the sufferings of Christ for his Church : in another passage, repeating the same thing, he says, it is for the confirmation of believers. If a question is raised as to Paul's meaning, (as under pretext of the former passage the Papists transfer part of our redemption to apostles and martyrs,) are we to overlook the explanation which is volunteered in the latter passage ? To say, therefore, in regard to a matter so clear and notorious, that they appeal to the Son of God, is absurd.

No less futile is their rhetoric, that Christ is not an unlearned, raw, or stammering judge, being on account of his utterance called the Logos : that he is not crafty, not double-tongued, not corrupted by bribery, no respecter of persons. Of what use is this loquacity but to show how well and at what length the Magdeburgians can prattle ? Everything which proceeded from the sacred lips of Christ we reverently adore as well as implicitly embrace : but his authority, which is above all exception, is injuriously impaired when they continue to assert it out of season, as if it were doubtful.

They manifest similar folly in citing their witnesses. Of what use was it, pray, when adducing passages of Matthew, Mark, Luke, and Paul, to add the ridiculous proviso, Always excepting the judgment of their superior, that is, Christ himself ; as if there were a danger lest Christ should deny himself in the organs of his Spirit. Let the thing then be distinctly announced. We acknowledge that those four authentic scribes of God have, with the most perfect good faith, stated the ordinance of Christ—an ordinance so clearly mystical, that any one denying it to be so is fit only for Anticyra. We are entitled then to inquire what analogy the bread bears to the body. The Magdeburgians, however, in order to have the flesh of Christ inclosed under the bread, refuse to admit that there is any mystery. What is to be gained by omitting the state of the question, and giving only a bare narrative ? How vain and futile the attempt to conceal the real controversy, by calling the evangelists clear, eloquent, and true ? Surely he who seeks an interpretation

of these words does not charge them with any want of
utterance. Nay, the true respect for them is not to fasten
at random and without consideration on everything they say,
as if we would tie them down to individual words and syllables, but attentively to consider their meaning, in order
that by a proper exposition of their words we may without
controversy embrace what they truly intended.

It is, therefore, mere petulance and falsehood to assert
that we appeal from Christ and the apostles to third parties.
Hence it is no wonder, if intoxicated with scurrility, they
expose their own disgrace when they say that they will come
with us to a third set of judges. Will they then, to gratify us,
do Christ the wrong of abandoning his tribunal and consent-
ing to leave the final decision to mortals? They premise that
they stand by the two former judges, and will never yield,
though angels from heaven should give a contrary decision.
Still if they saw that men were erecting a tribunal to overturn
the judgment of Christ, they ought not to have moved one foot.
I willingly relieve them from their offer of sacrilegious submission, for we ought sooner by a hundred deaths to confirm
the authority of Christ than yield to any human judgments.

Nothing of the kind, however, is done when the name of
interpreters is given to the fathers. If for them to perform
this office is to make them judges over Christ, let their
writings, as thus derogating from the sovereign authority of
the Son of God, be accursed. Meanwhile they declare that
they have no doubt of the support of the fathers, though
they deny the accordance of the phraseology employed by
them with the words of Christ. They do well and providently,
however, in leaving the decision to children of four years old.
Had they appealed to children of seven, they would easily
have detected such silly trifling as the following: "Let
neither part here have recourse to mere jangling, but let us
set down the words of Christ and his Apostles on the one
hand, and compare them with those of the fathers on the
other, in this way: Christ says, This is my body, and the
Apostles repeat the same thing; the fathers affirm that the
bread is the body. Child of four years old, guess and say
whether these modes of expression differ widely from each

other. To continue the comparison, Christ says, This is my body ; the fathers affirm that the bread is a symbol, sign, and figure of the body. Again, child of four years old, judge whether these phrases agree."

Surely if religion had any serious hold of their minds they would scarcely have stooped to such puerile trifling. The fathers occasionally in this ordinance retain the mode of expression used by Christ, as when the majesty of the doctrine is to be asserted, they quote the passages of Scripture *verbatim*, and yet they do not omit the office of interpreters as often as the occasion requires. Hence their fuller and more explicit statement, that as the bread is a sacrament of the body, it is in a manner the body. If there is any doubt as to their meaning, whether is it to be removed by the concise statement or by the added light of interpretation ? How then dare the Magdeburgians, under the pretext of one expression, obscure a clear statement and explanatory paraphrase ?

The *thirty-eighth* argument is taken from Augustine, who terms it a foul affair to eat the flesh of Christ corporeally. They answer, that Christ having ordered this, there is nothing flagitious in it. Were the antithesis real, wo to Augustine for having dared thus to asperse the Judge of the world. But as that holy man was no less commendable for modesty than piety and erudition, we must see whether he has indeed charged Christ with a crime. On the contrary, being aware that wicked and profane men were calumniating every expression of a harsher nature which occurs in Scripture, and that the foolish often without judgment and choice insisted too rigidly on the mere words, he, in order to defeat the malice of the former, and cure the error of the latter, prescribes a rule of sound interpretation. And as when Christ orders us to eat his flesh, there would be manifest absurdity in the literal sense, he teaches that the expression is not simple but figurative. The Magdeburgians, to disentangle themselves, must therefore prove two things—that Christ ordered his body to be eaten corporeally, and that Augustine does not speak of this corporeal eating.

In the *thirtieth* place, they relate a statement which I have made, that seeing the opposite party say that Christ is contained by the bread, just as wine is by a tankard, we too may be permitted to give an appropriate interpretation of the words of Christ. Here they accuse us of calumny ; as if their books were not extant. Although I attack no one, and would rather suppress this than furnish materials for new strife, the simile was not invented by me, but certainly proceeded from certain among themselves who thought it plausible.

The *fortieth* argument as set down by them is faulty. It is, Christ will return to final judgment as he was seen to ascend : Therefore, he is not corporeally present in the Supper. The complete statement should be, The same Christ, who was withdrawn from the view of man and taken up to heaven, will, as the angel declares, come in like manner as he was seen to ascend, and is, as Paul declares, to be looked for as the Redeemer from heaven : Therefore, he is not now on the earth bodily. The Magdeburgians answer, that he will come in a visible form. But there is no such distinction in the words either of Paul or the angel, and yet nothing would have been more appropriate than to have added the comforting consideration of his invisible presence, were it real. As their language speaks of Christ simply, how presumptuous is it to imagine that he is at the same time visible and invisible ? The sense in which he promises to be present with his disciples, I have elsewhere expounded in the words of Augustine ; though the expression itself is too clear to require an interpreter. For what can be more preposterous than to wrest what is said of grace, virtue, and assistance to the essence of flesh ?

The *forty-first* argument is, Stephen sees Christ sitting in heaven : Therefore, he does not dwell bodily on earth. The Magdeburgians answer, that that which Christ instituted in the Supper is not taken away by a special revelation. Nay, but that which was revealed to Stephen most completely refutes their fictitious error. For if at that time the presence of Christ alone could give Stephen invincible constancy of faith, it would have been much better to set him before him, so that he had only to stretch forth his hand, than to exhibit him at a distance. Therefore, just as the heavens were then

opened, let the Magdeburgians learn to open their eyes and
recognise that Christ though sitting in heaven is yet united
to believers on earth by the boundless and incomprehensible
energy of his Spirit. Their idea that Christ's dwelling in
Stephen at the time when he saw him in heaven cannot be
otherwise reconciled, is too ridiculous, Christ having himself
distinctly stated that in the same manner in which his Father
dwells in us, he too dwells. This manner Paul explains to
be by faith. There is nothing to perplex in the doctrine
that Christ dwelling in heaven in respect of his flesh, still
as Mediator fills the whole world, and is truly one with his
members, as their life is common.

The *forty-second* argument is, The body of Christ was inclosed in the womb of Mary, suspended on the cross, and
laid in the tomb : Therefore it is not immense and everywhere. They answer that it is just as Christ declares, and
therefore that he both wills and can make it to be in one
place and at the same time in every part of the world. But
this is no better than if some anthropomorphite were bab-
blingly to say that God has nostrils because he declares that
he smells sacrifice. Here indeed they are finely caught.
They say that we often reason fallaciously and sophistically
from the properties of body in the abstract to the person of
Christ. This calumny is easily disposed of. We do not
teach that because the body of Christ is finite, he is himself
confined within the same dimensions ; nay, we assert that he
fills all things, because it were impious to separate him from
his members. But as the question is concerning the flesh,
we insist on it. In short, we fully illustrate the distinction
between the flesh of Christ in the abstract and his person,
while they most perversely confound it. For in order to
prove that the flesh of Christ is immense and everywhere,
they are ever and anon insisting that there is one person in
Christ, and that he therefore fills heaven and earth in respect
of his flesh as well as his divinity. Do they not drag the
body of Christ in the abstract as it were by the hair, in making it follow the divinity wherever it extends ?

The *forty-third* argument I will state somewhat more
faithfully than they do, thus : Christ's promise to be in the

midst of us should be understood of his spiritual presence : but the thing promised is of all others the most desirable ; therefore faith can rest satisfied with spiritual presence. They answer, that we finish ourselves by this clear sentence, by inferring from it that Christ is present with us as he then was, that is, both as God and man. . What if I maintain, on the contrary, that he is not corporeally present as he then was, unless he is present visibly ; for, if I mistake not, this is to be ranked as a most proper and inseparable quality of body ? But as nothing is plainer than that Christ there joins himself to us as our Mediator and Head, the whole dispute is at an end the moment it is agreed that Christ, in the person of Mediator, or, if they prefer it, the whole person of the Mediator, is truly and essentially in the midst of us, although the flesh of Christ, or, which is the same thing, Christ is, in respect of his flesh, in heaven. For when mention is made by us of the spiritual presence, the other ought to be restricted to the flesh. After they have emptied themselves of a large stream of words, the whole comes to this, that the flesh of Christ remains in heaven though he dwells in us in his capacity of Mediator.

The *forty-fourth* argument is, If the substantial body of Christ is given in the Supper, it is received and swallowed indiscriminately by believers and unbelievers. Who has spoken in this way, I know not. I, for my part, would attach no weight to this argument. All the time I was under the strange delusion that the very substance of the flesh was given under the bread, I shuddered at the idea of its being prostituted to the ungodly. And the monstrous results with which that error is replete, nay, swollen even to bursting, I think I have elsewhere more than sufficiently demonstrated. Christ said, Eat, this is my body. What if the sacred bread is devoured in mockery by a Turk or a Jew ? Will it be no profanation of the body of Christ to allow it to pass into the stomach of a despiser ? The Magdeburgians answer, that as the words of Christ imply that it does so, they are not moved by any absurdity. But I supposed, that as the promise and the command are united to each other by an indissoluble tie, the former is not fulfilled

unless the latter is obeyed. And, indeed, since Luther
taught that the bread is the body only during the act of
celebration, while they themselves insist that the bread is
not a symbol, but the true and substantial body, I should
like to know how they are to escape from this dilemma?
Suppose that, according to their custom, one hundred mor-
sels are prepared for the use of the Supper, and the number
of actual guests is fewer than an hundred; when the celebration is finished, is that which remains over the body of
Christ, or does it, at the conclusion of the ordinance, cease
to be body? Provided I am allowed to enjoy the body of
Christ with all the pious, I will make them welcome to share
their imaginary body with Judas.

The *forty-fifth* argument is, We teach nothing at variance
with the confession of Augsburg, and therefore they have no
cause for quarrelling so bitterly, or rather, so savagely. If
there is any doubt as to this, we appeal to Philip (Melancthon) who wrote it. As the Magdeburgians speak hesi-
tatingly in their reply, I, trusting to a good conscience,
venture freely to repeat what I said. Let Philip, as often
as it is thought proper, be called upon to explain his own
meaning. Meanwhile, they only prove themselves contumacious by dissenting from their confession.

The *forty-sixth* argument is, If Christ is believed to be corporeally in the Supper, the transubstantiation of the Papists
cannot be firmly opposed. They answer, they are not to do
evil, that good may come. Where they got this argument, I
know not; but I willingly give it entirely up to them : nay,
its futility is apparent from our writings. For while we refute transubstantiation by other valid arguments, we hold
this one to be amply sufficient, that it destroys the analogy
between the sign and the thing signified; for if there be not
in the sacrament a visible and earthly sign corresponding to
the spiritual gift, the nature of a sacrament is lost.

The *forty-seventh* argument is, As the imagination of a corporeal presence gave occasion to the idolatry of the Papists,
and still confirms it, it ought not to be maintained. They
answer, that a consequence drawn from an accidental vitia-
tion is not valid. But what if we assert that the two things

are connected ? We not only deny the corporeal presence for
the purpose of discountenancing idolatry, but the better to
make it manifest how detestable the fiction of a corporeal
presence is, we show that it necessarily carries an impious
idolatry along with it. When they affirm that the body of
Jesus Christ is not to be worshipped although it be in the
bread, because Christ does not receive worship there, their
answer would be good if all men would admit its validity.
They pretend that no command has anywhere been given
as to worshipping the body of Christ. It is certainly said
properly of Christ as man, God hath exalted him, and given
him a name which is above every name, that at the name of
Jesus every knee should bow. Accordingly, Augustine justly
and shrewdly infers from this, that the flesh of Christ is to
be worshipped in the person of the Mediator. But I am
surprised that the Magdeburgians so liberally concede to us
what the rest of their party tenaciously retain. What does
Luther mean in writing against the doctors of Louvain, by
speaking of the holy and adorable sacrament, if the body is
not to be worshipped in the bread ? Here let them at least
agree among themselves, and subscribe once more to their
friend Westphal, if they would not deal deceitfully with the
cause of which they are advocates.

The *forty-eighth* argument is stated incorrectly and un-
faithfully. For we do not infer that there would be one
substance (*hypostasis*) of the flesh and bread, if the flesh is
in the bread, but if the bread is the flesh, as they insist, properly and without figure. For while they constantly inculcate, that it is only with a view to explanation they say that
the flesh is given under the bread, but that in the meantime
we must hold by the words of Christ, that the bread is flesh,
I should like them to tell me how the subject and predicate
are to be reconciled if there is not one substance. Therefore, however closely they study concealment, their secret
will be forced out of them. They stand convicted of a manifest contradiction in now admitting what they formerly denied, viz., that the body is conjoined with the bread. For,
under their twelfth head, they compared together the two
passages, The word was made flesh, and, This is my body.

In the *forty-ninth* place, in order to accuse us of mendicity, they give utterance to some strange fabrication of their own,—Nothing useless is true; the doctrine of a corporeal presence is useless: therefore it is not true. Here they tell us, that like persons famishing for hunger, we scrape together food not only from the abodes of dialecticians, but from the fields of rhetoricians also. As I would be ashamed to be rhetorical in such a style, I leave them what is their own. Meanwhile let them defend themselves against Paul, who condemns all questions from which no edification arises. Certainly if their doctrine is useless, it follows that they are wrong in raising such contests about it. It is evident that they are more friendly to the Papists than to us. If it is because of a frivolous question, let them consider how they shall one day render an account of their truculence. Wherefore, in order to refute the major, there was no need to vent foul blasphemy against the law of God. But they contend that what is useless is sometimes true. To prove a thing to be without doubt the law of God, is of no use to them. The Apostle had said that the ceremonies, as being shadows, did not profit the worshippers—that is, did not profit by themselves. Is therefore the whole law useless, while its utility is apparent even in passing sentence of condemnation on men? It remains now to see what benefit is produced by the figment which they obtrude upon us. The passage, " The flesh profiteth nothing," has already been expounded. But though we were not to found on any passages of Scripture, still as our doctrine contains the entire union of Christ with his members, in which our whole salvation and felicity consist, while they insist on a promiscuous eating by Peter and Judas, it is clear that they are quarrelling for nothing.

In the *fiftieth* argument they employ a gloss, and hence it is easy for them to dissipate shadows of their own raising; but I should like them to answer the argument when I state it thus, The communion of the substance of the flesh of Christ which they maintain, is either temporary or perpetual. If they say it is perpetual, Christ will remain in the most abandoned, in the fornicator, the murderer, the man stained by abominable crimes. If it is temporary and only for a moment, of what avail is it to receive Christ, and leave him in the same place the moment you withdraw your foot from the table? Assuredly if there be not a perpetual communication beyond the act of communicating, nothing more will be conferred than the remembrance of something lost. And it is certain, that what the Lord elsewhere affirms of his perpetual abiding in us, and what Paul teaches as to his dwelling in our hearts by faith, is sealed in the Supper. Hence we infer that the communion of which we are partakers in the Supper is perpetual. I may now therefore argue thus, The promise of Christ's dwelling in us is special, and is addressed to believers only; therefore none but believers obtain possession of Christ in the Supper. See how attentive our good censors are to the cause, while they tell us to give it a more attentive consideration.

The *fifty-first* argument is, A doctrine carrying many absurdities with it is not true: the doctrine of the corporeal presence of Christ is involved in many absurdities; therefore it follows that it is not true. The major they deny to hold universally, because there are various species of absurdities, and in theology every thing is not to be held absurd which is repugnant to human reason. But whether or not those which we produce are of that description, let our readers judge from the following:

In the *fifty-second* head they mention the first absurdity. It is absurd that the body and blood of Christ should be everywhere: but the corporeal presence in the Supper requires ubiquity. The Magdeburgians answer, that it is absurd to human reason only, not to faith, because it never can be absurd to believe Christ. Had they proved that we have not to attend to what is suited to the nature of the sacrament, they might now perhaps produce a doubt, but as we have proved a hundred times, that though the presence of the flesh of Christ does not lurk under the bread, due reverence and credit are given to his words, the difficulty is not yet removed. An argument which they obscure by stating it in brief and equivocal terms, is very stringent against them. Either the whole body of Christ is given under the bread or only a part: if the whole, the bread is no less blood than flesh. The same may be applied to the cup, so that the wine is not less body than blood. If they pretend that the body of Christ is without blood, and hold that the blood is extracted apart from the flesh, could any thing be more monstrous? We are not here speaking of common meat and drink. I ask, in what way they suppose that they eat the body and drink the flesh of Christ in the Supper? If they answer that the whole is in every part, why do they consider the bread rather than the wine to be the body? and why the wine rather than the bread to be the blood? If they answer, that the mode has not been revealed, why do they decide so boldly on the presence of the substance? It is this which plunges them into the abyss. Should they choose to mutter that the absurdity is merely physical, none but those who are more than fatuous will be persuaded that the substance of the blood can be dissevered by Christ from the substance of the flesh. It is said that their union is repugnant to the words. But though Christ remain entire in heaven, there is nothing to prevent him from giving his flesh as meat and his blood as drink, and from nourishing and vivifying us separately by each.

As in the *fifty-third* place they mutilate and corrupt our words, let the reader attend to the following absurdity. Seeing it is derogatory to the celestial glory of Christ that his body should be inclosed under earthly elements, he is insulted when he is placed corporeally in the bread. The Magdeburgians will perhaps object, that in a natural view this may seem insulting to Christ, but in a theological it is not so. What? When that is asserted of Christ, which no mortal man but God himself declares respecting him, will they not be ashamed to flee to that miserable asylum? I know that it was not disgraceful to Christ to be suspended on the cross, on which, triumphing over death and the devil, he sat as it were sublime in a triumphal chariot. But here, when he is drawn down from his celestial seat and fastened to an earthly and corruptible element, how different is the case? When he was hanging on the cross it was not the Father's pleasure that he should yet enjoy a blessed immortality in heaven, but now he has removed him from the earth that he may be exalted above all heavens. Wherefore let the Magdeburgians cease from telling us that the wisdom of God is foolishness to the world—let them not, under the blinding influence of their own sense, presume to throw everything into confusion.

They follow their usual practice under the *fifty-fourth* head, but the sum is, Any doctrine, which leads to contradiction in the Scriptures, is false ; but if the corporeal presence of Christ in the Supper is admitted, the Scriptures will contradict themselves ; this error therefore is justly repudiated. As to the major, they mention that disputes often arise from true doctrine ; as if we were saying that the doctrine is vicious for any other reason than for making Scripture self-contradictory. Their denial that Scripture is set at variance by their fiction is not to be wondered at ; for nothing is easier for them than to reconcile heaven with hell. When they deny that there is any contradiction in saying that the body of Christ is everywhere and yet in a particular place, that it is finite and immense, visible and invisible, mortal and immortal, whole and partial, in what else can any contradiction be found ? But I beseech pious and sober readers not to allow giddy men to seize upon the Spirit of concord and unity, to set him at variance with himself, and rend the Scriptures, that they may be able thereby to fabricate a multiform Christ.

The *fifty-fifth* argument it pains me to mention, but I must briefly inform the reader of their incredible impudence in presuming to construct an absurd argument without any plausibility, and then throwing it in our face. For who ever thought of arguing, that as Christ assumed our flesh he does not give it to us to eat ? On the contrary, our uniform doctrine is, that he assumed our flesh for the very purpose of giving life to our souls by communication with it. We teach that, inasmuch as he was made man, he is bone of our bone and flesh of our flesh. Let the Magdeburgians then assail their own falsehood as they will, but let not us be burdened with any share of the obloquy or disgrace.

The *fifty-sixth* argument is, It is a contradiction to say, that Christ in his flesh left the world and was received into heaven, and to say also, that in his flesh he lies hid under the bread. They answer, that there is no variance between these things in the view of faith, though, by our spirit of giddiness, they become what is easily said but not so easily proved. When they say that faith does not measure the works of God by the capacity of reason, but renders praise to his truth and omnipotence, although we admit it to be true, yet seeing the truth of God is simple and undivided, it does not follow that faith transfigures God, and makes him at variance with himself. The testimony of God is, that Christ was received into the heavens, and behoves to be contained by the heavens until he is to come as Redeemer, and that we should seek him there. As this doctrine is altogether inconsistent with the fiction of a corporeal presence, what can they gain by attempting to disguise the inconsistency ? Place must be given to the omnipotence of God, especially when a simple and easy explanation tells us how Christ sitting in heaven may give himself to be enjoyed by us on earth. With how much greater plausibility are we entitled to maintain that it is preposterous to exercise faith in a carnal eating of Christ, seeing it is far more congruous to his nature that we should rise upwards in order to enjoy Christ spiritually ?

The *fifty-seventh* argument is akin to the last. It is, There is an inconsistency in the assertion that there is a flesh of Christ which, invisible in heaven, is invisibly and insensibly eaten under the bread. Their statement, that it is incongruous to hold that Christ who has flesh and bones is eaten without flesh and bones, though they represent it as ours, we leave to themselves. For what has this to do with a debate as to the eating of his flesh ? When they answer, that there is no repugnance as far as faith is concerned, it is just as if the anthropomorphites were to allege that when they believe, on the words of Scripture, that God has eyes, nose, mouth, ears, arms, and feet, they shut their eyes to all absurdities, because faith surmounts all contradiction.

In the *fifty-eighth* place they betray their absurdity not less than their malice. I had said that the petulance of Westphal and his fellows could not but be odious to learned

and right-hearted men ; all the most learned of Luther's
friends and disciples having declared their satisfaction with
my doctrine.   I mentioned two, Gaspar Cruciger and Vittus
Theodorus.   Here the Magdeburgians fix me in a dilemma,
as if I had actually drawn the inference that we have therefore a good cause, and all the Saxon doctors ought at once
to pass over to our view.   These worthy men, who so roll
themselves in the mire, are grieved forsooth at the stigma
which I have thus thrown on the dead.   Now, that they
may not appeal in vain to the Church of which Theodore
was minister, I again repeat that I said nothing which I
cannot prove by his own handwriting whenever it shall be
necessary.   As to Cruciger's consent, not to go further, I
take Philip himself to witness, whose authority with his
disciples ought to be above exception.

The *last* of the arguments enumerated is, We sacramentarians have written on this subject more splendidly than
those of the opposite opinion are able to do ; we therefore
hold the truth, and our opponents should be silent.   First,
in pretending that we admit the name which they themselves
have wickedly imposed upon us as a stigma, nothing can be
more senseless than their trifling.   Let them call me sacramentarian whenever they please, it shall move me no more
than the barking of a dog.   But they even employ themselves in bringing a charge against us to which they are truly
and justly liable.   For as those who insert false legacies
or substitute false heirs are called Testamentarii, do not
these worthy men, when they substitute a fictitious body
contrary to the mind of the testator, deserve the same name?
There is certainly no colour for applying it to us.   But without regarding their absurdity I come to the subject.   I said,
I admit, and I do not repent having said, that I have spoken
more splendidly of the sacred Supper and its entire virtue,
that I have explained its dignity and efficacy better and
more faithfully than all who are like Westphal, and that
therefore it is unjust for any one to pretend that he is fighting against me in defence of the Supper.   And indeed
what can be more unworthy than for turbulent men, induced
by mere moroseness to disturb the Church of God, to come

forward under the fallacious pretence of defending the sacred Supper against us, who no less honourably assert its dignity than lucidly treat of its whole nature and virtue? To omit all my books, in which I distinctly teach that Christ by no means deceives us with bare and empty signs, but truly performs what he figures, does not our Agreement contain the same thing? And yet these men cease not to cry that we make void the holy Supper.

At present they furthermore object that I am not serious in leaving them to decide. But if they would look more closely to the judges to whom I have appealed, they would see that there is no place for them in the list. Faithful servants of Christ, grave and moderate men, I decline not as judges, but no reason admits of such authority being given to proud, obstinate, and contumacious despisers of the brethren. And yet they compare themselves to infants by whom God perfects praise, while they calumniously charge us with a vile attempt to terrify them by vile ostentation. I wish they were endued with a spirit of meekness and modesty, so as to prove themselves at least to be men. Where can greater and vainer ostentation be found than in themselves? Hence their Thrasonic boast in this very place, that they will make our ears tingle and our hearts tremble by their cries. See the humble children who so arrogate everything to themselves, that they leave not a particle of the Spirit to servants of Christ by whose labours, if they possessed one particle of docility, they ought to profit. Still harsher is their calumny that we resist the truth contrary to conscience. That the iniquity of this calumny may be known to the whole world, I appeal to thee, O Christ, the Son of God, supreme Judge of the world, whose authority is dreaded by devils themselves, that thou wouldst make it manifest now and on that day whether my mind has ever entertained the mad thought of tainting thy doctrine by any falsehood or corruption. But if thou seest me to be free and most remote from this crime ; nay, if thou art my faithful witness, that I sincerely and from the heart profess the faith which I have learned from thy sacred holy gospel, be pleased to suppress the diabolical slander of men who are so blinded by obstinacy or pride as to be incapable of any discrimination.

I again address my speech to you, pious readers, and beseech you all not to allow your senses to be stupified by that tingling of which the Magdeburgians boast. An expression constantly in their mouths is, that there is no room for discussion, when Christ the only Master and Teacher has clearly taught what is to be believed—no room for debate, when the same supreme Judge has distinctly given forth his decision. This they say, because they see that nothing would subject us to greater odium or be more plausible in their favour than to persuade the unskilful that no question can be raised as to this ordinance without overthrowing the authority of Christ. It is part of the same artifice to keep ever and anon crying that there is no less danger in listening to human reason than is incurred by him who listens to the blandishments of a harlot and gets entangled in her deadly snares. Though they use this language for the sake of procuring favour, we have no cause to fear that a knowledge of the fact will not wipe away all their glosses, and therefore there is nothing we more desire than that all should be able to form their judgment from the case itself. In this way it will at once be seen that our only reason for seeking an interpretation for the words of Christ is, that they may be engraved with due reverence on our hearts; that discarding human reason, and raising our minds above the world, we receive this high mystery with due faith, and hold it in the highest admiration. The smoke by which they would most iniquitously blind the eyes of the simple being thus dispersed, the false and invidious charges in which our opponents place the substance of their defence, quickly disappear.

But what do the men of Bremen on their part adduce? To retain quiet possession of their status, they pronounce high eulogiums on the magnanimity of Luther. These I readily admit, provided they do not wickedly and unworthily abuse the name of this justly celebrated teacher for their own advantage, or rather their own caprice. If any defect mingled with the lofty virtues of Luther, I would bury it in oblivion. Whatever it may have been, reverence and love for the gifts with which he was endowed would make me refrain from exposing it ; but to extol his defects as if they were virtues is foolish and preposterous affectation. Still less excusable is the fervour of their rash zeal in basely and shamefully corrupting Scripture in order to adorn LUTHER with the spoils of John the Baptist. For though they deny not that in John the Baptist was fulfilled what Malachi had foretold of Elias that was to come, they insist that this prophecy is also to be understood of Luther, who is that Elias who was to restore all things, and that that which was once accomplished by John the Baptist, the prophets as well as the testimony of Christ not obscurely intimate to have been again repeated in Luther. By this false assertion they dishonour the name of Luther not less than the Egyptians did the body of Jeremiah by worshipping his sepulchre. Admitting that the name of Elias may be given to Luther, it is sacrilegious temerity to assert that he is the last Elias, as if the hand of God were shortened, and he were unable hereafter to send forth an equal or a greater. What oracle revealed to them that the treasures of divine power were so exhausted or impaired by the formation of one individual, that none like him can come forth from his boundless and incomprehensible fulness ? I have no doubt that Satan purposely excites these insane eulogists in order to furnish profane scoffers with a longed-for opportunity of slander. I wish that the hand of him who could only subscribe by the single letter T, had been as unable for the whole writing as for that one word.

LUTHER having always held the principle, that it was not permitted either to himself or to any other mortal to be wise above the word of God, it is strange and lamentable that the Church of God should be so imperiously bound down to his decrees. They will deny that they intend this. Therefore let the name of Luther rest for a little until we have discussed the point with calm and placid reason. Their caution to beware of false teachers I too give, the object of our admonition being to guard the children of God against their pestiferous delusion. But what of the thing itself

They pronounce magisterially that they receive the words of Christ, This is my body, not symbolically or metonymically, but in the meaning which they naturally import. I hold that there is a metonymy, because the name of body cannot apply to the bread, unless in respect of its being a symbol. This view is completely confirmed by the analogy which the Scriptures uniformly preserve between the sign and the thing signified. If you ask the reason why, with gross absurdity they fasten upon the bare literal sense, they answer that nothing is more unjust or foolish than the question. Of what use is it for them daily to lift up their voice in the pulpit, if the interpretation of Scripture is denied to the Church? But they say that a clear text needs no exposition. Certainly not, provided they would admit that a sacrament is a sacrament. When Paul declares, that the Church is cleansed by the washing of water, the truth of the declaration is universally admitted. If they infer from it that the impurities of the soul are cleansed by the corruptible element of water, the Sun of righteousness himself will be obscured. Another declaration by Paul, that believers put on Christ, will be assented to by all. But if the men of Bremen transfigure Christ into a garment, what darkness will be substituted for clearness? And yet we hear what the words literally import. Moreover, in regard to the interpretation I should like them to point out the hostile standards under which they falsely pretend that we are at war among ourselves: although any diversity in the teaching of some from that of others is nothing to the point.

Let the reader then consider whether the sacramental mode of expression, because it does not please the men of Bremen, is to be altogether repudiated. There are four reasons which will not allow them to give up their opinion. The first is, that Jesus Christ, true and perfect God and man, is inseparably united in one person. But the union of the human nature with the divine does not confound the unity of both, nor does unity of person mix up the divine nature with the human, so as not to leave each its peculiar properties. Surely the soul of Christ approached nearer

to divinity than his body, and yet Luther did not on this
account admit that Christ, as man, had always a foreknow-
ledge of all things. Their second reason is, that the right
hand of God, on which Christ sits, is everywhere ; as if we
denied that Christ, the Mediator between God and man,
fills all things in an ineffable manner, so as to be everywhere
entire, and yet in respect of his flesh occupies a seat in
heaven. Their third reason is, that the word of God is not
fallacious or lying. But the question is not as to any falsehood in the word, but as to their stubborn obstinacy which
prevents them from giving any place even to the first rudiments of Scripture. For would they peaceably allow a place
for the rule, which, whether they will or not, is observed in
regard to all the sacraments, all disputes would at once ter-
minate. Their fourth reason is, that God has manifold and
various ways of existing in a place. But this variety cannot have made the body of Christ, when he instituted the
Supper, to be in one place visible, finite, and mortal, and at
the same time in several places, invisible, immense, and
immortal. See how truly they boast that the reasons which
they adduce to establish their error are certain, firm, and
unrefutable. It is stupor only that makes them acquiesce
in it ; they certainly cannot rest in it in safety. When they
object that the figure of the body was not delivered, nor the
sign of the blood poured out, we have a still clearer proof
how boldly these little fathers fight with their own shadow.
For what is the effect of the metonymy on which we insist,
but just to make the bread to be in a sacramental manner
the true body of Christ that was sacrificed for us, and thus
be truly communicated to us ? We do not found merely on
physical arguments, but wish that which Scripture plainly
teaches concerning the flesh of Christ to remain firm and
inviolable ; just as I a little ago observed, that we do not
give the words of Christ a forced meaning, but that which
similar passages demand.

The men of Bremen get finely out of the difficulty by saying, that as it is written, "In vain do they worship with the
commandments of men," the door is shut against all arguments. How irrelevantly they arm themselves with the

specious *dictum*, that the word of God must always be opposed to human reason, I think I have already clearly shown. For as we willingly follow without lifting our eyes any course to which God by his own voice calls us, so we are unwilling by a brutish stupor to confound ourselves with the unclean animals which do not cleave the hoof. That this memorable epistle might not be without its due weight, Christian Haveman appends his name. To him is added another who subscribes himself John T., A., and by his single celebrity supports all the others. For the words are: To take advantage of the opportunity of sending by the faithful members of Christ who were to visit you by the way, we could not procure the written subscriptions of all the pious brethren. Some were out of town, others not at home: meanwhile, that the truth may be confirmed in the mouth of two witnesses, I declare, &c. I am not now surprised at their lifting their heads so disdainfully under pretext of the words of Christ, since they hold the whole world bound to believe them on the first letters of their names. In another place, however, the same individual is not only more literal in expressing his name, but also by a silly and absurd addition, wishing to be thought facetious, says, I, John Teman of Amsterdam, pastor of the Church of Bremen, in Martin's Church, or, if the Sacramentarians will, in the Church of St. Martin, Bishop of Tours. This specimen of gravity will doubtless have the effect of procuring credit to the man.

Weary of all this folly, I would now pass to others, were I not detained for a little by another confession, which they say has been absolutely forced from them, by my having dedicated my trifles to them. As I perceive, that not only the men of Bremen, but others also of the same faction, are very indignant at my having performed my duty towards them, I must briefly tell them that they have put themselves into a passion for nothing. They clamorously express their high displeasure at my having dared, under a show of respect, to obtrude my book on the churches of Saxony. I may be pardoned for having thought them men, though they now breathe nothing but the ferocity of wild beasts. I have, however, a better excuse. I had no intention to dedicate my book to the followers of Westphal, nor have I, by any expression, manifested such an intention. The dedication is, To all honest ministers of Christ, and sincere worshippers of God, who observe and follow the pure doctrine of the gospel in the churches of Saxony and Lower Germany. To this class they certainly do not prove themselves to belong. With them, pride occupies the place of piety, ferocity is substituted for every humane feeling, and mere obstinacy leaves no room for any thing like moderation. Their confession is, That the true body of Christ is given to be substantially eaten in the Supper. We not less distinctly maintain true communion (κοινωνια) with the flesh of Christ of which Paul speaks. The only question is as to the mode. They say they care not how the thing is done, because they simply believe the words of Christ. I answer, that we too simply believe the words of Christ, but do not voluntarily quench the light of the Spirit by neglecting the gift of interpretation. This disposes of their specious excuse, that they feel constrained by the testimonies of Matthew, Mark, Luke, and Paul. Our doctrine does not refuse credit to their testimony, but faithfully and fully elucidates what others absurdly involve in darkness. Whether or not all four affirm distinctly and without any interpretation that the bread is the true and natural body of Christ, let their words show. The men of Bremen extract this meaning from the context. We too, therefore, may extract from the same context that the body and blood of Christ are offered to us in the Supper in a different way from that which they imagine. What do Luke and Paul affirm to be given in the cup? A covenant in the blood. As the same thing must be true of the body, it follows that nothing else can be inferred from the words of Christ, than that under the bread there is the ratification of a covenant in the body of the Son of God which was crucified for us. We are ordered to eat the body which was crucified for us ; in other words, to become partakers of the sacrifice by which the sins of the world were expiated. If they insist that the two things are conjoined, viz., the fruit of the sacrifice and the communion of the flesh, I myself press the very same point—that since by the

same law and in the same words the Son of God offers his
body, and the covenant in the body, the one is not to be
taken without the other. As it was said, Eat, this is my
body, they insist that the body of Christ is eaten substantially by all men whatsoever. Why might not I, on the
other hand, insist that all men whatsoever receive the covenant by drinking of the cup ? From this it would follow,
that all who approach the table truly and spiritually communicate with Christ. Let the men of Bremen loose this
knot if they would not be strangled by it.

But although the true body of Christ is eaten in the Supper, this is no ground for holding, as they do, that spiritual
interpretation is excluded. This interpretation would define the mode, and show the two things to be perfectly re-
concilable, viz., that the same body which was once offered
as a victim is given to us, and yet is not eaten in a carnal
manner. Certainly in the age of Augustine and Jerome no
man doubted that the body of Christ was one. The former,
however, to obviate a gross imagination, introduces Christ as
saying, I have committed an ordinance to you, which, spiritually understood, will give you life. The latter declares
more harshly, that the flesh of Christ which we eat in the
Supper is different from that which was offered on the cross,
and the blood drunk different from that which was offered ;
not that he really thought the natures of the flesh and blood
to be different, but that he might more distinctly express
that they are eaten in a mystery, that is, that it is owing to
the secret agency of the Spirit that the true and spiritual
flesh of Christ gives life to us. Formerly, it was sometimes
denied that the body of Christ, which is given us for spiritual
food is spiritual ; as if the dignity of Christ's glorious body
at present were inferior to that which will one day be possessed by all his members. Paul, speaking of the general
resurrection of the righteous, says, that that which is now
an animal body will then become a spiritual body, because
mortality will be swallowed up of life. But the perverseness
of the men of Bremen, not contented with one error, wholly
excludes the spiritual mode and interpretation.

Still more grossly do they infer from the term *breaking*,

that the bread which is distributed in the Supper is the true and natural body of Christ. Paul, I admit, says in one place, that the bread is broken, and in another, This is my body which is broken for you. But I wonder that those worthy teachers of the Hebrew tongue, who shortly after convert the pronoun *Hoc* into the masculine *Hic*, because the Hebrew has no neuter, do not understand what boys learn in their rudiments, that the present tense should be resolved into the future. Paul certainly says the same thing as the evangelists, who make no mention of daily breaking, but speak merely of a delivery which took place on the cross. The *breaking* of Paul is therefore equivalent to immolating, except that he alludes to the mystical act, which is a vivid mirror of the death of Christ. The fiction which the men of Bremen obtrude for the genuine sense, viz., This is my body which is broken for you or distributed in the bread, is nothing better than a brutish profanation, which will I hope excite the disgust of all the godly against them and their error, which they cannot defend without perverting every thing.

There is no reason why they should insist so much on the term κοινωνια. It signifies participation. What then ? If they infer from this that the body of Christ is substantially eaten, we in our turn will say that the substance of the altar was devoured by the priests, and the idol swallowed substantially by its worshippers, as Paul applies the term κοινωνια to both in the same passage. They altogether scout the introduction of the symbols and figures of the Old Testament ; but while I admit that the distinction should be observed between shadows and the body, still I hold that we ought not to disregard a resemblance which the Holy Spirit distinctly asserts. Above I have fully shown with what justice they pretend to have the support of the primitive and more modern Church : nor is it necessary to give a new refutation of what they allege in regard to the omnipotence of Christ. Their assertion that all who teach that the words of Christ contain a metonymy, which gives the sign the name of the thing signified, and makes the bread to be symbolically the body of Christ, charge Christ himself with falsehood, is barbarous in the extreme: especially when they at the same time give utterance to a furious anathema, consigning to the lower regions all who say that it is by virtue of the Holy Spirit that our souls are spiritually fed by the substance of the flesh of Christ, and who bid us rise to heaven in order to be admitted to this communion. In this way they certainly doom to perdition the whole primitive Church, which, in celebrating this mystery, regularly began with exhorting those present to raise their minds upwards. If the metonymy is not only accursed, but teems with blasphemy, what will become of poor Augustine, whose words we formerly quoted, viz., that the bread of the Supper is in a manner the body of Christ, because the sacraments, if they did not receive the name of things which they figure, would not be sacraments? The sense in which ancient writers occasionally say, that the body of Christ is taken by the carnal mouth, we have elsewhere explained to be the same as the sense in which they at the same time add that it is consumed. Should the men of Bremen, trusting to these words, follow out the process of digestion to the last, who would not be revolted by the monstrous idea? To conclude, If from the words of Christ, This is my body, it is inferred, that the substantial body of Christ is received by the carnal mouth, it might with equal force be argued that the divine essence of the Spirit was seen by the carnal eye, because it was said, Upon whom ye shall see the Spirit of God descending. Hence it will follow, that the Spirit of God was transformed into a visible dove.

Next come the men of Hildesheim, who say that they approach the cause with great confidence, because they are supporting Christ, and denounce impending destruction on us whose minds they describe as swollen with self-admiration, and completely carried away by pride—a magnificent exordium, provided the result corresponds with the outset. But we shall soon see that this sounding boast comes to nothing. The confession which they subjoin, that Christ instituted the Supper to be used as a perpetual ordinance in the Church, I could regard as tolerable, did they not immediately after corrupt it by a vile commentary.

That a command and a promise are therein contained, that
the corruptible material of bread and wine is set before the
eye, and that the true body of Christ is at the same time
given, is beyond controversy, and therefore the whole dispute
relates to the definition. As they attack me directly, by
defending Westphal, all I have to do is to maintain my
cause. Away, then, with the odious names of sects. With
what face do they say that I leave no mystery, no spiritual
fruit, in the Supper, but hold only that there are bare elements, which differ in no respect from other bread and wine?
I uniformly testify, that as Christ is by no means fallacious
in his signs, so the reality is annexed to the visible element ;
and the thing which the bread and wine figure is truly performed inwardly by the secret virtue of the Spirit. Shortly
after they are forced to confess that there is much which we
properly teach concerning spiritual eating, in which, if there
is no consolation or fruit, where can consolation be found ?
If they do not perceive this, how disgraceful is their stupor ?
But the advocates of a bad cause, having their confidence
only in calumny, must of necessity be thus carried to and fro.
If their purpose is to amuse one another with silly jests, and
try who can utter the greatest falsehoods against us, let them,
if they will, enjoy the sport to satiety. But how blind is it
not to see, that by disseminating and publishing their falsehoods, all they gain is to make the whole obloquy, which
they would fain throw upon us, fall back upon themselves.

It is notorious, that we do not strip the ordinance of Christ
of its reality, nor give the name of simple bread to that which
has been sanctified for a peculiar use. For we clearly teach
that whosoever receives the sacred bread with true faith is
nourished unto spiritual life by the flesh of Christ, just as
the body is sustained by earthly bread. Of what use,
then, is it to darken the cause, by raising smoke which can
be so easily dissipated ? Why do they not rather ingenuously maintain that our sentiments are plainly repugnant to
each other ? We acknowledge, on both sides, that the true
communion of the flesh and blood of Christ is held forth in
the Supper ; but when, in explanation of the mode, we add,
that it is owing to the secret and incomprehensible virtue of

the Spirit that Christ truly feeds our souls from heaven with
the substance of his flesh and blood, and that the bread and
wine are true pledges of the heavenly things which they
figure, because everything which the minister promises according to the command of Christ is fulfilled by its author,
the men of Hildesheim here begin to recoil. As it is no
wish of mine to retaliate injury, I acknowledge that they
speak with more moderation and modesty than those we
have hitherto heard. Worship, and kneeling at the sacrament, are distinctly condemned by them : they hold it superstitious to be in terror of conscience, lest the bread fall to
the ground, or any similar accident occur : and they do not,
like the Magdeburgians, dread the terms mystery and symbol. In short, whether they allow it or not, they have many
things in common with us. Our whole controversy with
them hinges on their affirmation of the two following things
—that the body of Christ is not only spiritually eaten in the
Supper, but is also substantially enclosed under the bread,
and is received not by believers only, but promiscuously by
all. If their purpose is to discuss with me, let them hereafter confine themselves within these limits. If they assail
me with calumny, I presume that the dishonesty of so doing
has already been sufficiently established. They are, therefore, the less to be borne with in charging us with craft—the
only charge by which they attempt to give a plausibility to
their cause ; though the impudence is too gross to deceive
any man of sound mind.

Let us now attend to the terms in which they oppose me.
It is blasphemous derision, they say, to represent that the
body is called and invited forth from heaven, or is fixed to
the bread. Were we speaking of the ordinance of Christ, I
admit there would be an impious scoffing in these words ;
but what blasphemy can there be in stigmatizing gross
errors ? They insist that the flesh of Christ is taken by the
carnal mouth and chewed by the teeth ; they contend that
the same body is immense, and lies invisible under the
bread ; and they will have it that the bread is truly and
properly the body. May not one, without blasphemy, attack

these monstrous errors ? Wherefore there is no ground for
charging us with impudence when we employ some marks to
distinguish the sacred ordinance of Christ from their senseless and absurd figments. As to the ordinance itself, they
will not find any among their party who speak of it more
reverently. How do they prove us to be blasphemers ? Because Paul teaches that the bodies of the pious are temples
of God, and that Christ dwells in their hearts by faith ; as if
in these cases where God the Father and Christ have chosen
us as mansions for themselves, the mode of inhabitation were
not spiritual. If there is any doubt as to this let Paul be
the interpreter of his own expression. He says, Ye are the
temples of God, for his Spirit dwelleth in you. A third passage shows what religious reverence they have in quoting
Scripture. That Christ is the hope of glory to the Colos-
sians Paul terms a mystery hid from eyes. Is he here
including the substance of the flesh of Christ in us ? It is
not either in imagination only, or by general power, that
Christ dwells in us, though we do not eat the substance of
his flesh with our mouths. For that peculiar method not
only more than distinguishes us from brute beasts (a charge
which those Cyclops, with their usual candour, bring against
us,) but from all the profane, while God sanctifies us as
temples for himself, and Christ ingrafts us into union with
his own body, so as to give us a common life with himself.

Were we disposed to vie with them in giving bad names,
we should not want words, but our nature is averse to it, and
our soul utterly abhors it. I would far rather be tongueless
than rival these people in evil speaking. They make themselves chaste and uncorrupted virgins, and liken us to har-
lots who proclaim their shame. They exclaim that we are
unworthy of a place on the earth ; that if we are not suddenly exterminated from the world, the mildest treatment
that can be given will be to banish us to the Scythians or
Indians : they accuse princes of slothfulness, in not employing the sword forthwith to cut off our memory, because we
say that Christ, having left the earth in respect of his flesh,
has been received into heaven. Though from thinking in
their petulance that any liberty may be taken with us, they

misrepresent our words, still let them foam as they may, they will not prevent our doctrine from standing forth clear, viz., that though Christ as God and man, and the Mediator between God and men, whole and undivided, fills heaven and earth, yet in respect of his flesh, he is only in heaven. I have elsewhere mentioned the common saying of the schools, that Christ is everywhere whole, but not wholly, (Lib. 3. Sentent. distin. 23.) Had this been known to these good theologians, it might have calmed their rage. What insult, I ask, is offered to Christ, when the flesh which he assumed, and in which he suffered, is said to have been taken up to heaven just as it was enclosed in the sepulchre? They exclaim, that nothing more atrocious could have been said by Jews or Saracens. Why then do they not turn their rage against the angels, for having presumed to argue that Christ was not in the tomb after he had risen? If Christ is everywhere in the flesh, because of his Divine nature, it was a foolish answer, He is risen, he is not here. Peter, too, deserves to be more severely punished than all blasphemers, for having given utterance to the worst of all blasphemies, viz., that Christ must be contained in the heavens. What shall I say in regard to antiquity? It is certain that all ancient writers, for five centuries downwards from the Apostles, with one consent support our view. Here they bedaub us with the slime of their own Osiander, as if we had any kind of affinity with him. Be it that Osiander, in his insane pride, despised a humiliated Christ; what is that to us, whose piety is too well known to be defamed by such vile falsehoods? Nay, with the best right I throw back the empty talk at their own heads. By denying a humiliated Christ, they extinguish the whole substance of our salvation, and impiously abolish an incomparable pledge of the Divine love toward us. If Christ was not emptied of his glory when he hung on the cross and lay in the sepulchre, where is the humiliation? They pretend that he was then possessed of celestial blessedness, and not only so, but that that flesh in which he suffered sat immortal in the heavens. All this shows that their only purpose is to stupify the mere populace by the noise of their thunder.

They say that the Son of God, our only glory and salvation, reigns in heaven, is most free, is not affixed to the bread, nor tied to the spheres. This, too, is our faith and profession; only let them concede, that the flesh of Christ is invested with heavenly glory, not divested of its own nature. Hence it is that the same man, Christ, who endured a most painful and horrible kind of death for us on the cross, now obtains a name which is above every name, that before him every knee should bow. Herein consists the true and full liberty of his authority and power, that as head of the Church he fills all things. But it is preposterous to wrest this into a proof of the immensity of his flesh. It is much more august while inhabiting heaven, in respect of his flesh, to exhibit his presence both above and below, by the agency of his Spirit, as seems to him good, than to have his power of working necessarily astricted to the presence of his flesh. We say, that Christ, the Mediator, is not prevented by distance of place from infusing life into us from his flesh, and exerting the present efficacy of that flesh in which he once reconciled us to the Father: we declare that flesh gives life to us, just as our body is nourished by earthly bread. This proud faction of giants acknowledges no presence of Christ, unless his flesh is actually placed before them. Is not this to force him into narrow limits? How he came out of the tomb, when it was closed, and came in to the disciples when the doors were shut, I have elsewhere explained, making it clear that they argue ignorantly and erroneously, in inferring from hence, that the ascension of Christ was a mere delusion. And yet while they set no limits to their slanders, they pretend that the thing on which they are wholly intent, is to lead us to a knowledge of the subject.

Meanwhile, some one having happened to charge them with Scythian barbarity, they boil so tumultuously at the expression as to lose sight of the cause, saying, that they are thus unworthily charged because of that doctrine in which they are supported by Christ, the Apostles, and all orthodox writers. But the first point to have considered was, first, whether Christ by saying, Eat, this is my body, transformed his own body so as to make it at the same

moment mortal and immortal, visible and invisible, circumscribed by place and yet immense; and, secondly, whether
posterity were entitled to employ the words of Christ in
support of the monstrous fiction, that those to whom the
bread is given in the Supper eat substantially of the flesh of
Christ. Until they prove this they are not liberated from
the charge. But what can be more impudent than their
shameless boast of the consent of the primitive Church,
which has so often been shown to be against them? They
refuse to admit any trope, alleging, that there cannot be one
in words so clear as, This is my body; as if there was not
equal clearness in the words, On whom you shall see the
Holy Spirit. Were we disposed to indulge in such empty
garrulity, what might we not make of the term *see*, and the
name of *Spirit?* If they say that the form of a dove was
the Spirit, nothing can be more absurd. They here falsely
accuse us of devising a trope, because the extent of our reason is not equal to the height of the mystery. Does that
incomprehensible communion which we assert fall within the
reach of sense? If they cease not to indulge in such impostures, I fear they will only expose their disgrace, which had
better remain hid. So far am I from taking pleasure in
exposing their folly, that I feel ashamed of it. I can easily
allow all the opprobrious epithets which they vent against
us to be read without any defence on our part; only let our
doctrine be at the same time borne in mind, as from it will
at once appear how causelessly they charge us with introducing a trope into the words of Christ merely in deference
to human reason. As I have always loudly enough declared
that Christ is communicated to us in the Supper in an incomprehensible manner, and that we ought accordingly to
adore this mystery which far surpasses our highest conceptions, what is meant by the rabid and dishonest assertion
that we believe nothing but what human reason dictates? I
have already shown, that we hold there is a metonymy in the
sacraments, in accordance with the common and perpetual
usage of holy Scripture, and that, consequently, we have been
compelled to adopt the interpretation which they impugn, not
so much by physical arguments as by the heavenly oracles.

It seems to them plausible to exclaim : Do you hear, O flesh ? Do you hear, O reason ? Consider the letter, consider the sense—that those who eat unworthily, while they comply with the ordinance, are called guilty of the body and blood of the Lord : the Spirit lies not, but every man is a liar ; every one who would dissever the reality from the sign should be placed in this class. But while it is agreed that the body of Christ is truly offered under the symbol of bread, and that his blood is truly offered under the cup, it is mere childish talk to inveigh with so much vehemence against the flesh and reason. How much more appropriately might we reply, Do you hear, O barker ? Do you hear, O frantic, O brutish man ? We assert a true communion of the flesh and blood of Christ in the holy Supper. To what end then all your tumultuous clamour ? How can you expect to pluck the eyes out of your readers, and prevent them from seeing what is so manifest ?

In regard to promiscuous eating, their error has been refuted too clearly to make it necessary to add a word. I hold that profaners of the Supper are guilty of the body of Christ; that is, his offered body, though they receive it not ; just as the Apostle testifies, that the despiser of the gospel tramples the blood of Christ under foot, for no other reason than because Christ by his own voice invites us to a participation with himself. In repeating so often, that the unbelieving and perfidious obey the ordinance of Christ, though they think it acute, they merely trifle. This no doubt is the reason why at the outset they separated the ordinance from the command and the promise ; as if Christ in instituting the Supper did not add the other two things along with it. Nay, what else was the institution of the Supper than a command to perform the ordinance, with the intervention of a promise ? Certainly the institution of Christ is the true law and rule for performing the Supper. But who can say that the rule prescribed by Christ is followed by those who, passing by the command and suppressing the promise, feign some imaginary thing of their own ? It would seem that the obedience of these worthy theologians consists in the illusory and fallacious performance of a naked ceremony without faith.

Tileman Cragius boasts that he is happy at having written these frivolities. I wish that instead of being so carried away to vapid clamour, by the immoderate tide of his joy, he had handled this very serious topic with becoming sobriety and temperance. He flatters his companion Westphal for having incurred so much odium by collecting the passages of Augustine against us. Let him look at the contrary passages which I have here adduced, and it will be strange if he does not fall down from very shame. Though from my love of rectitude and true candour, I confess that I am disgusted with such perverse tempers, yet this trifler is false in alleging that I hate men for whose salvation I purposely consult in the very sharpness of the terms which I employ. For having formerly tried in a friendly epistle what effect meekness and lenity might have upon them, I think I can now only hope for their repentance by repressing their insane pride more harshly.

I believe I have now performed my part in regard to all, unless I were to weary out the reader by repeating the same thing ten times over; indeed I fear I have already prolonged my discourse more than I ought. For what need was there to refute the men of Bremen, who had brought forward almost nothing except an inclination to hurt? After violently oppressing their colleagues at home, the only reason they pretend for spouting their venom upon me at a distance is, because I have condemned the Saxons as drunkards. But if they are not of the number, of what use was it for them to put themselves into such a passion? From this, however, it is apparent that these good Areopagites to save themselves the annoyance of seeing the light, write their decisions in the dark. I had chanced somewhere to speak of Westphal as temulent, having no intention, as I have already explained, to charge him with drunkenness, but merely to apply the language of the Prophet, who speaks of certain persons as drunken but not with wine, namely those who struck with stupor or seized with giddiness, have fallen from a sound mind.

To wrest this which was said of an individual and apply it to a whole nation, is truly a mark of blind temulence.

Let them henceforth learn to be more cautious and not to be borne headlong by blind revenge. How secure they have felt in handling this cause is clear from the simple fact that they lay claim to the victory merely from having proved the eating of the true body without saying anything of the mode. I never made it a question, whether the true body of Christ is eaten in the Supper: I only wish them to consider how it is done. How ridiculously they have paid their court to Westphal, is manifest from the silliness of the subscriptions, on which it pains me to animadvert. In particular, that man of Hildesheim who exults with insane joy, was not worthy of a word, which would have made my replies cumulative by adding two more than was required. Let the others, when they see that any objection which seemed to them plausible has been fully refuted, though they may not have been specially replied to, set it down as an advantage. How eager they are for contests to disturb the whole world, appears from their furious incentives: for they do not disguise that nothing vexes them more than their inability to involve as many as they could wish in the quarrel. The only thing which prevents them from charging all who differ from us with treachery, is the fear of incurring disgrace by disclosing the fewness of their own numbers. Though we should not remark it, the silence of those who, notwithstanding of their disagreement from us, cherish peace, is a sufficient condemnation of Westphal's faction. For they prudently consider what indeed is true, that when we are agreed on both sides that Christ in the Supper offers us his body and blood that our souls may be fed with their substance, and differ in sentiment only as to the mode of eating, there is no just ground for fierce quarrel. Were a just comparison made, there are many things which might impel us to fight more keenly. But so long as any hope of pacification appears, it will not be my fault if mutual good-will is not maintained. Though from being unworthily provoked I have been more vehement in this writing than I was inclined to be, still were a time and place appointed for friendly discussion, I declare and promise that I will be ready to attend, and manifest a spirit of lenity which will not retard the desired success of a pious and holy concord. I am not one who delights in intestine dissension, nor am I so tickled by the gratulations of those who subscribe to me, as to catch at strife as furnishing the materials of victory. On the contrary, I lament that those who ought to have interposed their authority to repress contention have by their delay left me no alternative.

Rumours of some pacificatory convention have been often circulated : and it cannot be believed that princes are so careless as not to feel solicitous to provide some remedy for this calamitous rending of the Church. Therefore as I have no doubt that the subject has been repeatedly agitated in their councils, so I know not what has caused the delay ; only with great sorrow I see that while some pertinaciously cleave to their own views, and others indulge in uncharitable suspicions, this most useful measure is neglected or even spurned. But I feel assured that in the event of a friendly conference, those who can now tolerate a candid defence of the truth would become still more impartial. Henceforth, therefore, let these men rage as they will, my determination is by delivering sound doctrine calmly and without contention, rather to consult for the sober, docile, and modest, than waste words on the petulant, disdainful, and obstinate. Meanwhile, I will beseech my Saviour, whose proper office it is to gather together all that lies scattered throughout the world, that while our adversaries give no hope, he himself would find a remedy for this unhappy dissension.

CLEAR EXPLANATION OF SOUND DOCTRINE

CONCERNING THE

TRUE PARTAKING OF THE FLESH AND BLOOD OF CHRIST IN THE HOLY SUPPER,

IN ORDER TO DISSIPATE THE MISTS OF

TILEMAN HESHUSIUS.

TRUE PARTAKING

OF THE

FLESH AND BLOOD OF CHRIST.

I MUST patiently submit to this condition which providence has assigned me—petulant, dishonest, rabid men, as if they had conspired together, must make me the special object of their virulence. Other most excellent men indeed they do not spare, assailing the living and lacerating the names of the dead ; but the only cause of the more violent onset which they make on me, is, because Satan, whose slaves they are, the more useful he sees my labours to be to the Church of Christ, stimulates them the more strongly to attack me. I say nothing of the old ravers, whose calumnies are already obsolete. A foul apostate of the name of STAPHYLUS has lately started up, and without a word of provocation, has uttered more calumnies against me than against all the others who had depicted his perfidy, bad morals, and depraved disposition. From another quarter one named NI-COLAS LE COQ, has begun to neigh against me. At length from another sink comes forth TILEMAN HESHUSIUS, of whom I would rather have the reader to form a judgment from fact and from his writings than express my own opinion.

O PHILIP MELANCTHON ! for I appeal to thee who art living in the presence of God with Christ, and waiting for us there until we are united with thee in beatific rest : Thou hast said a hundred times, when weary with labour and oppressed with sadness, thou didst lay thy head familiarly on my bosom, Would, would that I could die on this bosom ! Since then, I have wished a thousand times that it had been our lot to be together ! Certainly, thou hadst been readier to maintain contests, and stronger to despise obloquy, and set at nought false accusations. Thus, too, a check had been put on the naughtiness of many who were emboldened in insult by what they termed thy softness. The growlings of Staphylus, indeed, were severely chastised by thee; but though thou didst complain to me privately of Le Coq, as thy own letter to me testifies, yet thou didst neglect to repress his insolence and that of his fellows. I have not indeed forgotten what thou didst write. I will give the very words: I know that with your admirable prudence you judge from the writings of your opponents what their natures are, and to what stage of display they look.

I also remember what I wrote in reply, and will in like manner quote the words: Rightly and prudently dost thou remind me that the object of our antagonists is to exhibit themselves on a stage. But though their expectation will, as I hope and believe, greatly disappoint them, yet were they to carry the applause of the whole world along with them, the more intently must we be fixed on the heavenly Captain under whose eyes we fight. What? will the sacred company of angels, who both animate us by their favour, and show us how to act strenuously by their example, allow us to grow sluggish or advance with hesitation? What of the whole band of holy fathers? will they add no stimulus? What, moreover, of the Church of God which is in the world? When we know that she both aids us by her prayers, and is animated by our example, will her suffrage have no effect upon us? Mine be this stage. Contented with its approbation, though the whole world should hiss me, I will never be discouraged. So far am I from envying their senseless clamour, that I make them welcome to the stale glory of their obscure corner for a brief season. I am not unaware what it is that the world applauds and dislikes, but to me nothing is of more consequence than to follow the rule prescribed by the Master. And I have no doubt that this ingenuousness will ultimately be more acceptable to men of sense and piety, than a soft and equivocal mode of teaching betokening empty fear. As thou acknowledgest that thou owest thyself to God and the Church, I beseech thee to pay the debt as soon as possible. I do not insist in this way, because I trust to throw part of the obloquy upon thee, and so far ease myself. Nay, rather from the love and respect I bear thee, I would willingly, were it allowable, take part of thy burden on my own shoulders. But it is thy own business to consider without any suggestion from me, that if thou do not quickly remove the doubts of all the pious who look up to thee, the debt will scarcely ever be paid at all. I may add, that if this late and evening crowing of the cock does not awaken thee, all men will justly cry out against thee as lazy.

For this appeal to his promise, he had furnished me with an occasion by the following words: I hear that a cock from the banks of the Ister is printing a large volume against me ; if it shall be published, I have determined to reply simply and without ambiguity : this labour I think I owe to God and the Church ; nor in my old age have I any dread of exile and other dangers. This is ingenuously and manfully said ; but in another letter he had confessed, that a temper naturally mild made him desirous of peace and quietness. His words are : As in your last letter you urge me to repress the ignorant clamour of those who are renewing the contest about the worship of bread, (ἀρτολατρεία,) I must tell you that some of those who do so are chiefly instigated by hatred to me, thinking it a plausible occasion for oppressing me. The same love of quiet prevented him from discoursing freely of other matters, the explanation of which was either unpleasant to delicate palates or liable to perverse construction. But how much this saint was displeased with the restlessness of those men who still cease not to rage against us is very apparent from another passage. After congratulating me on my refutation of the blasphemies of Servetus, and declaring that the Church now owed and would to posterity owe me gratitude, and that he entirely assented to my judgment, he adds, that these things were of the greatest importance, and most necessary to be known, and then jestingly subjoins, in speaking of their frivolities, All this is nothing to the Artolatria. Writing to me at Worms, he laments that his Saxon neighbours, who had been sent as colleagues, had left after exhibiting a condemnation of our Churches, and adds : Now they will celebrate their triumphs at home, as if they had gained a Cadmean victory. In another letter, weary of their madness and fury, he does not conceal his desire to be with me.

The things last mentioned are of no consequence to Staphylus, who hires out his petulant tongue to the Roman Antichrist, and for the professed purpose of establishing his tyranny, confounds heaven and earth after the manner of the giants. This miscreant, whose base defection from the faith has left him no sense of shame, I do not deem of importance enough to occupy much time in refuting his errors. The hypothesis on which he places the whole sum and substance of his cause openly discovers his profane contempt of all religion. The whole doctrine which we profess he would bring into suspicion, and so render disreputable, on the simple ground, that since the Papal darkness was dissipated, and eternal truth shone forth, many errors also have sprung up, which he attributes to the revival of the gospel: as if he were not thus raising a quarrel with Christ and his Apostles, rather than with us. The devil never stalked about so much at large, vexing both the bodies and souls of men, as when the heavenly and saving doctrine of Christ gave forth its light. Let him therefore calumniously charge Christ with having come to make demoniacs of those who were formerly sane. Shortly after the first promulgation of the gospel, an incredible number of errors poured in like a deluge on the world. Let Staphylus, the hireling rhetorician of the Pope, keep prating that they flowed from the gospel as their source. Assuredly, if this futile calumny has any effect on futile erring spirits, it will have none on those on whose hearts Paul's admonition is impressed, There must be heresies, in order that those who are approved may be made manifest. (1 Cor. xi. 19.) Of this, Staphylus himself is a striking proof. His brutish rage, which plainly enough is the just reward of his perfidy, confirms all the pious in the sincere fear of God. The main object of this impure man, who is evidently an infidel, is to destroy all reverence for heavenly doctrine : nay, the tendency of his efforts is not only to vilify religion, but to banish all care and zeal for it. Hence his dishonesty not only fails by its own demerits, but is detested, like its author, by all good men. Meanwhile, the false charge, by which he would throw obloquy on us, is easily retorted on himself. Many perverse errors have arisen during the last forty years, starting up in succession, one after another. The reason is, because Satan saw, that by the light of the gospel the impostures by which he had long fascinated the world were overthrown, and therefore plied all his efforts, and employed all his engines, in short, all his infernal powers, either to overthrow the doctrine of Christ, or defeat its progress. It was no slight attestation to the truth of God that it was thus violently assaulted by the lies of Satan. While the sudden emergence of so many impious dogmas thus gives certainty to our doctrine, what will Staphylus gain by spitting at it, unless it be with fickle men, who would fain destroy all distinction between good and evil?

I ask, whether of the many errors about which, for the purpose of throwing obloquy upon us, he makes so much noise, there was no mention made before Luther? He himself enumerates many by which the Church was disturbed at its very commencement. Had the Apostles been charged with engendering all the sects which then sprung up, would they have had no defence? But any concession thus made to them will be good to us also. An easier mode, however, of disposing of the reproach of Staphylus is to reply, that the delirious dreams by which Satan formerly endeavoured to obscure the light of the gospel are now in a great measure suppressed; certainly, scarce a tenth of them has been renewed. Since Staphylus has advertised himself for sale, were any one to pay more for him than the Pope, would he not be ready, in his licentious spirit, to upbraid Christ? Whenever the gospel is brought forward, it brings along with it or engenders numerous errors. Never was the world more troubled with perverse and impious dogmas than at his first advent. But Christ the eternal truth of God will acquit himself without defence from us. Meanwhile, a sufficient answer to the vile charge is to be found in the fact, that there is no ground for imputing to the servants of God any part of that leaven with which Satan, by his ministers, corrupts pure doctrine; and that, therefore, to form a right judgment in such a case, it is always necessary to attend to the source in which the error originates.

Immediately after Luther began to stir up the camarilla of the Papacy, many monstrous men and monstrous opinions suddenly appeared. What affinity with Luther had the Munsterians, the Anabaptists, the Adamites, the Heblerites, the Sabbatarians, the Clancularians, that they should be regarded as his disciples? Did he ever lend them his support? Did he subscribe their most absurd fictions? Nay, with what vehemence did he oppose them, in order to prevent the spreading of the contagion? He had the discernment at once to perceive what noxious pests they would prove. And will this hog still keep grunting, that the errors which were put to flight by our exertion, while the Popish clergy did not at all bestir themselves, proceeded from us? Though he is hardened in effrontery, the futility of the charge will not henceforth impose even on children, who will at once perceive how false and unjust it is to blame us for evils which we most vehemently oppose. As it is perfectly notorious that neither Luther nor any of us ever gave the least countenance to those who, under the impulse of a fanatical spirit, disseminated impious and detestable errors, we are no more bound to bear the odium of their impiety than Paul was to bear that of Hermogenes and Philetus, who taught that the resurrection was past, and all farther hope at an end. (1 Tim. ii. 17.)

Moreover, what are the errors by which our whole doctrine is to be covered with ignominy? The wicked falsehoods which he utters against others I need not refer to: he assigns to me one sect of his own invention. He gives the name of Energists to those who hold that the virtue of Christ's body only, and not the body itself, is in the Supper. He, however, gives me Philip Melancthon for an associate, and to establish both assertions, refers to my writings against Westphal, where the reader will find that in the Supper our souls are nourished by the real body of Christ, which was crucified for us, nay, that spiritual life is transferred into us from the substance of his body. When I teach that the body of Christ is given us for food by the secret energy of the

Spirit, do I thereby deny that the Supper is a communion of the body? See how foully he employs his mouth to please his patrons.

There is another monstrous term which he has invented for the purpose of throwing a stigma upon me. He calls me Bisacramental. But if he would make it a charge against me that I affirm that two sacraments only were instituted by Christ, he should first of all prove that he makes them sep-teplex, as the Papists express it. The Papists obtrude seven sacraments. I do not find that Christ committed to us more than two. Staphylus should prove that four more emanated from Christ, or allow us both to hold and speak the truth. He cannot expect that his bombast is to make heretics of us, while we found on the sure and clear authority of God. He classes Luther, Melancthon, myself, and many others, as new Manichees, and afterwards, to lengthen the catalogue, repeats that the Calvinists are Manichees and Marcionites. It is easy indeed to pick up these reproaches like stones from the street, and throw them at the heads of unoffending passengers. He, however, gives his reasons for comparing us to the Manichees, but they are borrowed partly from a catamite, partly from a cynical buffoon. Of what use then were it for me to clear myself from the most absurd figments in which he indulges? I have no objection, however, to the challenge with which he concludes, namely, to let my treatise on Predestination decide the dispute: for in this way it will soon appear what kind of thistles (*staphyli*) are produced by this wild vine.

I come now to the Cock, (Le Coq,) who with his vile beak declares me a corrupter of the Confession of Augsburg, be-cause denying that in the holy Supper we are made partakers of the substance of the flesh and blood of Christ. But it is declared in my writings more than a hundred times, that so far am I from rejecting the term substance, that I ingenu-ously and readily 'declare, that by the incomprehensible agency of the Spirit, spiritual life is infused into us from the substance of the flesh of Christ. I also constantly admit that we are substantially fed on the flesh and blood of Christ, though I discard the gross fiction of a local intermingling. What then? Because a cock has thought proper to ruffle

his feathers against me, are all minds to be so terror-struck
as to be incapable of judgment ? Not to make myself ridiculous, I decline to give a lengthened refutation of a writing
which proves its author to be no less absurd than its stolid
audacity proves him drunk. It certainly proclaims that
when he wrote he was not *compos mentis.*

But what shall I do with Tileman Heshusius, who, magnificently provided with a superb and sonorous vocabulary, is
confident of prostrating by the breath of his mouth anything
that withstands his assault ? I am also told by worthy
persons who know him better, that another kind of confidence inflates him ; that he has made it his special determination to acquire fame by advancing paradoxes and absurd
opinions. It may be either because an intemperate nature
so hurries him, or because a moderate course of doctrine
leaves him no place for applause, on which his whole soul is
bent even to madness. His tract certainly proves him to be
a man of turbulent temper, as well as headlong audacity and
presumption. To give the reader a sample, I will only mention a few things from the preface. He does the very same
thing which Cicero describes to have been done by the silly
ranters of his day, when, by a plausible exordium stolen from
some ancient oration, they gave hopes of gaining the prize.
In like manner this fine writer, to seize upon the minds of the
readers, collects from his master Melancthon apt and elegant
sentences by which he may ingratiate himself or give an air
of majesty, just as if an ape were to get clothed in purple, or
an ass to cover himself with a lion's skin. He harangues
about the huge dangers he has run, though he has always
hugged his delicacies no less securely than luxuriously.
He talks of his manifold toils, though he has large treasures
laid up at home, has always sold his labours at a high rate,
and by himself alone consumes the whole. It is true, indeed,
that from many places where he wished to make a quiet
nest for himself, he has been repeatedly driven by his own
restlessness. Thus expelled from Gossler, Rostoch, Heidelberg, Bremen, he lately withdrew to Magdeburg. Such ex-
pulsions were meritorious, had he been forced repeatedly to
change his soil from a constant adherence to the truth ; but

when a man full of insatiable ambition, addicted to strife
and quarrelling, makes himself everywhere intolerable by his
savage temper, there is no ground for this complaining of
having been injuriously harassed by others, when his luxu-
rious habits were disturbed by his own unseasonable conduct. Still, however, he was provident enough to take care
that his migrations should not be attended with damage ;
nay, riches only stimulated him.

He next bewails the vast barbarism which appears to be
impending ; as if any greater or worse barbarism were to be
feared than that from him and his fellows. To go no further
for a proof, let the reader consider how fiercely he sneers and
tears at his master, Philip Melancthon, whose memory he ought
sacredly to revere. He does not indeed mention him by name,
but whom does he mean by the supporters of our doctrine who
stand high in the Church for influence and learning, and are
most distinguished theologians ? Indeed, not to leave the
matter to conjecture, he, by his opprobrious epithets, points to
Philip as it were with the finger, and even seems, in writing
his book, to have gone out of his way in search of materials
for traducing him. Well, he could not treat his preceptor
more modestly than by charging him with perfidy and sacrilege ! He hesitates not to accuse him of deceit in employing
ambiguous terms in order to please both parties, and thus
attempting to settle strife by the arts of Theramenes. Then
comes the heavier charge, that he incurred the guilt of a
most pernicious crime in aiming to extinguish the confession
of faith, which ought to be conspicuous in the Church. Such
is the pious gratitude of the scholar not only towards the
master to whom he owes any little learning he may possess,
but towards a man who has deserved so highly of the whole
Church.

When he charges me with having introduced perplexity
into the discussion by my subtleties, the discussion itself
will show what foundation there is for the charge ; but
when he gives the name of Epicurean dogma to the explanation which we give, no less religiously than usefully, in regard to the ordinance of the Supper, what else is it than to
vie in licentious talk with pimps and debauchees ? Let him

look for Epicurism in his own habits. Assuredly both our frugality and assiduous labours for the Church, our constancy amid danger, diligence in the discharge of our office, unwearied zeal in propagating the kingdom of Christ, and integrity in asserting the doctrine of piety—in short, our serious exercise in meditating on the heavenly life, will testify that there is nothing less accordant with our disposition than a profane contempt of God, of which it would be well if the conscience of this Thraso did not accuse him. But I have said more of the man than I intended.

Leaving him, therefore, I purpose briefly to discuss the cause, feeling, that with such as he a more accurate discussion were superfluous. For though there is some show about him, he does nothing more by his magniloquence than vend the old follies and frivolities of Westphal and his fellows. He harangues loftily on the omnipotence of God, on putting implicit faith in his word, and subduing human reason, in terms he may have learned from other sources, of which I believe myself also to be one. I have no doubt, from his childish stolidity in glorying, that he imagines himself to combine the qualities of Melancthon and Luther. From the one he ineptly borrows flowers, and having no better way of rivalling the vehemence of the other, he substitutes bombast and sound. But we have no dispute as to the boundless power of God; and all my writings declare, that far from measuring the mystery of the Supper by human reason, I look up to it with devout admiration. All who in the present day contend strenuously for the candid defence of the truth, will readily admit me into their society. I have proved by fact, that in treating the mystery of the Holy Supper, I do not refuse credit to the word of God; and therefore when Heshusius vociferates against me for doing so, he only in the most offensive manner makes all good men witnesses to his malice and ingratitude. Were it possible to bring him back from vague and sportive flights to a serious discussion of the subject, a few words would suffice.

When he alleges the sluggishness of princes as the obstacle which prevents a holy synod from being assembled to settle disputes, I wish that he himself, and similar furies, did not

obstruct all means of concord.   This he does not disguise a
little farther on, when he denies the expediency of any discussion between us.   What pious synod then would suit his
choice, unless it were one in which two hundred of his companions or thereabouts, well-fed to make their zeal more
fervent, should, according to a custom which has long been
common with them, declare us to be worse and more execrable than the Papists.   The only confession which they want is
a rejection of all inquiry, and an obstinate defence of any
random fiction which may have fallen from them.   It is perfectly obvious, though the devil has fascinated their minds
in a fearful manner, that it is pride more than error that
makes them so pertinacious in assailing our doctrine.

As he pretends that he is an advocate of the Church, and
in order to deceive the simple by fallacious masks, is ever and
anon arrogating to himself the common character of all who
teach rightly, I should like to know who authorized him to
assume this office.   He is ever exclaiming: We teach ; This
is our opinion ; Thus we speak ; So we assert.   Let the farrago which Westphal has huddled together be read, and a
strange repugnance will be found.   Not to go farther for an
example, Westphal boldly affirms that the body of Christ is
chewed by the teeth, and confirms it by quoting with approbation the recantation of Berengarius, as given by Gratian.
This does not please Heshusius, who insists that it is eaten
by the mouth but not touched by the teeth, and greatly disapproves those gross modes of eating.   And yet he reiterates
his *Asserimus*, (we assert,) just as if he were the representative of an university.   This worthy son of Jena repeatedly
charges me with subtleties, sophisms, nay, impostures: as if
there were any equivocation or ambiguity, or any kind of
obscurity in my mode of expression.   When I say that the
flesh and blood of Christ are substantially offered and exhibited to us in the Supper, I at the same time explain the
mode, namely, that the flesh of Christ becomes vivifying to
us, inasmuch as Christ, by the incomprehensible agency of
his Spirit, transfuses his own proper life into us from the
substance of his flesh, so that he himself lives in us, and his
life is common to us.   Who will be persuaded by Heshusius

that there is any sophistry in this clear statement, in which
I both use popular terms and satisfy the ear of the learned?
Would he only desist from the futile calumnies by which he
darkens the cause, the whole point would at once be decided.

After Heshusius has exhausted all his bombast, the whole
question hinges on this, Does he who denies that the body
of Christ is eaten by the mouth, take away the substance
of his body from the sacred Supper? I come to close
quarters at once with the man who maintains that we are
not partakers of the substance of the flesh of Christ, unless
we eat it with our mouths. His expression is, that the very
substance of the flesh and blood must be taken by the
mouth; whereas I define the mode of communication without
ambiguity, by saying, that Christ by his boundless and wondrous power unites us into the same life with himself, and
not only applies the fruit of his passion to us, but becomes
truly ours by communicating his blessings to us, and accordingly conjoins us to himself in the same way in which head
and members unite to form one body. I do not restrict this
union to the divine essence, but affirm that it belongs to
the flesh and blood, inasmuch as it was not simply said, My
Spirit, but, My flesh is meat indeed; nor was it simply said,
My Divinity, but, My blood is drink indeed.

Moreover, I do not interpret this communion of flesh and
blood as applying only to the common nature, in respect that
Christ, by becoming man, made us sons of God with himself
by virtue of fraternal fellowship; but I distinctly affirm, that
our flesh which he assumed is vivifying by becoming the
material of spiritual life to us. And I willingly embrace the
saying of Augustine, As Eve was formed out of a rib of Adam,
so the origin and beginning of life to us flowed from the side
of Christ. And although I distinguish between the sign and
the thing signified, I do not teach that there is only a bare
and shadowy figure, but distinctly declare that the bread is
a sure pledge of that communion with the flesh and blood
of Christ which it figures. For Christ is neither a painter,
nor a player, nor a kind of Archimedes, who presents an
empty image to amuse the eye, but he truly and in reality
performs what he promises by an external symbol. Hence

I conclude that the bread which we break is truly the communion of the body of Christ. But as this connection of Christ with his members depends on his incomprehensible energy, I am not ashamed to admire this mystery which I feel and acknowledge to transcend the reach of my mind.

Here our Thraso makes an uproar, and cries out that it is great impudence as well as sacrilegious audacity to corrupt the plain word of God, which declares, This is my body—that one might as well deny the Son of God to be man. But I rejoin, that if he would evade this very charge of sacrilegious audacity, he must on his own terms become an anthropomorphite. He insists that no amount of absurdity shall induce us to change one syllable. Hence as the Scripture distinctly attributes to God feet, hands, eyes, and ears, a throne, and a footstool, it follows that he is corporeal. As he is said in the song of Miriam to be a man of war, (Ex. xv.,) it will not be lawful by any congruous exposition to soften this harsh mode of expression. Let Heshusius get into the heroics if he will, his insolence cannot withstand this strong and invulnerable argument. The ark of the covenant is distinctly called the Lord of hosts, and indeed with such asseveration that the Prophet emphatically exclaims, (Ps. xxiv.,) Who is this king of glory? Jehovah himself is king of hosts.

Here we do not say that the Prophet inconsiderately gave utterance to that which at first glance is seen to be absurd, as this fellow wickedly babbles ; but after reverently embracing what he says, we no less piously than aptly interpret that the name of God is transferred to a symbol because of its inseparable connection with the thing and reality. Nay, this is a general rule in regard to all the sacraments, which not only human reason compels us to adopt, but which a sense of piety and the uniform usage of piety dictate. No man is so ignorant or senseless as not to know that in all the sacraments the Spirit of God by the Prophets and Apostles employs this peculiar form of expression. Nay, one who will dispute this should be sent to his rudiments. Jacob saw the Lord of hosts sitting on a ladder. Moses saw him both in a burning bush and in the flame of Mount Horeb. If the letter is pertinaciously clung to, how could God, who is invisible, be seen ?

Heshusius repudiates examination, and leaves us no other resource than to shut our eyes and acknowledge that God is visible and invisible. But an explanation at once clear and accordant with piety, and in fact necessary, spontaneously presents itself, viz., that God is never seen as he is, but gives manifest signs of his presence adapted to the capacity of believers.

In this way there is no exclusion of the presence of the divine essence when the name of God is metonymically applied to the symbol by which God represents himself truly—not figuratively merely but substantially. A dove is called the Spirit. Is this to be strictly taken, just as when Christ declares that God is a Spirit? (Matt. iii. 13; John iv. 24.) Surely a manifest difference is apparent. For although the Spirit was then truly and essentially present, he however displayed the presence both of his virtue and his essence by a visible symbol. How wicked it is in Heshusius to accuse us of feigning a symbolical body is clear from this, that no candid man infers that a symbolical Spirit was seen in the baptism of Christ, from his having truly appeared under the symbol or external appearance of a dove. We acknowledge then, that in the Supper we eat the same body which was crucified, although the expression in regard to the bread is metonymical, so that it may be truly said to be symbolically the real body of Christ, by the sacrifice of which we have been reconciled to God. And though there is some diversity in the expressions, The bread is a sign, or figure, or symbol of the body; and The bread signifies the body, or is a metaphorical, or metonymical, or synecdochical expression for it, they perfectly agree in substance, and therefore it is mere trifling in Westphal and Heshusius to start difficulties where none exist.

A little farther on he starts off in a different direction, and says, that whatever may be the variety in expression, we all hold the very same sentiments, but that I alone deceive the simple by ambiguities. But where are the ambiguities, on the removal of which my deceit is to stand detected? Perhaps his rhetoric can furnish a new kind of perspicuity which will clearly manifest my alleged equivocation. Meanwhile he unworthily includes us all in the charge of teaching that the bread is the sign of the absent body, as if I had not long ago distinctly admonished my readers of two kinds of absence, to acquaint them that the body of Christ is indeed absent in respect of place, but that we enjoy a spiritual participation in it, every obstacle from distance being surmounted by his divine energy. Hence it follows, that our dispute relates neither to presence nor to substantial eating, but only as to the mode of both. We neither admit a local presence, nor that gross or rather brutish eating of which Heshusius talks so absurdly when he says, that Christ in respect of his human nature is present on the earth in the substance of his body and blood, so that he is not only eaten in faith by his saints, but also by the mouth bodily without faith by the wicked.

Without adverting at present to the absurdities here involved, I ask, where is the true touchstone, the express declaration of the word of God? Assuredly it cannot be found in the barbarous terms now quoted. Let us see, however, what the explanation is which he thinks sufficient to stop the mouths of the Calvinists—an explanation so senseless that it must rather open their mouths to protest against it. He vindicates himself and the churches of his party from the error of transubstantiation with which he falsely alleges that we charge them. For though they have many things in common with the Papists, we do not therefore confound them together and leave no distinction. I should rather say, it is long since I showed that the Papists in their dreams are considerably more modest and more sober. And what does he himself say? As the words are joined together contrary to the order of nature, it is right to maintain the literal sense by which the bread is properly the body. The words therefore, to be accordant with the thing, behove to be pronounced contrary to the order of nature.

He afterwards excuses their different forms of expression, when they assert that the body is under the bread or with the bread. But how will he persuade any one that it is under the bread, unless it be in respect that the bread is a sign? How, too, will he persuade any one that the bread is not to be worshipped if it be properly Christ? The expression, that the body is in the bread or under the bread, he calls improper, because the substantial word has its proper and genuine signification in the union of the bread and Christ. In vain, therefore, does he refute the inference that the body is in the bread, and therefore the bread should be worshipped. This inference is the invention of his own brain. The argument we have always used is this, If Christ is in the bread, he should be worshipped under the bread. Much more might we argue, that the bread should be worshipped if it be truly and properly Christ.

He thinks he gets out of the difficulty by saying, that the union is not hypostatical. But who will concede to a hundred or a thousand Heshusiuses the right to lay worship under whatever restrictions they please? Assuredly no man of sense will be satisfied in conscience with the silly quibble, that the bread, though it is truly and properly Christ, is not to be worshipped, because they are not hypostatically one. The answer will instantly occur, that things must be the same when the one is substantially predicated of the other. The words of Christ do not speak of anything accidental to the bread, but if we are to believe Heshusius and his fellows, they plainly and unambiguously assert, that the bread is the body of Christ, and therefore Christ himself. Nay, they affirm more of the bread than can be lawfully affirmed of the human nature of Christ. But how monstrous is it to give more honour to the bread than to our Saviour's sacred flesh? Of this flesh it cannot truly be affirmed, as they insist on affirming in regard to the bread, that it is properly Christ. Though he may deny that he imagines any community of being ($\mu\epsilon\tau o\upsilon\sigma\iota a,$) I will always force him to admit, that if the bread is properly the body, it is one and the same with the body. He subscribes to the sentiment of Irenæus, that there are two different things in the Supper—an earthly and a heavenly, namely, the bread and the body. But I not do see how this can be reconciled with the fictitious identity, which, though he does not express it in a word, he certainly asserts in fact, inasmuch as things must be the same whenever we can say of them, That is this, This is that.

The same reasoning applies to the local inclosing which Heshusius pretends to repudiate, when he says, that Christ is not contained by place, and can be at the same time in several places. To vindicate himself, he says, that the bread is the body not only properly, truly, and really, but also definitively. Should I answer that I cannot give any meaning to these monstrous contradictions, he will meet me with what he and his fellows bring forward on all occasions as a shield of Ajax—that reason is inimical to faith. This I readily grant if he is to be regarded as a rational animal.

Three kinds of reason are to be considered, but he at one bound overleaps them all. There is a reason naturally implanted which cannot be condemned without insult to God, but it has limits which it cannot overstep without being immediately lost. Of this we have a sad proof in the fall of Adam. There is another kind of reason which is vicious, especially in a corrupt nature, and is manifested when mortal man, instead of receiving divine things with reverence, would subject them to his own judgment. This reason is mental intoxication, or pleasing insanity, and is at eternal variance with the obedience of faith, since we must become fools in ourselves before we can begin to be wise unto God. In regard to heavenly mysteries, therefore, we must abjure this reason, which is nothing better than mere fatuity, and if accompanied with arrogance, grows to the height of madness. But there is a third kind of reason, which both the Spirit of God and Scripture sanction. Heshusius, however, disregarding all distinction, confidently condemns, under the name of human reason, everything which is opposed to the frenzied dream of his own mind.

He charges us with paying more deference to reason than to the word of God. But what if we adduce no reason that is not derived from the word of God and founded on it? Let him show that we profanely philosophize on the mysteries of God, that we measure his heavenly kingdom by our sense, that we subject the oracles of the Holy Spirit to the judgment of the flesh, that we admit nothing that does not approve itself to our own wisdom. The fact is far otherwise. For what is more repugnant to human reason than that souls immortal by creation, should derive life from mortal flesh? This we assert. What is less accordant with earthly wisdom, than that the flesh of Christ should infuse its vivifying energy into us from heaven ? What is more foreign to our sense, than that corruptible and fading bread should be an undoubted pledge of spiritual life ? What more remote from philosophy, than that the Son of God, who in respect of human nature is in heaven, so dwells in us, that everything which has been given him of the Father is common to us, and hence the immortality with which his flesh has been endowed is ours ? All these things we clearly testify, while Heshusius has nothing to urge but his delirious dream, That the flesh of Christ is eaten by unbelievers, and yet is not vivifying. If he refuses to believe that there is any reason without philosophy, let him learn from a short syllogism : He who does not observe the analogy between the sign and the thing signified, is an unclean animal, not cleaving the hoof; he who asserts that the bread is truly and properly the body of Christ, destroys the analogy between the sign and the thing signified ; therefore, he who asserts that the bread is properly the body, is an unclean animal, not cleaving the hoof.

From this syllogism let him know, that even though there were no philosophy in the world, he is an unclean animal. But his object in this indiscriminate condemnation of reason, no doubt was to procure license to his own darkness, and give effect to the inference, that as when mention is made of the crucifixion, and of the benefits which the living and sub-stantial body of Christ procured, the body referred to cannot be understood to be symbolical, typical, or allegorical, so the words of Christ, This is my body, This is my blood, cannot be understood symbolically or metonymically, but substan-tially. As if mere tyros did not see that the term symbol is applied to the bread, not to the body, and that the metony-my is not in the substance of the body, but in the texture of the words. And yet he here exults as if he were an Olympic victor, and bids us try the whole force of our intellect on this argument—an argument so absurd, that I will not deign to refute it even in jest. For while he says, that we turn our backs, and, at the same time, stimulates himself to press forward, his own procedure betrays his manifest inconsist-ency. He admits that we understand that the substance

of the body of Christ is given, seeing that Christ is wholly
ours by faith. It is well that he harmlessly butts at the air
with his own horns, and makes it unnecessary for us to be on
our guard. I would ask, if we turn our backs when we thus
distinctly expose his calumny in regard to an allegorical
body? But as if he had fallen into a fit of forgetfulness,
after he has come to himself, he brings a new plea, and
charges us with holding the absence of the body, telling us
that the giving of which we speak, has no more effect than
the giving of a field to one who was to be immediately removed from it. How dare he thus liken the incomparable
virtue of the Holy Spirit to lifeless things, and represent
the gathering of the produce of a field, as equivalent to that
union with the Son of God, which enables our souls to obtain life from his body and blood? Surely in this matter
he overacts the rustic. I may add, that it is false to say
that we expound the words of Christ as if the thing were
absent, when it is perfectly well known that the absence of
which we speak is confined to place and actual sight. Although Christ does not exhibit his flesh as present to our
eyes, nor by change of place descend from his celestial glory,
we maintain that there is nothing in this distance to prevent him from being truly united to us.

But let us attend to the kind of presence for which he insists. At first sight his view seems calm and sensible. He
admits that Christ is everywhere by a communication of
properties, as was taught by the fathers, and that, accordingly, it is not the body of Christ that is everywhere, the
ubiquity being ascribed in the concrete to the whole person
in respect of the union of the Divine nature. This is so exactly our doctrine, that one is tempted to think he means
to curry favour with us by disguising his own. Nor have
we any difficulty in agreeing with him, when he adds, that
it is impossible to comprehend how the body of Christ is in
a certain part of heaven, above the heavens, and yet the person of Christ is everywhere, ruling in equal power with the
Father. Nay, it is notorious to all, how violently I have
been assailed by his party for the defence of this very doctrine. And in order to express this in a still more palpable

form, I employed the trite dictum of the schools, that Christ is whole everywhere, but not wholly, (*totus ubique sed non totum ;*) in other words, in his entire person of Mediator he fills heaven and earth, though in his flesh he is in heaven, which he has chosen as the abode of his human nature, until he appear to judgment.   What then prevents us from adopting this evident distinction, and agreeing with each other ?   Simply, because Heshusius immediately perverts what he had said, and insists that Christ did not exclude his human nature when he promised to be present on the earth.   Shortly after, he says, that Christ is present with his Church, dispersed in different places, and this in respect not only of his Divine, but also of his human nature.   In a third passage he is still plainer, and maintains, that there is no absurdity in holding that he may, in respect of his human nature, exist in different places wherever he pleases. And he rudely rejects what he terms the physical axiom, that one body cannot be in different places.   What can now be clearer than that he holds the body of Christ to be immense, and imagines a monstrous ubiquity ?   A little before he had admitted, that the body is in a certain place in heaven, now he assigns it different places.   This is to lacerate the body, and refuse to raise his heart upwards.

He objects that Stephen was not carried above all heavens to see Jesus ; as if I had not repeatedly disposed of this quibble.   As Christ was not recognised by his two disciples when he sat familiarly with them at the same table, not on account of any metamorphosis, but because their eyes were holden ; so eyes were given to Stephen to penetrate even to the heavens.   Surely it is not without cause mentioned by Luke, that he lifted up his eyes to heaven, and beheld the glory of God.   Nor without cause does Stephen himself declare, that the heavens were opened to him, so that he beheld Jesus standing on the right hand of his Father. This, I presume, makes it plain, how absurdly Heshusius endeavours to bring him down to the earth.   With equal shrewdness he infers, that Christ was on the earth when he showed himself to Paul ; as if we had never heard of that carrying up to the third heaven, which Paul himself so magnificently proclaims. What says Heshusius to this? His words are: Paul could not be translated above all heavens, whither the Son of God ascended. I have nothing to add, but that no degree of contempt can be too great for the man who thus dares to give the lie to Paul when testifying of himself. But it is said, that as Christ distinctly offers his body in the bread, and his blood in the wine, all pertness and curiosity must be curbed. This I admit; but it does not follow that we are to shut our eyes in order to exclude the rays of the sun. Nay, rather, if the mystery is deserving of contemplation, it becomes us to consider in what way Christ can give us his body and blood for meat and drink. For if the whole Christ is in the bread, nay, if the bread itself is Christ, we may with more truth affirm, that the body is Christ—an affirmation not more abhorrent to piety than to common sense. But if we refuse not to raise our hearts upwards, we shall feed on Christ entire, as well as expressly on his flesh and blood. And indeed when Christ invites us to eat his body, and to drink his blood, there is no necessity to bring him down from heaven, or require his actual presence in several places, in order to put his body and his blood within our lips. Amply sufficient for this purpose is the sacred bond of union with him, when we are united into one body by the secret agency of the Spirit. Hence I agree with Augustine, that in the bread we receive that which hung upon the cross; but I utterly abhor the delirious fancy of Heshusius and his fellows, that it is not received unless it is introduced into the carnal mouth. The communion of which Paul discourses does not require any local presence, unless we are to hold, that Paul, in teaching that we are called to communion with Christ, (1 Cor. i. 9,) either speaks of a nonentity, or places Christ locally wherever the gospel is preached.

The dishonesty of this babbler is intolerable, when he says, that I confine the term κοινωνια to the fellowship which we have with Christ, by partaking of his benefits. But before proceeding to discuss this point, it is necessary to see how ingeniously he escapes from us. When Paul says, that those who eat the sacrifice are partakers of the altar, (1 Cor. ix. 13,) this skilful expounder gives as the reason, that each receives a part from the altar, and from this he concludes, that my interpretation is false. But what interpretation? Only that which he has coined out of his own brain; communion, as stated by me, being not only in the fruit of Christ's death, but also in his body offered for our salvation. But this interpretation also, which he regards as different from the other, is rejected by him as excluding the presence of Christ in the Supper. Here let my readers carefully attend to the kind of presence which he imagines, and to which he clings so doggedly, that he can almost regard the communion which John the Baptist had with Christ as a mere nullity, provided he is allowed to hold that the body of Christ was swallowed by Judas. I would ask this reverend doctor how, if those are partakers of the altar who divide the sacrifice into parts, he can exonerate himself from the charge of rending while he gives each his part? If he answers, that this is not what he means, let him correct his expression. He must, at all events, surrender what he regarded as the citadel of his defence, and desist from asserting that I leave nothing in the Supper but a right to a thing that is absent, seeing I uniformly maintain, that through the agency of the Spirit there is a present exhibition of the thing, though it is absent in respect of place. Still, while I refuse to subscribe to the barbarous eating, by which he insists that Christ is swallowed by the mouth, he will continue, as before, to give vent in invective to his implacable fury. Verbally, indeed, he denies that he inquires concerning the mode of presence, and yet he insists no less absurdly than imperiously on the reception of his monstrous dogma, that the body of Christ is eaten corporeally by the mouth. These, indeed, are the very words he employs. In another passage, he says, We assert not only that we become partakers of the body of Christ by faith, but that also by our mouths we receive Christ essentially or corporeally within us; and in this way we testify that we give credit to the words of St. Paul and the evangelists.

But we, too, reject the sentiments of all who deny the presence of Christ in the Supper, and I therefore ask what the kind of presence is for which he quarrels with us ? Obviously that which is dreamt by himself and others who share in his frenzy. To cloak such gross fancies with the names of Paul and the evangelists is the height of effrontery. With them for his witnesses, how will he prove that the body of Christ is taken by the mouth both corporeally and internally ? He has elsewhere acknowledged that it is not chewed by the teeth nor touched by the palate. Why should he be so afraid of the touch of the palate or throat, while he ventures to assert that it is absorbed by the bowels ? What does he mean by the expression " within us ?" (*intra nos.*) By what is the body of Christ received after it has passed the mouth ? After the mouth, if I mistake not, the passage of the body is to the viscera or intestines. If he say that we are calumniously throwing odium on him by the use of offensive terms, I should like to know what difference there is between saying that that which is received by the mouth is taken corporeally within, and saying that it passes into the viscera or intestines ? Henceforth let the reader understand, and be careful to remember, that whenever Heshusius charges me with denying the presence of Christ in the Supper, the only thing for which he blames me is for thinking it absurd to hold that Christ is swallowed by the mouth, and passes bodily into the stomach. And yet he complains that I sport ambiguous expressions ; as if it were not my perspicuity that maddens him and his associates. Of what ambiguity can he convict me ? He admits that I assert the true and substantial eating of the flesh and drinking of the blood of Christ ; but he says, that when my meaning is investigated, I speak of the receiving of merit, fruit, efficacy, virtue, and power, descending from heaven. Here his malignant absurdity is seen not darkly, but as in open day, while he confounds virtue and power with merit and fruit. Is it usual for any one to say that merit descends from heaven ? Had he one particle of candour, he would have quoted me as either speaking or writing in such terms as these,—To our having substantial communion with the flesh of Christ there is no necessity for any change of place, since, by the secret virtue of the Spirit, he infuses his life into us from heaven. Distance does not at all prevent Christ from dwelling in us, or us from being one with him, since the efficacy of the Spirit surmounts all natural obstacles.

A little farther on we shall see how shamefully he contradicts himself when he quotes my words, The blessings of Christ do not belong to us until he has himself become ours. Let him go now, and by employing the term *merit* mystify the nature of the communion which I clearly teach. He argues that if Christ is in heaven he is not in the Supper, that instead of him we have symbols merely ; as if the Supper were not to the true worshippers of God a heavenly action, or a kind of vehicle which carries them above the world. But what is this to Heshusius, who not only halts on the earth, but does all he can to keep grovelling in the mire ? Paul teaches that in baptism we put on Christ. (Gal. iii. 27.) How acutely will Heshusius argue that this cannot be if Christ remain in heaven ? When Paul spoke thus it never occurred to him that Christ must be brought down from heaven, because he knew that he is united to us in a different manner, and that his blood is not less present to cleanse our souls than water to cleanse our bodies. If he rejoins that there is a difference between " eating" and " putting on," I answer, that to surround us with clothing is as necessary in the latter case as the internal reception of food is in the former. Indeed, nothing more is needed to prove the folly or malice of the man than his refusal to admit any but a local presence. Though he denies it to be physical, and even quibbles upon the point, he however places the body of Christ wherever the bread is, and accordingly maintains that it is in several places at the same time. As he does not hesitate so to express himself, why may not the presence for which he insists be termed local ?

Of a similar nature is his objection that the body is not received truly if it is received symbolically ; as if by a true symbol we excluded the exhibition of the reality. He ultimately says it is mere imposture, unless a twofold eating is asserted, viz., a spiritual and a corporeal. How ignorantly and erroneously he wrests the passages which relate to spiritual eating, I need not observe, as children may see how ridiculous he makes himself. In regard to the subject itself, if a division is vicious when its members coincide with each other, (and this is one of the first lessons which boys learn from their rudiments,) how will he escape the charge of having thus blundered? For if there is any eating which is not spiritual, it will follow that in the ordinance of the Supper there is no operation of the Spirit. Thus it will naturally be called the flesh of Christ, just as if it were a fading and corruptible food, and the chief earnest of eternal salvation will be unaccompanied by the Spirit. Should even this not overcome his effrontery, I ask, whether independently of the use of the Supper, there be no other eating than spiritual, which according to him is opposed to corporeal? He distinctly affirms that this is nothing else than faith, by which we apply to ourselves the benefits of Christ's death. What then becomes of the declaration of Paul, That we are flesh of the flesh of Christ, and bone of his bones? (Eph. v. 30.) What will become of the exclamation, This is a great mystery? For if with the exception of the application of merit, nothing is left to believers beyond the present use of the Supper, the head will always be separated from the members, except at the particular moment when the bread is put into the mouth and throat. We may add on the testimony of Paul, (1 Cor. i.) that fellowship with Christ is the result of the gospel no less than of the Supper. We saw a little ago in what terms Heshusius speaks of this fellowship: but the same thing which Paul affirms of the Supper he had previously affirmed of the doctrine of the gospel. Were we to listen to this trifler, what would become of that noble discourse in which our Saviour promises that his disciples should be one with him, as he and the Father were one? There cannot be a doubt that he there speaks of a perpetual union.

In making this absurd division, Heshusius is not ashamed to represent himself as an imitator of the fathers. He quotes a passage from Cyril on the fifteenth chapter of John: as if Cyril did not there plainly contend that the participation which we have of Christ in the Supper proves that we are united with him in respect of the flesh. He is disputing with the Arians, who, quoting the words of Christ, That they may be one, as thou Father art in me and I in thee, pretended to infer from thence that the unity of Christ with the Father was not in reality and essence, but only in consent. Cyril, to dispose of this quibble, answers, that we are essentially one with Christ, and in proof of it, instances the force of the mystical benediction. Were he contending only for a momentary communion, what could be more irrelevant? But it is no wonder that Heshusius thus betrays his utter want of shame, since he even claims the support of Augustine, who, as all the world knows, is diametrically opposed to him. He says, that Augustine distinctly admits (Serm. 2 de Verb. Dom.) that there are different modes of eating the flesh, and affirms that Judas and other hypocrites ate the true flesh of Christ. But if it shall turn out that the epithet *true* is interpolated, how will Heshusius exonerate himself from a charge of forgery? Let the passage then be read, and without a word from me, it will be seen that Heshusius in using the term *true flesh*, has falsified.

But he will say that a twofold eating is there mentioned: as if the same distinction did not everywhere occur in our writings also. Augustine there employs the terms *flesh* and *sacrament of flesh* indiscriminately in the same sense. (Ep. 23, ad Bonif.) This he has also done in several other passages. If an explanation is asked, there cannot be a clearer interpreter than himself. He says, that from the resemblance which the sacraments have to the things, they often receive their names; for which reason the sacrament of the body of Christ is in a manner the body of Christ. Could he testify more clearly that the bread is termed the body of Christ not properly, but because of the resemblance? He elsewhere says, that the body of Christ falls on the ground, but this is in the same sense in which he says that it is consumed: Did we not here apply the resemblance formerly noticed, what could be more absurd? nay, what a calumny would it be against this holy writer to represent him as holding that the body of Christ is taken into the intestines? It is long since I accurately explained what Augustine means by a twofold eating, namely, that while some receive the virtue of the sacrament, others receive only a visible sacrament; that it is one thing to take inwardly, another outwardly; one thing to eat with the heart, another to chew with the teeth. And he at last concludes that the sacrament which is placed on the Lord's table is taken by some unto destruction, by others unto life—that the reality of which the Supper is the sign, gives life to all who partake of it. In another passage, also, treating in express terms of this question, he distinctly refutes those who pretended that the wicked eat the body of Christ not only sacramentally but in reality. (August. Hom. 26 in Joan; De Civit. Dei, 21, c. 25; Contra Faust. 1. 13, c. 13; see also in Joan. Tract. 25-27, 59.) To show our entire agreement with this holy writer, we say that those who are united by faith, so as to be his members, eat his body truly or in reality, whereas those who receive nothing but the visible sign, eat only sacramentally. He often expresses himself in the very same way.

But as Heshusius by his importunity compels us so often to repeat, let us bring forward the passage in which Augustine says that Judas ate the bread of the Lord against the Lord, whereas the other disciples ate the bread of the Lord. It is certain that that pious teacher never makes a threefold division. But why mention him alone? Not one of the fathers has taught that in the Supper we receive anything but that which remains with us after the use of the Supper. Heshusius will exclaim, that the Supper is therefore useless to us; for his words are, "Why does Christ by a new commandment enjoin us to eat his body in the Supper, and even give us bread, since not only himself, but all the prophets, urge us to eat the flesh of Christ by faith? Does he then in the Supper command nothing new?" I in my turn ask him, Why God anciently enjoined circumcision and sacrafice, and all the exercises of faith, and also why he instituted baptism? Without his answer, the explanation is sufficiently simple, viz., that God gives no more by visible signs than by his word, but gives in a different manner, because our weakness stands in need of a variety of helps. He asks, How very improper must the expression be, " This cup is the New Testament in my blood," if the whole is not corporeal? To this we all long ago answered, that that which is offered to us by the gospel without the Supper is sealed to us by the Supper, and hence communion with Christ is no less truly conferred upon us by the gospel than by the Supper. He asks, How it is called the Supper of the "New Testament," if types only are exhibited in it as under the Old Testament? First, I would beg my readers to oppose to these silly objections the clear statements which I have delivered in my writings;—then they will not only find what distinction ought to be made between the sacraments of the new and of the ancient Church, but will detect Heshusius in the very act of theft, stealing everything but his own ignorant idea, that nothing was given to the ancients except types. As if God had deluded them with empty figures, or as if Paul's doctrines were nugatory, when he teaches, that they ate the same spiritual food with us, and drank the same spiritual drink. (1 Cor. x. 3.) Heshusius at last concludes—" If the blood of Christ be not given substantially in the Supper, it is absurd and contrary to the sacred writings to give the name of ' new covenant' to wine, and therefore there must be two kinds of eating, one spiritual and metaphorical, which was common to the fathers, and another corporeal, which is proper to us." It were enough for me to deny the inference which might move even children to laughter, but how profane the talk which contemptuously applies the term metaphorical to that which is spiritual; as if he would subject the mystical and incomprehensible virtue of the Spirit to grammarians.

Lest he should allege that he has not been completely answered, I must again repeat. As God is always true, the figures were not fallacious by which he promised his ancient people life and salvation in his only begotten Son. Now, however, he plainly represents to us in Christ the things which he then showed as from a distance, and hence Baptism and the Supper not only set Christ before us more fully and clearly than the legal rites did, but exhibit him as present. Paul accordingly teaches, that we now have the body instead of shadows, (Col. ii. 18;) not only because Christ has been once manifested, but because Baptism and the Supper, like sure pledges, confirm his presence with us. Hence appears the great distinction between our sacraments and those of the ancient people. This, however, by no means deprives them of the reality of the things which Christ now exhibits more fully, clearly, and perfectly, as might be expected from his presence.

His insisting so keenly and obstinately that the unworthy eat Christ I would leave as undeserving of refutation, were it not that he regards this as the chief bulwark of his cause. He calls it a grave matter, and one fit for pious and learned men to make the subject of a mutual conference. If I grant this, how comes it that hitherto it has been impossible to obtain from his party a calm discussion of the question? If discussion is allowed, there will be no difficulty in arranging it. The arguments of Heshusius are, first: Paul distinguishes the blessed bread from common bread, not only by the article but by the demonstrative pronoun: as if the same distinction were not sufficiently made by those who call the sacred and spiritual feast a pledge and badge of our union with Christ. The second argument is: Paul more manifestly asserts, that the unworthy eat the flesh of Christ when he says, that they become guilty of the body and blood of Christ. But I ask, whether he makes them guilty of the body as offered or as received? There is not one syllable about receiving. I admit, that by partaking of the sign they insult the body of Christ, inasmuch as they reject the inestimable boon which is offered them. This disposes of the objection of Heshusius, that Paul is not speaking of the general guilt under which all the wicked lie, but teaches that the wicked by the actual taking of the body bring down a heavier judgment on themselves. It is indeed true, that contumely is offered to the flesh of Christ by those who with impious disdain and contempt reject it when it is held forth for food; for we maintain, that in the Supper Christ holds forth his body to reprobates as well as to believers, but in such manner that those who profane the Sacrament by unworthy receiving make no change on its nature, nor in any respect impair the effect of the promise. But although Christ remains like to himself and true to his promises, it does not follow that that which is given is received by all indiscriminately.

Heshusius amplifies and says, that Paul does not speak of a slight fault. Nor is it a slight fault which an Apostle denounces when he says, that the wicked, even though they do not approach the Supper, crucify to themselves the Son of God, and put him to an open shame, and trample his sacred blood under their feet. (Heb. vi. 6; x. 29.) They can do all this without swallowing Christ. The reader sees, whether, according to the silly talk of Heshusius, I twist wondrously about, and involve myself in darkness from a hatred of the light, when I say that men are guilty of the body and blood of Christ when they repudiate both the gifts, to a participation in which eternal truth invites them. But he rejoins, that this sophism is brushed away like a spider's web by the words of Paul, when he says, that they eat and drink judgment to themselves: as if unbelievers under the law did not also eat judgment to themselves, by presuming while impure and polluted to eat the paschal lamb. And yet Heshusius, after his own fashion, vaunts of having made it clear that the body of Christ is taken by the wicked. How much more correct is the sentiment of Augustine, that many in the crowd press on Christ without ever touching him? Still he insists, and exclaims that nothing can be clearer than the declaration, that the wicked do not discern the Lord's body, and that darkness is violently and intentionally thrown on the clearest truth by all who refuse to admit that the body of Christ is taken by the unworthy. He might have some colour for this, if I denied that the body of Christ is given to the unworthy; but as they impiously reject what is liberally offered to them, they are deservedly condemned for profane and brutish contempt, inasmuch as they set at nought that victim by which the sins of the world were expiated, and men reconciled to God.

Meanwhile, let the reader observe how warm Heshusius has waxed. He lately began by saying, that the subject was a proper one for mutual conference between pious and learned men, but here he flames fiercely against all who shall presume to doubt or inquire. In the same way he is enraged at us for maintaining that the thing which the bread figures is conferred and performed not by the minister but by Christ. Why is he not rather enraged at Augustine and Chrysostom, the one of whom teaches that it is administered by man, but in a divine manner—on earth, but in a heavenly manner, while the other speaks *verbatim* thus, Now Christ is ready ; he who spread the table at which he sat now conse- crates this one. For the body and blood of Christ are not made by him who has been appointed to consecrate the Lord's table, but by him who was crucified for us, &c. I have no concern with the subsequent remark of Heshusius. He says it is a fanatical and sophistical corruption to hold, that by the unworthy are meant the weak and those possessed of little faith, though not wholly aliens from Christ. I hope he will find some to answer him. But he twists about, and tries to engage me in the defence of another cause, in order to overwhelm me with the crime of a sacrilegious and most cruel parricide, (such is his language,) because by my doc- trine timid consciences are murdered and driven to despair.

He asks Calvinists with what faith they can approach the Supper—whether with a great or a little faith ? It is easy to give the answer furnished by the Institutes, where I distinctly refute the error of those who require a perfection which is nowhere to be found, and by this severity keep back from the use of the Supper not the weak only, but those best qualified to receive it. Nay, even our children, by the form which is in common use, are fully instructed how to refute the silly calumny. It is vain for him there- fore to display his loquacity by running away from the sub- ject. That he might not plume himself by his performance in this respect, we think it proper to insert this much by the way. He says the two things are diametrically opposed, viz., forgiveness of sins and guilt before the tribunal of God ; as if the least instructed did not know that believers in the same act provoke the wrath of God, and yet by his indulgence obtain favour. We all condemn the craft of Rebecca in substituting Jacob in the place of Esau, and there cannot be a doubt that in the eye of God the act was deserving of severe punishment ; yet he so mercifully for- gave it, that by means of it Jacob obtained the blessing. It is worth while to observe in passing, with what acuteness he disposes of my objection, that Christ cannot be separated from his Spirit. His answer is, that as the words of Paul are clear, he assents to them. Does he mean to astonish us by a miracle when he tells us that the blind see it? It has been clearly enough shown that nothing of the kind is to be seen in the words of Paul. He endeavours to disentangle himself by saying, that Christ is present with his creatures in many ways. But the first thing to be explained is, how Christ is present with unbelievers, as being the spiritual food of souls, and, in short, the life and salvation of the world. And as he adheres so doggedly to the words, I should like to know how the wicked can eat the flesh of Christ which was not crucified for them? and how they can drink the blood which was not shed to expiate their sins? I agree with him, that Christ is present as a strict judge when his Supper is profaned. But it is one thing to be eaten, and another to be a judge. When he afterwards says that the Holy Spirit dwelt in Saul, we must send him to his rudiments, that he may learn how to discriminate between the sanctification which is proper only to the elect and the children of God, and the general power which even the reprobate possess. These quibbles, therefore, do not in the slightest degree affect my axiom, that Christ, considered as the living bread and the victim immolated on the cross, cannot enter any human body which is devoid of his Spirit.

I presume that sufficient proof has been given of the ignorance as well as the effrontery, stolidity, and petulance of Heshusius—such proof as must not only make him offensive to men of worth and sound judgment, but make his own party blush at so incompetent a champion. But as he pretends to give a confirmation of his dogma, it may be worth while briefly to discuss what he advances, lest his loud boasting should impose upon the simple. I have shown elsewhere, and indeed oftener than once, how irrelevant it is here to introduce harangues on the boundless power of God, since the question is not what God can do, but what kind of communion with his flesh the Author of the Supper has taught us to believe. He comes, however, to the point when he brings forward the expressions of Paul and the Evangelists ; only he indulges his loquacity in giving vent to the absurdest calumnies, as if it were our purpose to subvert the ordinance of Christ. We have always declared, with equal good faith, sincerity, and candour, that we reverently embrace what Paul and the three Evangelists teach, provided only that the meaning of their words be inquired into with becoming soberness and modesty. Heshusius says, that they all speak the same thing, so much so, that there is scarcely a syllable of difference ; as if, in their most perfect agreement, there were not an apparent variety in the form of expression which may well raise a question. Two of them call the cup the blood of the new covenant; the other two call it a new covenant in the blood. Is there here not one syllable of difference ? But let us grant that the four employ the same words, and almost the same syllables, must we forthwith concede, as Heshusius demands, that there is no figure in the words ? Scripture makes mention, not four, but almost a thousand times, of the ears, eyes, and right hand of God. If the same expression, four times repeated, excludes all figures, will a thousand passages have no effect at all, or a less effect ? Be it that the question relates not to the fruit of Christ's passion, but to the presence of his body, provided the term presence be not confined to place. Though I should grant this, I deny that the point on which the question turns is, whether the words, This is my body, are used in a proper sense or metonymically, and therefore I hold that it is absurd in Heshusius to infer the one from the other. Were any one to concede to him, that the bread is called the body of Christ, because it is an exhibitive sign, and at the same time to add, that it is called body, essentially and corporeally, what ground of quarrel would he have with him ?

The proper question, therefore, regards the mode of communication, though if he chooses to insist on the words I have no objection. We must therefore see whether they are to be understood sacramentally, or as implying actual devouring. There is no dispute as to the body which Christ designates, for I have declared again and again that I have

no idea of a two-bodied Christ, and that therefore the body
which was once crucified is given in the Supper.   Nay, it is
plain from my Commentaries how I have expounded the
passage, The bread which I will give is my flesh, which I
will give for the life of the world.

My exposition is, that there are two kinds of giving, because
the same body which Christ once offered for our salvation, he
offers to us every day as spiritual food.   All therefore that he
talks about a symbolical body is nothing better than the slander of a low buffoon.   It is insufferable to see him blinding the
eye of the reader, while fighting with the masks and shadows
of his own imagination.   Equally futile is he, when he says,
that I keep talking only of fruit and efficacy.   I uniformly
assert a substantial communion, and only discard a local presence and the figment of an immensity of flesh.   But this
blundering expositor cannot be appeased unless we concede
to him, that the words of Paul, "the cup is the new covenant
in my blood," are equivalent to "the blood is contained in
the cup."   If this be granted, he must submit to the disgrace of retracting what he has so pertinaciously asserted in
regard to the proper and natural meaning of the words.   For
who will be persuaded by him that there is no figure when
the cup is called a covenant in blood, because it contains
blood?   I do not disguise, however, that I reject this senseless exposition.   It does not follow from it that we are redeemed by wine, and that the saying of Christ is false;
since, in order to drink the blood of Christ by faith, the
thing necessary is not that he should come down to earth,
but that we should climb up to heaven, or rather, the blood
of Christ must remain in heaven, in order that believers may
share it among themselves.

Heshusius, to deprive us of all sacramental modes of expression, maintains that we must learn, not from the institution of the passover, but from the words of Christ, what it is
that is given to us in the Supper; and yet, in his giddy way,
he immediately flies off in another direction, and finds a proper phrase in the words, Circumcision is a covenant.   But can
anything be more insufferable than a pertinacious denial, that
in accordance with the constant usage of Scripture the words

of the Supper are to be interpreted in a sacramental manner?
Christ was a rock ; for he was spiritual food. A dove was the
Holy Spirit. The water in baptism is both the Spirit and the
blood of Christ, (otherwise it would not be the laver of the
soul.) Christ himself is our passover. While we are agreed
as to all these passages, and Heshusius does not dare to deny
that the forms of speech in these sacraments are similar,
why does he kick so obstinately when we come to the Supper? But he says that the words of Christ are clear. What
greater obscurity is there in the others?

On the whole, I think I have made it plain that he has
entirely failed, with all his empty noise, to force the words
of Christ into the support of his delirious dream. As little
effect will he produce on men of sense by his arguments
which he deems to be irresistible. He says, that under the
Old Testament all things were shadowed by types and figures,
but that in the New, figures being abolished, or rather fulfilled, the reality is exhibited. So be it ; but can he hence
infer that the water of baptism is truly, properly, really, and
substantially the blood of Christ? Far more accurate is St.
Paul, who, while he teaches that the body is now substituted
for the old figures, does not mean, that what was then shadowed forth was completed by signs, but holds that it was
in Christ himself that the substance and reality were to be
sought. Accordingly, a little before, after saying that believers were circumcised in Christ by the circumcision not
made with hands, he immediately adds, that a pledge and
testimony of this is given in baptism, making the new sacrament to correspond with the old. Heshusius, after his own
fashion, quotes from the Epistle to the Hebrews, that the
sacrifices of the Old Testament were types of the true. But
the term *true* is there applied not to Baptism and the Supper, but to the death and resurrection of Christ. I have
acknowledged already, that in Baptism and the Supper
Christ is offered otherwise than in the legal figures ; but if
the reality, of which the Apostle there speaks, is not sought
for in a higher quarter than the sacraments, it will not be
found at all. Therefore, when the presence of Christ is con-
trasted with the legal shadows, it is wrong to confine it to

the Supper, since the thing referred to is the superior manifestation wherein the perfection of our salvation consists.
Even were I to grant that the presence of Christ spoken of
is to be referred to the sacraments of the New Testament,
this would still place Baptism and the Supper on the same
footing ; and therefore, when Heshusius argues thus :

> The sacraments of the gospel require the presence of
> Christ :
> The Supper is a sacrament of the gospel,
> Therefore, it requires the presence of Christ :

I, in my turn, rejoin :

> Baptism is a sacrament of the gospel,
> Therefore, it requires the presence of Christ.

If he betakes himself to his last shift, and tell us that it
was not said in baptism, " This is my body," I answer, that
it is nothing to the point, which entirely depends on the distinction between the Old Testament and the New.   Let him
cease, then, from his foolish talk, that if the bread of the
Supper is the symbol of an absent thing, it is therefore a
symbol of the Old Testament.   The reader must, moreover,
remember that the controversy is not regarding every kind
of absence, but only local absence.   Heshusius will not allow
Christ to be present with us, unless by making himself present in several places, wherever the Supper is administered.
Hence, too, it appears that he talks absurdly when he opposes presence to fruit.   The two things perfectly agree.
Although Christ is distant from us in respect of place, he is
yet present by the boundless energy of his Spirit, so that his
flesh can give us life.   He is still more absurd when he says
that we differ in no respect from those under the Old Testament in regard to spiritual eating, because the mode of vivifying is one and the same ; and they received just as much
as we.   But what had he said a little before ?   That in the
New Testament are offered not the shadows of things, but
the reality itself, true righteousness, light, and life, the true
High-Priest ; that this testament is established, and the
wrath of God appeased by true, not by typical blood.   What
does he understand by spiritual, but just the reality, true
righteousness, light, and life ?   Now he insists that all these

were common to the fathers, than which nothing can be more absurd, if they are peculiar to the New Testament.

But lest I may seem more intent on refuting my opponent than on instructing my readers, I must briefly remind them that everything is subverted when he makes the fathers equal to us in the mode of eating; for though they had Christ in common with us, the measure of revelation was by no means equal. Were it otherwise, there would have been no ground for the exclamation, Blessed are the eyes which see the things which ye see, (Matt. xiii. 16;) and again, The law and the prophets were until John; Grace and truth came by Jesus Christ. (John i. 17; Matt. xi. 13.) If he answer, that this is his understanding, I ask whence spiritual eating is derived? If he admits that it is from faith, there is a manifest difference in the very doctrine from which faith springs: for the question here relates not to the quantity of faith which was in individuals, but to the nature of the promises under the law. Who then can tolerate him when, snarling like a dog, he endeavours to stir up odium against us, because we say that the light of faith now is greater than it was under the ancient people? He objects by quoting our Saviour's complaint, When the Son of man cometh, shall he find faith on the earth? (Luke xviii. 8.) To what end does he quote, unless he would on this pretext obtain pardon for his unbelief? So be it. Christ will not find faith in a thousand Heshusiuses, nor in the whole of his crew. Is it not true that John the Baptist was greater than all the Prophets, and yet that the least among the preachers of the gospel was greater than he? (Luke vii. 28.) The faith of the Galatians was not only small but almost stifled, and yet Paul, while he compares the Prophets to children, says, that the Galatians and other believers had no longer any need of a pedagogue, (Gal. iii. 25,) as they had grown up; that is, in respect of doctrine and sacraments, but not of men. So far from having profited in the gospel, Heshusius, like an ape decked out in silk and gold, surpasses all the monks in barbarism.

In regard to the eating of the flesh of Christ, how much better our condition is than that of the fathers, I have shown in expounding the tenth chapter of the first Epistle to the Corinthians. Still I differ widely from those who dream of a corporeal eating: for although life might be infused from the substance of a flesh which as yet did not exist, so that there was truly a spiritual eating, such as we now have, still a pledge was given them of the same communion. Hence it follows, that the expression of Augustine is strictly true, viz., that the signs which they had differed from ours in visible form, not in reality. I add, however, that the mode of signifying was different, and the measure of grace not equal, because the communion of Christ now exhibited is fuller and more abundant, and likewise substantial.

When Heshusius says that his controversy with me relates to the pledge, not to the reality, I wish my readers to understand what his meaning is. He admits that the fathers were partakers of spiritual eating in an equal degree with us, whereas I hold that it was proportional to the nature and mode of the dispensation. But it is evident that a pledge being interposed, their faith was confirmed by signs as far as the absence of Christ admitted. We have already said how our pledges exhibit Christ present, not indeed in place, but because they set visibly before us the death and resurrection of Christ, wherein consist the entire fulness of salvation. Meanwhile, Heshusius, contradicting himself, disapproves of the distinction which I make between faith and spiritual eating. If we are to believe him, it is a mere sophism. Accordingly, there is no part of it which he allows to pass without carping and censure. In this way it must be a mere sophism when Paul says that Christ dwells in our hearts by faith—that we are ingrafted into his body—that we are crucified and buried with him—in fine, that we are bone of his bones, and flesh of his flesh, so that his life is ours. He who sees not that these things are the fruits and effects of faith, and therefore different from faith, is more than blind. Equally blind is it to deny that the inestimable blessing of a vivifying communion with Christ is obtained by us by faith. But he cares not what confusion he causes, provided he is not forced to acknowledge that believers without the Supper have the very thing which they receive in the Supper. But he says that eating must differ from sealing. It does, but just in the same way as the sealing which takes place in baptism differs from spiritual washing. Are we not, independently of baptism, cleansed by the blood of Christ and regenerated by the Spirit? It is true, that to help our infirmity a visible testimony is added, the better to confirm the thing signified, and not only so, but to bestow in truth and more fully that which we receive by the faith of the gospel even without any external action.

He here gives a display of the malignity of his temper, by making it a ground of charge against me, that I teach in the catechism, that the use of the Supper is not unnecessary, because we there receive Christ more fully, though already, by the faith of the gospel, he is so far ours and dwells in us. This doctrine, if we are to believe Heshusius, is not only absurd, but insults the whole ministry of the gospel. Let him then accuse Paul of blasphemy for saying that Christ is formed in us like the fœtus in the womb. His well-known words to the Galatians are, My little children, for whom I again travail as in birth until Christ Jesus be formed in you. (Gal. iv. 19.) This is not unlike what he says in another place, Until ye grow up into a perfect man, to the measure of the stature of the fulness of Christ. There is no need of many words to prove this; for if Christ dwells in us by faith, it is certain that he in a manner grows up in us in proportion to the increase of faith. The objection of Heshusius is, What then is to become of an infant which, immediately after being baptized, dies without having received the Supper? as if I were imposing a law on God, or denying his power of working when he pleases, without the aid of the Supper. For I hold with Augustine, that there may be invisible sanctification without the visible sign, just as, on the other hand, there may be the visible sign without true sanctification. John the Baptist was never admitted to the Supper, and yet surely this did not prevent him from possessing Christ. All I teach is, that we attain to communion with Christ gradually, and that thus it was not without cause he added the Supper to the gospel and to baptism. Hence, though God calls suddenly away from the world many who are children, not in age merely but in faith, yet one spark from the Spirit is sufficient to give them a life which swallows up all that was mortal in them, as Paul, too, elsewhere declares. But in the eyes of Heshusius, Paul seems to be but a mean authority, since he charges him with teaching a doctrine which is absurd and impious. He indeed charges him in my name, but where is the difference, if the doctrine is taught in Paul's words? There is no ground therefore for his attack upon me for saying that the communion of Christ is conferred upon us in different degrees not merely in the Supper, but independently of it.

Though I deem it notorious to the whole world that our doctrine is clearly approved by the consent of the primitive Church, Heshusius has again opened up the question, and introduced certain ancient writers as opposed to us and in favour of his opinion. Hitherto, indeed, I have not handled this matter professedly, that I might not do what has been done already. This was first performed with accuracy and skill by Œcolompadius, who clearly showed that the figment of a local presence was unknown to the early Church. He was succeeded by Bullinger, who performed the task with equal felicity. The whole was crowned by Peter Martyr, who has left nothing to be desired. As far as Westphal's importunity compelled me, I believe I have satisfied sound and impartial readers in regard to the consent of antiquity, nay, I have said what ought to have stopped the mouths even of the contentious. But however solid the reasons by which they are confuted, it is like talking to the deaf, and I shall therefore be contented with a few brief remarks, to let my readers see that this new antiquarian is no less absurd and barren than Westphal was. It is rather strange that while he is ashamed to use the authority of Joannes Damascenus and Theophylact, he calls them not the least among ecclesiastical writers. Sound and modest readers will find more learning and piety in a single commentary on Matthew, which is falsely alleged to be an unfinished work of Chrysostom, than in all the theology of Damascenus. The writer, whoever he may have been, distinctly says that the body of Christ is only given to us ministerially. I thought it proper to mention this much, lest any one might suppose that Heshusius was acting liberally in declining the support of Damascenus. While I grant that he also repudiates Clement Alexandrinus and Origen, I wish my readers to remember that he has it in his power to select from antiquity whatever suits his purpose. He begins with Ignatius. I wish his writings were extant to prevent his name from being so frequently employed as a cloak by impostors like Servetus and Heshusius. For where is the candour in quoting an epistle which scarcely one of the monkish herd would acknowledge to be genuine? Those who have read that silly production know that it speaks only of Lent, and chrism, and tapers, and fast and festival days, which began to creep in under the influence of superstition and ignorance long after the days of Ignatius. But what of this fictitious Ignatius? He says that some reject the Supper and oblations because they deny that the eucharist is the flesh of Christ which was sacrificed for us. But what kindred or community with those heretics have we who look up with reverence to the eucharist, in which we know that Christ gives us his flesh to eat? But he will rejoin, that the eucharist is styled the flesh. It is, but we must see that it is so styled improperly, if we would not shut our eyes against the clearest light. The name of eucharist is derived either from the act of celebration or from both parts of the sacrament. Take which you please, certainly the literal meaning cannot be urged. That we may not be obliged repeatedly to dispose of the same cavil, let it be understood once for all that we have no quarrel with the usual forms of expression. Early writers everywhere call the consecrated bread the body of Christ: for why should they not be at liberty to imitate the only begotten Son of God, on whose lips we ought to hang and learn wisdom? But how very different is this from the barbarous fiction, that the bread is properly the body which is therein corporeally eaten.

With the same probity he classes us with Messalians and enthusiasts, who denied that the use of the holy Supper does either good or harm: as if I had not from the first spoken of the utility of this mystery in loftier terms than the whole crew who disturb the world by raging like bacchanalians

against me. Nay, they had kept perfect silence as to the
end for which the Supper was instituted and the benefit
which believers derive from it, until the reproaches of the
godly compelled them to make an extract from my writings
in order to escape from the odium of suppressing the most
important thing contained in it.   But he does not hesitate
to give us Schuencfeldius for an associate. Why do you, like
a cowardly dog, who is afraid of the wolves, only attack unoffending guests ?   When Schuencfeldius was infecting Germany with his poison, we withstood him boldly, and thus
incurred his deepest hatred; but now, if Heshusius is to be believed, it was we that fostered him.   Then, when he involves
us in the impious dogma of Nestorius, what answer can I give,
but just that one who slanders so wickedly refutes himself ?

He next comes down to Justin Martyr, whose authority I
willingly allow to be great.   But what in him is adverse to
our cause ?   He says, that the bread of the Supper is not
common.   The reason is, that he had previously explained
that none are admitted to partake of it but those who have
been washed by baptism and have embraced the gospel.
He afterwards goes farther, As Christ was made flesh, so we
are taught that the food which was blessed by him by the
word of prayer, and by which our flesh and blood are
nourished through transmutation, is the flesh and blood of
Christ himself.   The comparison of the mystical consecration
in the Supper with the incarnation of Christ, seems to
Heshusius sufficient to carry the victory : as if Justin were
making out that the one was as miraculous as the other,
while all he meant was, that the flesh which Christ once
assumed from us is daily given us for food.   For in confirming this opinion, he is satisfied with simply quoting the
words of Christ, and contends for no more than that this
benefit is imparted to the disciples of Christ alone who have
been initiated into true piety.

I grant, Heshusius, that Irenæus is a clearer expounder
of what is thus briefly stated by Justin.   I will not quote all
his words, but will not omit anything which is pertinent.
He inveighs against heretics who maintained that flesh is not
capable of incorruption.   If so, he says, neither has the Lord

redeemed us by his own blood, nor is the cup of the eucharist the communion of his blood, nor the bread which we
break the communion of his body. The blood comes only
from the veins and other substance of the man in which the
Son of God truly redeemed us. And since we are his members, and are nourished by the creature, and he himself con-
fers the creature upon us, making his sun to rise and rain to
descend as it pleaseth him, he declared that that cup which
is a creature is his body by which he nourishes our bodies.
Therefore when the mingled cup and broken bread have the
word of God pronounced, there is formed a eucharist of the
body and blood of Christ, by which the substance of our
flesh is nourished and consists. How is it denied that the
flesh is capable of the gift of God which is eternal life, seeing
it is nourished by the body and blood of Christ and is his
member, as the Apostle says, We are members of his body
and of his bones, &c.

Let the reader attend to the design of Irenæus. He is not
discussing whether or not we eat Christ corporeally : he is
only contending that his flesh and blood are meat and drink
to us, so as to infuse spiritual life into our flesh and blood. The
whole question cannot be better solved than by attending to
the context. The only communion which we are there asserted
to have with Christ in the Supper is spiritual, which is both
perpetual, and is given to us independently of the use of the
Supper. Heshusius insists that the only way in which we receive the body of Christ is corporeally and within us, and there
is nothing he can less tolerate than the doctrine, that believers
are substantially conjoined with Christ. For throughout the
whole book he insists on it as a capital article, that spiritual
eating is nothing but faith, and that the Supper would be
an empty show, were not corporeal eating added, and only
at that moment when the bread is introduced into the mouth.
This he repeats a hundred times. But what does Irenæus
say ? Surely all see, that in regard to the communion which
we enjoy in the Supper, he neither thinks nor speaks differently from Paul, when he says, that believers, both in life
and in death, are the members of Christ, flesh of his flesh
and bone of his bones. To overcome his stupidity, I must

speak in still plainer terms. He wishes to prove, from the words of Irenæus, that the body of Christ is received not only in a spiritual manner, but corporeally by the mouth, and that it is heretical to acknowledge only the spiritual eating of which our Saviour discourses in the sixth chapter of John, and Paul in the fifth chapter of the Ephesians ; because corporeal eating cannot lawfully be disjoined from bread. What does Irenæus answer ? That we are nourished by bread and wine in the sacred Supper, as Paul declares, that we are members of Christ. There is an end, therefore, to that distinction between corporeal and spiritual eating in which he boasted and gloried as the hingeing point of the whole controversy. Who will believe him, when he says, that this is sophistry ? Irenæus affirms that the two propositions, This is my body, and, We are the members of Christ, are the same both in degree and quality, whereas our censor exclaims, that unless the two be separated, all piety is subverted and God is denied. Nay, he distinctly applies the term Epicureans to those who think that nothing more is conferred in the Supper than to make us one body with Christ.

Our view is not affected by the doctrine delivered on the subject, with one consent, by Tertullian and Hilary, viz., that our flesh is nourished by the flesh of Christ, in hope of eternal life ; for they do not point to such a mode as Heshusius imagines. On the contrary, they remove all ambiguity, by referring to the perpetual union which we have with Christ, and teaching that it is the effect of faith, whereas, according to Heshusius, corporeal eating is confined to the Supper, and is as different from spiritual as earth is from heaven. Hilary says, (Lib. 8, de Trinitate,) As to the reality of the flesh and blood, there is no room left for ambiguity. For now, both by the declaration of our Lord himself, and our faith, they are meat indeed and drink indeed : and these when received and taken, cause us to be in Christ and Christ to be in us. Is not this reality ? He himself then is in us through his flesh, and we are in him, while that which we are with him is in God. That we are in him by the sacrament of communicated flesh and blood, he himself declares when he says, The world now seeth me not, but ye shall see me ; because I live, ye shall live also ; because I am in the Father, and you in me. (John xiv. 19.) If he wished unity of will only to be understood, why did he point out a certain degree and order of completing the union ? Just because, while he is in the Father by the nature of his divinity, we are in him by his corporeal nativity, and he, on the other hand, is in us by the mystery of the sacraments. Thus perfect union was taught by the Mediator : while, we remaining in him, he remained in the Father, and remaining in the Father, remained in us—thus, advancing us to unity with the Father, since while he is naturally in the Father in respect of nativity, we are naturally in him, and he remains naturally in us. That there is this natural unity in us, he himself thus declared, Whoso eateth my flesh and drinketh my blood, abideth in me, and I in him. (John vi. 56.) For none will be in him save those in whom he himself shall have been, having in himself only the assumed flesh of him who has taken his own. Shortly after he says, This is the cause of our life, that we who are in ourselves carnal, have life abiding in us by the flesh of Christ. Although he repeatedly says, that we are naturally united to Christ, it is apparent from this short sentence, that his only object is to prove that the life of Christ abides in us, because we are one with him.

No less clearly does Irenæus show that he is speaking of the perpetual union which is spiritual. He says, (Lib. 4, c. 34,) Our opinion is consonant to the eucharist, and the eucharist confirms our opinion. For we offer to him the things which are his, when consistently proclaiming the communion and union of flesh and spirit. For as that which is earthly bread, on being set apart by God is no longer common bread, but a eucharist consisting of two things, an earthly and a heavenly, so likewise our bodies, receiving the eucharist, are no longer corruptible, but have hope of resurrection. In the fifth book he explains more fully, that we are the members of Christ, and united to his flesh because of his Spirit dwelling in us. The reason why Heshusius charges us with extreme effrontery is, just because we deny that propositions which perfectly agree with our doctrine are adverse to it.

If a more familiar exposition is required Cyril will supply it; for, in his third book, when explaining our Saviour's discourse contained in the 6th chapter of John, he acknowledges that there is no other eating in the Supper than that by which the body of Christ gives life to us, and by our participation in it leads us back to incorruption. And in his fourth book (cap. 13) he says: Our Lord gave his body for the life of all, and by it again infuses life into us: how he does this I will briefly explain, according to my ability. For when the life-giving Son of God dwelt in the flesh, and was in whole, so to speak, united to the ineffable whole by the mode of union, he made the flesh itself vivifying, and hence this flesh gives life to those who partake of it. As he asserts that this takes place both in the Supper, and without the Supper, let Heshusius explain what is meant by " sending life into us." In the seventeenth chapter he says, Were any one to pour wax on melted wax, the one must become intermingled with the other. In like manner, when any one receives the flesh and blood of the Lord, he must be united with him: he must be in Christ and Christ in him. In the twenty-fourth chapter he distinctly maintains, that the flesh of Christ is made vivifying by the agency of the Spirit, so that Christ is in us because the Spirit of God dwells in us.

Heshusius, after making a vain and ridiculous boast of those holy writers, insolently applauds himself for leaving Clement Alexandrinus, because he is borne down by his authority. He also boasts, that he not unfrequently acts as our advocate and representative, by enhancing and amplifying, according to the best of his ability, everything advanced by us, that he may know whether anything forcible, &c. If this is true, he must not only be feeble, but altogether nerveless and broken down. Still, did he employ his abilities in judging aright, instead of using them entirely for quarrelling and invective, much of the intemperate rage with which he burns would cease. He certainly would not charge me with maintaining an allegorical eating, while I acknowledge that allegory is condemned by the words of Christ. But it is right that those whose pertinacious ambition hurries them into contest should be smitten from above with a spirit of giddiness, which makes them prostitute both their modesty and their faith.

It is strange, that while he is such a severe censor of Origen, that he will not class him among writers worthy of credit, he does not make a similar attack on Tertullian. We see with what implacable rage he burns against all who presume to interpret the words of Christ, This is my body, in any other but the strict and natural sense, holding those who do so guilty of a sacrilegious corruption. But when he feels himself struck by the words of Tertullian, instead of attempting to bear him down by violence, he rather tries to escape from him by means of tergiversation. Tertullian says: Christ made the bread, received and distributed to the disciples his own body, by saying, This is my body, that is, the figure of my body. Now it could not have been the figure were it not the body of the reality: for an empty thing, as a phantasm is, could not take a figure. Or, if he made the bread to be his body, because it wanted the reality of body, then he must have delivered bread for us. The vanity of Marcion would be gratified if the bread were crucified. Tertullian proves, that the bread was the true substance of the flesh of Christ, because it could not be a figure without being the figure of a true substance. Heshusius is dissatisfied with this mode of expression, because it seems dangerous; but, as if he had forgotten himself, he admits it, provided there is no deception under it. By deception he means, calling the bread the sign or figure of the absent flesh. That he may not gloss over the term absence in his usual manner, let the reader remember, as I formerly reminded him, that though Christ, in respect of place and actual inspection, is absent, still believers truly enjoy and are nourished by the present substance of his flesh.

All his quibbles, however, cannot deprive us of the support of Tertullian. For when he says, that the bread was made body, the meaning can only be ascertained from the context. To consecrate the blood in wine cannot be equivalent to the expression, To annex the blood to wine; but corresponds to the next sentence, where he says, that Christ confirmed the substance of his flesh when he delivered a covenant sealed with his own blood, because it cannot be blood unless it belong to true flesh. No man can doubt that the sealing which was performed on the cross is compared with the consecration by which Christ enters into an eternal covenant with his people. Heshusius makes no more out of the other passage, in which he says, that our flesh eats the body and blood of Christ, in order that it may be fed on God, in other words, be made a partaker of the Godhead. The sum is, that it is absurd and impious to exclude our flesh from the hope of resurrection, seeing that Christ deigns to bestow upon it the symbols of spiritual life. Accordingly, he ranks in the same class not only baptism but anointing, the sign of the cross, and the laying on of hands. But with strange stupidity, in order to prove that we do not become partakers of the flesh of Christ by faith alone, Heshusius quotes a passage from a tract on the Lord's Prayer, in which Tertullian says, That the petition for daily bread may be understood spiritually, inasmuch as Christ is our bread, inasmuch as Christ is our life, inasmuch as he is the word of the living God, who came down from heaven, and his body is held to be in the bread. Whence he concludes, that we seek perpetuity from Christ and individuality from his body. I ask whether, if it had been his intention to change sides, he could have given better support to our cause? See what ground he has for glorying in antiquity.

With similar dexterity he obtains the support of Cyprian. Cyprian contends that the blood of Christ is not to be denied to believers who are called to the service of Christ under the obligation to shed their own blood. What can he evince by this but just that the blood of Christ is given us by the cup as the body is given under the symbol of bread? In another passage, when disputing against the Aquarii, he says, that the vivifying blood of Christ cannot be thought to be in the cup if the wine is wanting, by which the blood itself is shown, he clearly confirms our doctrine. For what is meant by the blood being represented by the wine, but just that the wine is a sign or figure of the blood? Shortly after he repeats the same thing, saying, that water alone cannot express the blood of Christ, that is, designate it. But he says, at the same time, that the blood is in the cup:

as if the idea of local inclosing ever came into the mind of this holy martyr, who is only occupied with the question, Whether the mystical cup should be mixed with water only to represent the blood of Christ?

Another passage quoted by Heshusius is, How can they dare to give the eucharist to the abandoned, that is, profane the holy body of Christ, seeing it is written, Whoso eateth or drinketh unworthily, shall be guilty of the body and blood of the Lord? I neither think differently, nor am I wont to speak differently. But by what logic did this good man learn from these words that the body of Christ is given to the unworthy? All see that the word *giving* applies to the eucharist. Cyprian holds that if all are admitted indiscriminately, there is a profanation of the sacred body. See the ground on which our Thraso composes pæans. In another passage Cyprian says, That the wicked who, with impious hands, intrude to the Supper, invade the body of Christ; and he inveighs bitterly against the sacrilegious persons who take offence at priests for not at once receiving the body of the Lord with polluted hands, or drinking his blood with polluted lips: as if it were not hitherto known that this mode of speaking is common with early writers, or as if I had any objection to the same style, having many years ago quoted the same passage, and another similar to it, from Ambrose. Heshusius does not see the absurdity in which he is involving himself: for it will follow that Christ himself is exposed to the licentiousness and violence of the ungodly, since Cyprian there also says that they do violence to his flesh and blood.

Eusebius quotes a passage in which Dionysius of Alexandria maintains that it is not lawful to initiate, by a new baptism, any one who has long been a partaker of the flesh and blood of the Lord, and has received the sacred food. Heshusius argues, that if he who was baptized by heretics has received the body of Christ, it must be eaten without faith and repentance: as if there were no difference between thoughtlessness or error and impiety. He imagined that he was to gain much by pronouncing lofty encomiums on the ancient writers whose names he obtrudes, but he has only made himself more than ridiculous. He thunders forth their praises, and then, on coming to the point, finds they give him no support.

Athanasius, he says, is a divine writer worthy of immortal praise. Who denies it? But what is this to the point? Why, in stating that Christ was a high-priest by means of his own body, and by means of the same delivered a mystery to us, saying, This is my body, and, This is the blood of the New, not of the Old Testament, it is evident that he speaks of the true body and blood in the Supper. Do we then imagine it to be false blood, when we maintain that it is impossible without nefarious divorce to separate the words, The body which is delivered for you, and, The blood which is shed for the remission of sins? Rightly then does Athanasius teach that a mystery has been consecrated for us by the flesh and blood of Christ, nor could anything be said that was better fitted to explain our view; for had not Christ been possessed of true flesh and true blood, (the only point there delivered,) the consecration by which our salvation is placed in them would have been vain.

I have already shown how preposterously he opposes us with Hilary, when he distinctly treats of the vivifying participation of Christ, which demands not the external use of the Supper, but maintains perpetual vigour in believers. Heshusius says, that that is not the subject of dispute. Of what use then is it for him to twist his words against us, while they have no bearing on the point? Still more absurdly does he say that we are refuted by the single expression, that We receive the flesh of Christ under a mystery. As if *under a mystery* were not just equivalent to *sacramentally*. This again is most apposite for the confirmation of our doctrine. But lest any one should think that he errs through folly merely, he afterwards shows his malice by adding, that, according to us, divinity alone is given us in the Supper. This is his reason for saying that that one passage should suffice in the judgment of all to settle the controversy.

He exposes himself in the same way in quoting Epiphanius. That writer, discoursing how man is created in the image of God, says that, If it is understood of the body, there cannot be a proper likeness between what is visible and palpable, and the Spirit which is invisible and incomprehensible; whereas, if it refers to the soul, there is a wide distance, because the soul being liable to many weaknesses and defects, does not contain the divinity within itself. He therefore concludes, that God, who is incomprehensible, truly performs what he bestows upon men in respect of his image. He afterwards adds, And how many things are deduced from the like! For we see how our Saviour took into his hands, as it is contained in the gospel, how he rose up at the Supper, and took, and after giving thanks, said, That is this of mine. But we see that it is not equal or like either to a corporeal shape, or an invisible deity, or the figures of members. For this is round, and in regard to feeling, insensible. He meant to say, that by grace, That is this of mine; and no man refuses credit to his words. For he who believes not that he is true in what he said, has fallen from grace and from faith. Let the reader attend to the state of the case. Epiphanius contends, that though nothing like is the same, yet the image of God truly shines in man, just as the bread is truly called body. Hence it is plain that nothing is less accordant with the mind of this writer than the dream of Heshusius, that the bread is truly and substantially body. He asks, why does Epiphanius insist on faith in the words of the Supper, if the bread of the eucharist is not the body? Just because it is only by faith we comprehend that corruptible food is the pledge of eternal life. Meat for the body, says Paul, and the body for meat, but God will destroy both. (2 Cor. vi. 13.) In the bread and wine we seek a spiritual aliment, which may quicken our souls to the hope of a blessed resurrection. We ask Christ that we may be united to him, that he may dwell in us and be one with us. But Epiphanius treats not of the fruit or efficacy of the Supper, but of the substance of the body. How true this is, let the reader judge from his concluding words. Before speaking of the ordinance of the Supper, he says, The figure began with Moses, the figure was opened by John, but the gift was perfected in Christ. All therefore have that which is according to the image, but not according to nature. For in

having that which is according to the image, they have it
not in respect of equality with God.   For God is incomprehensible, a Spirit above all spirit, light above all light.   He
is not, however, devoid of these things which he has defined.
I wonder how Heshusius dares to make mention of faith,
while he maintains that the body of Christ is eaten without
faith, and bitterly assails us for requiring faith.

He boasts that Basil is on his side, because he applies the
terms abandoned and impious to those who dare with uncleanness of soul to touch the body of Christ.   This expression he uses in the same sense as that in which early writers
often say that the body of Christ falls to the earth and is
consumed, because they never hesitated to transfer the name
of the thing to the symbol.   I formerly acknowledged, that
Ambrose has spoken in the same way, but in what sense is
apparent from his interpretation of the words of Christ.   He
says, (in 1 Cor. xi.,) Having been redeemed by the death of
Christ, we commemorating this event by eating the flesh
and blood which were offered for us, signify, &c.   Shortly
after he says, The covenant was therefore established by
blood, because blood is a witness of Divine grace, as a type
of which we receive the mystical cup of blood.   Again, What
is it to be guilty of the body, but just to be punished for
the death of the Lord ?   He, accordingly, enjoins us to come
to the communion with a devout mind, recollecting that reverence is due to him whose body we approach to take.   For
each ought to consider with himself, that it is the Lord whose
blood he drinks in a mystery.   Heshusius has the effrontery
to produce this passage against us, though it supports us,
as if we had actually borrowed the expression of our doctrine from it.

But Heshusius opposes us even with verse.   Because Gregory Nazianzen, indulging the poetic vein, says, that priests
carry in their hands the plasma of the great God, he boldly
infers that the bread is properly the body of Christ.   My
answer, which I am confident will be approved by all men of
sense, is simply this, that Gregory meant nothing more than
Augustine has expressed somewhat more familiarly, when
speaking of Christ holding forth the bread to his disciples,

he says, He bore himself in a manner in his hands, an expression by which the difficulty is completely solved. For
when he says, (Serm. de Pasch.,) Be not impiously deluded
when hearing of the blood, and passion, and death of God,
but confidently eat the body and drink the blood, if thou
desirest life, Heshusius absurdly wrests his words to a
meaning foreign to them, since he is not there speaking of
the ordination of the Supper, but of our Saviour's incarnation and death, though I deny not that Gregory, in the
words eating and drinking, in which, however, he recommends faith, alludes to the Supper.

In regard to Jerome, there is no occasion to say much.
Heshusius quotes a passage, in which he says, that the bread
is the body of Christ. (In Malach. c. 1.) I make him welcome to more. For he writes to Heliodorus, that the clergy
make the body of Christ. Elsewhere, also, he says, that
they distribute his blood to the people. The only question
is, in what sense does he say this ? If we add the clause, in a
mystery, will not the controversy be at an end, since it is
clear, that in a mystery and Corporeally are antithetical ?
(In Ecclesiast.) As Jerome removes all doubt by expressing
this exception, what is to be gained by sophistical cavilling ?
I admit, that in another passage, (in Malach. c. 1,) Jerome
says, that the wicked eat the body of Christ, but, as he adds,
that they in this way pollute it, why seek for a difficulty where
there is none ? Unless, indeed, Heshusius is to make Christ
so subject to the licentiousness of the ungodly as to have his
pure and holy flesh polluted by infection from them. But
in another passage Jerome speaks more clearly : for he distinctly denies that the wicked eat the flesh of Christ, or
drink his blood. In like manner, he says, (in Hos. c. 9,)
The wicked sacrifice many victims, and eat the flesh of them,
deserting the one sacrifice of Christ, and not eating his flesh,
though his flesh is meat to them that believe. Why does
Heshusius childishly cavil about a word, while the thing intended is so transparent ? The substance of all his sophistical
jargon may be formed into a syllogism thus :

Whatever is called the body of Christ is his body substantially and in reality.

Irenæus, Tertullian, Cyprian, Justin, Ambrose, Jerome,
Augustine, and several others, call the bread of the
sacred Supper the body of Christ :
Therefore, the bread of the Supper is the body of Christ
substantially and in reality.

While Heshusius talks thus confidently, I should like to
hear his answer to a distinction, by which Jerome so completely dissipates and upsets his dream, that his words require to be softened down in an opposite direction. He says,
(in Ephes. c. 1,) The flesh and blood of Christ is taken in a
twofold sense ; either that spiritual and divine, of which he
himself said, My flesh is meat indeed ; or the flesh which
was crucified, and the blood which was shed by the soldier's
spear. I do not suppose, indeed, that Jerome imagined a
twofold flesh ; and yet I presume that he took notice of a
spiritual, and therefore different mode of communicating, to
guard against the fiction of a corporeal eating.

The passage which Heshusius has produced from Chrysostom I will run over slightly. Because that pious teacher
enjoins us to approach with faith, that we may not only receive the body when held forth, but much more touch it
with a clean heart, this able expositor infers that some
receive without faith with an unclean heart ; as if Chrysostom were hinting at the corporeal reception of a substantial
body, and not under the term body, commending the dignity
of the ordinance. What if he elsewhere explains himself,
and at the same time clearly unfolds the mind of Paul. He
asks, (in 1 Cor. Hom. 27,) What is it for one to be guilty of the
body and blood of the Lord ? Since he has shed it, he shows
that it was murder also, and not merely sacrifice. As his
enemies did not pierce him that they might drink, but that
they might shed, so he who communicates unworthily obtains no benefit. Surely even the blind may now see that
Chrysostom holds the wicked guilty, not of drinking, but of
shedding the blood. With greater folly Heshusius transfers
what was said by Chrysostom concerning the spiritual eating of the soul to the stomach and intestines. The words
are, The body is set before us, not only that we may touch
it, but that we may eat and be filled. Heshusius holds

this to be equivalent to saying that it is received into the bowels.

In producing Augustine as an advocate or witness, he passes the height of impudence. That holy person tells us to receive in the bread that which hung on the cross. According to Heshusius, nothing can be clearer than these words. They, no doubt, are so, if we are agreed as to the mode of receiving. Thus, when he says, in his Epistle to Januarius, that the order of the Church should be approved, requiring us to go fasting to the sacred table, in order that the body of Christ may enter the mouth before any other food, if we add, *in a mystery*, or *sacramentally*, all contention will cease. But Heshusius, absurdly laying hold of an ambiguous term, loses sight of the point in dispute. In his sermon on the words of the Apostle, by speaking of a two-fold eating, namely, a spiritual and a sacramental, he distinctly declares, that the wicked who partake of the Supper eat the flesh of Christ. Yes; but, as he elsewhere teaches, sacramentally. Let Heshusius say that we may as well deny that the sun shines at mid-day, as that these passages clearly refute our doctrine; I feel confident, that in my answer to Westphal, I so completely disposed of his calumnious charges, and those of his fellows, that even the contentious, in whom there are any remains of candour, would rather choose to be silent than to incur derision by imitating the petulance of Heshusius. He pretends that Augustine asserts the true presence of the body of Christ in the eucharist, because he says that the body is given in the bread, and the blood in the cup, distributed by the hands of the priests, and taken not only by faith, but by the mouth also; not only by the pious, but also by the wicked. I answer, that unless a clear definition is given of the sense in which Augustine uses the term body, Heshusius is acting deceitfully. But where can we find a better expounder than Augustine himself? Besides using the term eucharist or sacrament of the body promiscuously in the same passages, there is one which clearly explains his meaning, in which he says, that the sacraments, in respect of resemblance, receive the names of the things which they signify, and, accordingly, that the sacrament of the body is in a manner the body. (Ep. 23, ad Bonif.) Wherefore, as often as Heshusius obtrudes the ambiguous expression, it will be easy to rejoin, that Augustine, in so speaking, did not forget himself, but follows the rule which he prescribes to others. (Contra Adimant.) To the same effect, he elsewhere (in Ps. 3) calls the sign of the body a figure. Again, he says, (in Ps. 33,) that Christ in a manner carried himself in his own hands. Even were I silent, Augustine would clear himself of the calumnious charge. It is because of resemblance he transfers the name of the thing signified to the external symbol, and, accordingly, calls the bread the body of Christ, not properly or substantially, as Heshusius pretends, but in a certain manner.

The view which the pious writer took of the presence is perfectly apparent from the Epistle to Dardanus, where he says, Christ gave immortality to his flesh, did not destroy its nature. We are not to think that in respect of this nature he is everywhere diffused ; for we must beware of so elevating the divinity of the man as to destroy the reality of the body. It does not follow that that which is in God is everywhere as God. At length he concludes, that he who is the only-begotten Son of God, and at the same time the Son of Man, is everywhere wholly present as God, and in the temple of God, that is, the Church, is as it were the inhabiting God, and is in a certain place in heaven in respect of the nature of a true body. Of the same purport is the following passage, (in Joan. Tr. 50,) In respect of the presence of his majesty we have Christ always; in respect of the presence of his flesh it was truly said, Me ye have not always. There are similar passages in which the holy writer declares how abhorrent he is to the idea of a local presence. How miserably Heshusius quibbles, in regard to his assertion that the body of Christ is eaten by the wicked, is plain from a variety of passages. First, he opposes the virtue of the sacrament to the visible sacrament ; he makes an antithesis of eating inwardly and outwardly, of eating with the heart and chewing with the teeth. Were there any invisible eating of the body different from spiritual eating, he ought in expounding it to have used a threefold division. Shortly after he repeats the same antithesis, (Tr. in Joann. 26,) He who abides not in Christ, and in whom Christ abides not, unquestionably neither spiritually eats his flesh nor drinks his blood, although he press the sacrament of the body carnally and visibly with his teeth. Had Augustine approved of the fiction of Heshusius, he would have said, " although he eat the body corporeally." But the pious teacher is always consistent with himself, and here delivers nothing different from what he afterwards teaches when he says, (Tract. in Joan. 59,) That the other disciples ate the bread the Lord, whereas Judas ate the bread of the Lord against the Lord. This is well confirmed by another passage, (Contr. Faust. l. 3, c. 16,) where he again opposes, as things contrary to each other, *sacramentally* and *truly eating the flesh of Christ.* Hence it follows that it is not truly eaten by the wicked. In fine, what he understands by the expression sacramentally, (*sacramento tenus,*) he shows more fully when he declares that good and bad communicate in the signs. He says elsewhere, (Serm. 2 de Vert. Apost.,) Then has every one the body and blood of Christ, when that which is taken visibly in the sacrament is in reality spiritually eaten and drunk. If Heshusius objects that the wicked do not eat spiritually, I ask what Augustine means by the reality of which he makes believers only to partake? Moreover, if Augustine thought that the body of Christ is substantially eaten by the wicked, he ought to have represented it as visible, since nothing is attributed to the wicked but a visible taking. If, as Heshusius pretends, one sentence of Augustine is worth more in his estimation than ten prolix harangues of other fathers, every one must see that he is worse than a senseless trunk if these striking passages make no impression on him. And indeed when I see himself engaged with such a buffoon, I am almost ashamed at spending my time in discussing his frivolities.

Having performed this part of the play, he again flies off, and endeavours to lead us away from the subject. And, no doubt, while he goes up and down gathering invectives, as if he were making up a garland of flowers, he seems to himself a very showy rhetorician, while I, when I hear his frivolous loquacity, cannot help thinking of the shabbiest of orators. He pretends to discern in us the special characteristics of heretics, viz., that when we are unable to defend our error we clothe it with deceitful words. But when we come to the point, what deceptions does he discover, what subterfuges, what frauds, or cavils, or tricks does he detect? I omit the Greek terms which he would not omit, and in regard to which, by substituting adjectives for substantives, he betrays his ignorance. He admits that I reject metaphors and allegory, and have recourse to metonymy. As yet he has shown no cavil. Next he says, that I repudiate the sentiment of those who affirm that to eat the body of Christ is nothing else than to embrace his benefits by faith. This distinction also does not by any means substitute smoke for light, but is an apt and significant exposition of the subject. My maintaining that spiritually to eat the flesh of Christ is something greater and more excellent than to believe, he calls a chimera. What answer shall I give to this impudent assertion, but just that he is mentally blind, since he cannot understand what is so plain and obvious? When he represents me as substituting merit and benefit for flesh and blood, and shortly afterwards adds, that I acknowledge no other presence in the Supper than that of the Deity, my writings without a word from me refute the impudent calumny. For not to mention many other passages, after treating familiarly in my Catechism of the whole ordinance, the following passage occurs:—

" *M.* Have we in the Supper only a sign of the blessings which you have mentioned, or are they there exhibited to us in reality?

" *S.* Seeing that our Lord Jesus Christ is truth itself, there cannot be a doubt that he at the same time fulfils the promises which he there gives us, and adds the reality to the figures. Wherefore, I doubt not, that as he testifies by words and signs, so he also makes us partakers of his own substance, by which we grow up into one life with him.

" *M.* But how can this be, seeing that Christ is in heaven, and that we are still pilgrims on the earth?

" *S.* He effects this by the miraculous and secret agency

of his Spirit, to whom it is not difficult to unite things otherwise disjoined by distance of place."

Moreover, I say in my Institutes, " I am not satisfied with
those who, when they would show the mode of communion,
teach that we are partakers of the Spirit of Christ, omitting
all mention of the flesh and blood : as if it were said to no
purpose, ' My flesh is meat indeed,' " &c.   This is followed
by a lengthened explanation of the subject. Something, too,
had been said on it previously.   In the Second Book I had
refuted, as I suppose, with no less perspicuity than care, the
fiction of Osiander, which he falsely accuses me with following.   Osiander imagined that righteousness is conferred on
us by the Deity of Christ.   I showed, on the contrary, that
salvation and life are to be sought from the flesh of Christ in
which he sanctified himself, and in which he consecrates
Baptism and the Supper.   It will be there also seen how
completely I have disposed of his dream of essential righteousness.   I have got the same return from Heshusius that he
made to his preceptor Melancthon. The laws make false witnesses infamous, and enact severe punishments against calumniators.   The more criminal it is to corrupt public records,
the more severely ought the miscreant to be punished who, in
one passage, is convicted of three crimes—gross calumny,
false testimony, and corruption of written documents. Why
he so eagerly assails me with bitter invective, I know not,
unless it be that he has no fear of being paid back in kind.
I insist on the thing itself, which he would by no means
wish me to do.   I say that although Christ is absent from
the earth in respect of the flesh, yet in the Supper we truly
feed on his body and blood—that owing to the secret agency
of the Spirit we enjoy the presence of both.   I say that distance of place is no obstacle to prevent the flesh, which was
once crucified, from being given to us for food.   Heshusius
supposes, what is far from being the fact, that I imagine a
presence of deity only.   All the dispute is with regard to
place ; but because I will not allow that Christ is inclosed
under the bread, is swallowed, and passes into the stomach,
he alleges that I involve my doctrine in ambiguous expressions.   And to pretend some zeal for the piety he never

tasted, he brings forward Paul's exhortation to retain the
form of sound words. As if Paul's doctrine were expressed
to the life, or could have any affinity with such monstrous
dogmas as these—that the bread is properly and substantially the body of Christ—that the body itself is eaten corporeally by the mouth and passes into us. This worthy imitator of Paul, in a very short treatise, misinterprets about
sixty passages of Scripture so absurdly, as to make it manifest that not one particle of that living exhibition of which
Paul speaks had ever entered his mind.

In vain, too, does he endeavour to obtain greater license
for his petulance, by opposing us with the churches of
Saxony, and complaining of our having unjustly accused
him. For to omit many things which are obvious, I only
wish to know whether or not he and his fellows have not
been endeavouring for several years to pluck out the two
eyes of Saxony, the schools of Wittemberg and Leipsic.
After extinguishing these two lights, why, I ask, would he
boast the empty name of Saxony ? With regard to the accusation, my answer is, that I do not repent of having compared
to Marcion and the Capernaumites all who maintain the
immensity or ubiquity of the flesh of Christ, and insist that
he is in several places at the same time. When he compares
the two sentences, The bread is the sign of the absent body,
and, The body is truly and substantially present and is
given under the bread, it is easy to answer that there is a
medium between these extremes, that the body is indeed
given by the external symbol, but is not sisted locally. See
why he exclaims that we are Epicureans and inured to security. But the more causeless noise he makes, the more
clearly he discloses his temper, feelings, and manners. If
any man has in this age been exposed to great and perilous
contests, many know that it is I. And while we are still as
sheep destined to slaughter, this meek doctor of the gospel
insults in mockery over the terrors which press us on every
side, as if he were envying our quiet. But perhaps this provident man, who is carefully treasuring up the means of
luxury for a whole life, derides us for our security in living
from hand to mouth, and being contented with our humble

means. With the same shamelessness he fabricates strange understandings between me and all those whose errors I withstood single-handed, while he was sleeping or feasting. And to make it apparent how eagerly he is bent on calumny, having heard of the name of Velsius, which it is well known that I assumed and bore at Frankfort, he substitutes the name of Felsius, that he may be able to make me an associate of the man whom he allowed to go about raving at Heidelberg, because he dared not to engage with such a combatant. With the same candour and modesty he estimates our doctrine by its fruit, saying, that it induces contempt of the sacred Supper. Would that he and his fellows would come to it with equal reverence! When he charges us with setting no value on the use of it, I leave him to be put down by my Institutes, from which I quote the following passage *verbatim :*—" What we have hitherto said of this sacrament abundantly shows that it was not instituted to be received once a year, and that perfunctorily, as is now the common custom, but to be in frequent use among all Christians." After mentioning the fruits of it, I proceed thus:—" That such was the practice of the Apostolic Church, Luke tells us in the Acts, when he says, that the believers were persevering in doctrine, in communion, in the breaking of bread, &c. Matters were to be so managed that there should be no meeting of the Church without the word, prayer, and the communion of the Supper." After severely condemning this corruption, as it deserved, by quotations from early writers, I next say, " This custom of requiring men to communicate once a year was most assuredly an invention of the devil." Again, " The practice ought to be very different. The table of the Lord ought to be spread in the sacred assembly at least once a week. No one should be compelled, but all should be exhorted and stimulated : the torpor of those who keep away should also be reproved. Hence it was not without cause I complained at the outset that it was the wile of the devil which intruded the custom of prescribing one day in the year, and leaving it unused during all the rest." And yet this dog will still bark at me, as having cut the sinews of the sweetest consolation, and prevented believers

from recognising that Christ dwells in them—a subject on
which if he has any right views, he has stolen them from me.
But the proof which he has added sufficiently declares the frantic nature of his attacks, since the very thing which he had
detested he now seizes upon as an axiom of faith, viz., that
the hypostatic union of the divine and human natures in
the person of Christ cannot exist unless the flesh be at the
same time in several places. How could he prove more
plainly that he has no belief than by thus contradicting
himself? This levity and inconstancy indicates either excessive heat of brain, or variety of cups.

A still further degree of tedium must be endured, while I
make it plain to the reader, how acute, faithful, and dexterous he shows himself in refuting our objections. After
deluding the minds of the simple in the way jugglers do, he
says, that among our objections the one which seems most
specious is,—that a true and physical body cannot in substance be in several different places at the same time, that
Christ has a true and physical body in which he ascended
to sit at the right hand of the Father in a certain definite
place until he appear to judge the world, and that therefore
this body, which is circumscribed in heaven by a certain
space, cannot be in its substance in the Supper. He adds,
moreover, that there is no argument in which I place equal
confidence. First, how naughtily he lies in saying that I
thus confine the right hand of the Father to a narrow space,
is attested by several passages of my writings. But to forgive him this, what is more futile than to make the state of
the question to depend on a physical body, since often before
this I have declared that in this case I pay no regard to
physical arguments, nor insist on the decisions of philosophers, but acquiesce in the testimony of Scripture. From
Scripture, it is plain that the body of Christ is finite, and
has its proper dimensions. Geometry did not teach us this ;
but we do not allow what the Holy Spirit taught by the
Apostles to be wrested from us. Heshusius foolishly and
not without inconsistency objects that Christ sits in both
natures at the right hand of the Father. We deny not that
the whole and entire Christ in the person of the Mediator

fills heaven and earth.   I say *whole*, not *wholly*, (*totus, non totum*,) because it were absurd to apply this to his flesh. The hypostatic union of the two natures is not equivalent to a communication of the immensity of the Godhead to the flesh, since the peculiar properties of both natures are perfectly accordant with unity of person.   He rejoins, that sitting at the right hand of the Father is, according to the testimony of Paul, to be understood of eternal and divine majesty and equal power.   And what do I say ?   More than twelve years ago, my exposition, which quotes the very words of Paul, was published throughout the world, and bears, " This passage shows plainly, if any one does, what is meant by the right hand of God, namely, not a place, but the power which the Father has bestowed upon Christ to administer the government of heaven and earth.   For seeing that the right hand of God fills heaven and earth, it follows, that the kingdom and also the virtue of Christ are everywhere diffused.   Hence it is an error to endeavour to prove that Christ, from his sitting on the right hand of God, is only in heaven.   It is indeed most true that the humanity of Christ is in heaven, and is not on the earth, but the other proof does not hold.   For the words, *in heavenly places*, which immediately follow, are not meant to confine the right hand of God to heaven," &c.

He boldly persists in his impudence, and adding another passage from the same Epistle, pretends that it is adverse to me.   But my exposition is in the hands of the public.   I here insert the substance of it : Since to *fill* often means to *perform*, it may be so taken here.   For Christ by his ascension to heaven entered on possession of the dominion given him by the Father, viz., to rule all things by his power.   The meaning, however, will in my judgment be more elegant, if the two things, which though contrary in appearance agree in reality, are joined together.   For when we hear of the ascension of Christ, the idea which immediately rises in our minds is, that he is far removed from us.   And so indeed he is in respect of his body and human presence.   Paul, however, reminds us, that though withdrawn in respect of bodily presence, he yet fills all things, namely, by the agency of his Spirit. For wherever the right hand of God, which embraces heaven and earth, is diffused, there the spiritual presence of Christ, and Christ himself is present by his boundless energy, though his body must be contained in heaven, according to the declaration of Peter. Should any one ask, whether the body of Christ is infinite, like the God-head, he answers, that it is not, because the body of Christ, his humanity being considered in itself, is not in stones, and seeds, and plants. What is meant by this clause or exception, but just that the body of Christ naturally, when his humanity is considered by itself, is not infinite, but is so in respect of the hypostatic union? But ancient writers, when they say that the flesh of Christ, in order to be vivify-ing, borrows from his Divine Spirit, say not a word of this immensity, because nothing so monstrous ever came into their thoughts. While Heshusius admits that this is a dif-ficulty which he cannot explain, he gets off by representing things most dissimilar as alike. How the simple essence of God consists of three persons: how the Creator and the creature are one person: how the dead, who a thousand years ago were reduced to nothing, are to rise again, he says he cannot comprehend; but it is enough for him, that the two natures are hypostatically united in Christ and cannot be dissevered: nor can it be piously thought that the person of the Logos is without the body of Christ.

While I willingly grant all this, I wonder whence he draws the inference that the obscurity in the sacred Supper is the same. For who that is moderately versant in Scripture does not know what is and what is not the force of sacramental union? Moreover, as local presence cannot exist without ubiquity, he impugns my declaration, that the body of Christ is in the pious by the agency of the Spirit. This he does not in precise terms. He rather acknowledges that it is perfectly true, and yet he insists that the human nature of Christ is not less everywhere, or in several places, than his divine nature. I here ask, seeing that the habitation of Christ in believers is perpetual, why he denies that he dwells bodily without the use of the Supper? It seems to me there cannot be a firmer inference than this, If it is unlawful to dissever the flesh of Christ from his divinity, wherever the divinity dwells the flesh also dwells corporeally. But the deity of Christ always dwells in believers as well in life as in death ; therefore so dwells the flesh. Let Heshusius, if he can, dispose of this syllogism, and I will easily explain the rest.

I again repeat, As the divine majesty and essence of Christ fills heaven and earth, and this is extended to the flesh ; therefore, independently of the use of the Supper, the flesh of Christ dwells essentially in believers, because they possess the presence of his deity. Let him not cry that we dissever the indivisible person of Christ by not attributing the same qualities to both natures. For this being established, it will follow that the substance of the flesh is no more found under the bread than in the mere virtue of faith. I may add, that he declares his assent to Cyril, who contends that by the communion of the flesh and blood of Christ we become one with him, while Heshusius uniformly maintains that the wicked by no means become one with Christ, though they are corporeally intermixed with him ; and bringing together two passages from Paul, concludes that the presence of Christ, on which alone he insists, is not idle. There is still more ridiculous fatuity in what follows ; for from a passage in which Paul affirms that Christ speaketh in him, he infers that Christ is lacerated if we imagine him to speak by his divinity alone, to the exclusion of his flesh. After granting this, might I not justly infer that Christ was not less corporeally in Paul when he was writing than when he received the bread of the Supper ?

I have therefore gained all I wished, viz., that we become substantially partakers of the flesh of Christ not by an external sign but by the simple faith of the gospel. His quibbling objection, that the flesh is excluded from the Supper and from all divine acts when we teach that it is contained in heaven, is easily disposed of, since local absence does not exclude the mystical and incomprehensible operation of the flesh. Heshusius is under a very absurd hallucination when he imagines that fixture to a place implies exclusion, unless the body be inclosed under the bread. But he says, the Spirit is not with-

out the Son, and therefore not without the flesh. I, in my
turn, retort, that the Son is not without the Spirit, and that
therefore the dead body of Christ by no means passes into
the stomach of the reprobate. From this let the reader
judge where the absurdity lies. Nay, in order to drag the
body of Christ under earthly elements, he is forced to ascribe an immensity to the bodies of all believers, and tries
to play off his wit upon us, saying, that if each retain his
own dimensions, those who sit nearest to Christ after the
resurrection will be the happiest. Resting satisfied with the
reply of Christ, we wait for that day when our heavenly
Father will give each his proper station. Meanwhile we
abominate the delirium of Servetus, which Heshusius again
obtrudes.

His conclusion is, If the boundless wisdom and power of
God is not limited by physical laws; if the right hand of God
does not mean some small place in heaven, but equal glory
with the Father; if the human nature of Christ, from being
united to the Logos, has sublime prerogatives, and some
properties common to the divine essence; if Christ, not only
in respect of the Spirit, but inasmuch as he is God and man,
dwells in the breasts of believers, then by the ascension of
Christ into heaven his presence in the eucharist is secured
and firmly established. I, on the other hand, rejoin, If our
dispute is not philosophical, and we do not subject Christ
to physical laws, but reverently show from passages of Scripture what is the nature and property of his flesh, it is absurd
in Heshusius to gather from false principles whatever meets
his view. Again I infer, If it is plain, as I have most clearly
demonstrated, that whatever he has produced as adverse to
me concerning the right hand of God, he has borrowed from
my writings, he is proved to be a wicked calumniator. When
he says, that certain properties are common to the flesh of
Christ and to the Godhead, I call for a demonstration which
he has not yet attempted. Finally, I conclude, If Christ, in
respect of both natures, dwells naturally or substantially in
believers, there is no other eating in the Supper than that
which is received by faith without a symbol. He at last says,
in a cursory way, that all our objections with regard to the

departure of Christ, are easily solved, because they ought to be understood not of absence of person but only of the mode of absence, namely, that we have him present not visibly but invisibly. The solution is indeed trite, being not unknown even to some old wives in the Papacy; and yet it is a solution which escaped Augustine, by the admission of Heshusius himself, the chief, and best, and most faithful of ancient teachers. For in expounding that passage, he says, (in Joann. Tr. 50,) In respect of his majesty, in respect of his providence, in respect of his ineffable and invisible grace, is fulfilled what he said, I am with you always; but in respect of the flesh which the Word assumed, in respect of his being born of the Virgin, in respect of his being apprehended by the Jews, fixed to the tree, laid in the sepulchre, and manifested in the resurrection, ye shall not have me with you always. Wherefore? After he was conversant, in respect of the presence of his body, for forty days with the disciples, and they conducting him, seeing, but not following, he ascended into heaven, and is not here. He sits then at the right hand of the Father, and yet he is here; for the presence of his majesty has not retired. Otherwise thus: In respect of the presence of his majesty we have Christ always: in respect of the presence of his flesh, it was truly said to the disciples, Me ye shall not have always.

With what modesty, moreover, Heshusius says that I prove the eating of the flesh of Christ to be useless from the words of Christ, The flesh profiteth nothing; while I am silent let my Commentary demonstrate, in which I speak *verbatim* thus: Nor is it correct to say that the flesh of Christ profits, inasmuch as it was crucified, but the eating of it gives us nothing: we should rather say that it is necessary to eat it in order that we may derive profit from its having been crucified. Augustine thinks that we ought to supply the words *alone,* and *by itself,* because it ought to be conjoined with the Spirit. This is consonant to fact: for Christ has respect simply to the mode of eating. He does not therefore exclude every kind of utility, as if none could be derived from his flesh, but he only declares that it will be useless, if it is separated from the Spirit. How then has flesh the power of vivifying, but just by being spiritual ? Whosoever therefore stops short at the earthly nature of flesh will find nothing in it but what is dead ; but those who raise their eyes to the virtue of the Spirit with which the flesh is pervaded, will learn by the result and the experience of faith, that it is not without good cause said to be vivifying. The reader may there find more to the same purpose if he desires it. See why this Thraso calls upon the Calvinists to say whether the flesh of the Son of God be useless : Nay, why do you not rather call upon yourself, and awake at length from your sluggishness ?

Our *third* objection, according to him, is, The peculiar property of all the sacraments is to be signs and pledges testifying somewhat : and therefore in the Supper it is not the body of Christ, but only the symbol of an absent body that is given. Cæsar, boasting of the rapidity of an eastern victory, is said to have written, *Vidi, Vici*, I have seen, I have conquered ; but our Thraso boasts of having conquered by keeping his eyes shut. In our Agreement it is twice or thrice distinctly stated, that since the testimonies and seals which the Lord has given us of his grace are true, he, without doubt, inwardly performs that which the sacraments figure to the eye, and in them accordingly we obtain possession of Christ, and spiritually receive him with his gifts : nay, he is certainly offered in common to all, to unbelievers as well as to believers. As much as the exhibition of the reality differs from a bare and empty figure does Heshusius differ from our sentiments, when he pretends to extract from our writings falsehoods of his own devising. Hence as he is sole author of the silly quibble which he falsely attributes to us, I admit that he argues ill ; and as what he says of the absence of the body is cobbled by his own brain, though he is a bad cobbler, the fittest thing for him is to send him to his shoes with his frigid witticisms. Meanwhile I would have my readers to remember what was formerly said of a twofold absence ; for from thence it will be plain, that things which are absent in respect of place and of the eye, are not, however, far remote. These two kinds of absence Heshusius, from ignorance or malice, improperly confounds. It is at the same time worth while to observe how admirably he extracts the presence of Christ from the passage in which Peter calls baptism the answer (ἐπερωτησις) of a good conscience, though the Apostle there expressly distinguishes between the external symbol of baptism and the reality, saying, that our baptism, not the putting away of the filth of the flesh, but the trial of a good conscience by the resurrection of Christ, is similar to the ancient figure.

According to Heshusius, our *fourth* objection is, The sacraments of the New Testament, viz., Baptism and the Supper, are of the same nature, and entirely agree with each other: Therefore as in Baptism the water is not called the Holy Spirit except by a metaphor, so neither can the bread of the Supper be called the body of Christ, except allegorically, or, according to Calvin, metonymically. Our method of arguing will shortly be seen. Meanwhile let the reader observe, that Heshusius has again fabricated expressions which may furnish materials for fighting with shadows. Accordingly the " entirely agree" which he refutes is altogether his own; we have nothing to do with it, and hence I could easily allow him to knock down his own men of straw, provided he would cease from deluding the simple.

I now come to our argument. Since Scripture plainly declares (1 Cor. iii. 23) that we put on Christ in baptism, and are washed by his blood, we remark that there is no reason why he should be said to be more present in the Supper than in Baptism. The resemblance therefore is not placed in their being both sacraments of the New Testament, but in this, that Baptism requires the presence of Christ not less than the Supper. There was another reason. As they boldly rejected everything which was produced from the Old Testament, we showed that there was no room for this evasion in baptism. It is plain that they endeavoured to escape by a subterfuge, when they objected that there were only shadows under the law. The distinction was not unknown to us, nor was it destroyed by our doctrine, but we were thus forced to show, from the constant usage of Scripture, what was the force of sacramental modes of expression. But since their perverseness could not be overcome in any other way than by leaving the law out of view, and showing to these new Manichees, that in Baptism and the Supper, as being the sacraments of the New Testament, an analogy was to be observed, we clearly demonstrated, as was easy to do, that baptism is called the washing of regeneration and renovation in no other sense than that in which Christ called the bread his body.   I do not state all which the reader will find in my last admonition to Westphal, as at present it is sufficient to have pointed to the objections which Heshusius dilutes.   And yet I ought not to omit, that though he had read in the twenty-third article against the objectors of Magdeburg, what should have been more than sufficient to refute all his subtleties, he turns it over as if nothing had ever been written.

Next comes the *fifth* objection, in which he introduces us as speaking thus :—In the phrase, This is my body, we must have recourse to a trope, just as those phrases, Circumcision is a Covenant, The Lamb is a Passover, The Rock was Christ, cannot be explained without the help of trope, metaphor, or metonymy.   This may perhaps pass for wit with his boon companions, but all men of sense and piety must regard him as a falsifier, since this trifling is not to be found in our writings.   We simply say, that in considering the sacraments, a certain and peculiar mode of expression is to be observed in accordance with the perpetual usage of Scripture.   Here we escape by no evasion or help of trope : we only produce what is notorious to all but brutish minds that would darken the sun.   I acknowledge, then, our principle to be, that in Scripture there is a form of expression common to all the sacraments, and though each sacrament has something peculiar to itself, distinct from the others, yet all of them contain a metonymy, which transfers the name of the thing signified to the sign.   Let Heshusius now answer. His words are : It is not easy to admit that there is a trope in the words, The rock was Christ.   Still out of his facility he grants us this.   Here the reader will observe his difficult facility.   But how can he deny that the rock is figuratively called Christ ?   Is this all his great liberality ; to concede to us that Christ, strictly speaking, was not the mass of stone from which the water in the wilderness flowed? He goes farther, and says, it does not follow from this that all the articles of faith are to be explained metaphorically. But the question was concerning the sacraments. Let the pious and diligent reader turn over the whole of Scripture, and he will find that what we say of the sacraments always holds, viz., that the name of the thing signified is given to the sign. This is what is called by grammarians a figurative expression; nor will theologians, when they express themselves, invert the order of nature. With what propriety Heshusius flies off from Baptism and the Supper to all the articles of faith, I leave others to judge: every one must see, that like an unruly steed, he overleaps the goal. His answer, that individual examples do not form a general rule, is nothing to the purpose, because we do not produce any single example, but adhere to a rule which is common to all the sacraments, and which he in vain endeavours to overturn.

He is not a whit more successful in solving the other difficulty. We say with Augustine, that when a manifest absurdity occurs, there is a trope or figure in the expression. He answers, that in the judgment of reason nothing is more absurd than that there are three hypostases in the one essence of God, and yet no remedy of a trope is required; as if it were our intention, or had been that of Augustine, to measure absurdity by our carnal sense. On the contrary, we declare that we reverently embrace what human reason repudiates. We only shun absurdities abhorrent to piety and faith. To give a literal meaning to the words, This is my body, we hold to be contrary to the analogy of faith, and we, at the same time, maintain that it is remote from the common usage of Scripture wherever sacraments are spoken of. When Heshusius says that this opinion of ours is refuted by the name of New Testament, it is with no greater reason than if he were to deny that the Holy Spirit is metonymically termed a dove. He says, falsely and nugatorily, that insult is offered to Paul, as if we were rejecting his explanation, The bread is the communion of the body, whereas this communion is nowhere more fully illustrated than in our writings.

The rules of rhetoricians adduced by him show that he has never mastered the rudiments of any liberal study. But not to make myself ridiculous by imitating his silliness, I give the only answer which becomes a theologian,— that although a figurative expression is not so distinct, it gives a more elegant and significant expression than if the thing were said simply, and without figure. Hence figures are called the eyes of speech, not that they explain the matter more easily than simple ordinary language, but because they attract attention by their elegance, and arouse the mind by their lustre, and by their lively similitude make a deeper impression. I ask Heshusius, whether in our Saviour's discourse in the sixth chapter of John there is no figure? Surely, whether he will or not, he will be forced to confess that it was metaphorically said, Unless ye eat the flesh of the Son of God, and drink his blood. All, however, see more clearly what our Saviour meant to express, viz., that our souls, by a spiritual partaking of his flesh and blood, are nourished unto heavenly life. He makes it a ground of loud triumph over me, that when I saw that the grosser metaphors of others were exposed by the judgment of Luther, I craftily carved out a metaphor, which, however, is not at all consistent. He indeed admits the truth of what I teach, viz., that the sign is aptly expressed by the name of the thing signified, but holds that things unlike are here conjoined by a marvellous mode of expression. I hear what he would say ; but by what authority does he prove it ? He not only despises us, but rejects the interpretation of Brentius as confidently as he does ours.

Now then, although he persuade himself that, like another Pythagoras, he is to be believed on his own assertion, (αυτοπιστος,) in what way does he hold the body of Christ to be one with the bread ? He answers, in the same way as the Holy Spirit was a flame resting on the heads of the Apostles, and a dove which appeared to the Baptist. He means, then, that in an unwonted manner tongues of fire were the Spirit, and a dove was the Spirit. What need is there here for long discussion, as if the reader could not easily judge for himself which of the two is more con-

sistent—that the name of the thing should be applied to
the sign, or that the sign should be, strictly speaking,
the very thing ? The dove, under the form of which the
Holy Spirit appeared, immediately vanished : but as it
was a sure symbol of the presence of the Spirit, we say that
the name of the Spirit was correctly and aptly imposed on
it. Although this is displeasing to Heshusius, who maintains that however metonymy may be twisted, it cannot be
made to apply ; there is now no wonder that he is so much
in love with all kinds of absurdity, and hugs them as they
were his children, as he seems to be borne away by some
monstrous fondness for paradox, and can only approve of
what is absurd. Meanwhile, I receive what he grants, viz.,
that the bread of the eucharist is called the body of Christ
for the same reason for which the dove is called the Spirit.
I cannot have the least doubt, that in regard to the latter
expression, all will at once agree with me that there is a
metonymy. When, to defend his pride, he glories in mere
ignorance, the only thing fit for him is Paul's answer, He
that is ignorant, let him be ignorant.

If he feels that weariness, by which, according to Juvenal,
        Occidit miseros crambe repetita magistros,
why does he, in his *sixth* objection, inflict spontaneous misery upon himself, not only by useless repetition, but also by
vain fiction ? Our mode of arguing, though nothing of the
kind was ever in our thoughts, he pretends to be as follows :
Were the presence of Christ in the Supper corporeal, the
wicked would, equally with believers, be partakers of the
body of Christ. This inference, which Heshusius draws,
I reject as absurd. Hence it appears in what kind of wrestling he is exercising himself. But the reason is, that he was
unwilling to lose a verse of Menander, which formerly, when
talking tediously on this article, he had forgotten to insert.
I think I have clearly demonstrated how nugatorily he attempts to make a gloss of the immensity of God, that he
may thus separate Christ from his Spirit. God, he says, fills
all things, and yet does not sanctify all things by his Spirit.
But the reason is, that God does not work everywhere as
Redeemer. The case is different with Christ, who, in his

character as Mediator, never comes forth without the Spirit
of holiness.   For this reason, wherever he is, there is life.
Therefore, not to wander in vain beyond our bounds, let
Heshusius show that Christ, considered as born of the Virgin
to be the Redeemer of the world, is devoid of the Spirit of
regeneration.

In the *seventh* objection he makes it plain how truly I said
that those who inclose the body of Christ in the bread, and
his blood in the cup, cannot, by any tergiversation, avoid
dissevering the one from the other: for seeing no means of
evasion, he breaks out into invective, and calls me an Epicurean.   It is of no consequence to observe what kind of
scholars his own school has produced.   It is certain that the
stye of Epicurus does not send forth men who boldly offer
their lives in sacrifice, that they may confirm the ordinance
of the Supper by their own blood.   Six hundred martyrs
will stand before God to plead in defence of my doctrine.
For the same cause three hundred thousand men are this
day in peril.   Heshusius and his fellows will one day feel
how intolerable, before the tribunal of God, and in presence
of all the angels, is the sacrilege of not only fiercely lacerating the living servants of God, whose piety is placed beyond
a doubt by pious labours, watchings, and wrestlings, but also
of dishonouring innocent blood, sacred even to God, by cruelly
assailing the dead.   This is my brief answer to his reproaches.

As to the subject, let him at last give his own answer.   He
says, that without disseveration the flesh of Christ is eaten
in the bread, and his blood drunk in the wine, but that the
mode in which this is done is unknown to him.   In other
words, while he advances the most manifest contradictions,
he will not allow them to be examined.   But I press him
more closely.   As Christ does not say of the bread, This I
am; but calls it his body, and separately offers the blood in
the cup, it necessarily follows that the blood must be separated from the body.   It is a frigid sophism of the Papists,
that the body is in the cup, and the blood in the bread, by
concomitance.   Distinct symbols were not used without
cause, when he gave his flesh for meat, and his blood for
drink.   If the same thing is given by both symbols, then

substantially the bread is blood, and the wine is body ; and the bread, as well as the cup, will each be the whole Christ twice over. But if it was the purpose of Christ to feed his believers separately on spiritual meat and drink, it follows that there is neither flesh in the bread, nor blood in the wine, but that by these symbols our minds are to be carried upwards, that by eating the flesh and drinking the blood of Christ we may enjoy solid nourishment, and yet not dissever Christ. Though Heshusius, to darken this light, boldly defames, under the name of philosophy, a doctrine derived from pure theology, he gains no more than to make his obstinacy and arrogance detestable to all men of sense and moderation.

The *eighth* objection, concerning the worship of the bread, (αρτολατρεια,) though not faithfully stated, he adopts a very silly method of refuting. He maintains that the bread is not to be worshipped, because it is not the body of Christ by hypostatic union. Surely Philip Melancthon was not so ignorant of things and words as not to perceive this distinction. He saw, however, that if the bread was the body, it was to be worshipped without any reservation. Indeed, I have already shown, that were we to grant to Heshusius that it does not follow from his error that the bread is to be worshipped, he cannot, however, evade the charge of αρτολατρεια, because he cannot deny that Christ is to be worshipped in the bread, or under the bread. It is certain, that wherever Christ is, he cannot be lawfully defrauded of his honour and worship. What, then, is more preposterous than to place him in the bread and then refuse to worship him ? Nor have we to dispute about the matter, as if it were doubtful. For to what end is the bread lifted up among them ? Why do they fall on their knees before the bread ? If such gross superstition is excusable, the prophets did grievous wrong to the Gentiles when they said that they worshipped gold, silver, wood, and stones. All infidels thought that they were venerating the celestial Deity when they supplicated statues and images. They had no hypostatic union, but only a resemblance ; and though they annexed the power of God to images, they would never have ventured to assert that a piece of wood was substantially God. Shall we suppose that

those who unblushingly affirm the same thing of the bread
are not worshippers of the bread ?

His next sentence gives no obscure indication of the reverence with which he contemplates the boundless essence
of God. If it is so, he says, let us worship wood and stones
in which the true essence of God is. For although God
fills heaven and earth, and his essence is everywhere diffused,
the perverse fiction which Heshusius appends to this, and
his profane language concerning it, are abhorrent to piety.
The Spirit of God, he says, dwelt in Elias : why did not the
followers of Elias worship him ?   But what resemblance is
there between all the forms of divine presence of which
Scripture speaks, and this for which Heshusius contends ?
He is not entitled proudly to despise objections which he
is so unsuccessful in obviating. It is strange also why he
represents the arguments which overthrow his error as so
few in number. He is not ignorant that the objectors of
Magdeburg set them down at fifty-nine. Why then does he
pass the greater part of them without notice, but just because he would not advert to difficulties which he could not
solve without disgracing himself, and, seeing how the others
had been handled, the best course seemed to be to dissemble.

Though at greater length than I anticipated, I am not
sorry at having discussed the silly production of a man not
less wicked than absurd, if modest and worthy readers derive all the profit which I hope from my labour. It was for
their sakes I submitted to the weary task. The slanderer
himself was undeserving of an answer. That the whole
world may in future know more certainly with what title turbulent men so violently assail our doctrine, with what truth
they charge us with equivocation and imposture, with what
civility they load us with words of contumely, it has seemed
proper to append a brief summary of my doctrine. Perhaps
this right and true no less than lucid exposition may have
the effect of appeasing some individuals ; at all events, I am
confident that it will fully satisfy all the sincere servants of
God, since nothing has been omitted in it which the dignity
and reverence due to this ordinance demands. The paltry
censures by which Heshusius has endeavoured to excite

hatred or suspicion of my writings, I regard not, nor labour to refute, but rather am pleased that there should exist a notable specimen of the depravity and malevolence with which he is imbued, the stolid pride, and insolent audacity with which he swells. I do not now question his title to assume the office of censor against me. It is enough for me that while I am silent all sensible and moderate men will recognise under the character of the censor one who has the spirit of an executioner; so foully does he adulterate, corrupt, wrest, garble, lacerate, and subvert everything. Had he anything like candour or docility, I would clear myself from his calumnies, but as he is like an untamed bull I leave it to Beza to prune his wantonness, and bring him into due subjection.

THE BEST METHOD OF OBTAINING CONCORD,

PROVIDED THE TRUTH BE SOUGHT WITHOUT CONTENTION.

THAT no doubt or suspicion may delay and hinder CONCORD, we must, in the first place, explain what the points are on which we are agreed; for those points which, at the commencement of our contests, chiefly exasperated the minds of both parties, are now undisputed. What produced the greatest hatred was the allegation by one party that the grace of the Spirit was tied down to external elements; and, by the other, that only bare and empty figures resembling theatrical shows were left. This contention has now ceased, because we acknowledge on both sides,—

First, that THE SACRAMENTS are not only marks of outward profession before men, but are testimonies and badges of divine grace, and seals of the promises, giving a stronger confirmation to our faith.

That, therefore, their use is twofold—to sustain our consciences before God, and testify our piety before the world.

That God, moreover, as he is true and faithful, performs by the secret virtue of his Spirit that which he figures by external signs, and, accordingly, that on the part of God himself, not empty signs are set before us, but the reality and efficacy at the same time conjoined with them.

That, on the other hand, the grace or virtue of the Spirit is not inclosed by the external signs, because they do not profit all equally or indiscriminately, nor does the effect also appear at the same moment; but that God uses the Sacraments as to him seems good, so that they help forward the salvation of the elect, and instead of conferring anything on others rather turn to their destruction.

That, in short, the Sacraments are of no avail unless they are received in faith, which is a special gift of the Spirit, not depending on earthly elements, but on the celestial operation of the same Spirit. External helps are only added to meet the weakness of our capacity.

Particularly, in regard to the holy Supper of Christ, it is agreed, that under the symbols of bread and wine an exhibition of the body and blood of Christ is held forth; and we are not merely reminded that Christ was once offered on the cross for us, but that sacred union is ratified to which it is owing that his death is our life; in other words, being ingrafted into his body, we are truly nourished by it, just as our bodies are nourished by meat and drink.

It is also agreed, that Christ fulfils in reality and efficaciously whatever the analogy between the sign and the thing signified demands; and that, therefore, in the Supper communion with the body and blood is truly offered to us, or, (which is the same thing,) that under the bread and wine we receive an earnest which makes us partakers of the body and blood of Christ.

It remains to mention the articles as to which it is not yet clear either what view we are to take or how we are to speak.

Every man who, endued with a sound and correct judgment, possesses also a calm and well-ordered mind, will admit that the only dispute is in regard to the mode of eating. For we plainly and ingenuously assert that Christ becomes ours in order that he may thereafter communicate the blessings which he possesses to us: that his body also was not only once given for our salvation when it was sacrificed on the cross to expiate sin, but is daily given us for nourishment, that while he dwells in us we may enjoy a participation in all his blessings. In short, we teach that it is vivifying, because he infuses his own life into us in the same way in which we derive vigour from the substance of bread. Therefore, according to the different modes of eating adopted, disputes arise. Our explanation is, that the body of

Christ is eaten, inasmuch as it is the spiritual nourishment of the soul. Again, it is called nourishment by us in this sense, viz., because Christ, by the incomprehensible agency of his Spirit, infuses his life into us, and makes it common to us, just as in a tree the vital sap diffuses itself from the root among the branches, or as the vigour of the head is extended to the members. In this definition there is no quibble, no obscurity, nothing ambiguous or equivocating.

Some, not contented with this lucid simplicity, insist that the body of Christ is swallowed; but this is not supported by the authority of Scripture, or the testimony of the primitive Church, so that it is wonderful how men endued with moderate judgment and learning contend so pertinaciously for a new invention. We by no means call in question the doctrine of Scripture, that the flesh of Christ is meat indeed, and his blood drink indeed; because they are both truly received by us, and are sufficient for entire life. We also profess that this communion is received by us in the sacred Supper. Whosoever urges us farther certainly overleaps the proper bounds.

Moreover, to insist on the essential expression is not agreeable to reason, since the subject in question is the Sacraments to which Scripture assigns a peculiar mode of expression. Hence it follows, that the words, " This is my body," and also, " The bread which we break is the communion of the body of Christ," ought to be expounded in a sacramental manner. As some are suspicious of danger here, it is easy to obviate their fears. When the mode of expression is said to be sacramental, they think that the reality is overthrown by the figure. But they ought to observe that the figure is not set down as an empty phantom, but is taken grammatically to denote a metonymy; lest any one should suppose that the bread is called " The body of Christ," as absolutely as Christ himself is called " The Son of God." The term *body* is therefore figuratively transferred to the bread, and yet not figuratively as if Christ presented a naked and empty image of his body to our eyes, because the reality is not excluded by the figure, but only the difference is denoted between the sign and the thing signified. This is not repugnant to their union. Let cavilling only be laid aside, as it ought to be, in seeking concord, and it will be seen that there is nothing in this doctrine which ought to be odious or liable to misconstruction, and that it has ever been approved both by common sense and common usage.

First of all, it is necessary to remove the obstacle with regard to the immensity of the body. Unless it is admitted that it is finite and contained in heaven, there will be no means of settling the dispute. The idea of some, that there is no absurdity in supposing it to be everywhere, in consequence of its being united to the Divinity, is easily disposed of. For although the two natures form the one person of the Mediator, the properties of each remain distinct, since union is a different thing from unity. There was no dispute in ancient times as to this matter, for it was held with universal consent, that as Christ, the Son of God, the Mediator, and our Head, was once received into heavenly glory, so he is separated from us in respect of his flesh by distance of place, but still, by his Divine essence and virtue, and also spiritual grace, fills heaven and earth.

This being fixed, it will be lawful to admit forms of speech, by which, on account of their ambiguity, some are perplexed, viz., that the body of Christ is given us under the bread, or with the bread, because the thing denoted is not a substantial union of corruptible meat with the flesh of Christ, but sacramental conjunction. And there is no dispute among the pious as to the fact, that there is an inseparable tie between the sign and the thing signified in the very promise which makes no fallacious exhibition, but figures what is truly and in reality performed.

Moreover, it is in vain to dispute about a twofold body. There was indeed a change in the condition of the flesh of Christ, when received into celestial glory it laid aside all that was earthly, mortal, or perishable. Still, however, we ought to hold that no other body is vivifying to us, or can be regarded as meat indeed, but that which was crucified for the expiation of sin, as the words import. The same body, therefore, which the Son of God once offered to the Father in sacrifice, he daily offers us in the Supper as spiritual food. Only, as I lately hinted, we must hold in regard to the mode, that it is not necessary that the essence of the flesh should descend from heaven in order to our being fed upon it, the virtue of the Spirit being sufficient to break through all impediments and surmount any distance of place. Meanwhile, we deny not that this mode is incomprehensible to the human mind ; because neither can flesh naturally be the life of the soul, nor exert its power upon us from heaven, nor without reason is the communion which makes us flesh of the flesh of Christ, and bone of his bones, called by Paul, " A great mystery." (Eph. v. 30.) Therefore, in the sacred Supper, we acknowledge a miracle which surpasses both the limits of nature and the measure of our sense, while the life of Christ is common to us, and his flesh is given us for food. But we must have done with all inventions inconsistent with the explanation lately given, such as the ubiquity of the body, the secret inclosing under the symbol of bread, and the substantial presence on earth.

After these matters have been arranged there still arises the doubt as to the term substance, to settle which the easy method seems to be to remove the gross imagination as to the eating of the flesh, as if it were similar to corporeal meat which is received by the mouth and descends into the stomach. For when this absurdity is out of the way, there is no reason why we should deny that we are substantially fed on the flesh of Christ, because we are truly united into one body with him by faith, and so made one with him. Whence it follows, that we are conjoined with him by a substantial fellowship, just as substantial vigour flows from the head to the members. The explanation to be adopted will thus be, that substantially we become partakers of the flesh of Christ—not that any carnal mixture takes place, or that the flesh of Christ brought down from heaven penetrates into us, or is swallowed by the mouth, but because the flesh of Christ, in respect of its power and efficacy, vivifies our souls in the same way that bread and wine nourish our bodies.

Another controverted point relates to the term *spiritually*, to which many are averse, because they think that something vain or imaginary is denoted. Definition must there-fore here come to our aid. Spiritual then is opposed to carnal eating. By carnal is meant that by which some sup-pose that the very substance of Christ is transfused into us in the same way as bread is eaten. In opposition to this it is said, that the body of Christ is given to us in the Sup-per spiritually, because the secret virtue of the Spirit makes things which are widely separated by space to be united with each other, and accordingly causes life from the flesh of Christ to reach us from heaven. This power and faculty of vivifying might not improperly be said to be something ab-stracted from the substance, provided it be truly and dis-tinctly understood that the body of Christ remains in heaven, and that yet while we are pilgrims on the earth life flows and comes to us from its substance.

When some charge us with ignorantly confounding the two modes of eating, we deny that it is through ignorance we omit the notion which they have fabricated for themselves in regard to sacramental eating, which they insist to be an eating of the substance of the flesh without effect or grace. Nothing of the kind is either delivered in Scripture, or supported by the testimony of the primitive Church. For certainly the reality and substance of the sacrament is not only the application of the benefits of Christ, but Christ him-self with his death and resurrection. Wherefore, they are not skilful expositors who, on the one hand, make Christ de-void of the gifts of his Spirit and of all virtue, and, on the other, conjoin him with spiritual gifts and the fruit of eat-ing, because he cannot without insult be separated from his Spirit any more than dissevered from himself. Nor is any support given them by the words of Paul, that those who eat the bread of the Supper unworthily are guilty of the body and blood of the Lord, (1 Cor. xi. 27;) since the guilt is not ascribed to receiving, nor is it anywhere read, nor is it consonant to reason, that the receiving of Christ is the condemnation of any man. The condemnation is for reject-ing him. Let it be agreed, then, in regard to this article, that the body of Christ is eaten by the wicked sacrament-ally, not truly or in reality, but in so far as it is a sign.

This definition answers the question, What is it to receive the body of Christ in the Supper by faith ? Some are suspicious of the term *faith,* as if it overthrew the reality and the effect. But we ought to view it far otherwise, viz., That the only way in which we are conjoined to Christ is by raising our minds above the world. Accordingly, the bond of our union with Christ is faith, which raises us upwards, and casts its anchor in heaven, so that instead of subjecting Christ to the figments of our reason, we seek him above in his glory.

This furnishes the best method of settling a dispute to which I adverted, viz., Whether believers alone receive Christ, or all, without exception, to whom the symbols of bread and wine are distributed, receive him ? Correct and clear is the solution which I have given ; Christ offers his body and blood to all in general ; but as unbelievers bar the entrance of his liberality, they do not receive what is offered. It must not, however, be inferred from this, that when they reject what is given, they either make void the grace of Christ, or detract in any respect from the efficacy of the Sacrament. The Supper does not, through their ingratitude, change its nature, nor does the bread, considered as an earnest or pledge given by Christ, become profane, so as not to differ at all from common bread, but it still truly testifies communion with THE FLESH AND BLOOD OF CHRIST.

THE END OF VOLUME SECOND OF CALVIN'S TRACTS.

GENERAL INDEX.

A

ABRAHAM ate Christ spiritually, 431.

Absence, Present bodily, of Christ, 240.

Absurdities produced by too closely pressing the literal sense of Scripture, 433.

Absolution, The utility of, if private and optional, 321 ; should not be imposed by law, 321.

Abstinence and fasting laudable virtues, 149.

Administrator, The efficacy of the Sacraments depends not on the, 152, 233.

Adam, Our common ruin from, 131, 141.

Agency of the Holy Spirit, 50-53; efficacy of the Sacraments depend entirely on, 134.

Agonies, Fearful, by which our Saviour's soul was pierced, 46.

Agreement in regard to the Sacraments between the Churches of Zurich and Geneva, 221, 253 ; no ground for alleging it to be a fictitious, 273.

Allegory, Excessive fondness of the Fathers for, 435.

Ambrose, The Emperor Theodosius rebuked by, 437.

Angels and Saints not to be worshipped, 71 ; the proper office of, 71.

Anabaptists, Similarity of the arguments of, against infant baptism to those used in maintaining a local presence of Christ in the Supper, 305, 425; Servetus one of the, 265; detestable ravings of, 133.

Anthropomorphites argue like those contending for a local presence of Christ in the Supper, 299, 433, 508, 528.

Apostles' Creed, why so called, 39; four great divisions of, 39.

Arians, Source of the heresy of the, 301.

Ark of the Covenant, how called the presence of God, 430.

Artolatria, or worship of the bread, 498, 570.

Ascension, The body of Christ no longer on earth since his, 48.

Assurance of forgiveness, 146; not to be sought in predestination, 343.

Assemblies, Duty of holding Christian, 83.

Athanasius, The only point of resemblance between, and Westphal, 258; his high authority, 545; quoted, 545.

Augsburg, The Confession of, as published at Ratisbon, 225 ; high estimation in which held, 354 ; accordance of, with the Agreement between the Churches of Zurich and Geneva, 225, 261, 277, 306, 355.

Augustine, The drift of, in writing against the Donatists, 370 ; the chief, best, and most faithful of the Fathers, 562 ; quoted, 162, 225, 227, 230-232, 234-236, 264, 286, 304, 342, 358, 359, 362-365, 367-371, 374, 377, 378, 386, 388, 389, 410, 437, 449, 521, 522, 551, 562.

Auricular Confession part of the tyrannical yoke of the Pope, 133, 149.

Axioms, two articles forming a kind of, 147.

B

BAPTISM, Purposes served by formal profession of faith in, 34 ; how defined, 86, 153; title of infants to, 87, 88, 114, 115, 134, 154, 319, 320, 336-338, 425 ; how said to be holy, 320 ; how connected with regeneration, 86, 87, 336-340; form of administering, 113-118 ;

multiplicity of ceremonies in, rightly abolished, 117, 118; how it differs from the Lord's Supper, 92, 93, 446, 447, 564; proper uses of, 87, 114, 115, 337, 339; outward act of, not always accompanied by invisible grace, 237; absurdity of allowing women to administer, 319.

Barbarism with which Christendom threatened, 35.

Basil quoted, 547.

Believers, The imperfection of, 145; imperfection no ground of despair in, 178; receive Christ independently of the Sacraments, 236; Christ received only by, 302.

Berengarius, The alleged heresy of, 260, 362, 506; his recantation, 260.

Bethel, why called the gate of heaven, 296.

Beza, CALVIN leaves Heshusius to the correction of, 572.

Blasphemous prayers to the Virgin Mary, 145.

Blessings, Temporal, how far promised, 63, 64.

Body of Christ no longer on earth, 48, 49; locally in heaven, 220; how eaten in the Supper, 277.

Bread of the Supper, Christ not to be adored in, 220; not the sign of an absent body, 509; nor the body of Christ, 171, 172; an appropriate symbol of our Saviour's body, 89; called the body of Christ in the same sense in which baptism called the washing of regeneration, 565; Christ not to be adored in the, 220; what included under, 78, 498, 570.

Brotherly love, The Lord's Supper a strong inducement to, 173, 174, 177.

Bucer of blessed memory, 211, 281; his excellent writings, 262; attempt to destroy the reputation of, 262; accordance of his views on the Sacrament with those of CALVIN, 281; presence of, at Smalcald, 360.

Bullinger, his excellent writings, 262; attempt to destroy the reputation of, 262; local presence of Christ in the Supper refuted by, 535.

C

CÆSAR, The boast of, 563.

CALVIN, His care in preparing his Catechism, 34; reasons for writing his Catechism in Latin, 35; reasons for writing his Treatise on the Lord's Supper, 164; visits Zurich in company with Farel, 201; draws up the Agreement between the Churches of Zurich and Geneva, 201; his high respect for Luther, 224; Letter of the pastors of Zurich to, 201; exertions in order to produce concord, 201, 202, 246, 247; his labours for the edification of the Church, 250; unwillingly dragged into contest, 252; his familiar intercourse with the leading Protestants, 253; unjustly accused of violence by Westphal, 347; absurdly charged with bringing a general charge of drunkenness against the Germans, 256, 492; his attempt to reconcile Zuinglius and Luther, 277; attempt to depreciate his Commentaries, 278; kind of eloquence to which he aspired, 311, 324; success of his labours, 326; absurd charge of infidelity against, 329; no declaimer, 336; his views as to the punishment of heretics, 357, 358; his treatment of Servetus, 350; calumnious charge of resisting the truth against his conscience, 475; solemn appeal on this subject, 475.

Calvinists falsely charged as Marcionites and Manichees, 502.

Catechism, important uses of a, 34, 35; CALVIN's care in preparing his, 34; rules to be observed in framing, ib.; desirable that all Churches should have a common, ib.; pernicious consequences of a bad, 35; CALVIN's reasons for publishing a Latin, 35; extensive use of CALVIN's, 434.

Catechising neglected by the Papacy, 36; importance of, 37.

Capernaumites, a name properly given to Westphal's party, 362, 555.

Canonists, The, ashamed of the recantation forced from Berengarius, 260.

Carlostadt misinterprets the words of institution in the Supper, 267; the image war of, 322.

Celibacy, Imposition of, part of the tyrannical yoke of the Papacy, 133; unlawfulness of imposing, 149; abuses arising from, 149.

Ceremonies, Multiplicity of, rightly abolished, 117, 118, 317.

Ceremonies of the ancient law, why abolished, 191; absurd imitation of ancient, 192.

Christ, the eternal wisdom of the Father, 40; the offices of, 42, 43;

how the Son of God, 43; miraculous conception of, 44 ; why he assumed our nature, 44; why pronounced innocent before being condemned, 45; how he endured the wrath of the Father, 47; benefits from the resurrection and ascension of, 48; no longer bodily present, 48; the only spiritual nourishment of our souls, 166 ; the substance of the sacraments, 169; the only perfect sacrifice, 192 ; how communicated to us, 213; the body of, locally in heaven, 220 ; cannot be received without faith, 234; not placed under the bread, or coupled with it, 242 ; though not locally present, yet given substantially in the Supper, 277 ; spiritually eaten under the Old Testament as under the New, 293, 294; the flesh of, not immense, 385 ; our supreme, perfect, only, Master, 404 ; nothing impossible to, 416 ; why called the Passover, 428 ; how put on in baptism, 446 ; as the head of the Church fills all things, 489.

Christian assemblies, Duty of holding, 83.

Chalcedon, Council of, 130.

Chambery, Five Protestants burned at, 259.

Charity taught by the Lord's Supper, 177; duty of mutually exercising, 197.

Cherubim, The presence of God between the, 385.

Christendom threatened with barbarism, 35.

Chrysostom quoted, 366, 549 ; an unfinished work falsely attributed to, 535.

Church, the, Nature of, 50; why called holy, 50 ; the unity of, 51 ; how far visible, 51 ; why called Catholic, 51 ; no safety out of the, 52 ; government of, by pastors, 83; the whole spiritual government of, leads to Christ, 212 ; the duty of, in regard to careless ministers, 233; not to be disturbed on slight grounds, 244 ; difference between the Sacraments of the new and the ancient, 523.

Churches of Saxony and Lower Germany, 208; views of, in regard to the Sacraments, 208.

Churches of Switzerland, The doctrine of the, in regard to the Sacraments, 246.

Circumcision, What signified by, 338, 440.

Clemens, Alexandrinus, his authority, 541 ; quoted, 541.

Civil Government, The divine authority of, 135.

Cochlæus, A reference to, 258.

Commentaries of CALVIN, Attempt to depreciate the, 278, 279.

Commandments, Ten, how divided, 56; spiritual meaning of, 67.

Common sense, Mysteries of Scripture not to be tested by, 310.

Communicants, unworthy, Duty of excluding, 93, 120; partake only in the signs, 158; in what sense guilty of the body and blood of Christ, 234.

Communion, The requisites of, worthy, 176; the propriety of frequent, 179; grounds insufficient for abstaining from, 180, 181 ; enjoined only once a year under the Papacy, 188 ; in one kind only frivolous reasons for, 189; with Christians in the Supper not fictitious, 226; not confined to the Supper, 91.

Consubstantiation, Absurdity of, 159; almost as absurd as Transubstantiation, 272.

Confession of Augsburg, 225, 261, 277, 306, 354, 355.

Convention to settle disputes on the Sacraments desirable, 494.

Controversy, religious, Proper mode of terminating, 202.

Cornelius, The baptism of, 219 ; received the Holy Spirit before baptism, 219, 236, 339.

Conscience, Men cannot bind the, 147.

Confession of Faith, 130.

Council of Nice, 130 ; Ephesus, 130, 361; Chalcedon, 130 ; Tours, 159, 360 ; Vercelli, 360.

Confidence, The knowledge of God in Christ, the only foundation of, 38.

Corporeal presence of Christ in the Supper, Fiction of the, not of ancient date, 459.

Covenant, Ark of the, why called the presence of God, 430.

Creed, Apostles', why so called, 39; four great divisions of, ib. ; why punishment of hell not mentioned in, 53.

Crucifixion, Why of importance that Christ should die by, 46.

Conscience, Terrors of the awakened, 167, 168, 175.

Cruciger Gasper, Agreement of, with CALVIN in regard to the Sacraments, 313.

Cyprian quoted, 436, 543.
Cyril quoted, 435, 541.

D

DAILY bread, What included under, 78.
Damascenus, Joannes, a writer of no authority, 535.
Davidians, a sect of fanatics, 265.
Dead, Prayers to the, dishonouring to Christ, 147.
Death no longer terrible, 63; kind of, to be experienced by those alive at the last day, 49; premature, not necessarily a curse, 63.
Debate, Proper method of conducting, 255.
Debtor, God can never be our, 145.
Decalogue, how divided, 56; spiritual meaning of, 67.
Decree of God, Free and sovereign, 231.
Demonstrative pronoun, The use of, in denoting things absent, 405.
Descent of Christ into hell, What meant by, 46.
Devil wicked by nature, according to the Manichees, 133.
Devils and wicked men, how overruled by God, 41.
Dionysius of Alexandria quoted, 544.
Donatists, The drift of Augustine in writing against the, 370.
Doubt a bar to effectual prayer, 146.
Dove, how called the Holy Spirit, 171, 372.
Duty of excluding unworthy communicants, 93, 120.

E

EARTH, True happiness not to be found on, 52.
East Friesland, Dedication of CALVIN's Catechism to the ministers of, 34.
Eck, A reference to, 258.
Edward VI. of England, a king of the highest promise, 314; sudden death of, 314.
Elect, The Sacraments available only to the, 231.
Election, Lawful, necessary to confer the pastoral office, 133.
Elements of bread and wine become Sacraments only when the Word is added, 227.
Eighth Commandment, What implied in, 65.
Elias, Luther compared to, 477.
England, Discussion as to the Sacra-

ments in, 314; cruel persecution in, under Mary, 315; loss sustained in, by death of Edward VI., 314.
Ephesus, The Council of, 361.
Epiphanius quoted, 545, 546.
Epistles, Gospels and, Division of Scripture into, 322.
Error, People of God sometimes allowed to fall into, 194.
Eusebius, Dionysius of Alexandria quoted by, 544.
Eutyches, Heresy of, 131.
Evangelists, their different accounts of the institution of the Supper, 209, 243, 409, 420, 481.
Egyptian bondage, a type of the spiritual bondage of sin and tyranny of the devil, 57.
Eunomians, The heresy of, 141.
Empty shows, The Sacraments separated from Christ are only, 215.
Evangelical union, The advantages of, 35; strong inducements to, among Protestants, 251.

F

FAITH, Importance of unity in the, 34; definition of, 53; how produced, 53; benefits resulting from, 54; justification by, 54; proper root of all good works, 55; should continually increase, 85; the Scriptures the only rule of, 141; true nature of, 144; Christ received only by, 234, 303; the true modesty of, 239; body and blood of Jesus Christ received only by, 172.
Famine, Our spiritual, must be felt, that we may long for food, 176.
Fanatics, Abuse of the doctrine of predestination by, 143.
Farel, visit with CALVIN to Zurich, 201.
Farel, William, the indefatigable zeal of, 200; visits the Church of Zurich with CALVIN, 200; assists in drawing up the Agreement between the Churches of Geneva and Zurich, 221.
Fasting and abstinence laudable virtues, 149.
Fathers of the Church too much addicted to allegory, 435; their method of settling controversy, 202.
Father, What meant by the right hand of the, 49.
Feast days in honour of the Virgin Mary and saints, 322.
Filial confidence in God, on what founded, 75.

Fill in Scripture, often equivalent to perform, 558.

Fifth Commandment, What implied in, 63.

First-born among many brethren, Christ why called the, 44.

First Commandment, What implied in, 57.

Form of dispensing Baptism, 113-118.

Form of dispensing Lord's Supper, 119-122.

Form of celebrating Marriage, 123-126.

Form of visitation of the sick, 127, 128.

Forgiveness of sins, how obtained, 52, 79; figured by Baptism, 86; assurance of, 146; not to be dissevered from reformation of life, 132.

Flesh, prohibition of, under pain of mortal sin, unlawful, 149.

Flesh of Christ not immense, 385.

Fourth Commandment temporary, in so far as ceremonial, 61; given for three reasons, 61; how to be observed, 62, 63.

France, Confession of Faith by the Protestants of, 140; martyrdoms in, 259.

Frankfort, The Church of, 319; Diet of, to which French Protestants sent their Confession, 138.

Frequent Communion, The propriety of, 179.

Friesland, East, Dedication of CALVIN'S Catechism to ministers of, 34.

French Protestants, The loyalty of, 140; assent of, to all the articles decided by ancient councils, 140; constrained to take up arms, 140.

Fundamental principle of religion, A, 142.

Food, Our souls have in Christ their only, 157; how the word of God distributes this, 166.

Feelings indicating a fitness to receive the Lord's Supper, 178.

Frivolous grounds for abstaining from Communion, 180.

G

GEHENNA, Consciences how brought into a kind of, 175.

Geneva, Agreement of the pastors of, with those of Zurich, 201.

Genesis, CALVIN'S Commentary on, falsely charged with containing fierce invectives against Luther, 256.

Gentile idolatry, The nature of, 570.

Germans, CALVIN falsely accused of bringing a general charge of drunkenness against the, 256.

German Princes, always willing that their principles, as Protestants, should be examined, 316.

Germany, Churches of Lower, 208; views in regard to the Sacraments, 208.

God, The knowledge of, the chief end of human life, 37; wherein the true knowledge of, consists, 38; nothing worse than not to live to, 38; the method of duly honouring, 38; the knowledge of, in Christ the only foundation of confidence, 38; unity of the Trinity, 39; why called Father, 40; the providence of, not general, but particular, 40, 41; because the Father of Jesus Christ, our Father also, 40; devils and wicked men, how overruled by, 41; why called jealous, 59; how man can glorify, 76; how he blesses or punishes posterity, 52, 60; what comprehended under the love of, 67; how dwelt between the cherubim, 385.

Godhead, Three persons in the, yet God not divided, 39.

Good, wherein consists the chief, 37.

Good works, The necessity of, 55; the source of, 55; not meritorious, 143.

Gospel, The Sacraments appendages of the, 212.

Gospels and Epistles, Division of the Scriptures into, 322.

Government in the Church necessary, 94; leads to Christ, 212; civil, the divine authority of, 135.

Gregory Nanzianzen quoted, 334, 547.

Grisons, The Churches of the, 207.

Grains, The variety of, in bread employed as an illustration, 177.

Galatians, Strong language employed by Paul in rebuking the, 347, 348.

H

HAMBURG, inhospitable treatment of Protestant exiles at, 335.

Hand, right, of the Father, What meant by the, 49.

Happiness, True, not to be found on earth, 52.

Heart more especially required in prayer, 72.

Heaven, The proper idea of, 290.

Hell, The punishment of, why not mentioned in the Creed, 53; what meant by the descent of Christ into, 46.

Heresy of the Manichees, 130, 131 ; of Marcion, 131; Nestorius, 131; Eutyches, 131 ; Servetus, 130, 131 ; Schuencfeldius, 131.

Heresy sometimes originates with the unlearned, 328.

Heretics, mode of treating, 357 ; liable to punishment by the civil magistrate, 357.

Hebrew, Use of the present tense for the future in, 422, 483.

Heathen rites, several derived from the ancient patriarchs, 228 ; how the sacraments are converted into, 228.

Heshusius, The effrontery, stolidity, and petulance of, 527 ; CALVIN leaves Beza to correct, 572.

Holy living, The Lord's Supper a strong inducement to, 173, 174.

Holy Scriptures, how to be received and used, 82.

Holy Spirit, The agency of the, 50, 53; efficacy of the Sacraments depends entirely on, 134.

Human life, The chief end of, 37.

Human traditions, The danger of, 148.

Hypostatic union of the two natures in Christ, 558.

Hierarchy, Popish, a diabolical confusion, 134.

Hilary quoted, 435, 539.

Human reason, Proper province of, 422 ; different kinds of, 442, 512 ; mysteries of Scripture not to be measured by, 512.

I

IDOLATRY, Gentile, the true nature of, 570.

Idol, How the bread of the Supper converted into an, 220.

Ignatius, Spurious writings attributed to, 535 ; abuse of these writings, 535.

Illumination by the Holy Spirit, The necessity of, 53.

Images, Making and worshipping of, how prohibited, 58.

Immensity of the body of Christ, The figment of, 160, 241, 288, 311, 444, 529.

Impanation of Christ, The absurdity of the, 312.

Imputation of righteousness, 213.

Infants, The baptism of, 87, 88, 114, 115, 134, 154, 305, 319, 320, 336-338, 425; how said to be holy, 320.

Institution of the Supper, Reasons for the, 167.

Intentions, Good, not sufficient, 149; abuses founded on the pretext of, 149.

Interpretation of Scripture necessary, 478, 481, 482.

Irenæus quoted, 511, 537, 540.

Incomprehensible, Manner in which Christ is communicated to us is, 490.

Intellect, human, Mysteries of Scripture not to be measured by, 249.

J

JEALOUSY, How attributed to God, 59.

Jerome quoted, 410, 549.

Jesus, Meaning of the name, 42, 43.

Judaizing exemplified in regard to the Lord's Supper, 318.

Judas, How admitted by our Saviour to the last Supper, 93 ; in what sense the flesh and blood of Christ was received by, 297, 376, 417.

Justification, how received by faith, 54, 132, 145.

Justin Martyr quoted, 435, 537.

Juvenal quoted, 537, 568.

K

KINGDOM of Christ, The nature of the, 42.

Kingdom of God, Wherein consists the, 76 ; how said to come, 76, 77.

Knowledge of God, Wherein consists the, 38.

Κοινωνια, The proper meaning of, 269, 270, 414, 483, 516, 517.

L

LADDERS, The Sacraments a species of, 229.

Lascus, John á, The excellent writings of, 262, 267.

Law, The office of the, 68, 69 ; unregenerate cannot perform in any degree, 68 ; Christ the end of, 212.

Law, Ancient, the ceremonies appointed under the, 191.

Lawgiver, God the only, 148.

Le Coq, his attack on CALVIN, 496.

Leipsic, learned teachers at, 327 ; one of the eyes of Saxony, 396, 555.

Life, The chief end of human, 37.

Literal sense of Scripture, not to be pressed too closely, 433 ; words used in instituting the Supper not to be taken in the, 68.

Local presence of Christ in the Supper a mere figment, 218, 237, 240, 280, 384, 450-458.

Lord's Supper, True nature of the, 91, 157, 167 ; profanation of, 93, 94, 174 ; mode of dispensing, 105, 106; how it differs from baptism, 92, 93; union with Christ in, 91, 134; unworthy communicants receive the sign only, 158; danger of error in regard to the, 164 ; how made profitable to us, 167, 173; all the treasures of spiritual grace contained in, 168 ; in what sense the bread and wine in, are body and blood, 170 ; well fitted to remind us of our obligations to God, 173 ; a strong inducement to holy living and brotherly love, 173, 174; great guilt of profaning the, 174; errors in regard to, 182 ; not a sacrifice, 183; how abused under the Papacy, 187, 188; recent disputes in regard to the, 194.

Love of God, What comprehended under the, 67.

Loyalty of French Protestants, 139.

Luther, First views of, in regard to the Supper, 195 ; opposition of, to Zuinglius and Œcolompadius, 195, 252, 317; defect in his views, 196; his occasional vehemence, 224, 253, 258, 276, 277, 307, 330; respect of CALVIN for, 224; abuse made of his name, 276, 330, 333, 450, 477; his respect for CALVIN, 308; his magnanimity, 319; sometimes prudently accommodated himself to the times, 323; his learning, 327; compared to Elias, 477 ; sometimes mentioned in extravagant terms, 477; his implicit submission to the word of God not always imitated by his admirers, 477.

Laxity, The prevalence of, too great in admitting to the Communion, 321.

Lombard, Peter, quoted, 418.

Louvain, Luther's work against the Doctors of, referred to, 468.

Lyons, Martyrdom at, 259.

M

MAGDEBURG, Strong sympathy for, manifested by the Church of Geneva during its calamitous siege, 397.

Magnitude, definite, Our Saviour's body continues of a, 160.

Man, The natural misery of, 168; can-not seek to glorify God without advancing his own interest, 74, 75.

Manichees, Heresy of the, 133.

Manna, a symbol of spiritual food, just as bread and wine are symbols of the body and blood of Christ, 243, 293, 297, 391 ; a species of sacrament, 430.

Marpurg, The conference at, 253, 308, 360.

Marcion, The heresy of, 130; his absurd reason for assigning a heavenly body to Christ, 329.

Martyr, Peter, The excellent writings of, 262 ; a faithful minister of Strasburg, 314 ; his refutation of a local presence of Christ in the Supper, 535.

Martyrdom of Protestants at Chambery and Lyons, and other parts of France, 259 ; of six hundred persons holding CALVIN's views on the sacraments, 569.

Martyrs, communicate with Christ, though deprived of the sacraments, 236; celebration of the memory of, 322 ; antiquity of the celebration, 323 ; corruptions introduced in celebrating the memory of, 322.

Marriage, Design of God in instituting, 123 ; form of celebrating, 123-126.

Mary, Virgin, Blasphemous prayers offered to the, 145.

Mary, Why Jesus says to, " Touch me not," 455.

Mary, Queen, Bloody persecutions in England under, 315.

Mass, and other adulterations of the Lord's Supper, rightly abolished, 122 ; an execrable abomination, 135, 154 ; numerous corruptions connected with, 156, 183, 184, 191.

Matthew's Gospel, Commentary on, by an unknown author, 535.

Melancthon, Philip, justly esteemed by all princes and learned men, 355 ; appeal to by CALVIN, 355, 467; his love of peace sometimes excessive, 356 ; perfect agreement with CALVIN in regard to the Sacraments, 356 ; his presence at Smalcald, 360 ; CALVIN's solemn apostrophe to, 496.

Melchisedec, Christ sole and perpetual Priest after the order of, 156.

Member of the Church, How a man attests that he is a true, 52.

Merit, none in man, 145.

Metonymy, common in the Sacraments, 219.

Messalians, a sect of enthusiasts, 536.

Mimicry and buffoonery in celebrating the Supper, 193.

Ministry of death and condemnation, The law why called the, 69.

Monks, Evils of enjoining celibacy on, 133, 149.

Mortal sin, Absurd dogma in regard to the obstacle of, 217.

Moses, The model shown in the mount to, 228 ; his reception of divine unction without being circumcised, 236.

Murder in the sight of God, Anger, hatred, and any desire to hurt is, 64.

Mysteries of the faith not to be scanned by the human intellect, 249.

N

Nestorians, The heresy of, 131.

Neufchatel, The Pastors of, subscribers to the Agreement between the Churches of Zurich and Geneva, 201.

Nice, The Council of, 130.

Ninth Commandment, What implied in, 66 ; why public perjury specially mentioned in, 66.

Neighbour, What implied in the term, 69.

Number seven, The, implies perfection, 62.

Nuns, Evils of enjoining celibacy on, 149.

Nicolas, Pope, condemnation of Berengarius, 260.

O

Oaths, how far prohibited, and how far lawful, 60.

Œcolompadius, The views of, in regard to the Supper, 195, 267, 307 ; his views attacked by Luther, 195, 252; defect in his views, 196, 275; a faithful servant of Christ, 211 ; his refutation of a local presence in the Supper, 535.

Omnipotence of God not impugned by denial of Christ's ubiquity, 161.

Original Sin, the nature of, 131, 142.

Osiander despised a humiliated Christ, 488 ; his idea that righteousness is conferred on us by the deity of Christ, 554.

P

Pædobaptism, A plausible argument against, refuted, 340.

Papacy, Catechising neglected under the, 36; spurious sacraments of the, 36, 37, 134 ; gross abuses of, in regard to the Lord's Supper, 187, 188, 340 ; communion once a year only enjoined by the, 188 ; tyrannical yoke of, 133.

Papists, their absurd method of answering objections, 382.

Passion and death of Christ, the only perfect sacrifice, 192.

Pastoral office, Lawful election to, necessary, 133.

Pastors, Government of the Church by, 83, 133 ; subjection due to, 151 ; wherein consists the proper power of, 134, 135.

Pacification, Duty to aim at, by all lawful means, 493.

Passover, A lamb figuratively called the, 407; substituted for the Lord's Supper, 422.

Particular obligation on Christians to live in charity, 197.

Patriarchs, many heathen rites borrowed from the, 228.

Paul, Saint, How far the account of the Supper given by, agrees with that of the Evangelists, 209, 242, 243 ; strong language used by him in rebuking the Galatians, 347, 348.

Peace, The only kind of, desirable, 314.

People of God allowed to fall into error, 194.

Pestilence, war, and chastisements from God, 106.

Pope, The tyrannical ordinances of the, 133, 149 ; his primacy repugnant to Scripture and the primitive Church, 150 ; has encroached on the jurisdiction of God, 151.

Popish Hierarchy a diabolical confusion, 134.

Popish requisite of intention in the officiating minister, 233.

Posterity, how blessed or punished by God, 59, 60.

Prayer to be made to God only in the name of Christ, 70, 71, 73, 147 ; in what spirit to be offered, 72, 73; sluggishness in, how to be overcome, 72; ground of confidence in, 73, 146; proper subjects of, 74, 147; faith gives access to God in, 133 ;

God the only proper object of, 146; doubt a bar to effectual, 146.

Prayer, The Lord's, the model, but not the only form of, 83, 133.

Prayers to the dead dishonouring to Christ, 147 ; to the Virgin Mary, blasphemous, 145.

Presence of Christ, The nature of the, in the Supper, 289-291 ; scholastic distinction as to the, 418.

Predestination, The doctrine of, abused by fanatics, 143 ; assurance of salvation not to be sought in, 343.

Pretended unworthiness in fellow-communicants no ground for abstaining from communion, 181.

Priesthood of Christ, Nature of the, 42 ; benefits derived from, 43.

Primacy of the Pope, an enormous usurpation, 150.

Primitive Church, The doctrine of transubstantiation not countenanced by the, 185; accordance of CALVIN'S views on the Sacrament with those of the, 535.

Promise the thing chiefly to be regarded in the Sacraments, 215.

Pronoun demonstrative, The use of, in denoting things absent, 405.

Proper method of keeping back unworthy communicants, 181.

Prophet, How Christ is a, 42.

Propriety of frequent communion, 179.

Protestants generally agreed as to the leading doctrines of Christianity, 251.

Protestants, French, The loyalty of, 139; constrained to take up arms, 140.

Purgatory, The dogma of, derogatory to the finished work of Christ, 147.

Public perjury, why expressly mentioned in the ninth commandment, 66.

Perfection the mark at which we ought to aim, 69.

Philosophy, true, Wherein consists,161.

R

RATISBON, The confession of Augsburg published at, 225.

Reality in the Sacraments conjoined with the visible signs, 91, 135, 172, 225, 440.

Reality of Christ's human nature destroyed by the dogma of a local presence in the Supper, 187.

Reason, Human, Proper province of, 422; different kinds of, 442, 512;

mysteries of Scripture not to be measured by, 512.

Rebecca, The craft of, in substituting Jacob for Esau, 526.

Regeneration,how connected with baptism, 86, 87, 153, 218, 342 ; wherein it consists, 114.

Recantation of Berengarius, 260.

Religious controversy, proper mode of terminating, 202.

Remission of sins attested by baptism, 411.

Reformation, The, unjustly charged with the heresies which then arose, 499, 500.

Repentance, The definition of, 56.

Reproof, Severe, often justifiable, 349.

Resurrection, Order of the, 53 ; fanatically denied on the ground that we are to be partakers of the divine nature, 381.

Reprobates can only blame themselves, 232.

Reverence due to distinguished servants of God, 197.

Righteousness, The free imputation of, 213.

Right hand of the Father, What meant by, 49, 457, 559.

Rock in the wilderness, how said to be Christ, 242, 373, 432, 565.

Rulers, Civil, Submission due to, for conscience' sake, 135, 151; the authority of, subordinate to that of God the Sovereign Prince, 135.

Rites, Profane, how the Sacraments are converted into, 228; several borrowed from ancient patriarchs, 228.

Ridicule allowable in attacking error, 486, 487.

S

SABBATH, The observance of, how far still obligatory, 61, 62 ; mode of observing the, 61.

Sacraments, the, Definition of, 83 ; instituted in accommodation to our weakness, 84 ; the utility of, 84, 85, 225; how to be received, 85; number of, 86, 153; Christ Jesus the substance of, 169 ; efficacy of, not dependent on the administration, 152, 233 ; danger of despising the, 152; reality always conjoined with the signs, 162 ; the efficacy of, depends entirely on the agency of the Holy Spirit, 134 ; the promise the principal thing to be looked to in the, 215 ; effect nothing by, themselves ; gifts in, offered to all, but received by believers only, 217; believers communicate with Christ independently of the, 218 ; benefit of the, not always received in the act of communicating, but appears long after, 218 ; no local presence of Christ in the, 218, 219; the words of institution not to be taken literally, 219 ; the Spirit inwardly performs what is figured in the, 226, 238; not to be extolled above the word, 227 ; a kind of ladder to enable us to climb upwards, 229 ; unhappy disputes in regard to the, 246; how constituted by the words of Christ, 303.

Sacramental eating, what meant by, 373, 374.

Sacramental, mode of expression, 243, 250, 419.

Sacramentarians, a term of derision applied to those holding CALVIN'S views on Sacraments, 206, 211.

Sacrifice, a term anciently applied to the Supper, but improperly, 156; the Lord's Supper not a, 183 ; the death and passion of Christ the only perfect, 192.

Salvation, The mercy of God the only source of, 142.

Saints not to be worshipped, 70; feast-days in honour of, 322.

Satan, the true instigator of the disputes on the Sacraments, 309; his crafty policy, 206, 309.

Saxony and Lower Germany, The Churches of, 206 ; the views of, in regard to the Sacraments, 206, 309.

Saxony, Wittemberg and Leipsic, The two eyes of, 396, 555.

Schismatics, Who properly called, 151.

Scholastic distinction as to the presence of Christ, 418, 515.

Schuencfeldius, The erroneous views of, 131, 266, 537.

Scripture, The literal sense of, not to be pressed too closely, 433 ; division of, into Gospel and Epistle, 322, 323; necessary to keep within the limits of, 148; authority and use of, 82, 83 ; the sufficiency of, 133, 147 ; only rule of faith, 141.

Self-deception, Various forms of, 178.

Self-denial necessary in order to participate in the blessings of Christ, 175.

Self-examination necessary before receiving the Supper, 175.

Second commandment, What implied in, 58, 59; improperly made an appendage of the first commandment, 322.

Servetus an Anabaptist, 265 ; opposes Zuinglius and Œcolompadius on the Sacraments, 266; how treated by CALVIN, 358; his abuse of spurious writings attributed to Ignatius, 536 ; deliriums of, 561.

Seed, The Sacraments compared to, 342.

Seventh commandment, What implied in, 65.

Sick, Visitation of the, 127, 128; administration of the Supper to, in private, 320.

Seven, The number, implies perfection, 62.

Sixth Commandment, What implied in, 65.

Simon Magus, The baptism of, 341.

Sin, Original, The nature of, 131, 142.

Son of God, In what sense Christ the, 43.

Sorbonne, Subtle discussion of the Doctors of, 186; figment of, in regard to the Sacraments and mortal sin, 232.

Spirit, The agency of the, 50, 84; life transferred from the flesh of Christ by the, 249; necessity of being regenerated by, 144.

Smalcald, Conference at, 360.

Spiritual regeneration figured by baptism, 86.

Spiritual eating not opposed to sacramental eating, 373.

Stephen, The reference of, to the model shown on the mount, 228; vision of, 464, 515.

Sum of the ten commandments, 67, 68.

Strasburg, Peter Martyr, a minister of, 314, 319.

Superstition, Necessity of guarding against, 228.

Superstitious practices in regard to the Supper, 193, 237.

Supper, The, though received with little benefit at the time, may afterwards bear fruit, 218.

Switzerland, Doctrine of the Churches of, in regard to the Supper, 204.

Synodal Epistles designed to promote unity of faith, 35.

T

TAPERS, The use of, savours of Judaism, 318.

Taxes and tribute, The duty of paying, 135.

Temporal blessings, how far promised, 63, 64.

Temporary sacraments used in the days of miracles, 153.

Temptation, its nature, 80, 81; why we ask God not to lead us into, 81.

Tense, use of the present for the future in Hebrew, 422, 483.

Tenth commandment, What implied in, 66 ; imposes a law even on the thoughts, 67.

Terrors of the awakened conscience, 167, 168, 175.

Tertullian quoted, 542.

Theodosius, The Emperor, rebuked by Ambrose, 437.

Third commandment, What implied in, 60.

Tomb, Christ placed in, to make it more manifest that he underwent a real death, 46.

Tongue, Uselessness of prayer when conceived only by the, 71.

Tours, The Council of, 159.

Tradition, Human, The danger of, 148.

Transubstantiation, repugnant to the nature of a sacrament, 159 ; not countenanced either by Scripture or by the primitive Church, 185 ; absurdity of, 219 ; how refuted, 240 ; not more inconsistent than consubstantiation, 219, 272.

Transfusion of substance in the Supper a mere figment, 219, 239.

Treasures of spiritual grace contained in the Supper, 168, 169.

Tribute and taxes, Duty of paying, 135.

Types and figures not confined entirely to the Old Testament, 427-429.

Tyranny of the Pope, 133, 149-151.

U

UBIQUITY of the body of Christ, absurdity of holding the, 160, 161, 281; omnipotence of God not impugned by the denial of, 161; how refuted, 390.

Union, Evangelical, The advantages of, 35 ; strong inducements to, among Protestants, 251.

Unity of faith, The importance of, 34; of the Church, 51; Synodal epistles designed to promote, 35.

Unity of spirit, Duty of Christians to aim at, 197.

Unworthy communicants partake only of the signs, 158 ; in what sense guilty of the body and blood of Christ, 234.

Unbelievers shut out from all escape, 68.

Use, Common, of the Sacraments and the Gospel, 225.

V

VERCELLI, Council of, 360.

Virgin Mary, Blasphemous prayers to the, 146.

Virtue, none in the Sacraments per se, 216.

Visible sign always necessary in a Sacrament, 187.

Visitation of the sick, 127, 128.

Vitus Theodorus, Letter of, referred to, 31.

Vulgate version of the Scriptures, Ludicrous effect of an error in, 357.

Visible shape, Why God may not be represented by a, 58.

Volo, Absurd criticism on the use of the Latin word, 295.

Vivifying flesh of Christ, how, 507.

W

WAR, pestilence, and other calamities, chastisements from God, 106.

Water in baptism, a figure with the reality annexed, 87.

Weakness of faith, The Sacraments instituted in accommodation to our, 85.

Westphal, The intemperance of, 247, 254, 258, passim ; his party termed Capernaumites, 362, 555.

Wicked, Christ not received by the, 234.

Wittemberg, Faithful and learned teachers at, 326, 327, 360 ; one of the two eyes of Saxony, 396, 555.

Word, The, begotten of the Father from eternity, 130.

Word, should always accompany the dispensation of the Sacraments, 190 ; Sacraments not to be extolled above the, 227; all men invited but the elect only effectually called by the, 343.

Works, good, No merit in, 54, 143; the necessity of, 55, 143 ; of believers pleasing to God, 55.

Worthy communion, the requisites, 176.

Z

ZUINGLIUS, The views of, in regard to the Supper, 195, 308 ; the views of, attacked by Luther, 195, 252 ; defect in views of, 196, 275, 308 ; a faithful minister of Christ, 211 ; the excellent writings of, 262, 307.

Zurich, Visit of Calvin and Farel to, 200 ; agreement of the Pastors of, with those of Geneva, 221.

THE END.